*Edward M. Glaser*

*Harold H. Abelson*

*Kathalee N. Garrison*

# Putting Knowledge to Use

꩜

*Facilitating
the Diffusion of Knowledge
and the Implementation
of Planned Change*

 Jossey-Bass Publishers
San Francisco • Washington • London • 1983

PUTTING KNOWLEDGE TO USE
*Facilitating the Diffusion of Knowledge
and the Implementation of Planned Change*
by Edward M. Glaser, Harold H. Abelson, and Kathalee N. Garrison

Copyright © 1983 by: Jossey-Bass Inc., Publishers
433 California Street
San Francisco, California 94104
&
Jossey-Bass Limited
28 Banner Street
London EC1Y 8QE

The content of this book was prepared for the Mental Health
Services Development Branch, National Institute of Mental
Health, Department of Health and Human Services, under
Grant No. 5 R12 MH27566-03. Since grantees performing
research under government sponsorship are encouraged to
express their own judgment freely, the book does not necessarily represent the department's official opinion or policy.
Moreover, the grantee is solely responsible for the factual
accuracy of all material developed in the book.

**Library of Congress Cataloging in Publication Data**

Glaser, Edward Maynard (date)
    Putting knowledge to use.

    Bibliography: p. 437
    Includes index.
    1. Communication in the social sciences. 2. Knowledge,
Sociology of. 3. Technology transfer. 4. Thought and
thinking. 5. Reasoning (Psychology) I. Abelson,
Harold H. (Harold Herbert) (date). II. Garrison,
Kathalee N. III. Title.
H61.8.G58 1983    001    83-11281
ISBN 0-87589-572-7

Manufactured in the United States of America

JACKET DESIGN BY WILLI BAUM

FIRST EDITION

*Code 8319*

# The Jossey-Bass
# Social and Behavioral Science Series

# Preface

Researchers, practitioners, and administrators in many fields are perennially confronted by a major challenge, namely, to seriously consider the application of seemingly relevant, potentially valuable knowledge and exemplary practice in connection with their respective subject fields and, thereby, seek ways to improve methods of operation. In response to this challenge, they are producing an ever-growing literature that attempts to cast light on (1) barriers and gateways related to dissemination/transfer/utilization of validated, promising new knowledge and (2) strategies to facilitate desirable change in organizational and institutional settings. So numerous and dispersed are the articles, books, papers, and reports on these vital subjects that it has become imperative to condense and order the pertinent literature.

   With the encouragement, counsel, and practical assistance of the Mental Health Services Development Branch of the National Institute of Mental Health, the Human Interaction Research Institute has undertaken, first in 1971, then in 1976, and now in the present publication, the extensive task of distilling from the comprehensive literature the findings and proposals for meeting the above challenge. A concomitant task has been to provide a large and diversified bibliography on the subjects of knowledge utilization and innovative change. The need for putting together this updated volume became apparent as one perceived not only the amount and widened scope of new material but also its sophisticated quality with regard to interpretation and application. The further study of the subject, in addition to yielding new insights, turned up fresh areas of inquiry, such as the international transfer of technology, to which an entire chapter is devoted in the present volume.

While the genesis of the project upon which this publication is based was an effort to narrow the gap between knowledge and practice in the area of mental health, it soon became apparent that the writings of academics and practitioners in many fields were making contributions to the same underlying problems. Hence, the review of the literature was broadened to encompass such basic and derived disciplines as sociology and social work, political science and government, economics and industrial/business management, education and communication, anthropology, and systems analysis. The broadening of coverage, aided and abetted by computer search, provided an opportunity to achieve a cross-fertilization of generally useful ideas. It also has contributed to resolving the problem of how explanations, ideas, and suggestions need to be differentially considered in relation to specific settings.

This book is an effort to acquaint the reader with a vast and scattered literature and to facilitate the practical application of lessons that may be gleaned therefrom. A serious concern of the authors was how best to arrange the content in a way that would prove most useful to practitioners, consultants, researchers, administrators, teachers, and students in various fields directly or indirectly related to knowledge transfer and innovative change. Aside from an introductory and a concluding discussion, a three-pronged approach was selected.

First, it became apparent that numerous students of the subject were engaged in a search for *determining variables.* Hence, the several chapters in Part One are centered about an enumeration and analysis of such variables, classified under several types.

Second, much of the material was seen as dealing with the *stages* through which the process of transforming knowledge into changed practice evolves. Consequently, Part Two is devoted to the issues and suggestions related to each stage in the planning and execution of the process.

Third, a number of related topics were perceived as centering around the *linkage* of knowledge and practice but viewed from different vantage points. Thus, Part Three examines the operation of change agents and agencies, the communication media employed, transfer of technology across national boundaries, relationships between practitioners and researchers, and various perspectives and model frameworks.

It is hoped that this book will prove immediately useful and will also serve as a state-of-the-art point of departure for further study. The task of gathering insights concerning how knowledge may be more fully put to use, so as to achieve improved practice and needed changes in diverse fields of human endeavor, will long continue.

*August 1983*                                          Edward M. Glaser
*Los Angeles, California*


Harold H. Abelson
*Santa Monica, California*


Kathalee N. Garrison
*Los Angeles, California*

# Acknowledgments

This volume has been developed through the combined efforts of many persons.

First, the task could not have been undertaken without the many-dimensioned support of Howard R. Davis, acting associate director for knowledge transfer, Office of State and Community Liaison, National Institute of Mental Health (NIMH), and Susan E. Salasin, acting deputy associate director for knowledge transfer, Office of State and Community Liaison, NIMH. Their wise counsel, steadfast encouragement, and project management facilitation have been invaluable.

Special thanks are due to John E. Bell, former NIMH Region IX director, who first combed and summarized a large amount of literature beyond what had been identified for the 1976 volume, and who presented a preliminary draft that contributed significantly to the manuscript.

The outside content review consultants were Matthew B.

Miles, Center for Policy Research, New York; Donald C. Pelz, program director, Center for Research on Utilization of Scientific Knowledge, Institute for Social Research, University of Michigan; Jack Rothman, professor, School of Social Work, University of Michigan; Carol H. Weiss, professor, Graduate School of Education, Harvard University; and Gerald Zaltman, professor of marketing and director of research, Graduate School of Business, University of Pittsburgh. These consultants have contributed very knowledgeable, scholarly, and incisive editing that helped to separate wheat from chaff, and to improve the substance, organization, integration, and coherence of the entire document. Toward the end of the project Gerald Zaltman again reviewed the revised manuscript and added very valuable editorial input.

In addition to the consultants who reviewed the entire manuscript, certain chapters were reviewed by persons with specific content expertise in the given subject area. For example, Edward Wenk, Jr., professor of engineering and public affairs, University of Washington, prepared a complete rewrite on the chapter on international transfer of technology. And Karen E. Kirkhart, Department of Educational Psychology, University of Texas at Austin, and Ross Conner, Program of Social Ecology, University of California at Irvine, made major contributions as coauthors of the chapter on evaluation. Billie Gabel provided editorial and format suggestions that were most helpful in "smoothing out" portions of the manuscript.

We are grateful to all our colleagues for their respective contributions.

# Contents

Preface     vii

Acknowledgments     xi

The Authors     xv

1. Introduction: Nature and Scope of Knowledge
Utilization and Implementation of Change     1

**Part I: Factors Influencing Knowledge
Utilization and Change**     23

2. Determining Factors     27

3. Key Variables Influencing Acceptance of Change     55

4. Personal and Social Influences     68

5.   Organizational Factors                                    90

6.   Political, Economic, and Sociocultural Processes          123

**Part II: Stages in Problem Solving,
Knowledge Utilization, and Planned Change**                     151

7.   Stages in Processes of Knowledge Utilization
     and Change                                                155

8.   Assessing Needs and Developing Plans for Change           168

9.   Strategies for Achieving Change                           187

10.  Evaluating and Maintaining Planned Change                 221

**Part III: Linking Knowledge
with Potential Users**                                          253

11.  Roles and Activities of Change Agents                     255

12.  Means of Communicating Knowledge                          298

13.  International Transfer of Technical Knowledge              336

14.  Relating Research and Development to Practice             361

15.  Models and Systems for Facilitating Planned
     Change                                                    398

16.  Conclusion: Improved Knowledge Utilization—
     Highlights, Guidelines, and Prospects                     422

     Bibliography                                              437

     Name Index                                                605

     Subject Index                                             625

# The Authors

Edward M. Glaser is president of the Human Interaction Research Institute, a nonprofit organization, and managing associate of Edward Glaser & Associates, psychological consultants to organizations. He received his Ph.D. degree (1940) from Teachers College, Columbia University, in clinical and social psychology. On occasion he has been a visiting professor at the University of California, Los Angeles.

Glaser's main research activities have included studies of barriers and gateways to dissemination/utilization of knowledge stemming from promising R&D or exemplary practice findings; the refinement of qualitative and quantitative methods by which organizations can undertake self-evaluation of their programs; the facilitation of desired change; the development, implementation, and assessment of effective processes for improving quality of worklife and productivity in organizations; and generation of a paradigm for achieving and disseminating state-of-the-art consensus/synthesis in various subject fields.

In 1978 Glaser received the Gunnar and Alva Myrdal Prize for his work in the development of new approaches to qualitative evaluation of programs and systems and his testing of innovative methods for relating evaluative outcomes to needed improvements in the delivery of human services.

Glaser is a past president of the American Psychological Association (APA) Division of Consulting Psychology, past chairperson of the APA Committee on Scientific and Professional Ethics and Conduct, and past chairperson of the California State Psychology Examining Committee. Glaser has published over 100 professional papers and reports and two books: *An Experiment in the Development of Critical Thinking* (1941) and *Productivity Gains Through Worklife Improvement* (1976). He also is coauthor of the *Watson-Glaser Critical Thinking Appraisal* (rev. ed., 1980), a test that measures ability to reason analytically and logically.

Harold H. Abelson is dean emeritus of the City College School of Education, the City University of New York (CUNY), and senior staff associate at the Human Interaction Research Institute. He received his B.S. degree (1924) in education from the City College of New York and his M.A. degree (1925) and Ph.D. degree (1927) in educational psychology from Columbia University.

At the City College, aside from the deanship, he taught a wide range of courses, notably in educational research methods and in educational and clinical psychology. He developed and headed the master's training program in educational research, directed a child guidance educational clinic and a concomitant clinical school psychologist training program, and engaged in numerous educational and clinical research projects. He also held the position of acting dean of teacher education, CUNY. He has been a visiting professor at the University of Colorado, Cornell University, Hunter and Lehman Colleges of CUNY, and the New School for Social Research.

Abelson has served as consultant to a number of agencies, including the New York City Civil Service Commission, the Board of Examiners of the City's Board of Education, and the

Adjutant General's Office, U.S. Army. He has been licensed as a certified psychologist in New York State and is a fellow of the Divisions of Clinical and of Educational Psychology of the American Psychological Association and of the American Association for the Advancement of Science. He is a member of Phi Beta Kappa. In 1962 he received the Townsend Harris Medal from the City College Alumni Association.

In addition to his dissertation, *The Improvement of Intelligence Testing* (1927), and numerous articles and reports on educational and clinical psychological subjects, Abelson is the author of *The Art of Educational Research* (1933). This book represented an early attempt to bring together educational research and practice by elucidating a functional, problem-solving methodological system.

Kathalee N. Garrison is research associate and corporate officer at the Human Interaction Research Institute (HIRI). She received her B.A. degree (1941) from Eastern Michigan University in English and her M.A. degree (1946) from the University of Michigan in education, after which she taught school for several years.

She has served as administrative coordinator and editor on fourteen major research projects carried out by HIRI in the fields of education, health care, manpower and organizational development, and mental health. The primary focus of these studies was on planning and developing better ways of knowledge transfer on the parts of both the knowledge producers and those in the policy and practice arena. She compiled the source material for the widely distributed desk reference *Information Sources and How To Use Them* (1975), funded by the National Institute of Mental Health, and also assisted in the preparation of the 1976 edition of *Putting Knowledge to Use.*

# Putting Knowledge to Use

~~~

*Facilitating
the Diffusion of Knowledge
and the Implementation
of Planned Change*

# 1

# Introduction:
# Nature and Scope
# of Knowledge Utilization and
# Implementation of Change

## Seven Questions

The task and scope of knowledge utilization (and hence change) are presented in this introductory chapter under seven questions that serve as headings:

- What is meant by knowledge utilization and innovative change?
- Why study knowledge utilization and innovative change?
- How can a proposed change be examined analytically?
- How extensive is time lag?
- What differentiations are important in efforts to achieve utilization and change?
- What methods have been used in the study of knowledge utilization and innovative change?
- How does the review of literature presented here organize the subject of knowledge utilization and change?

1

1. **What Is Meant by Knowledge Utilization and Innovative Change?** For the purpose of this literature review, *knowledge* is broadly conceived to include (1) facts, truths, or principles, often associated with (but not limited to) an applied subject or branch of learning or professional practice, (2) information or understanding based on validated, broadly convergent experience, (3) reliably identified exemplary practice, including unusual know-how; (4) an item of information that a person certifies as valid by applying one or more criteria, or tests, and (5) the findings of validated research. The knowledge may take the form of an idea, a product, a process or procedure, or a program of action.

Technology is also covered in this literature review as the application to practical use of essentially scientific knowledge, often, but not solely, with reference to industrial arts, applied science, and engineering. Its meaning has been extended to include applications in design and organizational processes, whether in the industrial or the social field.

*Knowledge utilization* (or *technology transfer*), put simply, refers to the application of available knowledge or technology by a new user and, in some cases, to a new use. Utilization, then, implies use irrespective of intrinsic originality. Although this simple statement may serve as a "starter," the treatment of the subject as it unfolds in subsequent chapters will show it to be instead a complex process involving political, organizational, socioeconomic, and attitudinal components in addition to the specific information or knowledge.

*Utilization* and *change* are inextricably interrelated. *Adoption* typically refers to the initial decision to institute a particular change or to the early stages of acceptance. *Implementation* conveys the sense of a firm execution, at times in adapted form, of an "adopted" program, process, product use, or applied idea. (It should be noted that in the course of time the adopted or implemented element may be discontinued.)

*Dissemination* designates a wide dispersal or spreading in various directions, and refers often, but not exclusively, to the transmission of knowledge. *Diffusion* refers to deliberate (or, in the anthropological sense, to nondeliberate as well) spreading, especially by contact, of either innovations or established processes or products. *Adoption* and *implementation* reflect the intensity or depth of change, whereas *dissemination* and *diffusion* imply the extent or spread of information about a new or, at best, not commonly accepted concept or way of doing something in relation to meeting a given need or problem.

As implied, *change* may signify novelty in the sense of intrinsic originality, or it may simply refer to a new application of an old or common use. Of major importance is the distinction between *unplanned* and *planned* change. Implicit in most of the literature is a concern with planned change; nevertheless, realization of the impact of uncontrolled and uncontrollable impinging forces underlies many of the situations studied.

2. Why Study Knowledge Utilization and Innovative Change? The few statements that follow provide part of the answer.

"*Cresat scientia, Vita excolatur*" reads the motto on the seal of the University of Chicago: Let knowledge grow that life may be enriched. Yet, as our knowledge grows, our life is not automatically enriched by it. If knowledge is indeed to enhance our existence individually and collectively, that knowledge must reach the people who need it in a form that they can put to use. Putting what is known (and validated) to use is, indeed, the problem of our age (Glaser and others, 1967).

In a very practical way, the matter has been put succinctly by Glaser and Marks (1966, p. 6): "All over the world people struggle with problems and seek solutions. Often those who struggle are unaware that others face similar problems, and in some instances, are solving them. It is destructive and wasteful that people should be frustrated and often defeated by difficulties for which somebody else has found a remedy. . . . The gap between what we know and what we put to effective use bedevils many fields of human activity—science, teaching, business management, and organizations that provide health and welfare services."

In today's rapidly changing world, the need for more effective ways to meet new or continuing problems calls for the identification and rapid dissemination of the fruits of research, experimental, and demonstration projects and of validated exemplary practices.

The potential social benefits of scientific progress cannot be fully realized unless the knowledge is taken up by practitioners (potential users) at the decision-making level in government, agriculture, or industry or unless those benefits may serve to educate those who, now or in the future, may be expected to influence policy. Ultimately, the meaningfulness of all science, natural and social, rests in the ability and willingness to maintain a responsible dialogue between science and the society that sustains it (Burns and Studer, 1975).

A word of caution may be in order with regard to knowledge development and use. Knowledge by itself is always equivocal; it has potential for evil as well as good. It can be used for purposes that many consider socially harmful, and it can put new tools into the hands of misguided or oppressive, powerful people. And sometimes, when knowledge is used toward what are thought to be beneficial purposes, harmful secondary consequences occur. Frequently, as a technology becomes more widely diffused and used, such secondary consequences increase proportionately faster than the primary benefits. These often negative effects may lead to some degree of public reaction against technology and even against science itself. The primary benefits are often forgotten in the light of the discovery of undesirable side effects (Sieber, 1978). Consequently, the substantive evaluation of new knowledge and assessment of its complications for change are highly desirable.

3. **How Can a Proposed Change Be Examined Analytically?** Chapter Two contains sets of selected factors that can be used in the consideration of possible determinants of change. One of the widely used lists of variables is the set of eight factors (*A*bility, *V*alues, *I*nformation, *C*ircumstances, *T*iming, *O*bligation, *R*esistance, *Y*ield) under the acronym A VICTORY, later called "decision determinants analysis," offered by Davis and Salasin (1979). It serves as a procedural tool for (1) assessing an organization's readiness to adopt a proposed change, (2) identifying factors affecting successful adoption that may need to be attended to before any adoption attempt, and (3) guiding

the implementation process. Its application is illustrated in the incident described below, which took place in the office of the commissioner of public welfare in a Midwestern state. This incident illustrates how easy it is to propose seemingly sensible change, how difficult that change may be to implement, and how important it is to consider certain key determinants of change as a means for assessing the readiness of an individual, group, or organization to implement a proposed innovation.

The commissioner was responsible for the county welfare departments, which held legal responsibility for services to many patients discharged from state mental hospitals. His department also had authority for the state mental health programs, including the hospitals. Aftercare programs were of paramount interest at the time, and so he was an appropriate person to be approached about instituting a change in the statewide aftercare program.

The proposed change was an outgrowth of a major aftercare study recently completed. An important finding was that when patients were seen by the same worker during hospitalization and after return to the community, the probability of readmission would be significantly lowered. Stimulated by this research finding, a group of visitors, which included the head of the commissioner's own research program, together with consultants from the National Institute of Mental Health (NIMH) central office and regional office, called on the commissioner. They suggested a policy whereby county welfare workers would initiate relationships with patients several weeks before their expected discharge.

The visitors had little doubt that the commissioner would agree. He was known for progressive administration. Surely he would be grateful for this simple way to reduce readmission rates.

> After listening to the news, [the commissioner] merely lit his cigar, leaned back, and said nothing. So his visitors added that for aged patients included in the experimental group, their scores on the Minnesota Multiphasic Personality Inventory scale reflecting depression had dropped significant-

ly—again to a *statistically* significant degree. Even
with this exciting contribution, the commissioner
remained unimpressed. He had a few questions to
ask. They were essentially as follows, but the order
was a bit different:

"In your project, you used experienced
M.S.W. psychiatric social workers and public health
nurses with master's degrees. How do I know that
our county welfare workers will be able to match
the skills of your project workers? How will we
pay for the training programs necessary to prepare
the county workers to carry out the same aftercare
services? Where do I find funds to pay for their
travel expenses to state hospitals? Who will carry
out the work that they will be unable to accomplish while they are spending the required time at
the hospital helping the patients prepare for discharge?" (The commissioner was asking about the
ABILITY to produce the resources needed for the
change.)

"How will people in our hospital social service department feel about county workers coming
in and taking over a major portion of what they
have seen as their roles? And how will the counties
feel about extending the duties of their employees
beyond the responsibilities which they normally
carry?" (He was concerned with violating the assumed VALUES of the system.)

"Your findings sound almost too simple and
pat. How do you know the results you've obtained
did not stem from the high skills of the workers on
the project: and how do you know that their case-
load of only about six patients in any given time
wasn't the determining factor?" (The soundness of
the INFORMATION was being appropriately ques-
tioned.)

"In your project, your workers had their offices in a city very close to the hospital and the locations of the patients after discharge were also
fairly close. There aren't too many parts of the
state where things are that convenient. Will the
plan be feasible?" (The CIRCUMSTANCES, the commissioner was pointing out, would likely work
against the success of the change.)

"The counties aren't going to volunteer to

use their scarce resources for added service unless legislative and budget adjustments are made. The state legislature just met. How will I bridge things throughout the rest of the biennium?" (TIMING had not been given consideration.)

"Readmission rates already are respectably low. Who is so critically concerned about the problem that the increased expenditures would be warranted? Of course, I'd like to see readmission made unnecessary even for one patient, but it would help if the legislature, the governor, or at least some groups were concerned enough to back this change." (His point was that the OBLIGATION to change was not all that pressing.)

"The need for social workers in our hospitals would be considerably less. Some may lose their jobs. How will I handle their unhappiness? And the county workers are going to be raising Cain because of the hardships they will have to face, even if compensation is arranged. They'll have to stay away from their families during trips to the hospital, for instance." (The commissioner seemed to be reminding us that RESISTANCES had been overlooked.)

"The results are statistically significant, but will the improvement in the readmission rates be sufficient even to be noticed? Will anyone feel a sense of betterment for having gone along with this proposal?" (The reinforcing reward necessary to sustain successful change, the YIELD, admittedly was minimal.) [Davis and Salasin, 1978b, pp. 109–110]

The foregoing illustration argues for a cautious attitude toward the introduction of new knowledge. And caution needs to be tempered further with sensitivity to a series of factors (including resistances and barriers to change) such as are discussed in Chapters Three and Four. The totality of forces and events operative in a given situation may result in a phenomenon of delay termed "adoption time lag," if not outright rejection of the innovation or proposed change.

4. How Extensive Is Time Lag? An illustrative study of time-lag interval is that of the Battelle Columbus Laboratories

(National Science Foundation, 1973b) documenting the amount
of time required for ten innovative processes, products, or techniques to move from the point of conception to the point of
realization or culmination in terms of readiness for acceptance
in the marketplace. Obviously, these ten instances are not neces-

Table 1. Conception, Realization, and Time Lag for Ten Innovations.

| Innovation | Year of First Conception | Year of First Realization | Duration in Years |
|---|---|---|---|
| Heart Pacemaker | 1928 | 1960 | 32 |
| Input-Output Economic Analysis | 1936 | 1964 | 28 |
| Hybrid Corn | 1908 | 1933 | 25 |
| Electrophotography | 1937 | 1959 | 22 |
| Magnetic Ferrites | 1933 | 1955 | 22 |
| Hybrid Small Grains | 1937 | 1956 | 19 |
| Green Revolution: Wheat | 1950 | 1966 | 16 |
| Organophosphorus Insecticides | 1934 | 1947 | 13 |
| Oral Contraceptive | 1951 | 1960 | 9 |
| Videotape Recorder | 1950 | 1956 | 6 |
| Average Duration | | | 19.2 |

sarily typical of all innovations, and many good ideas *never* get
put to wide use. Conversely, many questionable changes are
made precipitously, without adequate "debugging" or assessment of undesirable side effects.

The factor of time lag is not a simple matter, reflecting
as it does complex psychological and social processes. Further,
the phenomenon varies in different settings. For example, a
study by Gee (1974) shows that the average time span for adoption or adaptation of promising innovations varies for different
countries—for example, 7.4 years in the United States, 7.7 years
in the United Kingdom, 3.4 years in Japan, and 5.2 years in Germany. The time lag also varies for different industries, technologies, product types, environmental conditions, and means of
financing.

Mansfield (1971) discusses the lag between invention and
innovation, noting that the lag may be expected to vary substantially because some inventions require changes in taste,

technology, and cost/capability of adoption before they can be used profitably, while others do not. Since the concepts of "invention" and "innovation" are not easy to pinpoint or date, Mansfield acknowledges that available data are extremely rough. However, he cites Table 2, prepared by Enos (1962a), who studied eleven inventions occurring in petroleum refining and thirty-five in other selected industries. It should be noted that

Table 2. Estimated Time Interval Between Invention and Innovation, Forty-Six Inventions, Selected Industries.

| Invention | Interval (years) | Invention | Interval (years) |
|---|---|---|---|
| Distillation of hydrocarbons with | | DDT | 3 |
| heat and pressure (Burton) | 24 | Electric precipitation | 25 |
| Distillation of gas oil with | | Freon refrigerants | 1 |
| heat and pressure (Burton) | 3 | Gyrocompass | 56 |
| Continuous cracking | | Hardening of fats | 8 |
| (Holmes-Manley) | 11 | | |
| Continuous cracking (Dubbs) | 13 | Jet engine | 14 |
| "Clean circulation" (Dubbs) | 3 | Turbojet engine | 10 |
| Tube and tank process | 13 | Long-playing record | 3 |
| Cross process | 5 | Magnetic recording | 5 |
| Houdry catalytic cracking | 9 | Plexiglass, lucite | 3 |
| Fluid catalytic cracking | 13 | Cotton picker | 53 |
| Gas lift for catalyst pellets | 13 | Nylon | 11 |
| Catalytic cracking (moving bed) | 8 | Crease-resistant | |
| | | fabrics | 14 |
| Safety razor | 9 | Power steering | 6 |
| Fluorescent lamp | 79 | | |
| Television | 22 | Radar | 13 |
| Wireless telegraph | 8 | Self-winding watch | 6 |
| Wireless telephone | 8 | Shell molding | 3 |
| Triode vacuum tube | 7 | Streptomycin | 5 |
| Radio (oscillator) | 8 | Terylene, dacron | 12 |
| Spinning jenny | 5 | Titanium reduction | 7 |
| Spinning machine (water frame) | 6 | Xerography | 13 |
| Spinning mule | 4 | Zipper | 27 |
| Steam engine (Watt) | 11 | Steam engine | |
| Ballpoint pen | 6 | (Newcomen) | 6 |

From Enos, J. "Invention and Innovation in the Petroleum Refining Industry." In Universities National Bureau Committee for Economic Research, *The Rate and Direction of Inventive Activity*. Princeton, N.J.: Princeton University Press, 1962, pp. 307-308. Copyright 1962 by Princeton University Press. Reprinted by permission.

Enos reported on what he considered important processes or products. The estimated time interval between invention and innovation averaged eleven years in the petroleum industry and about fourteen years in the others. As shown in the table, intervals varied markedly for different inventions.

A study by Lynn (1966), also reported by Mansfield, found that the "incubation period"—beginning with basic discovery and establishment of technological feasibility, and ending when commercial development begins—decreased (for twenty major innovations starting in the period 1885-1950) from thirty years (for 1885-1919) to nine years (for 1945-1964). The interval by type of market application was thirteen years for consumer type against twenty-eight years for industrial type. Private industry showed an incubation period of twenty-four years, compared with twelve years for the federal government.

A most striking case of time lag is reported by Mosteller (1981): In 1601, when the East India Company sent its first expedition to India, deaths from scurvy were reduced by serving three teaspoons of lemon juice daily to certain of the sailors. About 150 years later a somewhat similar experiment was successfully conducted. It took still another 48 years for the British navy to begin using citrus juice on a regular basis, thereby wiping out scurvy in the service. A delay of another 70 years— until 1865—resulted in similar application with equal success in the British mercantile marines. As it were, there was a total time lag of 264 years! Still, Mosteller cautions against haste in accepting newer practices without adequate evaluation.

An inventory of major advances in the comprehensive care and rehabilitation of persons suffering from chronic obstructive pulmonary disease found that many of the most promising treatment modalities and programs developed at some dozen medical centers in the United States were not widely known and used, although they had at least to some extent been reported in the literature (Glaser, 1968). Sometimes innovators, as they struggle to cope with difficult situations, are actually unaware that they have introduced a noteworthy innovation, so that no one ever reports the new design (Manela,

1969). In other cases, the research investigator is concerned with getting on to the next phase of his or her work and often begrudges the time required to write up the preliminary findings (Archibald, 1968; Bassett, Davison, and Hopson, 1968).

At a global level, the huge increase in the pool of knowledge may be an important factor in applicational time lag. *Twice* as much information was published in 1976 as in 1966. The number and size of journals, the documents in printed and nonprinted form, and the frequency of their issue have been growing (Lancaster, 1978a), although as Manten (1978) has shown, the number of scientists in the proliferating scientific fields has been increasing at a far higher rate. As the potentially available knowledge increases, the task of digestion and utilization becomes more and more difficult. Part of the difficulty lies in the great diversity of elements and circumstances involved, which reduces the likelihood of valid generalization.

5. **What Differentiations Are Important in Efforts to Achieve Utilization and Change?** Until recent years, too little attention has been paid to differentiations among the various types of knowledge utilization and change phenomena. Consequently, recommendations have often been expressed in too general a form to achieve practical effectiveness. Zaltman, Duncan, and Holbek (1973) stress the importance of reducing this generality by taking differentiations into account. One who plans to undertake a particular utilization effort must keep in mind the many considerations and circumstances affecting the particular case. It is then necessary to select measures in accordance with the characteristics of that case. Stated differently, each application of any principle that may evolve from a summation of individual studies of innovation is *contingent* on various characteristics that pertain to that application. This view has given rise to what has been termed contingency theory. An important question to bear in mind, then, is *"Under what conditions* does this or that strategy or procedure seem to be effective?"* The respective uses of various strategies are depicted in Zaltman and Duncan (1977).

Lieberman and Griffin (1976) affirm that studies in the field of utilization have been insufficiently specific. Hence, the application of known methods for using what has been learned about utilization requires (1) intentional and determined adaptation of methods to the particular case circumstances, (2) consistent and critical evaluation of their relevance and utility, (3) flexible analysis of feedback, (4) rapid, reasoned, and creative efforts to revise processes and procedures in the light of developing evidence of impact, (5) the relating of action to overall and specific objectives, and (6) thoughtful efforts to transmit to others the benefits gained from success or failure.

Warner (1974) presents a discussion of types of innovation in relation to selection of utilization strategies. But it is not enough, he asserts, to distinguish innovations solely on a physical or type basis. The *use* to which they are put constitutes a second dimension. Further, although profitability is an explicit determinant of the rate of diffusion of conventional market innovations, many quasi- and nonmarket innovations cannot be evaluated in dollars-and-cents terms; hence there are distinctions between profit and nonprofit activities such as are detailed in an entire volume edited by Zaltman (1979b) on management principles for nonprofit agencies and organizations.

The adopting unit constitutes another basis for differentiating among innovations, as do the characteristics of expected adopters and the origin of the innovation under consideration. Finally, Warner notes the distinction between modification of existing practices and installation of "new" innovations as a relevant factor in planning for utilization.

A sampling of literature depicting distinctions related to utilization and change—distinctions that might one day lead to a more systematic taxonomy—is marked by a diversity that makes classification difficult. Nonetheless, a crude categorization can be presented under two broad headings: (1) topical area and setting of the application and (2) character and scope of the change or transfer process.

*Topical Application Areas and Settings.* Literature on utilization exists within major disciplines and patterns of research and study (for example, physical sciences, social sciences); within areas of applied research such as government, business/industry, education, recreation, social programs and services; under diverse forms of organizations and operational programs; and in relation to programs of policy as well as operational development, technology, and administration. Each field puts its own stamp on the utilization process, for the particular area and setting strongly influence where, how, and why utilization occurs. Considerations such as (1) *geographical location* (urban, suburban, rural divisions), (2) *political organization* (local, county, state, nation) or (3) *form of political organization* (democratic, socialistic, authoritarian), and (4) *technological level* (developed or developing in areas of industry/business, education, or service) are all represented in the literature of utilization.

As an illustration of a distinction emanating from an area of application, it may be helpful to regard dissemination from two perspectives—as in the *economic model* developed by Ross (1974). Ross makes a useful distinction between two aspects of the dissemination process: (1) what he calls the "seller's" model, entailing the processes of initiating contact with potential users, sustaining that contact, and obtaining feedback by which an innovator works to achieve the transmission and use of the innovation by others, and (2) the "buyer's" model, the adoption of the innovative idea, product, program, or process by a "purchaser"—that is, the processes through which an innovation is sought after by a potential new user.

Applying these two models, one may then examine dissemination in terms of the process and problems at the interface between *producers and disseminators,* on the one hand, and *potential users,* on the other (Bhagat, 1977).

A further manifestation of interest in economics-type change is to be found in the wealth of literature dealing with *marketing.* Thus, the *Review of Marketing* edited by Zaltman and Bonoma (1978) provides varied coverage of the special problems and techniques affecting this form of change effort— namely, to induce modifications in consumer buying habits. That this objective has been made the subject of serious study is evidenced by the sophisticated coverage of systematic investigational techniques in a text on marketing research by Zaltman and Burger (1975). Wallendorf (1979) has studied the perception of clients of nonprofit agencies as consumers. The marketing approach has been extended to scientific and technical information in a treatise edited by King and Zaltman (1979), further demonstrating an economic view in much of the literature on change.

According to Udis (1976), while technology transfer is an ongoing process within most firms and industries, the obstacles to such transfer become more pronounced as one moves from industries to public services. Much of the criticism directed at technology in recent years springs from disappointment that critical social problems have not been much ameliorated by the application of advanced technology. Appreciable structural obstacles exist, particularly in the public sector. Public intervention through subsidy of research and development is unlikely to solve the problem by itself. Reexamination of sociopolitical values, priorities, and resource allocations in social institutions and in industrial organizations may be necessary before successful application of advanced technology in the social arena yields optimal results.

*Character and Scope of the Change or Transfer Process.* As might be expected, less radical changes are involved in borrowing an old idea or model for use in a new setting or activity than in introducing a completely new concept, procedure, or product.

The degree of change also affects the forms and means of dissemination and adoption. For example, to place a new machine to perform a particular function in a given setting is commonly seen primarily as an issue of capital expenditure. That focus may well lead to a neglect of the process through which proper utilization of the new machine may be achieved. Kraemer (1977) illustrates this very well in discussing the adoption and use of computers within local government. Without consideration of understanding and acceptance of the computers by those involved in its proper use, the potential benefits may not be realized. With thoughtful attention to those considerations, the investment may yield its potential.

Whitley and Frost (1972) note that technical changes involving marketable products are rather different from those that concern new ideas in service programs. The former give primary attention to semicommercial and full-scale production and distribution stages following a decision to engage in manufacture. The latter, especially if testing out a new program idea, usually emphasize the introduction of the program and tend to short-change aspects of evaluation, follow-up, and dissemination of the findings.

Egea (1975) differentiates the international transfer of "embodied" technology (such as products) and "disembodied" technology (such as concepts or production processes). For dissemination there is a distinction between the use of a *product* and the acceptance of a *process*. The communication and adoption of "disembodied" technology is the primary form of dissemination arising from the knowledge industries. In contrast, in business and industrial settings, dissemination more commonly refers to transfer and adoption of a product—a machine, a tool, or a technical program related to a setting or environment within which these sorts of "products" are used.

The Task Force on International and National Diffusion of Quality of Working Life Programs (1975), to guide the future of the quality of such programs, classified changes as (1) bringing about changes that *would not otherwise occur,* (2) *accelerating* some changes which were going to occur anyway but which the diffusers would like to see happen more rapidly, and (3) *preventing* changes which are coming on their own and which the diffusers would like to direct toward another outcome.

Haeffner (1973) asserts that the more *abstract* an innovation is in fact, or is made out to be, the more uncertain is the assessment of economic risks or expected profits. An innovation consequently will be accepted more easily if it is at what Haeffner calls a low "level of abstraction." However, a reading of his set of levels, given below, suggests that novelty also plays a part in the determination of abstractness, or the distinction between products and ideas.

- Level 1: An *existing* product, but cheaper.
- Level 2: An existing product that performs better in some respect.

- Level 3: A *new* product that performs the same function as an existing product, but is cheaper or performs better in some respect.
- Level 4: A new product that better satisfies another combination of functions than do existing products.
- Level 5: An *idea* for a product advantageous in ways that Level 3 products are advantageous.
- Level 6: An idea for a product advantageous in ways that Level 4 products are advantageous.
- Level 7: A product idea that in design or manufacture is based on a technical principle not previously applied in this way.
- Level 8: A product idea based on a new technical or scientific principle.
- Level 9: A product or process idea according to a physical or chemical effect not previously known.

The term "new product" means that the manufacturing method has been demonstrated in practice, and the term "product idea" that the manufacturing method has been demonstrated only in the laboratory [p. 24].

According to Fischer (1976), a significant distinction can be made between "horizontal" and "vertical" transfer. The former refers to the lateral shift of fully developed technology from one user context to another during the early stages of innovation, in which existing technologies are being brought to bear in creating a new technology. Vertical transfer, in contrast, is the adoption of a device that already fits the needs of the situation into which it will be put, thereby minimizing the problem of contextual fit. Otherwise stated, vertical transfer is the transfer of technology along the line from the more general to the specific, whereas horizontal transfer occurs through the adaptation of a technology from one application to another, possibly wholly unrelated to the first.

Gold, Peirce, and Rosegger (1975) set forth four specifications for differentiating new programs:

1. *Add a new* program—which may, according to Larsen and Agarwala-Rogers (1978), be a reinvented program.

2. *Displace an existing* program, usually because the present one has evidenced weakness or proved no longer adequate.
3. Continue a previous program but with *new operations* taking the place of the old.
4. Found an agency to begin a totally *new enterprise*—that is, one in which the agency as well as the program is an innovation.

Recognizing the nature of the new program allows the selection of appropriate strategies, thus determining the extent and form of efforts needed to integrate the new into existing programs and the extent of resources needed beyond those previously existing.

Munson and Pelz (1980) differentiate three levels of the innovative process: (1) primary innovating process, when no solutions to a problem are known to exist, called the level of *origination*, (2) secondary process, when a few prototype solutions exist elsewhere but are not well packaged—the level of *adaptation*, and (3) tertiary innovating process, when numerous well-packaged innovations exist—the level of *"borrowing,"* or *diffusion*.

In their introductory statement to a taxonomic overview of social change, Zaltman, Kotler, and Kaufman (1972) identify six types of social change according to a grid reflecting a short/long-term dimension on one axis and a threefold distinction concerning level of aggregation (micro, or individual; intermediate, or group; and macro, or society) on the other. At the individual level, Type 1 comprises short-term attitudinal or behavioral change, Type 2 a change in life cycle. At the group level, Type 3 is short-term normative or administrative change, Type 4 organizational change. At the societal level, Type 5 encompasses short-term invention/innovation or revolution, Type 6 long-term sociocultural evolution.

Barton (1975) presents four aspects of the interaction processes of research and social response:

1. Research to *measure needs,* leading to a decision whether or not to design a program.

2. Research that might lead to a *decision* on what kind of program to try—based on a study of the causes of the problem.
3. Research on reasons for and sources of *opposition to or support* for a program. Barton identifies three forms of reasons: program features, inadequate communication, and sociopolitical barriers.
4. Evaluation research to test *treatments,* leading to policy decision to continue, modify, or expand a program or not.

Citing earlier studies, Pelz (1978) reports on various distinctions in the types of knowledge available for policy making. Distinctions are made between relatively "hard" knowledge (typically research-based, quantitative, expressed in scientific language) and "soft" knowledge (non-research-based, qualitative, in lay language). Modes of use can vary from "instrumental" (assisting in devising a specific action or making a given decision) to "conceptual" (affecting a decision maker's overall understanding or thought about an issue) to "symbolic" (supporting an existing policy or discrediting an alternative).

From his vantage point as former deputy mayor and city administrator of New York City, Timothy Costello (1968) has analyzed the mechanism of change within the context of a political setting. Costello finds significant differences between the public and the private sectors. As types of change, he cites (1) planned change, (2) confluence of forces, (3) event-dominated change, (4) accidental innovation, and (5) external intervention.

Although this review covers a wide range in the literature of change phenomena, it touches only lightly on the types of sweeping discussion of societal or civilizational change to be found in such books as Peter Drucker's *Age of Discontinuity: Guidelines to Our Changing Society* (1968) or Alvin Toffler's *Third Wave* (1980); similarly with the extensive literature on futurology illustrated, for example, by Traub (1979). Such treatises provide stimulating background thought but fall beyond the more immediate practical considerations that constitute the scope of the present work.

**6. What Methods Have Been Used in the Study of Knowledge Utilization and Innovative Change?** The methodology used in the studies and articles reviewed has ranged from relatively objective experimental findings to empirical surveys of individual subjective judgment to conventional wisdom to generalization from a single striking case. A qualitative approach occurs more frequently than quantitative procedures. Highly sophisticated research techniques are the exception rather than the rule. The studies refer to *general processes* for facilitating knowledge validation, dissemination, utilization, and change, along with *specific efforts* for such facilitation in particular areas. Descriptive accounts share the limelight with prescriptive proposals. For the most part, concrete concerns predominate over theoretical considerations. Level of technicality varies. Modes of presentation suggest divergent intentions to reach a variety of readers.

The upshot of the foregoing summary statement is that the reader is left free to select material suited to his or her personal field of interest and preference for demonstrated proof. Not to be overlooked, however, is the thought-provoking potential inherent in the opportunity to share in the observations, findings, or conclusions offered by hundreds of thoughtful workers in the field of knowledge diffusion, transfer, utilization, and change as an outgrowth of their study of problems in various segments and complexities in that multifaceted field.

7. How Does the Review of Literature Presented Here Organize the Subject of Knowledge Utilization and Change? In this introductory chapter we have presented a number of references to distinctions leading toward a taxonomy of utilization and change factors as a necessary forewarning against overgeneralization. A further caution is in order because the separation of topics in the chapters that follow belie the central fact that the matter of knowledge utilization and innovative change is not a neatly arranged, step-by-step process but, rather, a "working together" of various factors at various stages, tailored to the situation at hand.

Thus, in Part One possible determinants of change are treated separately (or, at best, in the form of sets or lists) even though in live situations change-relevant variables interact in complex and subtle ways. Groupings within this part tend to separate the factors somewhat arbitrarily, according to (1) their primary reference to the individual project involved, (2) the characteristics of the participating persons, (3) organizational settings, and (4) the wider environment.

Part Two, which arranges the material under separate stages through which knowledge utilization and innovative change proceed, underemphasizes thereby the stage overlappings and interrelationships that normally occur. The stages depicted in Chapters Seven through Ten are somewhat artificially forced into a problem-solving mode as follows: awareness and assessment of needs; problem diagnosis and clarification; the search for pertinent knowledge; the consideration of alternative solutions; strategies for achieving change; evaluation, follow-through, and maintenance of planned change.

Part Three, though reflecting the general theme of linkage and communication, is even more diverse in its coverage. Here the work of change agents and agencies is first presented, followed by the general principles and the specific tactics of communication and information retrieval and dissemination. A chapter is then devoted to the international transfer of technology. Next considered are a number of issues and problems bearing on the relation of knowledge to practice, including the study of the impact of research on policy making. The last chapter of Part Three focuses on the extent to which elements of the utilization process have been synthesized or theorized to form systematic frameworks or models ranging from loose linkage of factors to highly integrated cybernetic systems.

The closing chapter serves to highlight some of the key insights that have been presented here and offers thoughts on future prospects.

## Summary Comments

There is an increasing availability of knowledge, capable—at least under certain conditions—of serving human purposes more effectively through the introduction of innovations that are better than standard practice. Generally, time lags between the various stages from conception of the new to development and widespread application are overly long.

Study of the phenomenon of dissemination/utilization of knowledge and exemplary practice, which implies change, has been undergoing change itself in recent years. More attention has been paid to this subject, and it has attracted a cadre of specialists. It is not a simple phenomenon, largely because of the great diversity of factors that enter into the acceptance, implementation, and institutionalization of change.

Beginning efforts to develop a taxonomy of the types of differentiations have been described in this chapter under two general headings: (1) topical application areas and settings and (2) the character and scope of the change or transfer process. This, however, is but a beginning. Change agents and change agencies are confronted by questions about the applicability of factors and of process principles to situations and circumstances reflecting particularity in so many respects as to bring into doubt the extent to which useful generalizations are possible except as applied to specified types of settings.

This chapter's preview of the several facets of the subject suggests further sources of complexity: (1) the interrelations among the various factors that bear on acceptance, implementation, and institutionalization of change and between the factors and the processes within which they operate, (2) the diverse conceptions of the stages of the utilization and change processes, (3) the numerous proposals regarding strategy and tactics, (4) divergent views on issues of linkage between knowledge production and use, and (5) varied theories embodied in conceptual frameworks or models of knowledge use and change.

Still another complicating factor is a lack of uniform terminology. The chapter opens with a brief statement of one sense in which such terms as *knowledge utilization, adoption, dissemination, diffusion,* and *change* may be conceived. However, the reader must still interpret from context the meanings ascribed to these and other terms as used by the several authors whose writings are reviewed. An equally important difficulty is the less-than-rigorous methods of investigation and analyses used in many of the studies and speculative writings reviewed. Several intrinsic circumstances account in large measure for the at times imperfect methodology used, among them limitations in resources for research, political pressures for predetermined conclusions, the multiplicity of causal factors in many situations, ethical restrictions on experimenting with possibly harmful factors, difficulties in measuring certain kinds of program outcomes, and differences in acceptable value criteria.

Despite these methodological limitations, the studies have served to clarify issues, generate hypotheses, and reflect a large body of valuable experience, evidence, and thinking.

# Part One

❧

# Factors Influencing
# Knowledge Utilization
# and Change

The effective use of knowledge or research findings to bring about needed improvements in conventional thinking, practice, and decision making (especially in organizations) is determined or at least influenced by many variables, functioning, as a rule, in combination.

These variables are treated in Part One, which is divided into five chapters. Chapter Two presents an overview of a wide range of influencing variables. These potential factors or leading emphases are then sorted out in the subsequent chapters. Chapter Three refers mainly to aspects of the new project, product, information, or procedure itself. Chapter Four considers associated personal or psychological characteristics that may influence innovative behavior, including resistant attitudes and how to deal with them. Chapter Five depicts the purpose, role, and character of the organizational setting into which the innovation is to be introduced. Chapter Six widens the inquiry to include surrounding political allocation of power and resources, economic and social forces, and ideological or cultural value considerations.

Many of the studies in Part One reflect the use of implicit

theoretical concepts. That is, they serve to identify certain key variables—grouped, perhaps, but not described as dynamically interrelated or connected with underlying principles, except by implication. These listings of variables, nonetheless, do not result from casual choice; one can readily "read between the lines" to sense, in most cases, a good deal of theoretical underpinning.

For example, the tenets of personnel psychology are sometimes seen in the discussion in Chapter Four of personal variables affecting innovative behavior. Although these variables are not ordinarily treated in an organismic, clinical fashion, dynamic implications can at times be seen behind the essentially "trait-type" treatment of the subject.

And so with many of the organizational variables referred to in Chapter Five. Here one recognizes the behind-the-scene influence of organizational theory, management theory, interpersonal psychology, motivational psychology, psychology of thought processes, social and political theory, communications theory, and industrial psychology.

Both speculative analysis and empirical data are included in the presentation of the determinants of knowledge utilization and innovative change. (These factors, treated separately in Part One, are considered more fully in terms of stage patterns and implementation in Part Two and in dissemination methods and the context of change theory or models in Part Three.)

It is only fair to say that innovation research that treats these factors as separate variables has come under sharp criticism (Eckensberger, 1972; Downs, 1978) because—

1. The so-called determinants of innovation have different impacts across innovations.
2. Determinants have a different impact across different decision units.
3. To speak of "an innovation" as if it had fixed form and content may be inappropriate, because it may not be immutable or represent exactly the same thing in different situations. (See also Rogers's, 1978, concept of "reinvention.")

Downs further questions the frequent assumption of linearity in the relationships of "determining" variables with the innovation variable. Methods used in conceptualizing, measuring, and interrelating variables in statistical terms are deemed inadequate for encompassing the complexity of the problem of explaining innovation, which is viewed as a *process* quite unapproachable by the correlational "variance" method. Mohr (1978) characterizes the approach as follows:

1. A process theory deals with events.
2. In process theory, time ordering among the contributing events is critical.
3. A process theory deals with a final cause, or end point, whose existence connotes the occurrence of prior events.

So, although for clarity we "take apart" the complex universe of knowledge utilization in Chapters Two through Six, the reader must keep in mind that the elements will be "reassembled" in context in Parts Two and Three as we discuss stage patterns, implementation/dissemination methods, and change theory or models.

# 2

# Determining
# Factors

Knowledge utilization and innovative change are undoubtedly determined or influenced by a variety of factors. It is not surprising that the literature contains many lists of selected variables. Some of these lists are considered by their authors as comprehensive, subsuming virtually all the determinants for predicting the outcomes of efforts or decisions to implement change. An account of a number of these selective inventories constitutes a good portion of the first part of the chapter. Then we consider barriers to transfer of knowledge or adoption/adaptation of innovations, among them the absence or inadequate presence of some essential determinants.

## Sets of Selected Factors

Lists of factors that bear on attempts to introduce change from current practice to something different, whether applied to projects, organizations, or concerned persons, have several purposes. Such lists can help to focus the attention of change agents—for example, researchers, research managers, inventors, knowledge disseminators, and practitioners or users of an innovation. Lists define key aspects of the total situation affecting the likelihood that a proposed change or innovation will receive serious attention. They (or selected relevant factors) also may serve a checklist function in the examination of particular situations for openness to consideration, adoption, or implementation of a proposed change. And they can aid in devising and applying strategies for facilitating the change process.

Although, as we have noted, the inclusion of variables in lists often reflects theoretical considerations, such sets of potential change determinants have come under criticism as failing to represent a theory of innovation or change. For example, Stolz (1981) states that whereas in applied behavior analysis, research is related to a coherent theory (reinforcement theory) and to a few powerful variables, in reports of the diffusion of innovation there are innumerable weak variables and no general theory. Referring to an earlier edition of the present review (Human Interaction Research Institute, 1976), Stolz finds not only lists of variables but, in fact, lists of the lists, which she regards as quite different from a general theory. Though recognizing that conclusions from an analysis of several instances of technology adoptions by government agencies actually constitute an additional list of likely effective variables, such lists do not provide a suitable overall theory. She urges a continuous search for such a theory. In this regard, she mentions the efforts of Stokes and Baer (1977) to develop a technology of generalization, "which they found implicit in the published literature, but which they had to draw out of that literature and then were able to summarize as a list [!] of techniques of varying utility" (Stolz, 1981, p. 502).

Despite the avowed limitations of "lists," what follows is a set of lists intended to identify the key factors that bear on the likelihood that an innovation will be adopted in a given setting. These lists provide the reader with a quick overview of likely influences affecting knowledge or technology transfer. A good many of the variables are treated in detail in later sections.

**Davis's Formulation of Change Factors.** Davis (1971; Davis and Salasin, 1975) has proposed the acronym A VICTORY as a mnemonic for encompassing the eight factors he considers necessary and sufficient to account for organizational behavior related to the utilization either of promising new knowledge or of validated innovative procedures/practices/products. These factors may be seen as determinants of how a given organization will respond to a particular proposed innovation. They are also relevant considerations to keep in focus during the process of implementing a given change or innovation.

The A VICTORY formulation, later termed the Decision Determinants Analysis and reduced to seven factors by combining Circumstances and Timing, evolved from a behavioral model of change, in turn adapted from learning theory embracing such considerations as drive or motivation, the ability or capacity of the learner, and circumstances or stimulus conditions (Davis and Salasin, 1979). A fuller treatment of the original form of the model is presented in Chapter Fifteen.

The factors, or elements, of the model have been defined briefly as follows:

A:  *Ability*—resources and capabilities of the organization (staff training, facilities, funds) necessary to implement, sustain, and evaluate the change.

V:  *Values*—the degree of accord between the values, cultural norms, and attitudes required by the proposed change and the organization staff's existing attitudes, values, philosophy, and operating style.

I:  *Idea/Information*—clear communication about the proposed innovation, including evidence for its validity and the techniques or actions needed for implementation.

C:  *Circumstances*—relevant factors operating in the organizational environment that may affect successful implementation, especially those active at start-up time.

T:  *Timing*—readiness to consider the innovation; timeliness for it to be implemented.

O:  *Obligation*—perceived need for or desirability of at least trying out the innovation, felt by relevant decision makers, preferably with support from influential staff members; "championship" for adoption stemming from decision makers.

R:  *Resistance*—inhibiting factors; organizational or individual disinclination to make the change, for whatever reasons.

Y:  *Yield*—expected (preferably measurable) benefits or rewards from utilization of the innovation as perceived by potential adopters and by those who would be involved with implementation at the operating level.

As the A VICTORY technique has been applied in a variety of studies and programs, particularly those associated with the improvement of mental health services, both the richness and the potential effectiveness of the model have been demonstrated (Davis and Salasin, 1975). The eight components of the model, for example, have been extended into a set of over forty questions one can ask concerning a potential change situation and a basic working list of about fifty prescriptive suggestions to which change agents can turn when approaching the task of achieving action or implementation of an acceptable idea for change (Davis, 1973a). NIMH also used the technique as a basis for organizing questions that can be asked in the conduct of program evaluation studies and, in collaboration with other agencies, has developed schedules or scales for use in assessing the likelihood of adoption of innovative programs by organizations or individuals (Davis and Salasin, 1975).

**Glaser's Formulation of Factors Related to Knowledge Transfer.** Glaser (1973) postulates four major factors as specifically related to knowledge transfer.

*Factor 1: Characteristics of the Innovation Itself.* Transfer is easier if the innovation has the following seven attributes in the acronym CORRECT:

- *Credibility,* stemming from the soundness of evidence for the value of the innovation or from its espousal by highly respected persons or institutions.
- *Observability,* or the opportunity for potential users to see a demonstration of the innovation or its results in operational practice.
- *Relevance* to coping with a persistent and sharply bothersome problem of concern to a large number of people (or to influential people).
- *Relative advantage* over existing practices (or yield, and incentive offered to change)—that is, the conviction that the

improvement will more than offset the considerable effort that change may require.

- *Ease in understanding and installation* as contrasted with difficulty of putting the innovation into operation or in transplanting it to different settings.
- *Compatibility* with potential users' previously established values, norms, procedures, and facilities.
- *Trialability, divisibility, or reversibility,* which permits a pilot tryout of the innovation one step at a time and does not call for an irreversible commitment by the system.

*Factor 2: Characteristics of the Potential Users.* The most relevant characteristics were found to be quite similar to the A VICTORY factors reported by Davis and Salasin (1979). One additional factor might be a leadership style that sets a role model of *willingness to entertain challenge* of one's own operation—a style that encourages a nondefensive, self-renewing organizational climate.

*Factor 3: Manner and Extent of Dissemination.*

- Early involvement of influential potential users in the planning, research, and development of the innovation is likely to help refine it, enhance acceptance, and increase the likelihood of utilization.
- Many potential users feel more comfortable in proceeding with implementation of an innovation if they can have technical assistance from a knowledgeable consultant.
- Personal contact between the innovator or knowledgeable consultant and potential users appears to be the primary source of learning about an innovative idea, and such contact contributes to successful adoption/adaptation.
- When potential adopters look for new ideas or products to meet a given problem, they need to feel that the search is legitimate; that is, they must not be inhibited by fear of being judged inept because they do not feel able to deal satisfactorily with the problem using only presently available resources.
- Innovations begun arbitrarily are apt to fall flat and be dis-

continued, especially if they are out of harmony with preferences of those affected. Nevertheless, a "fait accompli" technique can sometimes be effective if the change itself has
merit and needs to be experienced before its advantages become evident. Further, change is more likely to be adopted
where there is influential and persistent internal advocacy
for it, as contrasted with only outside advocacy.

*Factor 4: Some Additional Facilitating Forces.* Several of
the following forces that affect the probability of achieving
change apply to potential users as well as to the champions of
the innovation.

* *Leadership* that provides encouragement, positive reinforcement, direction, and timely follow-through for creative efforts to achieve improvement in operational performance.
* *Outside pressures* or environmental or administrative changes
  that impinge on an existing system and convince it that it
  needs to change—or force it to change.
* *An incentive system* that provides rewards for certain changes
  or types of behavior.
* *Strong dissatisfaction with the status quo*—widespread feelings of need for corrective action or change to overcome
  conditions that are perceived as seriously undesirable.

**Zaltman's List of Innovation Attributes.** Zaltman and
others (1973) offer the following list of attributes that are relevant to describing, explaining, and predicting responses to innovations:

1. *Cost*—financial and social, initial and continuing.
2. *Returns to investment*—tangible and intangible.
3. *Efficiency*—overall timesaving and avoidance of bottlenecks.
4. *Risk and uncertainty*—on the part of early adopters, lessened for later adopters.
5. *Communicability*—ease of dissemination and clarity of results.

6. *Compatibility*—consistency with "existing values, past experiences, and needs of receivers."
7. *Complexity*—of ideas and in actual implementation.
8. *Scientific status*—reliability, validity, generality, and so on.
9. *Perceived relative advantage*—the visibility and demonstrability of the innovation.
10. *Point of origin*—whether within or without the organization.
11. *Terminality*—point beyond which adoption becomes less rewarding, useless, or even impossible.
12. *Status quo ante*—reversibility and divisibility.
13. *Commitment*—prior attitudinal or behavioral acceptance.
14. *Interpersonal relationships*—impact on a disruptive/integrative continuum.
15. *Publicness versus privateness*—availability to all members of the social system.
16. *Gatekeepers*—number of approval channels.
17. *Susceptibility to successive modification*—ability to refine, elaborate, or modify the innovation.
18. *Gateway capacity*—opening of avenues to other innovations.
19. *Gateway innovations*—instrumental setting of stage for large-scale innovations.

These authors note that the attributes may apply differently to the different stages of the innovative process and to different organizations with diverse characteristics.

An essentially similar set of characteristics is presented in Lin and Zaltman (1973), with a chart listing characteristics of innovations as discussed in a number of articles published between 1962 and 1971.

**Havelock and Lingwood's List of Change Variables.** Havelock and Lingwood (1973) have proposed another set of project or change variables as a rating schema for diagnosing problems in the communication of new knowledge or innovations from any sender to any receiver. This set of concepts follows the acronymic designation HELP SCORES:

1. *Homophily*—similarity of characteristics of sender and receiver.
2. *Empathy*—understanding and feeling for the other and the other's situation.
3. *Linkage*—contact or relationship between persons or groups.
4. *Proximity*—placement of persons or groups near each other.
5. *Structuring*—evidence of planning, ordering, systematic arrangement.
6. *Capacity*—sign of affluence, talent, experience, wisdom.
7. *Openness*—sign of willingness to listen, receive, give, tell.
8. *Reward*—provision of financial support, security, esteem, status.
9. *Energy*—investment of time and effort, persistence, aggressiveness.
10. *Synergy*—coming together of forces, orchestration, synchronization.

High ratings on each of these dimensions are related to more successful communication and utilization of research knowledge, according to Havelock and Lingwood.

**Comparison of Adoption Factors.** Although all four lists we have discussed are couched in different terms, they are related in many respects, as Table 3 (pp. 36–37) suggests. To be sure, the meanings differ somewhat from list to list, but there is appreciable overlap.

**Other Suggested Change-Factor Listings.**

*The Battelle List.* The Battelle Columbus Laboratories (National Science Foundation, 1973b) studied twenty-one factors of probable importance to the direction and rate of the innovative process. These factors were selected from the general literature on the subject of variables influencing the adoption of innovations. Each factor was rated for degree of importance to each decisive event in the history of the ten outstanding scientific or technical innovations listed in Table 1, Chapter One. In order of significance, as measured by the percentage of decisive events to which they applied, the twenty-one factors were these:

1. Recognition of technical opportunity.
2. Recognition of the need.
3. Internal R&D management.
4. Management venture decision.
5. Availability of funding.
6. Technical entrepreneur.
7. In-house colleagues.
8. Prior demonstration of feasibility.
9. Patent/license considerations.
10. Recognition of scientific opportunity.
11. Technology confluence.
12. Technological gatekeeper.
13. Technology interest group.
14. Competitive pressures.
15. External direction to R&D personnel.
16. General economic factors.
17. Health and environmental factors.
18. Serendipity.
19. Formal market analysis.
20. Political factors.
21. Social factors.

The authors group or relate the factors to one another as follows:

Factors 1, 2, and 10 are related to various *motivational influences.*

Factors 3, 4, 5, and 19 involve *action taken consciously by management.*

Factors 6, 8, 9, and 12 *may involve management in some sense* but do not necessarily imply specific action by management.

Factors 7, 13, 14, and 15 describe *peer-group* forces that impinge on the R&D scientist.

Factors 11 and 18 are circumstances that are usually *unplanned or accidental.*

Factors 16, 17, 20, and 21 refer to the *general environment* within which the innovative process takes place.

Table 3. Factors Influencing the Likelihood of Adoption or Adaptation: Integrated Findings.

| Davis (8 Factors) | Glaser (19 Factors) | Zaltman and others (19 factors) | Havelock and Lingwood (10 Factors) |
|---|---|---|---|
| *Ability to carry out the change* | Capability of staff and availability of necessary resources | Financial and social costs | Structuring/planning Capacity/experience |
| *Values or institutional/cultural norms* | Compatibility with user's norms Leadership that encourages efforts to improve operational performance; willingness to entertain challenge | Compatibility Publicness vs. privateness Impact on interpersonal relations | Homophily Empathy |
| *Idea or information about the qualities of the innovation* | Credibility Observability Ease in understanding and installation Trialability/divisibility/reversibility Availability of technical assistance Adequate personal interaction between innovator and potential users | Communicability Divisibility and reversibility Complexity of concept or of implementation Susceptibility to successive modifications Scientific status Point of origin Terminality | Openness/willingness to listen |
| *Circumstances that prevail at the time* | Strong dissatisfaction with the status quo Pressures requiring structural or procedural change | Gateway to other innovations | Proximity |

| | | | |
|---|---|---|---|
| Timing or readiness for considering the idea | Sensitivity to context factors<br>Early involvement of potential users | | Linkage<br>Synergy |
| Obligation or felt need to deal with a particular problem | Relevance<br>Shared interest in solving common problems; internal advocacy<br>Need to feel that interest in change is legitimized | Commitment | Energy/investment of time and effort |
| Resistance or inhibiting factors | Skill in working through resistances | Risk and uncertainty<br>Gatekeepers or approval channels | |
| Yield, or perceived prospect of beneficial payoff from adoption | Relative advantage<br>Incentives/rewards for change | Efficiency of innovation<br>Perceived relative advantage<br>Gateway capacity<br>Return on investment | Reward/provision of financial support, esteem, status |

The above order of importance ascribed by the Battelle study to the twenty-one identified factors is probably specific to scientific and technical innovations.

*Havelock's Factors.* In another study that may be cited in contrast, Havelock (1974b) asked school superintendents to rate a series of statements pertaining to innovative procedures. The listing of procedures affecting the success of innovative projects in education, according to Havelock's factor analysis of superintendents' ratings, is as follows:

1. *Factor I:* Problem-solver perspective
   a. Maximizing chances of participation by many groups.
   b. Finding shared values as a basis for working.
   c. Providing a climate conducive to sharing ideas.
   d. Stressing self-help by the users of the innovation.
2. *Factor II:* RD&D perspective
   a. Systematic evaluation.
   b. Solid research base.
   c. Systematic planning.
   d. Adequate definition of objectives.
   e. Adequate diagnosis of the real educational need.
3. *Factor III:* Strategic manipulation
   a. Participation by key community leaders.
   b. Taking advantage of crisis situations.
   c. Involvement of informal leaders of opinion outside the schools.
4. *Factor IV:* Open advocacy and humane dialectic
   a. Confrontation of differences.
   b. Resolution of interpersonal conflicts.
   c. Creating awareness of the need for change.
   d. Creating an awareness of alternative solutions.
   e. Providing a climate conducive to risk taking.
5. *Factor V:* Financial capacity
6. Complex items
   a. Selecting a competent staff to implement change.
   b. Using a variety of media to get new ideas across.
   c. Persistence by those who advocate the innovation.

*Zaltman's Forces For and Against Change.* A book on dynamic educational change by Zaltman, Florio, and Sikorski (1977) describes in considerable detail, with frequent references to the literature, the following sets of forces for and against change in education:

1. Forces for change in education
   a. Performance gaps—discrepancy between what is and perception of what ought to be.
   b. Unrealistic expectations—of yield from product or service.
   c. Upward adjustment of expectations—dissatisfaction with present level.
   d. New personnel—with different and perhaps higher expectations.
   e. Awareness of pertinent new knowledge and technological change—stimulating pressure to apply.
   f. Change in power relationships—entailing different assessment criteria.
   g. Reference groups—comparison of accomplishment or rewards.
   h. Social value of output—resulting from changes in external conditions.
   i. Client group pressures—demands by students, parents, and public.
   j. External forces—social, economic, political pressures.
   k. Personal frustration—feelings of dissatisfaction; underutilization of resources.
   l. Other factors—such as changing type of personnel, more venturesome staff.
2. Resistance to change in education
   a. Cultural barriers—the "culture" of the school, cultural ethnocentricity, and the like.
   b. Organizational rigidity—highly standardized and routinized procedures.
   c. Social barriers to change
      1. Group solidarity—interdependence of members of a group.

2. Conformity to norms—guidelines of behavior deemed essential to stability.
3. Conflict—internal fragmentation militating against concerted action.
4. Constricted group insight—lack of awareness of interpersonal processes.
5. Hierarchy and social structure—inhibiting implementation of initiated programs.
6. Other factors—poorly defined authority, lack of rewards for initiative, and so on.

d. Psychological barriers to change
1. Perception—failure to "see" problems or possible solutions.
2. Insecurity—unsureness about self-performance, expectancies, and so on.
3. Homeostasis—tendency to return to complacency level when disturbed.
4. Conformity and commitment—prior allegiance to established ideas or ways.
5. Other causes of resistance—unavailability of resources, personal shortcomings.

It will be noted that Zaltman presents negative factors along with positive ones. He makes much of the concept of *performance gaps* as a stimulus to change, defined, in keeping with Downs (1967), as the discrepancy between what an individual or group is doing and what decision makers believe the individual or group ought to be doing.

On the opposite side, resistance to change (which Zaltman considers healthy under certain circumstances) is defined as any conduct that serves to maintain the status quo in the face of pressures to alter it.

*Roessner's Factors.* Using sources such as Gruber and Marquis (1969), Havelock (1969a), and Rogers and Shoemaker (1971), Roessner (1975) compiled the following list of factors likely to affect the success of technology transfer/research utilization programs:

1. Characteristics of successful transfer organizations
   a. Transfer organization credibility.
   b. Extent of priority setting; selectivity of products for transfer.
   c. Extent of resource organization orientation to user needs.
   d. Resource organization capacity: financial, personal, and motivational.
   e. Resource organization openness; responsiveness to user needs.
2. Nature of readiness of the item for utilization by others
   a. Product versus information.
   b. State of development.
   c. Extent of field testing.
   d. Extent of adaptation to user requirements.
   e. Visibility of results of application.
3. Characteristics of transfer agents and their activities
   a. Training and experience of transfer agents.
   b. Role of top officials in the field.
   c. Extent of person-to-person contact.
   d. Client/agent ratio.
4. Characteristics of potential recipients (users)
   a. Industry or service-area size and structure.
   b. Degree of competition.
   c. Nature of decision unit (organization or individual).
   d. Size of user group.
   e. Number and range of user needs.
   f. Dispersion of user locations.
5. Features of the transfer system as a whole
   a. Government regulation in industry or service area.
   b. Congruence of federal research priorities and user needs.
   c. Congruence of goals and incentives of transfer agents and user groups.
   d. Degree of difference between producer and user roles and interests.

Roessner used this list as a partial basis for a study of factors influencing the effectiveness of federal knowledge or technology transfer/utilization programs. Roessner noted that some of the factors could be changed through policy or program management decisions; others could not. He also noted that some factors could be used as preliminary formative measures of program effectiveness.

*Rothman's List.* Perhaps the largest list of potential change factors has been assembled by Rothman and his staff (Rothman, 1974) in a study sponsored by the National Institute of Mental Health. From a pool of 921 carefully chosen research reports on planning and organizing for social change, some 228 "generalizations" relative to change variables were derived. For example, a generalization on "personnel" notes that role orientations may be differentiated depending on whether the milieu is professional, bureaucratic, or client-centered. The descriptive statements, which are accompanied by "action guidelines" and supportive material from the sources examined, are presented in chapters bearing the following titles:

1. Practitioner roles—variables affecting role performance.
2. Practitioner roles—some dynamics of role performance.
3. Organizational behavior—contextual factors.
4. Organizational behavior—technology and personnel.
5. Political and legislative behavior.
6. Participation—voluntary associations and primary groups.
7. Participation—social movements, political action, client organization.
8. The diffusion and adoption of innovations.
9. Movement and assimilation of populations.
10. Research utilization as a process.

*Abelson's Set of Factors.* In conjunction with a study of teachers' responsiveness to psychoeducational ideas, Abelson (1970) analyzed the problem of transforming ideas into practice. He offers the following elements as a checklist of determining factors for examining the movement from idea to realization:

1.  *The ideas themselves*—their soundness, validity, significance, relevance, realism, source of support, relation to other ideas.

2.  *Communication and dissemination of the ideas*—complexity, precision, expansiveness in expression; "generalizability"; overtness, ease of practical illustration; manner of linguistic expression, style; form of publication; prestige of communicator.

3.  *Training and learning aspects*—the teaching or supervisory role of the transmitter; the role of the recipient; human and nonhuman communication media; characteristics of the teacher and the learner; attitudes toward ideas, old and new; style of coping with learning tasks, curriculum sequencing; preservice and in-service training; readiness and ability of the learner or practitioner to translate ideas into behavior.

4.  *Feasibility of executing the ideas*—sufficient time, money, effort, human resources; available logistics for delivery services embodying the ideas.

*The Central Theme Approach.* Some writers seek out a central emphasis, such as a theme, an idea, an area of interest, or an aspect associated with the complex phenomenon of utilization and change. Although these separate emphases may lack the desideratum of integration, they serve a useful expository purpose and draw attention to significant elements in the process as a whole.

The attempt of Sieber (1974b) and many others to present viewpoints concerning utilization and change processes suggest a number of approaches that focus on central themes or emphases. These are listed by Sieber as follows:

1.  *User-centered approach*—illustrated in the work of Fullan (1972) and the evaluation of the Pilot State Dissemination Program (Sieber, Louis, and Metzger, 1974).

2.  *Compliance-centered approach*—perhaps the sharpest contrast to the user-centered conception (Kritek, 1976).

3. *Administrative-imposed* or *management-centered approach* —closely related to the compliance-centered approach (Goldman and Moynihan, 1976).

4. *Change-centered conceptions*—sometimes reflecting basic motivations toward change on the part of key persons as a dynamic toward inducing change (Weiss, 1977b).

5. *Research-centered approach*—a logical outcome in the very conduct of research.

6. *Process-centered research approach*—drawing attention to the trend in recent years for researchers to pay explicit attention to the *implementation process* itself (Kritek, 1976).

7. *Economics-centered approach*—in which the profit incentive operationalized in monetary terms is a legitimate and dominant factor in change promotion (White, 1977; Hood, 1973).

8. *Resource-centered approach*—responsive to access to research and development funds.

9. *Organization-centered approach*—determined by the organization within which a change is to be induced as a spinoff from the organization's developmental needs.

10. *Expansion- or dissemination-centered approach*—represented especially in *technology transfer* on both domestic and international levels, where the very existence of a technological advance invites utilization.

11. *Resistance-centered approaches*—stressing employees' resistance to planned change within an organizational setting based on the structure of employee needs (Mealiea, 1978).

12. Finally, *person-centered approaches* emphasizing attention to personal elements that might be overlooked within other forms of change inducement.

*Other Leading-Idea Approaches.* Still another listing of what might be called leading-idea models is that of Ross (1974), who illustrates a variety of strategies that reflect the following specific emphases:

1. *Strong leadership:* Adopt innovations under the direc-

tion, and insistence if necessary, of the administrative head (such as president, superintendent) or functional head (such as controller, curriculum coordinator) of the target organization.

2. *Rational change process or management by objectives:* Adopt innovations by having the target organization or its consultant (a) sense problems or needs or state objectives and priorities, (b) develop alternative solutions, perhaps from prior research or experience, (c) evaluate alternatives using specified criteria, (d) select and adopt one alternative, and (e) follow up to observe achieved results.

3. *Response to a need or squeaking wheel:* Adopt innovations only after a need or problem, located either in the market or in the organization itself, is clearly recognized; then tailor the innovation to the need.

4. *Internal change agent:* Adopt innovations as a consequence of the active influence of one or several persons working within a given organization who facilitate communication and group attention to the value of certain innovations in better serving organization and group objectives.

5. *Adopting or copying:* Adopt innovations by observing a demonstration of the practice in a similar organization, then modify or copy it for use in the target organization; cause target organizations to adopt innovations by demonstrating the innovation in actual, operational use.

6. *Outside agent:* Cause the adoption of innovations by creating an agency outside the target organization whose special role is to introduce innovative practices in the target organization, usually through consultation but sometimes through requirements of law or other regulation.

7. *Incentives for change:* Make changes by offering financial support of a temporary or continuing kind on condition that the target organization adopts a specified innovation or any change drawn from a class of specified innovations.

The long array of determining variables and leading ideas, while reflecting versatility and inventiveness, presents a challenge to workers in the field of knowledge utilization and change to seek order out of diversity.

## Miscellaneous Factors

The above lists do not exhaust the variables associated with knowledge utilization or innovative change presented in the literature, as our brief sample of but a few miscellaneous additional illustrations will show.

The National Seminar on the Diffusion of New Instructional Materials and Practices (Social Science Education Consortium, Inc., 1973a, 1973b, 1973c, 1973d, 1973e) deals with the following questions that involve change factors:

1. Are there characteristics of particular *subject matters* that make products based on them more or less likely to be adopted?
2. Are there characteristics of *developers* that tend to inhibit or encourage use of their ideas and products?
3. What characteristics of *educational products* make them more or less likely to be diffused?
4. What characteristics of *schools* discourage or encourage the introduction and use of new ideas?
5. What *mechanisms within the diffusion system* encourage or discourage the diffusion of innovation?

Manning (1976) has developed a "Trouble-Shooting Checklist" (TSC) in two forms as a diagnostic and predictive instrument to aid educational change agents, faculty members, and administrators in estimating the effects of particular variables on an institution's potential for successfully adopting innovations. Checklist A deals with *dimensions of the institution.* Checklist B covers dimensions predictive of *suitability of an institution for a particular innovation.* Both checklists cover organization structure, personality and leadership styles, nature and type of communication used, levels of usage of modules and other instruments, and description of prospective teachers.

The Office of R&D Policy in the U.S. Department of Transportation found that effective transfer of research knowledge into useful processes, products, or programs occurred in two directions: vertical (from one governmental or industry level to another) and horizontal (from one functional area to another). Several factors contribute to successful transfer: awareness of user needs, user technical sophistication, supplier technical sophistication, reduction of risk-aversion tendencies, market aggregation, and program coordination. A number of mechanisms are available to accomplish this, including direct assistance, tailored documents, training, and demonstrations.

As has been noted, the aforementioned lists of change factors differ in their relative emphasis on determinants of change as they affect a particular innovative project, its organizational setting, and the persons concerned with the change. But they also vary in their usefulness to the several types of persons who may be interested in change processes. Those who are engaged in an immediately practical field situation may require a pithy, succinct set of considerations by which to work. Researchers in the area of change phenomena may wish to explore the possibilities of a larger number of variables, including those for which validity has not yet been fully established.

Both researchers and practitioners will have to consider the problem of interaction among variables (and combinations of variables) in producing innovative effects, including the study of forces operating for and against change. Further, the relation between a variable and its change effect need not be linear; there may be sharp cutoff points marking change from non-change.

Considerations such as these need to be kept in mind as studies of single variables are reported in Chapters Two through Six.

### General Deterrent Factors

Approaching the question of determinants negatively, a number of writers refer to the deterrents or barriers to transfer of knowledge or adoption of innovation. Others point to the uncertainty or "luck" factor. Still others emphasize what can be learned from a study of failures.

Many obstacles and resistances stand in the way of success in utilization efforts. Just as the study of successful utilization is instructive, so also the study of problems and failures may facilitate planning, adaptation, correction, and success.

The record of new program advances, though demonstrating many significant successes as well as failures, mostly reports developments that are only partial in their success or failure. Kotter and Schlesinger (1979) claim that most efforts encounter problems; they often take longer than expected and desired, they sometimes weaken morale, and they often cost a great deal in terms of managerial time or emotional upheaval (Luke and others, 1973; Miles, Fullan, and Taylor, 1978a; Zaltman and Duncan, 1977).

Hence, it should be recognized that plans may go wrong. This is not necessarily a reflection on the need for planning or on the adequacy of the plans. New or unpredictable factors may intrude and, in fact, most probably will. The dynamics of program implementation of themselves also introduce unexpected changes.

Mirvis and Berg (1977) and Berg (1977) performed an especially useful service in highlighting and analyzing instances of failure of innovative organization development programs. Mirvis and Berg note that programs fail because of such factors as incomplete theories, inaccurate diagnoses, inappropriate change technologies, intractable organization members, incapable change agents, and inflexible organizations. Such failures are often ignored or covered up, which prevents their analysis and precludes learning from them, thus leading to generalizations about methods and results that may be inadequately founded. Exploration of failures can challenge such generalizations and deepen the understanding necessary for both theoretical and practical gains.

As a commentary on these issues, Matthew Miles (personal communication) notes that, illuminating as analysis of failure can be, there is no guarantee that it will lead to understanding the conditions of success. Much "analysis" of failure is only speculative, of the "if only we had not done so-and-so" variety. In the absence of clear and precise linkages between actions and results, negative cases give weaker knowledge than successful ones. In most situations involving knowledge utilization and complex changes, "there are a thousand ways to fail but only a few to succeed."

Miles further observes that to illustrate this point, one might invoke the literature on school improvement. Historically, this literature has involved countless litanies of the supposed "negative" factors blocking learning, from "lack of readiness" to "cultural disadvantage" to "lack of discipline" to "dyslexia" to "student alienation" to "pseudo professionalism" to "outdated curriculum." The list is nearly infinite and has proved nearly infinitely unuseful. In contrast, the recent literature examining *effective* schools and schooling has identified a series of concrete factors that make a difference—high expectations for student achievement; a coherent, orderly environment; longer student time on task; and so forth (Rutter and others, 1979). Such factors are subject to control. In short, knowing what *not* to do does not necessarily tell one what *to* do. At the same time, we need to be aware that when things go right, we do not always know that it was because of what we did; an unplanned event may have saved us.

Because innovation is subject to many external influences that are uncontrollable by the innovator, serendipity and luck play a significant role in determining success or failure (Gee, 1974). Similarly, Gold (1975b) cites the solution of hitherto unsolved problems as involving a considerable amount of groping, with success perhaps more attributable to luck than to sheer magnitude of investment or to objectively demonstrable differences in staff quality.

Rosenberg (1972) points out that the "old" technology often continues to be improved after the introduction of the "new," thus postponing even further the time when the old technology is clearly outmoded. Adoption may be slowed as a result. Yet, curiously, it is a very general practice among historians to fix their attention on the story of the new method as soon as its technical feasibility has been established and to terminate all interest in the old. The result is to sharpen an often mistaken belief in abrupt and dramatic discontinuation of the old technology.

**Deterrent Factors in the Education Field.** Anthony (1974) discusses some barriers to change in secondary schools. He stresses organizational framework or structure as one frequently overlooked barrier to constructive change, asserting that many secondary schools are organized and operated like factories and that this structure is inappropriate for a school's focus, purpose, and goals because it is too hierarchical and rigid.

Avery (1977) evaluated the failures in efforts to implement an innovative educational program, Project Developmental Continuity. He found that factors contributing to failure included (1) inadequate planning by program managers, (2) incongruent local political, economic, and cultural environments, (3) lack of interorganizational communications, (4) poor reinforcement and follow-up, and (5) negative dispositions among implementers.

Ayscough (1976) sees the process of change in an educational center as learning to overcome such obstacles or blocks as (1) a predisposition against serious consideration of the innovation, (2) failure to understand what the innovation is and what it can do, (3) lack of recognition that the innovation is relevant to one's own needs, (4) rejection of evidence of the value of the innovation, (5) unwillingness to learn how to use it, and (6) inability to identify how each potential user can make a personal contribution. The head of a department or institution will also need to consider additional factors, such as cost (which does not normally concern the individual), effects on curricula, effects on other staff members, and relevance to objectives and attitudes at the departmental level.

Barriers to the implementation of an innovation in an experimental low-income school involving a "catalytic role model" for teachers, as contrasted with the more traditional authoritarian approach, are listed by Gross, Giacquinta, and Bernstein (1971) as follows: (1) the teachers' lack of clarity about the innovation, (2) the teachers' lack of required capabilities, (3) the unavailability of necessary instructional materials, and (4) the incompatibility of organizational arrangements with the innovation. The authors comment that the literature on change tends to focus on organizational conditions existing prior to the planned effort but gives relatively little attention to the period during which the implementation effort takes place. Since the time of their study, however, the importance of the implementation stage in planned change has received increased recognition (for example, Berman, 1980; Glaser, 1980a).

Deterrent Factors Affecting Innovations in Organizations. Myers and Sweezy (1978) studied 200 process or product innovations that passed initial screening but later failed commercially. They report that the majority of these were scuttled because of either uncontrollable market factors or poor management. Capital and technology problems, together with government regulatory procedures such as patent laws and antitrust concerns, accounted for most of the remaining failures.

Rothwell (1977) found that failures and delays in successful innovation adoption are associated with poor internal and external communication, poor quality of management and bad management practice, paucity of marketing effort, failure of interaction with potential customers, and poor development work. Management may back a loser. If so, little can be done at the operational level to retrieve the situation other than to terminate the project. This highlights another quite significant point, the *need for a set of "termination criteria."* Otherwise, projects have a tendency to continue under their own, often considerable momentum with a consequent, and needless, waste of resources.

There is no more effective stimulant for technological innovation than a clearly perceived market "pull" (Arthur D. Little, Inc., and Industrial Research Institute, 1973a, 1973b). At the same time, it was noted that the important barriers to innovation are more often related to marketing, finance, corporate organization, and the impact of government policy on industry than to technological factors such as availability of scientific information, uncertainty in solving technical problems, and limitations of scale-up and design.

In attempting to bring about equal employment for women in industry and business, Gery (1977) deals extensively with the types of barriers to change. She too speaks first of organizational structural barriers that include the policies, practices, personnel systems, benefits, communications, expectations, and accountability and reward systems within the total organization and within each operating unit. These factors must be confronted at multiple levels of the organization, since in many companies practices and interpretation of corporate policies and implementation of corporate systems vary so significantly by unit or location.

Beyond structural obstacles to change, problems may result from *interpersonal relations* among the members of an organization. These are not necessarily independent of the structure, but since they often cross identified structural boundaries, they may bridge or deepen chasms between structural components and, as a consequence, facilitate or impede changes.

David (1977) points to *over*planning and *over*management as barriers to innovation. As an illustration, an *undue* length of time for regulatory decisions may impede innovation, although intensive but expeditious planning and management do not.

### Summary Comments

At first blush, the number and range of possible determinants of utilization and change cited in this chapter are likely to overwhelm the reader. Various writers have tried to facilitate grasp by setting forth selective lists of determining factors. A table is included to show the overlapping of factors in four of these lists.

The reader may wish to consider how factors in the other detailed lists and additionally indicated approaches relate to those shown in the chart. A second strategy is to consider a particular situation involving transfer/utilization of some valuable knowledge, idea, exemplary practice, or innovative product and test the lists of utilization determinants against it.

Sets of factors, as such, have been branded as atheoretical. Nevertheless, lists are not unrelated to theory, in that (1) individual items are often borrowed from theories emanating from one source or another, (2) elements of a list may serve as the building blocks from which a connected theory may be constructed, and (3) a short list, such as the A VICTORY factors, or a selection of items from a longer list, such as Zaltman's list, may serve as a meaningful framework for ascertaining readiness for adoption or for planning implementation of a given program or project.

In any case, the lists are the products of careful study. The origin of the A VICTORY list, for example, may be attributed to considerable experience with mental health projects and to the stimulus of a highly respected learning formula that takes into account components of behavior such as capacity, self-expectancy, drive, stimulus conditions, and inhibitors. The Battelle list evolved from the abstraction of variables influencing adoption of ten outstanding scientific and technical innovations after the rating of each factor according to the degree of importance of decisive events in the histories of the respective innovations. Havelock's list grew out of ratings by a group of school superintendents of statements pertaining to innovative procedures. A number of the lists are based on surveys of pertinent literature.

Whether a list rests on empirical data, experience, or speculation, one may still ask to what extent the included elements "hang together" and what *kinds* of factors they represent. As to the first question, it has been noted that the A VICTORY formulation reflects the components of an acceptable learning or behavioral theory; in the remaining lists an integration of elements must be extracted inductively. (Havelock's list is notable in that he attempted to establish an orderly relationship through factor analysis.)

The question of the kinds of factors included may be approached by raising two types of questions. First, what is the nature of the influence or causation implied? Selection for inclusion in a list may be based simply on the observation of association without supporting evidence of causal relation. Where causation is implied, where does it reside: In the nature of the product, project, or process that is regarded as the "innovation"? In the probability that qualities of people who use or apply the innovation can readily exert an influence on its effectiveness? In the characteristics of the organizational or politico-sociocultural setting in which it is to function? These distinctions form the basis for the separate consideration of factors in the four chapters that follow, but it must be noted that the categories are not mutually exclusive.

Second, to what extent and by what mechanism is a given factor connected with other factors in producing whatever effect it may have: Can it operate singly, or must concomitant factors be present? Must it fit into a given order or time sequence—is it especially operative at one stage or another of the utilization and change process? Is the curve of its influence linear or curvilinear? These are the subtleties that need to be examined if the dynamic nature of a given factor is to be understood. The literature has addressed itself only partially and tangentially to these questions.

Deterrents, too, like positively stated factors, vary with setting and may be expected to entail similar interrelationship qualifications. Attention is drawn to them, typically, in conjunction with unsuccessful programs. Incidentally, an interesting question has been raised: whether one learns more from analysis of "failure" or from analysis of "success" in the application of innovative projects.

The conceptual and practical problem facing utilization researchers and practitioners is large—namely, how to make sense of such a voluminous set of variables. As the report of the literature (together with interpretive comment) continues in succeeding chapters, we hope the picture will become increasingly clear.

# 3

# Key Variables Influencing
# Acceptance of Change

This chapter distills from the literature those analyses and suggestions having to do with the variables related to the adoption or transfer of products, practices, or ideas (and their associated utilization strategies).

The presentation is made in two parts:

1. Studies of variables that are descriptive of or associated with given types of projects, programs, products, or information, placed for convenience under the following headings: relative advantage or yield; compatibility of values; comprehensibility; capability in terms of available skills, resources, and attitudes; demonstrability and trialability; championship by influential persons; and appropriateness of timing and circumstances. The reader will note that these variables are closely related to those included in the A VICTORY formulation. Resistance, covered in that formulation but not treated here, is discussed in Chapter Four.

2. Three illustrations, one from the education field and two from the mental health field, showing how multiple factors work in any particular situation.

## Interrelationships of Change Factors

In examining the characteristics of individual R&D projects or products or exemplary practices of any particular type, it is necessary to note two considerations: (1) the interaction of project, product, or program variables with one another and (2) the association of a given feature with elements of the change process as a whole. For example, the relative advantage of a new practice may depend on the timeliness of its introduction; the compatibility of a new procedure with user values may vary not only with the user's established values but also with the strategies used in attempts to modify existing value preferences. In other words, an innovative change of any kind is not an independent entity; it needs to be considered in context. This realization should prove helpful in analyzing project or practice characteristics as determinants of utilization and in devising strategies for facilitating appropriate utilization in a given case.

**Relative Advantage or Yield.** The greater the perceived likelihood of an innovation's achieving desired results in dealing with a persistent and vexing problem of concern to a great many people, the more likely it is to spark interest and to be adopted.

Innovations that appear to potential adopters to have relative advantage over existing practices, especially when espoused by highly respected opinion leaders, are more readily adopted than when relative advantage is not altogether clear (Hovland, Janis, and Kelley, 1953; Rogers, 1962a; Coleman, Katz, and Menzel, 1966b).

In the industrial or commercial field, the objective of achieving advantage through relevant and validated innovation, while possibly yielding benefit to numbers of consumers as well as producers over time, may be outweighed in the short run by the attraction of a low-risk profit incentive (Miles, 1964c; Glaser and Taylor, 1973). For example, a certain change in factory machinery might be an improvement but would be worth less than the cost of introducing it; therefore, in such a case it would have no relative advantage.

Changes that are inexpensive and can be accomplished

with already available materials, persons, and skills can be quickly introduced. As a rule, those that require large investments of money, time, and energy will come more slowly (Miles, 1964c).

Innovations in the social services may be hindered because their relative advantage is often difficult to assess (Rogers, 1968). "Advantage" includes psychological as well as economic or material factors, including remunerative considerations. Psychologically, an innovation also may have consequences for prestige, convenience, and satisfaction that are perceived as advantageous by the adopter. Or an innovation may subsequently require changes in the social structure of an organization that might be perceived as disadvantageous to those who feel their status is adversely affected. Economic factors appear even in public-sector settings. Bowman (1959), analyzing the motivation for community action in mental health, discovered that sometimes the beneficial "side effects" became important enough to obscure the original goals. For example, the funding allowance for "overhead" in a research grant may be more important in the mind of an administrator than the ostensible purpose of the research.

In general, some aspects of profit, as defined by those involved, are anticipated in any program or project initiative. Rosenberg (1972) defines profit in economic terms and from his long-term historical perspective demonstrates the diffuse and gradual development of economic gains from a typical innovation, its implementation, and the changes in its basic nature over time (a gradual downward slope of real costs). Social and educational program innovations presumably perceive profit as external (in terms of clients, pupils, or society, for example) rather than as internal to an organization, although certain types of profit motives within the organization may actually be more potent in decision making than those that are external.

Trattner (1977) addresses himself to the interactions between economic and social problems in the collection of, selection among, and ranking of ideas for research and development at national and international levels. He has adopted a formula, which he calls the "rule of the three Es," for selecting and ranking research or development ideas. According to the formula, *efficiency* is present when the *effects* produced are greater than the *efforts* to achieve them, or Efficiency = Effect ÷ Effort > 1. He adds forecasts of time frame and level of outcome in choosing goals and methods of intervention. Ideas for development are passed through a series of specific sieves to determine (1) whether the particular problem has already been solved, (2) the potential for obtaining needed research staff and funding, (3) the potential for efficient/effective implementation, and (4) the objectives to be reached (national economic, national social, and international). Each sieve leads to a forced yes/no (or go/ no-go) decision.

With regard to change in educational practice, Firestone (1977) supports the idea that effective change requires sophisticated understanding of the costs and benefits (and techniques) of change by those in positions of power. Yet, a decision to innovate may also be made on less than an objective or rational basis or for individual careerist reasons. Innovations are often selected without adequate consideration of how they will contribute to the solution of identified problems in particular or local settings.

**Compatibility of Values.** Innovations are more acceptable if they seem compatible with the user's previously established values, norms, procedures, and facilities (Rogers, 1962a; Miles, 1964c; Niehoff, 1966; Davis, 1971; Zaltman and others, 1973). A new drug "fits in" easily with customary medical practice; rather freewheeling use of subprofessional staff is a different matter and may be quite different from customary practice in some settings. A related point is that a potential adopter's main occupational interest seems to have a "halo" effect in contributing to rapid adoption of innovations most closely allied to that interest (Fliegel and Kivlin, 1966).

With regard to compatibility of value considerations, Becker (1970b) presents two positive characteristics in determining the adoption potential of medical programs: (1) practical value in the minds of professionals and (2) ease of communication to other professionals. Becker also lists six negative characteristics: (1) if the new program represents a major departure from traditional public health activity, (2) if it conflicts with important values in the health field, (3) if it might be opposed by the county medical society, (4) if it might be opposed by interested groups in the community, (5) if its use would threaten the health officer's reputation, and (6) if it would threaten or conflict with established economic interests.

Compatibility appears to be an important variable in the adoption of innovations in the field of mental health. For example, one study based on interviews with twenty-five practicing psychiatrists found very little impact of recent developments in neurophysiological research on private practice, although the psychiatrists were generally aware of these recent developments (Rose and Esser, 1960). This finding was attributed to the fact that the psychodynamic theoretical framework of most psychiatrists at the time of the study was not compatible with the theoretical assumptions on which the research was based.

Glaser and Ross (1971) also comment that for an innovation to be acceptable, it must be assimilated within the professional ideology of the potential adopter. They note that the field of mental health service delivery tends to be characterized by schools or ideologies to which staff are committed—for example, psychoanalysis, nondirective counseling, or behavior modification. The ideological orientation of an agency implies a coherent and congruent set of principles and techniques with which the proposed innovation must be compatible. Suggested changes to improve the effectiveness of administration, intake procedures, or treatment scheduling that do not challenge the prevailing ideology may sometimes be made by administrative fiat; but those that run counter to the existing school of thought, such as the introduction of group procedures in an agency oriented toward individual psychoanalytic therapy, would require a change in ideological acceptance before introduction.

It is a common observation that innovative practices are frequently in conflict with existing attitudes, customs, and values of both the researcher and the practitioner. When this is so, it discourages adoption. On the issue of conflict with the values and behavior of practitioners, Rosenblatt (1968) and Berlin (1969) note that much basic research is considered inapplicable in many settings and hence is likely to have quite limited impact.

Much of the material in Chapter Six on political, economic, and social factors also pertains to the matter of compatibility.

Comprehensibility. Other things being equal, a change that is easy to understand and to implement is more likely to be adopted than one that is complex and difficult to learn or to put into operation. Communicability of an innovation, especially in terms of having visible results, affects comprehension and hence influences adoption (Rogers, 1967; Rogers and Svenning, 1969).

Abelson (1970) reports that the "technicality" of a prescriptively stated psychoeducational idea, as judged by the investigator, is inversely related to its importance and its application to teaching practice, as judged by teachers.

Zaltman and others (1973) note (as have other authors) that complexity of ideas, as well as difficulty in their implementation, is a deterrent to the adoption of innovations.

Of course, information must be valid, adequate, and credible, as well as comprehensible.

In a wider sense, comprehensibility pertains to the subject of communication, discussed in Chapter Twelve.

Practicability Given Available Skills, Resources, and Attitudes. As noted by Davis (1973a), for a desired change to become actualized, there must be staff skills and knowledge appropriate to the change. In general, where skills are not already available, it is necessary to examine a projected innovation with a view to its teachability or its learnability.

Kraemer (1977), speaking of transferring a product such as a computer into a firm, specifies the need for competent personnel to assess the application and its suitability and to supervise its use.

Argyris (1974) has attributed the failure of most innovative experimental schools largely to the fact that those staff and board members who espouse freedom, mutual trust, and community decision making are usually unaware that they have been "programmed" throughout their lives for a behavioral style that tends toward controlling, winning, and avoiding negative criticism. In a later work, Argyris and Schön (1974) offer a prescription for the training necessary to bring actual behavior of teachers and administrators into accord with their professed theories.

**Demonstrability and Trialability of Proposed Practices.** Innovations also differ in the extent to which rewards are observable. The more obvious and tangible the gains, the greater the probability of adoption (Mansfield, 1963b; Glaser and Taylor, 1973). When people can see the results of using a new idea, they are more apt to adopt it. Hence, at least within the practical frame of reference of these studies, nonmaterial ideas have been found to diffuse more slowly than material innovations.

Changes that can be tried on a pilot basis in a few situations are more readily accepted than those that make an all-or-none demand on the entire system. This characteristic, sometimes called "trialability," reduces the perceived risk of an innovation and lessens resistance (Bright, 1964; Rogers and Svenning, 1969; Glaser, 1973).

The extent to which a proposed change is known to be reversible if it does not prove desirable may affect its adoption. Not all innovations can be discarded later with impunity; the bridges back to the status quo ante may have been burned. Situations in which the user need not "play for keeps" provide more opportunity for innovation (Miles, 1964c; Lippitt and Havelock, 1968; Zaltman and others, 1973).

In a research study on sociotechnical worklife conducted in Norway under a steering committee of the national unions, the national employers' confederation, and the government, the researchers protected both the workers and management by minimizing the extent to which either would be committed to long-term acceptance of experimental changes (Thorsrud, 1968).

If a proposed change is divisible, so that it can be introduced one step at a time, with opportunity to assimilate each stage before the next begins, it will arouse less resistance than more wholesale change would (Rogers, 1962a; Fliegel and Kivlin, 1966).

Before anticipating long-term benefits, Liston and Smith (1974) recommend the promotion of short achievable stages in implementing a long-chain innovation and reaching its ultimate goals. If each step is a clear-cut gain, motivation to continue taking next steps is engendered.

To counteract the concentration of attention only on the nature and qualities of the product (often the main emphasis in knowledge dissemination), Roberts and Frohman (1978) centered their attention on seeing the innovation in terms of *changes* of activities and *consequences* of these activities for the potential adopter. They viewed potential users as affected by the uncertainty involved in changes and their unknown consequences. They aimed communication directly toward reducing resistance generated in those prospective users who tend to become more conservative in the face of possible risk.

**Championship by Influential Persons.** Championship (or advocacy by influential persons), whether internal or external, may be added to the list of characteristics affecting the adoption of innovations. McClelland (1968) notes that almost no ideas or projects are accepted solely on their own merits. Fairweather, Sanders, and Tornatzky (1974) conclude that it seems necessary to locate small change-oriented groups within an organization—groups desirous of change in the organizational status quo—and then consistently to support their movement in this direction. Unless there is persevering action behaviorally directed toward change, no change occurs.

Of special relevance to championship is the point made in the National Science Foundation (1973b) Battelle study, cited in Chapter Two, that a technical entrepreneur (an individual within the performing organization who champions a scientific or technical activity) ranked sixth in importance for innovation, considerably higher than the twelfth-ranked technological gatekeeper (an individual who identifies scientific or technical information of relevance to the interests and activities of the researchers). As the technological gatekeeper would have a more intimate and continuing relationship with the R&D team, one might expect his or her influence to be higher than the technical entrepreneur's, but the data show otherwise.

Fairweather's studies (1971, 1973; Fairweather, Sanders, and Tornatzky, 1974) indicate that change is unlikely without outside pressure and guidance as well as inside championship. Davis (1972) came to a similar conclusion based on a study of NIMH projects. He found a need for pressure or advocacy outside the particular projects from the beginning if the projects are even to be reported in full, much less adopted. For example, before 1966 no grant-project monitoring or control system was in use for applied research at NIMH after the grant award determination. An attempt to assemble all the findings of mental health projects funded by the institute yielded final reports from only 40 percent. After the institute began (in 1966) to exert legitimate pressure through closer project monitoring at the *outset* of project activities, the percentage of final reports submitted rose gradually to 95 percent, where it has remained.

Numerous authors (for example, Halpert, 1966, 1973; Fairweather, 1971; Davis, 1972) have commented that many of the persons involved in testing or demonstrating innovative mental health delivery techniques are practitioners rather than scientists, and their primary goal is to provide good service, not to assess and disseminate project results, according to Davis's findings. Continued reminders of the importance of the project payoff are more important in service research than in fundamental research. Thus, the external champion needs to supplement the other project factors discussed above.

**Appropriateness of Timing and Circumstances.** The expression "an idea whose time has come" epitomizes an important determinant of "project" adoption. As an example, Manning and Rapoport (1976) examined the initial mixed reception to the latter's book *Community as Doctor,* based on a research project in a therapeutic community and published in 1961, at a time when scientific and policy interests in social-psychiatric ideas were declining. Later, however, it was found that the book had a quite widespread influence, and it was eventually embraced by the therapeutic community as a problem-solving guide. Several lessons, expressed as maxims, were learned—for example,

- The chances of direct utilization by subjects of an applied research study will be enhanced if the research formulation is collaboratively arrived at and the research results are fed back interactively.
- If, for any reason, collaborative formulation and interactive feedback are incompletely achieved, a defensive *rejection phenomenon* can be expected.
- Overt rejection does not preclude covert acceptance of many aspects of the research, particularly if there are mediating individuals in the action groups.

The significance of the timing of research and the report of its findings has been stressed particularly with regard to utilization of social science research by policy makers, especially those associated with legislative bodies. As van de Vall (1975) puts it, "Important for enhancing the project's impact is the researcher's ability to 'co-align' the stream of research information with the sequence of decisions in the policy-making process" (p. 23). Even research mandated by Congress or its agencies has often gone unused because its results have not been available at the time that budgeting or other legislative decisions had to be made.

Van de Vall also notes that pressures from an organization's external environment (socioeconomic, cultural, political, governmental, and pressure group) and from the "internal" environment (customer needs, employee demands, competing organizations, and task-supporting units—that is, sources within the organization's span of control) give salience to certain problems, thereby inducing change at a given time and circumstance.

## Multiple-Factor Studies

The vast majority of reports of research or speculation on knowledge utilization and innovative change are devoted not to single determinants but to multiple factors, often derived implicitly from descriptions of change programs. Three illustrations of this approach are presented next, to draw attention to the way determinants of knowledge utilization/innovative change are treated in sets rather than individually and the inseparability (in most instances) of *project* characteristics from *process* considerations, such as implementation strategy.

As an observer of the long-range attempt (beginning in the sixties) to revitalize the teaching of social studies, Marker (1976) suggests:

1. Considerable attention should be paid to *awareness of the potential innovation* among early adopters.
2. *Small trials* of the innovation, rather than systemwide or even departmentwide trials, should be encouraged at first.
3. Account should be taken of the *perception of relative advantage* from the adopter's point of view.
4. The more *complex* an innovation, the more difficult it is to push it into its trial stage.

Larsen and Nichols (1972) conducted a study to identify means of increasing the conditions that facilitate awareness and utilization of innovations by potential users. The study covered superintendents of 162 mental health institutions, 663 innovations, 577 innovators, 97 librarians, and 88 administrative assistants.

Results of the survey support the following hypotheses: (1) practitioners depend primarily on personal contacts for new information, (2) innovators rely on professional conferences for information and stimulation, (3) lack of funds often limits their attendance at conferences, (4) experience is regarded as more important than formal published research in contributing to development of an innovation, but in later planning and implementation stages the published works of others assume equal importance, (5) the degree of innovation is related to the amount of encouragement by administrators, (6) innovations are more likely to succeed when supported by persons who are to implement them, and (7) there usually is little interaction between innovators and the research department in institutions.

Greenberg (1977) reports on a three-year study that entailed, among other procedures, visits to a stratified sample of ninety-nine mental hospitals. The purpose of the study was to

ascertain the major factors associated with the change process in
state hospitals participating in the federal Hospital Improvement Plan (HIP), a program of federal subsidies designed to
assist individual hospitals in upgrading their care and treatment
programs. Among the observations made by Greenberg and his
colleagues are the following: (1) Paradoxically, the HIP program, which was designed to bolster a group of "have-not" organizations, has contributed to a widening of the disparity in
the competence of hospitals because of the tendency of the better institutions to take advantage of the HIP opportunity. (2) In
many cases relatively little planning was devoted to the HIP
projects. (3) In this study the HIP program was perceived by
hospital staffs as the most significant factor, among a large array
of factors, in influencing change in state hospitals. (4) Several
measures of project effectiveness were developed, including
success in meeting project objectives, impact on hospital, staff
reaction to HIP, project viability, diffusion, and a measure of
"generalized program achievement." (5) Project effectiveness
was significantly related to a number of predictor variables,
such as an institutional climate perceived as facilitating change,
pressure felt by staff for community contact, pressure for decentralization of authority and treatment, and staff attributes
such as increased competence and cooperativeness.

## Summary Comments

This chapter has examined in some detail several key, or
frequently cited, variables that in a sense are *primarily* attached
to the innovative element itself, although it is impossible to
separate such attachment completely from psychological, organizational, or politico-economic-sociocultural implications. In
most instances, the factor needs to be considered anew in conjunction with each of these categories.

Consequently, the full meaning of a particular determinant, such as "relative advantage," is fleshed in by various writers who treat the concept from different angles and as applied
in different settings. For example, assuming given qualities of
the persons involved, of organizational features, and of politico-

economic-sociocultural conditions, we need to ask: What is the likely impact of variations in the project factor designated relative advantage, or yield?

Since the resulting possible combinations will prove numerous indeed, the exercises will have to be limited to a few combinations of component considerations. As a practical matter, investigators and practitioners tend to use the suggested type of analysis with the limiting understanding that a given program characteristic will operate under conditions that apply to persons functioning under typical American organizations and institutions.

It is of interest to note that a number of the variables chosen for special treatment in this chapter were first introduced by Rogers in his reports of the diffusion particularly of new agricultural methods. The factors described in the chapter are also related to the A VICTORY characteristics, which, like Rogers's variables, have stood up under considerable testing in explaining and predicting practical adoption and implementation outcomes.

The treatment of these factors in the present chapter is supplemented by references elsewhere in this review. For example, in the discussion of the taxonomy of factors in Chapter One, the distinction between product, or "embodied," variables versus process, or "disembodied," variables bears on the subject of project characteristics. Similarly, a number of deterrents referred to in Chapter Two also pertain to project qualities. Individual factors emerge again in the treatment of the stages of the utilization/change process, in the account of the linkage between knowledge production and use, and in the references to the search for underlying theories.

# 4

# Personal and Social
# Influences

Characteristics of people, their social roles, possible vested interests, and attitudinal resistance may strongly affect the readiness of individuals or organizations to adopt an innovation, with its accompaniment of change. From initial knowledge production to ultimate utilization and change, people form a chain of weak and strong links. Transmitters and receivers alike play active or passive roles to a varying degree. Leaders and followers are involved, as are individuals and groups. The phenomenon of psychological resistance often overlays the process.

Studies reported in this chapter touch on these and related matters.

## Psychosocial Considerations

**Age, Tenure, and Vested Interest.** Several studies (for example, Rogers, 1962a) report that younger people are more attracted by innovation than their elders are, but more recent observations have tended to reduce the stereotype of senior citizens as adhering to the "good old days" (and ways). Marcum (1968) found younger educators in the more innovative schools; however, Lippitt and others (1967) reported the middle-age range most tradition-minded, older as well as younger teachers being more responsive to innovative proposals.

Although discussion abounds of the alleged decline in productivity with tenure, we located few reports on the relation of tenure to innovativeness. In a theoretical discussion, Griffiths (1964) proposes that the number of innovative programs or procedures is inversely proportional to the tenure of the chief administrator in an organization. He also asserts that change is more likely to occur if the successor to the chief administrator is from outside the organization.

In a study of the relation between school administrative and faculty turnover and the diffusion of educational innovations, Keith (1975) found that the continuity provided by low rates of administrative succession was not a necessary condition for the implementation of innovations. Turnover at lower levels of the organization proved to have clearer negative effect on the diffusion of innovation than turnover in the administrative hierarchy.

Strong vested interests can obviously constitute powerful barriers to the introduction of change (Watson and Glaser, 1965; Glaser and Ross, 1971). A tendency to preserve the status quo in methods of operation, whether for psychological, economic, ideological, political, or other reasons, may be present at various levels within an organization.

In a controlled study among junior high school teachers, O'Reilly and Fish (1976) found that resistance to educational innovation, as measured by the Educational Innovation Attitude Scale (EIAS), developed by Ramer in 1967, becomes more pronounced with tenure status (from school personnel records). Also in the study by O'Reilly and Fish, on a twenty-item dogmatism scale developed by Troldahl and Powell in 1965, the longer-tenured teachers had, on the average, scores indicating greater dogmatism than shorter-tenured teachers. However, to discover the intrinsic relations between age and innovativeness, it would be necessary to partial out associated factors such as presence of long-established lesson plans, improved status, and increased possessions that reflect vested interests.

**Economic and Social Status.** As with the "capacity factor" in organizations, an above-average economic status seems to encourage positive attitudes toward innovation. Rogers and Svenning (1969) found that persons with higher social status and more education were more likely to learn of an innovation and to try it. Moreover, studies of social revolutions have shown that leadership does not come from the most deprived individuals but from those already on their way up. Preoccupation with survival exhausts the energies of the very poor.

The fact that the National Teacher Corps (which was set up to train teachers to improve the quality of education in low-income area schools) attracted young, liberal, and unconventional trainees outside the usual group of prospective teachers is said to have contributed to the innovativeness of that program (Corwin, 1972b).

**Professional Qualities and Social Contacts.** Becker (1970b) applied the technique of the sociogram, developed by Moreno (1953), to reveal communication networks among colleagues in the study of diffusion of innovation among professionals. Using this technique in the study of public health officials, Becker (1970a) found that the well-respected scientist or professional tends to become an opinion leader and hence exerts an influence on innovative adoption.

Success in one's work bears examination, however. Although a feeling of personal security is often a prerequisite to accepting innovation, successful practitioners in any profession often feel little need to change (LaPiere, 1965; Berlin, 1969). A person may be eager for innovative change because he or she has been unsuccessful in the status quo, but more frequently it is because the individual's earlier innovative efforts have attracted attention and helped his or her upward mobility (LaPiere, 1965).

"Cosmopoliteness," or orientation and contact outside a particular social system, is another characteristic of innovative persons (Katz, 1961; Rogers, 1962a). The remark attributed to E. L. Thorndike is relevant here: "The mother of invention is not necessity; it is the knowledge of other people's inventions." Contact with a stimulating number and variety of persons and institutions provides a good background for conceiving fresh combinations. Coleman, Katz, and Menzel (1966a, 1966b) found that earlier adopters of a new therapeutic drug were doctors who read more journals and went to more professional meetings. A similar point was made about school superintendents by Hemphill, Griffiths, and Fredericksen (1962). A study of university faculty members found that proinnovation faculty members had taught at more institutions than those who showed significantly less interest in proposed innovations (Evans and Leppmann, 1968).

A variant of "cosmopoliteness" may be found in the concept of "role accumulators" as illustrated by Zaltman and Wallendorf (1979) in referring to a marketing study of influential persons with respect to new fashion buying. The authors assert that while innovators, opinion leaders, and gatekeepers are important people in the marketplace, there is yet another important, discernible group: role accumulators. They are members of many nonoverlapping social networks and thus "get around more" with many different types of groups. Literature is reported in support of the following propositions:

1. The greater the degree of role accumulation, the earlier (relative to the time of introduction) the person will become aware of the innovation and will adopt it.
2. The greater the degree of role accumulation, the more frequently a person will initiate interpersonal communications about innovations.
3. The greater the degree of role accumulation, the more frequently others will communicate about innovations with the role accumulator.
4. There is less overlap in role-accumulator ratings than between any pair of the following three: innovators, opinion leaders, or gatekeepers.

Whether the role-accumulator influence in fashion matters can be generalized to other marketing or wider contacts is a matter for future research.

Lippitt and others (1967) and McClelland (1968) both note that innovators are aware of more sources of information and are more familiar with research than noninnovators. It may be that the higher sense of personal security that tends to characterize innovators is based in part on confidence in their own knowledge.

Keeping up with the literature in one's field is evidently related to professional attitude. In a survey of some 3,000 engineers and scientists, mainly for the purpose of determining how scientists and engineers in industrial research and development acquire technical information useful in their work, Rosenbloom and Wolek (1970) found that those with a high degree of commitment to the job tended to pursue formal education and to use professional publications more often, and local sources of information less often, than the average respondent.

Rogers (1967) suggests that the professionalism of potential adopters is an important influence on diffusion of innovation. An interesting twist is suggested by a study of organizational factors affecting the success of innovative staff proposals submitted to line management in business organizations. Among the characteristics of organizations in which proposals were more likely to be successful were (1) a higher degree of professionalization of staff personnel and (2) a lower degree of professionalization of management (Evan and Black, 1967).

Havelock (1969a) indicates that the main effect of professionalism of staff is the entry, or input, of new knowledge into the organization. Further support for this idea is provided by Aiken and Hage (1968). These investigators found that the amount of extraorganizational professional activity (probably related to cosmopoliteness) was highly and positively correlated with organizational rate of new-program implementation. Amount of professional training in itself, however, did not appear significantly associated with rate of innovation.

However, using *professionalism* in the sense of professional status in an organization, Beyer and Trice (1978) found that top-level professionals, compared with lower-level personnel, tended to be somewhat indifferent to implementation of two federally mandated laws, one affecting alcoholism among federal employees and the other dealing with equal employment opportunity.

**Personality and Role of the Leader.** Mansfield (1963b,

1968b), after extensive studies of innovation among industrial firms, suggests that the personality traits, interests, training, and other characteristics of top and middle management may significantly determine how quickly a firm introduces an innovation. The same is true of knowledge dissemination, according to Havelock (1969a) and Glaser (1973).

In studying a plant in which successful change occurred, Guest (1962) placed considerable stress on the role of a new manager, because in this instance the formal structure of the plant and a number of other features remained unchanged. On the basis of his experience in studying this plant and his review of the literature, Guest concluded that (1) the head of an organization should induce all concerned to focus on organizational requirements rather than particular requirements of the head person, (2) achievement of goals requires an interdependence between the leader and subordinates, (3) to achieve results, the leader has to integrate other needs of subordinates with the requirements of top management, (4) the leader's authority needs to be exercised in playing the dual role of the group's representative to higher management and higher management's representative to the group, (5) the leader should be aware of and utilize horizontal as well as vertical communication, (6) the leader should encourage the enlargement of his or her own "span of cognition" as well as that of subordinates, and (7) he or she should encourage the generation of many decisions from the interaction of primary groups within the organization.

Whether the *manager* or the *organization* should be the primary target for change is the subject of an article by Burke and Schmidt (1971). While comparing the respective difficulties and characteristics of the two thrusts, the authors stress the reciprocal relation between the two and the importance of attending to both the manager and the organization.

The context in which a leader functions is further considered by Rubin, Plovnik, and Fry (1974), who comment that the leader's role as an innovator may be circumscribed by various conventions and circumstances. For example, the role of administration in a community health center may be influenced by the fact that the administrator, if not a physician, may be sub-

ordinated to an M.D. with set views. Feedback is usually limited
to responses of individual patients, who are not likely to be
aware of larger-scale organizational matters. Moreover, in such
agencies the bringing out into the open of any existing conflicts is seldom good politics or an effective way of raising
needed funds.

Although the characteristics of organizational leaders appear to influence organizational innovation significantly, it may
be erroneous to regard the "innovativeness" of officials as only
a matter of their own personal traits. They are required to be
functionaries. They occupy a certain position in a system and
are expected to act the corresponding role (Sieber, 1968). They
are subject to sanctions for unacceptable deviations (Rubin,
Plovnik, and Fry, 1974). As Carter (1968a) observes, all too
often the "gatekeeper" of change in educational and other social institutions is politically rather than professionally oriented.
That such persons become more alert to shifting pressures than
to research findings would seem to follow.

In any hierarchical organization, subordinates become
highly sensitive to the values and preferences of persons in higher positions. Rogers (1962a) asserts that there is a positive relationship between the rate of collective innovation and the degree of power concentration in a system. In any case, support
by top leadership will be a strong factor in bringing about
change (Mansfield, 1963b; Sieber, 1968; Glaser, 1973).

Somewhat offsetting the strategy of change from the top
down is the fact that subordinates often can and do subvert
changes of which they disapprove, while appearing to conform.
Changes instituted by the authoritarian approach are more
likely to be discontinued than those that evolve from a participative approach (Rogers and Shoemaker, 1971). Glaser (1976)
confirms this finding.

If there is a sensing unit to report emerging needs for
change, the critical question then becomes the relationship of
this intelligence service to the responsible decision makers who
are the gatekeepers of innovation (Glock, 1961; Paisley, 1968).
If the gatekeepers of innovation (often top management of the
organization) truly provide a nondefensive climate that encour-

ages and rewards challenge from within, and at all levels, then essentially all members of the organization are encouraged to become sensing units and, further, to participate in developing responses to identified problems or needs (Glaser and Taylor, 1973).

Glaser and Ross (1971), aware of the need for internal advocacy to overcome barriers, note that adoption strategy should be designed with the creation of internal advocacy in mind. Effective innovation is seen as involving intervention by leaders who focus staff attention on agency problems, stimulate initiative, support risk taking and experimentation, and provide recognition of innovative staff members. In formulating innovation and utilization strategies, the inclusion of leaders skilled in the above practices is an important consideration.

Along with effective internal leadership, championship and support by an outside change agent or knowledge specialist is helpful (Fairweather, Sanders, and Tornatzky, 1974). The combination of innovative leadership involving outside and inside personnel was found to be the leading factor in a list of factors studied by Corwin (1972b) in conjunction with a review of ten Teacher Corps programs in urban and rural areas.

Leadership in the diffusion of innovation is not limited to hierarchical leadership. Certain influential individuals within colleague reference groups or peer groups function in the role of opinion leaders. Involvement of opinion leaders as advocates of new ideas is an effective strategy of planned change (Rogers, 1962a; Rogers and Shoemaker, 1971).

The significance of the role of opinion leaders in furthering innovation is treated in a number of studies. For example, Becker (1970a) found a high correlation between the centrality of a health officer in the communication network and his cosmopoliteness.

Andrews and Farris (1967) report the results of two analyses exploring the relation between supervisory practices and scientific performance. The findings suggest that the supervisor may play an important role in enhancing or depressing innovation. Greatest innovation occurred under supervisors who knew the technical details of their subordinates' work, who could critically evaluate that work, and who could influence work goals. If a supervisor's technical competence has become obsolete or if less favorable conditions surround the work situation, the data suggest providing substantial freedom to subordinates. Further, freeing supervisors from responsibilities in the human relations and administrative areas may enhance innovation.

**Staff Morale and Cohesiveness.** Several studies relate high staff morale to organizational innovativeness (Chesler and Fox, 1967; Glaser and Ross, 1971). Actually, high morale would appear to be another effect of the same factors that facilitate organizational innovativeness. Level of staff morale, then, might serve as a good indicator of organizational climate.

Staff cohesiveness appears positively related to innovative organizations (Miles, 1965). Like high staff morale, this characteristic would seem to be a product of a positive organizational climate.

Miles and others (1971) studied survey feedback as a method of planned organizational change. When presentation of collected data was made at survey feedback meetings of work-related groups, the resulting interaction increased mutual liking among the interacting parties and, at the same time, increased pressure for conformity to group norms. If these norms favored change, then change became more likely.

Physical and social distance between members and subunits of an organization and between sources of innovation and potential adopters impedes innovation and diffusion (Rogers, 1967; Havelock, 1969a).

A qualifying consideration is the finding that satisfying social relations among staff may operate against change and may be characteristic of a "closed" organizational climate (Aiken and Hage, 1968).

As even this brief reference to the relation of morale and cohesiveness to change potential may suggest, behavior is likely to be influenced in subtle ways by social relationships.

The relation between interpersonal attitudes and actual behavior is not a simple one. Although generalizations may not be in order, an indirectly confirming study by Mann (1971) notes that classroom-type training in human relations does not assure translation of such learning to job performance and, in the situation studied, had little effect on the behavior of plant foremen. Related to this is the observation by Fairweather (1973; Fairweather, Sanders, and Tornatzky, 1974) that change-oriented attitudes do not necessarily result in change-oriented behavior.

O'Keefe, Kernaghan, and Rubenstein (1975) detail the use of the concept of group cohesiveness (and the activity of information gatekeepers) to predict the adoption or nonadoption of a new information system introduced experimentally into the work environments of twelve existing scientific groups (biomedical researchers and clinicians) within six metropolitan hospitals. Group cohesiveness was highly correlated with the presence of a gatekeeper, often the group's supervisor. Even where the gatekeeper was not the supervisor, group cohesiveness tended to facilitate utilization of the new information system. Cohesiveness was also highly correlated with a high adoption rate. In sum, the results of the study suggest that the degree of group cohesiveness, coupled with the influence of the group's gatekeeper and supervisor, were important determinants of the willingness of the scientists to use the new information system.

As a general principle, staff members have many differing roles in selecting and implementing new programs and projects. Johnson and Johnson (1977), expressing an interest in stimulating change in criminal justice operations, suggest that persons working to achieve organizational change from below the management level, though deprived of authority, have several strategic options open to them, such as collaboration and negotiation. Involvement usually differs, and probably should, between those who are placed in positions that will be directly affected by an innovation and those who will experience only repercussions from its introduction.

In reference to maintaining staff morale, Mealiea (1978) adds to the picture of complexity of role changes by pointing out that to remain viable, the employee is forced to upgrade old skills or develop new ones. However, this may not be feasible because of time constraints, lack of support facilities, or inability of the employee to learn. As a result, employees often see change as a threat to their existence within the organization. Rules, policies, and procedures frequently become habits for the individual and are relied on for both guidance and protection; that is, they act as a zone of security for the individual. When introduced, change typically reduces the applicability of established habits, and the employee must now face a changed and unfamiliar job environment without a zone of security. This demand is likely to increase a feeling of vulnerability and thereby reduce the feeling of control and understanding of the job environment.

Psychological Attributes. In analyzing incentives to innovation, Barnett (1953) stresses the concept of *wants,* conceived of as self-ordered drives of various types even where they carry the impression of being imposed externally. Barnett describes three categories of wants responsible for innovation: *self-wants, dependent wants,* and *voluntary wants.*

Shifting to another aspect of the innovation-adoption process, Barnett notes various assets that advocates of change may have which are favorable to acceptance control. These include prestige, an appealing personality, skill in personal relations, and majority affiliations.

Halpin (1962) suggests (without much empirical support) that a high need for affiliation on the part of many teachers and school administrators acts as a barrier to change. Need for affiliation is thought to produce a desire for sameness or equality among practitioners, who are afraid that being different will affect their status in the peer group. Because innovators appear to have a high need for achievement and to be less concerned with conformity to traditional patterns, according to McClelland (1969) they are often regarded as "deviates," or as being marginal, within their organization.

Programs for heightening a sense of personal security and an openness to ideas and for fostering personal and professional growth are often integral parts of research utilization strategies. Lippitt and Fox (1967) emphasize that innovators are open to adapting and modifying practices. They are relatively nondefensive and are not afraid of evaluation or possible failure. They tend to be nondogmatic and are oriented toward personal and professional growth.

Kelman and Warwick (1973) see social psychology as bridging variables at the micro, or psychological, level and those at the macro, or sociological, level in the study of social change. Thus, significant changes in the attitudes, values, or action orientations of individuals can best be understood in terms of the sociocultural context in which they occur. Similarly, if a program of planned social change, such as the adoption of new methods of farming, is to succeed, it must be accepted by the population.

Taking a psychodynamic point of view, Marmor (1975) sees resistance to change as entailing unconscious as well as conscious personality factors. On the conscious level, there may be a real or perceived threat to a segment of society. When a social or scientific change tends to challenge long-standing beliefs or practices of major importance in a particular cultural, social, or psychological way of life, significant resistance can be expected.

According to Marmor, unconscious factors such as irrational anxieties; intolerance for ambiguity; rigid, repressive, and authoritarian patterns that have dominated early life; and threats to the sense of wholeness may all account for resistance to scientific or other change.

Security is a factor closely related to the mood that favors creativity. When people feel anxious and threatened, they tend to regress to past patterns of action associated with more security. Change easily seems threatening; even new information that disagrees with previous assumptions may be upsetting (Marmor, Bernard, and Ottenberg, 1960; Zander, 1962; Watson and Glaser, 1965; National Science Foundation, 1969). Most psychotherapists recognize that while patients remain fearful and anxious, they cling to well-worn defenses. Only after they achieve a sense of security in the therapeutic relationship are they free to build new responses (for example, Rogers, 1969).

Viewing the problem of self-renewal on a grand scale, Gardner (1964) analyzes the individual as a source of change. He points up the value of commitments beyond self that presume an optimistic but not unrealistic attitude toward the future. Also emphasized is the need for a consensus on social values. Gardner sees the productive individual as facing problems with

moral seriousness and argues that society must help people find
constructive outlets for their commitments.

## Resistance to Change

It is a common observation that proposals to develop new
programs or to advance in new directions lead to resistance, at
least by some involved persons. Such resistance is normal (Dimock, 1978) and not necessarily undesirable (Organization for
Economic Cooperation and Development, 1973). Resistance
arises for many reasons, some not easily recognized.

Sieber (1968) warns that resistance may be seen as having
personal sources when it is actually imposed by system, position, and role. Moreover, resistance may indicate a real impracti-
cality of the proposed change. Rogers and Shoemaker (1971)
cite the hazards of *overadoption* because of insufficient knowledge, inability to predict consequences, or a mania for the new.

When resistance does occur, it may seriously block or
undermine an innovation. An understanding of the possible
sources of resistance may therefore be critical to the success of
efforts to implement innovation.

In an overall analysis of factors accounting for resistance
to change, Watson (1973) distinguishes between *resistance in
personality* and *resistance in social structure.* Under the former
rubric he considers the following factors: homeostasis, habit,
primacy, selective perception and retention, dependence, illusion of impotence, superego, self-distrust, insecurity and regression, deprivation, and anxiety. Factors in social systems that
contribute to the resistance of change are listed as conformity
to norms, systemic and cultural coherence, the sacrosanct, rejection of "outsiders," hierarchy, affluence and leeway, restricted communication, and the nature of the innovation.

One of the most frequently found generalizations regarding resistance is that *resistance occurs when those affected by a
change perceive it as threatening* (Bright, 1964; Havelock,
1969a; Becker, 1970b). In this context, resistance is viewed as
a device that functions to protect the individual against fears
and anxieties aroused by the implications of the proposed change.

More specific instances of resistance based on fear are suggested by the literature.

Karmos and Jacko (1977) observe that fatal weaknesses occur frequently in the early stages of implementation in relation to recommended and/or expected role changes. Expectations of the need to unlearn traditional roles and relearn new ones can produce uncertainty, concern, and even fear.

Behind the resistance to some changes are long histories of attitude and orientation. Luke and others (1973) tried to assist in changing the organizational structure of a large supermarket chain. Most executives had worked their way up from stockboy level under a management structure of close supervision. For many, the consultant approach "disconfirmed" the merit of the previous management style, which they had skillfully learned and mastered over the years and on which a large measure of their positive self-image undoubtedly rested. There was an element of risk in the project for managers, and the project was imposed on them; they had no real option to say no. Resistance was reduced when the organization underwent a change from close control of the managers to a form of training and consultation. The final success of the project as gauged by sales achieved and positive attitudes showed that involvement and commitment of people at various supervisory levels are required.

*Fear of loss of status or prestige or power* is often cited as a major reason for resistance (Marmor, Bernard, and Ottenberg, 1960; Bright, 1964; Berlin, 1969). Persons who have benefited the most from an existing order are unlikely to welcome a major change (Costello and Zalkind, 1963). A study of staff response to a mental health innovation concluded that the intensity of the negative reaction of professionals appears related to the extent to which the power and prestige of local service chiefs are threatened, the extent to which existing informal work relations are disrupted, and the extent that coercive pressures are applied to require marked deviations from traditional procedures (Blum and Downing, 1964). Fear of loss of status and prestige appeared to be a significant factor in a study of a hospital practices innovation that, despite initial acceptance and apparent technical success, was eventually rejected after several months. One possible explanation is that the innovation disrupted the social organization of the nursing unit and resulted in some loss of authority for the head nurse (Coe and Bernhill, 1967).

People resist changes that *threaten job security; innovation may threaten devaluation of the knowledge or skills presently required* (Bright, 1964). This, plus threatened status, may be the source of the frequently found resistance of mental health professionals to the employment of subprofessionals.

To support an innovation may mean that one will be seen as deviant (Cartwright, 1962; Rogers, 1962a; Borman, 1965) and spotlighted as a target for attack (Cawelti, 1967).

*Resistance is aroused when proposed change threatens or challenges currently held beliefs and values* (Anderson and McGuire, 1965). Some persons cannot seem to hear or understand proposals that appear to run counter to long and firmly held beliefs (Lewin and Grabbe, 1962; Watson, 1973). Berlin (1969) points out that learning new methods of work, or using new models and concepts, are likely to be resisted if they are perceived as threatening to one's established orientation and practice. Since the practitioner's theoretical framework is essentially his or her professional value system, all components are likely to be protected with some fervor.

*Fears of loss of self-esteem or sense of competency and/ or fear of exposure of weak points* can arouse very strong resistance (Berlin, 1969; Havelock, 1969a; Glaser and Ross, 1974). Similarly, one study in a mental health setting reports that resistance emerged because of the researchers' failure to acknowledge currently successful efforts (Poser, Dunn, and Smith, 1964). This source of resistance may be an important factor in the difficulties often encountered in the conduct and subsequent application of evaluative research.

Another fundamental generalization is that *people resist changes they do not understand* (Spicer, 1952). LaPiere (1965) points out that there is a pervasive fear of the unfamiliar among humans. Fear of the unknown can supersede even acute physical pain. Relatedly, studies of teacher rejections of innovations in teaching media found that some rejections occurred because of lack of adequate information. Innovations were claimed to be too complex to be understood (Eichholz, 1963; Eichholz and Rogers, 1964). This finding might suggest that resistance can stem either from a lack of understanding of the effects of a change or from inadequate understanding of the nature of the change itself.

A fundamental principle of resistance is that *people resist being forced to change* (Spicer, 1952).

LaPiere (1965) distinguishes between *rational resistance*, whether overtly or covertly expressed, and *irrational antagonisms*. A rational objection might be, for example, that others who tried an innovation have abandoned it. Irrational factors include apprehension about the unknown and rigid adherence to certain traditions. A threat to vested interests is rational; suspicion of a secret, worldwide conspiracy may border on the paranoid.

Klonglan and Coward (1970) offer additional insights into resistance through their analysis of adoption as a two-phase process, *symbolic adoption* (acceptance of the idea) and *use adoption*. This suggests that the source of resistance might be pinpointed: symbolic rejection would be related to sociological variables (compatibility and the like), while economic variables would be involved in resistance to use adoption (trial rejection).

In an organization, desired changes in one part may bring corresponding but unwelcome changes elsewhere in the system. These *side effects* may not have been expected, and they may stir strong resentment (J. B. Taylor, 1968).

Zaltman and others (1973) present as follows some factors affecting resistance to innovation:

1. Among the possible determinants of resistance are (a) the need for stability, (b) the use of foreign jargon, (c) impact on existing social relationships, (d) personal threat, (e) local pride, (f) felt needs, and (g) economic factors.
2. Structural factors affecting resistance include (a) stratification, (b) division of labor, and (c) hierarchical and status differentials.
3. Individual resistance factors include (a) perception, (b) mo-

tivation, (c) attitude, (d) legitimization, (e) accompaniments of trial, (f) results of evaluation, (g) actual adoption or rejection, and (h) manner of dissonance resolution.

In a later treatise Zaltman and Duncan (1977) categorize factors in group resistance to change as directly or indirectly psychological in character, as follows:

1. *Cultural barriers*—(a) cultural values and beliefs, (b) cultural ethnocentrism, (c) saving face, and (d) incompatibility of a cultural trait with change.
2. *Social barriers*—(a) group solidarity, (b) rejection of outsiders, (c) conformity to norms, (d) conflict or factionalism, and (e) group lack of insight.
3. *Organizational barriers*—(a) threat to power and influence, (b) nonsupportive organizational structure, (c) adverse behavior of top-level administrators, (d) unhealthful climate for change, and (e) technological difficulties.
4. *Psychological barriers*—(a) failures in individuals' perception or retention, (b) need for homeostasis, (c) tendency toward conformity and past commitments, and (d) nonproductive personality factors.

Goldman and Gregory (1977) illustrate a situation in which *resistance may result when program or process innovations are addressed to components of an organization where needs are visible.* Some organizational groups outside the target unit may be affected without perceived benefit or with disagreeable consequences that produce resistances. Recognizing and coping with these resistances may not seem central to an innovation but may become crucial to successful adoption within an organization.

The authors note, as well, that compliance does not necessarily indicate concurrence with objectives and programs. Hidden resistance, expressed elsewhere in informal situations, may fail to be revealed in formal evaluations. Such resistance may be so hidden that its eruption in the long term appears out of context, as when it becomes an issue in collective bargaining or in response to other change initiatives.

## Reducing Resistance to Change

Influences opposing change, such as deterrent factors or barriers to innovation, and certain personal characteristics as determinants of change are discussed in Chapters Two and Three of this volume. The present section focuses on the task of overcoming resistance where resistance is undesirable. The reader is reminded that resistant tendencies may be justified in some instances, as when a proposed change lacks valid support or is inappropriate in a particular setting. Immunity may prove to be a useful defensive mechanism socially as well as physiologically.

According to Lorsch (1976b, quoted in Kotter and Schlesinger, 1979), all other factors being equal, the greater the expected resistance, the more slowly the development must be paced in order to reduce resistance, and the more a manager will need to move toward involvement of others to find ways to reduce it. A further consideration is the position of the initiating manager vis-à-vis the resisters, especially with regard to power. The less power the initiator has with respect to others, the more the initiating manager must move rapidly, clearly, with little involvement of others, and quickly attempt to overcome resistance.

Kotter and Schlesinger (1979), observing that the strategic options available to managers can be usefully thought of as existing on a continuum, offer the following anchor categories to describe the approaches, along with instances in which they are commonly used:

1. *Education + communication*—when there is lack of information (or misinformation) and analysis.
2. *Participation + involvement*—when initiators need more information to design the change and when others have considerable power to resist.
3. *Facilitation + support*—when individuals resist because of adjustment problems.
4. *Negotiation + agreement*—when an individual or group "loses out" if the change is implemented and that group has considerable power to resist.

5. *Manipulation + cooptation*—when other strategies fail or are too expensive.
6. *Explicit + implicit coercion*—where speed is of the essence and the initiators have considerable power.

At one end of the continuum, the change strategy is a gradual, participative type of process designed to reduce resistance to a minimum. At the other end of the continuum, the strategy is one of very rapid implementation and little involvement of others. Resistance is mowed down and, at the extreme, this strategy results in a *fait accompli*.

Most persons and organizations are in "quasi-stationary equilibrium," with some forces driving them toward change and others resisting it. To reduce the resistance creates forward movement with less tension than if effort is made only to override it (Lewin, 1962; Cottle, 1969; Watson, 1973).

It is often hard for the advocates of a new idea to empathize with those who do not go along. It is helpful to recognize the important social role of the defenders who try to conserve the valuable elements of the old in the face of a tumult (Klein, 1968). Empathizing with them, the progressives can enter a dialogue that may result in amendments that permit broader support of the new idea. Failure to respect differences in values is likely to bring a backlash of increased resistance.

In his article on "how to change things," Reddin (1969) cites seven techniques for overcoming resistance: (1) diagnosis, (2) mutual setting of objectives, (3) group emphasis, (4) maximum information, (5) discussion of implementation, (6) use of ceremony (ritual), and (7) resistance interpretation.

In discussing resistance to change, Watson (1973) outlines the life cycle of resistance to an innovation and the psychological factors of individuals and groups that affect resistance. According to Watson, the life cycle of resistance entails the following:

1. Undifferentiated resistance.
2. Differentiated resistance.
3. Mobilized resistance, resulting in a showdown.

4. Sufficient success so that only conspicuous error could re-
   mobilize the resistance, with supporters of change taking
   power.
5. One-time advocates of change becoming resisters of emerging change.

Watson spells out sources of resistance in individuals and social
systems and offers thirteen recommendations about resistance
to change, grouped under three categories: (1) Who brings the
change? (2) What kinds of change succeed? (3) How is it best
done?

   In many organizations, the techniques of group dynamics
create a climate of mutual trust and openness, which dramatically dissipates resistance to change. Procedures for developing
this kind of relationship are variously called T-groups, L (for
*laboratory learning about leadership*) groups, sensitivity training, and encounter groups. The usual procedures are well described in Rogers (1968) and in Schein and Bennis (1965).
Beckhard (1966, 1971) offers case studies of their uses. Another treatment of group dynamics will be found in Cartwright
(1962).

   Schindler-Rainman and Lippitt (1972) demonstrated an
increase in the effectiveness of individuals or teams as agents of
planned social change in local communities, indicating the need
for concerted effort in overcoming community resistance to
change. As a result of the team training of professionals, paraprofessionals, and volunteers from a community working together to effect social changes in specific problem areas, performance improved notably. The training consisted of guidance
and feedback from professional trainers, interaction among
team members, and consultation between and among teams.

   In a study of the effects of various incentives for overcoming resistance to family planning in Asia, Rogers (1973a)
compared the offering of incentives directly to potential adopters of innovations with the use of intermediary persons in attempts to influence adopters. In effect, the intermediaries served
as a continuing bridge to persuasive communication, resulting
in improved family planning.

It is particularly important that participants feel free to express their doubts and negative feelings. Some promoters of a change find it hard to believe that a frank facing of disagreement and obstacles may win more converts than eloquent exhortation in favor of their proposal. Yet, this has been the experience of many consultants on change (Zander, 1962; Glaser, 1965; Glaser and Taylor, 1973). Conflict of opinion followed by sincere, skillful attempts at conflict resolution may be more productive than bland agreement, which is often unaccompanied by any sense of concern or commitment.

Resistance encountered in development of a program may, of course, also continue to have an effect during its continuation. Goldman and Gregory (1977) make the point that resistance to continuation of an innovative program will often reflect parallel resistance to its initiation but may surface in different ways and under different auspices.

Important as general strategies for overcoming resistance to change may be, it would seem imperative that a particularized study be made of resistance factors in the specific situation in which change efforts are to be made. This task is included in the statement of functions of change agents in Chapter Eleven. It has also been treated in Chapter Two as a phase of the application of the A VICTORY model to the determination of readiness to adopt new programs in mental health and, by extension, in other fields.

### Summary Comments

It is quite impossible to separate personality characteristics from project characteristics and from organizational settings in their influence on knowledge utilization in the interest of change. Nonetheless, there are variations in the makeup and status of the individuals who are the actors in the drama of change phenomena, and these variables are worthy of directed study, both as positive and as negative forces.

With regard to standard descriptors such as age, tenure, and social status, the available evidence is relatively sparse and nongeneralizable. Professional qualities, notably leadership status, are seen to be quite clearly influential in the use of knowledge. The subtler psychological qualities, notably those associated with personality dynamics (needs, wants, self-image, and so on), are also highly significant, whether viewed in terms of individual or group behavior. For those who attempt to institute and manage change—particularly the change agent—achieving a well-rounded understanding of the operation of psychological factors may be critical to the success of a change intervention program.

In considering a person's psychological openness or resistance to change, it is well to note the inseparability of psychological and social factors. A notable illustration is the significance of role and self-image as individual characteristics that are largely socially induced. But the interrelationship goes further; organizations and social institutions reflect individual psychological characteristics and, in turn, affect the individual's reaction to opportunities for change.

Just as it is people who are responsible for change, so it is people who resist change or who fail to put worthwhile knowledge to use. Although a distinction has been made between resistances that are embedded in social structure and those that are produced by personality characteristics, the psychological overlay is evident in either case.

The latter part of this chapter listed and described some of these psychological factors and methods of overcoming such resistances. That presentation needs to be supplemented by the consideration of practical and other barriers to change emanating from the wider organizational, social, and cultural environment.

# 5

# Organizational
# Factors

Whether one thinks of a small, definitive unit such as a clinic, school, or office or of a complex social institution such as a school system, factory, or governmental unit, it is clear that the nature of the organizational setting plays a large part in determining openness to change and the manner and effectiveness with which innovations are likely to occur and prosper. The present chapter considers the characteristics of organizations as they affect and are affected by change efforts.

R. A. Cooke (1979) notes that change in an organization may involve alterations in any of its facets, including its tasks, technology, structure, or components. Forces inside or outside the organization can generate change and also complicate its management.

Boundaries between component elements of the organizational setting cannot be sharply drawn. The breakdown presented in this chapter is largely for convenience of exposition. First we enumerate characteristics associated with organizational climate or organizational health. Then we present the following aspects of the subject: (1) organizational goals and planning, (2) organizational structure, (3) organizational communication and decision making, and finally (4) miscellaneous organizational factors related to innovation and change.

## Organizational Climate

**Nature and Components of Climate.** Organizational climate, as defined by Litwin and Stringer (1968), comprises the perceived subjective effects of the formal system, the informal style of managers, and other important environmental factors related to attitudes, beliefs, values, and motivations of people who work in a particular organization.

Litwin and Stringer observe that major differences in climate can be found among different organizations, even among the subunits of the same organization. In fact, different individuals in the same subunit may have different perceptions of the climate. (This, among other factors, makes organizational climate a very difficult concept to optimize and measure.) The dimensions of climate that tend to distinguish organizations are (1) perceived degree of structure and constraint, (2) degree of warmth, support, and encouragement that is experienced, (3) emphasis on reward or punishment, and (4) perceived performance standards set by management.

Litwin and Stringer argue that different climates may affect innovation by stimulating or arousing different kinds of motivation, generating distinctive attitudes about a person's relationship with others, and strongly influencing both feelings of satisfaction and performance level. The model they propose depicts a flow from (1) the organization system to (2) the perceived organizational environment to (3) aroused motivation to (4) emergent behavior to (5) consequences for organizational productivity and effectiveness in relation to mission.

Chakrabarti (1973a) summarized as follows the advantages of using the concept of organizational climate: (1) It permits analysis of the determinants of motivated behavior in actual complex social situations. (2) It simplifies the problems of measurement of the situational determinants by allowing the individuals in the situations to think in terms of bigger, more integrated chunks of their experience. (3) It makes possible the characterization of the total situational influence of various environments so that they can be mapped and categorized, thus permitting cross-environmental comparisons.

Benedict and others (1967) present organizational climate

under ten "dimensions" of organizational health, grouped under three headings, as follows:

1. Task accomplishment
   a. Reasonably clear, accepted, achievable, and appropriate *goals.*
   b. Relatively undistorted *communication flow* horizontally, vertically, and to and from the environment.
   c. *Optimal power equalization,* collaborative and based on competence rather than position.
2. Internal integration
   a. *Resource utilization,* reflecting a good fit between personal dispositions and role demands.
   b. *Cohesiveness,* or "organizational identity."
   c. *Morale,* feelings of well being and satisfaction.
3. Growth and active changefulness
   a. *Innovativeness,* tendency to grow, change, diversify.
   b. *Autonomy,* ability to act "from its own center outward."
   c. *Adaptation,* changes in response to organization/environment contact.
   d. *Problem-solving adequacy,* ability to sense problems and effect solutions.

One of the authors of the above-mentioned study has written on the development of innovative climates in educational organizations (Miles, 1978a). As a phase of the total process of improvement, he discusses the significance of climate as a general atmosphere of inventiveness, creativity, willingness to take chances, or excitement. Of special interest in the present context is the notion of innovativeness—or openness to consideration of innovation—as a group norm.

The literature calls attention to a number of staff factors related to organizational climate. For example, sufficient time should be provided for problem-solving and change-related activities. In order to create an organizational climate conducive to innovation and change, staff members must have some time free from the pressures of routine in which to engage in communication, problem solving, or pursuit of research input (Costello and Zalkind, 1963; Lippitt and others, 1967; Marcum, 1968).

Staff members who operate in organizations in which there have been changes are more open to further change (Bright, 1964). This seems particularly true when subsequent innovations are closely related to those preceding (Sapolsky, 1967). Innovations seem to come in clusters (Arthur D. Little Inc., 1963). However, Mansfield (1963b) found that a firm that is a leader in introducing one innovation may be slow to introduce the next.

Organizational forces are patently interactive. Glaser (1973) comments on the interplay of such factors as a leadership open to change, outside pressures for change, aroused will to change in response to crises, information feedback that stimulates desire for goal attainment, incentive systems, organizational rearrangements, shared interest in learning and problem solving, and even the increased readiness for change born of boredom or discontent with current commitments or modus operandi.

**Quality of Worklife.** The concept of organizational climate is closely related to the concept of quality of worklife (QWL). There is evidence (*Work in America,* 1972; Katzell and Yankelovich, 1975; Srivastva and others, 1975; Glaser, 1976, 1981b; Hackman and Suttle, 1977; Hinrichs, 1978; Hackman and Oldham, 1980) on the effects of participative management in which personnel at all levels are sincerely encouraged to have meaningful voice in the design, structure, and organization of their work. In general, employees are likely to recommend constructive changes that (if properly implemented) lead to enhanced job satisfaction, greater productivity, and improved quality of the organization's product or service.

When dealing with people under voluntary arrangements who are more or less free to "opt out" if they are sufficiently dissatisfied or have what they perceive as better alternatives open to them, decisions for change in which they have a meaningful say are more likely to be supported and to endure than authoritatively, arbitrarily handed-down decisions. Maier (1963) expressed this concept in the equation ED = Q $\times$ A: an *Effec-*

tive *Decision* = its *Quality* X *A*cceptance by those who are needed to implement it.

To illustrate various ways of designing systems that lead to greater employee output, Hinrichs (1978) presents twelve case studies classified under three broad categories of innovations: (1) behavioral reinforcement for the setting of target performance goals, with feedback and rewards, (2) redesign of jobs and working conditions, and (3) "humanistic," or QWL improvement, orientation.

It was found that all three types of system innovations showed significant productivity gains; furthermore, three years after initial implementation, in seven of the twelve cases the programs were still operative and were achieving various degrees of positive results. The author sets forth the main factors or conditions that seem to distinguish the more durable/viable instances from those that "petered out," including strong management support, permeation of the participative management style throughout the organization, guarantee of work, simultaneous installation of change on a number of fronts, tailoring to the nature and needs of employees, and a "something for everyone" approach.

If a management style that encompasses QWL improvement efforts can yield such constructive outcomes, and if that method of operation has been well described in the literature (as it has), one might expect rapid and widespread adoption. Not so. Walton (1977a) reported a study focused primarily on barriers and gateways to the diffusion of seemingly successful QWL experiments. He studied the extent to which experiments in work restructuring that had been applied to one section of eight large firms in the United States, Great Britain, Canada, Norway, and Sweden were subsequently adopted by other sections of those firms. He found that the extent of diffusion and adoption varied widely. In four companies, spread was nonexistent or nearly so. In three companies, somewhat more diffusion occurred; however, the rate either was slow or had not been sustained. Only in one company was diffusion/adoption truly impressive.

Elements that were considered relevant to the overall failure of diffusion were as follows:

1.  Regression in the pilot project itself.
2.  Use of a poor model for change.
3.  Confusion about what was to be diffused.
4.  Inappropriateness of the concepts used.
5.  Deficient implementation and follow-through.
6.  Lack of top-management commitment.
7.  Union opposition.
8.  Bureaucratic barriers.
9.  Threatened obsolescence.
10. Self-limiting dynamics, such as envy of rewards to the experimental group ("star" envy).

The author observed further that careful and extensive planning is required to ensure positive results and that problems of increased local autonomy and threatened roles are not easily resolved.

In general, the character of organizational climate, including such attributes as openness to internal challenge of modus operandi and suggestions for change, coupled with structural arrangements that encourage ego-involved caring about quality and efficiency of the organization's task performance, is likely to have significant bearing on organizational effectiveness.

## Organizational Goals

Whether goals are set *for* an organization or *by* an organization, certain considerations apply.

**Clarity of Goals.** As conceived by Miles (1965), in a healthy organization, which also provides for distortion-free communication and an equitable distribution of influence, the goals of the system are reasonably clear to the system members and reasonably well accepted by them. Goals should also be achievable with existing or available resources and should be appropriate. The ambiguity and diffuseness of educational goals, for example, diminish the effectiveness of educational organizations and impede institutional change (Halpin, 1962; Sieber, 1968).

Sieber (1968) identifies two consequences of goal diffuseness in relation to education: (1) reinforcement of the effects of status insecurity and vulnerability concerning innovation and (2) difficulty in measuring the attainment of goals, which makes it hard to reach consensus on the efficacy of particular programs, methods, or skills.

As an aid toward the setting of group goals, Jenks (1970) recommends the use of a Q-sort, a technique whereby respondents sort statements of possible goals according to their degree of acceptability. The resulting judgments may then be subjected to discussion and reconciliation.

Another aid toward the setting of group goals is the use of a modified form of the Delphi technique (Dalkey, 1967; Sackman, 1975). This technique was originally developed by Olaf Helmer and his associates at the Rand Corporation (Helmer, 1967) to facilitate the arrival at a consensus of expert judgment. As its name signifies, it is ordinarily applied to the prediction of developments and events in the future. It entails a procedure of written feedback regarding given questions which is iteratively shared anonymously among a group of knowledgeable and concerned persons, leading to reevaluation and further refinement. This procedure, however, can be applied to other matters, such as the clarification of the goals of a society, institution, organization, or project.

Still another aid toward establishing and clarifying goals is through goal-attainment scaling (Kiresuk and Sherman, 1968). The procedure involves the setting of goals—preferably (but not necessarily) goals agreed on by both the decision makers in an organization and the persons who perform the work required for goal attainment. Then, at periodic intervals, goal attainment is rated in comparison with expected attainment. New goals are then set for the next agreed-on time period.

Regarding the clarity and appropriateness of organizational goals, Rogers (1967) raises an interesting point about how the "case closure" orientation of vocational rehabilitation agencies acts to divert attention from consideration of innovative ideas. An emphasis on the quantity of closed cases rather than the quality of services rendered leaves counselors with little time to "fool around" with research results and also supports a focus on short-range goals, whereas the more significant gains from innovations are more likely to be reflected in long-range results.

**Goal Statement Versus Job Description.** When an organization such as a rehabilitation agency can hammer out its optimal program outcomes, set up process or time dimensions for instituting *agreed-on* specific controls or performance criteria related to those optimal program outcomes, measure performance, provide timely feedback, and offer rewards for superior performance in goal attainment, the agency then has an input-process-output frame of reference that provides a system of accountability. This is likely to result in a closer relation between goals and the means of achieving them (Glaser and others, 1967).

Written statements of organizational goals and proximate targets have been found helpful in reducing anxiety about change and in imparting a sense of security during the introduction of new procedures (Watson and Glaser, 1965; Bobbe and Schaffer, 1968; Schmuck, 1968).

In contrast to written goals, sharply defined job descriptions have been found to characterize organizations that are reluctant to innovate (Aiken and Hage, 1968). In the situations studied—namely, rehabilitation organizations—the two observations combine readily in the idea that the best work is done when participants share the objectives but are relatively free to do their share of the common task in their preferred way.

**Social Expectancies.** Organizations of whatever type are seldom, if ever, wholly autonomous. They operate within a context of customers or clients, communities, governmental controls, and public opinion. The way an organization perceives its relationship to its larger social context is an important determinant of the kinds of change it wants or can accept (Lippitt, Watson, and Westley, 1958). Any organization must protect ties to a supporting population and a client population. These relationships set limits beyond which the institution cannot go if it is to survive. The perception of the limits may, however, be inaccurate. One service of a change agent is sometimes to investigate the validity of the perceived limits.

The pressure of social or political demand or expectancy undoubtedly varies with the innovation under consideration.

For example, in the Battelle Columbus Laboratories study of factors associated with technological innovations (National Science Foundation, 1973b), such external considerations as political and social factors and health and environmental factors ranked relatively low. However, as Schön (1967) points out, this matter is a function of the country involved. In some countries (Japan, the Soviet Union, Great Britain) the government is a leading participant in technical innovation; in the United States, in contrast, the government tends to set rules and policies that may affect innovation and only rarely participates in the actual technical effort.

It should be noted that Schön published his view in 1967. The U.S. government has since made a number of attempts to stimulate greater efficiency in the task performance of some federal agencies. These efforts have, unfortunately, had little impact in reversing the overall declining rate of productivity in the United States.

Chapter Six will discuss more fully the influences that social, political, and other societal institutions exert on change.

Organizations obviously differ in their *vulnerability* to pressures from environmental, and especially social, forces. Vulnerability may be defined as the degree to which an organization is subject to power influences from its environment irrespective of organizational goals and resources (Sieber, 1968). For example, health agencies dependent on voluntary local support must be concerned with public opinion and politics more than privately endowed or nationally financed agencies. Sieber provides some good examples of the effects of organizational vulnerability—for example, (1) changes in practice that might disturb the local community tend to be shunned, (2) the adoption of innovation often depends more on political feasibility than on educational value, (3) innovations receiving wide publicity through the mass media become candidates for adoption, irrespective of their educational value, and (4) internal relationships of a vulnerable system may be so affected as to limit the planned experimentation.

The characteristics of the community served by an organization affect its ability to innovate (Havelock, 1970). Not infrequently, the leaders of a school or a church or other social agency outrun the tolerance of the constituency, and they are then reprimanded, constrained, or discharged (Ross, 1958).

The external and internal pressures affecting organizational change are vividly portrayed by Goldberg (1980) in her detailed analysis of the course and outcome of an attempt to change the orientation of the Community Service Society of New York from one that offered traditional casework for a predominantly lower-middle-class clientele to one that stressed multidisciplinary community programs in problem-ridden urban neighborhoods. Factors inducing the agency's trustees to seek to effect the change included (1) a perception of rising urban problems, (2) social welfare activities of the federal government, (3) declining support for family service organizations, and (4) the impression gleaned from several well-publicized studies that casework was ineffective with the poor.

Organizations pursuing objectives that are controversial in the larger setting have a conflict between their goals and their desire to be accepted in the community. A study of local affiliates of Planned Parenthood concluded that those units that were most concerned with keeping on good terms with other community agencies were less productive in achieving the objectives of the national agency. A degree of independence in pursuing the organization's own targets was deemed more effective and more congruent with its functions (Rein, 1964).

Reporting on a conference of social scientists principally concerned with innovation, Manela (1969) stated that some organizations (and some persons and teams within the same organization) are oriented primarily toward output and reception of their product by clients. Others attend mainly to the internal operations and bureaucratic functioning. Those persons, sections, and institutions that, by choice or by necessity, attend carefully to the market are apt to be more responsive to the need for change. The more an organization is wrapped up in its own machinery and operations, the less likely it will be to innovate.

## Organizational Structure and Associated Variables

The critical examination of the structure of an organization includes not only the distribution of power within it but also its bureaucracy, occupational specialties, size and capacity, organizational inertia, and capability for self-renewal. A summary of these factors is presented below.

**Distribution of Power.** On the basis of evidence he has accumulated, Rogers (1973b) places emphasis on the importance of the effect of a system's social structure on the diffusion of innovations. He sums up his position in nine propositions, as follows:

1.  Social structure acts to impede or facilitate the rate of diffusion and adoption of new ideas through system effects.
2.  Diffusion can change the social structure of a social system.
3.  Power elites act as gatekeepers for entering a social system, while favoring functioning innovations that do not immediately threaten to change the system's structure.
4.  A system's social structure helps determine the nature and distribution of an innovation's consequences.
5.  Top-down change in a system, which is initiated by the power elites, is more likely to succeed than bottom-up change.
6.  Bottom-up change involves a greater degree of conflict than top-down change.
7.  Bottom-up change is more likely to be successful at times of perceived crisis in a system.
8.  Bottom-up change is more likely to be successful when a social movement is headed by a charismatic leader.
9.  The role of the charismatic leader in a social movement decreases as the movement becomes institutionalized into a more highly structured organization.

Rogers indicates that his propositions are not limited in their applicability to such specific behaviors as the diffusion of innovations, social movements, and the like: They deal with change and structure in a more general sense, including broad social movements.

Power and status distribution within the organization affect its ability to innovate (Lippitt, Watson, and Westley, 1958; Rubin, Plovnick, and Fry, 1974). The organization may be too centralized or too diffuse or spotty. The literature, however, is less than conclusive regarding this variable. Chesler and Fox (1967), for example, urge the decentralization of administrative decision making in educational institutions in order to accommodate greater participation by staff. Similarly, both Rogers (1967) and Havelock (1969a) indicate that a highly developed organizational hierarchy impedes communication necessary for diffusion. Griffiths (1964) forthrightly states that "the more hierarchical the structure of an organization, the less the possibility of change" (p. 434).

However, Sapolsky (1967) concludes that the decentralized structure of the department store may serve as a major barrier to the institution of change. When interunit communication is good in such an organization, it allows for mobilization of forces against the tactics used to reduce resistance. Still another study reported that, possibly because adoption entails less risk than innovation, teachers in schools with a diffuse social structure *innovated* more, while those in a hierarchical structure *adopted* more (Lippitt and others, 1967). (To be sure, some changes may have foreseeable undesirable consequences and *should* be resisted.)

Barnes (1969), after pointing out that there are four main variables in an organizational change (the task, the technology, the people, and the structure), notes that differences in power distribution (for example, unilateral power versus shared power) can affect how changes can be initiated and implemented.

Davis (1973a) offers advice concerning a balanced attitude toward the use of power by the mental health administrator faced with the need to induce organizational change commensurate with the increasing tempo of societal and individual change. He points to the assumption made by some administrators that using power, authority, or money is easier than using what might seem to be more tedious change-management techniques. Simplistic adherence to this viewpoint has often resulted in false economy. However, he asserts, the belief that a sufficiently worthy new product or procedure will naturally be adopted on its own merits fails to take into account the hidden jungle of conflicting personal motives that can subvert even the most promising innovation.

Certain kinds or characteristics of power structure can limit effective adaptation and change. For instance, Pincus (1974) asserts that educational institutions are less likely to adopt innovations that change existing authority roles or significantly alter institutional structure.

**Bureaucratic Structure.** Thompson (1969) makes the point that modern bureaucratic organizations, theoretically considered, are intrinsically resistant to innovation because they are monocratic, they stress conformity rather than creativity, and they are conservative in orientation. Thompson believes that the bureaucratic structure is slowly evolving in the direction of greater flexibility. He suggests that this trend toward flexibility could be accelerated by looser structure, freer communications, decentralization, greater reliance on group processes, and modification of the incentive system (stressing the internal rewards of gratification rather than such external rewards as upward movement in the hierarchy).

Bennis (1971) basically agrees with Thompson, believing that the bureaucratic form of organization is out of joint with contemporary realities and that drastic changes in the conduct of corporations and managerial practices are necessary. He argues that managerial goals should be integrated with individual needs, and sources of power redistributed. Bennis predicts that the bureaucratic structure of organizations will be replaced by adaptive, problem-solving temporary structures with diverse specialists linked together by coordinating and task-performance-evaluating professionals.

According to Abbott (1965), there exists in education a hierarchical bureaucratic structure that makes it difficult to decide when new programs are needed and inhibits their generation. In order to produce a more innovative educational structure, it will be necessary to alter the traditional hierarchical organization, wherein the status of the administrative personnel is elevated above that of the teachers.

House (1976), in a study of factors related to educational innovation, noted how the implementation of change in school systems was affected by the politics of the central office staff within a district. The members of the central office staff, interacting with the superintendent and the school board, played a key role in promoting or inhibiting an innovation within the district. Before an idea could be presented to the school board, it had to gain the support of a small group, then advance to a major group and achieve a consensus there, and so on up the hierarchy until it was presented to the administrative council and finally to the school board. Proposals to the school board by outside groups were intercepted by the staff or, if not, were routed back to the central office staff for consideration. For any new idea to reach the stage of policy action, it had to go through the central staff. A new superintendent coming into a district could upset the informal patterns of the central office staff, thus allowing different ideas to enter.

In analyzing the often-overlooked consideration of depth of change, Downs (1967) recognizes four "organizational layers": (1) specific actions taken by the bureau (a principal characteristic of which is that the major portion of its output is not directly or indirectly evaluated in any market external to the organization in voluntary *quid pro quo* transactions), (2) the decision-making rules it uses, (3) the institutional structure it uses to make those rules, and (4) its general purposes. Downs has set down over 180 propositions or hypotheses regarding the life cycle, characteristics, officials, communication patterns, control problems and processes, search and change mechanisms, and other ideological factors in the operation of bureaucracies. A number of Downs' principles and hypotheses have a bearing on innovation and change in organizations, such as the following:

1. One way to spread the adoption of a given change is to design it so that it affects the smallest possible number of persons.

2.  Opportunities for change presented by purely internal developments are less likely to be utilized than opportunities presented by external developments.
3.  Rivalry leads to the greatest amount of creativity whenever the rival bureaus all receive appropriations from one budgetary authority but have separate personnel structures.
4.  The greater the diversity of viewpoints among bureau members, the greater the rate at which innovations will be suggested by bureau members.

Jermakowicz (1978) perceives the main challenge in the management of R&D activity as the integration of this activity with that of production and with the creation of organizational climate conditions favoring full consideration of promising new ideas or innovative approaches to removing impediments to optimal task performance. The answer, he maintains, lies largely in the sphere of organizational structure, mainly in the proper mix of characteristics of the innovative and the productive types of activity.

Differences between the two types are, for example, the following: (1) output of ideas versus goods and services, (2) unique versus reproductive character, (3) irregular versus regular processes, (4) nonregular versus regular forecasting and planning, (5) unmeasurable versus measurable outcomes, and (6) high versus relatively low risk. The competencies and the duties of managers vary between the "project matrix" innovative type of activity and the "production matrix" production type of activity, as does the predominant organizational arrangement of the two types. Communication patterns also differ, innovative activity entailing full and circular networks while productive activity leans toward chain or leader networks. Recognition of these differences and the advantages and disadvantages of the features associated with each variant may serve as the basis for devising the most effective combination for achieving both the project development and the production objective.

Many structural factors account for barriers to innovative change. A notable example is found in large government bureaucracies, where systemic rigidities within the agency become established and are maintained with tenacity. Many factors account for these rigidities—creation of the organization by law; formalization of operating procedures; employment of staffs under inflexible personnel systems affecting hiring, placement, promotion, transfer, demotion, discharge, and retirement; standing formal procedures for day-to-day operations; external control of budgets and funding that limits change. In some cases, however, "rigidity" may reflect stability in terms of maintaining that which has been found to work well, and it can be a strength and a virtue. Change should be considered only when the established procedure no longer works as effectively as available innovative alternatives.

Drawing on data from twenty case histories of specific innovations in medical school departments in Syracuse and Rochester, New York, Lambright and Carroll (1977) ascertained factors associated with the successful completion or the curtailment of the innovative process. They found that (1) full incorporation was related to whether the innovation actually worked as claimed, the process was reversible, improved service ensued, and cost savings were realized, (2) the head of a local line agency who functions as a "bureaucratic entrepreneur" proved significant, (3) a high capacity to innovate within the local bureaucratic structure was also significant, (4) a strong, locally based bureaucracy-centered coalition of involved individuals or groups facilitated innovation, (5) relationships of the given agency with other bureaucracies at the federal, state, and local levels proved influential, (6) success was related to locally defined and widely perceived need, (7) clear or categorical federal funding was helpful, and (8) state laws or regulations can spark successful innovation.

**Occupational Specialization.** Another factor of the organizational structure that appears related to innovation is occupational specialization, which may be a function of size, centralization, and other variables. A study of vocational rehabilitation agencies, for example, found a high positive correlation between the rate of acceptance and implementation of new programs and the number of occupational specialties within the organization (Aiken and Hage, 1968). Moreover, the number of occupational specialties was one of the best predictors of future program innovation. Similarly, a study of medical schools found that innovative schools had a larger number of departments in the basic sciences and clinical areas (Carrole, 1967). According to these studies, such intraorganizational diversity appears to foster creative exchange among staff.

Havelock (1969a), however, considers division of labor (specialization) to impede communication between organizational subunits in three ways: It fosters the formation of unique coding schemes, it stimulates interunit competition, and it encourages the formation of separate and incompatible group norms.

A key factor in determining the effects of specialization might be the extent to which specialized organizational subunits are autonomous or interdependent. Thus, Carrole's (1967) study found that the innovative medical schools reflected a lessening of the traditional departmental autonomy. The fading of departmental autonomy was attributed to a shift of funds allocation from department to the broader school unit. Similarly, the agencies in Aiken and Hage's (1968) study that had a high number of different occupational specialties and were the most innovative were also those most likely to have many cooperative relationships with other agencies. This might suggest that the focus of staff was on professional or organizational goals rather than departmental self-interests.

In a later study, Hage and Aiken (1970) pointed out that organizational complexity and emphasis on job satisfaction were positively correlated with a *high* rate of change; centralization, formalization, stratification, and concern with volume production and efficiency were positively correlated with a *low* rate of change. That is not to say that a high rate of change is necessarily better or more productive than a low rate. A high rate may make for instability and inefficiency in some situations.

Moch and Morse (1977) studied a sample of several hundred nonfederal hospitals with respect to size, functional differentiation of tasks, specialization of personnel, and decentralization. In considering the relation of these factors to innovation, they stress the importance of differentiating the type of innovations adopted—namely, those compatible with the interests of lower-level decision makers as against those that are not compatible. They emphasize, also, the need to take into account the interrelations among the four independent variables. Moch and Morse found that—

1. Larger size has a significant, though small, positive impact on the adoption of both types of innovation.
2. Decentralization and its interaction with size (the larger the hospital, the less centralized) appear to affect only the adoption of innovations compatible with the interests of lower-level decision makers.
3. The same is not true of functional differentiation; hospitals with a high degree of functional differentiation were more likely to have adopted innovations noncompatible with lower-level decision makers' interests.

Viewed from another angle, the matter of occupational specialization ties in with the experimental sociotechnical system such as has been sponsored by the Tavistock Institute in England, whereby relatively small work groups are given responsibility for relatively large tasks compared with the more detailed and specialized work required. In the sociotechnical system there is emphasis on optimizing the social (human) and mechanical components of work systems to enhance both. One such experiment entailing the redistribution of specialized jobs in a loom weaving factory in India is reported as successful by Rice (1971). In Norway, Thorsrud (1968) describes several equally successful experiments in the regrouping of job activities and skills involving increased responsibility (job enrichment and job enlargement by smaller, more autonomous work groups) by less-supervised workers. "Successful" in this context is defined in terms of greater job satisfaction *and* greater productivity. Glaser (1976) has summarized many such experiments in the United States, Europe, and Japan.

**Size and Capacity.** In spite of the popularly held assumption that larger organizations are slow and cumbersome in changing, evidence indicates that more change actually takes place in larger organizations. For example, Carrole (1967) found that larger medical schools were more innovative. Mansfield (1963b), in a study of 294 industrial firms, found that when profitability was held constant, the chances were good that a large firm would be quicker to use a new technique than a small firm. In a later study (1968b), he suggests that the largest organizations will do a disproportionately large share of the innovating under the following conditions: (1) when the investment required to innovate is large relative to the size of the organization that could use the innovation, (2) when the minimum size of the organization required to use the innovation is large relative to the average size of similar organizations, and (3) when the average size of the largest organizations is much greater than the average size of all potential users of the innovation.

Schön (1967) notes that innovation within the textile industry is quite limited because the individual firms are too small to support research and development; consequently, new developments come from outside the industry—that is, from related feeder industries such as chemicals.

Generally it would seem logical that the more successful, internally secure, and financially prosperous organization would be in a better position to risk innovation. Havelock (1969a) refers to this as a "capacity factor." Several studies have related organizational affluence to innovativeness (Richland, 1965; McClelland, 1968). The findings of Mansfield's (1963b) extensive empirical investigation of industrial firms, however, cast serious doubt on the certainty of this relationship. His study of 294 organizations found that a firm's financial health, as measured by profitability, liquidity, and growth rate, bears no close relationship to how long it waits before introducing a new technique. Havelock (1969a) makes note of this ambiguity.

The relation between size and such factors as financial success and organizational dynamics needs to be taken into account before size *per se* can be intrinsically associated with degree of innovativeness.

Gee (1978), in a study of innovations that succeeded in reaching commercial realization, found that firms with 101–

1,000 people required a shorter average innovation period by almost two years than firms with 1,001-5,000 people. But small firms (1-100 people) and those with over 5,000 employees exhibited an innovation period of intermediate length. The medium-sized firms may have shared the disadvantages of both small and large organizations without fully realizing the associated advantages, as indicated by their longer average innovation period. Factors conceivably associated with the relation between innovation and size may be the flexibility of a small organization and the greater resources and economies available to large organizations.

**Organizational Inertia.** This is the characteristic that has given large organizations a "bad name" with regard to organizational size and innovation. Actually, organizational inertia, which might in part result from an institutional hardening of the arteries, appears to be largely a function of the age of the organization and its failure to encourage deliberately a spirit of self-renewing challenge from its own staff and from those it serves. Large institutions appear most susceptible to this condition. Over a period of time, procedures, regulations, activities, and attitudes become routine, habitual, and cemented (Glaser, 1965; Havelock, 1969a).

Guest (1962) points out that the length of time required for an organization to improve its performance as it moves from one pattern of behavior to another is a function of (1) its size in terms of number of staff, (2) the number of specialized service, reporting, and control groups, (3) the number of levels in the hierarchy, (4) the complexity of technical operations, and (5) the intensity of personal insecurity and interpersonal hostility.

The bringing in of new blood may be significant in achieving innovation, as is illustrated in the case of the National Teacher Corps, where the conventional organization was "invaded by liberal, creative, and unconventional outsiders with fresh perspectives" (Corwin, 1972b, p. 441).

Complex organizations are described by Hage and Aiken (1970) as having a pervasive static or dynamic "style," reflecting the distinction between the "mechanical" and the "organic" models commonly used in the sociology of organizations. Inertia may be viewed as a manifestation of static style ordinarily related to an overall static environment.

Schön (1967) sees the corporation as caught in a dramatic ambivalence regarding innovation. The social system within the corporation attempts to maintain a stable state while under pressure for technical change that might be destructive of the stable state. Internal dissension between the R&D and the marketing arms of the corporation often reflects this ambivalent condition. This conflict tends to reduce innovation.

**Self-Renewal.** A characteristic related to organizational structure is the concept of organizational self-renewal, or the organization's ability to change its structure to adapt to new internal or external circumstances. Gardner (1964) asserts that we must learn to "organize for freedom"—that is, design and build organizations that help individuals to develop themselves.

Self-renewing organizations provide structures for sensing internal and external changes that call for creation of new procedures (Watson, 1973). Miles (1965) identifies a similar characteristic as a dimension of the healthy organization that he terms "problem-solving adequacy." This includes structures and procedures for detecting problems, inventing possible solutions, choosing solutions, implementing them, and evaluating their effectiveness. The apparatus to perform these functions may take the form of an office for research and development or a setup for problem sensing, such as an ombudsman, interview survey, or regular consultant service. The absence in an agency of any unit that is designed especially to detect internal trouble before it becomes serious, and external trends before they become generally evident, makes it unlikely that the organization will succeed in continuous self-renewal. It can only alternate between costly lag and overdue spurts of reorganization.

Related to self-renewal is self-examination. Davis (1972) found that organizations that carry out program evaluation tend to be more innovative than those that do not. However, Havelock and Havelock (1973a) found a slight negative relationship between emphasis on evaluation and number of reported innovations in U.S. school districts.

In a study in which the focus was explicitly the mental

health service delivery agency, Glaser and Ross (1971) formulated a set of operating conditions that would provide an organizational vehicle for effecting change: carrying out periodic reviews of agency mission, assessing program effectiveness, disseminating knowledge about promising alternative practices for carrying out various types of functions, providing opportunity for advocacy, providing a means for input to decision making by all concerned insofar as practicable, providing a way of sustaining commitment, having control over sufficient resources. These conditions can be considered functions of organizational climate and goals as well as structure.

## Organizational Communication and Decision Making

An organizational climate that supports the concept of self-challenge in a quest for renewal and rewards the contribution of new ideas is conducive to successful innovation. Marcum (1968), for example, compared the organizational climates of high- and low-innovating schools and found that the schools involved in innovating showed more open climates. Numerous others affirm and confirm this principle (Glaser and others, 1967; Watson, 1967; Schmuck, 1968; Glaser and Taylor, 1973).

Several features of organizational climate conducive to open-minded consideration of ideas for change are related to communication and decision making.

Open Communication. An essential ingredient of a healthy climate for change is free communication, both formal and informal, flowing up and down the hierarchical lines and horizontally among colleagues (Miles, 1965; Marcum, 1968; Glaser, 1973).

Survey feedback, a special form of communication (discussed, for example, by Mann, 1971), involves systematically reporting results of surveys of employee and management attitudes and perceptions on such issues as employee/management relations and work conditions. The feedback system has been found to be highly effective in increasing understanding and communication between employees and in modifying supervisory behavior.

Miles and others (1971) analyzed a process of survey feedback wherein a client system examined data about itself. They found that meetings to consider such data with a view toward making and implementing action decisions have the effect of encouraging new behaviors and developing norms that facilitate productive work.

In an intricate study of the relation between six forms of organizational intervention and measured outcomes in organizational climate, managerial leadership, peer leadership, group process, and satisfaction, Bowers (1973) found that survey feedback, when thoroughly followed through, was the only treatment associated with across-the-board positive changes in organizational climate.

Bowers analyzed his data as follows (p. 31): "For each treatment [intervention], two sets of scores are given for each variable category. One comparison is labeled 'Whole Systems,' and refers to grand response mean gain scores for all respondents combined within organizations receiving that treatment for the first and second waves of measurement (ordinarily one year apart). The other comparison is labeled 'Capstone Groups' and refers, within the Interpersonal Process Consultation, Task Process Consultation, and Laboratory Training treatments, to persons in groups that actually received that particular treatment. For comparison purposes, persons in groups of a similar nature (ordinarily the top management groups) are presented for the Survey Feedback, Data Handback, and No Treatment clusters."

In the twenty-three organizations studied, Bowers obtained the following results with regard to the six intervention or control strategies used:

1.  *Laboratory training* was negatively associated with change in organizational climate both for the systems as a whole and for the "capstone groups" receiving special attention.
2.  *Interpersonal process consultation* reflected a number of significant positive changes, especially in the managerial and peer-leadership areas.
3.  *Task process consultation* was associated with little change, except for decision-making practices and among capstone

groups, and only negative changes for the systems group as a whole.

4.  *Survey feedback,* as noted, reflected positive and significant changes for capstone groups in every area except managerial leadership, and in no case did it show negative change for the systems groups.

5.  In the case of mere *data handback,* which is not truly a change treatment, peer leadership and some aspects of managerial leadership improved, but all other measures showed essentially no change. Overall, organizational climate was viewed as becoming worse.

6.  *No treatment,* the control "treatment," was associated with general negative change for capstone groups and whole systems.

Gross, Giacquinta, and Bernstein (1971) report on an educational change study in which staff members were highly motivated to attempt implementation of a "catalytic role model" by which teachers were to become less directive. A major reason for unsuccessful results (at least during an initial period of several months) was the failure to establish and use feedback mechanisms to uncover barriers to change that arose during the attempted implementation, according to the authors. Also responsible was the director's failure to bring into the open the several types of difficulty the teachers were likely to encounter in the ghetto elementary school in which the experiment was conducted.

Dykens and others (1964), while advocating the importance of informal channels of communication, point out that a system of informal exchanges among staff members, by itself, is probably unlikely either to generate change or to compel interest in change in any systematic or important way; nor, they maintain, is it by itself likely to encourage creativity in thinking about long-range, complex, and demanding goals. Informality would seem to be adaptive when gradual modification is desired, rather than stimulative of markedly creative change. Lippitt and others (1967) mention a variable related to communication that may be critical: Organizational norms must support asking for and giving help. Thus, not only are the quantity, form, and direction of communication important, but the content must be related to the desired goals of problem solving in order for the organizational climate to be conducive to change.

Open communication enables access to new and developing ideas and innovations. Some persons are constantly exposed to concepts and programs and have access to those who not only are able to provide detailed information about them but also can sanction the development or application of an innovation. Others are removed from such stimuli, as House (1976) points out in the case of teachers who are limited by time constraints, by the expense of professional contacts, and by pressures to attend to daily classroom programs and are little rewarded for innovation.

In discussing the sharing of responsibility for decisions, Coleman (1976) cites two communication problems that are likely to affect change. The first is the problem, existing only in political democracies, of ensuring that each citizen or group of citizens has the effective right to express opposition to the government or its policies. The second is a problem that exists for any large corporate body, whether it is democratic or not: to have sufficiently accurate feedback from policy actions so that those who do have political power—however broadly or narrowly that power is distributed—can efficiently achieve their policy goals.

Research is rarely initiated by stockholders, workers, or customers. In nearly every instance in which information relevant to decision making is obtained, the design, execution, and publication of the research attend solely to the information needs of the central policy makers, not to the interests of other parties who may be affected. From these considerations, Coleman has made some suggestions about appropriate structures for generating research that will reflect the legitimate interests of all those who will be affected.

**Administrative and Colleague Support.** An administrative system of rewards or sanctions that motivate problem-solving efforts should exist, point out Costello and Zalkind (1963), who describe the administrator as a reinforcement agent. They state that positive reinforcement of correct responses is essential and recommend that the administrator place emphasis on extrinsic reinforcements such as salary and fringe benefits.

Lippitt, Benne, and Havelock (1966) found that teachers who perceived a principal as supporting innovation did in fact innovate more often. That the perception of administrative support is related to supportive activity (not just words) is also suggested by this same study, which found that more than one third of the teachers who viewed the principal as bringing educational literature to their attention adopted new practices, while those who viewed him or her as never bringing such literature to their attention did not adopt new classroom practices.

The attitude of colleagues toward change can exert a strong force that inhibits or facilitates innovativeness within an organization. Chesler and Fox (1967), for example, point out that new teachers in a system, fresh from college or advanced training, may enter a school eager to try new ways, only to be blocked by an established culture dominated by older teachers who do not welcome the suggestions. Lippitt and others (1967) found that teachers who perceived colleague support in adoption efforts were more likely themselves to be adopters of new practices.

**Participation in Decision Making.** Extensive participation by all persons concerned in the identification and solution of organizational problems is conducive to change (Watson and Glaser, 1965; Chesler and Fox, 1967; Glaser and Ross, 1971; Glaser, 1976, 1981b). Rigid, authoritarian structures and coercive controls reduce trust and retard innovation. Forced or authoritative decisions are more likely to be circumvented and/or discontinued; group decision making is a longer process but is more likely to result in lasting change (Rogers, 1967). Coch and French (1958) conducted a classic experiment on this thesis, involving the introduction of a changed product in a textile factory. Later replication supported the conclusion that the greater the involvement of workers or other stakeholders in planning the coming change, the better their acceptance of it (French, 1960; Marrow, 1969; Glaser, 1976, 1980a; Schrank, 1978).

According to White (1977), all groups in an organization

concerned with the complete operation cycle should be involved in the decision process before moving from an idea or research to development. In the case of new technology, it is important that even those who will not take part until the later phases of the operation, as, for example, in manufacturing or service, participate in the transition, because lead times for their participation might be quite long. In the setting where White works in development of diagnostic methods and equipment, the research phase is planned within a three- to five-year research period, and the total period from the beginning of the research to manufacturing operations is six to eight years.

Dykens and others (1964), in a study of strategies of mental health change, conclude that participation in change efforts by those affected may lead to positive and constructive feelings and can further enthusiasm for change.

A follow-up study after four years of a two-year organizational change program in a company that shifted from a highly centralized, authoritarian system toward a participation system (Seashore and Bowers, 1970) revealed an evidently continuing progression toward the participative pattern, accompanied by an increase in profitability. Suggested explanations for the success of the program included the thesis that reasonable assumptions about values and motives of individual workers were taken into account in making structural changes in the organization, thus "locking in" the central characteristics of the system.

In an earlier work, Marrow, Bowers, and Seashore (1967) report a change program initiated when a successful manufacturer acquired a less successful competitor. Changes introduced cut across organizational structure, policies, work methods, and technology and included the building of a new organizational climate with the introduction of participative management at all levels. The treatise carefully documents how applied behavioral science brought about change and provides a comparative study of the effects of two differing managerial styles on human behavior and task performance. As noted earlier, participation by workers in decision making is exemplified in the "sociotechnical" experiments conducted in Norway by a committee of workers, management, and government (Thorsrud, 1968). These experiments lessened supervision by foremen and increased worker responsibility through small-group operation on larger-scale tasks.

Although studies indicate that in most situations wide participation in decision making is preferable, Watson and Glaser (1965) suggest that the judicious use of executive or administrative power can be successful in what is referred to as the *"fait accompli."* This can be considered suitable when an authoritative decision is needed to overcome emotional, rather than rational, resistance to a change. An example cited is President Truman's order to integrate personnel in the Armed Forces and to open advancement opportunities for qualified members of minority groups.

But enforced changes can backfire. Sometimes, the greater the push, the stronger the opposition pull, as Marmor, Bernard, and Ottenberg (1960) observe. Enforced change can succeed only when opposition is relatively weak compared with the strength of the promoters.

Writing from personal experience as assistant secretary for administration in the Department of State, Crockett (1977) noted that, in that situation, efforts to introduce organizational change by directive without staff participation in decision making tended to result in hostility, suspicion, defensiveness, and a mobilization of both overt and covert opposition.

Firestone (1977) supports the principle that *how* a project is planned with personnel may determine its outcome more than their examination of its concepts and purposes does. As an illustration, he points to a workshop to consider personalized education that teachers were *required* to attend, thus seriously attenuating potential enthusiasm or motivation to attend the workshop.

He suggests that opposition to change may be reduced and made manageable by trade-offs between opposing forces—for example, exchanging staff support for centrally developed plans, in return for administrative help in furthering staff-initiated ideas. As Likert (1961) points out, this procedure may not by itself create staff support for change, but it can serve to eliminate the need to dilute innovators' ideas in order to avoid disappointments that add to subordinates' resistance.

Goodridge (1976), evaluating factors that entered into a

decision to adopt a highly individualized teaching program labeled Individually Guided Education (IGE) in eight schools,
made observations such as the following about the limited extent of decision sharing:

1.  Principals were the major decision makers, although in a
    majority of schools this decision was shared with teachers.
2.  Superintendents were not participants in any of the schools
    where the major decision makers were the principal and the
    staff.
3.  Board members, office personnel, and parents were mini-
    mally involved in the decision process.
4.  School boards were often prepared to let others decide
    about educational programs if no extra cost was involved.
5.  In none of the cases was decision making shared among
    board members, superintendents, principals, staff, and par-
    ents. When decision making was shared, it was between no
    more than two levels in the organization.
6.  When the research data were collected, many decision mak-
    ers considered that the amount of information available to
    them had been inadequate, although at the time of adop-
    tion they had considered themselves well informed.
7.  Visits to IGE schools had a positive effect on the decision
    to adopt IGE.

### Miscellaneous Factors

A number of other factors directly or indirectly related
to organization have been studied in relation to innovation and
change. For example, in a survey of several hundred school districts, Havelock (1973a) found a number of variables to have a
low but statistically significant correlation with an index of
school district innovativeness, notably the number of pupils,
per-pupil expenditure, utilization of media specialists and centers, in-service training, utilization of lay advisory groups, frequency of teacher strikes, and student unrest. (The last five
variables might well constitute "pressure forces," which, in
turn, lead to responsive change by the school district.)

The Institute for Development of Educational Activities

(I/D/E/A), in its 1970 annual report, addressed itself to problems of inducing change by setting up demonstration schools rather than working for reform within the school system. Successful programs tend to have considerable autonomy, to have entailed a long-term financial stake, to have employed a widely spread expenditure of energy, and to have developed a local constituency of parents, students, teachers, administrators, and community members.

Zaltman and others (1973) present the following five organizational factors as possibly affecting the innovative process in various ways:

1. *Complexity*—the number of occupational specialties and their professionalism.
2. *Formalization*—emphasis placed within the organization on following specific rules and procedures in performing one's job.
3. *Centralization*—the locus of authority and decision making within the organization.
4. *Interpersonal relations*—including degree of impersonality.
5. *Ability to deal with conflict*—over whether to innovate and how to innovate; differences in goals, perceptions, and so on; and intrapersonal, interpersonal, organizational, and interorganizational differences.

Rothman (1974), in an extensive literature survey, depicts organization variables of many kinds. In keeping with his interest in social work on a broad community action level, he considers the relations of organizations to their environment, along with the usual concerns regarding organizational goals, structure, bureaucracy, and operations. The roles of both professionals and paraprofessionals are given considerable prominence in the discussion of organizational change phenomena. The product of this investigation, Rothman's extensive list of generalizations and action guidelines relative to change variables pertaining to planning and organizing social change, has been referred to in Chapter Two.

More recently, Rothman (1980b) has prepared an action-oriented presentation of ideas on research-knowledge utilization in organizations. His study is based on social science research, supported by particular reference to a questionnaire and interview study of twelve British social service departments in and around greater London. He organizes findings and suggestions under four major headings: (1) structural factors conducive to research utilization, (2) the research process and research utilization, (3) organizational climate: attitudes and relationships, and (4) reports and products of research.

As an illustration of how research utilization is facilitated by the *structural connection of researchers to applied personnel,* Rothman suggests structured access of the research unit to the top planning functions, to the director of the agency, and to the senior management team. Regarding the *research process,* he suggests that operational personnel participate in carrying out the research. Illustrative of the importance of *organizational climate* is the observation that utilization of research is facilitated when researchers make interpersonal contact in operational situations. With regard to *reports and the products of research,* a number of ideas such as are discussed in Chapter Twelve on communication and dissemination are presented, including, for example, that research reports be made relevant to agency problems and concerns, exhibit credibility, and employ a style of presentation suited to agency personnel.

Cherns (1977) notes that the traditional ways of looking at organization design are often out of step with contemporary social conditions and technical advances. Whereas the crucial areas of change were formerly technological and economic, now the critical areas are political and social, as businesses and industries try to cope with political action and controls, consumer demands, environmental concerns, and generally better-educated employees and the public.

Baldridge and Burnham (1975) analyzed the results of two research projects on organizational change, one covering 20 schools in 7 districts and the other covering 264 large school districts. They point out that more attention to organizational features is needed because organizations are now the major adopters of social innovations and because organizational dynamics are the major independent variables that influence the number, rate, and durability of innovations.

Chakrabarti and Rubenstein (1976) examined the effects of seventeen variables (seven technoeconomic factors, the extent of top management support, six dimensions of organizational climate, and three modes of joint decision making) in the adoption of NASA innovations by sixty-five commercial organizations. In all, seventy-three cases of potential adoption were studied—twenty-eight process cases and forty-five product cases.

After reporting in detail on the various associations, the authors review the implications of the findings for organizational design, noting the relation of successful adoption of products to the availability of personnel to implement the technology, the difficulty of obtaining resources necessary for implementation, and the importance of top-management support of the technology.

Aldrich (1979) explains change in organizations on the basis of the distribution of resources in the organization's environment rather than of internal leadership or participation in decision making. His *population ecological approach* draws on economic history, industrial economics, the social psychology of organizations, organizational psychology, and political sociology. Organizations are perceived as undergoing three stages: variation, selection, and retention (or survival). Some organizations are selected over others because of their better fit with environmental requirements.

Kotter and Schlesinger (1979) recall that in 1973 the Conference Board asked thirteen eminent authorities to speculate on what significant management issues and problems would develop over the next twenty years. One of the strongest themes that run through their subsequent reports is a concern for the ability of organizations to respond to environmental change.

## Summary Comments

A major problem faced by those who set out to change any given element embedded in, or to be incorporated into, an organization is to determine the extent to which other elements of the structure and functioning of the organization need to be addressed, including its organizational climate.

The literature has much to say about organizational climate, the opening topic of this chapter. The characteristics included in climate are stated in ideal and idealized terms. Some of these characteristics are discussed also in conjunction with the quality-of-worklife literature, which presents some support for the positive terms mentioned in the treatment of organizational climate. The underlying issue in the consideration of this topic is the sharing of decision making. A participative and responsive management that involves employees in decisions that affect them and encourages them to identify and solve problems is likely to see an improvement in organizational effectiveness.

Elements of organizational climate crop up as various aspects of the organization are discussed—the setting of organizational goals; controls imposed by social expectancies; organizational structure; distribution of power; specialization; and related factors of size and capacity, organizational inertia, and self-renewal. Communication and decision making are also discussed as they relate to innovation and change. Factors specific to these various components need to be considered, and answers to questions about them may have to be differentiated according to settings, personnel involved, and conditions in general, but the underlying attitude toward organizational climate remains a central issue to be faced by those concerned with effective utilization of knowledge and skill and with the implementation of worthwhile change.

Regardless of the nature of the approach to organizational improvement, several authors have zeroed in on the question whether the enhancement effort should be directed primarily at the manager or at the organization.

A further distinction of special significance has to do with the order of approach—namely, whether one attempts general changes in an organization as a prelude to achieving a specific substantive change or whether one directs one's attention to the specific, without trying to modify the organization in any other way. In either case, as various writers have indicated, those involved in bringing about a change effort need to know the organization and the factors within it that are likely to militate against or to facilitate the desired change.

# 6

# Political, Economic, and Sociocultural Processes

An account of the determinants of the utilization of knowledge and the introduction of innovative change would not be complete without reference to influences associated with political, economic, and sociocultural institutions. In some instances the influence is patent, specific, and direct; in others, subtle, diffuse, and circuitous. The literature is replete with data and interpretations bearing on the subject. We shall present but a small sample of available references as a way of alerting the reader to the host of institutional factors that may affect the likelihood of innovation in industry, government, education, social services, and other aspects of individual and social life.

The special subject of research and policy formation, which affects decision making in these several fields, is treated in Chapter Fourteen.

### Political Factors

Governmental influences on the production and utilization of knowledge and the stimulation of innovative change are presented under four headings: government subsidy and regula-

123

tion, the process of governmental influence, effects on government agencies, and government policy issues. These topics are obviously interrelated and overlapping, as is the whole subject of political factors with those designated as economic and socio-cultural.

**Government Subsidy and Regulation.** Nelson, Peck, and Kalachek (1967), in a report sponsored by the Rand Corporation and the Brookings Institution, note federal government expenditures for R&D as far back as 1964 of well over $13 billion (in 1981 they were about $29 billion). Over $7 billion of this sum went to the Department of Defense; over $3.5 billion to NASA; and over $1 billion to the Atomic Energy Commission. The Department of Health, Education and Welfare received three quarters of a billion, most of which was allocated to the National Institutes of Health.

The report describes government policies regarding the advancement of technology as "vast and heterogeneous." Two broad objectives for such policies are stated: (1) to create advances needed by government agencies themselves in performing particular functions and (2) to stimulate progress to benefit either a particular private sector or the economy as a whole. To attain these objectives, the government also relies on privately supported R&D in the sense that these functions are often carried out by private firms that serve as suppliers to government agencies. The government may strongly influence this innovative process, however, by setting specifications for purchases and competitive bidding, for example.

Patent policy is another source of government influence on technological advance. On the positive side, according to Nelson, Peck, and Kalachek, the patent system has been an important social device for enhancing the rewards for invention and innovation by increasing the cost and difficulties of imitation and by making private property out of what otherwise, in the absence of secrecy, would be in the public domain. On the negative side, the system grants the inventor a monopoly that may either inhibit more widespread use of the innovation or add to the cost to the consuming public. Despite its limitations, no realistic substitute for the patent system has yet been proposed.

The authors of the report conclude their treatment by making several proposals, the most distinctive of which is the establishment of a National Institute of Technology designed in part to introduce a more orderly development and execution of public policy on technical advance.

Writing subsequently about issues similar to those raised by the Rand Corporation/Brookings Institution report, Mansfield (1971) notes a significant increase in the amount of attention devoted to public policies on technological change. Additional points made by Mansfield are that (1) the patent system was designed for the individual inventor, but most research and development is now performed by institutions, (2) patents are considered of limited importance to corporate innovation because most of the profits from many types of innovation can be captured before imitators have a chance to enter the market, (3) certain fields, such as electronics, chemicals, and drug industries, make extensive use of patents, while the automobile, paper, and rubber industries do not, (4) a President's Commission on the Patent System recommended a number of changes in the legal superstructure of the system, including speeding up patent approval, tightening the standards of patentability, and reducing the cost of challenging and defending patent rights.

Mansfield discusses other issues regarding the role of government, including the effects on technological change of antitrust policy and, in a later article (Mansfield, 1982), the bearing that tax policy may have on R&D and other innovative activities. In general, there has been a continuing debate around the combined issue of government subsidy and regulation of industry, as such measures have an impact not only on productivity but on innovative progress.

Similarly, in certain fields, notably education, sides have been formed regarding the degree to which federal subsidy may enhance or inhibit local initiative. Chapter Eleven considers the extent to which, and the agencies through which, federal efforts influence educational research, development, and dissemination.

Although Gerstenfeld (1977a), in a study of 107 successful and unsuccessful projects in eleven industries in Maine, noted instances in which government regulation had acted as a deterrent to innovation and had caused added expense, he found that, by and large, performance regulations were cited as a direct or indirect source of innovations. In 36 percent of the cases studied, the role of government was cited as a major factor affecting the innovation. The influence was especially noteworthy in the areas of pollution, safety, and energy. Federal regulations, at times in conjunction with state regulations, were most frequently associated with successful projects, there being very few local regulations among the instances studied. Variations in the effects of government regulations have been reported for various industries and types of products. For example, increased stringency in federal regulation of the drug industry has resulted in fewer new drugs becoming available in this country, compared with other countries; however, uniform airline pricing regulations resulted in an emphasis on service-improving innovation.

The Charpie Task Force Report, Section III (U.S. Department of Energy, 1978), analyzes the temporary energy-market demonstration project that the task force sponsored as a commercializing incentive to the introduction of new technology. It considers the necessary conditions for commercialization, the role of federal participation in the energy market, the characteristics of demonstrations, the past federal record in sponsoring technical demonstration projects, and the primary audiences for federally sponsored demonstrations. It is evident from this list of topics that a thorough and many-sided analysis of potential relations between government and industry is essential to a true understanding of governmental influence on a significant industrial field.

In an article in *Science,* Smith (1980b) summarizes certain of the views expressed in two books by Ramo (1980a, 1980b). Ramo is quoted as stating that the country is experiencing an "almost uncontrollable imbalance between rapidly accelerating technological advance and lagging social progress" (quoted in Smith, 1980b, p. 1331). What is needed to reduce inflation and enhance productivity, according to Ramo, is a more favorable climate for innovation. Specific measures are proposed whereby the government would permit accelerated depreciation of plant and equipment, eliminate income taxes on savings interest and capital gains, and reduce the tax on corporate income. Ramo's treatises include many other substantive proposals, but the fundamental point made in relation to innovation is that overregulation generally hampers corporate innovation and that the right balance of government and private participation needs to be sought in every technological undertaking. (The 1981–1982 tax laws seem to move in the direction that Ramo has proposed.)

Null (1976) reports an interesting illustration of the way in which governmental intervention may influence change. He indicates how the Federal Water Pollution Control Act Amendments of 1972 established the responsibilities of the U.S. Environmental Protection Agency for the drafting of regulations and of grant procedures for allocating some $300 million that had been appropriated for the program. The guidelines called for a definition of user needs and a clear and practical response to each of these needs. The regulations placed limits on freedom in the choice of solutions. They also served to frame the general form and scope of the government-supported project.

Examining federal dissemination policy in education, Raizen (1977) criticized three aspects:

1.  The variety of viewpoints on what constitutes dissemination, ranging from one-way flow of information to all possible activities that might result in desired educational improvement.
2.  The complexity of the structure and mechanics for dissemination induced by federal legislation. Fifty-four individuals and agencies had responsibility for dissemination in education—from the president to state and local agencies.
3.  Funding for dissemination. In fiscal year 1975, R&D funding represented less than 0.5 percent of the total investment in education. The funding for dissemination was 10 percent of all R&D. There was also a mismatch, according to Raizen, between agency responsibility and agency funding level.

**Legislative Enactments Process.** Legislative enactment is an obvious force for change, but one that is qualified by implementation factors. Beyer and Trice (1978) addressed the question of the extent and nature of the implementation of two federal legal mandates: the 1970 Hughes Act relative to problems of alcoholism among federal employees and the 1972 Equal Employment Opportunity Act. They found that legislation as an external impetus to change was qualified by community, organizational, and union advocacy or support, as well as by key actors such as installation directors, policy facilitators, and supervisors.

The importance of broad consensus underlying legislative proposals of comprehensive scope is illustrated by Swan (1976). Reporting on an effort to pass comprehensive legislation to decentralize the state hospitals in Minnesota, Swan concluded that a proposal of major scope has little chance of passage in a legislative body (even when the research is competent and cogent) if it has only limited support from executive authorities and, more important, if it lacks consensus on state policy (in this case, relating to deinstitutionalization). Without bipartisan consensus on goals, legislation must be drafted on a piecemeal basis—with individual items prepared in cooperation with the department involved and with coalitions of persons and groups supporting the effort.

The complexity that may be involved in emphasizing the legislative process to bring about change is illustrated in an attempt reported in *Science* (Smith, 1980a) to influence government policy toward support of a very large-scale R&D project. Smith reports a successful multifaceted effort made by a member of the House Science and Technology Committee to obtain congressional approval of a bill that provided for a demonstration nuclear-fusion installation (development of which may require $20 billion), projected to be operating within twenty years. The bill also provided resources for a test facility to tackle the most severe engineering problems that might be encountered within the decade. The strategy for bringing about such a large change in government support for fusion R&D included the following component tactics:

1. Persuasively *highlighting the promise of exceedingly worthwhile payoff.* Representative Mike McCormack (D–Wash.)

was a credible sponsor because he was a former scientist with the Atomic Energy Commission. McCormack promised that fusion would yield "an absolutely unlimited supply of cheap energy in a practical form for all mankind forever" (Smith, 1980a, p. 290) and alleged that it would provide energy independence for all the nations of the world, improve the economic posture of the United States, and lessen international strife in the Middle East and elsewhere.

2. *Building a powerful, influential supportive coalition.* After an unsuccessful attempt to increase fusion funds, McCormack impaneled his own advisory committee of distinguished scientists and atomic engineers, set up to counter a Department of Energy (DOE) committee that had been considerably less fervent in supporting the proposal. The new committee members included officers of companies doing fusion research with federal funds. A key staff member of the committee (Dr. Allan Mense) was a nuclear physicist then working at Oak Ridge National Laboratory.

This advisory committee heartily recommended acceleration of the program. Several months later, the same conclusion was reached by separate panels of the Atomic Energy Forum and the International Atomic Energy Agency.

3. *Building further support by personal contact with the decision makers.* With the powerful recommendations and sponsors mentioned above, the first goal was simply to provide members of Congress and their staff aides with information about fusion and its potential. McCormack signed up most of his colleagues on the House Science and Technology Committee as cosponsors, and Mense provided detailed technical information for the congressional staffs, including expected technological spinoffs.

Outside assistance was solicited and obtained from an industry trade association that provided a knowledgeable full-time lobbyist to work on the bill, and the number of congressional cosponsors was increased. Vigorous lobbying and letter writing were undertaken at the thirty or so universities where fusion research is now underway, and they, in turn, contacted their respective senators and representatives. Members of Congress from key states, including House and Senate majority and minority leaders, were contacted by constituents and senior scientists from DOE's national laboratories. Most of those personally contacted agreed to become cosponsors.

With this show of strength, McCormack had little difficulty persuading the House and Senate leadership to bring the bill up for a quick vote, despite the crowded calendar just before the October 1980 recess.*

This example illustrates the powerful confluence for support of major change (in support of fusion R&D in this case) that can be achieved by (1) credibly clarifying the worth, need, and attractiveness of the proposed change, (2) obtaining the backing of distinguished persons in the given subject field, and (3) having these respected, influential individuals and powerful groups make personal contact (lobby) with the decision makers to facilitate their appreciation of the important benefits that the investment promises—aside from the personal advantage that might accrue as a by-product from visible leadership as a cosponsor.

**Governmental Policy Issues.** Governmental concern with the need for change in a wide range of fields is demonstrated by Walsh (1979), who reports on an unpublished options paper prepared at President Carter's request by a year-long task force under the title "Domestic Policy Review of Industrial Innovation."

The fullness and diversity of input led to many recommendations, often contradictory. The complexity of innovation, cutting across many fields, was noted. Changes in tax policy, patent and antitrust laws, and governmental procurement policies were suggested. Small business put in a claim for more attention. Health, safety, and environmental interests perceived the federal role differently than business interests, as did labor people, who were suspicious of innovations that might cause the displacement of workers. Public-interest advisory groups urged the promotion of innovations to further the goals of society in line with social and human needs.

---

*Although the bill has been funded, at this writing it is in a "research mode only" category at DOE.

There was agreement that American productivity is lagging but little consensus on how to remedy the situation other than the proposal for direct federal support for research and development.

In addition, the apparently ever-widening gap between university and industrial communities was reckoned as a cause of the diminishing influence of universities on innovation, and government help in fostering collaboration was recommended.

Government regulatory processes may block many good innovations (Myers and Sweezy, 1978). For example, the government could provide advisory guidance concerning the applicability of a regulation and the means by which the items in question could be adapted to meet regulatory requirements. In the absence of such advice, firms often discover too late that their innovations must be adapted at great expense to meet regulatory requirements that they had misinterpreted.

In an attempt to set forth the factors likely to encourage individual invention and large-scale innovation, Quinn (1977) has proposed guidelines for a new institutional system to be applied to such major problems as energy, environmental improvement, health care, public transportation, and low-cost urban housing. His chief suggestion relates to potential partnership transactions between business and government that would (1) create or guarantee an initial demand, (2) reduce operational bottlenecks, (3) aggregate demands, (4) aggregate resources, (5) extend time horizons, (6) take unusual but worthwhile risks, and (7) provide incentives.

Quinn's suggestion applies mainly to big business. He would combine the better characteristics of individual entrepreneurs and smaller enterprises, which he describes in terms of incentives, risk taking, long-time horizons, and competition, with those of large-scale innovative programs, such as the approaches used by the Bell Telephone laboratories.

At the request of the Joint Economic Committee of the U.S. Congress, the program-level managers of federal R&D activities presented suggestions for improving the innovative process with respect to government-sponsored R&D. Salasin (1978) reports the findings of the survey, which included questionnaire and conference proceedings. Major barriers to improving program management were found in failure to provide an adequate interface between the R&D program and the diffuse networks of researchers, users of results, policy officials, and other "stakeholders" in an R&D effort. Other barriers include lack of information about the effect of changing management practices and lack of adequate resources available for program management.

Three major themes run through comments made by research managers at the conference:

1. Policy making must provide an appropriate environment for research efforts.
2. Policy makers, in general, may lack an understanding of problems of research and its utilization.
3. Bureaucratic "layering" and mission fragmentation have proved deterrents to progress.

Two steps toward improving the capability of federal R&D programs to foster innovation were proposed: first, a wide-scale survey of program R&D managers within the federal government to provide additional information about the relative importance of the various barriers impeding innovation (especially those identified in the study) and suggestions for overcoming the barriers; second, experimental employment and comparison of efficacy of different management approaches and policy guidelines within several agencies or programs.

Drawing on studies of barriers to technology transfer carried out by the National Science Foundation (1973a) and the National Academy of Engineering (1974), Gartner and Naiman (1976) offer two specific proposals affecting government action: (1) the creation of public policy that provides incentive to small and large firms for overcoming barriers to technology transfer and (2) the creation of a federal structure to define needs and markets, to study the impact of implementation, and to help innovators, users, and suppliers utilize technology available from federal and nonfederal sources.

Bingham and McNaught (1975b) raise two issues regarding the adoption of innovation by government agencies: (1) Why do some local government units readily accept technological innovations, while others virtually ignore them? (2) What are the processes usually followed in adopting an innovation? These questions were applied to four public agency areas: school districts, public housing authorities, public libraries, and two common functions of city government. The specific innovations studied included computer systems in housing authority management and videotape records for educational instruction in secondary schools.

The study found that innovations do not tend to spread readily from one city to another, although there are some regional (but no national) patterns of diffusion. Characteristics of size, socioeconomic status, conservatism, and nature of organization seemed to have little or no relation to adoption, but federal and state assistance and user demand did show such a relationship. *Incentive proved a highly important determining factor.*

Among the recommendations included in the report are (1) a decrease in emphasis on adoption of *product* innovations in favor of programs to support transfer of *process* or service innovations, (2) a federally supported program to certify public and private service innovations, and (3) federal support for "process grants" to provide seed money for developing process innovations in local government settings.

## Economic Factors

In several respects economic factors may operate in a manner similar to political factors. For example, industrial firms often provide support for R&D that is only remotely related to immediate commercial interests, as in the case of a reported $50 million, 10-year grant by a German corporation to Massachusetts General Hospital for research on genetic engineering (Sun, 1981). In turn, research influences industrial innovation. In addition, industry sets up its machinery for making decisions about the conduct of research and the utilization of the knowledge resulting from it. A major difference between governmental and industrial influences on the production and use of knowledge is the relative importance assigned to profit motivation.

**Profit Motive as a Factor in Innovation.** Historical studies by Wilson (1961) and by Gold, Peirce, and Rosegger (1975) examine the extent to which the profit motive has served as a determinant of innovation. Wilson studied how agricultural research was communicated and put to use by American farmers during the first half of the twentieth century. The profit motive was found to be a significant incentive to information utilization. The more practical the information the farmers received, the more they tended to give it serious attention. The process of acceptance went through the stages of awareness, interest, evaluation, trial, and eventual adoption or rejection of ideas.

*Industrial Research* magazine has sponsored an annual competition "to select the 100 most significant new technical products of the year." Questionnaires were sent to each of the persons responsible for the selected products from 1965 through 1974. Three hundred cases from this survey made up the sample for a study from which Goldhar, Bragaw, and Schwartz (1976) developed their analysis of the relative importance to innovation of a number of stimuli. A general market need is reported as having the greatest stimulus value, and a respondent's own recognition of a new technical possibility as being worthwhile is almost equally important. An offer of specific new technical information and a particular client's need are also influential but of modest importance.

Several studies have suggested that what competitors do tends to stimulate other firms or agencies to respond by developing new products or programs. Souder and Chakrabarti (1978b) question this, however. In their investigations they have found that what competitors may do or what competitors actually do is not a primary impetus toward innovation. They found, as did Goldhar and associates, that a desire to enter a new market or expand one's own proprietary lines provides greater impetus.

Determining profit advantage for high-technology product-line programs, according to Moore (1976), requires long-range forecasting, including consideration of factors specifically related to the product line in question. Moore identifies the pertinent factors as (1) the accuracy of estimates of the number of potential customers, (2) the accuracy of assumptions relating to product acceptance, (3) the probability of concurrent market introduction of competitive alternates, (4) the economic capability of potential customers to buy at a price that will yield a fair profit to the producer, (5) the attempts of competitors to "corner the market" by destructive price cutting, and (6) the actual protection achievable by assumed proprietary positions based on patents, trade secrets, marketing advantages, and financial strength.

More indirect, but of equal importance, are the effects on markets, costs, shortages, cost of capital, and availability of labor exerted by world, national, and industrywide economic conditions. Other indirect influences that should be considered are the political outlook, inflation, and currency exchange rates in foreign countries that must be depended on either as customers or as suppliers of essential materials and/or labor. Likewise, high-technology management must be alert to trends in legal controls and regulations that restrict operation or affect costs of high-technology products.

**Intensive Study of Particular Industries and Innovations.** Duchesneau, Cohn, and Dutton (1979, 1980) illustrated how change factors operate in the economic area, conducting a two-phase, in-depth study of the adoption and diffusion of technological innovations in fifty firms (and twenty control firms) in the footwear manufacturing industry. Two major questions were addressed: (1) What are the determinants of innovation; that is, what causes firms to use or not use a given innovation or sets of innovations? (2) What is the nature of innovation decision making in the firms studied?

Using the criterion of innovations adopted, Duchesneau and associates found significant antecedent factors to be as follows:

1. *Economic*—firm size and existence of a technical or engineering group.
2. *Managerial*—the number of managers above the level of foreman, the number with engineering degrees, the use of market research, managerial attitudes, and the use of consultants.

3. *Bureaucratic structure*—number of specialties and amount of extraorganizational activity.

4. *External communications*—frequency of contact with supplier representatives, number of trade journals read, and attendance at trade associations and trade shows.

5. *Intrafirm communications*—presence of interdepartmental managerial committee.

6. *Decision-making procedures*—performance gap (as perceived by principal respondent) and presence of a unit to evaluate new machinery.

In another phase of the study, it was found that awareness of a performance gap was a more significant factor with reference to major innovations than to minor ones.

A predominantly economic approach to the study of factors potentially associated with the rate of diffusion (in terms of market penetration or adoption) of some forty-one industrial innovations is evident in a study by Martino, Chen, and Lenz (1978), as the following list of principal factors included will show: relative advantage, investment cost, industry concentration, age of work force, age of facilities, capacity utilization, industry growth rate, profitability, compatibility, regulatory encouragement, professional work force, sales per employee, growth in productivity, capital investment per worker, and research and development.

The forty-one innovations were applicable to fields as diverse as chemical processes, aircraft, railroads, energy, coal mining, machinery, computer control, materials, and agricultural processing. Extensive data were gathered from trade and technical journals, industry association publications, and various reports and publications of the federal government.

The general conclusions of the study are presented in two parts. First, that mathematically determined diffusion prediction models were regarded as having sufficient power to be easily used by individuals wishing to apply them to particular industries in order to predict rate of diffusion in terms of market penetration. Second, and less intricate to follow, is the conclusion that among the strongest variables in the models were regulatory encouragement, market share, and compatibility with the work force. Although the total mix of variables as measured seemed to display reported predictive value, the majority of variables, taken individually, failed to reach statistical significance. Nonetheless, both the methodology of the study and the qualitative analysis of findings provide a forward step in the effort to account for industrial diffusion rates.

**Comparison of Successful and Unsuccessful Projects.** To study the influence of various aspects of the environment, Utterback and others (1976) asked firms to name a successful and an unsuccessful project. Associated with success were such factors as (1) need for some new, improved product or procedure, (2) initiation by top management of the firm, (3) more highly structured and sophisticated planning, and (4) initiation because of governmental actions or regulatory constraints. Variations in influential factors were found to be associated with the stage of development of the innovation.

According to Utterback, innovations can be conceived as a function of a firm's environment, including (1) technical, market, economic, governmental, and other components, (2) communication between the firm and its environment, (3) the firm's resources, and (4) its organization of resources, including financial and human resources, technology, and information.

Gerstenfeld (1977a), in seeking the sources of success or failure of inventions, directs attention to the outside forces that promote demands and stimulate the development and shape of innovative projects and programs. Although external demand and internal need may simply be two views of the same motivation, he focuses attention on demand. He cites especially the impact of government regulations on invention within 107 projects, 68 of which were successful. He found that the regulations did not serve primarily as a stimulus for invention; rather, they affected the *direction* of a significant number of the innovative projects. This was especially true where regulations expressed demands such as those for safety and pollution control.

**Trends in Economic Innovation.** The history of invention and of technological development casts considerable light on the factors that determine change, according to Rosenberg

(1972, 1978), who has reviewed the diffusion of technologies that have extended over centuries rather than over recent decades. He describes inventive activity as a gradual process of accretion; a cumulation of minor improvements, modifications, and economies; a sequence of events in which, in general, continuities are much more important than discontinuities. Even where it is possible to identify major inventions that seem to represent entirely new concepts and therefore genuine discontinuities (that is, sharp and dramatic departures from the past), pervasive technological as well as economic forces are usually at work tending to slow down and to flatten out the impact of such inventions on the rise of productivity returns.

Most inventions, at first recognition, are relatively crude and inefficient. They are, of necessity, badly adapted to many of the uses to which they will eventually be put.

In addition, Rosenberg notes the importance of developing skills and facilities not only in using new techniques but also in machine-making itself. This issue involves the broadest questions of industrial organization and specialization and lies at the very heart of the industrialization process.

The state of development of the capital goods industries, more than any other single factor, determines whether and to what extent an invention is ahead of its time. Each important invention goes through a gestation period of varying length, while the capital goods industries adapt themselves to the special needs and requirements of the new technique.

Rosenberg would therefore encourage a broad view of the total process of invention and utilization and the deepening of insight into the factors that speed up or slow down its pace.

The chapter by Gold, Peirce, and Rosegger in a data-packed volume (Gold, 1975b), largely on economic impacts and implications of technological innovations in various industries, uses a 100-year historical survey approach to statistical diffusion data on fourteen major innovations in the iron and steel industry and its material-supplying branches.

The percentage of total output accounted for by an innovation is considered to be a better indication of utilization than the number of firms adopting it. Inconsistent results were found with regard to whether diffusion rates, measured by the percentage-of-output method, were higher in recent years than in earlier decades. The same inconsistency surfaces about rates during periods of expansion or contraction of output levels.

The increasing complexity and sophistication of the problems of the impact of knowledge transfer and technological innovation on the environment and social life are illustrated in a report of the Organization for Economic Cooperation and Development (1980), reviewed in *Science* by Walsh (1980) under the title "Is There a Catch to Innovation?"

The OECD report shifts from earlier reports that tended to concentrate on the relation between R&D and innovation to the structural problems facing the economy and the social dimensions of innovation. As an illustration, the report notes that implicit in technological change is the replacement of labor-intensive by capital-intensive industry, entailing the displacement of labor and a flare-up of the automation scare, with its implications for unemployment. Yet, the report suggests an increase in the pace of technological change, provided adjustment mechanisms are available for managing innovation in a growing economy. The problem is said not to lie in the potential of science and technology as such but, rather, in the capacity of our economic system to make satisfactory use of that potential.

## Sociocultural Factors

**A Framework of Sociocultural Factors and Theories.** Lauer (1977) suggests that to grasp the full meaning of change, one must be aware of its pervasive presence and must also recognize the various levels of analysis at which it operates, as shown in Table 4.

Citing details and examples, Lauer presents the mechanisms or determining factors of change in terms of five perspectives:

1.  The mechanistic perspective, in which *technological development* is seen as the major source of social change.

Table 4. Levels of Analysis in Social Change.

| Level of Analysis | Some Representative Areas of Study | Some Representative Units of Study |
|---|---|---|
| Global | International organization; international inequality | Gross national product; trade data; political alliances |
| Civilization | Life cycle of civilizations or other patterns of change (evolutionary or dialectical, for example) | Artistic, scientific, and other innovations; social institutions |
| Culture | Material culture; nonmaterial culture | Technology; ideology; values |
| Society | Stratification system; structure; demography; crime | Income, power, and prestige; roles; migration rates; murder rates |
| Community | Stratification system; structure; demography; crime | Income, power, and prestige; roles; population growth; murder rates |
| Institutions | Economy; polity; religion; marriage and family; education | Family income; voting patterns; church attendance; divorce rate; proportion of people with college education |
| Organizations | Structure; interaction patterns; authority structure; productivity | Roles; friendship cliques; administration/production ratio; output per worker |
| Interaction | Types of interaction communication | Amount of conflict, competition, or neighboring; identity of frequent and infrequent participants in interaction |
| Individual | Attitudes | Beliefs about various matters; aspirations |

From *Perspectives on Social Change* by R. H. Lauer (2nd ed., p. 5). Copyright 1977 by Allyn & Bacon. Reproduced by permission.

2. The idealistic perspective, whereby *ideologies* are viewed either as facilitators of change or as principal impediments or barriers.

3. The perspective of *interactional mechanisms of competition and conflict,* including violence, as pervasive forces inducing change.

4. The perspective of *government and "status anguish,"* or discrepancy between actual and expected status, as sources of change.

5.   The perspective of the role of *special categories,* notably of elites and of youth, in producing social change.

The various mechanisms of sociocultural change merge into several patterns that describe the "how" of change. Lauer groups these patterns under two heads:

1.   *Cultural patterns*—stressing anthropological views and depicting the processes of evolution, diffusion, and acculturalization.
2.   *Societal patterns*—stressing industrialization and modernization (and their relation to urbanization, secularization, and bureaucratization).

Lauer concludes his otherwise extensive treatment of social change with a brief discourse on what he terms *strategies of change.* Some of the previously presented theories on the sources of change imply a kind of helplessness in the face of the broad sweep of history, but in this section Lauer stresses "willed history," or planned change. Returning to the concept of levels of analysis, in a discussion of targets of change, he includes the individual, the group, and the social structure. He notes as a strategy the wisdom of aiming low—that is, aiming at short-run and realistic targets. The familiar topic of change agents and that of the change strategies of power, as opposed to attitude influence, are touched on. The consideration of strategies ends with a brief comparison of violent and nonviolent approaches to the achievement of social change. It is evident that Lauer envisages his subject on a large canvas.

Kotler (1973) presents a five-faceted framework for describing the determining variables and conditions of social change, which he defines as the occurrence of an alteration in the form or function of a significant group, institution, or social order. The five elements of the paradigm are as follows:

1.   A *cause*—a social objective or undertaking that change agents believe will provide an answer to a social problem.
2.   A *change agency*—an organization whose primary mission is to advance a social cause.

3. *Change targets*—individuals, groups, or institutions designated as targets of change efforts.
4. *Channels*—ways in which influence and response can be transmitted between change agents and change targets.
5. A *change strategy*—a basic mode of influence adopted by the change agent to affect the change target.

Taken as a whole, Kotler's five-element framework does not purport to distinguish the building blocks of the process but, rather, to enter into the dynamics of the social planning of change.

Coleman (1973) notes qualifications that need to be taken into account in considering certain conflicting theories of factors that determine social change. Thus, *legal* action at the federal level, as regards incorporation law, is watered down by the fact that incorporation is done by individual states, and corporation managers tend to select for incorporation purposes the state that offers the most favorable terms. The provision of additional *economic* resources as a basis for changing social conditions has had mixed results, according to Coleman, notably in foreign aid. Theorists who stress *achievement orientation and individualism* fly in the face of the norms of certain societies that stress the power of collectivity (family, clan, tribe) in preventing the individual from adopting new ways. In contrast to the individualist theory, *revolutionary theories* depend on a total commitment to the revolutionary movement. They, like the other theories, require concomitant and pertinent changes in the educational system, broadly viewed, which are often lacking in providing both the skills and the attitudes necessary to implement the designs of the several theories of social change.

**Sociocultural Settings.** The sociopolitical character of an agency or setting has considerable bearing on its receptivity to and implementation of program change proposals. For example, in a rural setting, to introduce educational change requires sensitivity to the distinctive aspects of a social and political setting that tends to inhibit innovation (isolation, traditions and localized values, shortages of resources) and affects the appropriateness of selected change strategies (Boyd and Immegart, 1977).

From their field studies in rural Appalachia and rural communities in New York State extending over a five-year period, Boyd and Immegart have identified a number of faulty assumptions inherent in typical attempts at educationally oriented innovation by state and federal authorities in depressed rural areas.

The "faulty assumptions" are (1) that rural people will be glad to accept outside advice, help, and charity, (2) that they will regard change, as such, positively, (3) that large-scale infusion of *outside* resources and ideas will produce change, (4) that educational changes by themselves are an effective means of fostering broader social change, (5) that outside experts can penetrate the rural sociopolitical structure and affect decision making, and (6) that dramatic and significant progress can best be achieved by introducing the latest techniques and ideas.

The rural environment is by no means the only setting where assumptions about the character of the environment can have an impact. According to Kritek (1976), even in the well-structured and highly efficient setting of a large research-based industrial, educational, or social service program, environmental issues affect the decisions to be made. The appearance of value-free judgments is an illusion created by the complex set of values represented in the variety of components and personnel within an organization and of formal mechanisms for choice and operations. These mask the underlying values that lead to decisions.

Sutton (1974), in an attempt to ascertain the relation between political/cultural context and change-agent organization for innovation, first classified the U.S. mainland states as traditionalistic, moralistic, or individualistic. (The Southern states, for example, tend to fall in the first category.) He then obtained data on state planning through a mail questionnaire addressed to appropriate agencies.

Sutton concluded that the following factors increase as one considers the preceding classification: (1) the level of innovation in the state government, (2) the level of financial support provided change-agent organizations, (3) the tendency for change-agent activities to have a long-run product or outcome, and (4) the likelihood that there will be a specialized structure associated with the change-agent organization to protect it from its environment.

Sarason (1971) indicates how the cultures within and around a school affect a school's functioning and shape and how they control changes. The author stresses the need for an explicit diagnosis of environmental and cultural features of an institution or program, noting that in many studies of change such diagnosis is not explicit, and the features of the internal and external cultures are insufficiently defined.

While noting various institutional blocks to professional leadership in the actual implementation of educational change, Stiles and Robinson (1973) point to several major forces or determinants that tend to induce change, as follows:

1.  Pressure from minorities for rights and justice—for example, from ethnic and economic groups; from parents of children who are mentally, emotionally, or physically handicapped; and from students protesting against exclusion from the policy-making processes of society.
2.  Crisis conditions, such as reaction to the Soviet launching of Sputnik.
3.  New discoveries of knowledge and technology, such as findings on how children learn to read or respond to behavior reinforcement or the development of newer teaching technologies.
4.  Economic or political conditions, illustrated by changes in educational practices resulting from increases or decreases in available funds.

Stiles and Robinson see these forces as operating through the allocation of funds, modification of policies, legal enactments, court mandates, and research.

**Miscellaneous Psychosociocultural Factors.** Barnett (1953) approaches the subject of innovation by means of an intensive psychological analysis of cultural anthropological data. He perceives the invention, discovery, and diffusion processes as ubiquitous and richly manifested among all cultural groups, including primitive and ancient peoples. He interprets innovations as ideas rather than as things; hence, he stresses the mental aspect of the processes of innovating and accepting innovations. Cultural changes are initiated by individuals, but individuals live amid a milieu of ideas. The *size and complexity of the cultural inventory* that is available to an innovator establish limits within which he or she must function. The accumulation of ideas provides only a minimum condition for innovation. There must be a *concentration of ideas* in the personal experience of the innovator: The likelihood that a new idea will develop is enhanced where there is a *collaboration of effort,* a condition that varies with cultures.

Barnett also notes that the opposition of different "idea systems" may stimulate new ideas—for example, where different cultural groups mix or when missionaries operate in a given cultural setting. That which is different may be imitated, or a combination of elements from two cultures may result from such divergences.

Barnett goes on to detail the operation of innovation-determining factors inherent in a given cultural background, including (1) the extent to which change is an expected occurrence in the culture, (2) freedom from dependence on restrictive authority, (3) the presence of competition as an incentive, (4) the widespread existence of deprivation of essentials (in the sense of unavailability of something that a person believes he or she has a right to expect), and (5) the side effect of other changes (such as may be imposed by a conquering group or voluntarily adopted from an outside source). According to Barnett, the operation of each of these factors can be readily demonstrated by reference to anthropological data.

Morrison (1973) has studied the use of *relative deprivation* explicitly or implicitly as a central variable in the explanation of social movements and hence of social change. Relative deprivation is viewed in terms of what one *wants* rather than what one *has*. The concept of social movements employed in conjunction with examination of the role of relative deprivation is that of a primarily power-oriented movement—a deliberate effort to organize people to act in concert to achieve group influence to make or block changes. Further, for relative deprivation to be suitably described, the desires involved must become legitimate expectations and must be perceived as blocked. Changes in aspirational deprivation, and in extent of deprivation also influence the strength of the variable. Those who occupy positions well off the bottom but far from the top of the stratification system are more likely to be involved in social movements stimulated by aspirational deprivation than those in the lowest stratum.

Morrison holds that the following conditions make more likely the emergence of a power-oriented movement resulting from the experience of high relative deprivation:

1.  A large population experiencing the deprivation.
2.  Close interaction, communication, and proximity.
3.  Commonality in role and status.
4.  A stratification system with clear stratum boundaries and visible differences between the strata.
5.  The presence of much voluntary association or group effort in a society (often resulting in a residue of leadership and organizational skills).

In sum, Morrison notes that social movements create social change, but they are also created *by* social changes that take away opportunities or create expectations faster than opportunities for reaching the expectations are created, resulting in relative deprivation.

An obvious determinant of social change of various sorts is a set of demographic factors associated with population growth (Sprehe and Speidel, 1973). Population growth and the resulting age and geographical distribution have consequences for employment, economic development, urbanization, education, public health, the family, and environmental quality, among other facets of the economic, political, social, and cultural life of a society.

The two-way relation between social structure and diffusion is the subject of an article by Rogers (1973b), who summarizes his views in a series of propositions, such as follows:

1. *Social structure acts to impede or to facilitate the rate of diffusion and adoption of new ideas through system effects.*

*System effects* refers to norms, social statuses, hierarchy, and so on.

2. *Diffusion can change the social structure of a social system*; for example, the initiation of a marketing research department in a business firm may affect the rate of future innovation diffusion within the system.

3. *Power elites act as gatekeepers to prevent restructuring innovations from entering a social system while favoring innovations that do not immediately threaten to change the system's structure.* The power elites thereby channel innovations so that their consequences accrue disproportionately to certain favored individuals.

4. *Top-down change in a system, which is initiated by the power elites, is more likely to succeed than bottom-up change,* the latter often involving a greater degree of conflict. (This proposition is qualified by the fact that, except for work on the social psychology of social movements, research on social change has dealt predominantly with types of change that were promoted or at least favored by the power elite in the system.)

5. *Bottom-up change is more likely to be successful at times of perceived crisis,* such as an economic depression, a political or military setback, a competitor's breakthrough, or a status threat.

6. *Bottom-up change is more likely to be successful when a social movement is headed by a charismatic leader* (whose role decreases as the movement becomes institutionalized).

These propositions are considered to fall in a "middle range" between strict empiricism and general theory—that is, drawn from research findings and observations but only partway to the abstracted level of theoretical statements about social change. Nevertheless, they are perceived as applying to broad social movements as well as to more specific innovative practices.

Hawley (1978) uses a large canvas to depict a set of fundamental concepts and theories that have been employed in the description and explanation of social-change phenomena. In skeletal outline, his views can be summarized in a series of topic sentences:

1. The notion of directionality in social change rests on the assumption of irreversibility.
2. Irreversibility is an elemental assumption in the theory of evolution.
3. Expansion characterizes social growth, because cumulative change denotes an increase in the number and variety of roles and relationships, ordinarily accompanied by an increase in population and complexity.
4. Distinguishable components of technology are often staggered in their development, the tool in some instances appearing before an effective organization for its use.
5. The course of history has progressively reduced the utility of an evolutionary model in the explanation of cumulative change, but the accumulation of information in storage facilities is so vast that generations will pass before its potential uses are exhausted.

### Summary Comments

The small sampling in this chapter of the literature on political, economic, and sociocultural forces that affect the process of knowledge utilization and innovative change can serve only to alert the reader to a very large subject—one that has intrigued anthropologists, sociologists, historians, philosophers, economists, political scientists, educators, and a host of others in scholarly and applied fields of study. Each discipline has confronted issues bearing on the opposition between forces for stability and for change. Manifestations of the wider drama are present in matters ranging from the changing of an individual's hairstyle to the modification of the mores underlying society's family structure. Yet, each scholar or practitioner must allow his or her needs to determine the scope of inquiry or practice in any given enterprise, while always retaining a background awareness of the complex transactionalism of all the major influences at work.

Few would deny the general significance of the political, economic, and sociocultural environment in matters of knowledge utilization and innovative change. However, a general awareness is not enough; it is necessary to tease out the specific operative factors and to study the way they operate. This, in a limited way, is the objective of this chapter.

*Governmental factors* are depicted as existing on a two-way street: Through subsidy and regulation, government influences knowledge production, dissemination, and resulting change; it may itself be affected by information dissemination and by change efforts. This two-way process needs to be understood in viewing governmental functioning and pertinent policy.

The subject of the relations of politics to knowledge-related activities and innovative change raises debatable issues such as whether subsidy may result in undue control and whether regulation encourages or inhibits innovation. The way government operates when it tries to be helpful to knowledge utilization or innovative change has come under critical study. Questions have been raised concerning imbalances in the distribution of largess and the less-than-effective spreading of assistance over the several stages of the research-to-diffusion process. Notwithstanding criticisms, the literature as summarized in this chapter and in Chapter Eleven on linkage and diffusion bears testimony to the sizable impact of governmental factors.

The accounts of *economic variables* tend to rest on somewhat steadier ground. Although the element of risk is present, the profit motive, the study of contemplated innovations, the firm's resources, and consideration of moves by competitors are some of the definite, specific factors that have come under study. Since the objectives of information gathering and innovation tend to be more clearly defined in the economic field, investigators can devote their time more fully to the means, and less to the ends, of the process. The importance of the subject of management in commercial and industrial establishments explains the high degree of overlap between economic influences and organizational factors.

Highly detailed studies of single industries have contributed to the specificity with which economic factors are set forth. The objectivity with which the success of an innovation can be measured has lent added objectivity to comparative investigations of successful and unsuccessful projects. Only as eco-

nomic considerations are viewed in conjunction with the introduction of the broad and often undetermined effects of technological advances does intangibility prevail to any extent.

We truly enter the realm of subjective judgment when
*sociocultural factors* are made the focus of our studies. This is
particularly so when historically oriented students of change
attempt to evolve broad, long-range theories of civilizational dynamics, whether the course of history is seen as cyclical or uni-
directional. Anthropologists, sociologists, and social psychologists have also come forward with their accounts of the nature
of change and, for that matter, of the forces for stability. Although it is often difficult to tie the insights derived from these
sources to immediate tasks faced by change agents, one has only
to read a sampling of the literature of these fields to sense the
real impact of the wider environment on individual change efforts, particularly in the area of social change. Obviously, the
more attention change agents give to ethical and philosophical
issues, the more they are likely to be concerned with sociocultural factors.

The choice of desirable and effective strategies is likely to
differ when the target of change lies in the sociocultural area.
The issue of coercion, for example, takes the form in some instances of a choice between violent and nonviolent strategies.
In the various sociocultural settings, the literature includes data-
packed studies, notably by anthropologists, as well as far-reaching speculative inquiry. Enriched insights into change factors
and processes are likely to result as the diverse literature of the
sociocultural area is consulted and placed alongside the analyses
of previous chapters relative to project, psychological, and organizational factors.

With this chapter, the broad survey of factors associated
with knowledge utilization, technology transfer, and innovative
change ends. However, additional determinants are embedded in
process stages through which the phenomena in question pass.
These are presented in Part Two. The treatment in Part Two
of the staging of the utilization and change process and in Part
Three of modes of linking and disseminating knowledge and use
is designed to steady the hand of those concerned with change
as they weave a course through the maze of influencing factors.

# Part Two

⁓⁓⁓

# Stages in Problem Solving, Knowledge Utilization, and Planned Change

The summary of literature in Part Two bears on a fundamental question: To what extent are the processes of problem solving, of knowledge utilization, and of the resulting change marked by stages, and how can such stages be best characterized and put to use in understanding and applying these processes?

Although stages are virtually universally considered present, they are often perceived as fusing into one another in an irregular sequence. One is reminded of the query: Which came first, the chicken or the egg? Those who stress the problem-solving approach see felt need as the initiator of the thought-action sequence. Knowledge utilization advocates, though not denying a problem-solving orientation, often place knowledge and its development at the beginning of the series. Weiss (1977a) succinctly notes that utilization processes can take different sequences: those that are "knowledge-driven" (information in search of a user), those that are "problem-driven" (a need in search of a solution), or those that involve a reciprocal dialogue between a user system and a resource system.

Traditionally, the phenomenon of change has been studied by persons in numerous disciplines, such as geology, biology,

151

anthropology, history, sociology, and psychology. In each of these fields change has rarely, if ever, been perceived as a straight-line affair, although debates have raged between adherents of gradual change and believers in saltatory development. The differences of viewpoint on the role and quality of change have a bearing on both the problem-solving and the knowledge utilization processes. A thoughtful reference to theories that emerge from the disciplines mentioned will confirm the subtlety and complexity of the task of stage designation and establish the presence of various issues regarding the nature and enumeration of stages.

1. *Stage analysis needs to be contextually applied.* Just as a taxonomy of determinants of change needs to be developed, so a taxonomy of stage analyses is necessary to reflect the types of situations to which they are applied. The introduction of a modified national energy program can be expected to proceed through far different stages from those required for the introduction of a new commercial product.

2. *The extent to which a change strategy is planned will affect the stage analysis.* As noted more fully in Chapter Nine, Berman (1980) discusses two schools of thought and practice regarding the design of implementation strategies. One may be called *programmed implementation,* characterized by explicit preprogramming, and the other *adaptive implementation,* whereby initial plans are adapted to unfolding events and decisions. Obviously, the staging of the process will need to vary according to leanings toward one or the other position—or according to which position seems more suitable in relation to a given kind of change effort in a particular type of situation.

3. *Although unplanned and unintended changes are not deliberately "staged," they may manifest stages.* These may be subjected to analysis that, in turn, may throw light on the planning of change (Rich and Zaltman, 1978). To illustrate the lead statement, whereas social evolution (when influenced by human intention) entails planned staging to an extent, biological evolution (exclusive of the injection of human experiments) does not, but may instead follow its own unfolding stages.

4. *To the extent that the stage process analysis repre-*

*sents a one-way linear approach, it may be subject to the criti-*
*cism of Schön (1967), who comments that the perception of*
*the rational model of innovation as an orderly, goal-directed,*
*risk-reducing process is a myth.* Advance planning of the process becomes unfeasible because of unexpected twists and turns.
Further, innovation produces uncertainties owing to such factors as the technical feasibility of the idea, the novelty of the
idea, and the market reaction. In fairness to the stage approach,
it should be noted that most of the proposed patterns provide
for a monitoring procedure that permits flexibility of action
along the line as deemed necessary on the basis of what is
learned from the monitoring. The cycling or reiteration of
stages is commonly required.

To apply these several thoughts to the literature summarized in Part Two: The bulk of the writings refer to planned
change. Context is not always made explicit; hence, generalizations may be made only with caution. By and large, preprogramming is implied, with insufficient attention to the relative
uncontrollability of unforeseen variables affecting the change
process. Finally, the vast domain of unintentional change remains almost entirely outside the scope of the literature covered
by this volume.

A knowledge of the stages of utilization and change, even
in the simplified form employed by many writers, may serve at
least two practical purposes when cautiously used:

1. A planner can use such knowledge, at least tentatively, in
   ordering and executing activities.
2. Differentiations can be applied either to factors that determine knowledge utilization and change (as noted in Part
   One) or to strategic measures for facilitating utilization (referred to in Parts Two and Three) according to the stage of
   the process or program involved. Such considerations are
   dealt with in later discussions.

Part Two attempts to provide a convenient way of presenting the literature on the subject. Consequently, although
the knowledge-to-use sequence is also evident, essentially a

problem-solving approach is pursued in the next four chapters. Following an overview of stage enumeration in Chapter Seven, Chapter Eight carries the treatment from the stage of initial need awareness or concern through clarification or diagnosis and knowledge search to the consideration of alternatives and the selection of a preferred solution. Chapter Nine examines strategies for implementing and otherwise achieving the selected solution or actualizing planned change. Chapter Ten discusses problems of evaluation, follow-through, and the stabilization or institutionalization of desired changes.

# 7

# Stages in Processes
# of Knowledge Utilization
# and Change

## General Considerations

Considerable interest has been shown in depicting the stages
through which knowledge utilization or an innovative program
progresses. The presentation of stages in the first section of this
chapter is limited to a more general discussion centering primarily
on a problem-solving pattern. Subsequent sections set forth arrangements that refer respectively to (1) commercial and technological stage patterns, and (2) social and related stage patterns.

**Problem-Solving Approaches.** Writers who subscribe either
implicitly or explicitly to the problem-solving mode of stage
analysis, though using varying terminology, tend to follow the
same pattern. Nearly all begin with a need, a concern, a problem, a discrepancy between new ideas and conventional practice, or some other pressure for change; all move to diagnosis,
analysis, or clarification of the problem; all recognize a need for
obtaining pertinent knowledge (which may involve identification of existing knowledge or R&D to find new knowledge),
and most move to a stage of creating and considering alternative

interpretations or courses of action; most describe an action or implementation phase; and many see a need for evaluation and follow-through for refinement/improvement.

Earlier writers who pursued this general outline include Lippitt, Watson, and Westley (1958), Jenkins (1962), Jung and Lippitt (1966), Watson (1967), Greiner (1967), and Rubin (1968).

In an unpublished paper, Abelson (1964), building on Dewey's five-stage analysis of problem solving, has incorporated psychodynamic factors into the consideration of the five stages, designating them perplexity, problem viewing, solution seeking, solution testing, and resolution. Problems are seen as emerging from the matrix of daily living and as being resolved, temporarily at least, when the person "has had enough of the problem" and is ready to apply a chosen solution or pseudo solution, either in a real-life situation or simply in a mental rather than an actional context.

Cherns (1972a) sets forth the following phases in the process of relating research to policy making: (1) identification of the problem, (2) clarification of existing options and, as a possible outcome, the revelation of new, previously unsuspected options, (3) selection from available options, and (4) realization of the option selected. In each of these phases, the type of research called for receives varying emphasis.

Van de Vall (1975) presents what is essentially a problem-solving approach. The experience of conflicting pressures (a problem) and a diagnostic stage lead to awareness (and eventually a solution). A design based on alternative policy considerations and reflecting the organization's resources and goals contributes to the solution. Development of change policy responsive to abilities and motivation of persons affected by the change results in the acceptance of a program and eventually a given change.

Of special interest is van de Vall's observation that the three major stages of the change process—*diagnosis* (increasing awareness and understanding of the problem), *design* (exploring alternative solutions by scanning the range of policies available to the organization, and *development* (facilitating organizational change by stimulating the implementation of a chosen solution)—have been appropriated respectively by the separate disciplines of sociology, public or business administration, and social psychology and policy science. Van de Vall advocates an interactive approach calculated to penetrate the boundaries of the three major stages.

In the face of attempts to describe organizational behavior as following an orderly problem-solving mode, Cohen, March, and Olsen (1972) present what they term a (computer) "garbage-can model of organizational choice" (p. 1) as befitting certain types of organizations, notably those that can be considered as displaying "organized anarchy" (p. 2).

In the "garbage-can model," various kinds of problems and solutions devised by participants are dumped as they are generated into an explicit computer simulation model of a garbage-can decision process. Participants arrive at an interpretation of what they are doing and what they have done while in the process of doing it. The description is capped by the statement that, from this point of view, an organization is a collection of choices looking for problems, and solutions looking for issues to which they might be the answer.

The reader may wish to consider this account as a counterpoise to an overacceptance of the more rational, systematic type of problem-solving behavior as ordinarily described. With this caveat we return to descriptions of less iconoclastic presentations of the subject.

**Other General Approaches.** Gray and Roberts-Gray (1979), departing somewhat from a literal problem-solving approach, see the utilization of technology or applied R&D as a six-stage progression—namely, (1) research, (2) development, (3) later development, (4) delivery and initiation, (5) implementation, and (6) institutionalization.

Zaltman and others (1973) distinguish between the initiation stage and the implementation stage of the innovative process. They also suggest substages as follows: (1) Initiation stage: (a) knowledge-awareness substage, (b) attitude formation substage, (c) decision substage. (2) Implementation stage: (a) initial implementation substage, (b) continued-sustained implementation substage.

In a somewhat similar manner, Berman and McLaughlin (1976) boil down the innovation process to three stages: initiation, implementation, and incorporation.

The innovation model of Munson and Pelz (1980) described in Chapter Fifteen refers to the following stages: (1) the diagnostic stage, (2) the stage of design, (3) the stage of implementation, and (4) the stage of stabilization.

Davis and Salasin (1979), in a further development of Davis' A VICTORY model termed "Decision Determinants Analysis," refer to four stages in the change process: (1) assessment of change determinants, (2) establishment of goals, (3) action to manage determinants, and (4) follow-through and evaluation.

With regard to school mental health consultation, Alpert (1976) sets forth four stages: (1) entry and relationship building, (2) diagnosis and definition of overt and covert problems, (3) resolution of problems, and (4) termination.

Hage and Aiken (1970) envisage four stages of organizational change: (1) evaluation, in which the need for a new program is assessed, (2) initiation, management's decision to implement the new program, (3) implementation, the actual carrying out of an innovation, and (4) routinization, the organization's attempt to stabilize the effects of the new program.

## Broad Sampling of Stage Patterns
## from Varied Settings

According to Gee (1974), innovation in a commercial situation extends from the point of first invention or basic discovery through various stages of research and development, testing, design engineering, manufacturing, market analysis, marketing, and commercial introduction. To a large extent, the length of the innovation period is affected by a host of nontechnical factors, such as the availability of capital, the nature and structure of the market, management policies, government regulatory practices, energy and material resource availability, and human behavior. Obviously, many innovations are aborted before even reaching the point of commercial realization.

Gruber and Marquis (1969) developed a pattern, based on

the R&D perspective, that provides a sequential series of steps on which success in technology transfer depends: (1) generation of ideas, (2) research, (3) development, (4) production, and (5) marketing. Myers and Marquis (1969) defined this process as one of probabilities in estimating product or process success, cost, time, commercial success, and return to the firm.

Aneja and Aneja (1977) detail three stages in the development of an innovative process and product in relation to three well-defined component systems of a company's operations. Transforming a concept for a new or modified product into a full-scale marketable product involves the following: (1) Preparation for and conduct of a bench-scale operating test within a research component. (2) Process development through a semiworks or pilot-plan demonstration unit within the process development component. (3) Full-scale commercial production of a marketable product through the production component.

Long (1976) described the development of the laser in the Western Electric Company and its eventual incorporation into processing systems. The development progressed through five stages: (1) the *curiosity stage* (1961-1962), principally one of witnessing the unfolding of the discovery in the laboratory, (2) the *seed stage* (1962-1965), one of questioning the utility of lasers in order to provide a basis for the decision making involved in allocating resources for basic studies, (3) the *fundamental stage* (1965-1969), a time of building the foundation of basic knowledge in order to formulate and evaluate industrial applications, (4) the *applications stage* (1969-1973), the time of actual introduction of laser processing into manufacturing operations, and (5) the *maturity stage* (1973-    ), a period characterized by keeping abreast of the latest developments to ensure their incorporation into industrial use where appropriate.

Long attributes the success of the laser development to two conditions: (1) the smooth working relations between research and manufacturing and (2) the joint development program that links research and manufacturing and continues inclusion of the research component for technical assistance and problem solving as long as needed.

The importance of an awareness of developmental stages

is apparent in high-technology enterprise. Merrifield (1976) identifies each stage in planning: idea, feasibility demonstration, process development, pilot plant, semicommercial stage, and full-stage production. For each of these stages careful planning is done in research, engineering, marketing, legal, and financial components of the firm. A scoop by another firm that develops a superior technical approach may indeed be the result of failure by the original firm to engage in such planning, according to Myers and Sweezy (1978).

The Denver Research Institute (1970), in its Quarterly Report #4 of an NSF project, delineates four relevant steps in technology transfer: (1) recognition of opportunity and search for additional information to determine the relevance of the technology to organizational activities, (2) laboratory verification of materials or techniques, (3) market testing of prototypes or actual use of new technology in operational activities, and (4) marketing of technical products or processes.

Von Hippel (1978b) presents a four-stage user-dominated innovation pattern in which the user (1) perceives the need for the product innovation, (2) conceives of a solution, (3) builds a prototype device (if he or she has the capability of doing so), and (4) proves the value of the prototype by using it. Sometimes a fifth stage follows in which an inventive user diffuses (intentionally or unintentionally) detailed information to other potential users and to firms that might be interested in manufacturing the device commercially.

Robbins and Milliken (1976) have developed a pattern of the flow or transfer of technology that they assert is applicable to policy and practice at the national, industrial, and corporate levels. A critical aspect of the pattern is the constant assessment of nontechnological factors such as marketing, capital, and human resources during the entire course of the innovation cycle, which includes the following elements: innovative sources, idea generation, research mode, product or process, conception, management, technological stages, marketing decisions, and transfer to another division or firm. This conception is counter to the notion that transfer is essentially a communications or applications process following already-developed technology.

The authors insist that user knowledge and requirements must be blended in with the transfer process. This is tantamount to saying that the transfer process is itself an innovative process.

Although developed by Albala (1975) with special reference to the chemical industry, the following stage pattern is evidently applicable to many R&D situations.

### Exploratory Stage

1. Development and dissemination of new knowledge.
2. Recognition of the potential relevance of developed knowledge to an opportunity to use it productively.
3. Linkage of knowledge to specific development aims.
4. Acknowledgment of a precommitment to apply the knowledge if feasible.
5. Discovery and clarification of what information is needed that would bear on a firm decision about whether to proceed with an effort (including investment of resources) to apply the knowledge.
6. Clarification and evaluation of potential development issues and problems as they may relate to personnel, capital investment, available resources and technology, yield, and other influencing factors—both subjective and objective.

### Applied Research and Development Stage

7. Projection of possible applications and the forms of their design along with the processes that would be needed to achieve application.
8. Choice of particular aims and a program for reaching an application.

### Operational Development Stage

9. Implementation of the program decision and program development through change strategies that serve to clarify *what* an organization wants to become, followed by planning and tactics for *how* the organization goes about becoming the what. This includes use of necessary personnel

and nonpersonnel resources and work on other problems
that may be involved.

10. Consolidation and evaluation of the developed program
and its operations.

11. Planning and action toward program continuation, maintenance, expansion, and/or transformation.

12. Termination by incorporation into other programs or by
abandonment.

These stages imply a linear development. In action, however,
they represent frames that surround forward and backward
moves, the pursuit of advancement down side paths, the bypass-
ing of irrelevant steps, and pauses while new ideas are being formulated and circumstances change. The framing stages assist in
planning, reviewing and checking, evaluating, and identifying
steps in the operational process. They also mark points in program advancement.

Fairweather (1971) has developed a *model of experimental social innovation.* In delineating the attributes of social innovative experiments, he starts with the *definition* of a significant
social problem; this process includes engaging in naturalistic
field observations (diagnosis) to describe the parameters of the
problem in its actual community setting. The next step, *innovation,* creates and formulates different solutions as innovative
subsystems. These subsystems then go through the process of
*comparison,* whereby an experiment is designed to determine
the efficacy of the different subsystems in solving the social
problem. The innovative subsettings are implanted in appropriate social contexts so that they can be evaluated in their natural
habitat. In the *evaluation* phase, the subsystems are continued
in operation for several months or even years to allow for adequate outcome and process evaluation.

Throughout, participants in the subsystems are included,
and a cross-disciplinary approach is used. The model follows the
logical stages of (1) concern, (2) diagnosis, (3) formulation of
alternatives, (4) implementation, and (5) evaluation.

Rothman (1974) puts what is essentially a research re-
trieval-diffusion-utilization model to use in the very conduct of

his extensive attempt to achieve a fuller utilization of social science studies relative to the planning and organizing for social change. The earlier stages of the model were actually used by Rothman and his associates. The full model consists of the following components:

1.  A basic research pool is postulated.
2.  Retrieval, codification, and generalization activities are undertaken, resulting in:
3.  Consensus findings in the form of generalizations (abstract statements).
4.  Through a translation and conversion process there result:
5.  Generalized applicational principles (abstract statements).
6.  These are operationalized to yield:
7.  Applicational principles in delimited form (concrete statements).
8.  Initial implementation through field testing is attempted, resulting in:
9.  Practical and policy outcomes, refined and elaborated applicational principles, and the construction of diffusion media.
10.  Wide diffusion follows, leading to:
11.  Broad use in practice by clients, consumers, constituents, and so on.

In a later report Rothman (1978b) develops his model further, stating that to harness research to serve social service practice, it is necessary to improve methods of retrieving relevant research reports and to introduce new methods of conducting research. To do this, six basic stages and five intermediate steps are required. The author proceeds to detail and illustrate each phase of the process by reference to a long-term action project, the Community Intervention Project.

Rothman borrows from an engineering orientation of Etzioni in which small-scale models are first prepared and then lead to the production of one or a few full-scale prototypes, with accompanying stage modifications before any mass production. Also notable in the procedure are several specific principles

—for example, the use of a preliminary small-scale, tentative try-out with limited personnel and the "packaging" of affirmatively evaluated outcomes in convenient dissemination and implementation form.

How to transform a social science research finding or generalization into an application concept that can guide practice is the subject of another article by Rothman (1978a). Two steps are identified: conversion and design. *Conversion* entails use translation from descriptive to prescriptive form. *Design,* as similarly used by engineers, is defined as "the use of scientific principles, technical information, and imagination . . . to perform prespecified functions with a maximum of economy and efficiency" (p. 118).

Among the key characteristics of the conversion/design process are the following: (1) it involves synthesis of different and, at times, apparently contradictory ideas, (2) it is a blend of science and art, both critical and creative in character, (3) it is tentative and exploratory, subject to subsequent validation of findings, and (4) it employs a set of readily defined factors, such as identifiability, quantifiability, and empirical accessibility.

The conversion and design approach may benefit from certain suggestions, such as providing written rules to structure applicational functions, providing for training, and enhancing creative functioning through brainstorming and other stimulating techniques.

Rogers and Shoemaker (1971) describe five processes in the development and implementation of innovation: (1) stimulation, (2) initiation, (3) legitimation, (4) decision making, and (5) execution.

Presenting a model with special regard to early interventions in a large system by a consultant, Beckhard (1975) sets forth the following four functions, stages, or phases with particular reference to planning:

1. *Defining the change problem,* including the organizational change needed or desired and the *type* of change desired.
2. *Determining readiness and capability for change,* including

motivation and capability, and entailing a diagnosis of dissatisfaction.

3. *Identifying the consultant's own resources and motivations for change,* including congruence with organizational needs.

4. *Determining the intermediate change strategies and goals,* including an indication of targets and measuring points en route to the larger change objectives.

With regard to the foregoing, Beckhard considers it important to examine the accessibility of each subsystem and the linkage of the subsystems to the system as a whole.

Eveland, Rogers, and Klepper (1977) describe a model of innovation processes based on a review of the use of a data management and analysis tool sponsored by the U.S. Census Bureau in fifty-three cases of innovation in fifty-three local government agencies. The model rejects a commonly perceived dichotomy between "adoption" and "implementation," suggesting instead a continual shaping by specific small-scale decisions concerning the innovation. Five general stages are identified: (1) *setting the agenda*—perceiving a problem in an organizational unit, (2) *matching*—sensing new ideas for providing the solution to the problem, (3) *redefining*—stating the innovation in terms meaningful to the members of the organizational unit, (4) *structuring* —establishing the innovation within the structure of the organization, and (5) *interconnecting*—relating the innovation to parts of the organization outside its initial locus.

In relating information search to decision making and change in government bureaus, Downs (1967) asserts that a decision maker generating a new nonprogrammed action goes through the following thirteen steps: (1) perception of new information, (2) assimilation of new information, (3) assessment of performance, (4) formulation of alternatives, (5) analysis of alternatives, (6) evaluation of alternatives, (7) formulation of strategy, (8) selection of appropriate action, (9) continual acquisition of data, (10) evaluation of action impact, (11) feedback on action, (12) assimilation of feedback, and (13) reassessment of performance and possible modification in light of the reassessment.

The motivation to search for alternative actions arises from a significant discrepancy between what the bureau is doing and what it "ought" to be doing.

## Summary Comments

The accomplishment of significant change cannot be left to fortuitous behavior. Although some changes are seen as beyond human control, planned change has assumed a large place in recent literature. Effective planning requires familiarity with the stages of the entire process of knowledge production and use in the interest of change.

Whether employed by knowledge producers or users, a problem-solving paradigm (popularly expressed in John Dewey's five phases as applied to the thinking process of individuals) has been the accepted pattern in modern times. However, social or group problem solving carries the possibility of a division of labor in that some persons may engage in knowledge collection while others are assigned responsibility for other phases of the problem-solving process, such as the application of selected solutions. Although researchers and practitioners are inclined to follow Dewey's set of stages, the division of labor in the social setting has resulted in a debate over whether research and development can be fruitfully separated from the consideration of the needs of potential users of knowledge. The treatment of topics in this chapter varies between the "problem-driven" emphasis and the "knowledge-driven" approach. In any case, the literature contains many stage formulations as aids to planners and interpreters of the process under discussion.

Some writers start with the assumption that when something new and worthwhile—a program, a product, or knowledge —becomes available, the "marketing challenge" that remains is to initiate its adoption and ensure its implementation and, if positively evaluated, its institutionalization. Some other writers begin with what is typically seen as the first phase in problem solving—the discovery and assessment of need, next followed by an attempt to clarify a given problem, to set up procedures for gathering pertinent information, and to stimulate "creative" thinking designed to identify or generate promising solutions, from which one or more can be selected for "validation" and application.

Despite the diversity and disagreements in the attempts to designate stages, these efforts have the following positive values:

1.  To the extent that certain factors are found to recur in various studies and analyses, they show promise of significantly high potency in effecting utilization and change within a given degree of generality.
2.  There is evidence of a growing realization of the synergic operation of components of successful utilization and change efforts, as well as the importance of the contingency principle, or variation in the application of the several elements at different stages of the process and the necessity of tailoring that application to the needs and climates of different settings.
3.  The orderly presentation of components and stages of change provides source material for generating hypotheses about when and how to inject measures related to the determining variables.

On balance, it is fair to say that considerable progress has been made in the search for both descriptive and prescriptive stage patterns that may provide helpful in the task of putting knowledge to use and of increasing the likelihood of promising changes in diverse areas of human endeavor.

# 8

## Assessing Needs
## and Developing Plans
## for Change

Although stage analyses of the utilization and change process take a variety of forms, the elements of the process can be conveniently located under the rubrics of (1) need awareness, (2) diagnosis and problem clarification, (3) the search for pertinent knowledge, (4) consideration of alternative solutions, (5) strategies for effectuating promising solutions, (6) evaluation, and (7) follow-through of applied solutions. The present chapter considers the first four of these components as reviewed in the literature.

### Awareness and Assessment of Need

One of the most frequently advocated principles regarding innovation and change is that in order for change to be successful, it must be in response to a felt need. The need may be experienced either before or after acquaintance with the innovation, such as stimulation through the efforts of a producer or sponsor or a linking or change agent or through "sales" information that draws attention to the value of the innovation (Rogers, 1962a; Watson and Glaser, 1965; Glaser and Taylor, 1973).

Three aspects of the development of a need for change can be identified: an awareness of the problem, a recognition that the condition might be improved as the result of change, and a willingness to seek outside help, if needed, in bringing about the change.

Niehoff (1966) proposes that there are three types of felt need: (1) *solicited*—a need of which the recipients are fully aware to the extent that they solicit assistance from the change agent, (2) *demonstrated*—a need in which the recipients have demonstrated their interest to the extent that they have tried to solve their problem by their own efforts without outside assistance, and (3) *ascertained*—a need that, though already existing when the change agent arrives, is only latent within the local social group and must be ascertained or developed by both the innovator and the recipient.

Both administrators and other practitioners within an organization must perceive a need. Lippitt, Watson, and Westley (1958) state that outside help must be viewed as meaningful. An implication for research utilization is that practitioners may require persuasion in order to perceive research findings as potentially helpful.

The evidence is persuasive that to try to introduce new methods where there is no felt need is to court failure (Coe and Bernhill, 1967). Fairweather, Sanders, and Tornatzky (1974) stress the role that an outside agent and knowledge specialist can play in helping to nourish a sense of need for change. The best type of consultation is that which starts from the client's needs and helps the client to become an effective user of relevant R&D findings to meet those needs (Lippitt, 1962).

The importance of practitioners' transmitting their problematic concerns to researchers is shown in the emphasis that Havelock and Lingwood (1973) give to two sets of criteria they used in the critical analysis of four research and dissemination agencies. One set had to do with the agency's concern for developing the user's need awareness, self-sensing, and related qualities of problem sensitivity. The other set concerned the definition, transmission, and transformation of user needs in such a manner as to further appropriate knowledge utilization.

Sometimes the felt need is mainly for information rather than for some particular innovation or change to meet a given problem. The title *Developing a Sensing Network for Information Needs in Education* suggests the significance that Paisley and others (1972) ascribe to awareness of the concerns of practitioners. Paisley and others used (and analyzed) five alternative methods of ascertaining information needs bearing on the educational process, educational content, and human variables:

1.  Statewide surveys in which questionnaires were distributed to personnel in selected school districts and state educational agencies.
2.  A follow-up investigation in which educators who had requested information from central and local information centers were surveyed by questionnaire.
3.  An "information specialists" study in which expert personnel of ERIC clearinghouses and local information centers attempted to project the needs of their clients.
4.  A "hotline" study in which educators across the country were invited to call a toll-free long-distance number to request information.
5.  An "educational serials topic trends" study in which the periodical literature of the field of education was monitored at four time points so as to detect changes in topic preference rankings.

Among these five procedures, the statewide surveys, the follow-up study, and the information specialist study showed high consistency in results. The hotline study and the educational serials topic trends study tended to agree with each other (but to a lesser degree) in reflecting the nature of the information needs across method of data collection and in respect to the characteristics of the respondents (teacher, principal, counselor, and so on, on the one hand, and school level, on the other).

Some studies have revealed that the need for information is sometimes recognized only after the information has been encountered. For example, Rosenbloom and Wolek (1970), in a study of engineers, asked respondents to identify a recent instance of technical information which they had learned about from a source outside their immediate section or work group and which had proved valuable in their job. In one sixth of the instances in which useful information had been received, the need for (or appreciation of the value of) that information was recognized only *after* it had been encountered.

Trends in health care systems focus on specific needs that suggest the direction of possible innovation in that field. Beckhard (1974) lists such needs and presents illustrative problems as seen from different vantage points—that is, by deans of medical schools, directors and faculties of other health schools, hospital administrators, community health center directors, and hospital interns and residents. He finds a keen interest in the application of behavioral science and technology but also finds marked suspicion and doubt about its functional utility. The report reveals a flesh-and-blood picture of problems and perceptions of problems confronting the prospective innovator.

Many R&D personnel continue to support the importance of felt need as a determinant of knowledge utilization but also include wider sources of demand (for example, Berman and others, 1975; Howes and Quinn, 1978). Thus, Howes and Quinn, for example, confirm the idea that *readiness* to seriously consider an innovation, shown in an individual's felt need or an organization's readiness for a change program, is the most important element in a decision to adopt an innovation.

Chakrabarti and Rubenstein (1976) analyzed seventeen variables in the outside adoption of NASA innovations and determined that the degree of success in adoption was due in part to the specificity of the relation between a technology to be transferred and some existing and recognized problem or need.

Kelman (1975) makes similar points about the process by which international agencies give aid. In focusing on the aid program, it is important to look for a project directly related to people's immediate needs—an aid program that deals with a problem they face all the time and recognize; a project that can be executed simply and is likely to have rapid results; and a project for which the recipients have the skills and facilities to take it over. When such a project uses the recipients' special knowledge, experience, and skills and has potential for being taken over by the people themselves, it demonstrates the high esteem in which the recipients are held and actually raises their status, increases their skills, and leaves them less dependent.

It is evident, however, that not all persons, agencies, or firms have the capacity to develop clear conceptions of their own needs. Udis (1976), after study of the transfer of technology from military to civilian uses in seven major industrialized countries of Western Europe, finds that one of the common problems standing in the way of transfer is the inability of civil sectors to specify and understand their own needs. Many firms depend on outside potential "customers" to suggest their needs and the products that will meet them. Responsible personnel in these firms then recognize (as Rosenbloom and Wolek, 1966, had noted in an earlier study) the validity of the needs drawn to their attention and are duly appreciative of the value of this information. Cherns (1967), carrying his ideas back to a wartime period, attributes the awareness of need to three factors: (1) a crisis, (2) a handy supply of people able and ready to undertake research, and (3) a sponsor and potential user.

Basing his argument largely on quantitative findings of previous studies of patents granted, industrial applications made, and economic growth, Haeffner (1973) presents a case for heightened emphasis on need-oriented research institutes, as against "basic research" support. Haeffner also reports on a study of 567 commercially successful innovations from 191 companies in five distinct branches of industry; it was found that one third of the innovations could be classified as modifications of existing techniques, while the other two thirds were completely new products. Moreover, three quarters of the successful innovations could be classified as having been need-stimulated.

The importance of tuning in to user need is raised by Zaltman (1979a) in an article on utilization as a type of planned social change. He reviews a wide range of concepts pertaining to potentially applicable characteristics of the innovation or knowledge itself—for example, (1) organizational settings and practice, (2) knowledge users and use, and (3) other aspects of the utilization process. He summarizes his approach by noting that the various concepts identified in the article and their accompanying guidelines and propositions display an orientation that has the user rather than the "product" itself as the major focus in knowledge utilization.

Goldhar, Bragaw, and Schwartz (1976) identify two types of stimuli for innovation: a "demand pull" concept, in which knowledge of a need leads to a search for the appropriate technology, and a "technology push" or "solutions looking for problems" concept, in which the initial stimulus is the technical means and the information search then centers on identifying needs for that technology or "solution."

### Need and the Preassessment of Research

So that needs will be met, a contemplated research or innovation project requires careful preassessment—that is, the judging of its potential worth.

According to Souder (1978), the preassessment process itself is undertaken against a background in which the real world of innovation often differs strikingly from the world as conceived in management science. In Table 5 Souder contrasts his conceptions of these differences.

A deliberate preassessment involves four main steps:

1. Consideration of the bases for selection of a particular change objective and program.
2. Preevaluation of the processes and methods that might be necessary to effect change.
3. Predetermination of the resources that might become necessary or at least advantageous.
4. Anticipation and specification of the gains that might be achieved as an outcome of the change program.

Preassessment intrinsically entails prediction and often involves preliminary trial.

Rothwell (1977) urges a readiness to look ahead and attempt to make meaningful forecasts about the use outcome— and, in the case of manufacturing, specifically about sales. To

Table 5. The Real-World Environment Versus
the Management Science View.

| The Viewpoint That Management Science Models Seem to Take | The Real-World Environment |
|---|---|
| 1. A single decision maker, in a well-behaved environment. | 1. Many decision makers and many decision influencers, in a dynamic organizational environment. |
| 2. Perfect information about candidate projects and their characteristics; outputs, values, and risks of candidates are known and quantifiable. | 2. Imperfect information about candidate projects and their characteristics; outputs and values of projects are difficult to specify; uncertainty accompanies all estimates. |
| 3. Well-known, invariant goals. | 3. Ever-changing, fuzzy goals. |
| 4. Decision-making information is concentrated in the hands of the decision maker, so that he or she has all the information needed to make a decision. | 4. Decision-making information is highly splintered and scattered piecemeal throughout the organization, with no one part of the organization having all the information needed for decision making. |
| 5. The decision maker is able to articulate all consequences. | 5. The decision maker is often unable or unwilling to state outcomes and consequences. |
| 6. Candidate projects are viewed as independent entities, to be individually evaluated on their own merits. | 6. Candidate projects are often technically and economically interdependent. |
| 7. A single objective, usually expected value maximization or profit maximization, is assumed, and the constraints are primarily budgetary. | 7. There are sometimes conflicting multiple objectives and multiple constraints, and these are often noneconomic. |
| 8. The best portfolio of projects is determined on economic grounds. | 8. Satisfactory portfolios may possess many noneconomic characteristics. |
| 9. The budget is "optimized" in a single decision. | 9. An iterative, re-cycling budget determination process is used. |
| 10. One single, economically "best," overall decision is sought. | 10. What seems to be the "best" decision for the total organization may not be seen as best by each department or party, so that many conflicts may arise. |

Adapted from Souder, W. E. "A System for Using R&D Project Evaluation Methods." *Research Management,* 1978, *21*(5), p. 33. Reproduced by permission.

achieve this, it is usually necessary to search, and gain an understanding of, user needs. However, anticipating relevant factors in the *process* toward an outcome may prove to be even more important than forecasting the outcome itself. A worthwhile goal is desirable, but if it is not possible to reach, it may still be profitable to pursue it with the prospect that side effects from explorations in the process may prove to be of moment. In general, of course, resources are ordinarily insufficient for investing in development work only for the sake of possible serendipitous benefits.

With regard to the possibility of serendipitous benefits, it may be well to note that outcomes of a given innovation may be either beneficial or harmful and may spread out in many directions and have second- and higher-order effects, as indicated in the discussion of technology assessment in Chapter Ten. Hence, the treatment of technology assessment and the various techniques for predicting and clarifying consequences referred to in that discussion are applicable to the preassessment of research and other programs.

Goldhar, Bragaw, and Schwartz (1976) speak of the overabundance of information and a surfeit of choice, as in a supermarket. Individuals planning to initiate new-program activities become consumers of information and develop shortcuts and behavior patterns to help them cope with the overabundance —for example, engaging in discussions with technical colleagues in the firm. For managers of development activities, Goldhar and colleagues urge the answering of two useful questions:

1. Is the R&D effort organized to promote informal interchange of both technical and economic/market information?
2. Are the R&D people making enough use of external sources of economic and, especially, technological information (Utterback, 1971), or are they almost solely dependent on internal data? (The latter condition limits ability to match technological means with economic-need information in order to create a "design concept" that can be considered for support.)

Merrifield (1976), speaking from a management perspective, spells out the work of various components of a business—research, engineering, marketing, legal, and financial—in the pre-assessment of an idea for development. This relatively comprehensive review reduces the likelihood of an encounter with unexpected snags, can prove economical in time and financial investment, and strengthens confidence in the potentialities of a development—even though it may not prevent all unforeseen difficulties later in the project development.

White (1977), a research director in a major pharmaceutical firm, illustrates the heavy emphasis on assessment in his own research program. A project does not ordinarily become a candidate for large expenditure (say, more than $100,000 annually) until feasibility is demonstrated to senior laboratory personnel and the project proposal is compared with other projects in a portfolio process. That is, yearly, at a time coincident with the beginnings of the budget cycle, all research projects are compared for potential, risk, expenditure, and, very importantly, any "position effect" (halo effect) on other projects.

In the same direction, Gold (1975b) exercises caution in expecting a major developmental benefit from technological innovation when examining preassessment needs. Although the risks are often high and occasionally payoffs are dramatic, most efforts to develop and use innovations produce only modest gains, if any, and the products gain market shares only slowly. This recognition has led Gold to offer the following perspective:

1. Most top managers have a reasonably stable order of preference as among the means of improving or maintaining profitability, growth, market position, security of assets, stability of operations, and a favorable public image.
2. Their first preference is generally for continuation, or only moderate intensification, of familiar operations involving little risk to established organizational structures and patterns or resource allocation.
3. The generation or pioneering adoption of major technological innovations is likely to rank low because it tends to involve heavy investments, substantial risks and readjust-

ments in existing organizational arrangements, and budgetary allocations affecting many functions and operating divisions.

4. Such lower-ranking preferences are seldom resorted to except (a) when more-favored means prove inadequate, (b) when extramarket factors such as governmental pressures or subsidies alter the relative potentials or costs, (c) when technological advances by competitors threaten mounting disadvantages, or (d) when continuing internal technological development programs yield unexpectedly substantial potentials.

### Diagnosis: Problem Clarification

In the diagnostic phase, original perceptions concerning the problem are sharpened, relevant data are collected, the problem or need is redefined, and the organization takes a new look at it (Lippitt, Watson, and Westley, 1958; Jenkins, 1962; Jung and Lippitt, 1966; Watson, 1967; Greiner, 1967; Rubin, 1968).

Perhaps the earliest step after sensing an impulse toward new program developments is to define the problem to be overcome or the objectives that the proposed program is to accomplish. Souder and Rubenstein (1976) regard this phase as that of *idea development*. Definition of the program or of the problem may prove advantageous even though it is one of the most neglected steps. Servi (1976) regards it as highly critical. Information to explode myths and reduce or remove biases should be sought. As a result, a program planner will be able to avoid axiomatic or unsubstantiated statements and to move toward sounder definition of the problem to be solved or of program objectives.

Halpert (1973) suggests that researchers and administrators should get together and think hard about the questions that need to be answered by research before the former conduct studies and the latter try to apply the resulting findings. Research workers often focus on answerable questions that are not relevant to the critical issues confronting program administrators. Some program people are at times dazzled by the hardware of research and fail to specify their real information needs. A number of writers (Havelock and Lingwood, 1973, for example) draw special attention to the importance of transforming user needs into problem statements and researchable questions.

Problem clarification may require penetrative thinking. The account of innovations in Gabor (1970) makes it evident that vitally important human problems or "side effect" problems are often hidden and frequently go unheeded in the interactive rush to initiate change, to react to the consequences of change, and to adapt to changing circumstances.

Havelock (1973a) states that persons responsible for inducing change, after establishing an appropriate relationship, must guide clients in making a diagnosis that involves identifying the problems, identifying the opportunities that are open, and ensuring that the agent thoroughly understands the client's system. Common pitfalls of the diagnostic stage include spending too much time on diagnosis, using destructive confrontation, imposing the change agent's favorite diagnosis, and responding to the client's pressure for a crash program.

Van de Vall (1975), after a study of 120 projects of applied social research in the Netherlands, concluded that diagnostic studies of a social problem increase awareness and understanding of the problem by analyzing it in exact, detailed, and objective terms but that such studies are of value to policy makers in decision making only when they have experience with the problem to be solved and have recognized a real and felt need for research information.

Beyond the issues of diagnosis as applied to defined problems or programs, diagnosis also is used effectively to anticipate potential development areas. Trend studies are often made by government agencies as well as industrial, business, and labor groups.

Cherns (1972b) warns about dangers in diagnostic efforts that may result from unstated, unrealized, and thus overlooked ideological preferences and assumptions that determine which data to collect and the way conclusions are drawn from them. He points also to the preference for obtaining data through "hard" methods rather than by assessing people's nonverbal behavior, admittedly a more difficult task. He notes the common overvaluation of what can be counted and pithily illustrates this by noting that the counting of heads is implicitly based on the assumption that heads are equal.

McCool and Schreyer (1977), in discussing utilization of wildlife recreational research, stress the importance of a two-dimensional exchange of information between scientists and practitioners concerning problems, problem definitions, policies, procedures, viewpoints, and philosophies. Such exchanges and effective cooperation and communication are especially critical at the problem-definition stage (Schweitzer and Randall, 1974).

## Search for Pertinent Knowledge

As particular project plans are being formulated and consolidated, the need for further information, whether of a research or common-sense nature, keeps emerging.

Havelock (1977) speaks of such inquiries as "the search for solutions." He recommends that in this process the use of library and information services be given the highest priority; he advocates a search of what could be called "the resource universe" as an automatic part of every problem-solving strategy. Such a search would obviously include information in books, indexes, journals, and other published resources. However, a comprehensive search strategy has many aspects that go beyond the realm of print. For example, people with special expertise in the problem area might very appropriately be contacted, and there are other steps that could be taken as a part of "search" that have not traditionally been included in the librarian's role but could be an integral part of the expanded role and function of media supervisors and information specialists as change agents.

Mitroff, Kilmann, and Barabba (1979) contend that *solving* a problem is easier than identifying the correct problem or asking the key questions. With regard to raising questions, management information systems are often too narrow, limited, and sometimes misleading. Technical questions are overemphasized at the expense of the conceptual and human aspects. For example, the value of consulting all stakeholder groups involved in or affected by a given problem is often overlooked.

The remedy, according to the authors, lies in substantially enhancing the components or the "banks" that are employed in the management information system (MIS). With reference primarily to nonfinancial dimensions of value, the incorporation of an *assumption* bank, a *problem* bank, an *action* bank, and a *decision-maker* bank in addition to the customary data bank is proposed as a means of optimizing MIS and minimizing the possibility of a management *mis*information system (MMIS).

The role of persons becomes important in the exploitation of the contribution these banks can make to the problem-solving decision-making process. The authors explain how participants can be identified and divided into groups for developing a list of critical research questions, developing a MIS to answer the research questions, conducting debates on assumptions, and negotiating and synthesizing points of view.

The search for pertinent information is not limited to one stage in the process of knowledge utilization. And as Ettlie (1976) has noted, search behavior also appears in varying forms at different times. Ettlie believes that impersonal, external sources of information are most likely to account for the awareness of new production technology in advance of adoption of an innovation, whereas internal, personal sources are depended on increasingly during the first six months of implementation.

Whitley and Frost (1972) have categorized the tasks of idea development according to how scientific tasks are selected and problems defined. They point out that the group or community that influences task definitions will also be important in providing information or acting as a referral source.

Rosenbloom and Wolek (1970) found that scientists tend to make substantially more use than engineers do of sources outside the corporation in which they work. For industrial scientists, only about half the information gathered resulted from a specific search by the respondent. In nearly one third of the cases, the information was acquired because someone pointed it out without being requested to do so. In about one fifth of the cases, the respondent's intent in seeking information was to develop his general competence, rather than to acquire some particular knowledge. The authors conclude that "information looking for the man" is nearly as frequent as "man looking for information."

Efforts to shift the locale of mental health care from institutions to local communities were found to be hampered by limitations of existing information or of retrieval mechanisms (Swan, 1976). Swan noted a tendency among users to select information to support predetermined positions and to read into the information value judgments assumed to be implicit. He accordingly recommended that in policy research the value judgments that underlie analyses should be made explicit.

Swan further reflects on the relevance of twelve research reports designed to provide necessary decision-making information to staff in a state agency. He suggests that (1) recognition of the value judgments underlying analytical reports is necessary in order to anticipate and meet the conflicting interpretations of the findings that will be made within the legislative processes and (2) ultimate decisions will depend on achieving sufficient policy consensus—which research, no matter how competent, cannot achieve.

Davis and Specht (1978) regard information as basic to citizen participation in community mental health programs. They claim that before group process (the "how" of citizen participation) can be dealt with, the information necessary for decision making must be identified. This identification must be made before dealing with group-process issues.

According to Servi (1976), forecasting always implies uncertainty in implementation. Consequently, most of the questions for collecting ideas, argues Servi, should be formulated in such a way that they can be answered by three kinds of estimates—pessimistic, realistic, and optimistic. With respect to the first, candidly presented negative information about a proposed project is as important as positive information, especially to management as it makes adoption decisions.

## Consideration of Alternative Solutions

In generating alternative solutions to problems, including the choice of implementation strategies, a solid background of knowledge is usually considered necessary, along with qualities of open-mindedness and ingenuity. This stage of the process requires the translation of diagnostic data and insight into possible strategies of action and selection of the most feasible strategy (Lippitt, Watson, and Westley, 1958; Havelock, 1970).

Alternative solutions to problems or program goals to be considered are of three major types:

1. Direct translation from precedents to present programs and operations (doing what others have done and found helpful).
2. Invention of a new model to achieve selected goals (breaking away and moving in new directions).
3. Adaptation (modification) through change in characteristics of the existing model (finding other fitting ways to change the model).

It is important to retrieve or construct a number of alternative possible solutions from which a choice can then be made. The criteria for such choice may be many, but there are at least three that are fundamental and must always be applied (Havelock, 1977).

1. Does the proposed solution really go very far toward solving the problem? In other words, does it promise significant *benefits*?
2. Is it *workable*? Is there a reasonable chance that it can be implemented with the resources available? Will it actually deliver the promised benefits?
3. Assuming both benefit and workability, will it be an *acceptable* solution for both those to be benefited and those charged with implementation?

**Clarification of Available Alternatives.** Choice depends on having alternatives. Clarification of the alternatives available can help to direct choice. Gold (1975b) describes four alternatives for technological advancement that may apply. The first two are the most common: (1) programs seeding a stream of *small, evolutionary advances* in products and processes and (2) those aiming at *extraordinary advances.* The former have the advantage of relatively small risk in return for a high probability of successive small payoffs without long delays.

The two additional alternatives in commercial situations warrant careful consideration. One of these involves concentration on seeking the economies of production offered by *increases in the scale of operations.* The other consists in *adopting a total program developed elsewhere* to use whatever technological advances achieved by others seem to offer significant improvements in competition or use.

In comparing these alternative strategies, Gold notes five characteristics that seem important: (1) relative costs of development, (2) relative likelihood of success, (3) relative time to achieve such success, (4) relative magnitudes of resulting rewards, and (5) the extent of attendant costly disruptions in organizational arrangements, capital allocations, materials requirements, labor relations, and distribution patterns.

**Methods of Stimulating Creative Thinking.** In view of the role of creative thinking throughout the innovative problem-solving process, the literature calls attention to a number of methods of stimulating it.

Souder and Ziegler (1977) describe and illustrate twenty operational techniques for generating innovative ideas and stimulating creativity. Some of the procedures are widely known, such as brainstorming, synectics, free association, and heuristics; others are quite esoteric, at least in name if not in substance, such as bionics, morphological analysis, and the Buffalo method. The authors attempt to synthesize information about the twenty techniques by charting their characteristics in relation to problem and solution combinations arranged according to (1) type of problem (open-ended or closed-ended), (2) type of solution sought, (3) how well the problem is understood, (4) whether there are single or multiple solutions, and (5) whether participants are able to freewheel or are constrained by rigid, albeit logical, discipline.

Souder (1975a, 1975b, 1977a) describes in detail a method for considering alternatives called the Q-sort/nominal-interacting process. This process combines the use of psychometric methods entailing ratings and controlled group interactions. For example, a number of choices may be listed on cards and sorted by individuals anonymously, tabulated on a tally sheet, and then displayed to the entire group on a projector. The rating and the display are repeated several times. A group consensus tends to emerge.

The reiterative approach just described is reminiscent of the Delphi method, originally devised to obtain consensus on predictions by a group of experts.

An entire book by Sackman (1975) has been devoted to a critique of the Delphi technique. Its initial primary concern with scientific and technological forecasting has spilled over into the fields of business, education, medicine, and other areas, both broad and specialized. It has been extended beyond the function of prediction to include other aspects of complex problem solving as well. Sackman sums up the range of application objectives as including any type of rating scale used for the generation of quantitative estimates from a set of participants or for the achievement of qualitative evaluations.

Sackman sees the advantages of conventional Delphi as "primarily low cost, versatile application to virtually any area where 'experts' can be found, ease of administration, minimal time and effort on the part of the director and panelists, and the simplicity, popularity, and the directness of the method" (p. 32). Nevertheless, he states that the disadvantages outstrip the advantages, raising such questions as whether remote and private opinion is superior to face-to-face encounter, whether anonymity reinforces accountability, whether Delphi responses are precise and meaningful, and whether Delphi is uncritically isolated from the mainstream of scientific questionnaire development and behavioral experimentation. Sackman's overall conclusion is that "the massive liabilities of [conventional] Delphi, in principle and in practice, outweigh its highly doubtful assets" (p. 74). Despite the numerous and varied applications of the technique summarized in his book, he recommends that "conventional Delphi be dropped from institutional, corporate, and government use until its principles, methods, and fundamental applications can be experimentally established" (p. 74). He does concede that some see it as a heuristic vehicle to be used as an exercise for generating many insights.

The subject of stimulating creativity is treated by Stein (1975) in two volumes; the first is devoted to procedures to be used by or with individuals, the second covers group methods. Although procedures used in the empirical study of the effects of efforts to induce creative thinking have varied in their validity, Stein reports evidence of effectiveness for the several techniques. Both the techniques and their presumed outcomes differ in emphasis on cognitive versus personality factors and are appropriate in varying degrees to different purposes, persons, and settings.

Of particular significance to practical aspects of innovative change as it might be achieved through creative stimulation, Stein decries the fact that the treatment programs tend to confine themselves to what goes on *in* the creative individual and typically fail to examine what goes on *between* the creative individual and others from the time the individual has completed his or her "work" to when others have accepted it—or when they pay too little attention to it. This thought serves as a transitional consideration as we turn to Chapter Nine, with its emphasis on strategies for implementing change.

### Summary Comments

Two considerations are paramount as one considers the "earlier" stages of the problem-solving process as applied to knowledge utilization and innovative change. First, these aspects of the process, though tending to manifest themselves at relatively earlier periods, may be interspersed throughout the enterprise. Second, despite a tendency to differentiate between knowledge producers and knowledge users, and between change initiators and change implementers, the thought processes and activities described are entered into by all participants.

Further, the various components are reflected in the several levels—individual, group, organizational, and societal—although the underlying dynamics necessarily differ among the levels. Societal need awareness, built though it may be on individual consciousness of need, takes its own forms. As noted elsewhere, the opportunity for a division of labor permits wider scope for an organizational search for knowledge as distinguished from possibilities open to an individual. Similarly, a group can come up with a richer set of alternative solutions than an individual can, and these alternatives can be subjected, as a rule, to sounder group judgment.

# 9

# Strategies
# for Achieving Change

This chapter sets forth some guiding principles and methods that concern the achievement of desired objectives with regard to utilization and change, particularly the implementation phase. (Particular strategies that may be used by change agents or change agencies are also discussed in Chapter Eleven.) The present chapter illustrates the bearing of various general principles on implementation; cites their application to fields such as mental health, public services, education, and industry; and considers the place of power, as contrasted with persuasion, in achieving change.

## General Considerations

**Principles Implicit in Strategy Enumeration.** Several writers have set forth lists of strategies and, in so doing, have enunciated various underlying principles.

Applying Kurt Lewin's model of social change to organizational settings, Benne and Birnbaum (1960) suggest three strategies for achieving change: (1) to increase the driving forces, (2) to decrease the restraining forces, and (3) to combine the two methods. From the model, the authors extrapolate a number of principles for effecting institutional change.

1. To change a subsystem, relevant aspects of its environment must be changed.
2. To change behavior at one hierarchical level, complementary and reinforcing changes at other levels are usually necessary.
3. The place to begin is at points where strain exists and dissatisfaction with the status quo is a motivating factor.
4. In diagnosing possibility for change, the degree of stress and strain where change is sought needs to be assessed.
5. In a bureaucratic structure, change should ordinarily start with the policy-making body.
6. Both the formal and the informal organizations of an institution must be considered in planning change.
7. The effectiveness of planned change is related to degree of participation of all hierarchical levels in factfinding, diagnosis of needed change, and formulation and testing of program goals.

There are three types or categories of strategies for change, as presented by Chin and Benne (1969), each with its historical and philosophical base. *Empirical-rational strategies* are based on the assumption of the rational person who changes his or her behavior on the basis of research-based information and knowledge in response to environmental stimuli. *Normative-reeducative strategies* are based on the view of the individual's value relationship with the social environment, along with awareness of the individual's inner motivations and creative problem-solving ability. *Power-coercive approaches* view power as a source of all human action and seek to mass economic and political power behind change goals by nonviolent tactics, use of political institutions, and recomposition and manipulation of power elites. Methods for implementing these three strategies are presented and discussed, and relationships among the strategic types are delineated.

Chin and Benne list the following specific "strategies of deliberate changing" under their three types of general strategies.

*Empirical-Rational*

    Basic research, including basic social research
    Universal educational opportunity
    Personnel selection and replacement
    Scientific management
    Applied research and linkage systems and diffusion
    Practical utopian thinking
    Clarification of language

*Normative-Reeducative*

    Integration of differences
    Social intelligence
    Action research
    Problem solving
    Data-collection feedback
    Research training action
    National training laboratories
    Sensitivity (T-group) training
    Nonrational components of action
    Group sociotherapy
    Counseling
    Conflict labs
    Industrial sociology
    Organization structuring

*Power-Coercive*

    Conflict confrontation
    Nonviolent strategies
- Strikes
- Sitdowns
- Negotiations

    Administrative rulings
    Use of political institutions
- Ballot laws
- Compromise
- Judicial decisions
- Administrative decisions

Changing power elites
Influencing power deciders
Building countervailing power against established power

For most of the above "strategies," the authors list the names of persons associated with the given approach.

Glaser and Ross (1971) identify four strategies of advocacy formation: the fiat model, the platonic (rational appeal) model, the apostolic model, and the conversion model.

1. *Advocacy by fiat,* or change by force of power, administrative regulation, or law, leads to change resulting from decisions of those in authority, as in military, hierarchical, and bureaucratic organizations.

2. The *platonic model* assumes that potential users can be persuaded through education and rational appeal to use particular research-based information or innovative procedures. As evidenced by both Fairweather (1973) and Glaser and Ross (1971), this approach apparently leads to intellectual adoption more than to behavioral modification.

3. The *apostolic model* attempts to stimulate conviction and motivation toward behavioral change through testimony and personal presentation and discussion in addition to written persuasion. Glaser and Ross (1971) found that many potential innovators appeared to appreciate intellectual stimulation afforded by such discussions, but the discussions did not necessarily dissipate the participants' doubts concerning implementation.

4. The *conversion model* has a stronger emotional component, seemingly based on a more profound reordering of the conceptual frame of reference, with conversion facilitated by firsthand participation in a change-effort experience with a mutually reinforcing group of peers.

In the introduction to a collection of articles on the processes and phenomena of social change, Zaltman (1973) presents a table depicting types of change strategies. (See Table 6.)

In a later treatment of the subject, Zaltman and Duncan (1977) have prepared a book on strategies for planned change on the basis of their own experience as well as an extensive re-

Table 8. Typology of Change Strategies.

| Strategy | Description |
| --- | --- |
| Coercive strategies[a] | Nonmutual goal setting and one-sided deliberativeness |
| Normative strategies[a] | Compliance achieved through the issuance of directives based on values internalized as proper and legitimate |
| Utilitarian strategies[a] | Control over the allocation of resources serving as rewards and punishments |
| Empirical-rational strategies[b] | Provision of rational justification for action |
| Normative-reeducative strategies[b] | Change of attitudes, values, skills, and significant relationships |
| Power-coercive strategies[b] | Application of moral, economic, and political resources to achieve change |
| Power strategies[c] | Use and/or threat of force |
| Persuasive strategies[c] | Bias in the structuring and presentation of a message; use of reasoning, urging, inducement based on rational and/or emotional appeals |
| Reeducative strategies[c] | Communication of fact and relearning through affective and cognitive change |
| Individual change strategies[d] | Use of change among individuals as a means toward social or organizational change |
| Data-based strategies[d] | Collecting and presenting data to initiate problem-solving activity and to provide a basis in which to root decision |
| Organizational development[d] | Creating a supportive climate or culture for organizational change |
| Violence and coercive strategies[d] | Actions designed to inflict personal injury or property damage |
| Nonviolence and direct-action strategies[d] | Attempts to change attitudes and/or behavior |
| Manipulation[e] | A deliberate act of changing either the structure of the alternatives in the environment or personal qualities affecting choice without the knowledge of the person involved |
| Persuasion[e] | Interpersonal influence in which one person tries to change the attitude or behavior of another by means of argument, reasoning, or, in certain cases, structured listening |
| Facilitation[e] | Attempts to increase the ease with which individuals or groups can implement their choice or satisfy their desires |

[a]Garth N. Jones, *Planned Organizational Change.* New York: Praeger, 1969.
[b]Robert Chin and Kenneth Benne, "General Strategies for Effective Changes in Human Systems." In W. G. Bennis, K. D. Benne, and R. Chin (Eds.), *The Planning of Change.* New York: Holt, Rinehart and Winston, 1969.
[c]Gerald Zaltman, Philip Kotler, and Ira Kaufman, *Creating Social Change.* New York: Holt, Rinehart and Winston, 1972.
[d]Harvey A. Hornstein and others, *Social Intervention: A Behavioral Science Approach.* New York: Free Press, 1971.
[e]Donald Warwick, "Ethical Issues in Social Intervention." Working paper, York University, 1972.
Adapted from Zaltman, G. (Ed.). *Processes and Phenomena of Social Change.* New York: Wiley, 1973.

view of the literature. They place hindering factors largely under (1) cultural, (2) social, (3) organizational, and (4) psychological barriers. Strategies for inducing change are classified as (1) reeducation, (2) facilitation, (3) persuasion, and (4) use of power.

In listing common methods for bringing about change, Davis (1971) refers to change (1) by fiat, (2) brought about by the provision of special funds, (3) by sociopolitical exigencies, (4) by charisma of a leader, (5) resulting from intolerable problems, and (6) swept in by broad trends throughout the field.

Jones (1965) examines successful cases of planned organizational change in traditional societies and isolates, defines, and classifies strategies and tactics that perform critical roles in change processes. His strategies (some of which are the same as those listed by Chin and Benne and by Zaltman and Duncan) are grouped as follows:

*Coercive strategies*—characterized by nonmutual goal setting and resting on sanctions or the threat of sanctions. These strategies may include—

- A *strategy of pressure*—use of a show of force to fulfill predetermined objectives.
- A *strategy of stress induction*—efforts directed toward disturbing the equilibrium of an organizational system to prepare it for change.

*Normative strategies*—emphasizing normative power or compliance based on the internalization of directions accepted as proper and legitimate. These strategies may include—

- A *strategy of participation*—involving the concerned individuals in the decision-making process before the actual change is introduced.
- A *strategy of education/training*—providing training in basic skills required, assuming that underlying habits, attitudes, and ways of thought and behavior have been created.

*Utilitarian strategies*—controlling material resources and

rewards through the allocation of increased contributions, benefits, and services. The strategies may include—

- A *strategy of placement*—assuring affected members of a group that they will be taken care of in case the changes have such effects as work displacement.
- A *strategy of empiricism*—involving objective and empirical proof of the value of the new system introduced.

In addition to the three major types of strategy of planned organizational change, Jones lists the following tactics, applicable in conjunction with the several strategies, as used in the sample of cases studied:

The *tactic of action research*—in which research personnel become directly involved as manipulators in the change process.

The *tactic of technical modification*—in which changes in the traditional structure of the organizational system are induced as a means of increasing overall performance.

The *tactic of marginality*—in which persons such as acculturated bilinguals sharing value systems of their own society (or group) and that of the innovating society (or group) bridge the gap between the two.

**Strategic Factors Affecting Change.** Strategies and tactics for bringing about change are affected by four considerations (Kotter and Schlesinger, 1979): (1) the persons (and their roles) who use the particular strategies and tactics, (2) the nature of the strategies employed, (3) process conceptions, and (d) program aims. These considerations are so intertwined that an effort to differentiate them and deal with them separately would be not only very difficult but also probably unproductive.

Howes and Quinn (1978) cite twelve factors most often related to successful implementation of change programs:

1. Introducing the change over sufficient time.
2. Making the advantage of the change visible.
3. Showing organization members that their efforts will be supported.

4. Showing members that the change can easily be institutionalized.
5. Showing that immediate superiors support the change.
6. Clearly identifying the roles of all those involved in the change process.
7. Providing supportive services.
8. Setting up formal training for members' roles.
9. Rewarding the use of communication channels.
10. Relaxing standard operating procedures in changing units.
11. Integrating members with managers and change agents.
12. Making members feel adequately involved.

A study by Unco, Inc. (1973a), of the utilization of four advanced management techniques in state welfare departments incorporated a communication model into an adaptation of the problem-solving model of research utilization. From the combined model and from interviews with welfare personnel in three states, the investigators devised a set of twenty-five principles of research utilization, which they later presented in a separate report (Unco, Inc., 1973b). These principles, or guidelines, deal with various aspects of the communication/utilization process.

With respect to the communication cycle, the content of the messages needs to be clear to users of innovations, although excessive communication should be avoided. Suitable language needs to be employed, and written messages used with a realization of their limitations. A well-specified communication structure is critical. Definite links must be provided, and feedback made an intrinsic part of the process. The translator role is significant in achieving effectiveness.

With regard to the utilization cycle, the guidelines draw attention to the awareness of user need and to the articulation of the problem, as well as to the necessity of choosing solutions that are within the constraints of the user's organization, are responsive to economic, political, and social conditions, and are technically valid. Demonstrations need to be realistic as well as technically valid and must be responsive both to the user's methods of operation and to changing situations. The same is true of the implementation stage proper, following demonstration. User involvement and contingency planning are also stressed.

**Adaptation in Implementing Strategies.** A highly influential book of readings edited by Bennis, Benne, and Chin, first published in 1961 and revised in 1969 (and again in 1976, with K. Corey), emphasized the *planning* of change as an antidote to a laissez faire, "natural law," noninterventionist position in human affairs. By implication, if not explicitly, planning and careful control of the process were stressed. Several recent writers, however, have drawn attention to what might be termed gradual, adaptive, and developmental implementation of innovative ideas or practices rather than detailed planning and control.

Berman (1980), who has stressed the weaknesses of the implementation stage as a major source of lack of discernible success in many innovative attempts, suggests that a fruitful approach may result from the *matching* of strategies to situations depending on whether they call for *programmed,* or precisely planned, implementation, as against *adaptive* implementation. The programmed approach calls for clearness and specificity of the planned change effort, to be strictly followed, once a final adoption decision is made, by all levels of the organization involved. Precise, detailed, and presumably consistent objectives formulated by officials are to be followed by lower-level personnel. Resistance is handled by limiting discretion, monitoring behavior, and allocating incentives, particularly of an extrinsic nature. The innovations tend to be "packaged."

Adaptive implementation, in contrast, allows for policy to be modified, specified, and revised according to the unfolding interaction of the policy with its institutional setting. It seeks only general, perhaps vague, or even tacit agreement on goals and permits diverse participants to bargain and compromise positions on objectives and means in the course of implementation. It allows for considerable discretion. It seeks to achieve motivation through participation in decision making. Adaptive implementers would ideally use evaluation to further adaptation rather than as a monitoring device on the fidelity of application of a predetermined program.

Berman seeks to clarify his thesis of situationally differentiated application of the two approaches by first charting structured and unstructured types of policy situations. He then hypothesizes that the programmed approach is appropriate when *all* elements of the structured situation are present—that is, when (1) the change is incremental in scope, (2) little risk is involved, (3) the level of conflict is low, (4) the implementing system is tightly coupled with the institutional structure, and (5) the environmental setting is stable. If for any of these conditions the opposite condition is present, then an unstructured situation exists, and elements of adaptive implementation strategies are needed to cope with such problems as may arise.

Having set forth a rather sharply defined paradigm, Berman concludes with the observation that implementation strategies may well take a "mixed" form.

Eveland, Rogers, and Klepper (1977) offer four key propositions on which their model of the innovative process is based and which also relate to a more flexible position concerning planning, as follows:

1.  An innovation is made up of many elements with more or less specificity at any given point.
2.  Innovation is a process by which a general idea is translated into organizational action, a process that gradually reduces the degree of ambiguity with which the innovation is understood and permits individuals to interpret the idea within a wide range of meanings.
3.  Two major categories of decisions must be made in the course of the innovation process: (a) those relating to the innovation itself—the tool and its shape—and (b) those relating to the innovation's *application*—how it is to be used.
4.  Innovations are not constant in their various adoptions; the frequency of adaptation raises a fundamental question about the assumption of past diffusion research that innovation is a fairly standard item to those who adopt it.

From our viewpoint and experience, the approaches suggested by Bennis, Benne, and Chin, on the one hand, and by

Berman and by Eveland, Rogers, and Klepper, on the other hand, are not necessarily in opposition. It may be very desirable to involve representatives of all "stakeholder" groups in the planning and implementation stages and *together* iterate, revise, and adapt the plans in response to what is discovered as the process moves along in the implementation, monitoring, and institutionalization phases.

The process of adaptation has been the subject of several articles. For example, Glaser and Backer (1977), in arguing that durability of worthwhile innovations is more important than their strict adoption without change, cite evidence of the desirability of adapting innovations to local conditions if they are to be accepted and to achieve a likelihood of continuance, provided the innovation is maintained.

Rice and Rogers (1980) refer to adaptation as reinvention and detail a number of factors that may influence it. They note Larsen's and Agarwala-Rogers's observation (1977) that reinvention is more likely to occur when the innovation is more complex, when it is irreversible, and when an external consultant does not take an active role in the process. Rice and Rogers detail potential inducements to reinvention—for example, failure to match the system's problem, threats to political survival, resentment against an earlier form of an innovation, a wide definition of the problem, and a condition whereby an innovation consists of a collection of "loose" components, thus allowing for more flexibility.

Since Rice and Rogers perceive potential adopters as active participants in the adoption and diffusion process, they consider reinvention as not being necessarily bad.

In his treatise on strategies for change based on a four-year action-research project involving six liberal arts colleges and two universities, Lindquist (1978) also stresses adaptive change. His concluding summary calls for the following change agenda: (1) developing innovative models for adaptation rather than adoption, (2) strengthening diffusion channels and linking local leaders to them, (3) concentrating on thorough diagnosis of local goals and needs, (4) opening political gates to demands for change, (5) involving organization members not only in these earlier parts of the process but also in the thinking and formulation of proposals, (6) supporting the orientation and training of innovation implementers and leaders, (7) providing solid time, material, and facilities, (8) conducting both formative and summative evaluation, and (9) rewarding those who involve themselves in innovation and in intentionally disseminating the innovation internally and externally.

## Application of Strategies for Achieving Change in Special Fields

**Mental Health.** Balk (1978) draws twelve lessons leading into application strategies from a case study of the planning and implementation of comprehensive organizational change in a community mental health center (CMHC). The organizational difficulties created by environmental pressures from funding sources are analyzed. The planning processes used, responses within the organization to the planned change, and organizational lessons learned by the CMHC are presented. The reader may wish to review the twelve lessons, each of which discusses a single topic—for example, limited resources, dissension from within, confusion caused by change, self-interest, and knowledge versus behavior.

In the previously mentioned study by Fairweather, Sanders, and Tornatzky (1974), the factors facilitating adoption of a "lodge" program for aftercare mental patients (a house or facility outside the institution that can accommodate semi-independent living) included (1) nonpassive (in fact, aggressively active) presentation of the new idea, as through demonstration projects, (2) small change-oriented groups within the organization, fortified with the assistance of outside change agents, and (3) organizations where many people made the decisions rather than only a few at the top.

Sauber (1977) depicts the features of two types of strategic planning approaches for conducting an analysis of a community mental health program: *intraorganizational* and *extraorganizational*. The intraorganizational approach is characterized by program directors' making an initial assessment of a CMHC staff's desires and abilities and the distribution of resources and patient population, followed by a survey of community opportunities to utilize the center's strengths and achieve organizational goals.

The extraorganizational approach begins with a survey, forecast, and analysis of the external environment, followed by an examination of the organization's resources for serving the population and adapting to external environmental demands. Ideological and program variables with regard to the human services are analyzed. Sauber suggests that a major strategy for facilitating client access to a comprehensive range of coordinated human services and service organizations is to change the structure through which services are provided. He identifies four models that provide comprehensive neighborhood or community human services: the advice service, the diagnostic center, the multiservice center, and the human services network. Ecology and intervention strategies are suggested on six levels of intervention.

In a book on social change and the mental health of children, the Joint Commission on Mental Health of Children (1973b) outlines a broad program, one that reflects an analysis by Ronald Lippitt of barriers to change as existing in our assumptions, in our institutional and professional practices, and in the deficiencies of our knowledge and skills. The proposals for program development contain several special features that provide detailed strategies: (1) a design for youth involvement and participation in program planning and implementation, (2) the education of the young for participation in adult roles, (3) the recruiting and training of volunteers and paraprofessionals, and (4) the application of a self-renewal model for the development and maintenance of the several programs. In sum, along with the more traditional approaches, the report advocates an approach to mental health implementation that stresses developmental and preventive functions, as distinguished from curative measures.

An extensive case study of one of the largest mental hospitals in England is reported by Towell (1979), who, with colleagues, studied various aspects of the psychiatric program over a period of three years. Many factors of organization, personnel, and policies were examined by what was termed the Westville Assistance Group. These investigators unearthed a number of dilemmas, which, in turn, led to a strategy for achieving resolution and change in, for example, the following:

1.  Combining the local initiative required for creative problem solving with the central leadership, in order to overcome fragmentation.
2.  Achieving an effective balance between the exercise of discretion by professionals involved in delivery services and an appropriate system of managerial control.
3.  Seeking ways in which staff members' investment in traditional procedures can be made compatible with their active involvement in a process designed to achieve informed change.

In attacking these and other problems, the institution showed some tendency to cling to the past but made progress along limited lines. In recognition of the difficulties of changing long-established patterns, the Westville Assistance Group agreed with management on a role that would help staff members tackle problems and improve patient care in their own way.

In a summary chapter of a book on innovation and social process, Tornatzky and others (1980a) report on a series of empirical studies designed, on the whole, to test the hypothesis that change and innovation in the social field without human contact and interpersonal interaction are not likely to be beneficial or complete. More specifically and positively, they were able to demonstrate in a variety of experiments that participative decision making and group problem solving, when carried on with vigor, can make a difference in adoption. However, such involvement, entailing consultation, workshops, and similar techniques of organizational development, had to be "robust" to be effective, as distinguished from low-key, minimally intrusive intervention.

Another general conclusion of the many-faceted project described by Tornatzky and his colleagues is that the various types of intervention included *can* be empirically evaluated and should be subjected to further research.

**Public Services.** Rothman, Erlich, and Teresa (1976) have prepared a planning manual for service agencies, to help people promote change in organizations and communities. Specific strategies or action guidelines are offered. The action guidelines, derived from basic social science research findings, are general principles that can be used by a variety of people concerned with organizational and community change.

Four types of intervention, or action guidelines, are considered: (1) promoting an innovative service or program, (2) changing the goals of an organization, (3) increasing participation in organizations and groups, and (4) increasing effectiveness in role performance.

Rowe and Boise (1974) discuss three potential strategies for organizational innovation within public administration: organizational development, functional specialization, and periodicity.

1. *Organizational development,* Rowe and Boise suggest, can "train" individuals and related organization components to promote such organizational characteristics as structural looseness, changing of individual roles, professional and programmatic diversity, open communication, group decision processes, and limited competition.

2. *Functional specialization,* according to Rowe and Boise, refers to the typical practice of designing organizational units for specialized activities, such as those corresponding to the various stages of the process of innovation. Examples are the establishment of R&D units and of planning groups. The assumptions underlying structural-functional and systems theory provide a convenient rationale for this kind of compartmentalization.

A strategy of functional specialization may be the most feasible approach for organizations planning relatively nonradical innovations that will cover small amounts of organizational "space."

Where innovation is perceived as threatening to an organization's survival, compartmentalization of the new activities may in effect afford a measure of protection for at least a minimal innovative process.

3. *Periodicity* provides a third strategy. Here, alternating organizational forms are used, as when a variety of specialists and workers are assembled for a particular project, and a temporary organization is created that is disbanded when the project is completed, the workers being assigned elsewhere.

Rowe and Boise point out that one limit on the strategy of periodicity is the extent to which the same persons can assume a variety of roles and can function in different operational climates.

Glaser and Backer (1979) perceive organizational development as an evolving set of techniques, generally derived from the behavioral sciences, to strengthen staff communication and problem-solving capacities. As a general statement, the key objective is to help develop an organizational process whereby the stakeholders are encouraged to come together to share perceptions, define problems, generate or search out a range of possible solutions, select and plan to implement a solution, carry it out, and assess the impact of their actions. This type of diagnosis, intervention, and process maintenance can be implemented in some situations by internal staff alone; in other situations, inviting the help of a competent outside organizational development consultant may make the effort much more productive and acceptable to the participants.

Using two sample illustrations each in two state agency fields—highway transportation and air pollution—Feller, Menzel, and Engel (1974) studied technology diffusion in fifty states to determine patterns of adoption and the decision to adopt. They found systematic adoption of technologies in the air-pollution field but not in the field of highway transportation.

Little or no relation appeared between state adoption and eight variables, including size or prestige of the decision unit, professional orientation, interaction with agency personnel in other states, and agency autonomy. However, *federal agencies and external change agents offering support and technical assistance proved significant in inducing changes.*

The report offers a number of recommendations on conditions or methods favorable to the application of strategies, including (1) a sharper delineation at the federal level of objectives underlying development and diffusion of technology in the public sector, (2) federal promotion of objectives and standards, with only occasional specification of technologies, (3) federal support of evaluation activities, (4) studies of market strategies, including product innovations in industries that sell to the public sector, and (5) increased attention to various ways of facilitating the implementation phase.

Noting that the introduction of computerized hospital information systems may adversely affect employee satisfaction, efficiency, and productivity, Farlee (1978) proposes that administrators give consideration to the effects on staff of increased formalization, centralization, and stratification. The author suggests (1) avoiding making extensive changes in the roles of nurses or physicians or placing excessive restrictions on them, (2) allowing participation of those involved in the decision-making process, (3) avoiding excessive hierarchical changes, and (4) assuring those involved that the process of change is definite, continuous, visible, and in conformity with advance plans and schedules.

**Education.** Regarding education and social sciences generally, Kritek (1976) notes a shift in the literature on innovation and change from variables associated with the diffusion and initial adoption of innovations to those descriptive of the later implementation process. He sets forth a number of suggestions in line with increased stress on recognition of changing goals, continued and adaptable planning, provision for adequate resources, acceptance of new roles by the host organization, continuity of leadership, realization of the complexity often associated with new programs, incorporation of user input, and provision for monitoring and feedback mechanisms.

Karmos and Jacko (1977) assert that the literature on the evaluation and assessment of school innovations suggests that fatal weaknesses occur during the early stages of implementation. These weaknesses are often related to the effects of role changes on students, teachers, and administrators, since innovations usually require unlearning of traditional roles and relearning of new ones. Accordingly, the authors develop a series of rec-ommendations for each of the persons involved. By way of illus-tration: Central administrators are advised to involve teachers and specialists in decision making. On-site administrators are asked to provide guides for teacher training. Teachers are en-couraged to visit schools using the innovation. Consultants and specialists are expected to cooperate with administrators and teachers in formulating the roles for consultants and developers.

Goldman and Moynihan (1976), after noting that more and more school systems are engaging in educational planning that use such models as management by objectives, systems analysis, organizational development, and program and planning budgeting systems, report their conclusions from a study of planning in some seventy-five school districts in New York State. They note in particular, as others have noted, that the movement from planning to implementation is complex, as is the process of diffusion, which involves, basically, both profes-sionals and a mix of professional and community groups. They offer observations and suggestions, including the following:

1.  The chief administrative officer is a key to the entire pro-cess; however, the importance of linkage to external (re-gional and state) agencies cannot be overlooked.
2.  Four major process variables related to diffusion effective-ness are identified: (a) gaining commitment to the need for planning and change, (b) gaining commitment to the par-ticular planning model adopted by the school district, (c) dealing with interface issues, and (d) managing the issues of communication and coordination.
3.  Attention paid to human and political issues could be criti-cal to the success of local educational planning. (This seems obvious but often is given insufficient attention.)

Scanlon and his colleagues (1973) examine decision-mak-ing processes in school districts and state education departments to develop a change capability that can initiate and sustain edu-cational improvements from the district level to the building level. To accomplish change capability, the following strategies have been used: (1) establishment of criteria to ensure commitment to and understanding about R&D products as instructional systems, (2) development of training programs for administrators, teachers, and school district central-office personnel, (3) establishment of demonstration centers with national representation, (4) development of a data network and feedback system that permits the monitoring of schools, and (5) inclusion of state education agencies and central-office administrators in the development of a capability for introducing and maintaining educational innovations.

Citing a study of an innovative program for early detection and prevention of school adjustment problems (the Primary Mental Health Project [PMHP]) diffused to 200 schools, Cowen, Davidson, and Gesten (1980) conclude that the following seem to have facilitated the present dissemination effort: direct experiential involvement of consumers, an action orientation by disseminators, perseverance, provision of continuous support for local change agents, development of materials and experiences that simplify and demystify program conduct, assurance of a credibility base through research, and the program's adaptability to multiple realities.

Under the sponsorship of the National Institute of Education (NIE), Moore and others (1977) studied six diversified assistance groups offering face-to-face help to teachers, administrators, parents, and/or students in attempts to bring about change in local schools. The study focused on the history of each group, its methods of internal functioning, its philosophy of change, and its role in the change process. The authors identified the following patterns or principles affecting the educational change process:

1.  Highly detailed, focused change is more likely to occur than "ripple effect" change.
2.  Effects of change strategies such as modeling or the provision of materials are related to the characteristics of the intervention situation.
3.  Strongly held value commitments play a central role in change efforts.

4.  A time frame of three to four years is requisite for signifi-
    cant change.

Wolf and Fiorino (1972) queried some 600 educators in
depth to determine their experiences with innovation, the influence of recognized diffusion agents on their adoption of innovations, characteristics of selected target audiences in relation to
the adoption of innovations, and the comparison of five distinguishable stages of innovation adoption described by rural sociologists with those described by randomly selected educators.
Among the many findings of the study were the following: (1)
Most of the innovations discussed were drawn from outside the
environment of the practitioner; some were used intact throughout, and others were later modified. (2) Personal, direct-involve-
ment diffusion strategies (colleague contact, workshops, institutes, courses) were more popular with adopters of innovations
than those that did not entail personal, direct contacts.

It was also found that the five-step pattern of innovation
diffusion commonly seen in agriculture (awareness, interest,
evaluation, trial, and adoption) was somewhat applicable to the
field of education.

Goldman and Gregory (1977), considering development
in schools, studied the application of the following procedures
of the Program and Planning Budgeting System (PPBS):

1.  Organizational goals are designed.
2.  Particular programs presumed to serve these goals are iden-
    tified.
3.  Objectives for each program are specified.
4.  Information about intended objectives and actual accom-
    plishments is recorded and disseminated.
5.  Future activity is planned through comparison of inten-
    tions with accomplishments.
6.  Input factors are measured in terms of precise monetary
    costs.
7.  Alternatives are evaluated in terms of least-cost maximiza-
    tion of objectives.

In addition, to develop the School Planning, Evaluation, and Communication System (SPECS), two further elements, particularly relevant to the situation of schools, were added: (1) the accounting stage of the system was extended beyond the administrative office and into the classroom by teacher preparation of planning and evaluation documents; (2) a procedure to determine community goals for the local school system was developed, along with a follow-up procedure that attempts to match these goals with the actual measured output of student performance.

According to Miles (1978a), the designing of new schools is a focused, comprehensive strategy that can avoid conservative constraints, permit more experimentation and curricular change, and engage participants actively. Miles developed case studies of six new schools, and he examines the tasks and dilemmas facing this type of enterprise.

As an illustration, the dilemma of innovative versus familiar choices is examined in terms of forces favoring one or the other pole of the distinction. Factors favoring innovation are incentives to innovate, a mandate to innovate, commitment to goals, and an investment of energy. Factors opposing innovation and favoring the retention of the familiar include such "forces" as vulnerability, opposition from traditional parts of the system and the environment, uncertainty, risk avoidance, reliance on past practice, and protection of vested interest. Similarly, each phase of the entire framework of planning and implementation is analyzed in detail.

In a later study Miles (1981) outlines an agenda for future endeavors in this area. The following needs are stressed: (1) more *directly descriptive data* on such matters as the actual modes being used by teachers, administrators, boards, and the local community, (2) more *contingent analyses* showing, for example, for what sorts of innovations and in what sorts of organizational and community contexts a "technology transfer" approach will work, (3) an analysis and testing of the *causal claims* of supposed antecedents of the regularities noted, and (4) a treatment of the *innovativeness* and school *effectiveness*

as dependent variables for many or all of the "noted regularities" under each dilemma.

One of the most elaborate evaluation projects with significant bearing on strategies was reported by Berman and
McLaughlin (1976), who, with colleagues at the Rand Corporation, reviewed over a five-year period certain federally supported
innovative educational programs (noted below) and their underlying assumptions. Four questions, in particular, were addressed:
(1) How should innovation and dissemination of new practices be
assessed? (2) How do school districts select, implement, incorporate, and spread different kinds of innovations? (3) How do
differences in federal programs, in project characteristics, and in
local settings affect how projects are carried out, continued
with local funding, and disseminated? (4) What should federal
policies be toward educational innovation in light of the political, financial, and organizational constraints that the federal
government faces in its dealings with the public schools?

The authors present detailed findings on the generally
limited outcomes of these programs and possible reasons there-
for. They stress the uncertainty of the implementation phase in
the face of the complexity of the educational organizational
system. In their recommendations, consequently, they emphasize this phase and later phases designed to incorporate projected changes. They note that the assumption that school districts take something like an R&D approach is not borne out
and point to needed modifications in federal aid policies in
keeping with this finding.

More to the point, Berman and McLaughlin reviewed 293
projects liberally supported by the U.S. Office of Education in
four aid-program fields (Elementary and Secondary Education
Act Titles III and VII; Vocational Education Act, Part D; and
Right-to-Read Program). Their study yielded repeated instances
of research findings that innovations produce "no significant
differences." According to Berman and McLaughlin, the project
as implemented often bore little resemblance to the project as
conceived. It is the view of the authors that innovations may result in disappointing outcomes, not because of inadequacies of
the innovative idea, but because of the difficult and uncertain

process of implementing innovative efforts in an educational system that retards change.

In cases of successful implementation, the districts were generally characterized by what the authors called a "problem-solving" orientation; that is, they had identified and frequently had already begun to attack the problem before federal money became available. Unsuccessful implementation seemed to be associated with an "opportunistic" orientation in which district budgets were simply augmented with money that happened to be available.

Other characteristics of successful implementations include (1) a rejection of "proven solutions" packaged too rigidly to permit local adaptation, (2) local development or adaptation rather than adoption of materials developed elsewhere, (3) continuous planning and replanning rather than a burst of planning at the outset, (4) training emerging from ongoing needs of the project and defined by project participants, (5) strong support from key school and district administrators, and (6) consistent and committed technical assistance.

The authors strongly recommend support of a research program on ways in which schools and districts can be helped to develop a problem-solving orientation and the organizational and managerial capacity to make it work.

Widmer (1975) investigated local takeover of federal education programs under the Elementary and Secondary Education Act by examining how adopted and nonadopted innovative programs differed in their development, organization, dissemination, local leadership, and state support. Data were gathered from a stratified sample of twelve of thirty-eight programs funded in Massachusetts for the three-year period 1971–1974. The study identifies particular strategies, roles, and procedures that aid or hinder the adoption of educational innovations. Among the factors associated with successful adoption are the following:

1. The more tangible the project and the more easily it could be explained to others, the greater was the likelihood of adoption.

2. Observable changes were more likely to be accepted than internal or attitudinal change efforts.
3. Adopted projects tended to have school committee support.
4. Project directors of adopted projects tended to have expertise in the subject area of the project.
5. Project directors experienced a satisfactory relationship with the local supervisors in relation to initiation of the project.

Corwin (1972c, 1973) addressed the problem of how organizations similar to the Teachers Corps can cope and survive in a political environment by identifying twenty-two processes that apply political-economy dimensions to the shaping of a program's fate. Value consensus, goal setting, persuasion, use and dispersal of resources, checks and balances, prestige of member organizations, development of latent subcultures, dynamic tension between autonomy and independence, organizational networks, reform as a political process of compromise—these and related ideas are all mentioned as applicable to the political adjustment process faced by the program.

House (1974), drawing on material from a number of disciplines, including geography, organization theory, technology, sociology, economics, and political science, attempts to interpret the underlying dynamics of educational innovation. Among his conclusions are the following:

1. Diffusion tends to follow geographical lines marked by openness of transportation and communication routes.
2. The organizational structure of schools tends to exclude teachers from decision making.
3. The trend in the spread of technology is from more highly developed centers to lesser-developed areas.
4. With the exception of certain instances, for example, in agricultural diffusion, innovations have tended to spread when incentives are provided by government grants or other funding, the pattern of spread being from large urban centers to smaller population centers and outlying districts.

5.   The planning, research, development, and diffusion model reflecting the earlier basis of sponsorship of educational innovations by the U.S. Office of Education has been largely replaced by a more user-oriented model.
6.   With the development of technologically advanced products in the form of both hardware and software, one can expect a trend from a labor-intensive to a capital-intensive base.
7.   Social pressures result in a priority of political considerations over purely educational ones with respect to project support.

Though professing that remedies for deep-seated barriers to meaningful and widespread educational innovation and diffusion are hard to find, House does offer several suggestions with qualified hope for success—for example, (1) greater stress on humanitarian considerations, as against cost, (2) recognition that all innovation, notably technological, is not necessarily beneficial, and (3) horizontal division of labor, placing teachers on an equal footing with administrators with regard to decision-making functions.

**Industry/Military.** Roberts and Frohman (1978) set forth several basic change strategies for industrial research utilization that take into account propositions such as the following:

1.   Staff members specifically charged with the responsibility for increased market transfer and success of new products and processes tend to enhance research utilization.
2.   New information can, at best, create new awareness but does not necessarily lead to behavioral changes (such as buying a new product).
3.   The movement of people, joint teams, and geographical or physical proximity permits intensive person-to-person contact between the generator and the user of research, thereby promoting more effective research utilization.

Dunn and Swierczek (1977) studied sixty-seven successful and unsuccessful business and industrial change efforts by examining each case study for support or negation of eleven hypotheses about the conditions of successful change efforts gleaned from a review of the literature. Only three of the hypotheses were supported (and then only moderately or weakly) —namely, (1) that the mode of intervention should be collaborative, (2) that the change agent should have a participant orientation, and (3) that standardized strategies should be employed that evoke high levels of participation.

Wright (1966) refers to the issue of active promotion versus passive dissemination, reporting on a two-phase program of the Office of Industrial Application (OIA) at the University of Maryland, which seeks to study the transfer of technical information to industry from the National Aeronautics and Space Administration (NASA). OIA examined the factors that impede and those that facilitate such transfers. Findings indicate that a critical point in the transfer and utilization mechanism is frequently the personal interaction between the intended user and the innovator.

The major reasons for rejection and inaction, according to Wright, were technical and were associated with indeterminate applicability and uncertain market potential. Almost eight times as much interest was generated by the possibility of improving an existing product or process as by the chance of acquiring a completely new addition to the inquirer's processes and products.

Technology transfer or dissemination programs of various federal agencies, including an intensive case study account of the NASA Technology Utilization Program, are the subject of a book by Doctors (1969). Although inherent difficulties are present in a mission-oriented federal agency, Doctors does make a case for a federally sponsored program whose objective is to enhance future attempts at technology transfer. It is suggested that ideally such a program should (1) be experimental in nature, (2) be concerned initially with systematic data accumulation, (3) work with technology users capable of providing feedback, (4) work visibly in the market, and (5) accept the reality that political pressures may affect allocation of benefits on a geographical or institutional basis.

Udis (1976), on the basis of a study of military-to-civilian transfer of resources in seven major industrialized countries of Western Europe, presents a varied set of observations on the subject of transfer of ideas, technology, and persons.

1. Although considerable evidence of actual spinoff was found, there is a fairly widespread belief that successful transfer from the military to the civilian sector would have to be consciously planned or even forced.

2. Doubts have been raised about the economic justification for many of the high-technology projects conducted during recent years. The view has been expressed that high technology rarely moves to lower levels of technology within a country but more readily moves horizontally across national boundaries. Nevertheless, there are some areas of successful spinoff within the country, including the rapid transfer of advanced managerial skills.

3. Technology transfer is more often accomplished by a movement of persons between organizations or of information concerning components or processes than by the transfer of a particular product.

4. Obstacles to technology transfer include (a) government regulation, (b) competition between government agencies, (c) separation of divisions within a company, (d) postwar political agreements, (e) structural imbalance and problems of communication between different levels of a nation's economy, (f) problems of commercialization and fragmented markets, (g) customer inability to specify needs, (h) differences in the scale of output, (i) problems in transferring redundant specialized military resources, (j) the high cost of quality, and (k) inadequate marketing skills.

5. Concerning the transferability of people and skills, the military experience may have been too specialized, and other particularized characteristics of that milieu may not have prepared personnel for the requirements of the transfer situation.

T. Gray and C. Roberts-Gray of Perceptronics, working with Glaser and Backer (1980) as consultants, have developed a systematic stage model that incorporates strategies for dealing with technical, organizational, administrative, and human-factors-based problems likely to arise in various types of technology-transfer efforts. Although the "taxonomy of strategies" is described as specifically related to the introduction by the military of a complex, technologically involved innovation in battle-simulation techniques, the model is offered as representing a prototype relevant to a broad range of innovation adoption/utilization situations.

In essence, the model depicts four stages (R&D, delivery and initiation, implementation, and institutionalization). Each stage is supported by selected strategies or tactics. Each of the strategies is carefully specified by way of (1) a general description backed by supporting principles from the literature, (2) its particularized application to the project at hand, (3) its purpose as described by a necessary process and desired outcomes, and (4) measures for checking or monitoring the actual implementation of the proposed process steps.

Table 7 (pp. 216-217) provides Glaser and Backer's summary presentation of the strategies applicable to each stage.

### Power Versus Persuasion

The choice of strategies often involves the application of varying degrees of power. Greiner (1967) has made a careful analysis of the uses of different kinds of power in implementing organizational change. He describes unilateral power, in which the executive decides; shared power, in which decisions are made jointly; and delegated power, in which decisions are turned over to subordinates, either singly or in groups. Whereas executive power by itself is often thought to be ineffective, the commingling of the several kinds of power is considered most effective for promoting change. Too often, the decision is permitted to fall between unilateral and delegated power, without the kind of interchange that shared power entails.

Using an analysis by French and Raven (1959) of the bases of power whereby a social agent can influence another person, a role, a norm, a group, or a part of a group, Mann and Neff (1961) indicate different types of power that the change agent needs to understand and be able to use: *legitimate power,* based on obligation or duty; *reward power,* based on giving or withholding reward; *coercive power,* based on potential for punishment; *expert power,* based on greater knowledge or ability; and *referent power,* based on attraction and/or identification.

Managers often deal with resistance coercively (Kotter and Schlesinger, 1979). Here they essentially force people to accept a change by explicitly or implicitly threatening them (with the loss of jobs, promotion possibilities, and so forth) or by actually firing and transferring them. As with manipulation, using coercion is risky because inevitably people strongly resent forced change. But in situations where speed is essential and where the changes will not be popular regardless of how they are introduced, coercion may be the manager's only option.

In organizations power is expressed in part through rules. But Weber (1968) noted that the probability of compliance with rules increases when a capable enforcing agent is charged with attending to the rules. In two experimental studies Gray and Roberts-Gray (1979) provided empirical support as well as further elaboration of this proposition. They found that compliance increased with the designation of an enforcing agent and even more so when sanctions were announced or accompanied the application of the rule.

According to Walton (1969), there are two systems of ideas about social change, especially where conflict is involved, that often present a dilemma to the practitioner. First is the tactic of power, which has as its objective the obtaining of concessions; second is the tactic of attitude change, which aims to reduce hostility. The two tactics can be further delineated in terms of contrasts, such as emphasis on power to coerce versus trust; threat versus conciliation; and stereotyping versus differentiation. Two solutions to the dilemma are proposed: (1) to use the two strategies in sequence, as in freeze-thaw tactics in international relations, and (2) to have the contradictory strategies implemented by different persons or subgroups.

The dilemma can be minimized further by selecting, from each of the strategies, tactics that reinforce, rather than detract from, the alternative strategy. An additional approach suggested by G. Zaltman (personal communication) would use different strategies simultaneously, as required, with different types of personnel in the same agency.

One approach to power approaches is the psychological

Table 7. Strategies for Actualizing Change: A Summary Chart.

| Strategy No. | Strategy/Tactic Title | Model Stage | Brief Description |
|---|---|---|---|
| 1 | Project Plan Draft | Research & Development | Provide enough detail in project plan to permit internal judgment of worthwhileness of investment |
| 2 | Potential User Consultant Panel | Research & Development | If judged worthy of pursuing, submit project plan to review/critique by potential users |
| 3 | Mini–Pilot Test of Prototype | Research & Development | When product prototype is ready, subject it to preliminary field pilot test |
| 4 | Joint Application Team | Delivery & Initiation | Organize and make available to potential users an expert technical assistance team that can provide familiarity with the innovation and how to apply it for achievement of the desired results; provide on-site training in operation and maintenance |
| 5 | Field Demonstration as "Tune-Up" for Implementation | Delivery & Initiation | Carry out an on-site trial run before full implementation; continue training |
| 6 | A VICTORY Readiness Assessment | Delivery & Initiation | After delivery and initiation activities, assess readiness for full-scale implementation, using Davis' A VICTORY model for measuring readiness for adoption of the innovation |
| 7 | Circulation of Draft Implementation Plan | Implementation | Invite input from stakeholders on draft implementation plan before finalization |
| 8 | Participant Observation of Implementation | Implementation | Have those responsible for installing, operationalizing, evaluating, and monitoring the new technology observe implementation activities, note any problems, and work out any needed remediation activities; continue training during implementation experience |
| 9 | Reducing Outside Technical Assistance | Implementation | Wean the user from outside technical assistance; test for and help attainment of self-sufficiency |

| 10 | Overall Utilization Directive | Institutionalization | Develop organizational leadership support for the innovation to ensure its longer-term success; communicate and monitor policy and supporting practice |
| 11 | Maintenance of Implementation Competence in the Face of Personnel Turnover | Institutionalization | Provide ongoing training capability to ensure that replacement personnel in user organization receive training in innovation use |
| 12 | Permanent Tracking and Monitoring System | Institutionalization | Set up system for long-term training, particularly of new personnel who will be involved with use of the innovation to be sure there is capability to detect and respond to possible maintenance problems |

persuasion or facilitation strategy, in which potential users are perceived as clients (Guba, 1968). Glaser and others (1967) used a number of methods of persuasion in inducing rehabilitation agencies to consider the applicability of a new technique for training retarded persons for work. The effectiveness of each method was then assessed. A popularly written, easily understandable description of the new practice was somewhat effective, but a conference coupled with a visit to the demonstration site, followed by discussion not only of the model practice *but also of the promising innovations developed by each agency represented at the conference,* was more effective. Visits to various agencies by a traveling consultant added little to these two strategies for facilitating utilization.

Zander (1962), noting that the common denominator of examples of resistance to change rests on a self-protective mechanism, gives a list of some of the obstacles persuaders may encounter and suitable strategies for overcoming them. Among the scores of empirical studies reported, one by Anderson and McGuire (1965) found that persuasion is more likely to succeed if the persuader first shows that he or she sees the logic of the current way of doing things and only later presents the seeming advantages of the proposed change. Maier (1963) suggests using what he calls the "risk technique," in which potential adopters of a proposed change are first invited to identify all the risks or possible objections they can think of and, after discussion of these, are asked to consider offsetting or trade-off benefits.

Lewin and some of his followers have provided an explicit theory of persuasion (Lewin, 1962; Lewin and Grabbe, 1962; Jenkins, 1962). Essentially, this entails taking action to reduce the resistance to change and/or the attachment to the present way of doing things. Rather than trying to make the new seem more attractive at once, the client is induced to look more critically at the old. The forces making for stability and those impelling change are analyzed. Then steps are taken to unfreeze the present situation, move it to a new level, and then stabilize the situation at the improved level. Lewin and associates see this as a process of reeducation and suggest that cognitive changes, changes in values, and changes in actions occur—pretty much in that order.

Persuasion to change behavior can operate at three levels. Kelman (1958) has called these *compliance, identification,* and *internalization.* One complies when one must; this usually means enforcement by sanctions and close supervision. Identification with an admired person may lead to a change that persists only so long as that attraction remains salient. Internalization, the most powerful and stable change pattern, requires that the individual really believe the message. Then he or she will need no policing or approval from authority figures. Glidewell (1962) has designated the same three patterns for conversion alliteratively as bargaining, belonging, and belief.

As noted elsewhere, Fairweather, Sanders, and Tornatzky (1974) found that active persuasion intervention by the change agent and having a group of "champions" within the hospital to spearhead the change effort were the essential ingredients in the successful adoption of an innovative procedure and program in returning mental hospital patients to the community. In a study by Mann (1971), the didactic, or classroom, training approach to human relations proved inferior to an interactive feedback procedure whereby attitudinal survey data were fed back to workers and supervisors. The latter technique was also used effectively by Miles and others (1971).

## Summary Comments

This chapter has considered a wide range of change strategies, again noting the importance of fitting the selected strategies to the given setting and its circumstances. Among the major distinctions among strategies is that between power or coercion and persuasion, education, or facilitation. Another differentiation is that between the rational, or intellectual, approach and an emotional, or "personality," approach, the former often using information in the form of feedback as a major device for facilitating change. The choice of targets is another basis for sorting out strategies—for example, whether individuals or groups are to be targeted and the extent to which groups will be categorized for differentiated approaches.

The appropriateness of strategies to the several stages of the innovation utilization process has also been studied—for example, those that pertain to adoption, implementation, diffusion, and institutionalization. A major issue has been the extent to which adaptations of programs to be adopted should be permitted or encouraged, if needed, during the implementation stage. A further issue concerns the distribution of support of efforts to bring about adoption and implementation of a program as well as efforts to assure its durability and institutionalization.

Viewed as a stage in the total process of knowledge utilization and innovative change, strategies (in their choice and implementation) depend in part for their success on the effectiveness with which the previous stages of the process are executed. Thus, a sound assessment of need, an insightful diagnosis of the problem and issues involved, a rich collation of pertinent information, and an imaginative and critical consideration of alternative solutions to the task at hand all serve as guidelines in the search for suitable implementation strategies for achieving designated ends. Similarly, inclusion in the planning phase of those persons whose understanding and support are needed to carry out a change, training in any new skills required, and monitoring and technical assistance to assure proper application of plans and skill training are all essential strategies to assure successful implementation.

Additional considerations need to be taken into account in the choice and application of strategies. Significant efforts may be required in combating resistances, somewhat different from those used to institute change in situations in which an attitude of acceptance prevails. Another distinction needs to be made according to whether the objective of change is to bring about a particular change or a changed approach to problem solving in general. Obviously, strategies will differ according to the distinction between these two goals.

The treatment of strategies in Chapter Nine moves into some of the measures that have been applied in the special fields of mental health, public services, education, and industry. In these discussions, while common or basic questions of strategy are involved, incidental reference is made to a number of tactical devices, although these are covered more fully in the section on linkage and dissemination, the subject of Chapters Eleven through Fourteen.

# 10

# Evaluating
# and Maintaining
# Planned Change

Chapter Eight described the process of knowledge utilization and innovative change as it moves from need awareness to identification and consideration of promising alternative ways of meeting a need or problem. Chapter Nine discussed the adoption or implementation of selected alternatives to address the problem. The present chapter analyzes the role of *evaluation* in planned change. It also carries the description of the change process further to address the *maintenance* of innovations that are deemed worthwhile.

### Evaluating Planned Change

The evaluation of planned change has much in common with the field of program evaluation in general. Hence, to analyze the role of evaluation in planned change, it is useful to consider several broad issues from the field of program evaluation:

Authors of this chapter are Karen Kirkhart and Ross F. Conner.

- Purposes of evaluation
- Timing of evaluation
- Scope of the evaluation
- Evaluation designs
- Assessment of unexpected side effects
- Utilization of evaluation research findings

These issues will be used to organize this section's discussion of the role of evaluation in planned change.

**Purposes of Evaluating Planned Change.** Evaluation of innovative change may be conducted to serve any of the following purposes:

1. To determine the worth or value of the innovation.
2. To identify the most and least effective components of the innovation.
3. To identify the strategies and/or context variables that contributed to the successful implementation of the innovative change.
4. To identify the strategies and/or context variables that contributed to the successful maintenance of the innovation.
5. To identify the strategies and/or context variables that contributed to the successful dissemination of the innovation.

Note that each of these purposes is related to a particular type of decision that could be made or question answered regarding the innovation, using the evaluation data, as shown in Table 8. Typically, evaluation of planned change is conducted to serve more than one purpose and hence can answer more than one type of question.

The *maintenance* of planned change is the focus of the next section of this chapter, and evaluations of this type are well illustrated by the studies of Yin and others (1978), Glaser and Backer (1980), and Glaser (1981a), to be described there. The *dissemination* of innovations is the subject of Part Three of this text. Therefore, the present section will focus on evaluation of planned change for purposes of determining the worth of an innovation, determining more and less effective compo-

Table 8. Potential Relationships Between Evaluation Purposes
and Associated Key Questions.

| Purpose of the Evaluation | Provides Information to Answer → | Related Question |
|---|---|---|
| Determine the innovation's overall worth or value | | Should the innovation be maintained, terminated, or disseminated? |
| Determine most and least effective components of the innovation | | How could the innovation be altered or improved? |
| Determine strategies/variables that contributed to successful implementation | | What are the key ingredients that generally must exist to achieve innovative change? |
| Determine strategies/variables that contributed to successful maintenance | | What are the key ingredients that generally must exist to maintain innovative change? |
| Determine strategies/variables that contributed to successful dissemination | | What are the key ingredients that generally must exist to disseminate the innovation? |

nents of an innovation, and determining strategies/variables that contributed to successful implementation of change or adoption of an innovation.

Although Table 8 implies a clear relation between certain types of evaluation and the decisions that may follow, it is important to note that the two are in fact quite separate issues. Unbiased evidence on the overall value or worth of a given innovation does not necessarily lead to unbiased decisions concerning adoption of the innovation. Weiss (1972b) clearly depicts this imperfect correspondence between evaluation and adoption/adaptation decisions while describing the evaluation process as it realistically contributes to policy making, as discussed in Chapter Fourteen.

Nor is the list of purposes of evaluation in Table 8 exhaustive. Suchman (1967), Fullan and Pomfret (1977), Anderson and Ball (1978), Cronbach and Associates (1980), and many other writers point to a far more expansive set of purposes for which evaluative studies are made. Aside from arbitrary legislative mandate, Anderson and Ball, for example, list the following purposes:

1. To contribute to decisions about program continuation, expansion, or "certification."
2. To contribute to decisions about program modification.
3. To obtain evidence to rally support for a program.
4. To obtain evidence to rally opposition to a program.

    Suchman (1967) expands the latter two points still further, enumerating six *mis*uses of evaluation: (1) the use of evaluation results to justify a weak program by selecting out of context only those results that appear successful ("Eyewash"), (2) the use of evaluation results to cover up program failures—for example, by presenting only testimonials to the exclusion of more objective data ("Whitewash"), (3) the use of an evaluation to "torpedo" a program and eliminate it ("Submarine"), (4) using an evaluation as a gesture of objectivity, assuming the pose of "scientific" research for political reasons only ("Posture"), (5) using an evaluation to forestall taking other action ("Postponement"), and (6) using an evaluation to shift attention from an unsuccessful major component to some lesser, but more positive, program aspect ("Substitution"). These potential abuses of program evaluation apply equally well to the evaluation of planned change. In both cases partisan political and material motivations are often present and have to be recognized.
    Some kinds of evaluation situations call for special considerations beyond those present in traditional operational program evaluation. A challenging illustration of such a situation is in connection with attempting to evaluate effective human services for victims of personal violence. There is a fascinating dialogue between Howard R. Davis and Susan E. Salasin in *Evaluating Victim Services* (Salasin, 1981a). In that dialogue Salasin asks, "Dr. Davis, what do you feel are the most promising contributions that the evaluator can undertake in the area of services for victims?" Davis replies that the first contribution is that of traditional operational program evaluation. Then he goes

on to say: "But, as Charles Figley (1980) has said, that sort of evaluation may be down the road a piece when we talk about programs for victims through health services settings. Those innovative services that are emerging are still nascent. You don't measure a baby's worth; you nurture it. Programs are now being mounted only through compassion, zeal, desperation, and hope. Of course, planning those new services so that they will become evaluable is critical, but putting them to the test may still be a bit premature at this time" (p. 143).

Evaluation can serve any of several constructive purposes in the process of planned change—from rendering a judgment of merit or worth of an innovation to providing feedback on components of the innovation and/or its context that can improve the adoption or adaptation of the innovative program or process. To a large extent, the purpose(s) that the evaluation will serve is linked (among other considerations) to the timing of the evaluation process.

**Timing the Evaluation of Planned Change.** Since change is by definition a dynamic process, the timing of the evaluation is of key importance. Three aspects of timing are relevant to the evaluation of planned change: (1) timing the evaluation process to fit the realities of the operations of the program or system undergoing change, (2) timing the measurements taken to capture the outcome of the innovation or change, and (3) timing the feedback of evaluation findings to facilitate utilization of the results. In the first case, for example, the evaluator must consider the annual schedule of an organization when laying out the time line for an evaluation. (This aspect of timing is discussed more fully in Chapter One as one of the A VICTORY factors proposed by Davis (1973a; Davis and Salasin, 1975.) It would not be prudent to schedule a series of training sessions on the use of a new data-collection form during a time when the majority of the staff will be taking vacations. In the second case, the apparent success of an innovation may be strongly influenced by the point in time at which the evaluation is conducted; the evaluation design must allow sufficient time to gain a representative picture of the innovation and to detect both expected and unexpected effects. Evaluation that emphasizes short-run outcomes may be both inadequate and misleading, since it cannot reflect either long-term or delayed ("sleeper") effects (Ferman, 1969). (This aspect of timing is discussed further below as one of the parameters of planned-change evaluation.) Third, the timeliness of the report often has a strong effect on the utilization of evaluation results by stakeholding audiences. Even the most rigorously designed, well-implemented evaluation may fail to influence policy if the findings are reported *after* the decisions concerning the next major funding cycle have been made.

The matter of short-run outcomes versus delayed effects has been studied by Larsen (1981), who followed up the results of technical assistance consultation in mental health organizations. The criterion of consultation effectiveness used was the extent of identified problem solution after a four-month interval and one of eight months. Although no statistically significant difference between the consultation and the nonconsultation groups was found after four months, organizations receiving consultation service reported statistically reliable higher degrees of problem solving after eight months. Larsen concluded that it takes time for the impact of consultation to make itself felt in an organization. Hence, the *timing* of an evaluation of a program can exert a critical influence on the evaluation findings, a conclusion supported by Ciarlo, Rossman, and Hober (n.d.) and by Rich (1977).

Scriven (1980) makes a useful distinction between *formative* and *summative* evaluation, which bears on this issue of timing.

> FORMATIVE EVALUATION. Formative evaluation is conducted *during* the development or improvement of a program or product (or person, and so on). It is an evaluation that is conducted *for* the in-house staff of the program (with feedback of findings that in turn can be used for program improvement) and normally remains in-house; but it may be *done by* an internal *or* an external evaluator or (preferably) a combination [p. 56].

> SUMMATIVE EVALUATION. Summative evaluation of a program . . . is conducted *after* comple-

tion and *for* the benefit of some *external* audience
or decision maker (for example, funding agency,
or future possible users), though it may be *done*
*by* either internal or external evaluators or a mixture. For reasons of credibility, it is much more
likely to involve external evaluators than is formative evaluation [p. 130].

Scriven (1980, p. 56) summarizes the distinction between formative and summative evaluation by quoting a comment of
Bob Stake's, "When the cook tastes the soup, that's formative;
when the guests taste the soup, that's summative." Guba and
Lincoln (1981) clarify that the distinction between formative
and summative evaluation hinges on the intended use of the
evaluation by the program or project being evaluated.

With respect to the evaluation of planned change, summative evaluation is often associated with the research/devel-
opment/diffusion model in which major evaluation conclusions
and reporting are part of the final application stage. The ongoing integration of evaluation and change is most evident when
the mode of evaluation is formative, and particularly in cases
in which the implementation of an innovation is adaptive in
character. In such instances, the monitoring function prevails
throughout the entire process (Halpert, 1973; Anderson and
Ball, 1978; Abt and Magidson, 1980; Cronbach and Associates,
1980; Patton, 1980).

Scope of Evaluation of Planned Change. The third general issue relevant to the evaluation of planned change is its
scope. This can be approached from two perspectives: as a discussion of scope as overall breadth or as a specification of the
components of any given evaluation effort—that is, the aspects
of the planned-change process that the evaluation will address.

On the first point, the nature of the sponsorship and of
the setting of the evaluation has much to do with its scope. For
example, many large-scale, federally sponsored educational programs of recent years tended to set overly specific goals, thereby limiting the scope of the evaluation. These limited evaluations were often unable to capture the effects of state and local
variations on the federal programs.

The scope of evaluation may also be limited by tendencies

to exempt certain types of ongoing programs from assessment once they have been legislatively or traditionally established. Fresh examinations of previously approved programs, such as are implied in sunset laws and a commitment to zero-based budgeting (ZBB) at federal and other governmental levels, can have powerful implications for the inducement of change, if only in the sense of discontinuance (Otten, 1979). Nevertheless, although traditional programs, products, and so on are sometimes made the subject of evaluation, it is the innovative change that is most likely to arouse interest and be subject to formal appraisal.

Conner (1980) presents a conceptual model to guide the evaluation of various kinds of knowledge utilization efforts. Slightly adapted, this model is especially useful in defining the parameters of evaluation of planned change or innovative change. Conner concurs with a major premise of this chapter: The evaluation of planned change has much in common with program evaluation. Specifically, he advises that an innovation or an instance of planned change may be viewed as an evaluator would view any type of program or project. That is, the evaluator should consider four general aspects of the innovation or planned change: its goals, inputs, processes, and outcomes. Under these four components, there are ten aspects of the planned-change process that an evaluator might well consider in his or her assessment:

1. Goals of the planned-change process.
2. Quality of the innovation.
3. Importance of the innovation.
4. Resources for the planned-change effort.
5. Pattern of planned change.
6. Rationale for planned change.
7. Capabilities and attitudes of the persons implementing the change or adopting the innovation.
8. Type of change or adoption of the innovation.
9. Organizational level of change or adoption of the innovation.
10. Timing of change or adoption of the innovation.

Taken together, consideration of these aspects will help to define the major components of an evaluation effort. This relationship is illustrated in Figure 1. Each of these ten factors is
discussed briefly below.

1. *Goals of the planned-change process.* The first factor
concerns the evaluation of the goals of the planned-change process. The evaluator of innovative change addresses two main
questions here: "Are there goals for the planned-change process?" "If so, are these goals appropriate and sufficient?" Conner notes that goal setting for the planned-change process is a
difficult but necessary step if an innovation or planned change
is to have much hope of success. Even if goals are set, they can
change, and the evaluator should record and document these
changes. These changes provide a picture of how and why important issues arose and fell and of their relationship to the
overall success of the innovation or planned-change effort. Such
documentation may also make valuable formative contributions
to the change process, as discussed above.

Factors 2–4 refer to the evaluation of various inputs to
the planned-change process.

2. *Quality of the innovation.* The main question here is
"What is the *evidence* concerning the value of the innovation?"
One of the purposes of evaluation discussed earlier in this chapter is to determine the value or worth of the innovation itself.
This may involve the evaluator's selecting a design that would
permit drawing valid conclusions about the causal effects of an
innovation, as discussed below. In some instances the evaluator,
rather than collecting original data, might conduct secondary
analyses of data to determine whether the existing proof for the
potential value of the innovation is valid. That is, one must consider the quality of *evidence* supporting the innovation in order
to make a judgment about the quality of the *innovation* itself.
In either case, the innovation is a key ingredient in the planned-
change process and, as such, merits careful evaluation.

3. *Importance of the innovation.* The evaluator's guiding
question here is "Does the innovation have significant implications for changes in policies or practices?" The answer to this

**Figure 1. Conceptual Model of an Evaluation Effort Related to Aspects of the Planned-Change Process.**

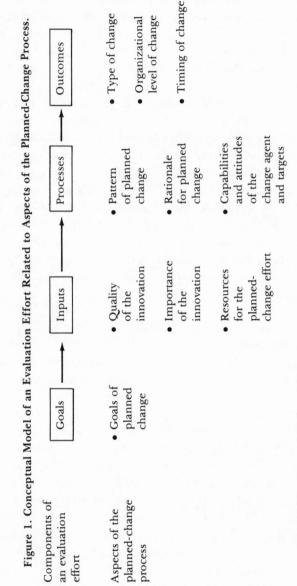

Components of an evaluation effort

| Goals | → | Inputs | → | Processes | → | Outcomes |

Aspects of the planned-change process

- Goals of planned change

- Quality of the innovation

- Importance of the innovation

- Resources for the planned-change effort

- Pattern of planned change

- Rationale for planned change

- Capabilities and attitudes of the change agent and targets

- Type of change

- Organizational level of change

- Timing of change

Adapted from Conner (1980), p. 642.

question is not absolute and will depend on the potential utilizers' judgment of the appropriateness of the innovation to their situation. If a considerable number of such potential utilizers feel that the innovation would not lead to significant changes, one would have to question the value of the innovation—or reexamine the content, format, and style of the method used for presenting its worth.

4. *Resources for the planned-change effort.* Conner notes that there are other resource inputs in a planned-change program besides the innovative idea or knowledge itself—for example, the materials or procedures to be disseminated, adopted, or adapted and the people who implement the change effort. The guiding evaluation questions here are "What is the quality of the instructional or explanatory materials (or technical assistance) to be provided in the planned-change process?" "What are the competencies, qualifications, and characteristics of the people who will be involved in the planned-change program (stakeholders, decision makers, participants)?" The materials should be judged for appeal, clarity, and appropriateness. The people who will be involved in the implementation should be assessed for the appropriateness of their skills and attitudes or readiness in relation to the planned change.

The third group of factors concerns the evaluation of the process of planned change. This aspect of evaluation is critical for a complete assessment of innovative change. The evaluator's primary task in evaluating knowledge utilization is to monitor and document the planned-change effort as it *actually* occurs. This monitoring can be done through observation as well as interviews or questionnaires and may employ one of the designs discussed below. The evaluator should be especially mindful of the pattern of planned change as it unfolds, the rationale for innovative change, and the attitudes of the persons implementing the change or adopting the innovation.

5. *Pattern of planned change.* The central question here is "What is the actual sequence of the planned-change (or adoption-of-innovation) process?" For example, the evaluator should be concerned with the path of any instructional or explanatory

material(s) and any discussions related to the innovation. Who reads and discusses what, and when? Uncovering this path may not be an easy task but will reveal much about the reasons for the success or failure of the change effort.

6. *Rationale for planned change.* "What are the *real* reasons, both overt and covert, for change or lack of change?" Knowledge can be used, or an innovation adopted, for a variety of reasons. For example, an innovation may be instituted solely for its intended effect or, instead, because it is a substitute for harder decision making or a way to discredit a current practice or policy. These latter rationales have been termed "symbolic" use and may not always constitute "*mis*use" as described by Suchman (1967). This motivation is something the planned-change evaluator will need to explore to fully understand the change process.

7. *Attitudes of the individuals implementing the change or adopting the innovation.* This aspect of the planned-change process refers to both the persons who will be the targets of change, or actual implementers of the innovation, *and* the manner in which the change is planned or the innovation implemented. The cooperative or recalcitrant attitudes of these people may well be a decisive determinant of the degree of change achieved, and these attitudes, in turn, may be affected by the way(s) in which the people are involved in the change process. For example, the extent to which the individuals are involved in planning for change may have a significant bearing on whether their attitudes will be cooperative or recalcitrant. Planned-change evaluators, then, must ask themselves, "What are the individual states (related to psychological and political/organizational factors) of the planned-change targets? What are the reasons for these states?" Note that, in the case of formative evaluation, these data themselves may be useful in formulating strategies to change people's attitudes and hence smooth the way for the planned-change process.

The final three factors concern the evaluation of the outcome of planned change.

This section addresses the central question of the evaluation process: Was the innovation in fact adopted, or the change implemented? To answer this question, the evaluator must assess the type, level, and timing of the change process.

8. *Type of change.* There are two guiding questions for the evaluator on this issue: "What kind of change or adoption of innovation occurred?" "What degree of change or adoption occurred?" Conner (1980, p. 634) explains this important factor with respect to the overarching concept of knowledge utilization: "Various writers have presented different conceptualizations of type of utilization (Caplan, Morrison, and Stambaugh, 1975; Knorr, 1977; Rich, 1977; Weiss, 1977c). Pelz (1978)* presents a framework which combines these different viewpoints. He distinguishes two types of knowledge: soft and hard. Soft knowledge is characterized as non-research-based, qualitative, and stated in everyday terms; hard knowledge is research-based, quantitative, and stated in scientific terms. These two types of knowledge are combined with three modes of utilization: instrumental, conceptual, and symbolic. The instrumental mode is direct, documentable use for decision making. The conceptual mode is indirect, intellectual use of research findings for the general enlightenment of decision makers. Rich (1977) has characterized these two modes as 'knowledge for action' and 'knowledge for understanding.' " (The third mode, "symbolic," was considered earlier, under "Rationale for planned change.")

These different types of knowledge utilization also apply to planned change and have implications for evaluation. For example, the targets for instrumental utilization are easy to identify, and the suggested actions are very specific; this is not true for conceptual or symbolic utilization. Because these types of use are independent of one another, the evaluator must watch for any or all of them.

9. *Organizational level of change.* "What organizational levels are not involved in the innovative change but perhaps should be?" This question is part of some of the other aspects of the planned-change process, but it is important for the eval-

---

*Further contributions by Pelz and others are discussed in Chapter Fifteen.

uator to think specifically about it, because it is sometimes hidden or overlooked and can be an important factor explaining success or failure in the adoption of an innovation.

10. *Timing of change.* "How fast—or slow—is the particular change to occur?" This aspect, too, is often overlooked but can be important in fully understanding the outcome of planned change. As discussed in the previous section, the timing of the evaluation itself is tied to the expected timing of change. That is, one must select an evaluation that is designed to look for change at the times (or during the time periods) when the change is expected to occur or unfold. If the evaluative "camera" is not ready at the proper time (or adjusted to the proper time-lapse setting), the complete picture of the change may not be captured.

Conner discusses how type of change, organizational level, and timing can be assessed in two main ways: using an "actual targets" approach (that is, surveying those people intended as targets of planned change) or a "potential targets" approach (that is, surveying evaluator-determined targets, whether or not intended). He also proposes an even more ambitious approach: an experimental test of various approaches to knowledge utilization with different groups of potential targets. The application of experimental and nonexperimental designs to the evaluation of planned change, and the respective advantages of each, are discussed below.

Evaluating planned change, as Conner's discussion shows, is often a complex task. The scope of evaluation of planned change involves the goals, inputs, processes, and outputs of a planned-change effort, as well as their interrelationships. There is no simple way to assess a phenomenon as multifaceted and multiphased as change. If one is seriously interested in putting knowledge to use, however, one must understand the planned-change process from start to finish. Evaluation can aid this understanding of the planned change. The following section discusses the range of designs available for such evaluation.

**Designs for Evaluating Planned Change.** As with any evaluation, the design selected to evaluate planned change must match the purpose of the evaluation, the types of questions one is seeking to answer, and the subsequent decisions to be made.

For example, if the purpose of the evaluation is to test the superiority of an innovation over a traditional protocol and to establish causal relationships, one might select a comparative experimental design wherein the effects of a given procedure, practice, or factor applied to one group or situation are compared with those of a control group or situation in which the experimental condition was not involved. If the purpose of the evaluation is to study the evolution of an innovation over time, one might select a sequential approach. Such a method monitors the effect of a sequence of interventions or activities, using multiple measures across time, and does not use a control group, although tests after initiation of the program or intervention may be compared with baseline measures (Rossi and Williams, 1972). In either case, one must consider the assumptions on which the judgments of value or worth are based, as well as the validity of the data used to support those judgments. It is important to be on the lookout for irrelevant or spurious accompanying factors that may invalidate the inferences concerning causal relationships and hence the judgments of value that were based on them.

Although a detailed treatment of experimental design is beyond the scope of this chapter, several excellent reviews on the subject are available. Cook and Campbell (1979) and Campbell and Stanley (1966) give detailed descriptions of numerous experimental and quasi-experimental designs. The application of such designs is well illustrated in the texts of Riecken and Boruch (1974) and Caporaso and Roos (1973). Miles (1980) provides a briefer treatment of the subject, and Kiesler (1973) discusses experimental methodologies more specifically in relation to the evaluation of social change programs.

The importance of developing alternatives to experimental methodology has been emphasized by Glaser and Backer (1972a) and by Guba and Lincoln (1981). Glaser and Backer (1972a) make a strong case for a *clinical approach* to program evaluation as an alternative or complement to traditional objective-quantitative evaluation design. The clinical approach is de-

signed to evaluate the program as a dynamic process or a complex entity consisting of interrelated components. It includes
attention to the thoughts, feelings, beliefs, perceptions, observations, experiences, and reports of all those concerned with the
project, taking particular note of convergent perceptions from
various viewpoints. Program outcomes are weighed against cost
factors, side effects, and the ordering of priorities. Consideration of the totality of the program, according to Glaser and
Backer, requires attention to its setting in its parent institution
and the community where it is situated. Programs are perceived
as dynamic, subject to changes accompanied by ongoing feedback of the assessment findings.

Similarly, Guba and Lincoln (1981) emphasize the limitations of the scientific paradigm of inquiry in the field of evaluation. They propose and describe a method which is based on the
themes of responsive evaluation and which uses naturalistic
methodologies in its application. The distinguishing characteristic of responsive evaluation is that it takes as its organizer the
concerns and issues of stakeholding audiences (and hence is "responsive" to those audiences). The term was first used by Stake
(1975), who suggests a number of iterative steps for conducting
responsive evaluation. First, the evaluator talks with a wide
range of stakeholders to gain an understanding of the purpose
of the evaluation and the nature of the programs to be evaluated. Next, the evaluator makes personal observations of what
actually goes on in the name of the program. On the basis of
these observations, he or she discovers the true purposes of the
program (both stated and unstated), as well as concerns about
the program and the evaluation. As preliminary data collection
continues, the evaluator begins to conceptualize the issues and
problems that the evaluation should address. Having identified
these issues and problems, the evaluator selects an appropriate
design, specifies the kinds of information needed and appropriate instruments (broadly defined to include observers, as human
instruments) for data collection. Data are then collected, pro-
cessed, and organized into themes, and the evaluator prepares
portrayals designed to communicate "in natural ways" and with
maximum direct personal experience. In reporting, the evaluator

matches both content and format to audiences. Formal reports, if used, are assembled as a final step.

Guba and Lincoln (1981) expand Stake's approach in several important ways and make a persuasive argument for the use of naturalistic measures within the responsive-evaluation framework. Particular emphasis is placed on qualitative methodologies and the "evaluator as instrument." Useful techniques include interviewing, observation, analysis of documents and records, and unobtrusive measures.

Alternatives to experimental evaluation methodology such as those described above are especially relevant to the evaluation of planned change. Sequential modes of evaluation often provide a better "fit" with the piecemeal social engineering that prevails in most private and public bureaucracies (Popper, 1945). For example, a sequential approach invites an administration to test planned innovations continually. When used in this way, evaluation can be developed into a sensitive instrument for the detection of decision points where minor adjustment may lead to major gains in goal attainment. Another advantage of sequential evaluation is its reversibility, which allows not only for tracing the effect of an innovation but also for tracing the effects of rescinding or modifying and improving a policy measure, program, or practice. The "incremental" nature of this method makes sequential evaluation a superior agent for combining organizational policies (Dahl and Lindblom, 1976; Etzioni, 1968).

Given that evaluations of planned change may be conducted for more than one purpose, as discussed earlier, the optimal evaluation design frequently involves a combination of experimental and nonexperimental methodologies. The successful integration of experimental and sequential approaches to the evaluation of planned change is well illustrated by the study of Benedict and others (1967).

Benedict and others (1967) studied the problem of inducing "organizational health" through analysis and the application of a case in which both clinical and experimental methods of intervention and appraisal were used. The experimental design followed a multiple time series with experimental and comparison

school systems. The "clinical-experimental" method entailed
(1) making theory-based general predictions, (2) clinical diagnosis by the change agent, (3) field (rather than laboratory) experimental design, (4) both experimental and clinical data collection, and (5) a clean-cut division of labor between persons
with change-agent responsibility for helping the client and those
carrying out assessment.

Benedict and her colleagues concluded from the total experience that the clinical-experimental method succeeded in
(1) allowing a relatively unbiased and objective measurement of
hoped-for changes in organizational variables, (2) assuring the
genuineness of whatever changes occurred, and (3) enabling the
investigators to study with some degree of richness and confidence the assumptions, plans, strategies, and effects of change
agents.

In sum, the evaluation of planned change draws on, and
often integrates, a rich array of evaluation designs ranging from
experimental to sequential approaches. Nonexperimental methodologies are particularly relevant to the evaluation of planned
change. As Lieberman and Griffin (1976) point out in their review of three books on educational change (Smith and Keith,
1971; Gross, Giacquinta, and Bernstein, 1971; Bentzen, 1974),
there is a need to broaden and clarify the methodology of
studying innovations. They emphasize that a necessary component of good evaluation is learning about what actually occurred, rather than what was supposed to occur. Since many
*actual* occurrences accompanying planned change may be unexpected, this aspect of planned-change evaluation warrants special attention.

**Assessment of Unexpected Side Effects.** As previously
mentioned, one important aspect of evaluating the outcome of
planned change is the evaluation of unexpected side effects of
change. It is precisely this issue that is addressed by the field
of *technology assessment.*

With the rapidly increasing pace and scale of societal
change, triggered in large part by revolutionary technological
developments, came increasing worldwide concern with the
need to assess *secondary or unintended consequences of new
technologies* in various fields. To meet this concern in the

United States, Congress established in 1972 the Office of Technology Assessment of the Subcommittee on Science, Research, and Development of the Committee on Science and Astronautics of the U.S. House of Representatives (Coates, 1974). In an earlier article Coates (1971) presented a succinct account of the rationale and scope of technology assessment, illustrated by describing a series of first- to sixth-order unintended consequences of three technological advances: the automobile, improved refrigeration, and television—the farflung, unplanned effects of which are widely known. Note that the term *technology assessment* includes *social* technologies and *social* effects.

In a later article Coates (1976) further develops the principles and procedures of technology assessment in terms of a "tool kit" containing such techniques as the Delphi method, trend extrapolation, decision trees, simulation, mathematical modeling, scenario and game construction, survey techniques, decision theory, and brainstorming. Space limitations prevent fuller treatment here; the interested reader is referred to Coates' article for an exposition of these approaches. Note, however, the commonalities between the tools of technology assessment and several of the tools of naturalistic evaluation referred to in the previous section.

Since the investment in time and money in technology assessments is considerable, critics of the approach are often found. David (1977) suggests that what seems to offer cautious control may in reality turn out to have the effect of arresting development. As an example, he cites the Office of Technology Assessment (OTA) itself, whose procedures, he alleges, tend to result in overplanning and overmanagement. Drucker (1974) proposes ongoing technological monitoring as an alternative to front-end technology assessment. This approach is modeled after the early detection of threats to health by use of epidemiological models, which can employ ongoing, existing health care systems to measure effects, collect data, and analyze them without interrupting operations or the chain of invention. Again, the importance of the timing of the evaluation is emphasized in the assessment of unexpected side effects just as in the evaluation of other aspects of planned change.

Clearly, the evaluation of unexpected side effects of

change can be highly complex, often entailing second- and third-order effects or even further consequences. The field of technology assessment, discussed further in Chapter Fifteen, shares many important issues and methodologies with the evaluation of planned change.

**Utilization of Evaluation Research Findings.** The final issue to be considered in the evaluation of planned change is the use of the evaluation data themselves. This issue is an especially interesting one in the context of this book for two reasons. First, evaluation findings may be used to influence the maintenance or dissemination of an innovation; hence, evaluation can become a tool in the change process itself. Second, in the field of program evaluation, evaluators have become concerned that their results are often not utilized; therefore, facilitating the use of evaluation data may itself become an instance of knowledge utilization. In both cases, evaluators become involved, reflexively, in the planned-change process!

In the first case, evaluation data can aid planned change by providing proof that an innovation is effective and therefore worth adopting or continuing. The role of evaluation in facilitating change is twofold: First, evaluation data may demonstrate the effectiveness of an innovation and/or document—the extent to which the innovation constitutes an improvement over previous conditions or procedures. If evaluation has proved that an innovation is in fact an improvement, the second way in which evaluation data can facilitate utilization should be considered: providing proof to persuade others to adopt the innovation. "Nothing succeeds like success," the saying goes, and it applies here too. Evaluative data can provide the evidence that an innovation is successful. With this type of evidence, one is in a good position to persuade others to follow one's lead, either those who might be involved in implementing the innovation with help or those who might want to adopt or adapt the innovation on their own. Note that this latter aspect of the role of evaluation in facilitating innovative change assumes that the evaluation data are *themselves* attended to and used. Unfortunately, this assumption is not always met—hence the second case of evaluators' becoming involved in planned change.

Like many innovative programs themselves, evaluation data constitute knowledge that may or may not be used. Recent studies by Braskamp and Brown (1980), Brown and Braskamp (1980), and Patton (1978) examine factors influencing the use of evaluation findings.

Although the role of the evaluator is subject to debate, Brown and Braskamp (1980) insist that evaluators must share with program developers the responsibility for utilization of evaluation information. To this end they need to collect information beyond the description of how well the program is meeting its objectives to include information about the setting in which the results may be used. This might include, for example, potential consumer opinion, staff morale, psychological as well as monetary costs, and similar background data related to the probability of utilization. Further, evaluators need to be aware of the organizational and political aspects of the motivation for the evaluative program as an aid to the promulgation of its findings.

Under the heading of external factors, Braskamp and Brown (1980) also refer to contextual and organizational considerations that tend to influence utilization of evaluative findings. Several major classes of factors have been identified: the characteristics of the potential audiences and users of the information, the structure of the organization that contains or is to contain the program being evaluated, the political context of the organization, and the nature and technical quality of the evaluation itself.

As with other areas of knowledge utilization or innovative change, the way the evaluation is conducted may well affect evaluation utilization. For example, Glaser (1980d), reporting in the Braskamp and Brown treatise, describes a state-of-the-art knowledge synthesis that involved scores of expert reviewers of early drafts of a document pertaining to the diagnosis and treatment of chronic obstructive pulmonary disease (emphysema, chronic asthma, and chronic bronchitis). The involvement of potential users in the evaluative process accelerated the utilization of the (positive) findings of the evaluation report. Brown and Braskamp (1980) also advocate a highly interactive consult-

ing relationship with key decision makers in the course of encouraging utilization. In Chapter Nine the general issue of participatory involvement has been described as a strategy for
achieving change.

In a similar vein, Brown and Braskamp recommend communication of evaluation information as an ongoing process
rather than as a one-time event. In formative evaluation, informal reports to key persons are suggested. The circulation of a
summative report for reaction is also proposed. Where feasible
and appropriate, face-to-face contacts, such as in meetings of
concerned persons, are likely to prove helpful.

Rieker (1980) notes the frequent disappointment experienced when positively evaluated research is not used by policy
makers. To enhance the likelihood of utilization, she offers an
interactive model of the federal evaluation/use process involving the roles and relations of the sponsoring agency, the research
organization, and the participants in the program being evaluated. Her design calls for a careful choice of the research agency,
clear but nonconstraining communication of objectives, appropriate translation of problems into research terms, translation of
findings in the research report into meaningful language, and coordinated dissemination efforts by researchers and sponsors.

Clearly, the recommendations cited above to facilitate
use of evaluation data mirror the strategies presented in Chapter
Nine to promote knowledge utilization and change in general.
Chapter Eleven examines such strategies in detail with respect
to change agents and agencies.

## Maintaining Planned Change

**Stages and Aspects of Follow-Through.** Four possible
ultimate outcomes of an innovation program can be identified:

1. *Incorporation* as an entity—wherein an adopted or adapted
   program or project has proved itself worthy of continuation, and gradual improvements have led to identified plans
   and provisions for its ongoing identity and status.
2. *Consolidation*—the innovation is joined with other programs

or projects into a new whole, wherein it may be identifiable, or it may lose its identity in the new entity.

3. *Expansion*—the initial project or program is extended in content, form, base of operation, scope of dispersion, and support provisions.

4. *Termination*—whether planned or not. Planning to terminate may be expected as a result of a negative evaluation, whether formal or casual, and often occurs when mistakes cannot be rectified and resources dry up.

Ultimately, all projects or programs may be said to terminate in one sense or another, at least in the forms in which they were initially conceived. Termination may be deliberately sought. Hence, one cannot simply equate the termination outcome with failure of the innovation.

A contributing factor to difficulties in innovation is the common failure to develop a follow-through plan for ensuring the continuance of demonstrated improvements. This can manifest itself in many ways, well examined in two publications* of the National Institute of Mental Health: *Innovations* and *Evaluation and Change*.

**Factors Affecting Follow-Through.** Every significant innovation is likely to run into some difficulties. There are "bugs" in the first model of every invention. Research utilization has inevitable elements of risk (Lippitt, 1965b) and corresponding need for extra encouragement. It is realistic to keep in mind that not all acceptance of innovation is enduring (and many innovations do not *deserve* enduring acceptance). An innovation may be discontinued because it has been replaced by a better idea or because of disenchantment with the results of the innovation or because of greater comfort with or vested interest in the previously established ways of performing the given function (Rogers and Shoemaker, 1971; Glaser and Backer, 1977, 1980; Glaser, 1981a).

A factor affecting follow-through and routinization is the phenomenon of "burnout," when the champions or devoted

*Discontinued in 1981.

"carry-throughers" of the innovative program become exhausted by their role. This problem has been observed in a great diversity of educational and community programs.

As programs expand, their coordination becomes an issue if changes are to be maintained. When a span of managerial control is narrow, there are few problems in coordination. However, when many agencies must be involved, some of which are complex, and where the span of control must be very broad, obstacles to coordination abound (McGowan, 1976).

**Durability and Routinization.** When the introduction of change involves a program that is regarded as an innovation, a stage of incorporation to ensure continuity and "delivering the goods" will need to follow (Manning and Rapoport, 1976; Glaser, 1981a).

*Correlates of Routinization.* How new service practices in an urban bureaucracy become routinized or part of standard practice is the subject of a report by Yin and others (1978), who studied the life histories of six types of innovations: computer-assisted instruction, policy computer systems, mobile intensive care units, closed-circuit television systems, breath testing for driver safety, and the firefighting jet ax. The specific organizational life-history events were conceptualized as *passage* (from one organizational state to another) or *cycles* (surviving over periodic organizational events). It was found that certain passages (for example, establishment of personnel classifications or certification) and certain cycles (for example, equipment turnover) were important in achieving utilization.

Yin and associates found that the degree of routinization (that is, adoption or use as standard procedure) was not related to the specific type of innovation or to external conditions such as financial and technical assistance. Major conditions leading to routinization appear to be internal and specific to the local agency. Early in its life history, an innovation must continually gain active support from agency practitioners, especially from top agency administrators.

In light of the findings, the authors were able to propose several strategies for promoting routinization in urban bureaucracy service programs. Among these are the following:

1. At the outset, it is important to get the new practice operating on a daily basis.
2. The new practice has to have concrete benefits for service practitioners.
3. If the new practice displaces an old one, specific steps need to be taken to eliminate the old practice.
4. Eventually the new practice has to be expanded to its fullest logical extent, or else it continues to be regarded as a "special project," which prevents it from becoming standard practice.
5. Because the time lags for achieving the various passages and cycles are different, it is important to get an early start on certain activities—for example, establishing the personnel classifications for any new job skills that might be required by the new practice—to ensure later routinization.

In their report on the longevity of OD programs in a large sample of United States and Canadian school districts, Miles, Fullan, and Taylor (1978a) note that 78 percent of the districts that had had at least eighteen months of sustained work expected more or less institutionalized continuance of the program. This positive reaction was explained in terms of results obtained, commitment and hard work, and top-management support. At the same time, heavily funded OD programs were *less* likely to become institutionalized, a finding that was confirmed by Berman and McLaughlin's (1976) study of federally supported change programs, which noted a tendency to discontinue a program when its external support was withdrawn.

In relation to vocational education demonstration projects, Hull and Bina (1977b) reported an exploratory research study of exemplary innovative projects. A key finding was that those sites most likely to continue the demonstration collected evaluation data more frequently than those sites less likely to continue. Project continuation was also associated with (1) an experienced project director, (2) weekly staff meetings, (3) one to six hours of staff in-service training, and (4) students and labor representatives on advisory committees.

*Three Suggested Frameworks.* The durability of innovations in human service organizations was the subject of a research study carried out by the Human Interaction Research Institute (HIRI) in collaboration with the Mental Health Services Development Branch of the National Institute of Mental Health (Backer and Glaser, 1979). The purposes of the study were (1) to find out and document why some reportedly effective innovations in provision of human services continue in viable and healthy form in some settings, while these same innovations do not survive in other settings, and (2) to develop a set of generalizations postulating conditions that facilitate the sustaining of worthwhile change in mental health organizations.

Data collection for the study included (1) site visits to long-surviving and short-lived adoption settings and (2) ratings by expert judges of potential durability variables at each site visited as applied to two innovative programs. Those programs were Goal Attainment Scaling (Kiresuk and Sherman, 1968) and the Fairweather Lodge program (Fairweather, Sanders, and Tornatzky, 1974).

In reporting the results of this phase of the study, Glaser (1981a) presents three conceptual frameworks for organizing factors bearing on durability.

1. The *first conceptual framework* is the A VICTORY analysis devised by Davis (1973a; Davis and Salasin, 1975). This approach is described in Chapter Two of the present volume. Most of Davis' factors were found by the site visitors (Glaser and Backer, 1980; Glaser, 1981a) to have a bearing on durability.

2. The *second framework,* which overlaps the first in a number of respects, sorts out selected factors more specifically according to whether the characteristics apply to the innovation itself, the host organization or setting, or the manner, timing, circumstances, and "dynamics" of the implementation process.

With regard to characteristics of *the innovation itself,* durability of innovation adoption was found to be facilitated if—

1. The innovation meets a real, well-defined need in the host organization that is acknowledged by at least some persons in the agency's leadership.

2. Modifications are possible and flexibility is permitted in response to local circumstances or preferences.

3. The innovation has the characteristics summarized in the acronym CORRECT: Credible evidence for its value; Observability, or opportunity for potential users to see a demonstration in an operational setting; Relevance to meeting a readily perceived need; Relative advantage or benefits over existing practices; Ease in understanding and installation; Compatibility with potential users' established values, procedures, and facilities; and Trialability, which permits a pilot tryout and does not call for an irreversible commitment by the system.

4. The innovation meets an objective need in a superior manner. It then may survive with little or no community support, so long as it receives sustained support from the host organization. However, community support is desirable and should be sought where appropriate.

5. The basic idea behind the innovation has sufficient independent viability so that even when the host organization goes out of existence, the original idea may be "repotted" in other, similar organizations.

6. An innovation is divisible so that parts of it may be sustained while other parts drop out (Glaser, 1981a, p. 179).

With regard to *the characteristics of the host organization,* durability is facilitated if—

1. The innovative procedure or program becomes well integrated into the host organization; it is most likely to survive if it becomes "systemic" to the organization's modus operandi and thus not dependent on the continued presence of special "champions."

2. The host environment is supportive, and the innovation is congruent with the values of at least some influential staff members.

3. There is maintenance of enthusiasm and "push" or championship of the innovative program *over time,* until it becomes systemic. Otherwise, initial success may not be sustained.

4. The host organization characteristically takes a constructive problem-solving approach to matters that arise on a day-to-day basis and holds periodic review meetings to encourage airing of problems and suggestions, including discussion of side effects of the change program.

5. There is widespread dissatisfaction with the status quo, which often makes for greater receptivity to consideration of change.

6. Adequate staffing and staff training (if needed) are provided to help develop skill and a sense of competence/security in utilizing the innovation.

7. The host organization has an administrative/managerial climate of "freedom to fail" and profit therefrom for improvement "next time."

8. The organization that adopts the innovation is characteristically self-challenging, self-evaluating, and generally open to serious consideration of promising new ideas, programs, products, and procedures (Glaser, 1981a, pp. 179–180).

With regard to *the manner and "dynamics" of implementation,* durability is facilitated if—

1. Efforts are made during the implementation phase to involve all stakeholders—particularly those on the host organization's staff—in discussions of pros and cons and, in general, participation with regard to planning for implementation.

2. Special funds and *technical assistance consultation to help get the program started* are available. After the innovation is established, technical assistance may no longer be needed.

3. An appropriate team of both champions and skeptics from a potential adopter organization can visit a respected site to observe the successful operation of the innovative program, procedure, or product.

4. Those who want to implement the change feel determined to make it succeed. Under those conditions, skepticism from some colleagues only serves to whet that determination.

5. Relevant community leaders are invited (if it is practicable) to participate as planning consultants and thereby become supporters.

6. There is a widespread perception that learning experiences from installation of the innovative program can have valuable spinoffs to/for other programs.

7. Adequate staff time is made available to plan and carry out the program properly.

8. Staff values are similar to those required for successful adoption of the innovation.

9. Implementation efforts take account of readiness for adoption or tryout of the innovation by those who will be instrumental to its initial success and long-term maintenance. Surfacing of resistances, questions, and any perceptions of risk should be respectfully invited and discussed in a problem-solving spirit.

10. The adopting organization shows interest in providing (and acquiring) *continuing updates* of information pertaining to successful application of the innovation.

11. The innovation receives endorsement and support from the top of the host organization.

12. There is evidence of intent to expand an innovation that has been adopted on a tryout basis.

13. Opportunity is provided to participate in a network of adopters and to observe other applications of the innovation.

14. Staff members receive frequent feedback about their progress in effectively operating the change program.

15. There is continuous reward to staff members for using the new method (Glaser, 1981a, pp. 180-181).

3. The *third framework* is designated as engineering/technology assessment because it combines an engineering orientation with sociotechnical considerations. The engineering approach involves attention to all phases of R&D endeavor: basic research, applied research or design, early (or front-end) followed by advanced (or back-end) development and field testing, and diffusion. The technology assessment aspect, as previously discussed, is concerned mainly with a deliberate attempt to con-

sider side effects or unintended consequences, both from a technical and from a human/social standpoint. Thus, to be durable, an innovation needs to go through an iterative development critique permitting "debugging" in the course of the process. Rothman's model, described in Chapter Seven, reflects this third orientation (Rothman, 1977, 1978a, 1978b).

There is much overlap among the three frameworks, and all three are valuable if skillfully applied.

From the foregoing reports of writings on the subject of durability and institutionalization of innovations, it is evident that concern for continuance requires the direct attention of the change agent. A change agent may wish to use the framework most congenial to his or her own orientation and the client's "set" or stage of readiness. The determinants of utilization and change treated in Part One may warrant review for additional light they may throw on problems of durability considered in this section of Part Two.

## Summary Comments

The difficulty of presenting problem-solving stages in the precise order of their application is evidenced in this chapter, which by its placement implies that evaluation is restricted to the later phases of the process. In truth, evaluative thinking accompanies every step in problem solving. The evaluation of planned change highlights the importance of formative evaluation—that is, the continuous study of events and outcomes as they emerge in the very course of the application of the program under study.

Related to this formative approach is the growing acceptance that, realistically, programs are not simply *adopted* uniformly in their initially stated form but are *adapted* by users in accordance with local circumstances and goals. The methods used in evaluation, in the study both of process and of outcome, reflect this more flexible approach. Particularly because of a concomitant realization that broad as well as narrow outcomes are important, evaluative modes of study and measurement have often been enlarged to include the less tangible characteristics along with the more objectively determined findings. In this connection, values, as well as quantitatively measured consequences, have been given a prominent place.

A further development has been the realization that innovations may have unforeseen and indirect outcomes. Hence, there is growing activity in the field of technology assessment, with its attempt to trace through second-, third-, and perhaps $n$th-order effects of technological advances.

Despite increased interest in evaluation, results of evaluation studies, even when commissioned, frequently are not utilized in decision making. Hence, a number of writers have emphasized what can be done to encourage the utilization (in whatever the suitable form) of evaluation results. Such proposals grow out of an examination of the role of the evaluator, the definition of utilization itself, the many factors that have been found to influence utilization, and the place of effective communication in achieving fuller use of evaluative findings.

A related problem reported in the literature is the finding that many projects or programs, including those described as successful, are discontinued before long for one reason or another. This finding has resulted in a set of proposals for increasing the likelihood of enhancing the *durability* of a promising innovation.

The section of this chapter on maintaining planned change serves as a fitting review of much of the material on the several stages of the knowledge utilization and innovative change process covered in Part Two. Perhaps the expression "As ye sow, so shall ye reap" sums it up best. Although special follow-up measures are required to assure durability, the maintenance of outcomes of change efforts depends not simply on what is done during the later stages of the introduction of a new program. Rather, it depends more on the procedures used at *every* stage of the process, beginning with initial project selection, followed by affording opportunity for stakeholder representatives to become involved in the planning, implementation, monitoring, and institutionalization of the planned change.

# Part Three

✦❦✦

# Linking Knowledge
# with Potential Users

Previous sections of this review have drawn attention to various aspects of the problem of linking R&D, exemplary practice, or improved technology with utilization in the conduct of human affairs—in mental health, education, public service, and private industry. Part One, in particular, set forth the wide range of factors, positive and negative, that may bear on the strength or efficacy of linkage efforts. Part Two depicted the stages through which the process is carried out for linking R&D findings and exemplary practices with felt needs. It also surveyed the strategies that may be used to facilitate dissemination and implementation of promising new knowledge in various potential user settings.

Here, Part Three picks up the threads of previous sections both by noting deliberate measures for inducing linkage and dissemination of knowledge and practice and by identifying intrinsic components of these processes. Within Part Three, Chapter Eleven presents the role and functioning of change agents, agencies, and networks; Chapter Twelve considers the place of personal and other means of communication in the dissemination/diffusion process, including reports on linkage through diffusion and transfer in several fields of application; Chapter Thirteen carries the subject beyond national boundaries by analyzing root issues in the international transfer of technology; Chapter Fourteen considers relationships between research and use and between researchers and practitioners as a possible source of time lag as well as a stimulus to constructive reduction of that lag; and Chapter Fifteen focuses on the extent to which elements of the utilization process have been synthesized, or theorized to form systematic frameworks or models.

# 11

### ᴬᶜᵌᴬ

# Roles and Activities
# of Change Agents

### ᵛᶜᵍᵛ

Among the many suggestions for facilitating appropriate utilization of promising new knowledge, the establishment of a linking mechanism in the form of a change agent (or agency in some cases) is strongly advocated by many writers.

Linkage is basically a series of two-way interactions that connect user systems with resource systems (Havelock, 1969a). The articulating mechanism can either overlap the two sides or bridge the gap between the researcher and the practitioner (Bhola, 1965a). As part of the mechanism, a "linker" may be an influential individual within the organization or (as in agriculture) an individual (or group) outside the organization whose mission is to translate promising research and to help practitioners adapt it to their situations.

Important as the contribution of the linking or change agent may be, the Battelle Columbus Laboratories sound a qualifying note in their study for the National Science Foundation (1973b) in which they explore the many factors that influence the decisive events leading to technological and scientific adoptions. The study concludes that innovation cannot be completely controlled or programmed by a change agent. Change agents in the form of the research-knowledge "gatekeeper" and the technical entrepreneur both exert some influence on adoption, as noted in Chapter Two. However, a number of factors other than the efforts of the intermediary were found to be higher on the list of determinants of change—for example, internal R&D management and availability of funding.

**Concept of the Change Agent.** The titles that are used for *middleman* vary as shown in Table 9 and suggest different concepts.

Table 9. Terms Used for *Middleman*.

| Term | Author |
|------|--------|
| 1. Social engineer | Watson (1945); Guetzkow (1959) |
| 2. Quasi-social engineer | Croker (1961) |
| 3. Change agent | Rogers (1962a) |
| 4. Linking agent | Lippitt (1965b) |
| 5. Knowledge linker | Schwartz (1966) |
| 6. Human link; change-agent team | Glaser and Wrenn (1966) |
| 7. Learning engineer | Mackie and Christensen (1967) |
| 8. Missionary | Glaser and others (1967) |
| 9. Behavioral scientist | Archibald (1968) |
| 10. Consultant | Lippitt and Havelock (1968) |
| 11. Research utilization specialist | Riley, Hooker, and Masar (1968); Engstrom (1969) |
| 12. Knowledge utilization specialist | Glaser (1973) |
| 13. Research translator | Mackie (1974) |
| 14. Intermediary | Munson and Pelz (1980) |

Havelock (1969a) and Glaser and Backer (1982) assert that the notion of the change agent is moving away from that of the agent as the conveyor of new facts, innovations, and research, as in the county agricultural agent model, toward a concept of the agent as *resource person, consultant, facilitator,* and *catalyst.* This would imply that the middleman would be serving much broader objectives than simply the spread of information and its linkage to practice.

The concept of knowledge production, once confined to

the researcher, is broadened by Short (1973) to cover the *integrator*, who, as a synthesizer or interpreter, brings together findings of a large number of studies; the *translator*, who identifies particular operational problems and invents solutions by transmitting, translating, or transforming already-existing solutions; and the *knowledge linker*, who bridges the gap between researcher and practitioner. Short adds that the roles are not mutually exclusive.

Roberts and Frohman (1978) regard change agents as organizational link-pins. Change agents become especially useful in facilitating communication passage through what Roberts and Frohman regard as the five stages of the adoption process—namely, (1) awareness, (2) interest, (3) evaluation, (4) actual or vicarious trial, and (5) adoption.

Practitioners (who may be citizen groups) are conceived in the role of the change agent by Rothman (1974), who attempts to depict the social-change roles of social work professionals, of paraprofessionals, and of lay groups.

**Types and Roles of Change Agents.** The functions of the middleman are numerous and tend to vary according to the nature of the role assumed. Havelock (1969a), in a typology of knowledge-linking roles, suggests the following possible functions: *conveyor* (transfers knowledge from producers to users), *consultant* (assists users in identification of problems and resources, provides linkage to appropriate resources, assists in adaptation to use, serves as facilitator, objective observer, process analyzer), *trainer* (instills in the user an understanding of an entire area of knowledge or practice), *leader* (effects linkage through power or influence in one's own group); *innovator* (initiates diffusion in the user system), and *defender* (sensitizes the user to the pitfalls of innovation; mobilizes public opinion, public sensitivity, and public demand for adequate applications of scientific knowledge). Not surprisingly, Havelock sees marginality and overload as the endemic problems of the linking role.

The linker operates between the resource system and the client system and serves both a knowledge/education function and a motivation function (Benne, 1962; Havelock, 1967; Sieber, Louis, and Metzger, 1974). The role of the middleman may take several forms: technical, professional, or applied scientific. Whether an applied-oriented scientist or a theory-oriented practitioner, this person must understand the ongoing change process in the organization and must present himself or herself in such a way as to be credible (Gallagher, 1965; Lundberg, 1966).

In comparing five change models (identified in Chapter Fifteen), Sashkin, Morris, and Horst (1973) place particular emphasis on the change agent's linking function—his or her mode of handling information and data. For example, in the *research, development, and diffusion model,* the key question is how the disseminator can identify the user population and select a means of communication that will result in acceptance of the new information, whereas in the *action-research model* the change-agent function tends to fuse with the research function in an ongoing interaction between knowledge production and user needs. What this analysis signifies is that a discussion of change-agent functions and roles should be qualified by the prevailing change model.

Bennis and Schein (1969) suggest that the role of change agent includes a number of elements. He or she (1) operates as a professional, guided by certain ethical principles and acting in the client's interests, (2) occupies marginal status without formal membership in the target system and often without the immediate supporting presence of colleagues, (3) plays an ambiguous role, often lacking in legitimacy and credibility, sometimes viewed with suspicion and hostility, (4) may be considered expendable, with few guidelines for his or her actions, and (5) almost always encounters resistances.

An active role of change agents in educational linkage is emphasized in a report of the Belmont Conference, sponsored by the National Institute of Education and the U.S. Office of Education. A summary of the position expressed at the conference will be found in Chapter Twelve.

P. Clark (1975) compares four types of intervention strategies affecting the relationship between the practitioner and the client. These strategies vary depending on the situational context and whether the focus is on single or multiple factors. The four types of intervention are as follows:

1. The *collaborative/dialogue approach,* entailing joint determination of goals and measures related to decisions and changes.
2. The *unilateral expert model,* whereby the expert provides the answers—an approach that is generally considered inappropriate in social science interventions.
3. The *delegated intervention approach,* typified by the training of full-time members of an enterprise to implement an innovation by themselves.
4. The *subordinate technician model,* which places the change-agent practitioner in a rather restricted role whereby he or she undertakes studies to discover information requested by the client, the latter deciding what steps to take in the light of the report rendered.

According to Clark, the determination of the appropriateness of each of the four intervention strategies rests on, for example, (1) whether the focus is on the manipulation of a single variable or multiple variables, (2) the depth of the interventions, (3) the narrowness or breadth of problem scope, (4) the degree of required formalization of procedures, (5) the predominant desire for learning, (6) the degree of awareness of problems, (7) client expectations, (8) the presence and extent of power centers, and (9) practitioner competencies.

In certain respects the categorization by P. Clark of types of change agents is related to distinctions made by A. Clark (1975) in his model, presented in Chapter Fifteen, of the client/practitioner relationship conceived of as a system.

On the basis of the responses of ninety-one professional change facilitators—consultants to organizations, social activists, and others—Tichy (1974) classified change agents into four types: (1) "outside pressure" (for example, a civil rights advocate), (2) "people-change technology" (for example, a job enrichment consultant), (3) "organization development" (for example, a specialist in system self-study and improvement), and (4) "analysis for the top" (for example, a university professor consulting on systems analysis for top management of a private company).

Demographic and value-congruence differences were found among the types of agents. As might be expected, the differences were found to be associated with incentive and reward as well.

Another type of role and structure for a change agent or consultant is presented by Dimock (1978). Concerned with the involvement of clients in efforts to implement change, Dimock and his colleagues developed the concept of Systems Improvement Research (SIR), whereby inside workers and outside consultants join in collecting data and making plans for change. SIR is essentially an action-research model using a data-based intervention strategy designed to evaluate organizational effectiveness, plan and implement change, and train participants in the use of organizational development (OD) technology.

Differences in demographic background and in value congruence (as between stated values and actions) were found among the several types of agents. For example, outside pressure agents had lower income, were more politically oriented, and had less formal education than the other types. They also evidenced the most congruence between stated values and actions.

Guskin and Chesler (1973), in discussing what they regard as the partisan nature of the scholar's diagnosis of social problems, insist "that the scholarly cloak of neutrality worn to protect one's professional status from democratic public consideration and attack is simply not visible" (p. 376). In short, value neutrality is deemed impossible. Guskin and Chesler see the theoretical alternative to diagnostic efforts, so-called pure research, as lacking social relevance and public accountability.

The authors also depict illustrative roles as guides to scholars participating in partisan social diagnosis:

1.  As brokers or gatekeepers of information itself.
2.  As serving directly the needs and desires of persons and groups in control.
3.  As information disseminators.
4.  As collaborators or consultants to various groups seeking humanitarian or organizational change.

5. As a linker between opposing groups by providing open access to, and understanding of, information.

Havelock (1970) weighs the relative advantages of the internal change agent and the outside consultant. The former has immediacy in his or her knowledge of the problems and has commitment; the latter is more likely to have perspective and expertise. The insider may be handicapped by being perceived as a stranger.

Zaltman and Duncan (1977) also treat the relative advantages and disadvantages of internal and external change agents. The latter are more objective and flexible in viewing change issues; the former, though possibly more biased, are likely to have more information with which to attack the issues. For example, Gluckstern and Packard (1977), at the University of Massachusetts and the Berkshire County House of Corrections, worked together toward reintegration of inmates into the community. The university-appointed project director (as external change agent) and a correctional officer (as internal change agent) provided an effective team strategy in collecting system information and offsetting personal judgment errors in implementing change. As an important contribution to the success of the program, the team relationship is discussed in terms of building mutual trust, training leaders, and transferring skills and responsibility from one agent to the other as the program evolved. Departure of the change agents marked the final stage of the program, in which the changes enacted were integrated within the system and perpetuated without the agents.

Aside from persons who are ordinarily labeled change agents, there are professional and semiprofessional groups that add to the number of types of change agents. These obviously include such persons as psychotherapists; members of the clergy; writers; teachers; politicians; stage, motion picture, and TV producers and performers; advertisers; and salespersons. Although indirect or implicit reference to them may have occurred in this volume, we have made no attempt to cover the literature pertaining to their role or functioning.

**Citizens as Change Agents.** Davis and Specht (1978) present a well-balanced version of a model of citizen participation in mental health programs—one that takes into consideration the citizens' level of understanding and potential for involvement. Successful involvement of citizens requires an increased recognition of their readiness and capacity for participation and a clearer identification of the decisions in which they can become productively involved. Otherwise, citizen participation may serve little more than a "puppet" function.

Davis and Specht also conclude that (1) citizens and professional staff do not hold the same definition of citizen participation, (2) health care personnel tend to resist citizen participative involvement in order to avoid their gaining decision-making control, and (3) the poor and disadvantaged in the community are not represented on citizen boards and advisory committees.

Daniels (1973) has described a comprehensive program of citizen involvement to help plan, implement, and monitor a community action type of change. He summarized experiences of the invited collaboration of potential users from the community with the University of Chicago Pritzker School of Medicine in development and administration of health and other services in urban, low-income, black communities on the south side of Chicago. Out of these experiences certain principles were derived:

1. Health services in low-income communities should have extensive citizen inputs in planning, organization, governance, and administration.
2. In order to acquire suitable advice, it may be necessary to expend large amounts of time and energy to inform the community of the possibilities for services.
3. If there is not a strong community organization, it may be necessary to support the creation of one.
4. Representatives of this community organization must not be the only community representatives involved with the start-up process.
5. If the community is inexperienced about governance, authority, and responsibility, it may be better to begin with an advisory structure, with training experience provided as needed, leading to the optimum eventual arrangement of governance by a board of directors.

6.  The maturity of the individuals and communities involved is probably closely related to the opportunity for the individuals to become responsible for the control of their own destinies.
7.  Although mistakes may be made, they probably cannot be greater than those made in the current system.

Further, on the subject of citizens' participating in the role of change agents, Goudy and Richards (1976) discuss legitimation of authority of the citizens' board as contrasted with professional staff. These authors studied a model-city multigoal "umbrella" poverty program in a Midwestern community. Professional staff and members of a citizens' board responded to an interview survey instrument that included sections on the role of citizen participation. The findings indicated disagreement between professionals and laymen on the relative degree to which the two types of persons represented public interests. However, such disagreement was not found to be evident in the two areas of program performance and power relations. Differing from the literature, which stresses hierarchical levels of authority, the professional and lay groups in the model-city program assumed responsibility for decision making as "partners." "Expertise" was reduced as a basis for authority. Thus, "new" aspects of social action programs, such as citizen participation, may best be conceptualized as intervening factors in the playing out of traditional organizational themes such as legitimation of authority.

Meyers and others (1974) sought to study organizational and attitudinal correlates of citizen-based accomplishment in mental health and retardation. They viewed accomplishment as reflecting four factors: (1) service creation and improvement, (2) outside resource mobilization, (3) local autonomy, and (4) coordination. Data were obtained from intensive interviews with the presidents of 37 citizen boards in Massachusetts and from 440 board members who responded to a mail questionnaire.

The data indicated that citizen-board accomplishment in mental health is somewhat related to a number of organizational, attitudinal, and social-role variables, including, among others, felt role ambiguity by board members, length of membership on the board, lay/professional cooperation within the board, the board's tendency to proceed democratically, availability of office space, close relationship with the local mental health administrator, and support by private local mental health associations.

According to Mogulof (1974), citizen participation in federally supported community organizations is best viewed as a policy goal in itself rather than as an instrument for achieving other goals. Mogulof sees citizen participation policy at the federal level as erratic, piecemeal, misunderstood, and possibly not really cared about. Nevertheless, this patchwork of federal attitudes and practices may have had great utility in contributing to federal and local experimentation with regard to participation in the 1960s. The form of participation at the end of that decade remained an issue warranting clarification and further development.

Winterton and Rossiter (1973) point out that although community or indigenous change agents have been increasingly employed in programs of directed change, the relation has often not been happy or productive for the agencies, agent, or client communities involved. To understand factors contributing to these difficulties, the authors conducted a study comparing the community agent and the external agent. They found that the community agent has a stronger community orientation than the external agent. Both agents suffer pressures of role definition and identify more strongly with the perceived social system of those to whom they are primarily accountable. The external agent is better suited to change situations and strategies that involve high levels of agent risk in the client community. The two types of agent are not interchangeable; both are successful in certain operations of the community, and both should be called on to effectively carry out programs of directed change.

**Functioning and Activities of the Change Agent.** According to Blake, Mouton, and Sloma (1969), labor/management conflicts and cleavages may be converted into a problem-solving approach on both sides by a change-agent team that works to involve management and labor in face-to-face confrontation designed to bring about conflict resolution. Eight phases of the conflict-resolving process are included: orientation, intergroup development of self-image and counterimage, exchange of images by management and union, clarification of image, intragroup diagnosis to achieve self-insight and understanding, consolidation of key issues, and planning for the next steps. The authors conclude that correcting a situation of long-term, chronic hostility requires continual and diligent follow-up efforts. They also found that the impact of the sessions was greater in treating new issues than in resolving old ones and that increasing interdependence among groups can breed hostility and disruptive conflict.

Lippitt (1962) identifies seven phases of the change agent's activities: (1) development of a need for change, (2) establishment of a consulting relationship, (3) clarification of the client problem, (4) examination of alternative solutions and goals, (5) transformation of intentions into actual change efforts, (6) generalization and stabilization of a new level of functioning or group structure, and (7) achieving a terminal relationship with the consultant and a continuity of changeability.

Mackie (1974) stresses the importance in increasing application potential of (1) collation and interpretation of research and (2) translation of research into practical terms. He considers the specially trained middleman as essential to the performance of these two activities.

The job of the change agent would appear to be difficult and demanding. According to Bennis and Schein (1969), the competence of the change agent should encompass conceptual diagnostic knowledge cutting across all behavioral sciences, knowledge of theories and methods of organizational change, knowledge of sources of help, orientation to the ethical and evaluative functions of the change agent's role, possession of operational and relational skills, and recognition of his or her own motivations.

Burke and Schmidt (1971) point out that the change agent may function in the development of either the organization or the manager.

Using case studies, Reddin (1977) illustrates typical errors made by organizational change agents working as management process consultants. The errors include initiating change from the bottom up, creating a change overload, raising expectations beyond what is possible, allowing inappropriate attachment, becoming trapped in one part of the organization, changing only a subsystem, inappropriately using behavioral interventions when structural interventions are more relevant, professional detachment in the face of needed change, and failure to seek help from persons with other types of needed expertise or information.

Ragab, Moriarty, and Guilmette (1977) describe a process they call Change Action Research (CAR). This is an approach to initiating and diffusing organizational change through influencing individual behavior, the overall organizational climate, and interpersonal style. The fundamental assumption of CAR is that if the individual or group is given the opportunity to compare espoused theory with the theory in action, as described by Argyris and Schön (1974), awareness of dysfunctional behavior and voluntary change will result. The CAR program consists of the following:

1.  *Organizational audit and feedback*—action is researched through personal observation, interviews, and surveys, and results are relayed to participants.
2.  *Development of change agents*—participants are exposed to inputs of fundamental knowledge in order to develop a group of experts within the organization.
3.  *Organizational reaudit*—to determine whether change has taken place. A multimedia case history is developed to increase momentum in a repeat change cycle.

The application of this approach to a Little League baseball team is presented, in which aims are clarified and contrasted, and action directives are formulated.

**Consultation.** Although the actual work of the change agent and the consultant are in many respects similar, there appears to have developed a distinct literature concerning consultation. We present the topic separately, largely as a matter of convenience.

Beckhard (1971) describes the process of consultation as entailing (1) initial contact by the client system, (2) defining the problem and establishing the relationship, (3) planning the first action steps, (4) assessing the facts, and (5) replanning and reestablishing the relationship. As a result of experience in a case situation, he concludes that—

1. It is necessary to establish a relationship with the several parts of the system before any effective problem solving can get underway.
2. It is important to establish a climate and procedure for feedback, both between the helper and the client system and among the parts of the client system.
3. The consultant needs to assess the readiness and capacity of the client system to change.
4. Since the change situation is mainly one of learning, the consultant should create conditions that favor learning.
5. Help offered should be in accordance with client, not consultant, need.
6. The consultant should be able to withdraw from the relationship, if necessary, to permit independence.
7. Provision should be made for evaluation.

Argyris (1970) describes a number of conditions that present different challenges to the consultant functioning as an interventionist vis-à-vis an organization. The consultant may face difficulties because of being a marginal figure. Often consultants encounter overlapping, conflicting, and at times antagonistic subcultures, and they may experience client mistrust and receive minimal feedback about the effectiveness of their efforts.

To meet these conditions, consultants must have confidence in their own intervention philosophy, have an accurate perception of stressful reality, be accepting of the client's attacks and mistrust, and bring their own experience of reality to bear on stressful environments.

*Types of Change and Consultation.* Several authors make distinctions among types and levels of change that may be of concern to change agents. For example, Morgan (1972) distinguishes among four types of change: (1) in technology, (2) in working methods, (3) in organizations, and (4) in people.

Beckhard (1975) differentiates among organizational targets that a consultant may stress. He lists the following ongoing social processes that may be affected: (1) interaction among individuals, (2) interaction among groups, (3) procedures for transmitting information, making decisions, planning actions, and setting goals, (4) strategies and policies guiding the system, the norms, or the unwritten ground rules or values of the system, (5) attitudes of people toward work, the organization, authority, and social values, and (6) the distribution of effort within the system.

Beckhard also distinguishes between *early intervention* and *maintaining change*. In the former aspect, he suggests a number of possibilities for where or how to start, such as the following: with the top team in the system, with a pilot project, with hurting systems, with the reward system, and with educational interventions. An organizationwide "health examination" may prove helpful in determining the first steps toward improvement.

Maintaining change in a large system requires conscious procedures and clear commitment. Among a number of interventions that are possible at this stage, notes Beckhard, perhaps the most important single requirement is for a continued feedback and information system, including such elements as periodic team meetings, organizational meetings to sense needs, problems, opportunities (or employee perception and opinion surveys for this purpose), meetings between interdependent units of the organization, renewal conferences, performance reviews, and periodic visits from outside consultants.

Blake and Mouton (1976) indirectly denote the nature of consultation by listing five main kinds of consultant intervention:

1.  *Acceptant*—gives the client a sense of personal security so that, when working with the consultant, he or she will feel free to express personal thoughts without fear of adverse judgment or rejection.

2. *Catalytic*—assists the client in collecting information to re-interpret his or her perceptions of how things are and to arrive at a better awareness of the problem and how to handle it.

3. *Confrontation*—challenges the client to examine how the present foundations of thinking, usually value-laden, may be coloring and distorting the way situations are viewed.

4. *Prescription*—telling the client what to do to rectify a given situation.

5. *Theories and principles*—offering theories pertinent to the client's situation, thus helping the client to internalize systematic and empirically tested ways of understanding it.

These modes of intervention may be used in combination. They may be directed toward an individual, a group, an organization, or a larger social system.

Caplan (1970) differentiates consultation (between mental health specialists and caregiving professionals or organizations) from other specialized methods such as supervision, education, psychotherapy, casework, and counseling, regarding it as the interaction between two professionals concerning a lay client or a program for such clients. He outlines four types of mental health consultation:

1. *Client-centered case consultation,* in which the consultee and consultant discuss a particular client case or group of cases.

2. *Consultee-centered case consultation,* which focuses on the consultee's difficulties in handling a case or cases.

3. *Program-centered administrative consultation,* which aims at planning or improving a program.

4. *Consultee-centered administrative consultation,* which deals with organizational difficulties, such as leadership or communication problems.

Caplan sees consultation also in an institutional sense, as when he discusses steps in formulating a consultation program in a community. The building of relationships, whether with an institution or an individual, is considered to be of paramount importance. Other recommended measures include (1) exploring goals with community leaders, (2) recognizing obstacles to communication—that is, conflicts of interest and distortions of perception and expectation, (3) clarifying the consultation contract, (4) arousing trust and respect, and (5) adjusting specific techniques to the type of consultation noted above.

In discussing the teaching of consultation, Berlin (1964) states that mental health consultation is different from consultation in agencies of an educative or technical nature. Mental health consultants may need to help an agency worker with problems produced by the worker's own conflicts. Consultant anxiety as well is an expected part of the process because of the many and varied implicit and explicit demands of the consultee. Administrators may be particularly difficult to engage in consultation because they may see it as a threat to their façade of adequacy. Problems of teaching consultation to administrators or agency workers center on helping the trainees to live through the inevitable frustration as they learn new techniques.

*Application Illustrations.* On the basis of a study of twenty-one voluntary youth-serving organizations that had *refused* standardized invitations to participate in a counseling assistance program, Strommen (1979) developed five guidelines for gaining access and securing cooperation:

1.  Seek access to a group through the introduction of a trusted colleague and encourage the leader's cooperation.
2.  If possible, convey your selection of strategies for group consultation through information supplied by a profile summary of how members perceive their group's readiness to effect needed change.
3.  Identify in advance a group's most troubling need and show how a change or innovation will meet that need.
4.  When planning a visit, assume that the more structured and goal-oriented groups will require a longer time to introduce and establish an innovative change.
5.  Prepare strategies for identifying and handling the obstacles that arise when certain innovations or changes are proposed.

Larsen and Norris (1978) have prepared a manual for consultants and consultee agency staff in mental health that offers a set of guidelines, procedures, and examples under three major headings: (1) a summary of guiding principles and behaviors contributing to effective consultation, (2) stages and steps to be followed before, during, and after the consultation visit by both the consultant and the organization, and (3) suggestions for effective consultant behaviors that may be of particular interest to prospective consultants. The treatise also contains a checklist (based on Davis's A VICTORY model) of questions for consultants and consultees as they plan, implement, and evaluate the process.

The summary of effective consultant behavior includes characteristics relative to the following propositions: (1) the consultant is *goal-directed,* (2) activities are directed toward *problem solution,* (3) the consultant encourages *consultee participation,* (4) the consultant is *active,* rather than passive, and (5) the consultant keeps in mind the center's *particular situation.*

Larsen, Norris, and Kroll (1976) attempted to identify factors in the consultation process related to utilization by analyzing information about consultant and mental health characteristics in a program involving ten consultants. Each consultant visited from one to three centers and spent one or two days at each organization. Utilization was related to a multiplicity of factors, less related to consultant characteristics than to organizational variables. *Degree of agency need proved the most dominant factor, combined with awareness of and agreement on the nature of the problem.* The most effective consultants took an active role, matched their expertise to the specific need of the organization, and provided concrete suggestions.

In an unpublished paper on technical assistance consultation regarding mental health programs, Larsen (1981) found the following four consultant characteristics (among eighteen variables tested) to have a statistically significant correlation with consultation effectiveness, defined as the extent of identified problem solution following consultation.

1. *Supportive*—the consultant generally highlighted the

strengths of the consultees and their organization and encouraged their efforts.

2. *Knowledgeable*—a consultant's most important attribute is
   having content expertise.

3. *Clarified problems and opportunities*—the consultant did
   not assume that the consultees were in agreement on the
   nature and importance of the problem that was the subject
   of the consultation.

4. *Presented multiple solutions*—the consultant generated a
   number of alternative solutions to the problem.

Butler (1975) reports on a visiting consultant program for
rehabilitation research utilization that involved the preparation
of a roster of individual files of 280 experts who might meet
stated agency consultation needs. The needs had been ascertained by means of a seventy-nine-item inventory responded to
by 178 persons in top administrative, middle-management, and
practitioner roles in state vocational rehabilitation and welfare
agencies. Preliminary evaluation with 84 recipient agencies
pointed to the value of the program.

**Organizational Development and Consultation.** The problem of transferring the principles and techniques of organizational development (OD) to mental health services is the subject
of an article by Glaser and Backer (1979). Four topics are considered: how mental health organizations implement OD strategies, difficulties in application of OD in mental health, its advantages and disadvantages, and action recommendations for
mental health administrators considering an OD approach.

Aimed at enhancing organizational effectiveness and job
satisfaction, OD activities include team, intergroup, total-organi-
zation, and personal, interpersonal, and group-process interventions. Difficulties in carrying OD strategies over from industrial
to mental health settings may arise because of differences in
professional values, greater government regulation, and bureaucratic tradition. Glaser and Backer detail potential benefits and
shortcomings of OD as applied to the mental health area. Among
the former are increased organizational capacity to manage
needed changes and greater sharing of responsibility for pro-

gram improvement among the staff. Among the latter are expense in staff time and money and the possible excessive diminution in the exercise of authority.

The authors also suggest measures the administrator can use to help decide whether an OD intervention might be relevant to a particular organizational setting.

As a social scientist and an outside consultant to organizations, Cherns (1977) attempts to understand and appreciate the organization's physical, political, social, economic, and technological environment and how its social system is constructed and operated. Noting that traditional ways of looking at organization design are often out of step with contemporary social conditions and technological advances, he suggests that managers use principles such as the following in dealing with "an increasingly turbulent environment":

1. Objectives should be specific, but specification of methods for achieving them should be minimal.
2. As far as possible, the design elements in an organization should allow for those who wish extensive personal participation, with responsibility, variety, involvement, growth, and so on.
3. When change occurs, whether by plan or naturally, the organization must be considered "in transition," and changeover organization designs must be developed alongside final designs.

Fullan, Miles, and Taylor (1978) conducted an extensive NIE-sponsored study of the state of the art of organizational development in schools. The investigations encompassed literature review, case studies, and empirical questionnaire surveys designed to portray OD work in school districts across the United States, including the number and background of consultants, the different types of OD approaches and programs, and factors associated with success or failure. The authors also clarify the meaning and significance of OD in schools and differentiate its application at the level of the school district, at the level of intermediate units such as states or provinces, and at the federal level.

Although schools are perceived as organizations, the following special properties pertain to them:

1. They are characterized by *goal diffuseness*—their mission is usually abstractly stated, and output measurement is difficult.

2. *Technical capability* is often suboptimal, with a weak knowledge base.

3. *Coordination problems* are typically present, with schools and school districts reflecting low-interdependent, "loosely coupled" systems.

4. Schools have *boundary management* problems, with vulnerability to pressure groups or dissatisfied stakeholders, such as parents.

5. Public schools in particular are *noncompetitive* for resources, with feeble incentives for innovation.

6. Schools form a *constrained, decentralized* system, with thousands of nominally autonomous units that nonetheless are subject to constraints exerted by standardized testing, a national textbook market, various accreditation and certification requirements, and legislation.

These characteristics tend to define and/or limit the work of OD in schools and have influential bearing on its success. Among requisites for success are carefully planned consultant entry procedures that involve top management and other potential participants, the establishment and use of internal OD consultants along with external consultative services, the use of survey feedback and other organizational efforts focused on particular problems, and participative and collaborative modes of intervention. Understandably, the assessment of the impact of OD on the schools varied appreciably, and its future was considered unpredictable in view of variations in the quality of its application and the many problems it confronts.

Using in part the findings of the NIE-sponsored study, the same authors have prepared an extensive state-of-the-art review of the literature on OD for the *Review of Educational Research* (Fullan, Miles, and Taylor, 1980; this article has been reproduced under the same authorship by National Institute of Education, 1981). Noting that the field of OD is badly in need of stock-taking, the authors assess the state of the art of OD in four ways: (1) critiquing and clarifying the values, goals, and assumptions of OD in general and as applied to education, (2) identifying and analyzing the various models and characteristics of OD in practice (conditions and strategies affecting its initiation, implementation, and continuation), (3) assessing the impact or outcomes of OD on achievement, productivity, and attitudes, and (4) reconsidering OD's future and suggesting policy implications for educational agencies at different levels.

In summing up the questions of the value and the future of OD, Fullan, Miles, and Taylor consider the probability that any given OD program will be "successful" in perhaps half the instances or less. They note that (1) "not a few" OD programs studied have been ineptly conducted, have focused on individual training rather than on OD, have dealt with superficial issues, have lacked a coherent model, or did not match interventions to diagnosed problems and (2) many studies of OD have methodological weaknesses, the avoidance of which might have presented an even less positive assessment of OD. Despite the less-than-favorable outcome of the studies to date, the authors express the view that the problems confronting OD are not intrinsic ones that would make it inapplicable to organizations generally or to schools specifically.

Schmuck and Miles (1971) treat in detail the specifics of OD strategy in schools (such as improving classroom group processes, using group problem-solving procedures, starting up a new senior high school, using survey feedback and consultation, using teams of change agents, and changing schools through student advocacy). These authors also present a generic scheme for classifying OD interventions. The model is expressed in the form of a cube, the three dimensions representing "diagnosed problems," "focus of attention," and "mode of intervention," as detailed below.

1. *Diagnosed problems* include goals, plans; communication; culture, climate; leadership, authority; problem solving;

decision making, conflict/cooperation; role definition; and other.

2. *Focus of attention* refers to a person; role; dyad/triad; intergroup (two or more); and total organization.

3. *Mode of intervention* entails training (educational); process consultation, coaching; data feedback; problem solving; plan making; OD task force establishment; and technostructural activity.

Thus, a single OD combination might entail the task force establishment designed to improve intergroup relations with regard to the problem of organizational communication.

The OD cube reflects, then, 9 X 5 X 8, or 360, mathematically possible but not always meaningful combinations, involving the three dimensions. It is intended to aid in categorizing specific efforts in school improvement.

Margulies, Wright, and Scholl (1977) review and evaluate research on the impact of OD. They note that proponents of OD feel that its tools and techniques can improve an organization's problem-solving ability, increase its adaptability to rapid societal change, and provide managers with updated concepts and methods for managing their organizations. Although an abundance of literature on OD was found, it is reported that little of the research on its effects could withstand rigorous testing.

Porras and Patterson (1979), building on work done with Berg (Porras and Berg, 1978), explore current OD assessment practices. They propose a model to help clarify assessment and offer guidelines for enhancing the assessability of change activities. Two types of impediments to assessment are presented: (1) the relative low interest in assessment on the part of both OD consultants and clients because of primary interest in the bringing about of change itself and (2) the lack of an agreed-on definition of assessment and the related issues of its role in decision making, its scope regarding involvement in change itself as contrasted to knowledge production, its stress on pure research as contrasted to meeting user needs, and its concern with values.

The model of assessment presented by Porras and Patterson includes a consideration of three aspects of the assessment *process* and their interrelationships: (1) the assessed target (situational factors and variable selection), (2) the assessor (roles and goals), and (3) the assessing procedure (type of change, methodologies, timing). In addition, the model provides for an examination of the assessment *product* (guides for current and future activities, theory construction).

The following guidelines are offered for more effective OD assessment (1) *variables selected for measurement and controls* (instruments and "experimental" patterns), (2) *use of eclectic research strategies* (for example, questionnaire surveys, operationalized measures, a time-series design, interviews, structured observations, and unobtrusive measures), (3) *assessing different types of change* (for example, changes in communication and in satisfaction or perception), (4) *use of data* (whether for action or for basic research), and (5) *the assessor* (whether internal, external, the intervener, or an unbiased party).

In checklist form the guidelines take the form of questions such as the following: (1) Are the variables I am measuring the same variables being assessed by the intervention? (2) Can I combine my data-gathering foci so that some of the information obtained can be fed back for action, some can be used purely for basic research, and some can be used for both? (3) Am I aware of the various expectations of the individuals involved as well as my own?

**Training of Change Agents.** Havelock and Havelock (1973b) take up the *training* of change agents, particularly in the field of education. The topics included are as follows:

1. Our contemporary knowledge of the change process.
2. Goals of training.
3. Some principles of good training design.
4. A framework for training designs.
5. Self-renewal within the school system.
6. Linking schools to outside resources.
7. Effecting political and structural change in schools.
8. Changing the larger system.
9. Sample model of a fully developed training design.

Hoberman and others (1977) describe a systems approach to management training in the mental health field designed to train and educate psychiatrists and related professionals in management and administration. The program is conducted in two stages, the first to increase participants' awareness and understanding of concepts, theories, and newer practices in management and administration, the second to meet at workshops to consider mental health policy and administrative issues. Topics included in training are long-range planning, leadership styles and administrative effectiveness, management by objectives, organization as a societal change agent, and implementation of organizational change. The program helps participants to develop solutions to actual operational problems, improve working relationships, expand understanding of the total mental health system, and develop and increase knowledge and understanding of theories and concepts of administration.

In the vocational rehabilitation field, the Rehabilitation Utilization Specialist (RUS) serves in a change-agent or linkage role. Usdane (1971), in summarizing development of the RUS role, notes that it was necessary to provide specific training to enable the RUS to acquire skills in teamwork, orientation toward problem identification and solution, and knowledge about resources useful to improve services to the disabled. Backer (1974) conducted an evaluation of the RUS project.

Miskel (1973) describes a pilot program with two major strategies for training personnel to develop, diffuse, and apply planning, monitoring, and evaluating techniques with respect to the change process in schools. The strategies comprise (1) a content phase covering such procedures as the Delphi forecasting technique, program evaluation and review, personal and interpersonal process laboratories, and the like and (2) a process phase in which personnel are brought together for an intensive resident conference, involving practical skill training in the above-mentioned procedures.

Banathy (1971) has developed a system designed to train individuals in the role of educational information consultant (EIC). The EIC serves as a linkage agent between the worlds of education research and practice by (1) negotiating with a client about information need, (2) retrieving pertinent information, (3) transforming the information, (4) communicating the information to the client, and (5) performing a self-evaluation. This EIC instructional system is intended for independent study by a learning team of three to five persons and is divided into seven instructional modules. Instructional activities in the modules proceed through four phases: (1) individual preparation, (2) team learning, (3) team application, and (4) individual and team performance evaluation. Included are instructions for compiling a "paper trail," a record of decisions and actions taken in serving a client.

Harrison and Hopkins (1969) present a detailed analysis of the inadequacies of conventional American higher education for training change agents where the ability to adapt to or act in unfamiliar and ambiguous social situations is required. Included in this category are all types of community development or community action work, at home or abroad. Principles embodied in a suggested inductive approach are listed:

1. Exposure to situations that require diagnosis, definition of problems, devising solutions, and taking action.
2. Orientation to immediate data, as distinguished from secondhand and abstract sources of information.
3. Exposure to situations where competing cultural values are involved.
4. Experience and action, as distinguished from understanding only.
5. Use of authority to promote experimentation, risk taking, and self-expression in the learner.
6. Use of expertise to teach problem-solving processes rather than supplying information.

Since Harrison and Hopkins' publication, numerous university programs have been developed that offer training of change agents and consultants, in addition to programs by University Associates, the National Training Laboratory (NTL), Organizational Consultants, Inc., and others.

## Change Agencies and Networks

Many of the functions and activities of change agents have been institutionalized in the form of recognized change-supportive agencies of one kind or another.

A perspective on the nature of several such agencies can be obtained by consulting Havelock and Lingwood (1973), who, using a set of major criteria derived from a "problem-solving dialogue" model, made a detailed analysis of four then-existing federal government research dissemination and utilization agencies: Division of R&D Utilization, Employment and Training Administration, U.S. Department of Labor; Research Utilization Branch, Social and Rehabilitation Service (now National Institute of Handicapped Research), U.S. Department of Health and Human Services; Mental Health Services Development Branch, National Institute of Mental Health, U.S. Department of Health and Human Services; and National Center for Educational Communication, Office of Education, U.S. Department of Health and Human Services, later transferred to the National Institute of Education.

The studies included interviews with staff, questionnaires, documented conferences, and literature survey. Criteria were applied to six areas of consideration: user self-service, need processing, solution building, solution processing, microsystem building, and macrosystem building. Recommendations for improvement of the several agencies in each of these areas are provided.

An indispensable reference tool for those seeking information about research utilization programs within the federal government is the *Directory of Federal Technology Transfer,* prepared under the auspices of the Federal Coordinating Council for Science, Engineering and Technology (1977). This volume presents capsule summaries of virtually every currently operating unit within a federal agency that is concerned with application of R&D findings or spread of existing technology. Each summary presents a brief history of the technology-transfer program, a description of service efforts or research studies it has undertaken, and a listing of contact persons from whom further information can be sought.

Governmental and, to a lesser extent, nongovernmental research utilization agencies have been established in a number of fields, such as mental health, rehabilitation, education, and science and technology. Several illustrations of such agencies are presented here.

**Mental Health.** The National Institute of Mental Health (NIMH), particularly in its Mental Health Services Development Branch and in its various publications, has performed significant linkage functions. Among its varied efforts is the sponsorship of a Network of Consultants on Planned Change and Knowledge Transfer (which can be reached through the above-mentioned branch of NIMH). The twenty-plus members of the network are persons who have done, and are engaged in, significant research on the nature and problems of putting knowledge to use in various types of settings or under given conditions and on barriers, gateways, and strategies related to knowledge transfer and change.

The 1980 meeting focused on mental health services for victims of crime, terrorist attacks, and the like. This subject is discussed in a report by Lund (1980), referred to later in this section.

Though not representing change agencies in the usual sense, two well-supported commissions on mental health sponsored by a host of mental health associations and organizations as well as by the federal government have served as powerful forces for change. These are the Joint Commission on Mental Illness and Health (for example, Robinson, DeMarche, and Wagle, 1960) and the Joint Commission on Mental Health of Children (for example, Joint Commission, 1969, 1973a, 1973b). Hundreds of specialists were involved in each commission, comprehensive surveys were undertaken, and scores of recommendations were made in the two sets of reports. Though one-shot affairs, they carried out on a grand scale the survey, monitoring, and recommendation functions often associated with change agencies.

Rehabilitation. Engstrom (1970) has described the Social and Rehabilitation Service as an agency whose mission has included the dissemination of new knowledge and the stimulation of research utilization and program change. In a brief, informative later article, Engstrom (1975) presents an overview of the policy objectives and specific activities of the research utilization program of the Rehabilitation Services Administration (RSA)—now the National Institute of Handicapped Research (NIHR)—from its inception in 1975. He emphasizes (1) participatory planning, (2) assessment of RSA R&D grants, (3) dissemination experiments offering alternatives to the printed word, (4) development of guidelines for final written reports, (5) attention to transferability of utilization findings, and (6) specific suggestions for project conceptualization, design, conduct, and implementation.

The concept of the Research Utilization Laboratory (RUL) as a change agent has been sponsored by the Social and Rehabilitation Service (name subsequently changed to Rehabilitation Services Administration), according to Usdane (1971), to select approved and effective research outcomes within a certain category, adapt them to a field laboratory setting, and, with at least one other similar agency, replicate the findings. The major concern is to simplify the recommended procedures and to make innovations more widely applicable. The laboratories established have been essentially field-testing, cross-validation stations where outcomes of promising research are incorporated into ongoing service systems with a minimum of additional staff.

The dynamic nature of a Research Utilization Laboratory designed to link research with practice is displayed in the report by Robinault and Weisinger (1975) of shifts in the objectives of one of the RULs sponsored by the RSA. The change was from an information, training, and resource consultant center to a unit whose mission was to stress the improvement of management practice. To be sure, the information dissemination function continued, but in somewhat different contexts, entailing evaluation and field studies.

Sadler and McDevitt (1979) report on a conference organized to help define a policy for the Division of Utilization of the RSA. Ideas proposed in the conference include the following:

1. The utilization program should define and delineate the different audiences to be addressed.
2. The program should include identification of user needs, demonstration, evaluation, dissemination, provision of technical assistance as required, maintenance, monitoring, and follow-up.
3. There should be a link with other relevant established programs.
4. Regional utilization units and core areas such as medical rehabilitation should be considered.
5. The RSA needs to provide direction, guidelines, and organizational definition of its program to aid in establishing a structure for the utilization division.

The potential tasks of the Division of Utilization were set forth to include the assembling of a knowledge base, planning for utilization, determining utilization readiness, developing dissemination and utilization strategy techniques, and evaluating utilization efforts. An appendix presents an annotated list of "significant rehabilitation utilization events and activities of the RSA from 1955 to the present."

**Education.** The importance that agencies of various kinds can play in "building capacity for renewal and reform" and in stimulating knowledge production and utilization is indicated in a report of the Task Force on Resources Planning and Analysis of the National Institute of Education (NIE) Office of Research and Development (National Institute of Education, 1973). The report is designed to describe the initiative of NIE in its attempt to build organizational capacity of the R&D community: to create information and alternative practices and products of value to educators, to increase the capacity of a variety of agencies to link research to practice, and to enhance the capability of schools and state agencies to engage in a process of continual improvement that makes the most effective use of local resources as well as products of external R&D. The report presents a series of recommendations under four categories:

1. Developing a monitoring system within NIE.
2. Strengthening the external R&D system.
3. Building a linkage and support system.
4. Building problem-solving capacity in the operating system.

The underlying philosophy expressed by the Task Force is indicated by its belief that the R&D system needs to include attention to how and by whom problems get formulated in the first place; to identification of possible resources for solving (or coping with) the identified problems; and to the existing inhibitors and facilitators within an organization's operating system that will affect the possibility of implementing the proposed solution to a problem.

Datta (1977) describes the role and the program of NIE since its inception in 1972. The institute was organized around six major problem areas: achieving educational equity; improving teaching, learning, and measurement of basic skill attainment; strengthening local problem-solving capacities; achieving greater equity and productivity in school financing; expanding knowledge utilization, dissemination, and educational research capability; and improving the relationship between education and work.

Among the units or programs sponsored by NIE and/or the Office of Education are the Educational Resources Information Center (ERIC); the Research and Development Utilization Program (RDU); the National Diffusion Network (NDN), which includes a Joint Dissemination Review Panel to evaluate projects or programs that seem worthy of dissemination through the network, as well as a publication called *Educational Programs That Work*; the Research and Development Exchange (RDX); and a State Capacity Building System. These and other federally sponsored dissemination activities are described in Chapter Twelve.

For up-to-date information on NIE, one may consult the institute's publication *NIE Information,* Winter 1980, which, in addition to listing the institute-sponsored Regional Education Laboratories and the National Research Centers, reports on various items relevant to the activities of NIE.

**Criminal Justice.** As an illustration of a major area in which attention has been called to the establishment of appropriate agencies and networks for effective knowledge exchange and planned change, the field of criminal justice may be mentioned.

The need for improving the performance of entrenched bureaucracies is illustrated by Chelimsky (1979) in a paper dealing with efforts to do more for the *victims* of crime. Chelimsky documents and decries the neglect and even abuse to which crime victims are subjected, while the legal system concerns itself mainly with the rights of criminals. She then goes on to indicate some types of knowledge or exemplary practices for aiding victims of crime that are not widely diffused or utilized.

Chelimsky attributes this general neglect of victims to both public apathy and bureaucratic agency self-interest, together with the tendency to regard the victim solely as an element (for example, as a witness) in the legal procedure of processing a crime. She notes the relationship of victimization to disadvantaged socioeconomic status.

As to what should be done about what she regards as a serious human welfare problem, the author notes five major implications for the enhancement of agency incentives for victim services:

1.  In creating new agencies, one should ensure that there is no basic rivalry between victim services and other agency goals.
2.  In expanding other agencies—mental health clinics, for example—to include victim services, care must be taken that the dominant agency perspective does not compete with, absorb, or distort the responsibility of service to the victim.
3.  In placing victim services in an agency, one should be aware of possible conflicts with agency self-interest.
4.  In implementing new services, strategies for change should

be chosen with an understanding of agency incentives and vigilance toward antichange behavior.

5.  Staffing of agencies to deliver victim services requires attention to potentially negative characteristics such as indifference or unresponsiveness.

To achieve change in this area, outside forces need to be mobilized, and a whole set of related tasks must be undertaken. In sum, the most important challenge with regard to victim services for the 1980s will be to develop a network of caring people who can muster the public and private support required. In this effort, evaluation and knowledge diffusion research are likely to play a major role.

The relations among mental health agencies, the criminal justice system, and knowledge utilization are forcefully illustrated in an article by Lund (1980) in an entire special 1980 issue of *Evaluation and Change* devoted to services for victims (or survivors) of crimes, terrorism, violence, and similar sources of unusual stress. Lund raises the question of how ready the mental health system is to adopt and expand both R&D, knowledge transfer, and services for victims. His response is based on a survey of thirty directors of community mental health centers and fifteen members of the 1980 session of the Network of Consultants on Knowledge Transfer and Change. Davis's A VICTORY model of determinant factors that influence organizations was used as an aid in the survey.

The study concluded that despite several positive indicators, such as a moderately well-perceived need, the mental health system, as presently constituted, is not yet at a point of critical readiness for major efforts to meet the needs of victims. Facilitative action by internal or external agents of change is needed to overcome the absence of specific pressure for such programs, the lack of available resources, and the incomplete state of current knowledge. Advice tends to lean toward some form of counseling, but opinion differs on whether victims of personal violence require treatment or types of service distinctive from a conventional approach.

**Science and Technology.** The program mechanisms of the

U.S. Environmental Protection Agency (EPA) operating as a technology-transfer agent are outlined by Crowe and Madancy (1974) as including the following.

1. *Organization mechanisms:* (a) The Technology Transfer Program functions as an office in the EPA's Headquarters Research and Development Organization, and (b) each of the ten EPA regions has a contact person for technology transfer.
2. *Production mechanisms:* (a) Needs are identified, and (b) careful evaluation is employed with respect to technology-transfer products.
3. *Dissemination mechanisms:* (a) Dissemination process is accomplished by means of headquarters staff activities and budget, and (b) the process is controlled to ensure rapid and efficient response to requests from users.

The Denver Research Institute (1974) prepared *Space Benefits,* a publication for the NASA Technology Utilization Office, to provide NASA with accurate, convenient, and integrated resource information on the transfer of aerospace technology to other sectors of the U.S. economy. The technological innovations derived from NASA space programs and their current applications in the following areas are considered: manufacturing consumer products, manufacturing capital goods, new consumer products and retailing, electric utilities, environmental quality, food production and processing, government, petroleum and gas, construction, law enforcement, and highway transportation.

A brochure entitled "Technology Utilization at Work" (National Aeronautics and Space Administration, 1976) describes, with pictorial illustrations, the "catalyzers of technology transfer" sponsored by NASA. In addition to detailing the many publications and information retrieval services offered by NASA, reference is made to the Technology Utilization Office, which arranges for multidisciplinary teams of professionals located at research institutes and universities to contact public-sector agencies or medical facilities to learn what significant problems might be solved by the application of NASA technology.

Rubenstein (1975) reported on a project conducted in cooperation with the Division of Science Information Service of the National Science Foundation to review the state of the art in various aspects of the field of information systems and utilization and to design some key experiments to be carried out in a large number of organizations as well as some "administrative experiments" to be carried out by individual managers of R&D or scientific and technical information (STI) to solve particular STI problems.

Other major sections of the report include a literature analysis, a survey of STI users, a survey of ongoing and proposed experiments by STI users, the development of a propositional inventory, the exploration of the feasibility of a framework for analyzing the STI process, and a list of working papers on the same project.

The Division of Policy Research and Analysis of the National Science Foundation has served a coordinating agency function for several years through its Working Group on Innovation Processes and Their Management. This group has been sponsoring research on technological innovation in a wide variety of public and private settings, including the diffusion and widespread utilization of technologically advanced products, processes, and services. Identification of potential leverage points for federal action has been a major goal of this NSF activity.

## Temporary Networks

A "temporary system" is at times set up to perform certain of the functions of the more permanently established network.

The use of temporary systems (Miles, 1964d, 1965; Moriarty, 1967; Havelock, 1968b, 1969a) to free up communication, enhance trust, and build more productive cooperation is widely advocated. Collaboration between research workers and practitioners can be facilitated by a few days of meeting together, away from their offices and duties, with the help of a skilled professional to guide the group growth process (Schein and Bennis, 1965; Havelock, 1969b). Likewise, the wish of management to introduce innovation may be much better accepted by other personnel if the decisions are reached after some team training (Marrow, 1969). Miles sees the special advantages of a temporary system in the fact that it is held only for a short time, at a place separate from the daily office pressure, so that people may experiment with new behavior under conditions of low risk and high learning. The norms that develop in such groups favor openness, authenticity, sharing, inquiry, and mutual aid. Periods of good experience in temporary systems can enable work teams to deal better with real problems in a constructive, creative way.

Glaser (1980e) describes a prototype for knowledge sharing on the part of a network of medical specialists in the field of chronic obstructive pulmonary disease (COPD). The paradigm, which in part was an outgrowth of an earlier pilot study, served a dual purpose: (1) to develop an authoritative synthesis of the state of the art in this field and (2) to develop procedures for achieving dissemination and utilization of the best available knowledge. The author outlines the process sequence as follows:

1. The need for a synthesis of the knowledge base regarding diagnosis and treatment of COPD was determined by consulting a number of professors of pulmonary medicine.
2. A substantial number of highly respected, influential researchers/practitioners in the field were recruited to work together on the state-of-the-art document, the project coordinator serving as process facilitator.
3. Shortly thereafter, a two-day meeting of the team was held to develop initial goals, identify potential user audiences, work out a content outline of the paper, and agree on a procedure for task accomplishment.
4. As the process of literature review, writing, and critique progressed, copies of each member's input were distributed to the rest of the team, whose comments were then further shared; in addition, whenever warranted, meetings of geo-

graphically proximate members were held to further personal contact and discussion.

5.  Outside critical inputs were obtained by virtue of the fact that team members had contact with other equally influential medical professionals across the country.

The state-of-the art article prepared by the project team was published in the *Journal of the American Medical Association* (Hodgkin and others, 1975). Over 8,500 requests for reprints were received, not counting requests to reproduce several thousand additional copies. The article invited criticism and suggestions, and more than 100 readers responded to that invitation. In light of these and other suggestions and questions, a monograph was drafted, which was circulated among team members, sent to distinguished professionals outside the project team, and published after an intermediate revision and a team conference. The monograph, which has had a second printing, has become one of the most frequently used resource publications for continuing education in the field of pulmonary rehabilitation. Also available is a forty-five-minute movie of the treatment in action.

This unusual project demonstrates the efficacy of combining features of such concepts as the temporary network system, close contact with the "invisible college" of distinguished researchers/practitioners in the subject field, and reiterative formulations of expert knowledge (illustrated also in the Delphi and nominal-group techniques). The resulting state-of-the-art document benefited further from multifaceted dissemination/utilization strategies. The project also demonstrated the possibilities of achieving certain network benefits without the establishment of permanent commitments often associated with formal agencies.

The *Report of the Task Force on International and National Diffusion* (as summarized by Davis and Cherns, 1975b) presents recommendations for the development of a center and an extended network that would guide the Quality of Working Life Program in the future. Aside from its substantive reference to working life, the summary report is significant in presenting an organized account of how a *network* of concerned social scientists might be established and might carry on its operations.

Five main aspects of the task are identified: determining (1) *what diffusion is,* (2) *who* is to engage in diffusion, (3) *what* is to be diffused, (4) *to whom* it is to be directed, and (5) *how* diffusion is to be conducted.

Diffusion is seen as transcending the mere transmission of information to include the influencing of change. Although the proposed network group of social scientists and close associates is to be primarily responsible, others will contribute to diffusion as well, but not in the role of publicists or reformers.

As to *what* is to be diffused that concerns the quality of working life, two broad headings are involved: (1) raising consciousness of the problem and (2) diffusing what can be done to influence the quality of working life. The scope of this concept has been variously interpreted—from increasing "compensation" for work in such terms as pay and shorter hours to wider psychological and social considerations to quality of life in general.

Diffusion to *whom* is considered in terms of audiences or publics such as *actors,* who make decisions; *influencers,* who influence actors; and *supporters,* on whom the influencers or actors act. Audiences may be further subdivided according to international, national, and local sectors or industries and still further in relation to power groups such as unions, enterprises, or associations.

Among suggestions on *how* diffusion can be conducted are (1) reaching key individuals, such as gatekeepers, (2) building a relationship of trust, (3) securing support of power groups, and (4) guarding against arousing internal conflicts within the group or organization where cooperation is sought.

As an overall approach, the report urges an attitude of open debate and collaborative learning.

## Social Network Analysis and "Networking"

A network is an interactive arrangement—formal or informal—of individuals, groups, or organizations for the purpose of sharing information, influence, power, or whatever they wish.

In recent years, considerable interest has been shown in the concept of social networks as they relate to the sharing of knowledge and worthwhile innovation. To be sure, interpersonal sets of relationships have been studied in the past in terms of sociometry, communication, organizational patterns, "invisible colleges," cultural diffusion, and the like; but the newer emphasis attempts to synthesize descriptive studies and make readily available exemplary practices and theoretical analyses relevant to the interest of the network members.

Network analysis may be said to address the question "Who interacts with whom concerning what, and when, where, and how?" Within this broad framework, networks (other than purely physical systems) take many forms.

A major distinction can be made between "natural" or "spontaneous" networks that are essentially informal and those that are deliberate and entail planned intervention. The latter are formal in their origin and organization. Kadushin (1977) considers this distinction as the first of three dimensions, terming it *emergent versus instituted.* His other dimensions are *interstitial versus single organizational* (dependent on whether the network links existing systems or is found totally within one system) and having *high versus low visibility* (that is, the extent to which it is fully known to persons inside or outside it). Schön (1977) sees three broad categories of informal networks: (1) *helping* networks, aimed at providing support or assistance in a personal sense, (2) *organizational ecologies,* which include both persons and organizations defined by a function (such as health care) or a geographical community, and (3) *secondary networks* composed of "providers, practitioners, interveners, and researchers" in some social policy domain (Miles, 1978b). The second of these types draws attention to the fact that networks may exist among organizations as well as individuals. Thus, Smith (1977) presents at some length an analytical case report of an elaborate effort to involve a number of organizations (including a national education center, a state department of education, several universities, and local school districts) in a multifaceted art education project.

Networks may be distinguished according to their underlying goal. For example, Miles (1978b) summarizes network "frames," or purposes, as overcoming (1) backwardness or obsolescence, (2) inequity, (3) stagnation, (4) isolation and resource poverty, (5) anomie or aloneness, and (6) unshared craft or competence. This distinction carries with it (1) differences in function (for example, modernization, cosmopolitanization), (2) differences in primary flow types (for example, knowledge, objects, power, affect), and (3) differences in expected change (for example, diffusion of new technology, energy or resource increase, shared value). The particular purpose, setting, nature of the existing network, types of persons involved, and so on will determine which strategies and tactics to apply—and, for that matter, whether to attempt intervention at all.

To address this last issue, a number of students of the subject suggest that it may be wise in some instances not to upset the operation of existing networks, especially of the informal and low-visibility types (for example, Schön, 1977; Miles, 1978b). Intervention, they argue, may diminish the "natural" energy, commitment, and vitality that many spontaneous, indigenous networks develop on their own. As a special case, where outside intervention supplies funds or other support on a temporary basis to such networks, withdrawal of aid may result in a collapse of the self-help potential of informal networks.

Several of the dissemination networks sponsored by the National Institute of Education are undergoing study by Louis and Dentler, with Rosenblum (1982), to assess actual implementation and impact. In the field of education in particular, formal intervention is often advised because of the generally loose organization of units in the hierarchy from teachers to school boards and because of the constraints and boundaries within and between the several components of the system. (See also "Multiple Dissemination Methods," in Chapter Twelve, for further discussion of the far-reaching and powerful effects of government-funded educational networks supported with technical assistance.)

Although it is not possible to generalize across goals, settings, and institutions, various guidelines for network-building strategies and tactics will be found in the literature. In general terms, a sampling of these proposals may be stated as follows:

1. Strategic choices will vary not only with respect to the broad "frame," or purpose, of the intervention but also according to (a) the type of change sought (for example, in particular types of human services delivery organizations, or in certain types of business/industrial organizations, (b) the type of network expected, and (c) the network participants (Miles, 1978b).

2. At the macrostrategy level, strategies will need to be adjusted according to whether (a) a new network is to be created, (b) an old one is to be enhanced or expanded, or (c) differential networks or subsystems are to be induced.

3. At a more specific, or micro, level, there are network functions toward which intervention efforts may be directed (Miles, 1978b). Of these, *input-related functions* include (a) problem diagnosis, (b) incentive definition, (c) recruitment, (d) resource mobilization, and (e) design. *Operations-related functions* encompass (a) linkage, (b) communication, and (c) education and training. *Output-related functions* refer to (a) projects, (b) materials, and (c) evaluation and replanning.

4. Networking strategies need to be applied with full awareness of the stages or developmental life cycle through which networks are likely to proceed. In a sense, the listing of input-, operations-, and output-related functions represents an enumeration of the stages of the process.

5. For each function, or stage, Miles (1978b) has identified structural approaches (network development through particular mechanisms, procedures, and durable arrangements that transcend persons), as distinguished from educative approaches (development through alterations of attitudes, beliefs, and knowledge of network members).

In sum, networks exist as a fact of organizational and social life. At the least, they are a means through which efforts to put knowledge to use or to achieve change can be facilitated. In some cases the objective of enhancing creative innovation efforts and utilization of promising knowledge that is already available but is underutilized may well be a network mechanism tailored to the needs, resources, and "linking readiness" of the organizations, groups, or individuals who wish to be involved in the network.

In the next chapter we turn to one of the major functions of change agents, agencies, and networks—namely, the task of communicating available information/knowledge bearing on given subjects or types of knowledge.

## Summary Comments

The first of the main sections of this chapter may be designated "the change agent in search of identity." The treatment of the subject of change agentry has been far from simple. The very *concept* of the change agent has varied, as indicated by the many titles assigned to such persons, including those that stress the knowledge side, the linking function, and the utilization aspect. The diversified *roles* assigned change agents reflect distinctions implied in those titles. Among the many titles expressive of roles are *teacher, integrator, translator, partner, insider, outsider, gatekeeper, broker, expert, technician, collaborator, interventionist, activist, advocate, manager, initiator,* and *strategist,* not to mention the popular term *consultant.*

Corresponding to the titles and roles of change agents are a host of *activities* that span a range from grand strategies to minor tactics. *Status* and relationships are perceived as important features accompanying the execution of functions. Official recognition varies from the hired expert consultant to the uninvited citizen interventionist. Advice on how change agents should behave to increase their effectiveness is plentiful.

*Consultants and consultation* come in for special treatment in the literature, perhaps reflecting a trend toward professionalism. Much of what is said under this topic overlaps the several discussions concerning change agents. But as one reads the several writings on consultation, one detects a firmer image of the professional participant in the process. This trend reaches its most formal expression with respect to the attempt to describe the work of the consultant in *organizational development* (OD), a much-used but not always uniformly applied enterprise. One set of coauthors concluded that the probability that any given OD program in education can be designated as "successful" is perhaps only 50 percent or worse, implying weaknesses in the way the essential features of the approach have been applied, rather than intrinsic inadequacies in the concept itself.

Several of the writings reviewed in this chapter urge that consultants, and change agents in general, should undergo thorough training for depth understanding of that role.

That the subject of organizational development (and the related topic of consultation) should not be taken lightly is suggested by the size of the body of literature devoted to it. This literature touches on many aspects of the process, including such considerations as types of OD consultants, implementation measures, obstacles to success, and successful and unsuccessful applications.

As noted in the second section of the chapter, *change agencies* have been established in a number of fields, including mental health, rehabilitation, education, and science and technology. These agencies have the advantages of pooled planning and operating resources, of extensive support (often from government), of continuity of effort, of wider participation, and of broader targets and objectives.

While change agents as "lone wolves" continue to perform important functions, the extensiveness of the task of utilizing promising knowledge and inducing needed change has caused a flourishing growth of *networks* of utilization specialists. Those networks often serve to identify promising R&D in given fields, along with exemplary practices, coupled with dissemination and information exchange services. They also may offer technical assistance or consultation where desired in connection with adoption consideration.

A number of examples of these more or less formal organizations designed either to assist individual change agents or to perform change functions directly are described in some detail. These agencies have themselves been responsive to change. One of the evident changes is a recognition of the place of temporary or semi-informal networks of persons concerned with one or another aspect of knowledge dissemination and interested in sharing experience and expertise. Whatever the limitations of these *temporary networks,* they have the advantages of flexibility of form, relatively modest administrative costs, and the capability of concentrating on one particular problem at a time.

Beyond the notion of the utilization network ordinarily established to coordinate efforts of change agents, there is the far broader concept of the social network as an inherent characteristic of organizational and social life. Although much of the newer literature on this phenomenon is largely a reformulation of older ideas, a "rediscovery of the wheel," it provides new insights, both descriptive and prescriptive, of potential use in the art of knowledge dissemination and change agentry.

Dealing as they do with the actors in the linkage process, the topics of Chapter Eleven serve as a fitting preliminary to a consideration of communication and dissemination, treated in the chapter that follows.

# 12

# Means
# of Communicating
# Knowledge

The various ways of transmitting knowledge can be considered under three headings: (1) *personal communication,* (2) *written communication,* and (3) *other forms of dissemination/diffusion.* The literature is replete with studies that demonstrate the efficacy of face-to-face contacts as an influence on knowledge utilization and change. And yet, the significance of written forms of knowledge storage, retrieval, and transmission cannot be gainsaid. A continuing problem is that of achieving ready accessibility to and easy identification of available information relevant to targeted questions or concerns. Further, communication and its concomitant effects on comprehension, attitudes, and behavior take a variety of other forms represented by diverse media and patterns of presentation.

The transmission of knowledge from producer to user may be viewed either from the vantage point of the *user* in search of needed knowledge or exemplary practice or from that of the *producer* seeking to make knowledge available to potential users. The process as a whole entails the interaction of the two thrusts.

The matter of targeting information toward particular audiences to serve distinctive needs has received the attention of investigators—for example, Magisos (1971) and Crowe and Madancy (1974). In a number of studies, questionnaires have been submitted to various categories of potential users of research or knowledge to ascertain their needs.

To be effective, the disseminator needs to be sensitive to the stages through which a message goes as the receiver reacts to it. In this regard, Paisley (1969) distinguishes the following ten stages through which a message progresses:

1. Awareness that a message is being sent.
2. Attention: the receiver tunes in.
3. Exposure: transference via the receiver's sense organs.
4. Comprehension: cognition of what is being communicated.
5. Retention: the message is kept—or lost—in competition with other messages.
6. Motivation: potential for acceptance.
7. Pretrial evaluation: judgment on whether to put it to use.
8. Trial: tentative tryout of idea.
9. Posttrial evaluation: examination of the results of the tryout.
10. Complete adoption: use of the idea after decision to adopt it.

It is evident that the mere sending of a message does not automatically ensure acceptance and application.

Effective dissemination is contingent on clear formulation of the information to be transmitted (Cherns, 1969, 1972a). Such formulation is related to the following six factors, among others: (1) level of concreteness, (2) form (pure, objective, operational, actional), (3) assumptions (open or implied), (4) volume, (5) contemporaneity (displacement of old knowledge), and (6) conceptual content. As noted in Chapter Two, comprehensibility and freedom from technicality are major determinants of project adoption.

According to Knox (1973), the most important changes in the technological information system within the fifteen to twenty years prior to 1973 were the following: (1) The advent of the technical report as a major record form, supplementing books and journals. (2) Development of the computer, electronic display devices, and microforms. (3) The creation, mostly by federal agencies or with federal subsidy, of computer-based files of abstracts and indexes for particular subjects, with subsequent distribution to particular user groups.

The other side of diffusion is the reception of new information and new programs. Whitley and Frost (1972) studied the inward flow of information, the formation of internal communication barriers in a division of a large government research establishment, and the way scientists, among others, function as gatekeepers for the transmission of external information. In the situation studied, the authors found, further, that information from internal reports, together with conferences, was more influential than that obtained from external sources.

### Personal Communication

**Power of Personal Communication.** A number of studies illustrate the power of personal communication. Two classic investigations reported findings that have subsequently been confirmed. The first investigation pertains to diffusion in reference to hybrid corn seed (Ryan and Gross, 1943). Almost half of the farmers interviewed cited personal contacts with salesmen as their earliest source of information; 10 percent named radio advertising as their first source. About 15 percent indicated that neighbors had provided the information, while 11 percent named farm journals. However, the findings indicated that although professional salesmen most often served the "introduction" function, neighbors were the most influential in activating adoption of the hybrid corn.

The second classic study (Coleman, Katz, and Menzel, 1966b) focused on the introduction of a new drug and its acceptance, over time, among prescribing physicians. Several channels of influence usually preceded use of the new drug by a physician, but a social intermediary (detail man or colleague), rather than impersonal media (journals, house organs, and so on), was frequently indicated as the major source of information leading to prescription of the drug. The sources of information reported by the physicians were as follows: 57 percent had first learned of the drug from the detail man, 18 percent from direct mail from drug houses, 7 percent from a professional journal, and 7 percent from another physician. Almost 90 percent of the doctors had sought or awaited word from at least one of the reported sources before first using the drug; 62 percent indicated that they had received the information from three or more sources before use.

A succinct chart showing the design and findings of the two classic studies (by Ryan and Gross and by Coleman, Katz, and Menzel) is reproduced in an article by Katz in Bennis, Benne, and Chin (1969).

A retrospective study (Roberts and Larsen, 1971) was conducted by identifying innovative programs already introduced in mental health institutions and tracing the innovation backward to the source of the information. Results indicate that the primary source for innovative ideas was personal contact. Formal communication channels, such as books, journals, and speeches, played a significantly smaller role. If the ideas that come from personal interaction provide the catalyst for information-seeking behavior, other sources of information will subsequently be used.

The potential value of person-to-person communication as a mechanism for facilitating change seems well established.

A study by Glaser and Taylor (1973) of successful, as contrasted to relatively unsuccessful, applied research projects sponsored by the National Institute of Mental Health emphasized the value of collaboration between knowledge developers and knowledge users. The study found that the successful research projects were characterized by a high level of communication with and involvement of potential users. The project staff of successful projects made efforts to induce interest and cooperation from a wide group of supporters and potential users. Potential obstacles became shared concerns. Resolution of these obstacles, by both research project staff and potential users, often provided unexpected benefits that strengthened the project. An investigation by Zaltman and Deshpande

(1979) that focused on interactions between market researchers and marketing managers in client organizations confirmed these findings in a private-sector context.

In a company studied by Udis (1976), it was found that many of the ideas on which certain innovations were based were brought into the firm as a result of a new person's joining the firm. Evidently, a new person tends, through personal contact, to serve as a carrier of new ideas.

In the field of mental health and mental retardation, Larsen and Nichols (1972) found an emphasis on word of mouth and personal contact as primary bases for the acquisition of information and the initiation of innovations by institutional personnel.

Informal Contact. Most practitioners learn mainly from face-to-face contact with other people (Rogers, 1962a; Coleman, Katz, and Menzel, 1966b; Niehoff, 1966; Havelock and Mann, 1968; Rubin, 1968; Roberts and Larsen, 1971). They learn most readily from "influentials" in their profession (Lazarsfeld, Sewell, and Wilensky, 1967; Becker, 1970b), from persons with contagious enthusiasm (Bowman, 1959), and from those with whom they have easy rapport.

After reviewing relevant literature on factors related to the successful transfer of R&D findings, Glaser (1973) concludes that, at least in some fields, the most effective single means for increasing information may be personal interaction and that the strategic contact is the "gatekeeper," or well-informed colleague who serves to channel information to co-workers. Roberts and Larsen (1971) report a similar finding. Obviously, the process of consultation places major emphasis on person-to-person communication, as noted in Caplan's (1970) treatise on mental health consultation, which discusses this mode of knowledge and judgment transmission in great detail.

Tracing the diffusion of knowledge of a new hybrid seed corn and of a new antibiotic, Katz (1961) found that information moved through previously established channels of personal communication. Although salesmen play an important role in providing early information, informal contacts (neighbor, professional colleague) often support the acceptability of that information.

Rich (1979b) interviewed some twenty-nine high officials in federal government agencies about (among other matters) the form of information they received in trying to formulate policy on the duration of unemployment benefits. Personal interaction, including conversation by telephone, was reported far more frequently than written sources of information.

Quite different and new possibilities for the dissemination of information from person to person are illustrated in the service provided by the University of Alabama Medical Center. Telephone inquiries on medical matters by health personnel located in other parts of the state are routed to qualified faculty members under a system called Medical Information Service via Telephone (MIST). The service, instituted in 1969, has grown annually to the extent that during the year 1976–77 over 20,000 calls were received, the majority from primary care physicians. In reporting on the plan, Klapper, Harper, and Bridgers (1978) indicate that the MIST system plays a vital role in improving health care for Alabamans, expands the information needed for statewide planning of services, curbs potential increases in medical costs, and has served as a model for other states.

Crane (1970) notes that the use of formal or informal channels of information by scientists depends on whether they are searching for knowledge in their specialized area or outside it, the latter being associated with informal channels. The scientific literature itself is seen as consisting of tightly knit cores, which the scientist explores through directive searching for specialized and specific information. Links to other cores result from random searching. How information moves from one group to another—the phenomenon of "scatter of knowledge," which the author regards as necessary for cross-fertilization—is revealed in studies of "invisible colleges," an elite of interactive, productive scientists in a particular subject area. Crane recommends that isolated scientists be brought into closer contact with scientists who are the foci of communication networks.

Rosenbloom and Wolek (1970) distinguish between formal information sources (principally the published literature) and informal sources. They note that professional orientation is usually associated with the use of formal sources, whereas mission orientation is related to the use of informal ones. The authors suggest that managers should exert effort toward the linking of professionally oriented and mission-oriented activity.

Parker and Paisley (1966) report that research workers depend heavily on informal information networks: interpersonal systems, "accidental" acquisition of useful information, "inefficient" and "irrational" information seeking, and the like. Accidental discovery of information in stimulating environments is especially useful to applied scientists who are in touch with *many* dissimilar colleagues and who have the advantages of unrestricted long-distance telephoning and travel.

Writing about the improvement of communications among scientists, Swanson (1966) urges that informal information practices be aided and amplified, first, by identifying the information-exchanging groups and, second, by improving and expanding the selective communication systems within these groups, with a high level of feedback to check on the value of the information dissemination. Swanson states that as much as 85 percent of useful scientific information is exchanged informally before the usual bibliographical sources are consulted to ascertain whether published information is available.

Niehoff (1967) discusses gossip and its positive and negative effects on the change process in endeavors such as community development projects. Positive gossip, favorable to project goals, is an index of the establishment of efficient information flow, both of communication input and of feedback, and also indicates a perception by local inhabitants that the project goals would benefit them. Moreover, change agents can deliberately use such gossip as a method of information dissemination. Negative gossip, or rumor-mongering, results from lack of information flow between the change agent and potential adopters and/ or failure of local people to perceive advantages from the project goals. A linear negative relationship between communication feedback and rumor-mongering is hypothesized; that is, when the degree of feedback is low, the chances for rumors will be high. Niehoff recommends that operations people monitor the "grapevine" as an index of communication flow and utilize the potential force of positive gossip for spreading ideas.

**Conferences, Seminars, and Workshops.** Conferences in which research findings and exemplary practices are presented and discussed in depth with practitioners are more influential than publications or other one-way reports (Glaser and Wrenn, 1966; Glaser and others, 1967; Carter, 1968a; Engstrom, 1969; Garvey and Gottfredson, 1976). A good illustration of the use of this type of conference in the medical field is the report by Glaser (1968) on promoting the use of a consensually recommended comprehensive care program for patients with chronic obstructive pulmonary disease. In another study, Glaser and others (1967) report the effectiveness of a combined conference/site-visit approach to increase awareness and promote utilization of an R&D-based procedure for training mentally retarded young adults to achieve a significantly improved vocational and social adjustment.

Cooper and Archambault (1968) report the success of a conference conducted in two parts separated by a four-month period during which reading lists and materials were distributed. Providing the participants with an opportunity to determine the program for the second part of the conference increased their involvement with the issues being considered.

Spooner and Thrush (1970) found that an interagency conference regarding a particularly successful innovation, during which implementation plans were worked out, with personal follow-up, aided appreciably in the dissemination of the particular findings and was instrumental in initiating institutional change.

Conferences have a two-way impact (Nagi, 1965). Practitioners face up to the implications of research findings, but researchers also profit from the feedback from those who would like more practical assistance.

Havelock and Markowitz (1973) found that well-organized topic-centered conferences on highway safety matters were a key element in binding together this applied R&D community. Such meetings were heavily attended both by R&D opinion leaders and by key national decision makers. Hence, they were a major factor in linking research to practice.

Beckhard (1978) demonstrated that a well-planned writing conference as a mechanism for technology transfer can be effective in speeding up the application of new knowledge. Meeting a set of prearranged conditions, a group of twenty-two experts conferred for three and a half days and produced, under Beckhard's direction, a 150-page manuscript on change processes in large systems and on knowledge areas needed by managers and change agents of institutions and organizations, by volunteers who run community organizations, and by political leaders. The document also contains outlines and designs for professional development programs and graduate courses.

The conference as a method for disseminating knowledge and inducing significant innovative change takes on added potency when supplemented by two features—namely, provision for (1) a planned and carefully edited publication of conference proceedings, especially where preliminary prepared papers are used as a basis for discussion, and (2) an annual series of meetings centering on a major topic of concern to a particular profession or group. The Vermont Conference on the Primary Prevention of Psychopathology may be cited as an example. Descriptive information on these conferences, held annually at the University of Vermont, is available from the University Press of New England.

**Demonstrations and Visits.** Many innovations are most convincing when demonstrated, largely because of such factors as personal contact and feedback communication by participants (Niehoff, 1966). Visits to situations very like those in which the visitor works back home, but where something new is being done, are likely to have transfer value (Miles, 1964d; Carter, 1968b). At times, however, observers who visit and admire radical innovations of experimental schools and colleges do not adopt them (Watson, 1964), especially when they see their own situation as basically different.

Glaser and Ross (1971) found that a site visit sometimes engenders enough advocacy so that visitors may aggressively sponsor the innovation when they get back to their home agencies. Such sponsorship would probably be more productive if two or more persons from the same agency visited the demonstration site and hence could reinforce each other on return to their own setting. Exchange of professional workers would facilitate this kind of diffusion (Cady, 1968), as would more released time and travel funds.

A study by Baer, Johnson, and Merrow (1976) examined various facets of the use of mainly technological demonstration projects. In this investigation the Rand Corporation, at the invitation of the U.S. Department of Commerce, analyzed twenty-four federally funded demonstration projects designed to improve the environment for innovation and the general vitality of the economy. The study purported to identify major factors associated with successful and unsuccessful project outcomes and to formulate guidelines for federal agencies for improving future demonstration projects.

In their report of the study, Baer, Johnson, and Merrow noted three types of measured outcomes—information success, application success, and diffusion success—citing illustrations drawn from case studies of the various types of projects. They also determined the relations among the three types of outcomes. Attributes associated with diffusion success were found to be (1) a technology well in hand, (2) presence of federal cost- and risk-sharing among local participants, (3) initiative for the project from nonfederal sources, (4) a strong technology delivery system, (5) inclusion of all active components of the technology delivery system, and (6) absence of tight time restraints.

Baer, Johnson, and Merrow present guidelines for federal agencies that might improve future demonstration projects under five headings to correspond with successive steps in demonstration activities, as follows: (1) strategies for demonstrations, (2) exploratory study, (3) planning and implementation, (4) management, monitoring, and evaluation, and (5) dissemination of results. The proposals are too numerous to present in full, but several illustrative suggestions will indicate their nature.

Regarding strategies for demonstration, the agency is advised to develop an overall strategy even before initiating an exploratory study. Some of the elements included in the strategy are (1) resisting political pressure to demonstrate before a technology is well in hand, (2) conducting several demonstrations in parallel, addressed to the same problem, if budgetary constraints allow, (3) including explicit plans for follow-through after the demonstration, and (4) allowing enough time in the demonstration's schedule for slippage, especially when undertaking large projects with significant technological uncertainty.

Glaser and Wrenn (1966), following the model so successful in the work of county agricultural agents, suggest that, where possible, demonstrations be set up within some influential institutions that might profit by adoption of the innovation. Another proposal is that pilot laboratories be established and assigned responsibility to try out (demonstrate) development based on recent research and to publish practical operating guidelines for use by other institutions (Engstrom, 1969).

Rein and Miller (1966) point out that, in the area of social action, demonstration projects are sometimes recommended as an excuse to postpone change rather than a way to facilitate it. They do, however, suggest that success of demonstration efforts can be enhanced by better planning with regard to the kind of influence a project is intended to have, the target group to be influenced, and how influence will be exerted. Similarly, Lippitt and Butman (1969), in a study of mental health demonstration projects, reported that projects profit from awareness of the needs of potential adopters and the means to assess and evaluate ways of communicating with them and that projects need help with planning and carrying out diffusion activities.

Richland (1965) reports a traveling seminar arranged by the System Development Corporation for 120 educators. After visiting schools where various innovations were in operation, the tour members had a day together to review, discuss, and generalize their observations. The project was evaluated by visits one year later to the schools run by these educators. In comparison with educators at similar control schools, the tour participants had introduced many more innovations.

In a major study supported by the National Institute of Mental Health (Larsen, Arutunian, and Finley, 1974), the

American Institutes for Research (AIR) provided expense-paid visits to be made by community mental health center staff to other centers to determine the effect on innovation of (1) site visitation alone as compared with (2) transmission of pertinent written material and (3) concurrent use of consultant assistance along with site visits. The researchers reported that staff reaction to all three diffusion techniques was extremely positive, ratings of "useful to some degree" ranging from 86 percent for the consultant's visit to 94 percent for the site visit. As to preference regarding type of diffusion technique, 79 percent indicated preference for interpersonal techniques as against 19 percent for written techniques, with 2 percent citing other techniques. The improvement of methods of communicating information about new practices to capture user interest was undertaken in a collaborative effort of NIMH and AIR to develop *Innovations* as a publication dedicated to the description of innovative programs. It was evident from the study that although centers that encourage staff visits to other centers are more likely to consider innovations than those that do not support such contact, appropriate written material *and* outside consultants add to the likelihood of carrying forward the innovative process.

Kunce and Hartley (1975) report on funded site visits by rehabilitation personnel to innovative projects in other states. The program described, sponsored by the Rehabilitation Services Administration (now National Institute of Handicapped Research), has gone under the name of Research Utilization Through Learning Experiences (RULE). The article presents findings from an evaluation of some 220 visits completed during a thirty-month period. The authors conclude that the RULE visits in many cases stimulated decision-making action at the agency level and that the methodology for the operation of the project could readily be transferred to other areas.

Sarbaugh and others (1973) undertook research to evaluate the degree to which a program of exhibiting display modules of new teaching methods influenced the adoption of those methods. The study examined (1) prior adoption level of display visitors, (2) amount of attention paid to different aspects of the displays, (3) reactions to displays, (4) ability of the modules to persuade teachers and administrators to adopt innovations, (5) effectiveness of combining consulting sessions with the display modules, and (6) the sources of information that people use to learn about these new methods. Results indicated that the displays and consulting sessions definitely promoted increased awareness and adoption of educational innovations.

## Written Communication

**Growth and Use of Printed Matter.** The amount of time a scientist or engineer devoted to interacting with the information system in science and technology, according to Knox (1973), had not changed during the past twenty-five years, even though the volume of technological information, as represented by the world's scientific and technical literature, increased roughly *sixteen times* between 1930 and 1970. Personal contacts have proliferated as the recorded information system has proved less able to satisfy the needs of users. Monographs and handbooks as a means of covering a number of journal articles are only partly effective in handling the information dissemination problem. The system also faces problems of speed of response and quality of material.

When a journal article or monograph on a given topic is developed through interactive collaboration among leaders in that subject field and published as a state-of-the-art document that is widely distributed through a prestigious professional specialty organization, utilization of the information is found to be significantly enhanced—at least in connection with recommended treatment of chronic obstructive pulmonary disease (Glaser, 1980e).

Manten (1978) used data on the annual production of published scientific contributions to develop a model of the growth of science and to infer implications for publishing. Analyses of publishing trends led to the projection that the rapid growth in output of primary contributions during this century (of such volume as to yield a scientific-knowledge doubling rate of about eleven years during the period 1950–1970) had begun to slow, so that during the period from 1973 through 1986 the doubling-time rate would be prolonged to fourteen years. He foresaw a corresponding reduction in publications, accentuated by increasing costs. For instance, he predicted that unsubsidized publication of the current large volume of research reports would decrease; selections would be more stringently controlled; the number of journals would begin to contract through merger or termination; and satisfactory new forms of dissemination for access would have to emerge.

The availability of knowledge to those who might apply it depends, of course, on the nature, extent, and effectiveness of the dissemination of the knowledge (Hagstrom, 1965; Chin, 1974; Collins, 1974). The transfer of knowledge has received much study by workers in repositories of knowledge, such as libraries or information centers (for example, ERIC centers), and by university and industrial specialists in communication. To date, one of the most comprehensive of these studies has been accomplished in the Center of Research in Scientific Communication at Johns Hopkins University under the leadership of W. D. Garvey and many colleagues (Garvey and Compton, 1967; Garvey and Griffith, 1972; Garvey, Lin, and Tomita, 1972a, 1972b; Garvey and others, 1972a, 1972b; Garvey, Tomita, and Woolf, 1974).

Garvey and Gottfredson (1976) summarized and interpreted a series of studies of the information-flow and dissemination systems of several scientific disciplines. Following Hagstrom (1965), who found that self-interest of individuals and groups controls the process, their studies demonstrated that interactive communication is the salient feature of the social system in research and the pursuit of knowledge. Collins (1974) notes that the nature of the informal communication network in a case of interchanges among and between laboratories in the United States and Canada took the graphic form of a sociometric chart.

The progression of research information dissemination goes from (1) informal talk among colleagues to (2) prepublication dissemination, such as some type of report of the main contents of future journal articles, to (3) scientific-meeting presentations, distribution of preprints, and face-to-face interaction to (4) transfer from the informal to the formal domain—namely, journal publication.

The publication of research findings does not necessarily result in widespread absorption of these findings by practitioners. It is estimated that half the articles in "core" scientific journals are each read by no more than 200 persons, although distribution of preprints and reprints augments this total exposure (Garvey and Griffith, 1964). Monographs, like books, usually attract the more academic reader and have a limited distribution. Thus, the potential for dissemination of new knowledge through the professional literature appears limited because of the small size of the audience in proportion to the actual number of practitioners in the given field.

An article by D. Greenberg (1967) revealed (as of the date of his study) limited use of NASA materials by commercial firms in certain areas, as reported by the Denver Research Institute in "The Channels of Technology Acquisition in Commercial Firms and the NASA Dissemination Program." Surveys were conducted of sixty-two firms in four industries—electric batteries, printing and reproduction, industrial controls, and medical electronics—and eleven vocational-technical schools. Few, if any, of these organizations were at the time vigorously seeking to utilize directly the vast outpouring of science and technology that the federal government was underwriting. Instead, the technologist with a problem was inclined to fall back on the already-familiar standard manuals and textbooks. Government publications were not perceived as major channels for acquiring technological information. The preferred channels were found to be professional journals and face-to-face contacts, especially in conventions and symposia. Highly specific subject matter conferences were valued most.

Dissemination to practitioners is further hindered by the fact that research reports are usually read and used by other researchers, seldom by practitioners (Havelock, 1969b). Roberts and Larsen (1971) report that few mental health practitioners make any large-scale and systematic effort to uncover research results that could serve as a basis for change; instead, they rely heavily on contact with colleagues to stimulate innovation.

Further, most innovations that are adopted emerge from the work experience of practitioners rather than from research results. Practitioners tend to be "doers," not "readers"; hence, they tend to rely more on oral communication than on publications (Halpert, 1966; W. Paisley, 1968).

This difference in information-seeking behavior between researchers and practitioners, between theory and practice, leads us into another dimension of the research utilization problem. One of the problems with most research reports is that they strike the practitioner as being unaware of and unappreciative of what has already been achieved. The reader will be in a more receptive frame of mind if the report begins by recognizing the successful work that has already been done (Likert and Lippitt, 1963).

**Improved Reports.** As a type of printed or otherwise reproduced material that has traditionally adhered to rather technical presentation, research reports are seen by a number of writers as most useful if they are brief and easily readable (Glaser and others, 1967; Carter, 1968a; Goldin, Margolin, and Stotsky, 1969). The same finding has more impact if it reaches the practitioner several times in slightly differing forms (Halpert, 1966; Garvey and Griffith, 1967, 1971; Glaser and Taylor, 1973).

A report is more effective if it focuses directly and explicitly on a decision that the professional or manager must make (Glaser, 1968). And it is important that the right bit of information get to the right person at the right time (Paisley, 1968).

Transferring research-based knowledge into innovative protocols for nursing practice is the subject of an article by Haller, Reynolds, and Horsley (1979). The article describes the gap between academic knowledge and nursing practice as perceived by nurses and depicts the research-based teaching or learning protocols as a bridge between the two. Close attention is paid to meaningful "packaging" of the information in the form of a product that nurses can use.

The New England Rehabilitation Institute recommends applying relatively active modes of dissemination to carefully selected targets—for instance, sending a follow-up questionnaire to persons who had been mailed a monograph and requesting their reactions to the report and its findings (Goldin, Margolin, and Stotsky, 1969). This contrasts with the more common practice of sending out a research finding, by means of an article or monograph, to the world in general (Archibald, 1968).

One suggestion for improving reports is that they should not begin with the usual review of the literature but should capture the interest of practitioners in their first few pages, stating problems in forms the user will recognize as familiar and perhaps summarizing some main findings (Goldin, Margolin, and Stotsky, 1969).

Consultants to a college administration who reviewed how many of their recommendations had been followed a year later found that (1) major points should have been put at the beginning rather than at the end of their report, (2) too many minor recommendations had been made, which lessened the impact of their main findings, (3) there should have been a more careful appraisal of the costs (in time as well as money) of the innovations proposed, and (4) the bulky appendix was a liability (Wilson, 1961).

One should, however, have realistically limited expectations for the effectiveness of even good reports in gaining acceptance for an innovation. At best, they stimulate interest; they rarely create active advocacy, particularly if the innovation presents discernible difficulties (Glaser and Ross, 1971).

**Readable Reviews.** Although printed materials are not the only source of knowledge, they represent a voluminous repository. Responding to the need to bring selected materials to the attention of users, disseminators have recognized the importance of periodic readable reviews of relevant literature directed toward particular audiences (Kadushin, 1964; Halpert, 1966; and others). Klein (1968) reports a system that condenses new findings in mental health, translates them into lay language, and makes them available to mental hospital workers. Another report (Matheson and Sundland, 1969) describes how a central information agency sends notices, followed by photocopies of published reports, to individuals according to their stated field of interest. Users of the dissemination service report a two-way benefit: to themselves in terms of time saved and to colleagues to whom they pass on pertinent information.

NIMH's publications *Mental Health Digest, Innovations, Evaluation and Change* (discontinued in 1981 for economy reasons), and, more recently, *Consultation* are examples of specialized media designed to provide mental health workers with needed information. NIMH also has published *Information Sources and How to Use Them* (prepared for NIMH by the Human Interaction Research Institute) as an aid to locating new knowledge in the literature.

During the middle sixties, several journals in sociology, psychology, and anthropology were launched to convey to practitioners aspects of behavioral science research that might prove useful to them. Klein (1968) sees a need for a pocket-size magazine, as readable as the *Reader's Digest,* to tell social workers what the scientists have recently discovered.

**Abstracts and Related Services.** The preparation of abstracts, bibliographies, and reproductions of literature, such as the examples briefly described below, facilitates the task of transmission somewhat.

Annotated and selected bibliographies of technology transfer and technological innovation were prepared by Forecasting International, Ltd., in 1973. The material has been categorized according to its relevance to federal and nonfederal activities as well as its significance for technology transfer or technological innovation. The annotated bibliography contains 315 entries relevant to federal government action, and all are of high quality. About 50 additional entries relevant to nonfederal action of similar high quality are included. The selected bibliography contains approximately 375 entries, categorized in the same manner.

For the National Science Foundation, Bungay (1976) collated approximately 200 abstracts summarizing the publications resulting from its Intergovernmental Science Program in state and local governments and in technologically oriented institutions around the country.

The National Technical Information Service (NTIS) within the Department of Commerce has set forth a comprehensive and systematic program for transferring technology to both private firms and public agencies. According to Gartner and Naiman (1976), no matter how carefully and thoroughly documents about technologies are prepared, many prospective users still require additional specific technical and economic information.

**Problems of Publication.** Problems in publication are growing (Bhagat, 1977), including delays in release and increases in costs of publications as a result of inflation. The changes emerging within the publishing industry and in libraries appear to be leading to transformation of the forms, processes, channels, and costs of the dissemination of knowledge, so much so that Lancaster (1978b) foresees a possible withering of libraries, to be replaced by electronic (paperless) modes of transmission and by computer terminals in homes, in offices, and elsewhere, thus removing the need for direct access to publications.

Bhagat traces the probable effects on libraries and publishers of the changing status of the information industry, of retrenchments in higher education, and of cutbacks in research funds. The crisis is especially severe in the humanities. To meet the situation of contractions and increased costs, he offers suggestions for the industry in general and for publishers, scholars, and libraries in particular. These suggestions include (1) review procedures for screening irrelevant information, (2) reduce ambiguity to users by careful labeling and indexing, (3) increase efficiency by avoiding duplication, (4) consolidate small journals, and (5) increase publication of specialized research in synoptic form. In sum, the proposals require an increase in flexibility of production, distribution, and use.

To meet the many problems that plague the current unintegrated journal situation, Garvey and Gottfredson (1976) recommend a delayed-integrative journal system whereby piecemeal articles would be delayed until a coherent series of research works could be synthesized into a single major article.

Time lag is another deterring factor with regard to published reports. A logjam exists in the formal communications system—that is, the flow of information through the professional journals. The process between the generation of a research development and its appearance in professional journals and abstracts can consume months or even years (Kaplan, 1958). In the field of psychology, for example, Garvey and Griffith (1967) found roughly a nine-month delay between submission of a journal article and its publication. Moreover, considerable time may elapse between the completion of a study and development of a manuscript for journal publication. Once submitted, the article may be rejected for lack of journal space (Kaplan, 1958).

The common delay in research publication may not always be bad. Delayed formal publication has the merit of being monitored or filtered information, which, when selectively cited in such reviews as the *Annual Review of Psychology* perhaps two or three years after publication, achieves acceptance as part of the pool of recognized knowledge. Garvey and Griffith (1971) note the different functions of formal and informal information transfer in psychology, viewed in terms of the published report and the working paper or technical report, respectively. The authors consider the working paper important because it often gives the most detailed account of procedures, instruments, and so on and because, being informal, it permits the researcher to speculate and to theorize more than the published article does.

**Computer Storage and Retrieval.** Vickers (1973), acknowledging a certain inevitability about the growing part that computers will play in future information systems and concerned about the costs of obtaining information, analyzed the operating budgets of eighteen computer-based information systems in Europe and the United States. He discovered that mechanized systems are more significantly affected by variations in management and staff costs than by technical factors such as depth of indexing, data preparation, or computer programming.

The phenomenal growth in automated information systems for science and technology is the subject of a striking article in *Science* by Doszkocs, Rapp, and Schoolman (1980). The authors assert that the rapid advances in computer technology in the 1970s have enabled large interactive scientific and technical retrieval systems to be implemented. The extent of this development is indicated by the statement that there are 528 publicly available bibliographical or bibliographical-related data bases containing 70 million citations or records spanning many subject areas.

Despite the impressive speed and flexibility of interactive retrieval systems, their impact has been less than it might be because of factors such as limited awareness of their existence, the uneven quality of retrieval devices, inadequate linkages among data bases, *"retrieval deluge" of material not found by researchers to be directly relevant to their interests,* and an inadequate supply of specially trained intermediaries.

The article by Doszkocs and associates presents further details concerning available bibliographical data bases, data banks, and "knowledge" bases. The last-named is the newest form of automated information retrieval system. It is based on analyzed or synthesized "knowledge" rather than on bibliographical records or numerical data.

Another article in *Science* (McGinnis, 1980) deals with the special problem of citation indexing in science, technology, and the humanities. McGinnis presents a critical review on the subject by Garfield (1979), who refers specifically to the Science Citation Index (SCI) and the Social Science Citation Index (SSCI). The idea behind the citation index is that authors reveal in the references they cite their judgment about the literature relevant to the topics they cover. Although citation indexes may serve other purposes, such as providing counts of the number of citations of works by given authors or institutions, the use most relevant to the utilization of knowledge relates to implications of the indexes for the location of pertinent information. For example, a network of researchers on a given specialized subject may conceivably emerge by consulting either of the indexes.

Wheeler and Foster (1977) briefly examine several technicalities in the use of computerized information searching in psychology. They review various stages in the procedure that a user of such a system adopts after choosing a data base, such as specification of either an overall category or a single term to structure the search for particular information. Advantages of an off-line output information retrieval system are enumerated: thoroughness, breadth of sources, speed, output format, Boolean combinations, productivity, recent references, and cost efficiency. Some limitations of computerized information searching are discussed with reference to recall, relevance, and searching skills.

In research settings, where there may be excessive involvement with elaborate data handling, Servi (1976) suggests that R&D managers can improve communication by being *more concerned with people and their ability to properly use complex data-handling technology than with data in the abstract.*

Johansen and DeGrasse (1979) report on the examination by a group of fifteen scientists of the effects of computer-based *teleconferencing* on working patterns. Computer conferencing is small-group communication through computers. Participants enter a conference by logging into a computer network and joining the discussion, which is recorded on an electronically stored transcript. In this study, questionnaires, usage statistics, conference transcripts, and interviews were used to gather data on working-pattern changes. Hurdles included psychological barriers to using keyboard devices as well as such practical problems as finding a terminal and paying for its use. However, assuming these initial barriers can be overcome, computer conferencing can increase accessibility to distantly located colleagues and information. It is concluded that although increased use of computer conferencing could encourage greater cooperation among researchers, it would require a definite change in a researcher's communication habits.

Kraemer (1977) takes a hard look at the actual value of computer technology transfer to local governments as compared with claims and expectations. He bases his evaluation on responses to questionnaires sent to data-processing managers and chief executives of several hundred cities and counties as part of the Urban Information Systems project supported by the National Science Foundation. He concludes that the appeal of technology transfer stems from several allegedly questionable notions, such as (1) that technologies are readily transferable from one site to another, (2) that high value is redeemable from

R&D investments through extensive "spinoff," (3) that users are able to transfer sophisticated technology without the need for making substantial development expenditures, and (4) that certain technologies, such as management techniques as instruments of reform, are capable of "modernizing" public administration.

Kraemer finds a number of disadvantages associated with differences between benefit claims and realities of actual transfer performance of computerized information systems in local governments:

1. Effective transfers occur only where there has been a great deal of early in-house development. It is when computing background is relatively undeveloped that governments are most often deceptively targeted for software transfer.
2. Shifts in budgetary expenditure occasioned by outside services may cause dislocations within the government organization.
3. Savings from computerized transfer occur only under the best of conditions.
4. Savings are meaningful only if the transfer-in application meets a real need in the government and is economical to implement, operate, and maintain.
5. Successful transfer requires technical sophistication by the host government.
6. In some instances, lack of standardized computer hardware and lack of programming languages are major barriers to application transfer among local governments.
7. The idea of some kind of national clearinghouse and resource center might be a good one, but such a center would be costly to build, would entail problems of updating, and would require local cooperation.

In sum, the author states that transfer is a logical idea and can have substantial benefits, *provided everything works right.*

Fortunately, the technology exists to improve communication, and already new institutions such as information analysis centers are evolving that may eventually permit a much more efficient and less costly utilization of the world's knowledge. The proportion of national budgets going into research will eventually necessitate such efficiencies, as will the growing recognition that basic scientific knowledge of a nonclassified, nonmilitary type might well be internationally shared. Such an improved information system will strengthen the interdependence of research institutions and confirm the value of a pluralistic institutional environment for research.

### Other Studies of Dissemination Means

**Comparative Studies.** Langrish and others (1972) examined the methods by which 102 technical ideas were brought into firms in the United Kingdom. They discovered that in all but a few cases the innovations were based on previous technology (sometimes quite old technology) rather than on scientific research, although scientists frequently were involved after the fact in the development and engineering phases of the innovation process.

Paine (1979) obtained data on the extent of use and the usefulness of a number of dissemination strategies employed by seventeen program developers in three types of settings: school (ten), home/residential (five), and work (two). The following list of eleven dissemination strategies is rank-ordered on the dimension of usefulness, with item number 1 the most useful. The number of program developers reporting the *use* (as distinguished from usefulness) of each is shown in parentheses.

1. Demonstration and training centers ($N = 11$)
2. Long-term training ($N = 13$)
3. Short-term training ($N = 17$)
4. Word of mouth ($N = 15$)
5. Nonprint media ($N = 14$)
6. Commercial publication ($N = 11$)
7. Publication list ($N = 12$)
8. Conference presentations ($N = 17$)
9. Professional communications ($N = 12$)
10. In-house materials ($N = 13$)
11. Professional publications ($N = 14$)

From the findings it is evident that extent of use and judgment of usefulness do not go hand in hand. For example, although demonstration and training centers were regarded as the most useful dissemination strategy, they were employed by only eleven of the seventeen program developers.

In an article on strategies for obtaining utilizable knowledge, Glaser (1980d), citing several approaches, consulted some forty persons, mainly practitioners such as physicians, nurses, rehabilitation counselors, and educators, on their information-seeking preferences when solving a problem. Consulting with knowledgeable people was found to take precedence over reference to written material. Access to an automated information retrieval system fell low on the list of responses.

Allen (1977) reports on a series of studies entailing two phases: (1) the determination of information patterns of about thirty-three research and development projects and (2) a study of person-to-person communication networks in thirteen R&D laboratories involving from 90 to 400 professionals. Eight sources of messages were designated: literature, vendors, customers, other external sources, laboratory technical staff, company research programs, analysis and experimentation, and previous personal experience. Data based on survey instruments (included as appendixes) were gathered on twin pairs of high- and low-achieving R&D projects. Various differences between pairs for both scientists and engineers were found in such factors as type of media employed, use of formal versus informal literature, degree of diversity of sources, and extent to which internal versus external sources were consulted. The role of the "technological gatekeeper" was found to be crucial.

The author suggests that more attention should be paid to the engineers and scientists as communicators. In studying barriers to internal and external communication, it was found that a "law of least effort" applied; geographical propinquity and architectual layout of laboratories affected communication flow.

Ettlie (1976) studied four types of information sources and their use during the whole innovation production process, basing his study on Ross's (1974) model of initiating and sustaining factors in utilization. Ross investigated four sources: impersonal external, personal external, impersonal internal, and personal internal. Ettlie demonstrates that the type of information use varies with the time of use within the process of innovation and utilization.

**Mass Media.** Mass media such as TV, radio, magazines, and newspapers are helpful in making the general public aware of problems or new approaches in social affairs, science, health, education, and many other fields, whereas interpersonal communication can build more credibility (Rogers, 1962a; Rogers and Svenning, 1969). Paisley (1968) observes that ideas are much more likely to be accepted if they come through channels that potential users respect but that actual application of innovative ideas depends more on ease of use than on the medium.

An informative review of "powerful research traditions" relative to mass media is provided in an article on communication and social change by Westley (1973). Embedded in these traditions are concepts such as the following:

1. Mass media have served as the communication instrument that human society needed to expand its frontiers, both intellectual and technical.
2. Mass media under certain conditions can serve as propaganda and can be manipulated to achieve conformity.
3. Power elites control the masses by controlling access to mass media.
4. Communications reflect the conditions of society and therefore cannot shape them.
5. Mass communication affects voting and other decisions through a two-step process, by first influencing opinion leaders, who then influence others.

Westley believes that the several traditions fail to give sufficient place to the already-formed values and preferences of the recipients of a communication. "Mass persuasion" needs to be viewed, as well, in terms of the way in which a culture provides for the resolution of problems in decision-making groups. Information not congruent with existing states is likely to be rejected.

Lin and Burt (1975) demonstrate the different parts played by three types of communication: the mass media, interpersonal channels, and local media. They define the last-named as those communication media that, though able to reach a large audience, are capable of customizing messages for different groups or geographical areas. The authors studied models of the three approaches in El Salvador. They report their findings as follows:

1. Mass-media users tended to be aware of an innovation earlier than other persons but had no greater tendency to adopt the innovation than those who were not mass-media users.
2. Persons who became aware of the innovation through the local media tended to be aware of the innovation late but were the only media users who subsequently tended to adopt the innovation.
3. Persons who became aware of the innovation through interpersonal sources as defined in this study tended to be aware of the innovation later than others and were less likely to adopt it than those who did not use interpersonal sources.

**Multiple Dissemination Methods.** It is apparent that dissemination efforts are frequently not limited to a single medium. The present section cites examples of multiple methods.

The channels of communication are not mutually exclusive, and several together are likely to have more impact than any one alone (Menzel, 1966b; Havelock, 1970). Designs for communicating significant research findings may include a combination of T-groups to increase mutual trust, factual presentations, discussion, brainstorming, role playing, and planning for action.

Manpower Science Services, Inc. (1974), has developed the concept of multimedia packaging of social science knowledge for dissemination purposes. In devising a manual on role modeling and role playing, for example, the agency assembled a set of audiotapes, workbooks on simulation, and a multimedia collection of workshop materials on group leadership techniques. The preparation of the package is based on a model comprising information retrieval, communication, diffusion, and adoption principles.

A "total dissemination push" is illustrated in the efforts of the U.S. Environmental Protection Agency to achieve technology transfer in the matter of municipal water-waste treatment facilities, as described by Crowe and Madancy (1974). The total program, which had demonstrable success, included seminars; publications in the form of design manuals, technical capsule reports, seminar publications, handbooks, process brochures, project brochures, newsletters; audiovisual media, including technical videotapes and nontechnical films; and presentations at professional conferences.

As part of an overall plan for achieving research utilization, Lippitt, in a report by Havelock (1974a), suggests the following implementation mechanisms:

1. Conference of technical resource people.
2. A technical resources panel on a regional basis.
3. An advisory committee.
4. Telephone contact.
5. A regional interagency exchange-of-practice-and-planning meeting.
6. Annual visiting committees.
7. Annual regional conference.
8. National products report.

It is evident that a diversified approach emphasizing interpersonal contact is favored.

Other illustrations of multiple strategies, together with their effects, will be found in Glaser and others (1967) and Fairweather, Sanders, and Tornatzky (1974).

The U.S. Department of Education has sponsored a variety of dissemination programs for the improvement of education. These measures initially reflected the pressure on education of the postwar "Big Science" knowledge explosion following the launching of Sputnik (Paisley and Paisley, 1973). Subsequently, the requirements of special groups (for example, racial minorities, the handicapped) exerted an influence on federal sponsorship of innovative programs and products. These efforts were backed by a number of laws, such as the Elementary and Secondary Education Act, Titles I, III, IV-C, V, and VII, that provided large appropriations for program development, modest amounts for research, and limited amounts for dissemination along with special services.

The pages that follow present brief descriptions and comments concerning some of the principal programs sponsored by the federal government.

1. *Educational Resources Information Centers (ERIC).* ERIC was established as a network of clearinghouses for acquiring, abstracting, indexing, and reproducing educational research information other than regularly published materials. The index material has become massive in scope.

Burchinal (1967) has proposed that, in addition to information services such as ERIC, there is need for small *local information services.* These would be staffed with information specialists who would be familiar with all the large information services, know the operational requirements of the systems, act as intermediaries between the user and the systems, and be able to provide feedback to the systems about information requirements of the user.

The idea of the use of field agents was picked up by Sieber, Louis, and Metzger (1974), who reported on the procedures and problems of retrieving and transmitting information from educational sources (such as ERIC) by means of field agents assigned to one urban and two rural school systems as part of a pilot state dissemination program. The authors note three aspects of the success of the agency program: (a) the program developed a model for future extension and retrieval programs in education, (b) field-agent generalists were shown to be superior to subject matter specialists, and (c) the majority of clients in all areas (70 to 90 percent) not only expressed the intention of using the service again but also recommended it to others.

2. *The National Diffusion Network (NDN).* The development of the National Diffusion Network (NDN) illustrates the

importance and the scope of efforts to achieve dissemination/ adoption in education (Magi Educational Services, Inc., 1975, and as later revised). The basic function of the NDN is to assist interested public and private schools in becoming aware of proven and successfully demonstrated, innovative educational ideas, products, and programs and in acquiring, through training and technical assistance, the competence necessary to adopt a proven educational program. The NDN involves the following:

- The Developer Demonstrators (DDs), usually Local Educa- tion Agencies (LEAs), including colleges and nonprofit insti- tutions that have developed exemplary education programs on the local level.
- State Facilitators (SFs), aiding other LEAs in their states to determine needs relative to NDN's pool of projects, perform- ing a linking function.
- The U.S. Department of Education, which provides the im- petus, funding, and technical assistance for establishing and maintaining the NDN and is responsible for monitoring and evaluating its implementation.
- LEAs and other educational institutions, including private schools, representing the terminals of the delivery system, the consumers whose needs are to be met through the adop- tion of the Developer Demonstrator projects.

3. *The Joint Dissemination Review Panel (JDRP).* The JDRP is the U.S. Department of Education's major internal quality control mechanism for its financially supported dissemi- nation activities. The JDRP's efforts help to identify programs of excellence for exemplary status. Its approved products and practices are used chiefly by the NDN.

The JDRP's *Ideabook* by Tallmadge (1977) describes this quality control mechanism. The *Ideabook* illustrates ways of gathering evidence of the effectiveness of educational innova- tions, thus serving as a guidebook for planning evaluations in an- ticipation of future submission to the JDRP, and it suggests how to bring current evidence of effectiveness together in a suc- cinct and forceful manner, thus enhancing the chances of JDRP approval and helping potential adopters compare products and their associated claims and match them with their educational needs.

The basic premise of the JDRP is that any claim of educational effectiveness must be established through compelling, objective, valid, and reliable evaluation of program results and data. Several conditions must be met in order to arrive at this determination. The panel's *Ideabook* and *Guidelines* have complete information about these conditions. The NDN annually publishes a catalogue of all JDRP-approved products and practices entitled *Educational Programs that Work*.

4. *The Research and Development Exchange (RDX)*, initiated in 1976 as part of the NIE's regional programs, is a network of regional educational laboratories and university R&D centers working to support state and local improvement efforts (Far West Laboratory for Educational Research and Development, 1979). The RDX supports local dissemination and school improvement groups by working through school districts, intermediate service agencies, state education agencies, and national education associations.

5. *Research and Development Utilization (RDU) program*. Yet another thrust of NIE in the interest of the utilization of educational R&D will be found in the institute-approved R&D Utilization (RDU) program, introduced in 1976. This program was designed to apply R&D *products or ideas* to school problems, to develop a *problem-solving process* whereby schools would systematically identify such problems and select and implement new ideas, and to organize a *linkage system* whereby national, state, and other external resources would be made available to school personnel (Louis, 1980). Thus, product dissemination and local capacity building were to be encouraged in an integrated way.

The RDU program differs from NDN in that the former is concerned equally with the use of R&D products *and* the development of local organizational capabilities to solve problems, while NDN aims primarily to diffuse exemplary practices and materials through reliance on empirical proof (provided through the JDRP) supporting claims for educational improvement. The

NDN also provides longitudinal training and technical assistance to potential adopters of procedures and materials within the product pool.

The number and variety of federally sponsored projects have resulted in various attempts at analysis and synthesis of findings. For example, a report by Emrick and Peterson (1978) summarizes and then synthesizes findings of the following major studies of various federally supported projects for educational dissemination and change:

- Sieber, Louis, and Metzger (1972): *The Use of Educational Knowledge: Evaluation of the Pilot State Dissemination Program* (2 vols.).
- Berman and others (1975/1977): *Federal Programs Supporting Educational Change*—Innovative Projects, ESEA Title III, Bilingual Education, ESEA Title VII, Vocational Education Act, 1968 Amendments, Part D, Exemplary Programs, and the Right-to-Read Program (8 vols.).
- Stearns and others (1975/1977): *Evaluation of the Field Test of Project Information Packages* (5 vols.).
- Emrick, with Peterson and Agarwala-Rogers (1977): *Evaluation of the National Diffusion Network* (2 vols.).
- Moore and others (1977): *Assistance Strategies of Six Groups That Facilitate Educational Change at the School/Community Level* (3 vols.).

The extensiveness of the federal support of the dissemination studies mentioned above is matched by the diversity of findings. However, the cross-study synthesis report did come up with the following five major generalizations:

1. Meaningful change occurs as a process, not as an event.
2. Directed personal intervention is by far the most potent technical support resource and may be a necessary condition for many forms of utilization.
3. Continuous personal participation of the implementing staff is needed to firmly root and sustain the utilization.
4. Administrators occupy a crucial role in supporting the utilization process.

5.  Descriptive, instructional, and support materials are needed, particularly for utilizations including organizational or instructional changes.

In another (unpublished) statement prepared in conjunction with a review of Emrick and Peterson's cross-study synthesis report, Spencer Ward (of NIE) depicts the five federally supported programs as (1) indicating program effectiveness in producing change in schools but failing to provide sufficient support for program continuation, (2) referring to capacity building only in the more limited meaning of ability to develop and sustain a given innovation, (3) underemphasizing the crucial role of the school administrator in the change process, (4) perceiving the functions of information provision, technical assistance, and helping the school system build its capacity to assess and improve education as external, separate, unintegrated roles with no attention to their interrelationships with school district specialists, evaluators, and staff development resource persons, (5) giving little attention to the nature and quality of the information to be conveyed to practitioners, and (6) shedding little light on the functions of the linking agent beyond emphasizing the importance of interpersonal contacts.

In sum, Ward suggests the need for long-term studies that simultaneously examine the program improvement process from the perspective of school personnel as well as the external resource system as the initiator of improvement.

Ward also served as commentator on the report (Bank and others, 1979) of a major conference on educational linkage —namely, the 1977 Belmont Conference jointly supported by the National Institute of Education and the U.S. Office of Education, now the U.S. Department of Education. In his statement Ward (1979) noted the significance of the management/leadership domain of a school system as it relates to linking and linkage support systems. The external linker stimulates information flow to and through people called "gatekeepers" at the various levels of the internal organizational hierarchy. Existing diffusion systems should be utilized as far as possible. A "functional complementarity" among schools and the resource support systems should be maintained. Financial support is a necessary concomitant. Local school and service centers may serve as a bridge to external resource systems.

In an epilogue to the Belmont Conference report by Bank and her associates, Ward sums up the support services needed for school functioning and practice improvement by listing four types of service—problem solving, resource finding, knowledge, and implementation support—all of which involve external and internal influence as well as personal and interpersonal skills. The four-way interactive model of dissemination implied above is seen as depicting a flexible linker role, whether enacted by an individual or by a group of linking personnel.

There have also been efforts to sort out and evaluate the several approaches. Among these may be mentioned studies by The NETWORK, Inc., which has announced a series of reports summarizing major federal programs (The NETWORK, Inc., 1981a, 1981b, 1981c, 1981d, 1981e, 1981f).

Dr. David Crandall, director of The NETWORK, Inc., has provided (personal correspondence) the following penetrating summary evaluation of the NDN's role and modus operandi as a network:

> The National Diffusion Network (NDN) provides us with a successful networking model in education. The NDN represents the first time among government programs that the charge of dissemination and spread of effective practices has been placed within a supportive network of actors. This strategy changes the locus of the initiative away from the government sponsors in Washington and places it instead in a multifaceted group of practitioners who take their cues as much from their clients and peers as from their monitors. The structure includes geographically dispersed process linkers called state facilitators, the originators of practices and products, and regional technical assistance units coordinated along functional lines by a partnership with designated federal program officers. No longer is dissemination and practice implementation left solely to the idiosyncratic notions of program developers and service providers whose

priorities are otherwise. Instead, rapid, widespread, and faithful program implementation is fostered by a network of linking agents who have endorsed a common agenda of their own making in concert with coordinated, consistent federal (national) leadership.

Some of the more prominent features of the NDN are as follows:

- *Sustained commitment to widespread diffusion of promising practices through the use of subnetworks on both content and process issues.* For example, the technical assistors constitute a subnetwork of *process* consultants who also use cadres of experts in matters of evaluation, publishing, and so on; through *content* subnetworks we (The NETWORK, Inc., Andover, Mass.), along with special education projects and Follow-Through programs, have banded together, thereby creating a "content" or problem-focused subnetwork.

- *Mechanisms for screening promising practices and selecting them for inclusion in the NDN, coupled with mechanisms for use by school-based practitioners.* The [Department of Education's] Joint Dissemination Review Panel reviews nominated projects for their educational and statistical significance. If a project is approved, it is eligible to compete for a Developer Demonstrator (D/D) grant. The users of the D/D programs (school-based practitioners) screen and select a project(s) for implementation in their school by matching their needs to the strengths of the different D/Ds; they do so through assistance from the linkers (process) and the developers (content) in awareness and training workshops.

- *A peer-to-peer training setup, whereby school-teachers and other local personnel help and train others like themselves.* This is markedly different from other government dissemination efforts, which relied primarily on practices and products developed by university and R&D staff who were usually not practitioners and not available to conduct training.

- *Arrangement for division of labor between pro-*

*cess (linkers) and content (developers) people.*
The effectiveness of the NDN's attempt to develop, disseminate, and supplement effective practices (Crandall & Associates, 1982) as compared with more complicated R&D efforts and commercial products and processes has been demonstrated and documented.

- *Setup of decentralized (regional) technical assistance function for all members of the network.* Through regional assistance centers, both developers and linkers can seek solutions to their problems and serve as consultants to their peers.
- *Provision of personalized attention to potential adopters,* for example, visible people in both developer and linker capacities helping the users select and implement their chosen innovation.

To summarize, then, the NDN is a successful, personalized, multilevel network. It encompasses identification of promising findings from R&D investments and a large variety of exemplary programs that are linked together by a system of subnetworks supported by a responsive technical assistance structure. Since its inception in 1974, it has maintained bipartisan support in Congress, with chief state school officers, and thousands of local educators. It has weathered a year with zero funding (1976) and has survived the current storm of budget cuts.

From the foregoing account of a number of the federally supported dissemination programs and mechanisms, it is apparent that a great body of experience with multiple methods has been accumulated. A challenge and opportunity now is for service delivery organizations in various fields to study these exemplary models for possible adaptation to their own interests and knowledge transfer needs.

## Summary Comments

Communication is obviously an essential mechanism for putting knowledge to use, for inducing desired changes, and for spreading knowledge and innovative change. This chapter skims the surface of the vast subject of communication but zeroes in on the practical findings and proposals reported in the literature as they pertain to the specific means for accomplishing the above-mentioned objectives.

Within the scope of the literature covered, one of the most prominent points made is the power of interpersonal communication for stimulating an interest in new ideas. Beginning with the early agricultural-extension-agent studies and moving into other areas such as the use of a new drug, a number of reports have stressed the importance of face-to-face communication. This includes informal contacts, conferences, seminars, workshops, demonstrations, trade fairs, and visits. An excellent summary regarding this general finding is offered by the Roberts and Larsen report (1971). To wit: Innovative ideas come primarily from personal contacts. Once an idea is initiated, however, many types of information sources are used even if they are inefficient. The single source of variance that could be manipulated to increase information utilization is personal interaction. If the ideas that come from such interaction provide the catalyst for information-seeking behaviors, other sources of information will be used.

Among reasons cited for the more limited use of written communication are (1) the overload created by a superabundance of printed matter, (2) the technical and limited nature of research reports, (3) the limited number of readable reviews, (4) the restricted quantity of abstracts and related services, (5) the increasing problems (especially in cost and delayed timing) of publication and library service, and (6) despite astounding technical advance, the problems of computer storage and retrieval.

The comparison between personal and written communication may be too pat and may reflect the limitation in outlook regarding the scope of change mentioned in the discussion of the change-agent/client relationship. Without denigrating the importance of personal contact, one wonders, for example, what medical progress would be like without medical textbooks and scientific reports in medical and other technical journals.

However, the problem of effective communication and

dissemination need not be viewed solely as a competition between one class of media and another. This is not to say that comparative studies of media should not be consulted. Rather, attention needs to be directed to the mix of the means for conveying desired messages, including the highly powerful potential of mass media of whatever type. The chapter closes with an account of several instances of multiple methods of achieving dissemination and cites the field of education as a prime example of a diversity of approaches.

# 13

**⁂**

# International Transfer
# of Technical Knowledge

**⁂**

The international transfer of technology is a process by which specialized technical information, management skills, or supporting resources from a supplier in one country (for the most part, a developed country) are coupled to the economic, social, and political mechanisms of a recipient country (for the most part, a developing country) to meet a defined set of the latter's needs. Two challenges thus arise: the harmonization of goals of the two concerned parties and the adaptation of appropriate structures and contractual arrangements to heighten goal achievement of each.

Serious difficulties arise because technology transfer is a nonintegrated innovation process—that is, not all the functions of innovation are conducted under a single integrated management (Robbins and Milliken, 1976; Brooks, 1967). Principles of facilitation are therefore needed to accommodate a wide range of technologies (for example, food production, supply and distribution of energy, public health), as well as to accommodate differences in socioeconomic characteristics of both supplier and recipient. Although the present review is concerned mainly with the process of knowledge utilization and innovation

336

change, certain substantive aspects of international transfer are included to give body to the discussion.

The transfer, borrowing, or diffusion of technology across national boundaries is as old as the use of fire and the crossbow. Nineteenth-century industrial development of the United States utilized technology from Western Europe. Several new features now characterize the international transfer process, however, and heighten its importance in world affairs. These include—

1. The conviction of developing nations that technology will facilitate large-scale and rapid industrialization to improve their standard of living and quality of life (Manzoor, 1977).

2. The growing ideological belief by developing peoples of their right to access of technology, parallel to rights of industrialized nations for access to their natural resources (Etemad, 1977).

3. Increased involvement by the United States, through its declaration on the New International Economic Order enunciating principles of equity, sovereign equality, and cooperation aimed toward global levels of economic/social development, as well as reduction of the increasing tension between developed and developing nations (Balasubramanyam, 1977).

4. The rapid and extensive internationalization of business, such as the multinational enterprise, increasingly centered in bases outside the United States (Clausen, 1972).

5. Decentralization of worldwide political power such as has been lodged in the United States and the Soviet Union relative to the growing importance of new nations and regional groupings (Clausen, 1972).

6. A modern revolution in global communications and transportation (Clausen, 1972).

7. Advances in the technology of information handling and dissemination that make use of computer-based services and satellite communication systems (Clausen, 1972; Hernandono, 1978; Adimorah, 1978; Price, 1975).

8. The increasing tendency to transfer sophisticated technology alone, instead of a packaged transfer of technology, capital, and managerial know-how (United Nations Conference on Trade and Development, UNCTAD, 1976).
9. The increased number of students receiving advanced scientific, technical, and managerial education in foreign countries (Kelman, 1974, 1975).
10. The growth in complexity and interdependence of public and private institutions involved in technology transfer (Wenk, 1979).

## Perspectives

Both developing and developed nations perceive technology as the crucible for future economic growth because it has proven capacity to generate wealth, to enhance material standards of living, to improve health, and to provide a wider range of personal options. Throughout this discussion, incidentally, technology is defined as more than technique—that is, more than science and engineering. It encompasses the totality of specialized means, including those of management, administration, and public policy, used to develop goods or services for human sustenance and comfort. Technology also has a deeper anthropological meaning. It is a key element of culture; it determines the relationship of a community with its natural environment and is the most concrete expression of values (Wenk, 1979). Sooner or later, each society that strives to upgrade its technical capability discovers that it is both unfeasible and socially counterproductive simply to paste a veneer of technology onto indigenous culture. Hence, transfers of technology require a high sensitivity to match technical resources congenially not only with social goals but also with infrastructure, or cultural/social foundations.

Four realities underpin a modern technological society, according to Wenk (1979). The first is that technology will be avidly sought as a touchstone toward progress. Second, technology acts as an organizing principle to concentrate power and wealth and thus plays a political role in our society; more and more key decisions involving technology transfer will result from government policy, rather than from classical market processes. Third, we are recognizing that technological initiatives induce capricious, unexpected, and unwanted side effects, often for innocent bystanders. Finally, natural resources, manufactured goods, information, and people freely cross the globe. So do pollutants, fads of youth culture, and the ethos of equality.

As consumer products project images of affluence and the mass media portray political freedom, an unintended result is that those less well off tend to instantly perceive their deprivation. They may then be stimulated positively to imitate or adapt, but they also may be stimulated negatively to nurse resentment, sharpening basic conflicts between the developed and the developing world. Although rhetoric at the United Nations often casts the issue in ideological terms, such conflicts must also be perceived as by-products of complexity, technological evolution, and mismatches in natural endowments and social norms. Those conflicts also may be perceived as stemming from devils, on the one hand, continuing colonialism under another name, and, on the other hand, a tendency to view industrial laggards as inferiors.

These conflicts have also been inflamed by debates on limits to growth. Beginning in 1972, a number of studies delineated global limits to food, minerals, energy, industrial capacity, and environmental resiliency. One study advocated a deliberate slowing of growth to avert catastrophe (Meadows and others, 1972). In the Third World, however, many saw this recommendation as a conspiracy of continued bondage and delay in self-realization. Fortunately, this attitude is softening. The United Nations Environmental Program (UNEP) announced a World Conservation Strategy in March 1980, involving both developed and developing nations. What this requires of recipient nations is a higher sensitivity in technical initiatives, to mitigate, moderate, or avoid inadvertent and unwanted external costs by anticipatory analysis. Technology assessment is one such form of preventive medicine. The greatest challenge, however, is how to get the patient into the doctor's office—that is, how to inculcate an appetite for impact assessment and for balancing long-term consequences against short-term rewards. Many of these issues were highlighted at the 1979 United Nations Conference on Science and Technology for Development.

## Technology Delivery Systems: A Social Process Model

Given these barriers to technology transfer, we are faced with idiosyncrasies in each that would allow few lessons from past enterprises for application to future problems.

Some holistic concept is required.

Wenk (1979) has proposed a technological delivery system (TDS) to explain the social processes involved. These incorporate inputs, outputs, organizational components, and information linkages. Inputs include specialized knowledge, capital, natural and human resources, and human values. Outputs include the intended goods or services and the unintended effects on social and physical environments. Distinctive organizations that play some role in shaping the desired output include research laboratories, firms, interest groups, governmental agencies and regulatory bodies, legislatures and the courts, and individual citizens. These organizations are laced by internal communications with widely dispersed points of decision making associated with goal setting, resource allocation, bargaining, conflict resolution, and performance analysis. Information thus constitutes the vital substance that animates components through an ensemble of market, political, legal, and social processes, so as to develop a coherent response to output demands.

In every TDS, government appears in key roles of authoritatively sensing and ranking priorities, generating policies and programs, and providing social support. Underpinning political behavior are traditions, customs, and values that both drive and modulate the behavior of bureaucratic apparatus.

Each specific purpose of consumer need defines a specialized TDS. Each TDS must satisfy three *functional criteria* (Robbins and Milliken, 1976): Technology must have a source; it must be produced; it must be delivered to achieve a social or economic profit. Wilkins (1974) classifies steps by which private companies of one nation transfer technology across international borders: (1) export of products, (2) export of patents, (3) technical assistance, and (4) extension abroad of the firm itself. Complementing these processes is another set, which depends on recipient initiatives: (1) importation of production processes, (2) commercialization of foreign patents in a domestic market, (3) arrangements to apply specialized technical assistance, and (4) acquisition of a complete technology with the assistance of a foreign investor.

In this transfer there need not be symmetry between the transmitting and the recipient organizations; one or the other or both may be public or private.

Finally, each TDS involves an array of such structures and processes as national policies, patents, codes of conduct, creation of technology centers, contractual and institutional arrangements, regional and subregional linkages, and support by international banking mechanisms or assistance from developed countries (Ewing, 1976).

The need for synthesizing activities involving technical information, technical assistance, and technology transfer is the theme of an article by Rubenstein (1976). The suggested umbrella term for all three is *technical exchange transaction* (TET). Varieties of TETs are depicted as reciprocal pairs, such as between source and receiver, and may be used by highly developed, intermediate, and less developed countries. The concomitant problems of transfer are detailed in each case. Units other than countries, whether they be organizations or individuals, are shown to follow similar patterns according to degree of technical sophistication.

The whole subject of coordinating the three components of TET is analyzed in terms of illustrative issues and research questions—for example, (1) How crucial is a common natural language to successful TETs? (2) Who pays for the TET and who benefits from it in time, energy, money, and lost opportunities? (3) Can (and how can) people be trained for the generalist role needed in the switching function of the TET process?

Discontinuity in the TET process is regarded as wasteful and possibly harmful; hence, research on and resolution of the problem of synthesis are regarded as imperative.

In presenting a basic position concerning the place of

communication in technological dissemination, particularly with regard to international transfer programs, Dar and Levis (1974) make the following points:

1. Communication with the country involved is required to help survey a new environment, raise people's aspirations, guide and control a dynamic process, and teach and share new skills.
2. The matter of identifying and encouraging key persons in various areas of endeavor is important.
3. Linkages between the parties concerned, particularly in oral rather than written form, need to be established.
4. In addition to key persons and gatekeepers, communication paths are necessary that involve political decision makers, planning and research agencies, various levels of administratration, and other persons or units.
5. A communication designed to convey necessary messages must make itself heard against competition by mass media and other communication channels.
6. Special emphasis and adaptation of the above considerations are particularly needed in a joint technology program across national lines.

### Models and Mechanisms of Technology Transfer

Technology transfer may be grouped under the following four models:

1. A *direct borrowing,* in which the government of a recipient country sets its development priorities and takes initiative to fulfill these objectives.

2. *Joint development* with collaboration between representatives of both the transferring and the recipient nation, with or without participation of third parties in planning and execution (Dar and Levis, 1974).

3. *The multinational enterprise* (MNE). Egea (1975) cites two mechanisms at the disposal of transnational corporations—first, direct investment by setting up wholly owned subsidiaries or joint ventures and, second, the licensing of technology to a wholly owned subsidiary or an independent party. The first

mode is preferred when technology being transmitted can be easily copied, the second when it can be subject to proprietary control.

Multinational enterprises attract considerable attention as technology suppliers, partly because they are a growing element of transfer, partly because of the potency of yield, and partly because of the perceived lack of symmetry in relationships with recipient countries, with the MNE having an unfair advantage in negotiations. Michalet (1976) has described their functioning as a production unit of scientific and technical know-how. The MNEs have the largest expenditures for development as compared with expenditures for either applied or basic research, but these enterprises are not necessarily the most inventive. A major share of their funds is spent for marketing research because they recognize that monopoly control of new products is short-lived and, therefore, returns from investments in innovation must be achieved rapidly.

With the evolving importance of MNEs as transfer agents, their power to circumvent or subvert intergovernmental relationships has been widely heralded. Of greater importance, however, is their interest in promoting world order and relaxation of nationalistic constraints. The uneasiness about multinationals stems largely from their relative immunity to accountability, for in their invisibility they are free to exploit weaknesses of individual nation-states that become dependent on them.

4. *Technical assistance of the sort provided by the United States through AID.* Such programs are often believed to involve the sending of money abroad, but this is not so. AID dollars buy from domestic sources (over 4,000 American companies) goods and services that are exported rather than funds. Such assistance is intended to foster psychological and technical independence by recipient countries, but in practice it may not (Bader, 1977). It has also been asserted that the foreign assistance does not always represent the best of American technology, often being obsolete, overpriced, and unsuited to the labor-intensive requirements of the nation. And such technologies are often standardized rather than custom-fitted to the particular needs and culture of the recipient.

## Social and Economic Aspects
## of Technological Transfer

The harmonious coupling of transferrer to recipient fundamentally involves a convergence of interests. For the former, these may include the promotion of research, advancement of foreign policy or commercial interests, and humanitarian and educational concerns, taken singly or in combination. A similar set of mixed motives drives the recipient country (Pontecorvo and Wilkinson, 1974). Although serious conflicts between these two sets of interests arise, as discussed later, many shortfalls in performance occur from ignorance, inexperience, human error, gaps in communication, fallibility, and accident.

**Preconditions and Barriers.** It is essential to inventory preconditions in the recipient country that enhance the prospects of a socially satisfactory transfer. Pontecorvo cites three preconditions: the severity of need, as defined in relation to GNP; the recipient's potential to muster human and material resources; and the recipient's full economic participation, involving government, industrial management skills, and the infrastructure capacity to absorb scientific and technical matter. Kojima (1977) and Vernon (1966) cite the following requisites: (1) the production function should require a significant input of labor, (2) products should have elasticity of demand, (3) production processes should not rely heavily on external economies, (4) products should be based on standard specifications and produced for inventory without fear of obsolescence, (5) items should be of high enough value to absorb freight costs, and finally, (6) the most suitable manufacturing industry would be one that is traditional, labor-intensive, well standardized, and price-competitive.

Jones (1976) approaches the question of preconditions by identifying two common engineering failings: inattention to critical detail during initial stages of a project and the need to adopt processes to minimize capital requirements. Plant reliability in a hostile climate with poor maintenance is a more important consideration than cost.

Wilkins (1974) recognizes at least twelve *barriers* to overcome for effective diffusion of technology: (1) insufficient demand, (2) lack of capital, (3) lack of natural resources, (4) cost of labor, (5) lack of sufficient technical skills or education to absorb know-how, (6) problems in economies of scale represented by mismatch in resources between transmitting and recipient organizations, (7) infrastructure barriers, (8) cultural barriers, (9) language barriers, (10) administrative barriers represented by mismatches in priorities, (11) inadequate business and management skills or organizational structures, and (12) basic management attitudes hostile to innovation. Time lags in the initial adoption and in the absorption of the technology by the host country provide evidence of weakness in the transfer process (Wilkins, 1974; Rogers, 1962a; Rogers and Shoemaker, 1971).

**Examples of Shortfall in Technology Transfer.** Shortfall in social performance of technology transfer can be defined more dramatically through specific examples than through abstract principles. Bucklin (1976) describes marketing of food products in rapidly growing urban centers as a major distribution challenge. Small, undercapitalized and weakly managed firms, clogged retail and wholesale terminals, high food spoilage rates, and pervasive distrust of middlemen are found to be sources of underachievement by recipient nations in delivering food to the urban poor.

To improve effectiveness requires certain *change agents* in recipient countries, coupled with the exercise of power to alter those patterns of social, political, or economic activity that enfeeble transfer. Bucklin (1976) and Rogers (1962a) suggest tests of potency with respect to such questions as these: (1) Is the system expanding proportionally to the population growth? (2) Are facilities being maintained to desired standards? (3) Are facilities available to all income groups? (4) Are the key institutions generating sufficient revenue to meet costs, both internal and external?

Hawthorne (1976) focuses attention on infrastructure, with the proposition that the level of technology that can be effectively transferred gravitates toward the level of the industrial structure into which it is to be absorbed. He then advances the notion of *technological multipliers* that improve infrastructure through carefully designed policy to produce results greatly in excess of the effort and cost involved in the infrastructure development. If savings from a technological transfer are evident on a national, state, or village level but not for the individual consumer, then Parikh (1978) urges a different strategy of incentive compensation to the user to win and maintain acceptance.

With both supplier and recipient, a balance is required between long- and short-term behavior of the sociopolitical system. Rather than long-range planning, aids to decision making require building into the transfer process ways and means of asking the question "What might happen if . . . ?" or "What may happen unless . . . ?," thereby forcing the identification of alternative tactics and strategies, the delineation of consequences of each, and their evaluation in order that choices will have a higher probability of producing the overall desired outcomes.

## Components of Technology Transfer

**Labor.** Economic history points to a progression as countries develop from labor-intensive toward more capital-intensive production. Associated with this transition is a movement from primary production—say, of natural resources—to manufacturing and then to service industries. Thus, the mix of labor and capital may change as nations become more technologically sophisticated. Another factor that conditions the appropriate mix is the interest rate for capital. At a time when interest rates are rising steeply, there is more incentive to moderate the role of capital-intensive production.

On the issue of labor productivity, Nelson (1968) points out that the value added per worker in manufacturing varies widely from one country to another. He concludes that the quality of labor does not alone account for all of the differences: Many are the consequence of the *mix* of the amount of capital and the quality of labor. Nelson then concludes that the emphasis in developing countries on low capital expenditures may inadvertently blunt the achievement of objectives.

**Capital.** Whatever the labor-intensivity, some accumulation of capital is necessary for adaptation of a technology. A great deal therefore depends on who makes the decisions and has the power to implement them with regard to the interest rate and the type of capital involved. Kaplinsky (1976) notes that, in conflicts or power struggles between supplier and recipient of technology, conflict resolution ultimately stems from the ability to mobilize the necessary technical and financial resources for the transfer function.

**Research and Development.** With technology so dependent on specialized knowledge, the production of new knowledge through scientific research and development is a significant factor in innovation. With 98 percent of all R&D expenditures being undertaken in highly industrialized nations, Egea (1975) argues that an aggressive and well-planned scientific and technological effort is urgently needed by the less developed nations. Increased capacity would reduce technological dependence, especially on multinational enterprises, and would improve the recipients' screening capacity in selecting technology targets. In addition, research and development are ingredients of the education and training system.

Further, Egea highlights the irrationality of the dissemination process: Information needed for development must be purchased under circumstances in which obtaining what is needed is dependent on knowing what is available. Lack of such knowledge tends to limit the choice of the developing country.

Properly integrated, the local science system may be both strengthened and linked with production units, rather than, as often happens, linked internationally with other scientists but isolated domestically. Sometimes a recipient industry might prefer foreign R&D because it gains access to knowledge that is technically less risky, is proven in practice, and is based on marketing experience, a handmaiden to successful transfer. But then, as N. Clark (1975) points out, prospects shrink for a viable indigenous alternative: Skilled personnel may leave for better overseas jobs and local laboratories turn more toward pure science. Science then becomes an intellectual consumption item enjoyed by an educated elite, and this tendency leaks over to the education system itself.

This issue points up the importance of differentiating between science and technology. New knowledge through basic research is generated worldwide and follows an ethic of open publication, so that the results of discovery are seldom regarded as proprietary. Clearly, scientists in a developing country must be competent to utilize the results of discoveries made elsewhere, but the great majority of such persons are not satisfied with simply interpreting others' results. They would prefer to engage in research themselves and gain the prestige of identity that goes with individual contributions to the scientific pool. Here we find a major distinction between scientists and engineers (Jones, 1976). The engineering profession focuses on application and adaptation, and its reward system emphasizes "making a machine work," rather than gaining personal identity. As developing countries nourish R&D, they are obliged to seek a balance between basic science and application.

Unfortunately, the problem is sometimes exacerbated when scientists in a developed country try to assist those in a less developed one by applying their own standards and ethos. For example, in the marine science field, with a tradition of international cooperation (Ross and Smith, 1974), joint programs were not always successful. Foreign scientists often had insufficient background and were inadequately funded; there were language and cultural barriers; a true spirit of partnership failed to develop; inadequate attention was given to enhanced training of scientists from developing nations; and collaboration among scientists from different countries was often conducted as a blend of two separate projects, rather than through integrated planning. Finally, scientists from developing countries often failed to distinguish unique characteristics of each recipient country—characteristics that should be taken into account to render partnerships viable.

Information. Since the main product of research and development is information or knowledge, its generation, storage, retrieval, dissemination, translation, and integration into the technology-transfer system are essential (Adimorah, 1978). The United Nations General Assembly, at its thirtieth session, in 1975, adopted a resolution on establishment of networks to exchange technological information, and in 1976 it established an Interagency Task Force on Information Systems (IATFIS). At its fifth session, IATFIS concluded that the concept of networks had been tested by studies at national, regional, and international levels and found valid at each level. Effectiveness of networks was said to depend on identification, by recipient nations and regions, of information relevant to specific needs and on the adaptation of existing dissemination systems, including telecommunication, to meet the needs of various specialized users.

These communication requirements indirectly reflect the fact that merely better technological aids to information handling are not enough. Rather, a human/machine interpretive system must be interposed between the client and the information pool in order that user needs can be interpreted, on the one hand, and technical information be selectively withdrawn and packaged, on the other. The task force concluded that the above concepts could be built into existing institutions and that no new international superstructure was required. Communication networking, incidentally, would also make it possible to decentralize information libraries, with access to all everywhere. Niehoff (1967) also emphasizes the need to match the information system to local cultural patterns and utilization behavior.

**Infrastructure.** The role of recipient infrastructure in facilitating transfer is widely recognized: The character of the value system and of the operational social, economic, and political systems, the professional capabilities for handling technical information, the presence of managerial skills, and the ability to bargain with technology suppliers all enter the picture. So, of course, does the expression of political power and political will. Indeed, as Helleiner (1975) points out, since social costs arising from the introduction of technology have to be reckoned with, and skills for government administration are increasingly available in recipient nations, traditional arguments against government controls are less persuasive. Hawthorne (1976) tabulates elements in technology transfer that are critically dependent on the technical infrastructure, such as engineering, product technology, manufacturing technology, and corporate organization.

**Education and Training.** From the foregoing it is clear that education plays a key role in accelerating processes of technology assimilation. Quintero-Alfaro (1972) proposes three principles to be kept in mind when trying to effect educational change in societies with less advanced technology:

1. The principle of economy, by focusing learning compatible with basic motivations of the recipient population.
2. The principle of cultural continuity.
3. The principle of human perspective, by active involvement of all citizens in the design and implementation of strengthened educational systems.

Havelock and Huberman (1978) have formulated a preliminary theory of how and why educational change occurs in different settings, with implications for managing such change. The issue is not simply one of more education but of what *kind* of education. In developing countries, educational innovation attempts often tend to be overambitious in the amount of time, energy, and material resources invested and the degree of rapid and massive changes expected. To survive, innovations must receive support from leaders; there must be active participation from below, including that of teachers, students, and the community. Smaller, well-planned, locally originated innovations appear to have a relatively high rate of success.

Dore (1975) challenges educational priorities in many developing nations that produce disastrous numbers of overeducated unemployed while failing to raise the overall educational level. He answers with two strategies. The first is to engage in *marginal measures* that would reduce salary differentials, increase the cost of higher education, provide loans rather than state subsidies for higher education, encourage employers to pay less attention to paper qualifications and more to job performance, switch resources from higher education to the primary level, intensify efforts to introduce relevant curricula in primary schools, and improve vocational education. His other alternative is to seek *structural reform* in the educational system. Such radical changes may be needed when tradition is too strong. Such reform can be accomplished by relying on apprenticeship more than formal precareer training and by relying on tests for aptitude for higher-level education and training in proportion to predicted employment opportunities. Then primary and junior secondary schools could concentrate on the needs of the majority of the population who would not proceed to further education, rather than on advanced students concerned only with getting the B.A. ticket of entry—who are not likely to succeed in finding jobs. A few countries, such as China, have already adopted this system.

The importance of training is illustrated by Husseiny (1977), who regards human capital as a major element in regard to nuclear technology transfer. He notes the importance of identifying requirements in various skill categories and of obtaining qualified personnel. Where foreign experts are employed, language barriers may be critical. Masters (1978), in dealing with the same question of nuclear energy training, found that often the most pressing needs do not revolve around highly sophisticated subject matter but on such mundane operations as organizing a filing system.

**Decision Making and the Control of Power.** The selection of which technology to transfer, the mobilization of the necessary input resources, the sensing of impediments to successful accomplishment, and ultimately the delivery of the intended product or service with a minimum of problems involve a series of complex decisions by all the major partners in the transfer enterprise. In turn, these decisions and the capability for their implementation depend on control of power in the system. Kaplinsky (1976) tabulates five such areas: entrepreneurial, organizational, financial, staffing, and invention. Distinctions must be drawn between the *substance* and the *appearance* of such control. For example, although equity considerations may be reflected in power distribution, they are seldom the source of power. As mentioned earlier, the test of viability is the capacity to accumulate resources, and this capacity may often be screened by or confused with appearances.

On the recipient side of the equation, attention is focused on the increased role of the host government. We find that technology contracts between recipient industries and representatives of supplier countries are appraised by public authorities who may refuse permission on the basis of price, restrictive conditions, local availability of comparable knowledge, or economic or social value to the country. Often the controlling role of government is achieved through industrial licensing, which restricts the number of firms and the degree of differentiation in each product or industry (Helleiner, 1975). Control of consumptive technology may be exercised, as well as control over production technology. Finally, government may seek to influence the overall strategy of development directly or indirectly through policies on taxes, tariffs, licensing, and government expenditures.

Most of these interventions by government are aimed at heading off abuses by multinational firms that supply technology. But in any scheme, potential exists for improper influence and corruption. Further, in government, expertise and administrative capacities may be limited.

Finally, it must be recognized that government plays a role of integrating heterogeneous class interests in recipient countries. The key questions, therefore, are not whether government intervention is increasing but what its character is and how much intervention is exercised.

## Appropriate Technology

Considering the needs and the capabilities of recipient nations, a good deal of attention has recently been focused on the notion of *appropriate technology*. This term and its equivalents, *alternative* and *intermediate technology*, have been variously defined (often pejoratively). Together these three terms, unfortunately, define a hierarchy between technologically advanced and less advanced nations (Helleiner, 1975). The endeavor in technology transfer is always to find the most appropriate medium and methods. Perhaps the best way to approach the issues of appropriate technology is simply to base the ultimate choices on a far more sensitive appreciation of all the elements involved in technological delivery systems and of controlling forces and to approach with candor the strengths and weaknesses of both recipient and supplier.

## Case Studies

Characteristics and problems of technology transfer can be illuminated through the examples of nuclear energy and of medicine. As to *energy,* it is universally recognized that industrialization increases demand. Aspiring nations are accordingly obliged to provide for their rapidly growing energy needs. Given their often meager resources of fossil fuels, they are bound to consider nuclear energy an attractive option. The technologically advanced nations with nuclear competence have not, at least in the early stages, developed policies and practices that would facilitate the transfer of nuclear technology in other than a piecemeal and disorderly manner (Etemad, 1977). The processes of transfer are also manipulated over the issues of dangers that accompany nuclear energy, the questions of safe disposal of radioactive waste, and, more prominently, the issue of proliferation of nuclear materials that have the potential of being diverted for weapons and their use or threat of use by irresponsible parties. Manzoor (1977) notes that nuclear energy carries with it a high dependency that supplier nations endeavor to preserve. He alleges unilateral and secretive decision making and club diplomacy by uranium suppliers.

Whatever the reasons, it is clear that there is an enormous demand among developing nations for the nuclear option. But smooth and effective transfer has not been achieved through existing techniques of control. Appeals to lubrication of this process through equity among nations, in the interest of the world order, are difficult to reconcile with the continued high threat of world terrorism. Leong (1978) takes the view that, at the operating level, the transfer of nuclear power-plant technology has been successful, so that the problem exists mainly at a high policy level.

The international transfer of *medical technology* is carried out through four transfer agents—medical education and research, multinational corporate transactions, technical assistance by the World Health Organization, and bilateral foreign aid programs. Bader (1977) sets forth a number of deficiencies: overemphasis on diagnosis and treatment of disease rather than prevention, exaggerated emphasis on research, depletion of resources for expensive equipment, the brain drain of professionals to developed countries, inappropriate promotion of pharmaceuticals and infant feeding formulas, and priority construction of capital-intensive teaching hospitals that serve a small, elite minority rather than the advocacy of preventive measures and health promotion among large populations.

To correct these practices, Bader proposes monitoring of international medical transfer, including codes of conduct, and developing intermediate technologies scaled to broader human needs, with relatively more emphasis on public health measures rather than interventions (Krishnan, 1975; Rich, 1973).

Key health factors such as endemic proportions of communicable diseases and parasitic afflictions often serve as barriers to economic development. (See also Kuhner, 1971; Griffith, Ramana, and Mashaal, 1971.)

## Side Effects

Whether in developed or in developing nations, a technology designed to produce particular goods or services is always accompanied by indirect effects. These effects are often not discovered until a considerable lapse of time from the start of the technological initiative, with the result that correctives are economically expensive or politically unfeasible. Sometimes the side effects are ecologically irreversible.

One of the most common impacts concerns adverse effects on the environment. Developing nations have been the least willing to make the necessary trade-offs that would either slow economic growth or entail costs of environmental protection, if the costs would limit the expected payoff.

It must be recognized, however, that the diffusion of technology into the fabric of a traditional culture is bound to have intense socioeconomic repercussions. Some can be absorbed gracefully, but some have the effect of destabilizing the internal social structure and thus, in the long run, defeating the intended accomplishments.

The importance of recognizing the potential side effects of technological initiatives, thus enabling mitigation or prevention, is highlighted by Wenk's (1979) concept of technology as an amplifier. Technology has long been understood to be an amplifier of human muscle through the lever and the wheel. More recently, its role has been recognized as an amplifier of the human mind. Now we find that technology is a *social* amplifier—of social appetites, of social complexity, of social conflict, of social "dis-benefits," of the role of governments (and, thus, an amplifier also of their weaknesses).

Here, then, lies the rationale for technology assessment, to provide those making decisions with systematic techniques to estimate side effects.

## Symbiosis and Conflicts

Assessing different interests of the technology supplier organization and the recipient inevitably discloses conflicts in goals, in motivation, in style, in technique, in timetables, and, of course, in the cultures themselves. Much attention is focused on reconciling the heavy-handed approaches of international firms with the disruptive political and economic policies under which they attempt to operate. Hostile attitudes of developing nations toward international business have long and well-documented historical precedents because of the repeated exploitation of developing nations. At the heart of these conflicts is a difference in ideological perspective. The developing nations hold that *both* natural resources and technology are essential legacies of humankind. Natural resources are geographically bounded, but this should not deprive any sectors of easy, equitable, and legitimate access. They hold the same point of view with regard to science and technology, in direct conflict with the viewpoint held by advanced nations (or firms within them) of nearly absolute sovereignty over the specialized knowledge involved (Etemad, 1977).

Much of the hostility toward industrialized suppliers is aimed at multinational enterprise. N. Clark (1975) analyzes how the MNE influences relationships with developing countries. Through different devices, such as the wholly owned subsidiary, joint-venture arrangements, and license contracts, the MNE may create dependence by modifying the balance of overseas payments, employment in modern and traditional sectors, income distribution, the structure of local capital markets, and, ultimately, the pace and pattern of economic development. Clark goes on to formulate a theory of dependence activities and effects:

1. Placing underdeveloped countries, especially the smaller ones, in a weak bargaining position, especially with highly complex technology.

2. Modulating the behavior of the local company or subsidiary through restrictive clauses built into license contracts, restrictions of exports to third countries, tying imports of intermediaries to those of affiliated companies, prohibition of diversification, nondisclosure clauses, limits on outputs and price, revocation of patent rights at the end of a specified period, minimal royalty clauses, and so on.

3. Imposing monopolistic rents that may soak up a sizable fraction of reinvestable surplus by repatriation of profits to parent-company countries. Then, technology, instead of increasing growth rates, lowers them through its channeling of the reinvestable surplus.

4. Affecting not only the pace of growth but also its pattern.

Internationally determined consumption patterns of elite groups create a climate in which the foreign-based MNE flourishes, so as to induce further inequality of income. In turn, such unequal income distribution alters the pattern of consumption in a way suited to the interests of the MNE but inimical to the long-term social and economic reform of the recipient country.

Many of these features are summed up in grievances evident in the declaration of the New International Economic Order at the United Nations. One overall strategy to meet these problems, and the one given highest priority in U.N. discussions, concerns the dissemination of information so as to increase access to multiple sources of technology and thus reduce monopoly controls. In turn, this anticipates the strengthening of science policy capabilities within developing countries, so that they may intervene in relationships of MNEs with those recipient-country firms that would otherwise accede to monopoly transfers.

To achieve their locally determined social and economic goals and at the same time maintain parity in negotiations with technology suppliers, the developing nations have tried to develop a number of strategies. Ikonicoff (1974) recommends three: industrialization to induce local substitution for imports, particularly of consumer goods that cater to the elite; deliberate choice of priorities for needs of the total population for economic growth; and labor-intensive, rather than capital-intensive, program methods. Ewing (1976) formulates somewhat different development strategies: emphasis on rapid industrial growth, with priority on intermediate and capital goods, with a view to transforming the entire structure of the economy; export-oriented industrialization; and development of the rural sector, both through agriculture and through medium scale-industry.

The United Nations Conference on Trade and Development (UNCTAD) Secretariat (1976) elaborates development strategies in terms of a disciplined sequence of related activities: (1) identification of technological needs, (2) information on alternative sources of such technology, (3) evaluation and selection of the most appropriate technology, (4) breakdown of the technology package into components that must be imported and those that can be locally supplied, (5) negotiation of the best possible terms and conditions for the technology to be imported, (6) adaptation and absorption of imported technology and development of indigenous capabilities, and (7) dissemination of newly acquired technology to other potential users.

## Conflict Resolution

Much of the literature concerned with achievement of a fair and symmetrical relationship between technology supplier and recipient focuses on the elegance in execution of management strategies and bargaining skills. Kelman (1974), however, draws on theories of *attitude change* that emphasize the role of positive attitudes in achieving the goals of each party with a minimum of friction. Development of effective relations involves providing new information about other countries and peoples, followed by explicit personal interaction between the nationals of the two countries involved. Both parties thus have opportunity and motivation to see the other in a favorable light; constructive perceptions usually follow friendly interactions.

In acting as the "group of 77," a body from the developing countries at the General Assembly of the United Nations, many nations adopt a far more structured and legalistic approach. They favor the establishment of a *code of conduct* (Roffe, 1977). Such a code would govern the acquisition, adaptation, and assimilation of technology through prohibition of restrictions on use or on further acquisition of technology, so as not to constrain continued importation, the purchase of equipment and spare parts, or the purchase of technical or managerial skills. Such a code would also deal with payments, so as to overcome (1) obligations of recipient nations to convert payments into capital stock, (2) constraints on the duration of transactions, and (3) practices that exempt the supplier from liability consequent on defects in goods produced by the recipient with the help of the technology acquired (Solo, 1976).

Drafts of a proposed code have been prepared by various parties and were found to differ over such issues as rights of access to technology; freedom of parties to determine the terms of arrangements, applicable laws, and a forum for settling disputes; extension of a code of transactions within and between related companies; international contractual arrangements; guarantees and responsibilities of parties, confidentiality; protection and defined terms of proprietary information; and legal character of the code of conduct.

Increasingly, *the U.N. has become an informal standard-making body* to govern technology-transfer relations between developing and developed nations. One of the major issues, according to Lall (1976), concerns the patent system. A major question is whether abuses of international systems of granting special protection to innovators can be reformed by more-stringent laws in recipient nations. Lall also notes that refinement and adoption of an improved international patent system will be more important to less developed countries that remain capitalist than to those that follow a socialist pattern. Put another way, the role of the patent system in the transfer of technology depends significantly on the political/economic structure of the recipient nation.

Dessemontet (1977) expands on the legal aspects of patent barter and arbitration, particularly examining implications of licensee law. Agreement seems widespread, however, that transnational patent laws do not fit into existing national systems of law and that far more imaginative solutions in dealing with patents may therefore be required. The literature is silent on the high transaction costs associated with patent litigation and the trade-offs that may be considered in order to minimize such nonproductive costs to all parties concerned.

## Summary Comments

This chapter has treated the subject of knowledge transfer and resulting change in a different manner than the other chapters of this review. Previous chapters remind the reader that substantive aspects of knowledge or change should not be neglected while treating procedural matters. This chapter, however, gives equal importance to substantive and procedural considerations. A discerning analysis may reveal that no essential procedural differences exist between international transfer of technology and strategies to facilitate knowledge utilization within a country, but at least on the surface, the special conditions of the transnational process lend support to separate treatment.

This chapter demonstrates variances in the details that call for consideration as particular programs for dissemination are studied or put into practice. Among the substantive and special aspects of international transfer of technology are such problems as organizing and managing an enterprise under two sets of governmental laws and regulations, diverse economic interests, cultural proclivities, language modes, personnel capabilities, and technological statuses.

The differences require various adaptations in the application of principles and procedures ordinarily suited to meeting the objectives of knowledge transfer and utilization and the introduction of change.

It may be well to note how political, economic, and cultural factors take on primary importance in the matter of international transfer of technology in a world geographically diverse in the distribution of technological information and of natural resources. Superficially, a process in interchange and leveling seems to be occurring, but the phenomenon is far more complicated than that of "water seeking its own level."

# 14

### Relating Research
### and Development
### to Practice

We next consider the role of universities as sources of knowledge, the interrelation of basic and applied research, the orientation of researchers and practitioners in relation to utilization, and collaboration in several illustrative fields. The discussion concludes with a consideration of the relation of research to policy making.

## Role of Universities

The way universities perceive their role and their policies in conducting applied research determines, to an appreciable degree, the extent to which knowledge is put to use.

Studies reported by Mulkay (1972a) support the observed primacy of the universities in knowledge production. Traditionally, utilization was looked on as a secondary process, capable of being isolated effectively from research and of being separately ordered. In this view, after the conclusions of research were derived, ways of utilizing them were developed.

361

Although knowledge continues to be valued for its own sake by many members of the academic community, increasing attention has been paid to the application of validated knowledge in political decisions, in economic planning, and in social affairs, to cite but a few examples.

The fact that the role of university faculty members in the transfer of technological information is being explored (Sincoff and Dajani, 1976) is in itself an indication of a changing relationship between developers of knowledge and users. These authors examined the factors underlying the transfer of technological information by university faculty members, the demands made on public agencies and institutions of higher learning, the tendency toward conflict between intradisciplinary and interdisciplinary cohesiveness among faculty members, and methodological approaches that can be used in achieving technology transfer.

Mulkay (1972a), in an analysis of various characteristics of the "research community," follows others in identifying the salient rewards within the university as attached to professional recognition. Rewards vary in accordance with the quantity and, more significantly, the perceived quality of information supplied to the scientific community (Cole and Cole, 1968). Consequently, although researchers may be motivated by the concern to solve certain socially defined problems or by desire for extra financial returns from grant/contract awards, it is likely that their contributions to knowledge will be rewarded mostly by various forms of desired recognition. Moreover, that recognition will depend on conformity to expectations of "appropriateness," operating within the research network.

Sanctions in the university encourage the development of knowledge for its own sake and the publication of knowledge as an end goal. These sanctions may inhibit the development of applied knowledge and the application of theoretical knowledge.

Branscomb (1973) believes that self-motivated university research alone cannot be relied on to solve major social problems, although with sufficient resources a university could, over time, develop or recruit the necessary range of talents and skills to do so. Typically, such an effort would be incompatible with the other missions of the university—the development of new conceptual knowledge and the education of students. But universities, coupled with action agencies, can contribute to a broad examination of the way problems are conceived and the identification of significant variables and major phenomena.

Provided that the support of political institutions is granted, according to Branscomb, university research can play an effective role in such areas as health care delivery, housing, environmental protection, and urban transportation. However, excellent university reports in these areas often go unread except by other university researchers or the intellectually alert segments of the general public. Consequently, they have little influence, states Branscomb, on political or administrative decision makers.

It might be of interest to note the role of the university in knowledge use in a communist-dominated country. The Technical University of Wroclaw, Poland, has worked out three organizational patterns of university/industry interrelations (Pelc, 1978):

1. The university undertakes individual research tasks on the basis of separate short-term agreements with industry.
2. The university, together with industry, designs complex projects and takes part in their execution up to final implementation on an industrial scale.
3. The university is a permanent partner of an industrial organization. On the basis of long-term agreements, it conducts continuous analysis of the technological level and conditions of manufacturing processes and initiates new undertakings, improvements, and even complex projects.

Each of these forms has some advantages. Application of each of them depends on mutual matching of the partners. For the most part, the first kind of cooperation is used initially. Variants 2 and 3 tend to occur after a period of further experience (usually a few years). Current information flow depends more on a system of personal contacts than on the official status of the agreements. In addition to the three variants mentioned above,

Pelc observes that it is possible to introduce a form of agreement in which institutional barriers between the partners disappear. For example, common innovation groups may be formed which employ the labor representing both partners, and in which the results obtained from the introduction of new products bring benefits both to the producers and to the university.

Pelc further proposes that—

1. Research projects should be consistent with the educational program and mission of the university.
2. Management of the university should approve the individual research project proposals, taking into account both the need for academic freedom and the motivation of research staff toward scientific projects. In addition, it should consider access to governmental and industrial funds and the correlation of projects with national and industrial goals.
3. Economic effectiveness of R&D activity in a university is not comparable with that in other research institutions, such as industrial ones, because of the importance the university places on long-term exploration of problems and development of new disciplines.

### Interrelation of Basic and Applied Research

The relation between knowledge and action is a subject that goes back historically to the ancient Greeks (at least). Rich (1979c) succinctly traces the history of the place of knowledge and action in human thinking.

In recent times the familiar pattern of research, development, and dissemination (RD&D) essentially reflects a knowledge-to-action ideology. However, the linear approach is increasingly being replaced by *circular* models, in which the extension of knowledge is initiated at any point on a holistic knowledge-utilization-knowledge circuit and is developed by forward and backward movements around the circle, with simultaneous processing of many variables. Servi (1976) calls this a reiterative mode, in which the process moves "backward" at some stages, as well as forward. He illustrates this pattern by the example of an inventor in an industrial research and development environment who is about to attack a new problem. The would-be inventor scans the available information and promptly moves to a creative task but then returns to the information storage system for more ideas; the reiterative mode recurs throughout the whole process from problem to diffusion.

Roberts and Frohman (1978) have expanded this concept of reiteration by pointing out how, in technological development, user demand is a primary stimulus to recognition of a problem and to invention.

Knowledge is of many types, and action entails many processes. Cherns (1972b) has made a systematic effort to examine the forms of knowledge in terms of purpose. He differentiates among four types of research and research agencies and notes their characteristics, related diffusion efforts, and the relevance of their findings to application. Briefly, these are as follows:

1. *Pure basic*—to provide knowledge for its own sake. Conducted mostly in universities, diffused in learned publications, and available for potential translation into action, if relevant.
2. *Basic objective*—to assist in understanding a problem in field applications. Often conducted through comparative studies by field agencies and diffused in professional publications. Its findings commonly lead to planned change but not by immediate prescription.
3. *Operational*—to tackle an ongoing problem within an organization and feed back information for comprehending the problem, without the aim of recommending changes in action, although such changes may ensue.
4. *Action*—to propose a change within an organization and the strategies to be used in implementing it. This is the thrust of many case studies in the organization development literature.

The relation between basic and applied knowledge rests, in good part, on one's conception of knowledge itself. In a penetrative, ideationally rich analysis, Holzner and Fisher (1979) present a sociological backdrop to the knowledge utilization scene. The concept of the *knowledge system* that characterizes any social structure is developed in relation to the following considerations: the distribution of knowledge-related activities, the way knowledge is differentiated and diffused in the system, the extent of trust in the knowledge system and in knowledge itself, the relation between rational inquiry and rational action, and the location of knowledge production, organization, storage, and use in the social system.

The structure of knowledge and the frames of reference of the participants in the knowledge "business" of inquiry and decision are viewed as taking different forms—for example, science, legal knowledge, pastoral knowledge, and "experiential knowledge." Knowledge utilization is, among other things, a process that transfers items of knowledge from one domain to another. Knowledge can be structured according to *need,* as when medical knowledge is organized on the basis of the examination of a patient, not on the basis of anatomical or physiological theory. The frame of reference, then, serves as an important determinant of use and affects tests of truth and relevance as applied to decision making. The same approach applies to the general processes occurring in knowledge utilization, such as knowledge maintenance, knowledge transformations, the determination of knowledge needs, and organizational learning capacities.

Price and Bass (1969), on the basis of an extensive analysis of current research into the roles of scientific research and technology in technological innovation, conclude that although new knowledge is not the typical *starting* point for the innovative process, interaction with new knowledge is frequently essential. They assert that the function of basic research can often be described as a meaningful dialogue between the scientific and technological communities. The authors describe the process within which the dialogue takes place as *coupling* and identify several general types of coupling:

1. *Indirect coupling,* which represents a lack of direct dialogue between the originators and the users of new scientific

knowledge. Under this type of coupling, technology users conduct surveys of the literature to locate pertinent items.

2. *Passive availability.* Here, scientists are open to approach by technologists desiring their advice but take no special initiative to stimulate the dialogues.

3. *Direct participation* in project work by scientists as consultants or advisers, which establishes a two-way partnership in problem-solving activities.

4. *The use of the gatekeeper function* whereby many organizations encourage coupling by direct action. Selected individuals are given responsibility for seeking an exchange of information between scientists and engineers and then bring about such exchanges either directly or through stimulation of the appropriate dialogues.

Price and Bass evaluated a number of studies on the frequency of use of these mechanisms and found in three studies that passive availability and direct participation were the dominant modes. These two models together accounted for three times the number of "coupling events" as did the indirect and gatekeeper modes combined.

Garner (1972) carries the problem of ascertaining the problems of users back to the very initiation of scientific research. Garner believes that too many researchers, in focusing their interest on supposedly "pure" research, overlook the potentially stimulating effect of responsiveness to user problems. He seeks to break down what he regards as a false dichotomy between pure and applied research, noting that applied research too can have generic value or lead to new theoretical insights. The same is true of serendipitous findings. In support of this position, he cites a number of instances of experimental psychology research originally stimulated by here-and-now practical problems but leading to a resurgence of basic scientific development in related areas.

Zaltman (1979a) views knowledge itself as part of the well-established topic of social change; he consequently adopts the perspective of a knowledge advocate or knowledge transfer agent. The basic approach of his article involves four activities:

Identifying social change practices, or guidelines, that appear to work; identifying the propositions from which a particular guideline appears to be derived; identifying the concepts found in separate propositions; and concluding with a perspective on knowledge utilization that emphasizes a user orientation, as contrasted with the more common "product" orientation.

Adopting an analytical (basic) rather than a prescriptive (applied) mode in a working paper prepared for a June 1980 conference on the political realization of social science knowledge, Zaltman declares that a better understanding of the nature of the concept of knowledge use and its measurement is essential. His paper assumes that there exist multiple dimensions and hence multiple conceptualizations of the term *use* and, similarly, multiple ways of measuring it. Further, many factors may influence the conceptualization and measurement of use in any one situation. Thus, there may be (1) positive use of knowledge by an R&D manager, (2) misuse of knowledge, (3) nonuse, (4) the selective use of knowledge dependent on the people who are to use it, and (5) perception of the knowledge by potential adopters. Knowledge is variously construed in its variety of uses and is susceptible to differing expectations concerning the consequences of an application of an idea.

Zaltman and Deshpande (1979) set forth action guidelines for enhancing utilization in accordance with a relationship between user need and research implementation. The main elements of the scientific and technical information (STI) model used are presented in a flow chart, with feedback connecting all the segments, entailing the following stages: (1) user needs assessment, (2) translation of needs into research questions, (3) conduct of utilizable research, (4) storage of research information, (5) translation of research into action implications, (6) implementation of action implications, and (7) evaluation of research application.

In essence, the guidelines call for direct and detailed attention to each stage of the process and for continuous contact and mutual responsibility involving researchers and users. User need is made the compelling determinant of the behavior of all concerned.

## Practitioner/Researcher Relationships

**Differences Between Researchers and Practitioners.** Researchers and practitioners, especially in the social sciences, seem to have inhabited two rather different professional communities, or "worlds." An investigator seeking basic knowledge may well have a different set of values, problems, norms, and reference groups than a practitioner seeking to help clients.

Many researchers have felt it necessary to communicate only with narrow publics of their intellectual discipline. As a result, the written reports of in-progress or completed research appearing in journals make excessive use of academic jargon peculiar to a particular specialty (Halpin, 1962; Kogan, 1963). Joly (1967) recognizes the gap between the researcher's language and the practitioner's and how it may result in mutual distrust and lack of communication. The academic orientation of many researchers, according to Archibald (1968), signifies their evident belief that they have completed their commitment when they have reported to the funding agency or have published an article in an academic journal.

Rodman and Kolodny (1965) describe the research investigator as logical, the practitioner as intuitive. Nagi (1965) contrasts the statistical skills of the research scientist with the clinical skills of the practitioner. Research attempts to discover common patterns in a population; the clinician views each case as unique. The scientist can live indefinitely with the tentative and hypothetical; the administrator wants to act with confidence. As Likert and Lippitt (1963) point out, the research worker asks questions in the form of "Why?," while the practitioner wants to know "How?"

According to Altman (1973), even the problem-solving styles of practitioners differ from those of behavioral scientists. Altman notes distinctions along the dimensions of criterion versus process orientation, analysis versus synthesis, and doing and implementing versus knowing and understanding.

Similarly, the manager or operator has tended to seek a prescription—what to do (Glock, 1961). Careful tests of credibility are commonly used in research but are less applied by practitioners (Flanagan, 1961). It seems that the practitioner, in order to improve his or her service, is likely to interpret and apply research findings beyond their limits of reliability and validity; disappointment and disillusionment may follow.

A number of critics believe that practitioners tend to rely on precedent, common sense, and intuition much more than on research findings (Pellegrin, 1965; Rose and Esser, 1960). Pellegrin perceives the effects of this orientation and behavior as contributing to a vicious circle existing in the field of education: Many educators do not think of the scientific method and research as having significant relevance in their work. This perception creates an atmosphere in which low priority is given to research endeavors or the utilization of results therefrom. Then, because of low evaluation and neglect, research continues to be regarded as a doubtful undertaking—and this view perpetuates the low esteem in which educators hold research.

Another example of the contrast in viewpoints arises when behavioral scientists try to set up "control groups." They soon discover that agencies and situations vary in so many dimensions that to control all but one factor would mean to fetter and cripple normal operations (and, indeed, thus render scientific findings dubious). Managers understandably resist such imposition (Nagi, 1965). The same kind of problem arises in attempts to replicate a social experiment (Manela, 1969). It is usually impossible to find a second setting that is enough like the original to warrant the expectation that changes just like those found the first time should appear also in the attempted replication. Scientists seek rigor; managers must be realistic.

The most regrettable outcome of this difference in viewpoint is that the problems attacked in many research studies appear trivial to most managers of human services delivery (Rosenblatt, 1968), while attempts to interpret significant research conclusions and to apply them in realistic social settings are viewed by most "pure" scientists as mere vulgar popularizations (Archibald, 1968; National Science Foundation, 1969). The general tendency of each side to stereotype, belittle, and reject the work of the other leads to avoidance and/or overt hostility (Schmuck, 1968).

To better understand linkage issues between R&D professionals and decision makers in highway safety, Havelock and Markowitz (1973) used a questionnaire to ascertain the comparative perspectives of the two groups. Also studied were the attitudes of researchers (including research opinion leaders, a subgroup who form a bridge between researchers and decision makers) and of the decision makers toward a series of "myths" about highway safety. For the most part, no dramatic differences were apparent in the beliefs of researchers and decision makers considered as total groups, but subgroups among researchers and decision makers had distinctive viewpoints. For example, it was possible to identify an "old guard" attitude syndrome that blamed the driver and a "new guard" syndrome that put more stress on a variety of factors, including the vehicle. Members of the old guard were more likely to be based in industry and in state and local government agencies; members of the new guard were more likely to be located in universities and the federal government.

Without indicating any similarities or differences that might exist in subgroups of "social scientists" and "decision makers," a study by Weiss and Weiss (1981) sought to ascertain through interviews the attitudes of the two groups toward each other and toward the role of social science research in public policy in the field of mental health. The social scientists (principal investigators and peer-group reviewers of research in mental health) and the policy makers (representatives of federal, state, and local mental health agencies or centers) agreed closely in their awareness of obstacles to the use of mental health research. In response to an open-ended question, they showed considerable agreement on what makes or could make research studies more useful. In ratings of the importance of twenty-six detailed research characteristics, statistically significant differences between the ratings by the social scientists and by the policy makers appeared for twenty-one of the twenty-six characteristics. Thus, although the perceptions of the two groups seem to show more overall agreement than conventional wisdom would admit, "fine-grained" differences emerge. Further, social scientists ascribed to the policy makers criteria of a more practical and less methodologically sound nature than those to which the policy makers themselves subscribed.

Drawing on experiences in working with both health centers and medical schools, Beckhard (1974) notes the clusters of perceptions, defenses, traditions, and stereotypes that impede collaboration between health workers and behavioral scientists. The former, for example, see the latter as missionaries rather than as hard scientists, as persons seeking to introduce change for its own sake; the latter assert that health systems do not welcome their intervention and are run by doctors who do not respect input from nonmedical disciplines.

Engstrom (1970) found considerable indications that part of the gap between research and practice is due directly to the difference in the value systems or orientation of researchers and administrators, including attitude toward research, and an accompanying lack of communication between them. Halpert (1973) attributes the gap in mental health services to a failure by *both* researchers and mental health administrators to analyze questions fully before looking to research for the answers.

Aronson and Sherwood (1967) reviewed the efforts to evaluate a group of demonstration programs dealing with juvenile delinquency and youth crime. Conflict, though not continuous, was evident in the interactions between researchers and program designers. The main source of difficulty between them —as seen by researchers—was the designers' preoccupation with the components of programs without reference to their objectives or to the connections between those components and the kinds of changes the program was intended to produce.

The current self-perception of scientists may be only a little more flexible, even though Useem (1976) regards the early reluctance of academic investigators to engage in applied social research as largely overcome by academe's condition of economic dependence ("Who pays the piper calls the tune"). Nonetheless, as Useem notes, many continue to believe that the integrity of their activity must be strenuously protected against what they perceive to be potentially serious threats from an unchecked, or perhaps ill-informed, limits-to-inquiry movement; limits are seen to conflict with a basic scientific ethic.

Scientists note also that much new knowledge is controlled in its release by proprietary rights or by security controls through "classification," reducing the accessibility (Klempner, 1973) and the intellectual confrontations that come in open discussion, thus preventing the operation of Weinberg's (1963) principle that relevance to a neighboring field is a central criterion for judging scientific merit.

From a study in Great Britain, R. B. Duncan (1972b) concludes that those who accept the academic version of science are much more likely to avoid or at least postpone employment in the outside world, thus affecting the tie between scientific knowledge and practice. Also interested in those scientists who became managers, he studied the attitudes of ninety scientists employed in research and development in a variety of British industrial firms and government research establishments. He found that career advancement usually entails the acceptance of substantial managerial responsibility. Many scientists disapprove of this state of affairs; those who approve, Duncan found, consider a certain amount of administrative responsibility unavoidable and essential. Scientists in managerial positions may still operate with a narrow "technicist" conception of management, however, and the "technicist," or nonadministrative, attitude is likely to be fostered by prevailing values in scientific education and by certain organizational characteristics that separate research and development from production and marketing.

McCool and Schreyer (1977) provide an analysis of the special problems to be studied with regard to dissemination, criteria transmission, and utilization of scientific knowledge between wildland scientists and recreation managers. Their article presents the view that utilization efforts are both *general* in framework and conception and *particular* with regard to a special field of application. In wildland settings, managers and researchers are isolated from each other, and hence there is a gap to be bridged; however, it is not practical to shift roles in the direction of a high degree of contact. As members of subcultures, those in each group share values and perceptions that inhibit effective interaction.

**Collaboration Between Researchers and Practitioners.** The collaboration of research scientists and practitioners in joint research projects appears to provide the greatest potential for maximum utilization of research findings. This potential is so strong because successful collaboration optimally results in research findings that not only are immediately available and understandable to the practitioner but also are relevant to the realities of the practice situation. Havelock (1969a) points out that, in many instances, the practitioner himself or herself is not the ultimate user but serves as linker with the consumers (a physician's patients, for example, or a teacher's pupils).

Of primary importance is the *identification and development of a research problem that reflects the interests and concerns of those affected by the research project* (Fairweather, 1967; Glaser and Taylor, 1973; Garner, 1972; Hodgkin and others, 1975). Furthermore, maximal utilization is likely when researcher and practitioner interests are parallel.

Another basic principle is that, *wherever feasible and appropriate, some knowledgeable and influential members of practitioner groups that appear to be potential users should be involved in all phases of the research*. Once an area of research need is identified, the collaboration should continue through problem formulation, study design, data collection, interpretation of findings, and application of the results (Van den Ban, 1963; Rodman and Kolodny, 1965; Glaser and others, 1967; Glaser and Taylor, 1973). The practitioner can make significant contributions to each of the research phases and can affect participation of the eventual beneficiaries of research in its design, conduct, and evaluation. Those who have a significant part in planning and decision making are not only better informed but also more committed to making use of the findings (Rogers, 1962a; Watson and Glaser, 1965; Glaser and Taylor, 1973; Glaser, 1976, 1980c, 1980e, 1981b).

An important consideration is the *need for the research team to contain a representative of the agency's top management.* Fairweather (1967) and Glock (1961) emphasize that the person representing administration must have policy-making power. Flanagan (1961) compares two studies, both of which included the users in the planning but one of which was better utilized than the other, and attributes the superior utilization to the origin of that study with the prospective user and the greater involvement of the management.

*Frequent honest and open communication* between researchers and practitioners reduces the likelihood of the emergence of stumbling blocks in the study and enhances the chances that research findings will be put to use (Van den Ban, 1963; Fairweather, 1967).

Another important step in preventing the development of problems is early *clarification of practitioner and administrator expectations for the research* (Chesler and Flanders, 1967; Fairweather, 1967; Wolfensberger, 1969). It is important for the researchers to make clear to the practitioners at the beginning that the outcome will probably not be clear dicta on how they should run the organization.

Normally, the flow of communication has been presumably from the researcher to the practitioner. It might be useful to try a reverse communication process—informing behavioral scientists on the existing state of the (practical) art (Glaser and Wrenn, 1966). Gaps in existing knowledge, or unmet needs for additional knowledge, might be pointed out; subsequent research then might have more to say to practitioners in response to their learning readiness or felt needs.

Glaser (1973) addresses the lag between the development of seemingly significant research findings and their cross-validation, dissemination, and eventual utilization. Intensive and supportive joint action is advocated between researcher and funding agency to facilitate effective end-product utilization, and a number of specific strategies are advanced. Case material from an ongoing demonstration project is presented to illustrate how research utilization can be strengthened through a collaborative partnership among funding agency, researchers, linking agents, administrators, and potential users.

Research is also more likely to proceed smoothly when, before starting the project, there is a very *explicit understanding between researchers and agency administrators regarding reciprocal responsibilities* (Fairweather, 1967; Glaser and Taylor, 1973).

Collaboration between scientist and practitioner need not take the form of a joint research project. For example, in studying the optimal conditions for implementation of existing educational research into classroom practice, Eash (1968) favors a "coaction" model that engages the researcher and practitioner in a joint problem-solving task. Interestingly, both case studies used to support this model involved the participation of not only the practitioners (teachers) but the consumers (pupils) as well. The additional involvement of the pupils seemed to be an important factor in bringing about change.

According to Duncan (1974), four identified types of interaction that affect the relations of researcher and manager may be present:

1.  The researcher and the manager are separate, and neither seeks to respond in an efficient manner relative to the needs of the other.
2.  The researcher and the manager are in communication with each other.
3.  The researcher and/or the manager are engaged in persuading each other.
4.  There are mutual responsiveness and support of each to the other.

In a report to the Marketing Science Institute on the comparative perspectives of managers and researchers, Zaltman and Deshpande (1979) surveyed responsiveness to a number of potentially influential factors in the use of market research. Among their findings and conclusions are the following:

1.  Managers and researchers need to be more aware of each other's paradigms or views about the marketing research enterprise.
2.  Special efforts will be necessary to widen researchers' understanding of the "political" implications of their findings and the managers' zone of acceptability of valid research.
3.  Personal interaction is very important in creating trust in

research results, the interpersonal climate affecting perceptions of the technical quality of research reports.
4. Managers should seek further exploratory research concerning more mature and especially declining products.

In sum, the report stresses personal perceptions and relationships as requisites if research knowledge is to be put to use
in the marketing field.

The organization of more research around issues of practical decision is a two-way process: The practitioners will need
to present their quandaries in researchable form; the investigators will more often have to choose problems that have clear
implications for practice (Lazarsfeld, Sewell, and Wilensky,
1967; Argyris, 1969). If researchers spent more time in the
field, they would better understand the situation. One suggestion is that sponsors who fund projects require some fieldwork
by the investigators (Mackie and Christensen, 1967). Field research usually has implications that can more readily be utilized in practice (Guba, 1968).

A special need exists to increase practitioners' appreciation of good theory. Theory is too often seen as the antithesis
of practice (Pellegrin, 1965; Jung and Lippitt, 1966). Warranting reiteration is Kurt Lewin's observation that nothing is so
practical as a good theory. Just as research alone may not result
in wise decisions, so experience may by itself not yield concepts
or wisdom (Lewin and Grabbe, 1962). Too often, a piece is
chosen out of a whole research enterprise and treated as an innovative "gimmick" apart from the theory that makes it meaningful (Dexter, 1965). Goldin, Margolin, and Stotsky (1969)
recommend that training be designed for practitioners that would
focus on the understanding and application of research results.
It may prove helpful if practitioners *and* researchers regard theory as essentially an explanation of experience (Holzner and
Marx, 1979).

Wolfensberger (1969) recommends that, before supporting
intra-agency research, the administrator scrutinize his or her
own attitudes toward research—what are sanctified areas in the
agency that cannot tolerate investigation, how well can the

agency survive controversy, and how prepared is the administrator to absorb a divergent, nonconformist creative researcher? On the other side of the coin, Goldin, Margolin, and Stotsky also suggest that the training of researchers include content on the principles of research utilization, with emphasis on the psychosocial aspects of innovation and change.

Using selected psychodynamic principles combining a Jungian approach with that of Berne's transactional analysis, Mitroff and Mitroff (1979) depict the several types of relationships that may exist between a "knowledge expert" and a recipient client. From transactional analysis are borrowed the distinctions among the "critical parent," the "mature adult," and the "anxious child." Jungian theory contributes the differences among concern with impersonal facts, impersonal possibilities, personal facts, and personal possibilities. The result is a 3 × 4 matrix of preferred attitudes toward knowledge, or transactional types, based on dominant personality characteristics. For example, the "anxious child, impersonal facts" attitude is "Unless I have knowledge that is based on impersonal facts and is statistically reliable, I am unable to function because of anxiety." Or the "critical parent, personal possibilities" attitude: "The only valid kind of knowledge is that which benefits the largest group of people or has meaning to the entire community."

The authors believe that awareness of the combined frameworks can be useful in analyzing individual and organizational behavior and hence in diagnosing and treating individual and organizational problems of communication for knowledge utilization.

For each of a series of barriers to collaboration between social scientists and community social work practitioners, including such considerations as communication difficulties, interprofessional conflict, and methodological assumptions, Rothman (1974) proposes "action guidelines" designed to achieve increased collaborative results. For example, Rothman suggests that the "change agent" use practice language or the actual words of practitioners similar to his or her "client" in presenting examples of how action guidelines may be implemented.

He further suggests that the specific action principle contained in the narrative example be clearly and simply explicated and that possible problems or pitfalls be outlined.

Sands and Glaser (1978) discuss recommendations from the 1977 National (Military) Symposium on Research Utilization with particular reference to collaboration through education and training. They note the following suggestions for improved utilization activity: (1) a more serious commitment to improved utilization, (2) greater interaction between research and user communities, (3) allocation of responsibility for functions affecting utilization in such a way as to make use of specialized competencies, (4) arrangements for ongoing dialogue between users and producers regarding R&D requirements, (5) improved methods of utilization management planning, (6) greater accountability for the success of the R&D activity *and* its utilization component, and (7) with regard to reporting and dissemination, a stronger focus on the translation of technical reports and usable results into "practitioner language."

The pattern of utilization set forth in the "Tavistock model" describes as follows the process whereby research actually gets into use (Tavistock Institute, 1964, quoted in Cherns, 1972b, pp. 25-26): "On the whole [the social scientist] has to reach his fundamental data (people, institutions) in their natural state, and his problem is how to reach them in that state. His means of gaining access is through a professional relationship which gives him privileged conditions. The professional relationship is a first analogue of the laboratory for the social sciences. Unless he wins conditions privileged in this way, the social scientist cannot find out anything which the layman cannot find out equally well, and he can only earn these privileges by proving his competence in supplying some kind of service. In a sense, therefore, the social scientist begins in practice, however imperfect scientifically, and works back to theory and the more systematic research which may test this, and then back again to improved practice."

**Examples of Collaboration or Agreement.** In recounting a case study of a government-sponsored effort to facilitate innovation in the U.S. shipbuilding industry, Jenstrom (1978) describes an exceptionally effective demonstration of cooperative governmental, professional, and industrial effort. Of particular interest is the program strategy for overcoming the several obstacles to cooperative efforts—namely, the essentially competitive nature of the industry, the low priority given research and development in it, lack of confidence and credibility in government's ability to assist, and industry's suspicion concerning legal entanglements with government agencies. These obstacles were largely overcome by (1) encouraging the shipbuilders to define their common needs and outline projects in keeping with these needs, (2) arranging for the projects to be housed within the industry itself, (3) providing mechanisms to ensure joint management of the projects, (4) sharing costs, and (5) encouraging implementation of the results of successful projects.

Garvey (1976), like Jenstrom, describes the unique ten-year federal/industry research innovation program designed to improve the productivity of the shipbuilding industry and reduce government subsidies. Garvey's report covers the first five years of the program and goes into some detail about the "lessons" that can be learned from the program. Among these lessons are the following:

1.  Technological improvements can reduce costs and improve profitability in the shipbuilding industry.
2.  Small, incremental improvements are more likely to occur than a major breakthrough.
3.  The major ingredients in the innovative process are the qualifications of the people, including those who know the basic technology as well as those who know practical shipbuilding.
4.  In addition to providing the resources and organization, management must provide the environment for an innovative process to be effective.

White (1977) describes a survey of scientists whose fields lie within the corporate interests of the firm where he is director of research. The survey is conducted at least once a year by senior research personnel in the corporation and one or more members of a business-oriented group such as marketing. The purpose of the survey is not to gauge markets but to ascertain scientific trends on which to base new research projects. The scientist-to-scientist approach removes much of the aura of commercialism attached to market surveys, and those persons who represent the corporation become more appreciative of the technological aspects. This has proved a very successful method of creating research projects leading to novel products and is particularly useful in quickly relating new research staff members to corporate interests with validation from external sources.

Collaboration is useful within the industrial field itself as well as between outside research and practitioners. Von Hippel (1978b) studied the comparative history of innovation development between product manufacturers and product users and drew the following conclusions:

1. Within the field of scientific instrumentation and process equipment (machinery used in the process steps of making a product) innovations, different findings ensued. Product users accounted for most new or newly commercialized products, whereas in the instances of polymers and polymer-additives industrial fields, all the novelties were accounted for by product manufacturers.
2. The key to the industrial modifications in which user groups played a dominant innovative part lies in the role of interface personnel—market researchers, salespersons, and technical service specialists.
3. Users need to search out and report back innovation needs, and innovative product users need to be separated from routine users, with provision by manufacturers for special relations with the former type of user.

To avoid the frustration of nonuse, according to von Hippel, most industrial laboratories place their advanced technology work under designated organizational units that develop particular products. Even in laboratories that are somewhat insulated from day-to-day commercial pressures, management works to increase the likelihood that research results will eventually be brought to the marketplace. Similarly, the most successful government laboratories closely integrate their in-house research efforts with external development contracts.

Despite the existence of problems between academicians and managers in the field of public administration, Bowman (1978), using an extensive survey instrument, found much overlap in the two groups' attitudes about the sources and dissemination of knowledge, objectives of research, barriers to its implementation, and methods used to link theory to practice, thus revealing a number of common interests between researchers and practitioners.

### Research and Policy Making

The matter of the relation between research and use in the sense of policy making has evolved as a significant topic of investigation. Weiss (1977a) has offered a penetrating, "true to life" analysis of the nature of the utilization of social research in public policy making in her introductory chapter to a book devoted to the subject. She regards as simplistic the "traditional wisdom" assumptions that (1) increased use of social research is necessarily bound to improve the quality of social decisions, (2) social research is not now well used by government, and (3) government officials could make better use of social policy research if some relatively modest reforms were made. Although these widespread beliefs contain elements of truth, the issues affecting research use in public policy need to be approached with a realistic understanding of the way policies are formulated and the actual interface of social research and the policy-making process.

Illustrative of this type of factual, differential analysis of the issues is the treatment of the subject in three chapters of the book edited by Weiss, dealing respectively with the place of research in congressional decision making (Dreyfus, 1977), in judicial policy making (Rosen, 1977), and principally in the executive branch of the federal government (Useem, 1977). Uncertainties in the findings and value orientations of the research, motivational divergences, practical pressures, political considerations, and traditional prerogatives, although they operate differently among the three branches of government, all serve as complicating factors that make a one-to-one relationship between social research and policy making untenable. Efforts to improve the relationship must take these factors into account.

The process whereby research knowledge may slowly or indirectly insinuate itself into policy or action decisions is the subject of a later article by Weiss (1980), who develops the concept of "knowledge creep." In Weiss' study, 155 high-level federal, state, and local mental health officials responded to interview questions in the conscious use of social science research and the circumstances under which they sought out research information when considering a policy or program. In essence, a clear majority of the respondents indicated use of research, but with varying degrees of specificity or consciousness. Furthermore, the nature of their use of research implied a variety of reasons (such as to lend support to or legitimize an already-accepted position) in addition to direct application to basic problems of service needs or program evaluation.

Thus, although the study concludes that public officials use research more widely than previously thought, its use tends to be *diffuse,* rather than in a direct "one decision to one research study" objective relationship. For one thing, public officials did not conceptualize decision making as an event or themselves as "making" decisions.

All these findings lend support to an overall conclusion that social research does have a pervasive influence, but one that lacks definitiveness and operates in an indirect and often slow fashion.

Using further responses of the mental health officials referred to in Weiss' report, Weiss and Bucuvalas (1980a) explored the frames of reference that decision makers employ in assessing the usefulness of social service research. In this study the respondents reacted to fifty actual research reports, thereby revealing salient frames of reference criteria, or dimensions of research as related to acceptance. Five frames of reference were manifest: relevance of research topic, research quality, conformity of results with expectations, orientation to action, and challenge to existing policy. All five factors were positively related to the likelihood of using a research study. They may be grouped under the two basic tests of *truth* and *utility*. Research quality and conformity with expectations provide alternative grounds for trusting a study (truth test); action orientation and challenge to existing policy are alternative bases for applying the results (utility test).

In a later report Weiss and Weiss (1981) tried to determine the usefulness of research in general, compared with its usefulness in particular cases, by having decision makers and social scientists read and evaluate actual research reports and also rate two studies on twenty-six research characteristics. A correlation was then computed between the degree to which a study possessed each research characteristic and how useful it was rated to be. The decision makers' self-reports of the twenty-six research characteristics matched quite well with the revealed importance of the characteristics in action ($r = .69$). The correlation between the social scientists' estimates of the importance of the various research characteristics and the revealed importance of the characteristics to decision makers was .44, less accurate than the .69 correlation for decision makers but hardly out of the ballpark.

The issues raised by Weiss and others concerning how knowledge insinuates itself into policy making need to be linked with the distinctions referred to in Chapter One between "hard" and "soft" knowledge as types of knowledge, on the one hand, and instrumental/engineering, conceptual/enlightenment, and symbolic/legitimate modes of utilization, on the other (Pelz, 1978). With Weiss, Pelz argues that the typical conclusion in the literature that public policy makers have made little use of social science in their decisions flows from an overly narrow definition of knowledge utilization—namely, one that overlooks "soft" knowledge and conceptual and symbolic modes of utilization.

Roessner (1980) has attempted an assessment of the extent to which the literature on the diffusion of innovations can help in resolving public policy issues involving governmental efforts to influence technological diffusion in the civilian economy. He pursues this purpose by listing national policy issues and problems concerning technology diffusion and outlining the types of knowledge and information required to address the problems. He then identifies the subareas of diffusion research requisite to providing the relevant knowledge and assesses the extent to which, in his judgment, the available research actually does so.

An illustration of a policy problem is contained in the question "What strategies should be used to disseminate information about new technologies to particular social and economic subsystems?" The knowledge required is stated in two parts: (1) Knowledge of the structure and dynamics of communication networks that link the subsystem population to sources of technological information. (2) Knowledge of the structure and dynamics of the communication networks that link members of the subsystem to one another.

Obviously, the listing of problems and requisite knowledge is only part of the total process of achieving research utilization in policy making. The task of linking research with use requires careful staging of the process. Roessner borrows from Eveland, Rogers, and Klepper (1977) in noting the following stages in the social science research process: (1) problem delineation, (2) identification of variables, (3) determination of relationships, (4) establishment of causality among variables, (5) manipulation of causal variables for policy-formation purposes, and (6) evaluation of alternate policies/programs.

The scope of the task would seem to be hopeless in view of its complexity. For example, Roessner notes that one study (Public Affairs Counseling, 1976) lists seventy-eight variables as possibly influencing the innovative behavior of individuals and organizations. But he suggests that policy analysts can make a contribution by becoming familiar with diffusion literature and then identifying and referring to the half-dozen or so pieces of research that are on subjects most closely resembling the technology, potential market, and institutional setting characterizing the particular policy problem at hand.

Lindblom and Cohen (1979) take a dim view of the role

of professional social inquiry (PSI) and of practitioners of PSI in the actual or potential determination of social problem solving. In a sweeping and sharp indictment of the self-perception and functioning of current PSI practitioners, they cite illustrations from several fields, such as government, commerce, and education, to show that the inputs of so-called rational and scientific findings of PSI practitioners are far outweighed (and intrinsically so) by those of "ordinary knowledge" and nonrational action (and interaction among interested parties) in realistic policy making and social problem solving. Without setting forth specifics of how effective problem solving can be accomplished, the authors recommend that social inquiry professionals assume a fresh perception of their role. They also urge them to seek out ways of interacting realistically with policy makers in situations entailing social problem solving.

Concerned with the process whereby social research may find its way into policy making, Davis and Salasin (1978b) offer suggestions for surmounting barriers to coordinated action. Among their findings and conclusions are the following:

1. A large proportion of policy makers rely heavily on in-house sources and public media, in contrast to R&D projects, often conducting studies *after* policy decisions.

2. The social R&D community has voiced complaints about the character of social research, including the alleged reluctance of social researchers to work on specific policy questions and the failure of federal-research-program managers to give scientists adequate incentives to work on policy-relevant research.

3. Barriers to maximum quality in mental health R&D include (a) inharmonious settings, (b) failure to cross-validate findings, (c) limited research design skill, coupled with limited value of classical experimental design, (d) too infrequent evaluation of the quality and consequences of federal projects, (e) insufficient collaborative arrangements in federally funded programs, and (f) a work overload on federal research administrators.

4. The authors suggest the following steps to strengthen the social R&D contribution to policy making: (a) Clarification of the policy-related innovation process by means of such analy-

ses as the Decision Determinants Analysis model (also called the
A VICTORY model). (b) Coordination among federal funding
agencies, using flexible mechanisms including shared responsibility of investigators and research managers. (c) Institution of review procedures likely to attract qualified research personnel.
(d) Encouragement of the use of improved research design. (e)
Bringing the policy world and the research enterprise together
by synthesizing material, furthering retrieval services, encouraging informal networks, sponsoring papers with policy implications, using newly designed specialized media, and developing a
corps of knowledge transfer specialists.

In another article Davis and Salasin (1978a) contend that
there is a shortfall in the application of potentially useful applied social research to improved delivery of human services.
They have set forth a number of suggestions for improved utilization of promising R&D in that field, including the following:

1. Encourage researchers to undertake thoughtful analysis of
   social needs and make clear their relation to social policy.
2. Clarify ways in which policy makers can use relevant human service knowledge.
3. Employ more widely the methods that exist for facilitating
   the utilization of policy-relevant research.
4. Overcome the occasional fear of researchers that support
   for further research will cease once a study is utilized.
5. Narrow further the still-broad communication gap between
   researchers and policy makers; for example, invite certain
   policy makers to critique drafts of policy-relevant research
   reports.
6. Make the subject of optimum transfer of social research
   into action a deliberate subject of social research into such
   matters as design, measurement, need assessment, analysis of
   policy-making processes, and diffusion and utilization practices.

Stolz (1981) also asserts that government policy makers
rarely or never adopt behavioral and social science technologies
as policies solely because of data from carefully designed out-

come studies. However, in examining three examples of adoption of technological innovations by governmental agencies, she found that certain key variables are likely to be of critical importance, as follows:

1.  Research data have shown that the innovation was effective.
2.  The technology meets the continuing mission of the adopting agency.
3.  The potential adopter has a pressing management problem.
4.  The availability of the dissemination to the potential adopter is timely.
5.  Potential adopters are able to view ongoing (model) programs.
6.  The adoption is proposed by the policy makers, rather than by researchers who developed the technology.
7.  The intervention is tailored to local conditions.
8.  Those who will have to implement the program are involved in the preliminary research and in asking for the adoption.
9.  Funds are available for dissemination.
10. A key person, trained, enthusiastic, and with significant social skills, persists through political infighting to protect the program from going under.

The relevance of social R&D to real-life policy issues and how that relevance is perceived by high-level policy makers are the subject of a treatise by Lynn (1978b). Illustrations of his findings are as follows:

•  Policy making tends to be concerned with immediate issues and problems and to be less interested in future-oriented research.
•  Criteria for relevance of social R&D to policy making can be specified—for example, actual use and influence.
•  Few, if any, criteria of relevance seem to be applied during the planning of social R&D by social scientists and funding agencies.

- Research management typically focuses on individual projects rather than on multiyear, multiproject research programs.
- If this analysis is correct, the solution to the relevance problem will have two aspects: (1) recognition of the complexity of the knowledge-into-policy process and realization that many criteria are appropriate for assessing the relevance of social R&D to policy making; (2) acceptance of the need to apply criteria of relevance consciously before projects are selected and funded.

If much of the output of policy research does not find immediate application, it still may well have influence (Bowman, 1978; Rich, 1977; Weiss, 1980). Through circuitous routes and over time, it enters the discourse of informed publics. It may surface in intellectual journals and magazines of opinion, in media coverage, through teaching in university departments and professional schools, in seminars sponsored by professional organizations, and in elite clubs. In time, as research provides new form, shape, and direction to a public issue, policy research can affect the climate of opinion or result in paradigm shifts. The once-accepted assumptions are challenged; the once-outlandish conclusions become familiar. In the doing, research broadens the range of acceptable ideas. When renewed crises arise and new steps must be taken, informed publics and government officials will have a greater readiness for significant change.

In a later treatment of the use of social science in public policy, Pelz (1980) reviews the work of Caplan, Morrison, and Stambaugh (1975), Rich (1975, 1977), and Knorr (1977) in rounding out the distinctions among the types of knowledge employed and the ways they are used. Pelz corroborates the finding that social science is more widely applied than is generally acknowledged in that, aside from the usual instrumental use in a particular action, it is important to consider its conceptual use (change in understanding or thinking) and "symbolic" use (legitimating an existing policy).

In two reports Rich (1977, 1980a) develops further the distinctions made between instrumental and conceptual use of

research or other information by noting the differences (1) between short-term and long-term research (with their respective
payoffs of investment) and (2) between first and second "waves"
of utilization (reflecting the difference in time for an agency to
digest the information). Moreover, he relates these distinctions
to three critical issues: What is the appropriate mix between
short-term and long-term research? What constitutes valuable information? What does utilization research teach us about effective organizational procedure?

Within the context of the manner of responding to research information, it is helpful to appreciate the characteristics
of many "bureaucrats"—jealous of position, protective of organizational interests, suspicious of new information and ideas, and
yet needing "expert" knowledge to maintain power (Rich,
1979c). To counter the forces against knowledge utilization and
change, there is need to develop the counteracting influence of
a newer breed—the modern, professionally oriented policy
analyst.

Further, strategies for the more effective utilization of information resources may well include the following considerations, according to Rich (1975):

1.  Policy makers should be involved in the decisions about
    what information to collect and how the information will
    be processed and used.
2.  Where policy makers are not familiar with the technologies
    or methodologies being used, an information broker is
    needed to encourage more effective utilization.
3.  There should be continuous feedback between policy mak-
    ers and the staff members providing information to them,
    both for in-house staff persons and for those outside the
    government.
4.  Researchers should seek ways to summarize their informa-
    tion, develop long-term indicators, and provide trend infor-
    mation.

Mitchell (1980) reports on an NIE-sponsored study that
focuses on social science utilization among state legislatures in

formulating basic educational policies. A total of 160 key legislative policy makers in Arizona, California, and Oregon were interviewed.

The responses were categorized according to (1) stages of the legislative decision-making process ("articulation" of the issue, "aggregation" of similar interests, "allocation" or ultimate outcome, and the "oversight" functions) and (2) type of resources identified as important in controlling the decision-making process. As decisions flow through the four *stages,* they are seen as being shaped and controlled by the use of particular *resources* available to key legislators, staff consultants, and other influential actors. Social science research was identified as one of the resources.

According to Mitchell, four broad factors influence orientations toward legislative decision making: reference group orientation, decision style orientation, decision mechanism orientation, and grounds for decisions. Social science utilization serves mainly but not exclusively with regard to the fourth factor—namely, grounds for decisions—as a type of authority used to "encourage, persuade, cajole, embarrass, or intimidate other policy makers into accepting a policy proposal" (p. 11).

"Experts" are perceived as having (1) legal, (2) political or legislative, (3) technical, or (4) scientific skills. Each type makes a different contribution to legislative decisions. The scientific specialists emphasize analysis and interpretation of data. With some exceptions, the respondents find social science cumbersome and not a very reliable source of guidance. Full-time professional staff tended to show greater appreciation and interest than did other respondents to the inquiry.

Mitchell suggests that the development of scientific advocacy be recognized as a *political* process, that scientific analysis be brought to bear *earlier* in the process, and that scientific utilization serves best to refine and criticize—not to replace—other, more fundamental mechanisms for defining and resolving public policy issues.

Under the title "Research Brokerage: The Weak Link," Sundquist (1978) presents a model for tracking the movement of scientific knowledge into policy. Defining research "brokers" as the "repackagers" of knowledge for consumption by decision makers, he asserts that in many decision-making settings research brokerage is often completely missing, badly organized, or poorly staffed. The President's Council of Economic Advisers, in contrast, is described as well organized and as having considerable official as well as informal power in moving the findings of economic research onto the national policy-making scene.

Caplan, Morrison, and Stambaugh (1975), using taped interview replies, investigated the uses of social science information by 204 officials in the executive branch of the U.S. government to assist in making policy decisions. They found such use frequent but centered predominantly on information produced within the government. Officials, like others, tend to use statistics selectively to buttress a favored point of view.

These findings were further elaborated by Caplan (1976a, 1976b), who studied the relation between social research and national policy by investigating the questions of what research gets used, by whom, for what purposes, and with what effects.

As to *what was used,* Caplan discovered that 32 percent of the instances of use of research methodology involving primary data entailed social statistics; 20 percent, program evaluation; 9 percent each, survey research and field experimentation; 8 percent, cost analysis; 6 percent, organizational analyses; and 1 to 4 percent, other forms of investigation. It was found that the extent of the use of social statistics varied with various policy areas and government units. Slightly more than half the data used came from in-house sources.

As to the characteristics of *those who used the research,* Caplan discerned three "orientations": a *clinical* orientation entailing political and social ramifications of the policies, an *academic* orientation held by experts in their fields who stressed the internal logic of the issues, and an *advocacy* orientation limited almost exclusively to extrascientific forces.

The *purpose of the use* included a broad spectrum of agency problems, eighteen fields being represented. Organizational management yielded the greatest percentage of instances of use, followed by education, health, crime, communications, public opinion management, welfare, the military, and employment at the top of the list, while international relations, research methodology, consumer affairs, and recreation were at the bottom of the list. The author concluded that the predominant purpose of knowledge utilization is to improve bureaucratic efficiency.

*Effect,* or impact, of social research on policy decision was determined by coding the 575 instances of use according to (1) an estimate of the number of people affected by the related policy decision and (2) the relative importance of the policy decision in their lives. Four levels of impact were noted: policy issues affecting the entire nation (13 percent), policy issues affecting large population segments (41 percent), policy issues affecting small population segments (9 percent), and administrative issues affecting government personnel (37 percent). Thus, over half the instances of use involved matters of considerable individual and social consequence that affected sizable segments of the nation's population.

In seeking to define the place of scientific knowledge in public policy formation in a democracy, Nelkin (1979) draws attention to two at times opposing forces, (1) populist demand for greater public participation in policy choices and (2) the use of scientific knowledge as a resource or commodity to be manipulated either by the politically powerful or by those best educated to understand the implications and appropriate utilization of the particular piece of knowledge. As background for understanding the place of these two forces in influencing decisions, she traces the history of the evolution of an expert "elite" and the subsequent insistence by the public on access to information and expertise. She also notes the growth of a "public-interest science" and a sense of social responsibility among scientists.

With regard to the phase of social research that refers to social indicators, Caplan and Barton (1978) assert that use by upper-level U.S. government officials is minimal. Further, the authors believe that use is not likely to be increased by improved measurement procedures, esthetically improved packaging, or more widespread dissemination of such information among persons who influence policy decisions unless deliberate effort is made to institutionalize the importance of social indicators into government policy making and operations.

Van de Vall (1975) advocates a diagnostic survey for social policy development. Such a survey is to be based on experiences of conflicting social pressures and to lead to research designed to present an exact analysis of the policy problem. However, policy makers must have a real and felt need for research information if they are to use it in decision making.

Van de Vall offers a model that depicts four major functions of applied social research in policy making while taking account of differences in discipline research and policy research throughout:

1. Providing feedback in health, education, and welfare between inarticulate demand and monopolized supply.
2. Diagnosing problems with the aim of designing and developing measures of planned social change.
3. Controlling the variables of input (planning), throughput (delivery), and output (evaluation).
4. Taking into account differences between internal and external researchers (that is, whether the researcher is a staff member of the organization or an outside consultant) and between internal and external problems (that is, whether the problem is within the organization or its task environment or beyond), thus making four researcher/problem combinations.

Holland, Holt, and Brewer (1978) provide an illustration of a common tendency to view the relevance of given research-based information to policy making from different perspectives. The authors, who are associated with the California Department of Corrections, studied decision making with regard to parole of prisoners. They found support for a hypothesis that the use of information in decision making about parole for individuals differs between prison caseworkers and parole board members. The former base their judgments on recidivism-related factors that include the component of the offense severity; the latter, on the severity of the offense and whether the length of the prison sentence was proportionate to the degree of severity.

Thus, it is evident that the literature is replete with analyses and exhortations designed to bring together research and practice as well as researcher and practitioner.

## Summary Comments

This chapter considers several issues bearing on knowledge/practice relationships.

One of these issues is the extent to which universities, as seats of learning, contribute to knowledge use and to some of the deterrents to fuller service in this regard. Another is the roles of basic and applied research in vitalizing knowledge; we considered in some detail several specific queries about how the one may relate to the other.

The chapter reviewed numerous reports on the relationship of practitioners and researchers, considering differences between them as well as modes and examples of collaboration. The differences include a tendency to live in two different professional communities, or "worlds"; distinctive cognitive styles; responsiveness to divergent rewards; and different beliefs about how knowledge can best contribute to human welfare.

Among the various collaborative measures suggested are working jointly on particular projects, identifying problems of common interest, placing representatives of both types on top-management teams, open communication, common involvement in the making of certain decisions, development of a more common terminology, and equalization of status.

An interesting and productive example of collaboration is an extensive, ten-year government/industry project in the shipbuilding industry in which representatives of scientific, engineering, and company management groups cooperated in planning and implementing scores of innovative means for improving productivity in United States shipbuilding.

The second half of the chapter presented a fairly extensive coverage of the newer literature on the relation of research to the formation of policy. The literature tends to rebut the widespread belief that research (particularly social science information) has had little effect in policy decision making. The limitation that has been found is that the findings of individual studies are often not consulted in particular decisions such as legislative actions but that, over a period of time, policies are influenced by the accumulation of research findings. This conclusion may be supported by a distinction between what is termed the "conceptual" and the "instrumental" use of knowledge. The latter refers to the use of specific information as a means of arriving at a decision about an immediately pressing problem, while the former refers to the building up of a frame of reference based on information as well as judgment as an aid in providing a more intelligent or "enlightened" foundation for decisions.

Obviously, the foregoing account is but a global statement of the relation between research and policy making. The literature goes into considerable detail. For example, one set of studies depicts varying uses of information by legislative, executive, and judicial branches of government.

As to the use of research in general, it has been described as "creeping" into policy making. Its use tends to be diffuse rather than direct. One extensive empirical study reported how government officials typically arrive at decisions; for example, legislators consult a good deal with colleagues and are responsive to popular pressures and political considerations.

Because of the circumstances under which they operate, legislators often use research for purposes other than objective assistance in framing policies—for example, as an excuse for delaying action on an unwanted piece of legislation or as post hoc justification for a previously agreed-on decision.

Yet, such research as is carried out is expected to meet criteria of truth and utility, the latter criterion including relevance, action orientation, and timeliness. "Soft" knowledge is distinguished from "hard" knowledge. Various sources of knowledge, such as opinion polls, population statistics, and other forms of research information, are reacted to selectively. Various types of knowledge are found to be more applicable to one stage of the legislative process than to another and, similarly, to one or another of the functions of legislation, such as the allocation of resources as against oversight of their expenditure.

In general, studies of the relation between social research and governmental and social policy have been investigated in terms of what research gets used, by whom, for what purposes, and with what effects. A number of writers address the question of what needs to be done to enhance the amount and effectiveness of utilization.

In retrospect, the treatment in Chapters Eleven through Fourteen of linkage and dissemination has ranged over a number of general and particularized analyses and suggestions bearing on the targets, settings, sources, and types of change efforts. This diversity of coverage gives added impetus to the need to develop synthesizing patterns of utilization and change phenomena, the subject of the next chapter.

# 15

❧

# Models and Systems
# for Facilitating
# Planned Change

❧

Much of the literature on utilization and change deals with ideas
and suggestions for practical application. Often these are empirically derived, but not infrequently they are based on impres-
sionistic evidence. At the same time, there is indication of a
strong interest in seeking underlying principles (often borrowed
from related disciplines) on which to base application and in
building systematic models of the process of utilization and
change.

Previous chapters, in which we have presented relatively
discrete lists of factors, themes, and stages in the process of
knowledge utilization and change, have alluded to more comprehensive or theoretical formulations. In this chapter we present a sampling of writings on (1) various overall perspectives
that have been applied to the subject and (2) systematic frameworks or models designed to show relations among selected
components of the process.

## Perspectives

**Academic Disciplines as the Source of Perspectives.** In a compilation of analytical articles on utilization and change (Radnor, Feller, and Rogers, 1978a), the varying perspectives of a number of academic disciplines are presented at length in a single source. In the concluding article of that treatise, Kranzberg (1978) describes a multidisciplinary approach as reflecting diverse positions. Thus, anthropologists and sociologists tend to focus on elements of sociocultural resistance to change and the interactions of different cultures with one another; geographers tend to concentrate on the spatial patterns of diffusions; psychologists on innovative behavior in organizations and individuals; economists on investment, labor or capital intensiveness, resource endowments, and so on; historians examine invention and technological advances in a time perspective and within a societal context. Following are a few illustrations of these varied perspectives.

Writing as an *economic historian,* Rosenberg (1978) asserts that the diffusion of inventions is an essentially economic phenomenon whose timing can be largely explained by expected profits. One of the factors that influence the rate of diffusion is that "old" technologies continue to be improved after the introduction of the "new," thus postponing the time when the old technology is clearly outmoded. Uncertainty, not only over the profitability of an innovation but also over whether a still more profitable one is likely to be made available at a later time, tends further to slow diffusion.

Feller (1978) also considers the applicability of *economic analysis* to the adoption of innovations but refers particularly to adoption by public-sector organizations. He notes that attention has been moving away from emphasis on the "determinants" of innovativeness, toward identification of the decision makers in the adoption process and toward analysis of the processes of search, match, and implementation that occur between an adopter's performance requirements and the characteristics of an innovation.

In evaluating the past and potential contributions of the *R&D management literature* to innovation diffusion research, Radnor, Ettlie, and Dutton (1978) assert that the impact of the management literature on the tradition of innovation diffusion research, though not readily visible, has great potential. They cite (1) specific organizational and innovation-related factors that emerge from the broad field of management literature, (2) particular diffusion/adoption studies, and (3) policy studies that have important implications for national innovation policy.

Among the implications suggested are (1) the importance of the structure of the supplier side of the diffusion paradigm, (2) the importance of the "innovation in an organization" unit of analysis proposed by Downs and Mohr (1976), (3) the emphasis on the process of reinvention suggested by Rogers (1978), (4) the viewing of the stream of innovations in and/or between organizations in their environments over time, and (5) the need for linking and synthesizing management policy and national policy. In sum, management policy, national policy, innovations, and institutions may all be relevant factors for consideration in connection with efforts to introduce innovative characteristics into a system.

The perspective of innovation/diffusion research in the *public policy field* is presented by Rich (1978), who raises questions about formal and informal decision-making structures, reward/incentive systems, uniqueness of problems, types of coordination and resource sharing, and the existence of particular decision-making styles. From his examination of empirical studies and speculative analysis of issues in this field, Rich concludes that a new approach to conducting research on utilization in public policy formulation and innovation must be developed in order to introduce change techniques that are more likely than traditional techniques to influence organizational change and decision-making processes. He contends that, for one thing, utilization should be seen as but one concern within the context of factors, conditions, and constraints affecting a given problem. For another, knowledge utilization in the sense of the direct use of information is only one consideration in the overall process of deciding whether an organization should adopt a new technique or process as part of its day-to-day operations. Hence, more attention needs to be given to conceptual utilization and the required methodology for relating research to the problem-solving aspects of policy formation.

Brown (1978) presents four viewpoints on innovation research: the adoption perspective, the market and infrastructure perspective, the economic history perspective, and the development perspective.

The basic tenet of the *adoption perspective* is the spread of the innovation across the landscape, as it were, primarily as the outcome of a learning or communications process. Rogers and Shoemaker (1971) and Hagerstrand (1967) represent this approach, which stresses adoption by households or individuals.

The *market and infrastructure perspective* focuses on the way innovations are made available to potential adopters through market-oriented diffusion agencies that take into account profitability, sales potential, or need for the innovation in given market areas. It implies effort by the diffusion agency to induce adoption in its market or service area. Like the adoption perspective, it addresses the problem of a particular innovation.

The *economic history perspective* recognizes the continually changing character of the innovation and the market or economy into whose competitive equilibrium it is introduced. This framework, treated more fully elsewhere (Rosenberg, 1972), encompasses (1) continuity of inventive activity, (2) development of technical skills among users, (3) development of skills in machine making, (5) complementary technologies, and (6) concurrent improvements in old technologies.

The *development perspective* considers both the role of the level of development in the diffusion process and the impact, over periods of time, of diffusion practices on individual and collective welfare. This pespective is concerned, for example, with the possibility of governmental and entrepreneurial practices that systematically favor certain types of individuals, households, or nations as innovations are developed and diffused or transferred from one unit to another.

Brown argues that although the several perspectives are not mutually exclusive in practice, the relative emphasis given to one or another is related to policy considerations, such as effects on collective and individual welfare, and the design of diffusion research, including prediction and evaluation models.

A paper by Pellegrin (1978) discusses the contribution of *sociology* to the study of innovation as applied to decision making. Although in the past sociology may be said to have been related to diffusion research through extensive anthropological studies and through one of its branches, rural sociology, the author admits that diffusion research has not been a major area of sociology, which has been concerned with the broader field of social change. Yet, in the author's opinion, a reconceptualization might clarify the relation of diffusion research to other types of studies of planned change in the sociology field. The proposed direction is a policy orientation for research that provides guides to decision making and action.

A *psychologist's view* of organizational innovation is presented by Yin (1978), who sees psychology as increasing the probability of innovation by contributing to the understanding of both the conditions that facilitate innovation and how decision makers become innovative or noninnovative.

Yin presents a critical review of the limitations of three traditional approaches for studying the innovative process: (1) the research, development, and diffusion approach, (2) the social interaction (diffusion) approach, and (3) the innovative organization's approach. He then offers the *organizational change approach* as probably the most useful context for analyzing organizational innovation and gives the following reasons. First, the three approaches just listed are viewed as misleadingly directing attention to innovations—that is, *solutions*—as the main unit of analysis. In contrast, the organizational change approach directs attention to the decision maker's *problems* in deciding how and when to innovate. Second, the three approaches, originally intended to apply mainly to adoptions, have been inappropriately applied to organizational characteristics. Third, because of an idiosyncratic data base, the three approaches fail to provide generalizations about organizational innovativeness.

Yin asserts that the organizational change approach can lead to more fruitful types of studies of organizational innovation and to different orientation than those reflected by the other approaches. The major recommended research method is the case study. Only case studies, Yin insists, can examine decision-making changes over time. Such case studies need to be carefully designed, conducted, and aggregated so that information can be reliably gathered and generalized. Key events *within* the organization, called "passages" or "cycles," need to be identified and examined. These include such items as equipment turnover, estabishment of stable arrangements for maintenance and supplies, changes in organizational governance, validation of training programs, and turnover of key personnel.

Yin contends that the organizational change approach is potentially useful for policy making in that, to the extent that the correct organizational events have been identified, it will be possible to direct the decision maker's efforts toward influencing such events in order to innovate.

Schön (1971) presents a perspective that stresses "learning systems" as a counterpoise to continually changing circumstances in individual, organizational, institutional, and cultural situations. In all these areas there is a need to maintain a "stable state" while responding to the forces of change. Businesses, government, and social institutions must become learning systems in order to adapt to ever-changing situations. Moreover, whereas earlier considerations of diffusion stressed the dispersion, usually of a product, from a central source to peripheral areas, the complexity of modern business and other systems entails the involvement of many peripheral and interconnected points in a wide matrix of factors. Ideas and attitudes are essential elements in the complex undergoing change.

The learning-systems perspective as applied to government, for example, is epitomized in the following passage: "If government is to learn to solve new public problems, it must also learn to collate the systems for doing so and to discard the structure and mechanisms grown up around old problems. The need is not merely to cope with a particular set of new problems, or to discard the organizational vestiges of a particular form of government activity which happen at present to be particularly cumbersome. It is to design and bring into being the institutional processes through which new problems can continually be confronted and old structures continually discarded" (p. 116).

Other disciplines have contributed to model building in the field of change and knowledge utilization. For example, psychotherapy is closely related to the change process as applied to individuals and groups, not to mention community impact. Education and the psychology of development and learning are rich in theories of change and of knowledge acquisition, to cite examples from a large list.

The subject of communication as linkage between knowledge producer and user provides another example of interdisciplinary dependence. Dahling (1962) cites Shannon's *information theory* to illustrate the spread of an idea through an amazing number of disciplines, including computer science, electronics, psychiatry, psychology, engineering, educational psychology, biology, physiology, radar, linguistics, biosociology, library science, optics, education, statistics, social science, and journalism.

An early book on the diffusion of innovations (Rogers, 1962a) notes the fields of anthropology, education, industry, and medical and rural sociology as traditional sources of research on diffusion. A later book (Rogers and Shoemaker, 1971) adds marketing and communication to the list of sources.

**Five Widely Cited Perspectives.** Additional perspectives have been set forth by Havelock (1969a) and Sashkin, Morris, and Horst (1973), among others. Of the following five approaches, the first three are described by Havelock, the last two by Sashkin and associates.

The first is the *research, development, and diffusion* perspective. This model assumes that there is a relatively passive target audience of consumers, which will accept an innovation if it is delivered through a suitable medium, in the right way, at the right time. It calls for a rational sequence of activities from research to development to packaging before dissemination takes place. It assumes large-scale planning and requires a division of labor and a separation of roles and functions. Evaluation is particularly emphasized in this model, in which there is a high initial development cost and which anticipates a high payoff in terms of the quantity and quality of long-range benefit through the model's capacity to reach a large audience of potential users.

The second is the *social interaction* perspective, which is more sensitive to the complex and intricate set of human relationships, substructures, and processes involved in the adoption and dissemination phases. This model stresses the importance of face-to-face contacts. It implies that a user can hold a variety of positions in the communication network and that people tend to adopt and maintain attitudes and behavior that they perceive as normative for their psychological reference group. The size of the adopting group is basically irrelevant in this model, which follows essentially the process stage of knowledge and research diffusion, with appropriate influencing strategies used at each stage.

Third is the *problem-solving* perspective, which starts with the user's needs as a beginning point for research, with diagnosis as an essential first step in the search for solutions. The outside helper, or change agent, in this model, is often non-directive, mainly guiding the potential user through his or her own problem-solving processes and encouraging the user to utilize internal resources. The model assumes that self-initiated and directed change has the firmest motivation and hence the best prospect of being maintained.

In the fourth model, the *planned change* perspective, information is considered useful only if it leads to action and is shared between the change agent and the client. The assumptive basis of this model is that change occurs through a consciously controlled, sequential, and continuous process of data generation, planning, and implementation. The changes made need to be stabilized and supported.

The fifth model is the *action research* perspective. Though similar in some respects to the problem-solving and planned change models, it is most distinctive in emphasizing the development of research within and by the organization. The type of research and its methodology are influenced by its being carried out concurrently with the ongoing activity of the organization. The results of the research, though intended mainly for the organization itself, may prove useful to others and contribute to behavioral science in general. The model assumes the action research to be a continuous process of research, action, evaluation, and more research enlightened by the evaluation findings.

It is evident that the various perspectives are not mutually exclusive and that they display similarities and differences. For example, all five of the models may entail the use of a consultant, but the models differ in their use of external and internal sources of assistance. In varying degrees, the several approaches may be seen as reflecting influences from such disciplines as applied physical science, sociology, psychology, management, and social science.

## Systematic Frameworks or Models: A Sampling

Many of the approaches to achieving knowledge utilization and change thus far described entail, implicitly if not explicitly, aspects of systems models. Such models are characterized by (1) interactive components of a system that includes inputs, transformations, and outputs, (2) a dynamic flow of "signals" (that is, messages) or "effects" (that is, influences), (3) feedback of information at a given stage in the process that modifies subsequent repetitions of prior stages, (4) boundaries of varying degrees of "permeability" between the system and the supersystem in which it resides and among the subsystems it contains, and (5) an "overseer," or controlling coordinating mechanism.

Systems models vary in abstractness, generality, complexity, and scope or comprehensiveness, along with other attributes. The following account of a few selected writings on the systems approach is meant to demonstrate varied patterns of thinking about knowledge utilization and change phenomena that incorporate one or more of the essential systems attributes. As noted in the discussion of their uses later in this chapter, models are intended to help organize one's thoughts about complex processes.

In the presentation that follows, the "system" is conceived in several senses to demonstrate the wide variety of forms that models may take: (1) as a relationship between a change-agent practitioner and a client (Clark), (2) as an informational search loop, a problem-solving dialogue (Havelock), (3) as a many-faceted approach to a change process (Pelz and Munson), (4) as a total organizational production effort (Souder and Rubenstein), (5) as a cybernetic social process (Etzioni), (6) as an overall cybernetic technological process at a national or international level (Dobrov), (7) as a social network, subject to technical, political, and cultural cycles (Tichy), (8) as a technological society facing an uncertain future (Wenk), and (9) as mathematically expressed relations among component functions of behavior or change (Davis).

Client/Practitioner Relationship as a System. At a fairly concrete level, A. W. Clark (1975) examines the client/practitioner relationship, considered in system terms, viewing it as an engagement between individuals, between an individual and a system, or between systems. The internal and external environments of the client and the practitioner systems, their collaborative arrangements, and the key characteristics of the social and technical systems are described.

Clark presents three models of client/practitioner systems and analyzes them in terms of interdependency in relation to their environments:

1. *Separate closed systems*—the client and the practitioner are separate, and each system is closed to the environment.
2. *Separate open systems*—the client and the practitioner are also separate but relate openly to their environments.
3. *Interdependent open systems*—the client and practitioner overlap each other in functions and relations, and both are open to the environment.

Clark studies these forms with regard to tasks, external forces, value systems, reward systems, and power systems. The study highlights the need for an exchange process in which there is sufficient give-and-take so that the payoffs for the various parties are satisfactory.

Closed Versus Bipolar Loop Problem-Solving Model. Havelock (1977) has made a significant distinction between two forms of search process: (1) a *closed-system loop,* in which an individual, group, or organization engages in search but only with itself, and (2) a *bipolar problem-solving loop,* in which the original problem solver is a user, and an outside helper is a resource person integrated into the search process, so that problem messages are heeded at the time of sending by the resource person, and solution messages are delivered at a time and in a manner such that they can be promptly attended to by the user.

Havelock provides a conceptual model depicting the linkage of the resource system with the user system during the problem-solving dialogue or process. Four components are shown: the client or *user system,* represented diagrammatically by a circle at the right, (2) the knowledge or research *resource system,* represented by a circle at the left, (3) the *need processing* system, represented by an arrow leading from the user system to the resource system, and (4) the *solution-processing system,* represented by an arrow leading from the resource system to the user system. The first two, it may be noted, are problem-solving systems; the last two represent the dialogue between the first two.

This model has been used as the framework for studying four federal research dissemination agencies (Havelock and Lingwood, 1973), for charting eight "operational modes" reflecting various possible emphases by a research development, dissemination, and utilization agency (Havelock and others, 1974), in examining resource linkage in educational innovations (Havelock, 1973a), and in determining the extent to which highway safety research communication can be considered to represent an effective system (Havelock and Markowitz, 1973).

**Stages, Level of Development, Actors, and Content in the Innovating Process: A Framework.** A comprehensive approach is offered by Pelz and Munson. A preliminary version (Pelz, Munson, and Jenstrom, 1978) has been expanded into a conceptual framework on innovating in organizations (Munson and Pelz, 1980) and summarized in Pelz and Munson (1980). As one aspect of the framework, the innovating process is seen to occur in stages, as follows: (1) At the *diagnosis stage,* a sense of unease or of aspiration is translated into a problem, so that action toward solving it may be undertaken. (2) At the *stage of design,* an innovative solution is developed, adapted, or adopted, and detailed guidelines for action are established. (3) At the *stage of implementation,* the innovation is put into operation and may be evaluated to decide whether to expand, modify, or discontinue it. (4) At the *stage of stabilization* (also called incorporation, routinization, or institutionalization), the innovation becomes accepted as part of standard operating procedure —and no longer an "innovation."

In the expanded framework (Munson and Pelz, 1980), the process of diffusion is seen as a repetition of the innovating process, which takes different forms depending on the *"level of development"* of the innovation: (1) Innovating occurs at the level of *origination* (earlier called initiation) when no solution to a problem is known to operate elsewhere, and the innovating organization develops a first-time solution. (2) Innovating occurs at the level of *adaptation* when a few prototype solutions exist but are not well packaged; the organization modifies these precedents to develop its own variation. (3) Innovating occurs at the level of *borrowing* when many well-packaged innovations exist; the organization copies one with little change.

Munson and Pelz include two other conceptual domains in their model: the actors involved in the process of innovating within each setting and the content of the innovation.

*Actors* include (1) the initial innovation source, (2) managers in the adopting organization, (3) workers, (4) social controllers, or (5) intermediaries, each characterized by their interests in the innovation and their power to influence the innovating process.

The *content* of the innovation includes (1) the technological content (the device or process that represents a change in the current methods of producing goods or services) and (2) its embedding content (arrangements needed for linking the technological content into an operating system). Each of these may vary in preparedness and complexity; embedding complexity, for example, includes both *depth* (extent of change in functions of organizational members) and *breadth* (proportion of the organization's members affected).

Under an analytical matrix in which the three levels of

development are arrayed against the four stages, the authors suggest that what goes on under each stage will differ in important ways depending on the level of development. For example, at the origination level, design is a core part of the innovating process, where the innovation itself takes form and shape, whereas at the borrowing level, design becomes much less significant because both technological and embedding content are well developed.

Under this model of four conceptual domains, the authors develop a series of propositions describing how the innovating process will vary within different parts of the framework. For example, with regard to actors: When power is concentrated and the interests of actors are congruent, tactics that soft-pedal power and encourage consultation are indicated. Or again, with regard to content: During stabilization, software innovations are more likely to experience continuous modification and "drift" than hardware innovations.

In their summary paper the authors stress three points:

1. An explicit attention to actors (or their organizational and societal roles) permits one to see conflicting interests in a more evenhanded way and to give more attention to the question of whom the innovation serves.

2. The concept of level of development helps one to understand what otherwise seem to be incongruous observations in the literature—for example, shifts in the function of change agents between the level of origination and the level of borrowing.

3. The distinction between the technological and embedding content of an innovation tends, for example, to clarify the linkage among the embedding complexity of an innovation, the power of the workers, and strategies for the implementation stage.

**Souder and Rubenstein's Innovation Factor System.** A host of stimuli, conditions, and formulations were brought together in a highly complex conceptual model developed by Souder and Rubenstein (1976). Their model was stimulated by a program initiated by the National Science Foundation in 1972; it was specifically developed in response to concern over the decline in productivity of R&D activities in the U.S. economy but aimed at a wider application—the development of models of the R&D innovation process. The process as conceived by Souder and Rubenstein incorporated four subsystems, all of which influence a firm's decision to innovate: the envirosystem, the perceived inducements system, the intervening variables system, and the policy/experience system. Each of these subsystems is described below.

*Subsystem #1: The Envirosystem.* This subsystem includes such factors as economic and market conditions, available technology, the legal environment, and, of course, competitive factors. Several studies suggest that the stimuli for innovations come from *outside* the innovating firm—for instance, from market needs rather than technological opportunities (Marquis and Myers, 1969; Baker, Siegeman, and Larson, 1971; Terreberry, 1973; Utterback, 1974). Feller, Menzel, and Kozak (1976) support the importance of the diffusion of new technologies as stimuli to innovation. They introduce a concept of *diffusion milieu*—those elements external to an organization which bring pressure on the firm or agency to alter its existing practices and which condition the information flow on the performance characteristics of the proposed innovation(s).

*Subsystem #2: The Perceived Inducements System.* The firm may perceive several factors external to it as stimuli to innovate. Souder and associates have found that the firm's perception of the urgency of a competitive threat to its basic technological position, its perception of new opportunities, and its perception of existing market needs are all stimuli, even though the costs of responding to the opportunities may be very high.

*Subsystem #3: Intervening Variables.* The organization's character, climate, and communication structure are noted here, as well as technology capabilities. Studies have indicated that smaller firms, by virtue of their less complex decision structures, may be inclined toward earlier internal innovation or adoption of available technologies. Other potential intervening variables include diversity of assignments, consultations outside the work setting, organizational risk strategy, and similar characteristics.

*Subsystem #4: The Policy/Experience System.* Whether the firm selects one particular idea over other alternatives depends to a great degree on its project selection process. This process, in turn, will be influenced by the risk orientation of the firm's project selection decision makers (who may not be the same persons as those who will either direct or carry out the work once the project is selected), the perceptions of the economic and market factors facing the firm, and the felt urgency for innovative activities. The position of the firm relative to its competitors, the nature of the industry, and the firm's experience with similar ventures in the past will all strongly influence the support it lends to RD/I activities. Similarly, the firm's perceptions of its technical capabilities will strongly influence its project selection/rejection decisions. Its perceived track record in moving similar projects to an expeditious and successful completion is also an important factor.

It is evident from the presentation of Souder and Rubenstein's model that it depicts the interactive influence of multiple factors on program change.

**Cybernetic Societal Guidance Model.** Etzioni (1965) proposes a theory of innovation, or societal guidance, based on an analogy with cybernetics. Applied now to a wide variety of fields, cybernetics originally stressed the control of mechanisms (including homeostasis) mainly through feedback signals. Four factors are present in a practical cybernetic system. The first is a *command post* of one or more centers that issues signals to the work unit. The second factor is *two-way communication* (or feedback)—lines that carry instructions from the center(s) to the working units and carry information and responses from the units back to the center. Although many cybernetic models omit the concept of *power*, some form of energy transmission, or "enforcement," is involved as a third factor: If the steering units cannot back up their signals with rewards or sanctions, they will frequently be disregarded. The fourth factor is the distinction within the command centers between subunits that absorb and analyze incoming information and those that effectuate selective action—that is, in a practical sense, between knowledge makers and policy makers.

When all these elements are available and functioning effectively, when communication lines are well integrated and not overloaded, when information and decision-making units have free access to each other, then we have an effective control system.

According to Etzioni, some engineers and managers think that a social system can also be run this way. The government is viewed as the cybernetic overlayer of society. In the United States, the command positions are exemplified by the White House, Congress, state capitols, and city halls. Universities, research institutes, government experts, and think tanks are the knowledge makers. The civil service, press, radio, and television are the two-way communication lines.

When a cybernetic model is applied to a social system, in Etzioni's view, then one must take into account—for both ethical and practical reasons—the fact that citizens cannot be coerced to follow "signals" (regulations and the like) unless those signals are, to a significant extent, responsive to individual values and interests. If the citizens are forced, the system violates rights and generates increasing levels of resistance. These become a major reason for society's inability to manage its affairs effectively. Effective societal cybernetics requires that the downward flow of control signals from the government to the people be accompanied by effective upward flow from the people to the government, as well as by the lateral flow of signals among citizens expressive of their values and needs.

In a later publication Etzioni (1968) develops further his model of social guidance as a theory of macroscopic action in presenting the cybernetic notion of *knowledge* as a subunit of the controlling mechanism of a social system. He sees four main theoretical dimensions as being derived from the cybernetic analogy, as follows:

1. The intraknowledge relation, or the relation among the various symbols and sets of symbols that constitute knowledge.
2. Knowledge and reality, or the relation between knowledge as a symbolic system and the external world.

3. Relations between knowledge producers and other controlling units, or the intrasocietal organization of the relations between the production and consumption of knowledge.
4. The effects of knowledge on societal action and interaction, or the effects of differences in the possession and organization of knowledge on the relations between societal actors.

Etzioni notes that the significance of knowledge as a variable that partly explains differences in societal conduct is increasing, particularly differences in the societal *organization* of the production and utilization of knowledge.

**Systematic Assessment of New Technology Model.** Dobrov (1978) develops the concept of the cybernetic systems model in terms of broad technological, social, and governmental development. He advocates, as others have, a method of systematic assessment of new technology (SANT) to direct overall technological policy and progress at national and international levels. SANT includes technology forecasting, technology assessment, alternative technologies (from which choices are to be made), evaluation of research, and a system of data on which to base science and technology management decisions.

Although the scope of his work is far beyond that in most treatments of knowledge utilization, the advocated methodology of systematic assessment is adaptable to all levels of innovation, according to Dobrov. He warns, however, that there is not and cannot be one universally good and "unified" method for technological progress. Rather, it is necessary to systematically select methods that meet the needs of particular organizational requirements, characteristics, or situations.

Along with input from management sciences, systems analysis, statistics, and political science, Dobrov uses cybernetics to develop a model for a national R&D system involving three zones: (1) legislative and executive power at the state level, (2) executive power at the level of operational management of R&D organizations, and (3) users, with feedback from the later to the earlier zones and internal interactions within each zone.

This generalized scheme of the interaction among the elements of the structure for management of national science and technology activity has been adopted by UNESCO and applied in various countries reflecting essentially different sociopolitical, economic, and technological contexts.

Social Network Technical/Political/Cultural Cycles Model. Reaching out into the broad social environment, Tichy (1980b) sets forth a model of organizational change that takes into account three interrelated cycles—technical, political, and cultural—based on the dynamics of social systems. Adjustments must be made in the face of dilemmas relating to technical design or production problems; political allocation, or power and resource, problems; and ideological/cultural mix, or normative/ values problems. Adjustments in each of these areas are conceived in cyclical terms. The cycles overlap and interact with one another, calling for strategies of varying degrees of action. Each cycle has its own level of uncertainty dependent on changing goals and environmental conditions, as well as on differences among organizational members.

Tichy notes that organizational cycles, interacting as a system, trigger one another, are affected differently by uncertainty-created events, and use different tools for dealing with uncertainty. The dynamic interrelationships among the parts of the organization must be analyzed from the three perspectives: technical, political, and cultural. Management of change consists in predicting, channeling, guiding, and altering the three cycles.

Tichy's account of the implications that organizational cycles have for change management (Tichy, 1980a) is incorporated into a far more detailed and complex presentation of a social network approach to organization development (Tichy, 1979). *Social network analysis,* described below, coupled with the examination of political, rational, and normative factors (the cycles approach), is offered as a means for coping with the multiple problems facing complex organizations. The coping procedure entails the use of some nine *leverage points for change,* such as mission, strategy, task, people, and emerging networks. Tichy proposes that the role of organization development be broadened to include attention to all the levers in the context of three traditional views of organizations and change:

the rational-economic perspective, the political-power perspective, and the normative perspective.

Network analysis is a means to the achievement of organizational change. Networks display transactional content, providing for exchanges of effect, influence, information, and goods and services. They entail various kinds of linkages between individuals. They are characterized by size (number of individuals), density (actual versus possible links), and other features worthy of study.

**Technology Delivery Crisis Model.** Wenk (1979) makes use of a systems approach in confronting the vast struggle for survival of our technological society. His analysis of the technology delivery system has been discussed in Chapter Thirteen. He sees threats to global survival in a system that may well get out of control unless a wide range of strategies is introduced to cope with the fast-moving course of events. Among these strategies are the following: (1) an inquiry into why the policy apparatus (public and private) has been deaf to the danger signals of the future, (2) the initiation of "survival training" as a major component of education for the future, (3) a new "coalition politics" entailing collaboration among scientists, engineers, and citizens, (4) crisis avoidance by technology assessment, (5) establishment of interinstitutional networks, which Wenk views as "a metaphoric fourth branch of government," and (6) development of mechanisms for conflict resolution.

**A Formula-Type Model.** Chapter Two described the A VICTORY formulation, designed to assess organizational readiness for the introduction of an innovation or change and also to guide the implementation process. Subsequently, the A VICTORY acronym has been subsumed under a working model termed Decision Determinants Analysis (DDA) and described in articles by Davis (1978) and Davis and Salasin (1979). The A VICTORY model within the DDA approach reflects a basic learning theory expressing the determinants of behavior in the formula

$$B = (Es + T + Sc)(P + Hs)(D \times C) - I$$

The equivalences between the elements of the behavior formula and the variables in the DDA or A VICTORY model are as follows:

| | | | |
|---:|:--:|:--|:--|
| Behavior | B | = PD | *Program Decision* |
| Capacity | C | = A | *Ability,* or resources required |
| Self-expectancy | $E_s$ | = V | *Values* that give purpose, perceptions, characteristics |
| Pattern | P | = I | *Information* for proposed action steps |
| Stimulus Conditions | $S_c$ | = C | *Circumstances* that prevail at the time |
| Timing | T | = T | *Timing* |
| Drive | D | = O | *Obligation,* the felt need or motivation |
| Inhibitors | I | = R | *Resistances* as they are relevant to the desired change |
| Habit strength | $H_s$ | = Y | *Yield,* or the rewards that the expected change may bring about |

Thus, we close the presentation of samples of models, or systematic frameworks, with a formulation that, in a sense, brings us back full circle to the consideration of elements that can be applied concretely and specifically to the study and implementation of programs for achieving knowledge utilization and innovative change.

## Uses of and Criteria for Models

As is evident from the presentation to this point, the term *model* is used in a number of senses. Most concretely, it signifies a miniature replica of a real thing, such as a ship or a working engine. More abstractly, it may mean a formulation of the structure and function of an intricate, intangible process, such as the form and operations of a government. The latter type of model is often depicted in graphic form, either as an organizational chart or as a flow chart. Implicitly or explicitly, the model builder in either case may draw on theory, experience, and, to a degree, validated evidence concerning analogies or relationships of one kind or another.

It is well to remember that models do not usually represent established laws or verities, but are, more often than not, hypothetical and heuristic. A model is to be judged not necessarily on its a priori capacity to reflect truth but, rather, on its fruitfulness in *leading* to useful knowledge and dependable outcomes. In the search for effective grasp of a phenomenon, it is important that models be treated as concepts, or as stepping stones or "conceptual scenarios" that may lead to increasing insight.

Several writers have set forth the criteria or component topics and elements that need to be considered in developing a systematic model.

Davis (1973a) and Davis and Salasin (1979) propose twelve characteristics (stated below) that a model of change should have if it is to be of use in everyday organizational situations. These writers note that the A VICTORY or Decision Determinants Analysis model is an attempt to incorporate all twelve features.

1.  The model, above all, should be practical.
2.  The parts of the model should be manipulable.
3.  Economy of use should be a primary consideration.
4.  Ease of communication is important.
5.  The model should be comprehensive.
6.  Synergism—the force of factors working together—is important to consider.
7.  The model should lend itself to intervention in phases.
8.  It should be possible to work with the individual components of the model.
9.  The model should call attention to how the change process influences the rest of the system.
10. The model should be flexible and versatile enough to apply to different organizational systems.

11.  The model should provide a basis for a subsequent evaluation of the effectiveness of change.
12.  The model should recognize the human characteristics of the participants involved.

Lippitt, Watson, and Westley (1958) refer to six content elements that might enter into a model of planned change, as follows:

1.  Problems of internal relationship within client systems.
2.  Problems of external relationships of client systems.
3.  Change forces and resistance forces to which client systems are exposed.
4.  The role of the change agent.
5.  Phases in the process of planned change.
6.  Particular "helping methods" applicable to each phase.

Similarly, Glaser (1973) offers a succinct summary of key factors that bear on the knowledge transfer process. His factor categories subsume the major components of a comprehensive model:

1.  Characteristics of the innovation or type of knowledge to be transferred.
2.  Characteristics and settings of potential users.
3.  Manner and extent of dissemination.
4.  Facilitating and inhibiting forces bearing on the given transfer effort.

In presenting the presidential address to the Division of Military Psychology of the American Psychological Association, McClelland (1968) set forth a list of considerations for evaluating change models that included the following factors:

1.  Mutual recognition of the change-agent and client-system roles.
2.  Means of affecting the direction, temper, and quality of change.
3.  Evaluation of cost effectiveness.

4.  Diagnosis of strengths and weaknesses.
5.  Definition of the time required for a continuing relation-
    ship.
6.  Ease of realistic communication without distortion.
7.  Inclusion of bases for assessing when the model is applica-
    ble and when it is not.
8.  Usefulness to people with different backgrounds.
9.  Means for detecting gaps in theory and practice.

According to Chin (1969), there are two major categories
of models that the practitioner can use as a diagnostic tool for
planning change: the *systems model* and the *developmental
model*. Chin defines typical major terms used in each type of
model. For the systems model these are *system; boundary; tension, stress, strain,* and *conflict; equilibrium* and *steady state;*
and *feedback*. The terms defined in conjunction with the developmental model are *direction, identifiable state, form of progression, forces,* and *potentiality.*

Chin raises five questions about the relationship of the
change agent to the model:

1.  Does the model account for stability and change?
2.  Where does the model locate the source of change?
3.  What does the model assume about the determination of
    goals and directions?
4.  Does the model provide levers for effecting change?
5.  How does the model place the change agent in the scheme
    of things?

Each general model type is examined in the light of these
questions. Chin asserts that a third model for change is emerging, one that incorporates features from both the systems and
developmental models. In that model, direct attention is paid to
the induced forces (for example, the added impact of a change
agent) producing change.

The foregoing indications of what a model should be or
do represent exploratory excursions into a large field of inquiry.
From these examples two major requirements emerge as most

significant: that the model work and that it serve to clarify important aspects of the several parts of the utilization or change process.

## Summary Comments

The two major sections of this chapter—*perspectives* and *systematic frameworks*—may be viewed in the light of the emergence of what is, in essence, a derived discipline that has as its province phenomena associated with knowledge utilization and innovative change.

Regarding perspectives, the treatment reflects an extension of Rogers' "research traditions," or borrowings from a small number of disciplines that have shown a concern with diffusion. The more recent writings add to the list of these "traditions" and lend additional theoretical insight in their application.

Regarding systematic frameworks or models, much of the pertinent literature parallels the growth of interest in supplying organizing principles to discrete phenomena in line with a systematic synthesis of their particular aspects or manifestations. These efforts are in line with "systems" thinking and use the expression *models* to designate frameworks that can be used in generating explanatory or programmatic hypotheses.

The writings reported in this chapter should tend to dispel any notion that views on determinants of utilization or change or efforts to achieve these outcomes arise out of thin air or that these phenomena are free from the operation of complex, interactive forces. The diversity of proposed perspectives and the plethora of models should serve as reminders that, despite numerous contributions at the practical level and considerable theoretical thought, the new "discipline" is very much in need of further development.

# 16

## Conclusion: Improved Knowledge Utilization—Highlights, Guidelines, and Prospects

### Key Determinants of Knowledge Utilization and Change

The material cited in this book points up the complex interaction of the determinants or clusters of variables bearing on effective use of knowledge or tryout of promising innovations. One very valuable way of subsuming key determinants has already been presented under the A VICTORY acronym (Davis, 1971; Davis and Salasin, 1975). Another way of presenting these determinants may be described under the following seven basic requirements.

The innovation itself, after review by those who have the power to decide for adoption, must seem, on net balance, *worthwhile*. And after initial trial, if the adoption is to be durable, it must also be deemed worthwhile by those in a position to decide on retention, modification, or discontinuance.

422

The person, agency, or organization that is considering adoption must be *willing* and *able* to adopt. In many situations there needs to be agreement (willingness) on the part of management to at least partly release from other duties a respected, influential member of the organization to be identified as internal change facilitator/coordinator. If a consultant from outside the organization is engaged to provide technical assistance in connection with adoption and implementation of the innovation, such assistance is likely to be much more effective when carried out with the help of an internal change facilitator.

Relevant members of the organization also must be *informed* realistically about what is involved and required in connection with effective implementation and monitoring if the innovative process, program, or method of operation is to be viable without the sustained imposition of powerful authoritative demand.

Whether the innovation fits well into the surrounding ideological/cultural/political value *orientation* in a given setting (or in the mind/feelings of an influential "gatekeeper") can significantly affect the likelihood of durable adoption.

The *circumstances/timing factors* that prevail at the time adoption is being considered can likewise have major influence on the chances of its durability.

Finally, manifest or latent feelings of *resistance* to adoption of the new product, policy, procedure, or activity need to be recognized, understood, and taken into account in the decision process regarding adoption and in tailoring of the implementation process.

Related to the above-mentioned factors bearing on effective use of promising new knowledge or innovations is the observation by Rogers, Eveland, and Klepper (1977) that utilization of an innovation is not necessarily adoption *per se* but a process in which organizational consensus on how the innovation can best be used in the given setting is gradually shaped. Innovations are not constant in their various adoptions; rather, *adaptation* is frequent.

The literature review in the preceding chapters has identified and reported various strategies or procedures that have been found effective under certain conditions for facilitating dissemination/transfer/utilization of exemplary practices developed in various subject fields and of promising findings derived from R&D studies. This literature on knowledge transfer bears on the critical and growing problem of how to span the oft-observed abyss between the discovery of "better ways" for meeting various types of problems and the assimilation or shaping of that knowledge into general practice, or having it serve as input to policy formulation.

To be significantly influenced by some new knowledge, program, or product implies change. Many readers of this volume may seek to learn effective means for accurately identifying barriers and then finding gateways to achieve various types of seemingly promising change, or at least to stimulate serious consideration thereof. In reporting numerous selected studies and findings on the many aspects of knowledge creation, diffusion, and utilization, we have provided various authors' suggested lists of relevant variables. In this wrap-up chapter we will try to recapitulate some key strategies and tactical considerations bearing on the successful adoption/implementation of innovative change. Different clusters need to be tailored to fit different contexts.

Let us first take the case of often-overlooked implementation considerations in connection with the introduction of new technology. The August 22, 1980, issue of *Science* published an editorial by Amitai Etzioni entitled "Reindustrialization of America," which rather quickly became a kind of new "buzzword" phrase at the time to identify and prescribe several of America's major ills. Etzioni stated: "How are we to see that our problem is not that of hyperinflation, or weakening of the dollar, or declining productivity, or exhaustion of oil, but an underlying structural problem which deeply affects all these and most other elements of our socioeconomic condition? We have overburdened our industrial machine, the modern American economy, that previous generations labored to put together. . . . Once the broader picture is drawn, the corrective practically suggests itself; a decade or so of reindustrialization of America, to shore up the key elements of its productive capacity, instead of tinkering with some and taking a stab at fixing others" (p. 863).

The reindustrialization Rx cited here may be helpful and justified. However, for it to work out effectively and efficiently (as we believe Dr. Etzioni would agree), some critical "directions for taking" need to be added to the prescription—namely, guidelines for implementation, monitoring, evaluation, refinement if needed, and maintenance. These would include tryout of prototype equipment or innovative procedures under normal operating conditions so far as practicable before permanent installation; installation by technical representatives from the developer/producer *working in conjunction with the user's team* that will become responsible for operation and maintenance; provision of on-site consultation assistance from the developer/ producer to help with training of user operating and maintenance personnel until they demonstrate proficiency in application; assignment of an interested, knowledgeable, influential person from within the organization to serve as internal colleague consultant; adaptation or shaping to the sociotechnical factors prevailing in the user's milieu; and encouragement of affected user personnel to offer suggestions, ask questions, and become ego-involved participants.

Unless adequate and timely attention is given to sociotechnical factors bearing on the user's understanding and acceptance of major technological change, the expensive investment in "reindustrialization" may fail to yield the expected advantages. Inadequate planning and faulty implementation can lead either to a nonproductive, costly, frustrating "debugging" experience in terms of both technical and human factors related to operational performance or to discontinuance.

A related, important factor in deciding on strategies designed to achieve effective implementation of an innovative policy or procedure is the match between characteristics of the given innovation and characteristics of the potential users. Does a *programmed* or packaged approach appear needed, or would an *adaptive*, developmental approach be more suitable? The former calls for clarity and specificity in handed-down directions for implementation—hence planning and control. The latter allows for unfolding interaction and perhaps negotiated adaptation between the developers or proponents of the innovation and the institutional setting of the user, where motivation is achieved through participation in decision making.

## Some Guidelines for Practical Action

The following four guidelines may be useful to facilitate planned change (shaping consensus for utilization/implementation) or consideration of knowledge input (relevant information) bearing on a proposed policy question:

*Guideline #1: Consider context, assess readiness, and provide incentives as well as consultation assistance for adoption or adaptation.* When developing a new technology or product or program, especially one whose adoption would require change in an organization's existing practice, study the factors in potential user settings that are relevant to successful adoption (such as incentives and readiness "for"; resistances of any kind "against"). Where feasible, involve a representative sample of hands-on participants or users and decision makers in the settings of potential users as consultants during the development and planning stages. Then, provide adequately sustained technical or consultation assistance at the time of delivery, setup, implementation, maintenance, and evaluation in the user context. Consider applying Davis' and Salasin's (1978b) Decision Determinants Analysis to assess readiness for adoption/implementation at a given site and to guide the implementation process. Bear in mind Norman Maier's pertinent equation: $ED = Q \times A$; an $E$ffective $D$ecision = its $Q$uality multiplied by its $A$cceptance by those who are needed to effect implementation.

*Guideline #2: In connection with efforts to use R&D findings to influence policy decisions, focus on altering the patterns of awareness or perception of relevant policy makers, and consider policy makers' interests, values, and constraints.* When trying to use knowledge from social science research to influence political/administrative policy, it is well to bear in mind that social problems and their proposed remediation involve *political judgments* and conflicts and thus are embedded in partisan content.

As reported in Chapter Fourteen, in connection with research designed to influence policy decision, Weiss (1980) carried out an interview study of 155 persons who held high-level positions in federal, state, and local mental health agencies with reference to two major questions: (1) whether and in what ways the respondents consciously use the results of social science research in reaching decisions on the job and (2) whether and under what circumstances they seek out research information when considering policy or program alternatives. She found that knowledge from social science research is used less to solve particular problems than to provide a background of information and ideas. Research knowledge tends to creep into policy deliberations in diffuse ways.

In a subtle, sometimes unconscious way, knowledge of research findings may change people's perception of a problem by shaping their interests, values, and understandings and thus influence their decisions. Cumulatively, this conceptual (rather than instrumental) utilization of R&D findings slowly builds up and eventually surfaces to influence program and policy decisions. Or, as Weiss has so well expressed this finding (personal communication, 1980): "The key point is that ideas, generalizations, and concepts from social science do not often influence policy and practice by direct application (adoption, instrumental utilization in decisions), but rather by changing the parameters of the discussion. Research generalizations and concepts alter people's understanding of the situation, highlight new issues, change the facets of the problem that they consider amenable to action, help to reorder their priorities, extend the range of alternatives they consider, allay certain uncertainties and anxieties, and create others. The effects of social science research are often subtle and difficult to detect but come about through alteration of patterns of awareness—which in time can have massive consequences."

A confounding aspect of research knowledge and utilization impact is, as Salasin has noted (1981b), that it "may be like water that often runs into underground rivulets, marrying unseen with other flows, not always of converging research information, but of the additional seven influencers of decision: available resources, felt needs, resistances, values, circumstances, timing, and perceived rewards. The confluence may surface miles away, with the unique contribution of research diluted beyond recognition. The absence of a good tracer to measure utilization is a serious problem in our attempts to find better ways to nurture the process" (p. 1).

When attempting policy-relevant research, one cannot assume that policy makers necessarily behave in ways that objectively assess the consequences of various alternatives in a comprehensive and deliberate manner. Try to understand the policy makers' special interests, constraints, values; then present the research findings in ways that (succinctly) make clear what may be gained from heeding the findings—over the short *and long* run—by the policy makers, constituents/supporters, the public, and so on.

An interesting example (Smith, 1980a) of strategy and tactics used to influence governmental policy toward support of a very large-scale R&D project has been summarized in Chapter Six and may be worth reviewing in this context.

*Guideline #3: Develop communication networks.* Many organizations operating in the same general field—public schools, for example, or community mental health centers—have certain common problems. Some organizations develop what to others may be innovative, unusually successful ways of dealing with those problems, at least in their particular settings. If these organizations and people are brought together in a network to share exemplary practices in an each-one-teach-others mode, they tend to set up a learning readiness and problem-solving exchange wherein there is receptivity also to presentations of new information from R&D studies.

During the last several years there has been significant growth in the establishment of communication networks involving an exchange of information among institutions engaged in common activities. In that context, problems or felt needs are identified, and information may be offered about existing or emerging relevant R&D findings or about unusually successful practices that some network members have developed to deal with those vexing problems. The National Diffusion Network

(NDN) sponsored by the U.S. Office of Education and the National Institute of Education is one example of such a network. It identifies (and validates) especially effective projects or practices for dealing with given types of problems, diffuses the information through the network, and couples this service with technical assistance consultation in the form of staff training for interested potential users.

Already, NDN has improved the education of millions of students and the teaching of thousands of teachers. Each year, more than 25,000 teachers, principals, administrators, and other staff members are trained to understand and use one or more NDN projects. This process facilitates spread of the good news of successful experiments.

Clifford and Cooper (1980) describe another illustration of network building for knowledge dissemination and information exchange in the mental health field. The arrangement is for six community health centers, one from each state in federal Region V, to provide technical assistance in the area of mental health program evaluation. Some findings that can be derived from three and one-half years of experience with this resource network are the following:

1. The task of identifying, linking, and mobilizing these resources is more important than providing technical assistance (over the long run).

2. Numerous organizations provide technical assistance or training as part of their missions. However, very often these missions operate in parallel, each one restricted to a particular group or level of government. By bridging the gaps between these missions, one not only economizes on the use of scarce resources but also creates networks, which, in turn, generate new resources. This bridging also contributes to the team-building and legitimation processes that are so often necessary for the utilization of new knowledge and skills.

3. Technical assistance activities exist in a "political" context, and one must be cognizant of this fact. Network building involves linking the various constituencies in the environment. Therefore,

the core group that is trying to build the resource
network must itself reflect and be able to move
among the multiple constituencies [p. 132].

In an editorial in *Science,* February 5, 1982, James B.
Hunt, governor of North Carolina, makes a noteworthy case for
an expanded network strategy. He proposes that state and local
governments take initiatives to collaborate with scientists from
universities and public and private research institutions to form
networks (possibly regional ones) that are likely to generate or
share information about technological advances or promising innovative practices that can better meet people's needs and desires. The examples he cites of such successful collaboration in
North Carolina are impressive.

If an easily readable state-of-the-art paper or monograph
can be prepared to bring together and synthesize the best of
what is known from R&D and exemplary practice bearing on
given subjects or problems, such a resource can be of great value
both to network members and to others.

*Guideline #4: Give major attention to possible ways of
kindling interest and support of potential users: Be clear about
cost-benefits, other existing evidence of worth, and feasibility
of adopting the new technology or procedure.* Inviting stakeholders in an organization to participate in planning, implementing, monitoring, and evaluating the innovative product,
procedure, or program can help to develop needed understanding and support.

The existence and role of the change agent or the change
agency do not obviate the need for developers of promising
new knowledge to think about how to increase the capability
and the motivation of potential users of an innovative program
or product to perceive its areas of relevant, cost-beneficial application. The efficacy of information flow depends in part on capability and motivation of both the developers/senders and the receivers of the information, sometimes aided by linking agents.
Sometimes developers (researchers) are disinclined to get involved in the dissemination (sender) role but may be glad to

have an appropriate linking agent or research agent or research utilization specialist take on that task.

A sometimes useful method for relating potential problem-solving efforts or processes to substantive needs or concerns is to lay out and fill in the boxes of a matrix. Figure 2 depicts a hypothetical matrix-outline example that would fit into the context of a mental health services delivery agency.

**Figure 2. Outline of a Matrix for Goals and Goal-Attainment Strategies.**

Possible Problem-Solving Activities

| Needs/Concerns | Provide technical assistance | Undertake networking | Establish information clearinghouse | Improve capabilities for self-evaluation | Convene concerned groups to develop action strategies for specific types of problems | Develop appropriate oversight procedures | Establish relationships with state and local legislators who control funding |
|---|---|---|---|---|---|---|---|
| Providing services for chronically mentally ill | | | | | | | |
| Ensuring professional accountability | | | | | | | |
| Providing continuity of care | | | | | | | |
| Improving evaluation of treatment outcomes | | | | | | | |
| Improving prevention efforts | | | | | | | |
| Integrating physical health, mental health, and social services | | | | | | | |

## Future Prospects

Despite an increasing store of practical wisdom on the subject of change, innovation, and knowledge utilization, as well as a recent expansion of an interest in conceptual models, there are many unexplored areas and insufficiently tested change strategies.

What, then, is the state of the art, and what are its prospects for the future? As previously noted, the summarized reports vary in character from statements of "conventional wisdom" to statistically or experimentally controlled empirical investigations. The resulting "findings" reflect this mixture of intuitive and objective inputs. One is left with the overall impression that whatever the underlying rational, intellectual basis for utilization of validated or at least promising innovations, there also is an essentially subjective overlay of sensitive interpersonal relations that can be cultivated to serve as strong links between researchers, administrators, and practitioners.

Further, one may inquire about the state of the development in which the art finds itself. The operative mode seems to be based largely on personal predilection and pragmatic experience. But there is also evidence of excursions into the use of theoretical models, and research validation of hypotheses and theories.

Further conceptualization and additional empirical research seem both to be needed and to be in the works, while there appears to be widening interest in the matter of applying already-known principles or guidelines for putting knowledge to use.

With regard to conceptualization, further exploitation of ideas derived from systems theory seems promising. Already, a number of models of research utilization recognize the existence of subsystems and suprasystems among the phenomena of change and utilization processes. This is true of the model reported by Havelock and Lingwood (1973), which, as previously noted, provides for a user system, a resource system, a need-processing system, a solution-processing system, a microsystem, and a macrosystem.

At the level of empirical research, there are countless top-ics that invite further investigation. The number of empirical studies reported in this distillation is relatively small compared with nonempirical studies. And many of the empirical investi-gations could well warrant cross-validation.

Studies conducted in one area of application may warrant repetition in each of a number of other fields. For example, in a study reported by Hodgkin and others (1975, 1979) and Glaser (1980e), the authors developed and widely disseminated a com-prehensive, repeatedly refined state-of-the-art synthesis/consen-sus paper (subsequently enlarged into a monograph), dealing with a family of biomedical diseases—namely, chronic obstruc-tive pulmonary diseases. The details of procedures (which we call "progressive iteration") for developing this state-of-the-art document, and the utilization strategies employed, along with their resulting major impact, are described in Chapter Eleven. This strategy for spreading information and enhancing utiliza-tion of state-of-the-art practices would seem equally useful in connection with other biomedical problems and probably would be just as applicable to a variety of subject fields.

Numerous other differentiations in variables affecting knowledge development, diffusion, and utilization call for in-vestigation. Interesting but untested hypotheses abound in the literature. In particular, there is a need for further compe-tent evaluation studies of various strategies for diffusion/utiliza-tion.

Large-scale cooperative studies that tap the talents of sea-soned researchers in the field of knowledge utilization seem es-pecially promising. Havelock (1974a) sought to find out how three teams of specialists in problems of knowledge utilization (Edward Glaser and colleagues, Ronald Lippitt and colleagues, Everett Rogers and colleagues) might address the same given problem. The three teams first work independently and then come together in conference. Havelock tried this approach in the course of an attempt to suggest an "ideal" research utiliza-tion pattern for the Social and Rehabilitation Service. The re-sult was that the three approaches were both overlapping and different, with a good deal of integration growing out of the exposition and critical review of the separate position papers at a two-day conference.

Some government agencies—for example, the Department of Defense—occasionally offer an equal amount of funds and time to qualified organizations for initial independent development of proposals designed to meet a complex problem or need. The most promising features of the several competing approaches may subsequently be integrated.

A similar procedure could be used within any organization or agency by inviting an appropriate group (or several competing groups) to develop strategies for facilitating the adoption (or perhaps refinement before adoption) of new concepts, programs, or products intended to meet some identified need. Each member of such a group could outline steps she or he would propose for gaining acceptance and developing implementation skills. Members would be asked to state their guiding principle or rationale for each proposed step. Then they would compare their outlined steps and discuss differences, usually reaching consensus in the process.

Glaser (1973, 1981b) has suggested what might be termed a strategy or "theorem" bearing on research utilization that can have relevance to various fields of operation in our own society. He points out that, for any problem confronted by many individuals, groups, organizations, or institutions, the range of response effectiveness approximates the normal bell-shaped distribution curve. If the qualities that characterize the most exemplary practices (the upper 1-2 percent of that curve) can be identified, and the *conditions* that seem to account for this relative excellence can be determined, we *may* find that this knowledge or procedure or product can (with thoughtful, skillful, sensitive application of appropriate knowledge transfer strategies) be made available for consideration and use by others. There is potential for upgrading the quality of life in many functional areas rather quickly by following such a procedure. At the same time, even the best available knowledge and practice may be deficient in various ways, thus calling for a continuing search for new and greater knowledge.

This concept and strategy seem to hold promise for expediting the spread of superior ways of dealing with many existing problems. Merton ([1948], 1982, pp. 264-265) offers a related observation: "In the world laboratory of the sociologist, as in the more secluded laboratories of the physicist and chemist, it is the successful experiment which is decisive [if it can be cross-validated] and not the thousand-and-one failures which preceded it. More is learned from the single success than from the multiple failures. A single success proves it can be done. Thereafter, it is necessary only to learn what made it work." To this we would add "and how it can most fruitfully be brought to the attention of potential users."

Currently, with our continuing concern with inadequate productivity and technical/political problems such as ineffective management of natural resources and of toxic and nuclear wastes, it seems clear that results of basic research generally do not diffuse through our economy fast enough or effectively enough to contribute as much as they potentially can.

The contemporary pace and scale of change will probably continue to accelerate, as Toffler and others have suggested. If they do, then a related problem already with us, and likely to become of increasing concern, may be that of achieving reasonable stability and conservation of those things that seem good, rather than just searching for promising innovative programs. In some areas of our lives it would appear that a most welcome change would be greater stability—for a change!

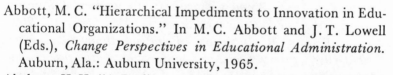

# Bibliography

Abbott, M. C. "Hierarchical Impediments to Innovation in Educational Organizations." In M. C. Abbott and J. T. Lowell (Eds.), *Change Perspectives in Educational Administration.* Auburn, Ala.: Auburn University, 1965.

Abelson, H. H. "A Rudimentary Analysis of the Problem-Solving Process." Unpublished paper, School of Education, City College, City University of New York, 1964.

Abelson, H. H. *Teachers' Responsiveness to Selected Psycho-Educational Ideas.* Report No. 70-71. New York: Division of Teacher Education, City University of New York, 1970.

Abernathy, W. J. *The Productivity Dilemma: Roadblock to Innovation in the Automobile Industry.* Final Report to National Science Foundation, Grant No. PRA-7420571. Baltimore: Johns Hopkins University Press, 1978.

Abernathy, W. J., and Townsend, P. L. "Technology, Productivity, and Process Change." *Technological Forecasting and Social Change,* 1975, 7(4), 379-396.

Abramson, M. A. *The Funding of Social Knowledge Production and Application: A Survey of Federal Agencies.* Washington, D.C.: National Academy of Sciences, 1978.

Abt Associates, Inc. *Urban Development Applications Project: Urban Technology Transfer Study.* (NTIS N75-30951.) Cambridge, Mass.: Abt Associates, Inc., 1975.

Abt, C. C. (Ed.). *The Evaluation of Social Programs.* Beverly Hills, Calif.: Sage, 1977.

Abt, P., and Magidson, J. *Reforming Schools: Problems in Program Implementation and Evaluation.* Beverly Hills, Calif.: Sage, 1980.

Achilladelis, B., Jervis, P., and Robertson, A. *Project SAPPHO: A Study of Success and Failures in Industrial Innovations.* Brighton, England: Science Policy Research Unit, University of Sussex, 1971.

Adimorah, E. N. O. "Scientific Information Transfer and National Development in Africa." *UNESCO Bulletin for Libraries,* 1978, *32*(5), 333-337.

Adler, N. E., and Coleman, D. "Goal Setting, T-Group Participation, and Self-Rated Change: An Experimental Study." *Journal of Applied Behavioral Science,* 1975, *11*(2), 197-208.

Agarwala-Rogers, R. *Diffusion of Impact Innovations from 1973-1976: Interpersonal Communication Networks Among University Professors.* (ED 143-316.) New York: Exxon Education Foundation, 1977a.

Agarwala-Rogers, R. "Why Is Evaluation Research Not Utilized?" In M. Guttentag (Ed.), *Evaluation Studies Review Annual.* Vol. 2. Beverly Hills, Calif.: Sage, 1977b.

Agnew, P. C., and Hsu, F. L. K. "Introducing Change in a Mental Hospital." *Human Organization,* 1960, *19,* 195-198.

Aiken, M., and Hage, J. *The Relationship Between Organizational Factors and the Acceptance of New Rehabilitation Programs in Mental Retardation.* Final Report to Vocational Rehabilitation Administration, Project RD-1556-G. Washington, D.C.: Social and Rehabilitation Service, 1968.

Aiken, M., and Hage, J. "The Organic Organization Innovation." *Sociology,* 1971, *5,* 63-82.

Albala, A. "Stage Approach for the Evaluation and Selection of R&D Projects." *IEEE Transactions on Engineering Management,* 1975, *22*(4), 153-163.

Alderfer, C. P. "Changing Processes in Organizations." In M. D. Dunnette (Ed.), *Handbook of Industrial and Organizational Psychology.* Chicago: Rand McNally, 1976.

Aldrich, H. E. *Organizations and Environments.* Englewood Cliffs, N.J.: Prentice-Hall, 1979.

Aleshire, D., and Strommen, M. P. *Effecting Utilization: Experimental Use of Consultants. Phase II Report.* Minneapolis, Minn.: Search Institute, n.d.

Aleshire, D., and Strommen, M. P. "Introducing Innovations into Volunteer Organizations: Factors Associated with Readiness to Change." *Innovations,* 1978, *5*(2), 23-26.

Alkin, M. C. "Naturalistic Study of Evaluation Utilization." In L. A. Braskamp and R. D. Brown (Eds.), *New Directions for Program Evaluation: Utilization of Evaluative Information,* no. 5. San Francisco: Jossey-Bass, 1980.

Alkin, M. C., Daillak, R., and White, P. *Using Evaluations: Does Evaluation Make a Difference?* Beverly Hills, Calif.: Sage, 1979.

Alkin, M. C., and others. *Evaluation and Decision Making: The Title VII Experience.* Los Angeles: Center for the Study of Evaluation, University of California, 1974.

Allen, T. J. *The Differential Performance of Information Channels in the Transfer of Technology.* Cambridge: Alfred P. Sloan School of Management, Massachusetts Institute of Technology, 1966.

Allen, T. J. *Roles in Technical Communication Networks.* Cambridge: Alfred P. Sloan School of Management, Massachusetts Institute of Technology, 1969.

Allen, T. J. *Managing the Flow of Technology: Technology Transfer and the Dissemination of Technological Information Within the R&D Organization.* Cambridge, Mass.: M.I.T. Press, 1977.

Alpert, J. L. "The School Psychologist as a Consultant to Schools." In B. B. Wolan (Ed.), *International Encyclopedia of Neurology, Psychiatry, Psychoanalysis, and Psychology.* New York: Brunner/Mazel, 1976.

Al-Timini, W. "Innovations-Led Expansion: The Shipbuilding Case." *Research Policy,* 1975, *4,* 160-171.

Altman, I. "Some Perspectives on the Study of Man-Environment Phenomena." *Representative Research in Social Psychology,* 1973, *4*(1), 109-126.

Altrocchi, J. "Mental Health Consultation." In S. E. Golann and C. Eisdorfer (Eds.), *Handbook of Community Mental Health.* New York: Appleton-Century-Crofts, 1972.

American Educational Research Association. *Some Propositions on Research Utilization in Education.* Washington, D.C.: American Educational Research Association, 1965.

Ammerman, H. L., Clukey, D., and Thomas, G. P. (Eds.). *The Oregon Studies in Educational Research, Development, Diffusion, and Evaluation.* Vol. 4. Monmouth, Oreg.: Teaching Research, 1972.

Anderson, L. R., and McGuire, W. J. "Prior Reassurance of Group Consensus as a Factor in Producing Resistance to Persuasion." *Sociometry,* 1965, *28,* 44-56.

Anderson, S. B., and Ball, S. *The Profession and Practice of Program Evaluation.* San Francisco: Jossey-Bass, 1978.

Anderson, W. A., and Dynes, R. R. *Social Movements, Violence, and Change.* Columbus: Ohio State University Press, 1975.

Andrew, M. D. *Teacher Leadership: A Model for Change.* Bulletin 37. Washington, D.C.: Association of Teacher Educators, 1974.

Andrews, F. M., and Farris, G. F. "Supervisory Practices and Innovation in Scientific Teams." *Personnel Psychology,* 1967, *20*(4), 497-516.

Aneja, A. P., and Aneja, V. P. "The Strategy of Process Translation." *Research Management,* 1977, *20*(6), 37-40.

Anthony, R. B. "Change in Secondary Schools: Some Important but Overlooked Barriers." *Indiana Social Studies Quarterly,* 1974, *27*(2), 33-35.

Applebaum, R. P. *Theories of Social Change.* Chicago: Markham, 1970.

Archibald, K. A. "The Utilization of Social Research and Policy Analysis." Doctoral dissertation, Washington University, 1968. *Dissertation Abstracts International,* 1968, *29,* 679A. (University Microfilms No. 68-10,771.)

Archibald, K. A. "Alternative Orientation to Social Science Utilization." *Social Science Information,* 1970a, *9*(2), 7-34.

Archibald, K. A. "Three Views of the Expert's Role in Policy Making: Systems Analysis, Incrementalism, and the Clinical Approach." *Policy Sciences,* 1970b, *1,* 73-86.

Arensberg, C. M., and Nickoff, A. H. *Introducing Social Change: A Manual of Community Development.* Chicago: Aldine-Atherton, 1971.

Argyris, C. *Organization and Innovation.* Homewood, Ill.: Irwin, 1965.

Argyris, C. "On the Effectiveness of Research and Development Organizations." *American Scientist,* 1968, *56*(4), 344-355.

Argyris, C. "Explorations in Consulting-Client Relationships." In W. G. Bennis, K. D. Benne, and R. Chin (Eds.), *The Planning of Change.* (2nd ed.) New York: Holt, Rinehart and Winston, 1969.

Argyris, C. *Intervention Theory and Method: A Behavioral Science View.* Reading, Mass.: Addison-Wesley, 1970.

Argyris, C. *Interpersonal Competence and Organizational Effectiveness.* Homewood, Ill.: Dorsey, 1972.

Argyris, C. "Alternative Schools: A Behavioral Analysis." *Teachers College Record,* 1974, *75,* 429-452.

Argyris, C. *Increasing Leadership Effectiveness.* New York: Wiley, 1976.

Argyris, C., and Schön, D. *Theory in Practice: Increasing Professional Effectiveness.* San Francisco: Jossey-Bass, 1974.

Armenakis, A. A., and Feild, H. S. "Evaluation of Organizational Change Using Nonindependent Criterion Measures." *Personnel Psychology,* 1975, *28*(1), 39-44.

Armenakis, A. A., Feild, H. S., and Holley, W. H. "Guidelines for Overcoming Empirically Identified Evaluation Problems of Organizational Development Change Agents." *Human Relations,* 1976, *29*(12), 1147-1161.

Aronson, S. H., and Sherwood, C. C. "Researcher Versus Practitioner: Problems in Social Action Research." *Social Work,* 1967, *12*(4), 89-96.

Arthur D. Little, Inc. *Patterns and Problems of Technical Innovation in American Industry.* Report to the National Science Foundation, No. C-65344. Washington, D.C.: National Science Foundation, 1963.

Arthur D. Little, Inc., and Industrial Research Institute, Inc.
*Barriers to Innovation in Industry: Opportunities for Public
Policy Changes.* Washington, D.C.: National Science Foun-
dation, 1973a.

Arthur D. Little, Inc., and Industrial Research Institute, Inc.
*Barriers to Innovation in Industry: Opportunities for Public
Policy Changes. Executive Summary.* Washington, D.C.: Na-
tional Science Foundation, 1973b.

Atkeson, B. M., and Forehand, R. "Parents as Behavior-Change
Agents with School-Related Problems." *Education and Urban Society,* 1978, *10*(4), 521-538.

Attkisson, C. C., and others (Eds.). *Evaluation of Human Service Programs.* New York: Academic Press, 1978.

Austin, C. J. "The MEDLARS Project at the National Library
of Medicine." *Library Resources and Technical Service,*
1965, *9,* 94-99.

Avellar, J. W., and others. *The Community Lodge Program.*
East Lansing: Michigan State University, 1978.

Avery, E. L. "Tug of War: Local Implementation of Federal
Educational Innovation." Doctoral dissertation, Harvard University, 1977. *Dissertation Abstracts International,* 1977, *38,*
4462A. (University Microfilms No. 77-30,673.)

Ayscough, P. B. "Academic Reactions to Educational Innovation." *Studies in Higher Education,* 1976, *1*(1), 3-9.

Backer, T. E. "Evaluation of Research Utilization Specialist
Projects in Vocational Rehabilitation." Doctoral dissertation,
University of California, Los Angeles, 1974. *Dissertation Ab-
stracts International,* 1974, *34,* 564B.

Backer, T. E. "Putting Research to Use: Some Guidelines for
Rehabilitation Professionals." *Proceedings of the February
1980 Region II Workshop, Putting Research to Use in Rehabilitation.* Washington, D.C.: George Washington University
Medical Center, 1980.

Backer, T. E., and Glaser, E. M. *Proceedings of the Research
Utilization Specialist Conference, September 1973, Pacific
Palisades, California.* (NTIS PB-253 509.) Los Angeles: Ed-
ward Glaser & Associates, 1973.

Backer, T. E., and Glaser, E. M. "Workshop on Research Utilization Specialist Model: A Report." *Rehabilitation Counseling Bulletin,* 1975, *19*(2), 396-404.

Backer, T. E., and Glaser, E. M. (Eds.). *Proceedings of the Advanced Workshop on Program Consultation in Mental Health Services, March 1977, Annapolis, Maryland.* Los Angeles: Human Interaction Research Institute, 1978.

Backer, T. E., and Glaser, E. M. *Methods for Sustaining Innovative Service Programs.* Final Report to the National Institute of Mental Health, Grant No. 5 R12 MH27566. Los Angeles: Human Interaction Research Institute, 1979.

Bader, M. B. "International Transfer of Medical Technology: Analysis and a Proposal for Effective Monitoring." *International Journal of Health Services,* 1977, 7(3), 443-458.

Baehr, P. R., and Wittrock, B. (Eds.). *Policy Analysis and Public Innovations: Patterns, Problems, and Potentials.* Beverly Hills, Calif.: Sage, 1981.

Baer, W. S. *University-Industry Interactions.* Santa Monica, Calif.: Rand Corporation, 1979.

Baer, W. S., Johnson, L. L., and Merrow, E. W. *Analysis of Federally Funded Demonstration Projects: Final Report.* Santa Monica, Calif.: Rand Corporation, 1976.

Baer, W. S., Johnson, L. L., and Merrow, E. W. "Government-Sponsored Demonstrations of New Technologies." *Science,* 1977, *196,* 950-957.

Bailey, S. K., and others. *Significant Educational Research and Innovation: Their Potential Contribution to Experimental School Design.* Syracuse, N.Y.: Syracuse University Research Corporation, New York Policy Institute, 1972.

Baire, K., and Rescher, N. (Eds.). *Values and the Future.* New York: Free Press, 1969.

Baker, E. L., and Quellmalz, E. S. *Educational Testing and Evaluation: Design, Analysis, and Policy.* Beverly Hills, Calif.: Sage, 1980.

Baker, N. R., Siegeman, J., and Larson, J. "The Relationship Between Certain Characteristics of Industrial Research Proposals and Their Subsequent Disposition." *IEEE Transactions on Engineering Management,* 1971, *18*(4), 118-124.

Baker, N. R., and Sweeny, D. J. *An Assessment of Modeling*

*Capability Related to the Process of Organized Technological Innovation Within the Firm.* Final Report to the National Science Foundation, Grant No. PRA-7517332. Washington, D.C.: National Science Foundation, 1977.

Balasubramanyam, V. N. "Transfer of Technology: The UNCTAD Arguments in Perspective." *World Economy,* 1977, *1*(1), 69-80.

Baldridge, J. V., and Burnham, R. A. "Organizational Innovation: Individual, Organizational, and Environmental Impacts." *Administrative Science Quarterly,* 1975, *20*(2), 165-176.

Baldridge, J. V., and Deal, T. E. *Managing Change in Educational Organizations: Sociological Perspectives, Strategies, and Case Studies.* Berkeley, Calif.: McCutchan, 1975.

Baldridge, J. V., and Tierney, M. L. *New Approaches to Management: Creating Practical Systems of Management Information and Management by Objectives.* San Francisco: Jossey-Bass, 1979.

Balk, D. "Change in a Community Mental Health Center: A Case Study with Twelve Lessons." *Group & Organization Studies,* 1978, *3*(4), 447-455.

Banathy, B. H. *The Educational Information Consultant. Skills in Disseminating Educational Information: A Training Manual.* (ED 149 725.) Washington, D.C.: Office of Education, 1971.

Bank, A., Snidman, N. C., and Pitts, M. "Perspectives on Evaluation, Linkage and Program Improvement." In A. Bank and others, *Dissemination and the Improvement of Practice: Cooperation and Support in the School Improvement Process.* San Francisco: Far West Laboratory for Educational Research and Development, 1979.

Bank, A., and others. *Dissemination and the Improvement of Practice: Cooperation and Support in the School Improvement Process.* San Francisco: Far West Laboratory for Educational Research and Development, 1979.

Banks, J., and Clark, R. F. "A Venture into Meta-Evaluation: OEO Region IV's Housing Study." *Policy Sciences,* 1976, *7*(3), 249-254.

Baranson, J. *Technology and Multinationals.* Lexington, Mass.: Lexington Books, 1978.

Bardach, E. *The Implementation Game: What Happens After a Bill Becomes a Law?* Cambridge, Mass.: M.I.T. Press, 1977.

Baritsch, H. "Review of Organization for Economic Cooperation and Development (OECD), *Case Studies in Educational Innovation.*" *International Review of Education,* 1976, *22* (2), 293-297.

Barnes, L. B. "Organizational Change and Field Experiment Methods." In V. Vroom (Ed.), *Methods of Organization Research.* Pittsburgh, Pa.: University of Pittsburgh Press, 1967.

Barnes, L. B. "Approaches to Organizational Change." In W. G. Bennis, K. D. Benne, and R. Chin (Eds.), *The Planning of Change.* (2nd ed.) New York: Holt, Rinehart and Winston, 1969.

Barnett, H. G. *Innovation: The Basis of Cultural Change.* New York: McGraw-Hill, 1953.

Barnett, H. G. "The Acceptance and Rejection of Change." In G. K. Zolischan and W. Hirsch (Eds.), *Explorations in Social Change.* Boston: Houghton Mifflin, 1964.

Barnett, H. G. "Laws of Socio-Cultural Change." *International Journal of Comparative Sociology,* 1965, *6*, 207-230.

Barringer, H. R., Blanksten, G. I., and Mack, R. W. (Eds.). *Social Change in Developing Areas: A Reinterpretation of Evolutionary Theory?* Cambridge, Mass.: Schenkman, 1966.

Barry, J. R. "The Promotion of Changes in Service Delivery." *Academic Psychology Bulletin,* 1979, *1*(1), 41-46.

Bartlett, M. H., and others. "Dial Access Library—Patient Information Service." *New England Journal of Medicine,* 1973, *2881,* 994-998.

Barton, A. H. "Applied Research in the Political Process." *Current Sociology,* 1975, *23*(1), 49-67.

Basiuk, V. *Technology, World Politics, and American Policy.* New York: Columbia University Press, 1967.

Bass, G. *A Study of Alternatives in American Education: The Implementation of Change.* Santa Monica, Calif.: Rand Corporation, 1978.

Bassett, G., Davison, W. P., and Hopson, A. *Social Scientists,*

*University News Bureaus, and the Public: Some Factors Affecting the Communication of Social Science Information.* New York: Graduate School of Journalism, Bureau of Applied Social Research, Columbia University, 1968.

Battelle Columbus Laboratories. *Interactions of Science and Technology in the Innovative Process: Some Case Studies.* Final Report to the National Science Foundation, Contract No. C-667. Washington, D.C.: National Science Foundation, 1973.

Bauer, R. A. "Social Psychology and the Study of Policy Information." *American Psychologist,* 1966, *21*(1), 933-942.

Bauer, R. A. *Second-Order Consequences: A Methodological Essay on the Impact of Technology.* Cambridge, Mass.: M.I.T. Press, 1969.

Beal, G. M., and Bohlen, J. *The Diffusion Process.* Special Report No. 18. Ames: Iowa Agricultural and Home Economics Station, 1967.

Bean, A. S., and Mogee, M. E. "The Role of the Purchasing Agent in Industrial Innovation." *Industrial Marketing Management,* 1976, *5,* 221-229.

Bean, A. S., and Roessner, J. D. "Assessing the Government Role in the Commercialization of Federally Funded R&D." Paper presented at American Chemical Society Symposium on Commercialization of Federally Funded R&D, Miami, Fla., September 1978.

Bean, A. S., Schiffel, D., and Mogee, M. E. "The Venture Capital Market and Technological Innovation." *Research Policy,* 1975, *4,* 380-408.

Becker, M. H. "Factors Affecting Diffusion of Innovations Among Health Professionals." *American Journal of Public Health,* 1970a, *60*(2), 294-304.

Becker, M. H. "Sociometric Location and Innovativeness: Reformulation and Extension of the Diffusion Model." *American Sociological Review,* 1970b, *35,* 267-282.

Becker, S. W., and Stafford, F. "Some Determinants of Organizational Success." *Journal of Business,* 1967, *40,* 511-518.

Becker, S. W., and Whisler, T. L. "The Innovative Organization:

A Selective View of Current Theory and Research." *Journal of Business,* 1967, *40,* 402-469.

Beckhard, R. "An Organizational Improvement Program in a Decentralized Organization." *Journal of Applied Behavioral Science,* 1966, *2,* 3-25.

Beckhard, R. "The Confrontation Meeting." In W. G. Bennis, K. D. Benne, and R. Chin (Eds.), *The Planning of Change.* (2nd ed.) New York: Holt, Rinehart and Winston, 1969a.

Beckhard, R. *Organization Development: Strategies and Models.* Reading, Mass.: Addison-Wesley, 1969b.

Beckhard, R. "Helping a Group with Planned Change." In H. A. Hornstein and others (Eds.), *Social Intervention: A Behavioral Science Approach.* New York: Free Press, 1971.

Beckhard, R. "ABS in Health Care Systems: Who Needs It?" *Journal of Applied Behavioral Science,* 1974, *10,* 93-106.

Beckhard, R. "Strategies for Large System Change." *Sloan Management Review,* 1975, *16,* 43-55.

Beckhard, R. "The Writing Conference: A Mechanism for Technology Transfer." *Exchange: The Organizational Teaching Journal,* 1978, *3*(3), 29-33.

Beckhard, R., and Harris, R. T. *Organizational Transitions: Managing Complex Change.* Reading, Mass.: Addison-Wesley, 1977.

Beckman, N. (Ed.). "Policy Analysis in Government: Alternatives to 'Muddling Through.' " *Public Administration Review,* 1977, *37,* 221-263.

Bee, R. L. *Patterns and Process: An Introduction to Anthropological Strategies for the Study of Sociocultural Change.* New York: Free Press, 1974.

Beer, M. *Organization Change and Development: A Systems View.* Santa Monica, Calif.: Goodyear, 1980.

Beer, M., and Huse, E. "A Systems Approach to Organizational Development." *Journal of Applied Behavioral Science,* 1972, *8*(1), 79-101.

Beigel, A., and Levenson, A. I. (Eds.). *The Community Mental Health Center: Strategies and Programs.* New York: Basic Books, 1972.

Bell, D. *The Coming of the Post-Industrial Society: A Venture in Social Forecasting.* New York: Basic Books, 1973.

Ben-David, J. "Roles and Innovations in Medicine." *American Journal of Sociology,* 1960, *65,* 557-568.

Benedict, B. A., and others. "The Clinical-Experimental Approach to Assessing Organizational Change Efforts." *Journal of Applied Behavioral Science,* 1967, *3*(3), 347-380.

Benne, K. D. "Deliberate Changing as the Facilitation of Growth." In W. G. Bennis, K. D. Benne, and R. Chin (Eds.), *The Planning of Change: Readings in the Applied Behavioral Sciences.* New York: Holt, Rinehart and Winston, 1962.

Benne, K. D., Bennis, W. G., and Chin, R. "Planned Change in America." In W. G. Bennis, K. D. Benne, and R. Chin (Eds.), *The Planning of Change.* (2nd ed.) New York: Holt, Rinehart and Winston, 1969.

Benne, K. D., and Birnbaum, M. "Change Does Not Have To Be Haphazard." *School Review,* 1960, *68,* 283-297.

Bennett, A. M., Rappaport, W. H., and Skinner, F. L. *Telehealth Handbook: A Guide to Telecommunications Technology for Rural Health Care.* Washington, D.C.: U.S. Government Printing Office, 1978.

Bennett, C. A., and Lumsdaine, A. A. (Eds.). *Evaluation and Experiment: Some Critical Issues in Assessing Social Programs.* New York: Academic Press, 1975.

Bennis, W. G. "A New Role for the Behavioral Sciences: Effecting Organizational Change." *Administrative Science Quarterly,* 1963, *8,* 125-166.

Bennis, W. G. *Changing Organizations.* New York: McGraw-Hill, 1966.

Bennis, W. G. "Theory and Method in Applying Behavioral Science to Planned Organizational Change." In W. G. Bennis, K. D. Benne, and R. Chin (Eds.), *The Planning of Change.* (2nd ed.) New York: Holt, Rinehart and Winston, 1969.

Bennis, W. G. "Changing Organizations." In H. A. Hornstein and others (Eds.), *Social Intervention: A Behavioral Science Approach.* New York: Free Press, 1971.

Bennis, W. G. "Bureaucracy and Social Change: An Anatomy of a Training Failure." In P. H. Mirvis and D. N. Berg (Eds.),

*Failures in Organization Development and Change: Cases and Essays for Learning.* New York: Wiley, 1977.

Bennis, W. G. *The Unconscious Conspiracy: Why Leaders Can't Lead.* New York: AMACOM, 1978.

Bennis, W. G., Benne, K. D., and Chin, R. (Eds.). *The Planning of Change.* (2nd ed.) New York: Holt, Rinehart and Winston, 1969.

Bennis, W. G., and Peter, H. W. "Applying Behavioral Science for Organizational Change." In Foundation for Research on Human Behavior, *Comparative Theories of Social Change.* Ann Arbor, Mich.: Foundation for Research on Human Behavior, 1966.

Bennis, W. G., and Schein, E. H. "Principles and Strategies in the Use of Laboratory Training for Improving Social Systems." In W. G. Bennis, K. D. Benne, and R. Chin (Eds.), *The Planning of Change.* (2nd ed.) New York: Holt, Rinehart and Winston, 1969.

Bennis, W. G., and others (Eds.). *The Planning of Change.* (3rd ed.) New York: Holt, Rinehart and Winston, 1976.

Bentzen, M. M. *Changing Schools: The Magic Feather Principle.* New York: McGraw-Hill, 1974.

Berg, D. N. "Failure at Entry." In P. H. Mirvis and D. N. Berg (Eds.), *Failures in Organization Development and Change: Cases and Essays for Learning.* New York: Wiley, 1977.

Berg, M. R., and others. *Factors Affecting Utilization of Technology Assessment Studies in Policy Making.* Ann Arbor: Center for Research on Utilization of Scientific Knowledge, University of Michigan, 1978.

Berger, B. *Societies in Change.* New York: Basic Books, 1971.

Berk, R. A. (Ed.). *Educational Evaluation Methodology: The State of the Art.* Baltimore: Johns Hopkins University Press, 1981.

Berke, J. S., and Moore, M. T. "The Education Policy Development Centers: A Case Study of an Institution-Based Approach to Policy Research." Paper presented at 66th annual meeting of American Educational Research Association, Los Angeles, April 1981.

Berkowitz, M., and others. *An Evaluation of Policy-Related Rehabilitation Research.* New York: Praeger, 1975.

Berlin, I. N. "Learning Mental Health Consultation History and Problems." *Mental Hygiene,* 1964, *48*(2), 257-266.

Berlin, I. N. "Resistance to Change in Mental Health Professionals." *American Journal of Orthopsychiatry,* 1969, *39,* 109-115.

Berlyne, D. E. "Uncertainty and Conflict: A Point of Contact Between Information Theory and Behavior Theory Concepts." *Psychological Review,* 1957, *64,* 329-339.

Berman, P. "Implementation of Education Innovation." *The Educational Forum,* 1976, *40*(3), 345-370.

Berman, P. "The Study of Macro- and Micro-Implementation." *Public Policy,* 1978, *26,* 157-184.

Berman, P. "Thinking About Programmed and Adaptive Implementation: Matching Strategies to Situations." In H. Ingram and D. Mann (Eds.), *Why Policies Succeed or Fail.* Beverly Hills, Calif.: Sage, 1980.

Berman, P., and McLaughlin, M. W. "Implementation of Educational Innovation." *The Educational Forum,* 1976, *40*(3), 345-370.

Berman, P., and McLaughlin, M. W. *An Exploratory Study of School District Adaptation.* Santa Monica, Calif.: Rand Corporation, 1979.

Berman, P., and others. *Federal Programs Supporting Educational Change.* Vol. 4 (abridged): *A Summary of the Findings in Review.* Santa Monica, Calif.: Rand Corporation, 1975.

Berman, P., and others. *Federal Programs Supporting Educational Change.* 8 vols. (Vols. 1-5, 1975; Vols. 6-8, 1977.) Santa Monica, Calif.: Rand Corporation, 1975/1977.

Bernhardt, I., and MacKenzie, K. D. "Some Problems in Using Diffusion Models for New Products." *Management Science,* 1972, *19*(2), 187-200.

Bernstein, I., and Freeman, H. *Academic and Entrepreneurial Research.* New York: Russell Sage Foundation, 1975.

Bertelsen, K., and Harris, M. R. "Citizen Participation in the Development of a Community Mental Health Center." *Hospital and Community Psychiatry,* 1973, *24*(8), 553-556.

Bertrand, A. L., and Von Brock, R. C. (Eds.). *Models for Educational Change.* Austin, Texas: Southwest Educational Development Laboratory, 1968.

Beyer, J. M., and Trice, H. M. *Implementing Change: Alcoholism Policies in Work Organizations.* New York: Free Press, 1978.

Bhagat, N. A. "Information Dissemination—A Systems Viewpoint." *IEEE Transactions on Professional Communication,* 1977, *22*(2), 76-79.

Bhola, H. S. *A Configurational Theory of Innovation Diffusion.* Columbus: Bureau of Educational Research, Ohio State University, 1965a.

Bhola, H. S. *Innovation Research and Theory.* Columbus: Bureau of Educational Research, Ohio State University, 1965b.

Bhola, H. S. *Configurations of Change: The Framework for a Research Review.* East Lansing, Mich.: Midwest Universities Consortium for International Activities, Inc., 1976.

Bhola, H. S., and Blanke, V. E. (Eds.). *Strategies for Educational Change.* Columbus: Ohio State University Research Foundation, 1966.

Bice, G. R. *An Analysis of Dissemination and Utilization of Vocational Education Research and Development Efforts.* (ED 130 153.) Washington, D.C.: National Research Council, National Academy of Sciences, 1975.

Bice, T. W., Eichhorn, R. L., and Klein, D. A. "Evaluation of Public Health Programs." In M. Guttentag and E. Struening (Eds.), *Handbook of Evaluation Research.* Vol. 2. Beverly Hills, Calif.: Sage, 1975.

Biggart, N. W. "The Creative-Destructive Process of Organizational Change: The Case of the Post Office." *Administrative Science Quarterly,* 1977, *22,* 410-426.

Bingham, R. D. *The Adoption of Innovation by Local Government.* Lexington, Mass.: Lexington Books, 1976.

Bingham, R. D., and McNaught, T. P. *The Adoption of Innovation by Local Government: A Summary.* (NTIS PB-247 192.) Milwaukee, Wisc.: Office of Urban Research, Marquette University, 1975a.

Bingham, R. D., and McNaught, T. P. *The Adoption of Innova-*

*tion by Local Government: Final Report.* (NTIS PB-247 193.) Milwaukee, Wisc.: Office of Urban Research, Marquette University, 1975b.

Bingham, R. D., and others. *Professional Associations as Intermediaries in Transferring Technology to City Governments.* Milwaukee: University of Wisconsin, 1978.

Binswanger, H. P., and others. *Induced Innovation: Technology, Institutions, and Development.* Baltimore: Johns Hopkins University Press, 1978.

Blackman, A. W., Jr. "The Rate of Innovation in the Commercial Aircraft Jet Engine Market." *Technological Forecasting and Social Change,* 1971, *2,* 214.

Blackman, A. W., Jr., Seligman, E. J., and Sogliero, G. C. "An Innovation Index Based on Factor Analysis." *Technological Forecasting and Social Change,* 1973, *4,* 3.

Blackman, C. A. *The Process of Change.* East Lansing: College of Education, Michigan State University, 1965.

Blair, J., Jr., and others. *Industry, Innovation, and the Municipal Market.* Final Report to the Economic Development Administration, U.S. Department of Commerce, Contract F-C3431. Philadelphia: Franklin Institute Research Laboratories, 1973.

Blake, R. R., and Mouton, J. S. *Building a Dynamic Corporation Through Grid Organization Development.* Reading, Mass.: Addison-Wesley, 1969.

Blake, R. R., and Mouton, J. S. *Consultation.* Reading, Mass.: Addison-Wesley, 1976.

Blake, R. R., Mouton, J. S., and Sloma, R. L. "The Union-Management Intergroup Laboratory: Strategy for Resolving Intergroup Conflict." In W. G. Bennis, K. D. Benne, and R. Chin (Eds.), *The Planning of Change.* (2nd ed.) New York: Holt, Rinehart and Winston, 1969.

Blanke, V. E. (Ed.). "Planning for Educational Change." *Theory into Practice,* 1966, *5* (entire issue).

Blanke, V. E. *Educational Change and Diffusion.* Columbus: Educational Development Faculty, Ohio State University, 1971.

Blanke, V. E., and others. *EPEC: Evaluating the Process of Educational Change.* Columbus: Evaluation Center, Ohio State University, 1972.

Blum, R. H., and Downing, J. J. "Staff Response to Innovation in a Mental Health Service." *American Journal of Public Health,* 1964, *54,* 1230-1240.

Bobbe, R. A., and Schaffer, R. H. "Mastering Change: Breakthrough Projects and Beyond." *American Management Associations Bulletin,* 1968, *120* (entire issue).

Boguslaw, R. *The New Utopians: A Study of Systems Design and Social Change.* Englewood Cliffs, N.J.: Prentice-Hall, 1965.

Bohlen, J. M. "The Adoption and Diffusion of Ideas in Agriculture." In J. H. Copp (Ed.), *Our Changing Rural Society: Perspectives and Trends.* Ames: Iowa State University Press, 1964.

Bolton, B. "Research Utilization of R&D Project Results with Severely Handicapped Deaf Clients." *Journal of Applied Rehabilitation Counseling,* 1974, *5*(1), 27-39.

Bolton, B. "Research Utilization." In B. Bolton (Ed.), *Rehabilitation Counseling Research.* Baltimore: University Park Press, 1979.

Booth, D. A. "Change and Political Realities." In R. I. Miller (Ed.), *A Multidisciplinary Focus on Educational Change.* Lexington: Bureau of School Service, University of Kentucky, 1965.

Borich, G. D. (Ed.). *Evaluating Educational Programs and Products.* Englewood Cliffs, N.J.: Educational Technology Publications, 1974.

Borich, G. D., and Jemelka, R. P. *Programs and Systems: An Evaluation Perspective.* New York: Academic Press, 1981.

Borman, L. D. "The Marginal Route of a Mental Hospital Innovation." Paper presented at annual meeting of Society for Applied Anthropology, Lexington, Ky., April 1965.

Boruch, R. F., and others. *Reanalyzing Program Evaluation: Policies and Practices for Secondary Analysis of Social and Educational Programs.* San Francisco: Jossey-Bass, 1981.

Boss, R. W., and McConkie, M. L. "An Autopsy of an Intended OD Project." *Group & Organization Studies,* 1979, *4*(2), 183-200.

Bottle, R. T. "Scientists, Information Transfer and Literature

Characteristics." *Journal of Documentation,* 1973, *29*(3), 281-294.

Boucher, W. L., and others. *Federal Incentives for Innovation. The Impact of EPA Administrative Practice on the Innovation Process in U.S. Companies: A Case Study of Regulatory Barriers to Innovation.* (NTIS PB-259 176.) Denver, Colo.: Denver Research Institute, 1976.

Bowen, D. "Value Dilemmas in Organization Development." *Journal of Applied Behavioral Science,* 1977, *13*(4), 543-556.

Bowers, D. G. "OD Techniques and Their Results in 23 Organizations: The Michigan ICL Study." *Journal of Applied Behavioral Science,* 1973, *9*(1), 21-43.

Bowers, D. G., Franklin, J. L., and Pecorella, P. A. "A Model for Systematic Approach to Organizational Development." *Journal of Applied Behavioral Science,* 1975, *11*(4), 391-409.

Bowers, D. G., and Norman, R. "Strategies for Changing an Organization." *Innovation,* 1969, *3,* 50-55.

Bowers, D. G., and Seashore, S. E. "Predicting Organizational Effectiveness with a Four-Factor Theory of Leadership." *Administrative Science Quarterly,* 1966, *11,* 238-263.

Bowers, D. G., and Seashore, S. E. "Changing the Structure and Functioning of an Organization." In W. M. Evan (Ed.), *Organizational Experiments: Laboratory and Field Research.* New York: Harper & Row, 1971.

Bowman, J. S. "Managerial Theory and Practice: The Transfer of Knowledge in Public Administration." *Public Administration Review,* 1978, *38*(6), 563-570.

Bowman, P. H. "The Role of the Consultant as a Motivator of Action." *Mental Hygiene,* 1959, *43,* 105-110.

Boyan, N. J. "Problems and Issues of Knowledge Production and Utilization in Educational Administration." In T. L. Eidell and J. M. Kitchel (Eds.), *Knowledge Production and Utilization in Educational Administration.* Eugene: Center for the Advanced Study of Educational Administration, University of Oregon, 1968.

Boyd, W. L. "The Public, the Professionals, and Educational Policy Making: Who Governs?" *Teachers College Record,* 1976, *77*(4), 539-577.

Boyd, W. L. "The Changing Politics of Curriculum Policy Making for American Schools." *Review of Educational Research,* 1978, *48*(4), 577-628.

Boyd, W. L., and Immegart, G. L. "Educational Innovation, Sociopolitical Culture, and Depressed Rural Communities." *Journal of Educational Administration,* 1977, *15*(1), 49-66.

Boyer, C. J. *An Analysis of the Doctoral Dissertation as an Information Source.* (ED 065 157.) Austin: University of Texas, 1972.

Boylan, M. "The Sources of Technological Innovations." In B. Gold (Ed.), *Research, Technological Change, and Economic Analysis.* Lexington, Mass.: Lexington Books, 1977.

Brager, G., and Holloway, S. *Changing Human Service Organizations.* New York: Free Press, 1978.

Brandl, J. E. "Policy Evaluation and the Work of Legislatures." In L. A. Braskamp and R. D. Brown (Eds.), *New Directions for Program Evaluation: Utilization of Evaluative Information,* no. 5. San Francisco: Jossey-Bass, 1980.

Branscomb, L. M. "Conducting and Using Research." *Daedalus,* 1973, *102*(2), 145-152.

Braskamp, L. A., and Brown, R. D. (Eds.). *New Directions for Program Evaluation: Utilization of Evaluative Information,* no. 5. San Francisco: Jossey-Bass, 1980.

Braunstein, Y. M. "Public Policy and Research on Economics of Information Transfer." *Proceedings of the American Society for Information Science,* 1976, *13,* 7.

Braunstein, Y. M. *Maximizing Efficiency and Effectiveness of Information Data Banks.* (NTIS AD-A041 595.) Paris: Advisory Group for Aerospace Research and Development, 1977.

Brewer, G. D. *Politicians, Bureaucrats, and the Consultant.* New York: Basic Books, 1973.

Brickell, H. M. "The Dynamics of Educational Change." *Theory into Practice,* 1962, *1*(2), 81-88.

Brickell, H. M. "State Organization for Educational Change: A Case Study and a Proposal." In M. B. Miles (Ed.), *Innovation in Education.* New York: Bureau of Publications, Columbia University, 1964.

Bright, J. R. *Research, Development, and Technological Innovation: An Introduction.* Homewood, Ill.: Irwin, 1964.

Brittain, J. M. *Information and Its Uses.* New York: Wiley, 1970.

Brodsky, S. L. "Go Away—I'm Looking for the Truth: Research Utilization in Corrections." *Criminal Justice and Behavior,* 1977, *4*(1), 3-10.

Brooks, H. "National Science Policy and Technology Transfer." In National Science Foundation, *Technology Transfer and Innovation.* Washington, D.C.: U.S. Government Printing Office, 1967.

Brooks, H. "Knowledge and Action: The Dilemma of Science Policy in the 70s." *Daedalus,* 1973, *102*(2), 125-143.

Broudy, H. S. "Criteria for the Theoretical Adequacy of Conceptual Framework of Planned Educational Change." Paper presented at Conference on Strategies for Educational Change, Washington, D.C., November 1965.

Brown, B. S. "The Crisis in Mental Health Research." *American Journal of Psychiatry,* 1977, *134*(2), 113-120.

Brown, H. J., Miller, J. K., and Pinchoff, D. M. "Study of Information Dissemination Service, Health Sciences Library, State University of New York at Buffalo." *Bulletin of the Medical Library Association,* 1975, *63*(3), 259-271.

Brown, L. A. "The Market and Infrastructure Context of Adoption: A Spatial Perspective on the Diffusion of Innovation." *Economic Geography,* 1975, *51,* 185-216.

Brown, L. A. "Diffusion Research in Geography: A Thematic Account." Studies in the Diffusion of Innovation Discussion Paper Series. Columbus: Department of Geography, Ohio State University, 1977.

Brown, L. A. "The Innovation Diffusion Process in a Public Policy Context." In M. Radnor, I. Feller, and E. Rogers (Eds.), *The Diffusion of Innovations: An Assessment.* Evanston, Ill.: Center for the Interdisciplinary Study of Science and Technology, Northwestern University, 1978.

Brown, L. A., Malecki, E. J., and Spector, A. N. "Adopter Categories in a Spatial Context: Alternative Explanations for an Empirical Regularity." *Rural Sociology,* 1976, *41,* 99-118.

Brown, M. *On the Theory and Measurement of Technological Change.* Cambridge, England: Cambridge University, 1966.

Brown, R. D., and Braskamp, L. A. "Summary: Common Themes and a Checklist." In L. A. Braskamp and R. D. Brown (Eds.), *New Directions for Program Evaluation: Utilization of Evaluative Information,* no. 5. San Francisco: Jossey-Bass, 1980.

Brown, R. H. "Social Theory as Metaphor: On the Logic of Discovery for the Sciences of Conduct." *Theory and Society,* 1976, *3*(2), 169-197.

Bruckmann, C. G., and Mandersloot, W. G. B. *Writing Informative Reports on Investigations in Science and Engineering.* (NTIS N78-24992.) Pretoria, South Africa: Council for Scientific and Industrial Research, 1977.

Bruyn, S. T., and Rayman, P. M. (Eds.). *Nonviolent Action and Social Change.* New York: Halstead, 1979.

Bryk, A. S., and Light, R. J. "Designing Evaluations for Different Program Environments." In R. A. Berk (Ed.), *Educational Evaluation Methodology: The State of the Art.* Baltimore: Johns Hopkins University Press, 1981.

Buchanan, G., Horst, P., and Scanlon, J. "Federal Level Evaluation—Improving Federal Evaluation Planning." *Evaluation,* 1973, *1*(2), 86-90.

Buchanan, P. C. "The Concept of Organizational Development or Self-Renewal as a Form of Planned Change." In G. Watson (Ed.), *Concepts for Social Change.* Washington, D.C.: National Training Laboratories Institute for Applied Behavioral Science, 1967a.

Buchanan, P. C. "Crucial Issues in Organizational Development." In G. Watson (Ed.), *Change in School Systems.* Washington, D.C.: National Training Laboratories, 1967b.

Bucklin, L. P. "Channel Change Agents in Developing Countries." *International Journal of Physical Distribution,* 1976, *7*(1), 59-68.

Bundegaard-Nielsen, M. "The International Diffusion of New Technology." *Technological Forecasting and Social Change,* 1976, *8,* 4.

Bundegaard-Nielsen, M., and Fiehn, P. "The Diffusion of New

Technology in the U.S. Petroleum Refining Industry." *Technological Forecasting and Social Change,* 1974, *6,* 1.

Bungay, J. *Intergovernmental Programs: Abstracts of Publications, 1967-1975.* (NTIS PB-254 485.) Washington, D.C.: National Science Foundation, 1976.

Burchinal, L. "Needed: Local, One-Stop Information Centers." *Educational Researcher,* 1967 (special supplement), 8-9.

Burke, W. W. (Ed.). *The Cutting Edge: Current Theory and Practice in Organization Development.* La Jolla, Calif.: University Associates, 1978.

Burke, W. W., and Hornstein, H. A. *The Social Technology of Organization Development.* Fairfax, Va.: National Training Laboratories Learning Resources Corporation, Inc., 1972.

Burke, W. W., and Schmidt, W. H. "Primary Target for Change: The Manager or the Organization?" In H. A. Hornstein and others (Eds.), *Social Intervention: A Behavioral Science Approach.* New York: Free Press, 1971.

Burns, E. M., and Studer, K. E. "Reflections on Alvin M. Weinberg: A Case Study on the Social Foundations of Science Policy." *Research Policy,* 1975, *4,* 28-44.

Burns, T., and Stalker, G. M. *The Management of Innovation.* London: Tavistock, 1961.

Burt, R. S. "The Differential Impact of Social Integration on Participation in the Diffusion of Innovations." *Social Science Research,* 1973, *2,* 125-144.

Bushnell, D. S., and Rappaport, D. (Eds.). *Planned Change in Education: A Systems Approach.* New York: Harcourt Brace Jovanovich, 1971.

Butler, A. J. "Visiting Consultant Program for Research Utilization." *Rehabilitation Counseling Bulletin,* 1975, *19*(2), 405-415.

Butler, M., and Paisley, W. *Factors Determining Roles and Functions of Educational Linking Agents with Implications for Training and Support Systems.* San Francisco: Far West Laboratory for Educational Research and Development, 1978.

Butler, M., and others. *Development of Training Resources for Educational Extension Services Personnel.* Palo Alto, Calif.:

Institute for Communication Research, Stanford University, 1973.

Buyukcolak, U. "Transfer of Technology: Factors Influencing Small Farmers in the Adoption of Modern Agricultural Technology Related to High-Yielding Varieties of Wheat Production in Turkey." Doctoral dissertation, Cornell University, 1977. *Dissertation Abstracts International*, 1978, *38*, 4512A. (University Microfilms No. 78-00,086.)

Cadwallader, M. L. "The Cybernetic Analysis of Change." In A. Etzioni and E. Etzioni (Eds.), *Social Change: Sources, Patterns and Consequences*. New York: Basic Books, 1964.

Cady, L. L. "The Philosophy of Inservice and Continuing Education." *Mental Hygiene*, 1968, *52*, 456-461.

Caledrone, G. E. *Statistics About Society: The Production and Use of Federal Data*. Beverly Hills, Calif.: Sage, 1974.

Calsyn, R., Tornatzky, L. G., and Dittmar, S. "Incomplete Adoption of an Innovation: The Case of Goal Attainment Scaling." *Evaluation*, 1977, *4*, 127-130.

Campbell, D. T. "Reforms as Experiments." *American Psychologist*, 1969, *24*, 409-429.

Campbell, D. T. "Assessing the Impact of Planned Social Change." In G. M. Lyons (Ed.), *Social Research and Public Policies*. Hanover, N.H.: Dartmouth Press, 1975.

Campbell, D. T., and Stanley, J. C. *Experimental and Quasi-Experimental Designs for Research*. Chicago: Rand McNally, 1966.

Campbell, R. "The Role of School Study Councils and Local School Districts in the Dissemination and Implementation of Educational Research." In K. Goldhammer and S. Elam (Eds.), *Dissemination and Implementation: Third Annual Phi Delta Kappa Symposium on Educational Research*. Bloomington, Ind.: Phi Delta Kappa, 1962.

Canon, L. K. "Self-Confidence and Selective Exposure to Information." In L. Festinger, *Conflict, Decision, and Dissonance*. Stanford, Calif.: Stanford University Press, 1964.

Capla Associates. *National Diffusion Network Skills Taxonomy*. Rochelle Park, N.J.: Capla Associates, 1977.

Caplan, G. "Types of Mental Health Consultation." In W. G.

Bennis, K. D. Benne, and R. Chin (Eds.), *The Planning of Change.* (2nd ed.) New York: Holt, Rinehart and Winston, 1969.

Caplan, G. *Theory and Practice of Mental Health Consultation.* New York: Basic Books, 1970.

Caplan, N. "The Use of Social Science Information by Federal Executives." In G. M. Lyons (Ed.), *Social Research and Public Policies.* Hanover, N.H.: Dartmouth Press, 1975.

Caplan, N. "Social Research and National Policy: What Gets Used, by Whom, for What Purposes, and with What Effects?" *International Social Science Journal,* 1976a, *28*(1), 187-194.

Caplan, N. "The Use of Social Statistics by Federal Executives with Special Attention to Policy Decisions in Education." In National Research Council, *Setting Statistical Priorities* (Appendix E). Washington, D.C.: National Research Council, 1976b.

Caplan, N. "A Minimal Set of Conditions Necessary for the Utilization of Social Science Knowledge in Policy Formation at the National Level." In C. H. Weiss (Ed.), *Using Social Research in Public Policy Making.* Lexington, Mass.: Lexington Books, 1977.

Caplan, N. "The Two-Communities Theory and Knowledge Utilization." *American Behavioral Scientist,* 1979, *22*(3), 459-470.

Caplan, N. "What Do We Know About Knowledge Utilization?" In L. A. Braskamp and R. D. Brown (Eds.), *New Directions for Program Evaluation: Utilization of Evaluative Information,* no. 5. San Francisco: Jossey-Bass, 1980.

Caplan, N., and Barton, E. "The Potential of Social Indicators: Minimum Conditions for Impact at the National Level as Suggested by a Study of the Use of 'Social Indicators 1973.'" In *Social Indicators Research 5.* Dordrecht, Holland: D. Reidel, 1978.

Caplan, N., Morrison, A., and Stambaugh, R. J. *The Use of Social Science Knowledge in Policy Decisions at the National Level: A Report to Respondents.* Ann Arbor: Center for Research on Utilization of Scientific Knowledge, Institute for Social Research, University of Michigan, 1975.

Caporaso, J. A., and Roos, L. L., Jr. (Eds.). *Quasi-Experimental Approaches: Testing Theory and Evaluating Policy.* Evanston, Ill.: Northwestern University Press, 1973.

Carey, W. D. *Intergovernmental Uses of Federal R&D Centers and Laboratories: Report to the Council of State Governments.* Lexington, Ky.: The Council of State Governments, 1973.

Carl, L. M., and others (Eds.). *The Oregon Studies in Educational Research, Development, Diffusion, and Evaluation.* Vol. 5. Monmouth, Oreg.: Teaching Research, 1972.

Carleton, W. *An Analytical Framework for Investigation of Financial Constraints of High Technology Ventures.* Final Report to the National Science Foundation, Grant No. PRA-7522652. Washington, D.C.: National Science Foundation, 1978.

Carlson, E. D., Grace, B. F., and Sutton, J. A. "Case Studies of End User Requirements for Interactive Problem-Solving Systems." *Management Information Systems Quarterly,* 1977, *1,* 51-63.

Carlson, R. O. *Adoption of Educational Innovations.* Eugene: Center for the Advanced Study of Educational Administration, University of Oregon, 1965.

Carlson, S. "International Transmission of Information and the Business Firm." *Annals of the American Academy of Political and Social Science,* 1974, *412,* 44-54.

Caro, F. G. "Issues in the Evaluation of Social Programs." *Review of Educational Research,* 1971, *41*(2), 87-114.

Carpenter-Huffman, P., Hall, G. R., and Sumner, G. C. *Change in Education.* Cambridge, Mass.: Ballinger, 1974.

Carrole, J. "A Note on Departmental Autonomy and Innovation in Medical Schools." *Journal of Business,* 1967, *40,* 531-534.

Carter, L. F. "Knowledge Production and Utilization in Contemporary Organizations." In T. L. Eidell and J. M. Kitchel (Eds.), *Knowledge Production and Utilization in Educational Administration.* Eugene: Center for the Advanced Study of Educational Administration, University of Oregon, 1968a.

Carter, L. F. *Research and Development: Its Application to*

*Urban Problems.* Santa Monica, Calif.: System Development Corporation, 1968b.

Cartwright, D. "Achieving Change in People." In W. G. Bennis, K. D. Benne, and R. Chin (Eds.), *The Planning of Change: Readings in the Applied Behavioral Sciences.* New York: Holt, Rinehart and Winston, 1962.

Cassel, J. "Social and Cultural Considerations in Health Innovations." *Annals of the New York Academy of Sciences,* 1963, *107,* 739-747.

Cates, C. S., and Ward, S. (Eds.). *Dissemination and the Improvement of Practice: Cooperation and Support in the School Improvement Program.* San Francisco: Far West Laboratory for Educational Research and Development, 1979.

Cawelti, G. "Innovative Practices in High Schools: Who Does What—and Why—and How." *Nation's Schools,* 1967, *79,* 56-88.

Center for Research in Scientific Communication. *Production, Exchange, and Dissemination of Information in Journal Articles on Sociology.* Baltimore: Johns Hopkins University Press, 1971.

Central Advisory Council for Science and Technology. *Technological Innovation in Britain.* London: Her Majesty's Stationery Office, 1968.

Cetron, M. J. "Technology Transfer, Where We Stand Today." In H. F. Davidson, M. J. Certon, and J. D. Goldhar (Eds.), *Technology Transfer.* Leiden, Holland: Noordhoff, 1973.

Cetron, M. J., Davidson, H., and Goldhar, J. (Eds.). *Industrial Applications of Technology Transfer.* Leiden, Holland: Noordhoff, 1974.

Chabotar, K. J., and Kell, D. G. *Linking R&D with Local Schools: A Program and Its Policy Context.* Cambridge, Mass.: Abt Associates, Inc., 1979.

Chadwin, M. L. "The Nature of Legislative Program Evaluation." *Evaluation,* 1975, *2*(2), 45-49.

Chakrabarti, A. K. "Organizational Climate as Causal Variable in Innovation." *Indian Journal of Social Research,* 1973a, *14*(2), 102-110.

Chakrabarti, A. K. "Some Concepts of Technology Transfer: Adoption of Innovations in Organizational Context." *R&D Management,* 1973b, *3*(3), 111-120.

Chakrabarti, A. K., and Rubenstein, A. H. "Interorganizational Transfer of Technology: A Study of Adoption of NASA Innovations." *IEEE Transactions on Engineering Management,* 1976, *23*(1), 20-34.

Chapanis, A. "Prelude to 2001: Explorations in Human Communication." *American Psychologist,* 1971, *26,* 940-961.

Charpie, R. L. *Technological Innovation: Its Environment and Management.* Washington, D.C.: U.S. Government Printing Office, 1967.

Charters, W. W., Jr., and Pellegrin, R. "Barriers to the Innovation Process: Four Case Studies of Differentiated Staffing." *Educational Administration Quarterly,* 1973, *9,* 3-14.

Chelimsky, E. *A Symposium on the Use of Evaluations by Federal Agencies.* Vol. 1. McLean, Va.: Mitre Corporation, 1977a.

Chelimsky, E. (Ed.). *Proceedings of a Symposium on the Use of Evaluation by Federal Agencies.* Vol. 2. Washington, D.C.: Mitre Corporation, 1977b.

Chelimsky, E. *Victims of Violence: Agency Incentives and Individual Needs.* Paper presented at annual meeting of Evaluation Research Society of America, Minneapolis, October 1979.

Cherney, P. R. (Ed.). *Making Evaluation Research Useful.* Columbia, Md.: American City Corporation, 1971.

Cherns, A. B. "Putting Psychology to Work." *Occupational Psychology,* 1967, *41*(2-3), 77-84.

Cherns, A. B. "Social Research and Its Diffusion." *Human Relations,* 1969, *22*(3), 209-218.

Cherns, A. B. "Relations Between Research Institutions and Users of Research." *International Social Science Journal,* 1970, *22*(2), 226-242.

Cherns, A. B. "Social Sciences and Policy." *The Sociological Review Monograph: The Sociology of Sociology,* 1972a, *16,* 53-75.

Cherns, A. B. "Models for the Use of Research." *Human Relations,* 1972b, *25*(1), 25-33.

Cherns, A. B. "Perspectives on the Quality of Working Life." *Journal of Occupational Psychology*, 1975a, *48*(3), 155-167.

Cherns, A. B. "Social Engineering in Britain: The Use of Social Sciences in Social Policy." *Current Sociology*, 1975b, *23*(1), 99-127.

Cherns, A. B. "Can Behavioral Science Help Design Organizations?" *Organizational Dynamics*, 1977, *5*(4), 44-64.

Cherns, A. B., and Davis, L. E. "Goal for Enhancing the Quality of Working Life." In L. E. Davis and A. B. Cherns (Eds.), *The Quality of Working Life.* Vol. 1. New York: Free Press, 1975.

Cherns, A. B., Sinclair, R., and Jenkins, W. I. (Eds.). *Social Science and Government: Policies and Problems.* London: Tavistock, 1972.

Chesler, M. A., and Barakat, H. *The Innovation and Sharing of Teaching Practices: A Study of Professional Roles and Social Structures in Schools.* Ann Arbor: Institute for Social Research, University of Michigan, 1967.

Chesler, M. A., and Flanders, M. "Resistance to Research and Research Utilization: The Death and Life of a Feedback Attempt." *Journal of Applied Behavioral Science*, 1967, *3*, 469-487.

Chesler, M. A., and Fox, R. "Teacher Peer Relations and Educational Change." *National Educational Association Journal*, 1967, *56*(5), 25-26.

Chesler, M. A., Schmuck, R., and Lippitt, R. "The Principal's Role in Facilitating Innovation." *Theory into Practice*, 1963, *2*, 269-277.

Chin, R. "Models of and Ideas About Changing." In W. C. Meierhenry (Ed.), *Media and Educational Innovation.* Lincoln: University of Nebraska Extension Division and University of Nebraska Press, 1964.

Chin, R. "Change and Human Relations." In R. I. Miller (Ed.), *A Multidisciplinary Focus on Educational Change.* Lexington: Bureau of School Service, College of Education, University of Kentucky, 1965.

Chin, R. "Some Ideas on Changing." In R. I. Miller (Ed.), *Perspectives on Educational Change.* New York: Appleton-Century-Crofts, 1967.

Chin, R. "The Utility of Systems Models and Developmental Models for Practitioners." In W. G. Bennis, K. D. Benne, and R. Chin (Eds.), *The Planning of Change.* (2nd ed.) New York: Holt, Rinehart and Winston, 1969.

Chin, R. "Applied Behavioral Science and Innovation, Diffusion, and Adoption." *Viewpoints,* 1974, *50*(3), 25-46.

Chin, R., and Benne, K. D. "General Strategies for Effecting Change in Human Systems." In W. G. Bennis, K. D. Benne, and R. Chin (Eds.), *The Planning of Change.* (2nd ed.) New York: Holt, Rinehart and Winston, 1969.

Churchman, C. W. *The Design of Inquiring Systems.* New York: Basic Books, 1971.

Ciarlo, J. A. (Ed.). *Utilizing Evaluation.* Beverly Hills, Calif.: Sage, 1981.

Ciarlo, J. A., Rossman, B. B., and Hober, D. "Awareness, Use, and Consequences of Evaluation Data in a Community Mental Health Center." Denver, Colo.: University of Denver, n.d. (Mimeo.)

Cicchinelli, L. F., and Halpern, J. *An Experimental Federal-State Technology Transfer Mechanism, Evaluation Status and Planning.* (NTIS PB-259 246.) Denver, Colo.: Denver Research Institute, 1975.

Clark, A. W. "The Client-Practitioner Relationship as an Intersystem Engagement." In L. E. Davis and A. B. Cherns (Eds.), *The Quality of Working Life.* Vol. 1. New York: Free Press, 1975.

Clark, D. L. "The Function of the United States Office of Education and the State Departments of Education in the Dissemination and Implementation of Educational Research." In K. Goldhammer and S. Elam (Eds.), *Dissemination and Implementation: Third Annual Phi Delta Kappa Symposium on Educational Research.* Bloomington, Ind.: Phi Delta Kappa, 1962.

Clark, D. L. "The Engineering of Change in Education." In D. Bushnell, R. Freeman, and M. Richland (Eds.), *Proceedings of the Conference on the Implementation of Educational Innovations.* Santa Monica, Calif.: System Development Corporation, 1964.

Clark, D. L., and others. *A Study of Teacher Education Institu-*

*tions as Innovators, Knowledge Producers, and Change Agencies.* Bloomington: Indiana University, 1977.

Clark, M. F. "Creating a New Role: The Research Utilization Specialist." *Rehabilitation Record,* 1969, *10,* 19-23.

Clark, N. "The Multi-National Corporation: The Transfer of Technology and Dependence." *Development and Change,* 1975, *6*(1), 5-21.

Clark, P. A. *Action Research and Organizational Change.* New York: Harper & Row, 1972.

Clark, P. A. "Intervention Theory: Matching Role, Focus, and Context." In L. E. Davis and A. B. Cherns (Eds.), *The Quality of Working Life.* Vol. 1. New York: Free Press, 1975.

Clark, T. N. "Institutionalization of Innovations in Higher Education: Four Models." *Administrative Science Quarterly,* 1968, *13,* 1-25.

Clarke, T. E. "Decision Making in Technologically Based Organizations: A Literature Survey of Present Practice." *IEEE Transactions on Engineering Management,* 1974, *21*(1), 9-23.

Clausen, A. W. "The Internationalized Corporation: An Executive's View." *Annals of the American Academy of Political and Social Science,* 1972, *403,* 12-21.

Clifford, D. L., and Cooper, S. "Technical Assistance and Building Resource Networks." *Knowledge,* 1980, *2*(1), 117-132.

Cline, M. G., and others. *Education as Experimentation: Evaluation of the Follow-Through Planned Variation Model.* Cambridge, Mass.: Abt Associates, Inc., 1975.

Clinton, A., and House, J. H. "Attributes of Innovations as Factors in Diffusion." (ED 038 347.) Paper presented at 55th annual meeting of American Educational Research Association, Minneapolis, March 1970.

Coates, J. F. "Technology Assessment: The Benefits . . . the Costs . . . the Consequences." *The Futurist,* 1971, *5,* 225-231.

Coates, J. F. "Technology Assessment." In McGraw-Hill Yearbook, *Science and Industry.* New York: McGraw-Hill, 1974.

Coates, J. F. "Technology Assessment—A Tool Kit." *Chemtech,* 1976, *6*(6), 372-383.

Coch, L., and French, J. R. P., Jr. "Overcoming Resistance to

Change." In E. Maccoby and others (Eds.), *Readings in Social Psychology*. New York: Holt, Rinehart and Winston, 1958.

Cochrane, J. L., and Zeleny, M. (Eds.). *Multiple Criteria Decision Making*. Columbia: University of South Carolina Press, 1973.

Coe, R. M. (Ed.). *Planned Change in the Hospital*. New York: Praeger, 1970.

Coe, R. M., and Bernhill, E. A. "Social Dimensions of Failure in Innovation." *Human Organization*, 1967, *26*, 149-156.

Coelho, G. V., and Rubenstein, E. A. *Social Change and Human Behavior: Mental Health Challenges for the Seventies*. Rockville, Md.: National Institute of Mental Health, 1972.

Cohen, A. *Attitude Change and Social Influence*. New York: Basic Books, 1964.

Cohen, D. K. "Politics and Research: Evaluation of Social Action Programs." *Review of Educational Research*, 1970, *40* (2), 213-238.

Cohen, J. "Factors of Resistance to the Resources of the Behavioral Sciences." *Journal of Legal Education*, 1959, *12*, 67-70.

Cohen, M. D., March, J. G., and Olsen, J. P. "A Garbage Can Model of Organizational Choice." *Administrative Science Quarterly*, 1972, *17*(1), 1-25.

Cohen, M. W. "Citizen Participation in the Decision-Making Activities of Formal Social Service Agencies: An Unreasonable Goal?" *Community Mental Health Journal*, 1976, *12*(4), 355-364.

Cole, N. S., and Nitko, A. J. "Measuring Program Effects." In R. A. Berk (Ed.), *Educational Evaluation Methodology: The State of the Art*. Baltimore: Johns Hopkins University Press, 1981.

Cole, S., and Cole, J. "Visibility and the Structural Basis of Awareness of Scientific Research." *American Sociological Review*, 1968, *33*, 397-412.

Coleman, J. S. *Policy Research in the Social Sciences*. Morristown, N.J.: General Learning Press, 1972.

Coleman, J. S. "Conflicting Theories of Social Change." In G. Zaltman (Ed.), *Processes and Phenomena of Social Change*. New York: Wiley, 1973.

Coleman, J. S. "Policy Decisions, Social Science Information, and Education." *Sociology of Education,* 1976, *49,* 304-312.

Coleman, J. S., Katz, E., and Menzel, H. *Doctors and New Drugs.* Indianapolis: Bobbs-Merrill, 1966a.

Coleman, J. S., Katz, E., and Menzel, H. *Medical Innovation: A Diffusion Study.* New York: Bobbs-Merrill, 1966b.

Coller, A. R. *A Taxonomy of Programmatic Tasks in an Educational Evaluation, Facilitation, and Coordination System.* (ED 051 283.) Northfield, Ill.: Cooperative Educational Research Laboratory, 1970.

Collier, K. G. "Review of Organization for Economic Cooperation and Development (OECD), *Case Studies in Educational Innovation.* Vol. 4: *Strategies for Innovation in Education.*" *British Journal of Educational Technology,* 1975, *6*(1), 79-80.

Collins, H. M. "The TEA Set: Tacit Knowledge and Scientific Networks." *Science Studies,* 1974, *4*(2), 165-186.

Collins, J. F. *Sources and Resources: An Annotated Bibliography on Inservice Education.* Syracuse, N.Y.: School of Education, Syracuse University, 1979.

Collins, S. M. "The Use of Social Research in the Courts." In L. E. Lynn (Ed.), *Knowledge and Policy: The Uncertain Connection.* Washington, D.C.: National Academy of Sciences, 1978.

Conner, R. F. "The Evaluation of Research Utilization." In M. W. Klein and K. S. Teilman (Eds.), *Handbook of Criminal Justice Evaluation.* Beverly Hills, Calif.: Sage, 1980.

Conner, R. F. "Measuring Evaluation Utilization: A Critique of Different Techniques." In J. A. Ciarlo (Ed.), *Utilizing Evaluation: Concepts and Measurement Techniques.* Beverly Hills, Calif.: Sage, 1981a.

Conner, R. F. (Ed.). *Methodological Advances in Evaluation Research.* Beverly Hills, Calif.: Sage, 1981b.

Conoley, J. C. (Ed.). *Consultation in Schools: Theory, Research, Procedures.* New York: Academic Press, 1981.

Conrath, D. W., and others. "An Experimental Evaluation of Alternative Communication Systems as Used for Medical Diagnosis." *Behavior Science,* 1975, *20*(5), 296-305.

Constantino, R. "Global Enterprises and Transfer of Technology." *Journal of Contemporary Asia,* 1977, *7*(1), 44-55.

Conway, M. E. "Clinical Research: Instrument for Change." *Journal of Nursing Administration,* 1978, *8*(12), 27-32.

Conway, R., and others. "Promoting Knowledge Utilization Through Clinically Oriented Research: The BENCHMARK Program." In C. H. Weiss (Ed.), Symposium on Research Utilization Quandary. *Policy Studies Journal,* 1976, *4*(3), 264-269.

Cook, T. D., and Campbell, D. T. *Quasi-Experimentation: Design and Analysis Issues for Field Settings.* Chicago: Rand McNally, 1979.

Cook, T. D., and Conner, R. J. "The Educational Impact of Six Months Viewing of 'Sesame Street': A Review of Seven Summative Evaluations." *Journal of Communication,* 1976, *26,* 155-164.

Cook, T. D., Levinson-Rose, J., and Pollard, W. E. "The Misutilization of Evaluation Research: Some Pitfalls of Definition." *Knowledge,* 1980, *1*(4), 477-498.

Cook, T. D., and Associates (Eds.). *Evaluation Studies Review Annual.* Vol. 3. Beverly Hills, Calif.: Sage, 1978.

Cooke, R. A. "Managing Change in Organizations." In G. Zaltman (Ed.), *Management Principles for Nonprofit Agencies and Organizations.* New York: American Management Associations, 1979.

Cooke, R. A., and Coughlan, R. J. "Developing Collective Decision-Making and Problem-Solving Structures in Schools." *Group & Organization Studies,* 1979, *4*(1), 71-92.

Coombs, P. H., Ahmed, M., and Israel, B. B. (Eds.). *Attacking Rural Poverty: How Nonformal Education Can Help.* Baltimore: Johns Hopkins University Press, 1974.

Cooper, C. *Science, Technology, and Development: The Political Economy of Technical Advance in Underdeveloped Countries.* London: Frank Cass, 1973.

Cooper, C. R., and Archambault, B. (Eds.). "Communication, Dissemination, and Utilization of Research Information in Rehabilitation Counseling." Proceedings of a Regional Conference sponsored by the Department of Guidance and Psychological Services, Springfield College, Springfield, Mass., May 1968 and October 1968.

Corbett, W. T., Jr., and Guttinger, H. I. "The Assumptions, Strategies, and Results of a Linkage Model for Dissemination." (ED 148 327.) Paper presented at 62nd annual meeting of American Educational Research Association, New York, New York, April 1977.

Corwin, R. G. "Organizational Structure and Educational Innovation in More and Less Modernized, Urbanized Regions of the United States: Some Directions for Cross-National Research." *International Review of Education,* 1972a, *18*(1), 85-94.

Corwin, R. G. "Strategies for Organizational Innovation: An Empirical Comparison." *American Sociological Review,* 1972b, 37, 441-454.

Corwin, R. G. "Strategies of Organizational Survival: The Case of a National Program for Educational Reform." *Journal of Applied Behavioral Science,* 1972c, *8*(4), 451-480.

Corwin, R. G. *Reform and Organizational Survival: The Teachers Corps as an Instrument of Educational Change.* New York: Wiley, 1973.

Corwin, R. G. "Innovation in Organizations: The Case of Schools." *Sociology of Education,* 1975, *48,* 1-37.

Costello, T. W. "Change in Municipal Government: A View From Inside." Paper presented at 76th annual meeting of American Psychological Association, San Francisco, September 1968.

Costello, T. W., and Zalkind, S. S. (Eds.). *Psychology in Administration.* Englewood Cliffs, N.J.: Prentice-Hall, 1963.

Cottle, T. J. "Bristol Township Schools: Strategy for Change." *Saturday Review,* 1969, *52,* 70-82.

The Council of State Governments. *Power to the States: Mobilizing Public Technology.* Lexington, Ky.: The Council of State Governments, 1972.

Cowen, E., Davidson, E., and Gesten, E. "Program Dissemination and the Modification of Delivery Practices in School Mental Health." *Professional Psychology,* 1980, *11*(1), 36-47.

Cox, F., and others (Eds.). *Strategies of Community Organization.* Itasca, Ill.: Peacock, 1979.

Cox, G. B. "Managerial Style: Implications for the Utilization of Program Evaluation Information." *Evaluation Quarterly,* 1977, *2*(1), 499-508.

Crain, R. L. "Fluoridation: The Diffusion of an Innovation Among Cities." *Social Forces,* 1966, *44,* 467-476.

Crandall, D. P. "The Relationship Between Innovativeness and Selected Elements of Group Structure." (ED 062 662.) Paper presented at 57th annual meeting of American Educational Research Association, Chicago, April 1972.

Crandall, D. P., and Associates. *People, Policies and Practices: Examining the Chain of School Improvement.* 10 vols. Andover, Mass.: The NETWORK, Inc., 1982.

Crane, D. "The Nature of Scientific Communication and Influence." *International Social Science Journal,* 1970, *1,* 28-41.

Crane, D. "Information Needs and Uses." In C. A. Cuadra and A. W. Luke (Eds.), *Annual Review of Information Science and Technology.* Vol. 6. Chicago: Encyclopaedia Britannica, 1971.

Crane, D. *Invisible Colleges: Diffusion of Knowledge in Scientific Communities.* Chicago: University of Chicago Press, 1972.

Crawford, E. T., and Biderman, A. D. "The Functions of Policy-Oriented Social Science." In E. T. Crawford and A. D. Biderman (Eds.), *Social Scientists and International Affairs.* New York: Wiley, 1969.

Crawford, R. "The Application of Science and Technology in Local Governments in the United States." *Studies in Comparative Local Government,* 1973, 7(2), 1-19.

Creighton, J. W., and Jolly, J. A. (Eds.). *Technology Transfer in Research and Development.* (ED 135 405.) Monterey, Calif.: Naval Postgraduate School, 1975.

Cremin, L. A. *The Transformation of the School.* New York: Knopf, 1961.

Cresap, McCormick, and Paget, Inc. *Developing a Framework for the Dissemination of Educational and R and D Products.* (ED 122 866.) New York: Cresap, McCormick, and Paget, Inc., 1976.

Crockett, W. J. "Introducing Change to a Government Agency." In P. H. Mirvis and D. N. Berg (Eds.), *Failures in Organization*

*Development and Change: Cases and Essays for Learning.* New York: Wiley, 1977.

Croker, G. W. "Some Principles Regarding the Utilization of Social Science Research Within the Military." In *Case Studies in Bringing Behavioral Science into Use: Studies in the Utilization of Behavioral Science.* Vol. 1. Stanford, Calif.: Institute for Communication Research, Stanford University, 1961.

Cronbach, L. J. "Beyond the Two Disciplines of Scientific Psychology." *American Psychologist,* 1976, *30,* 116-121.

Cronbach, L. J., and Associates. *Toward Reform of Program Evaluation: Aims, Methods and Institutional Arrangements.* San Francisco: Jossey-Bass, 1980.

Cronbach, L. J., and Suppes, P. *Research for Tomorrow's Schools: Disciplined Inquiry for Education.* New York: Macmillan, 1969.

Crowe, R. E., and Madancy, R. S. *The U.S. Environmental Agency's Experience in Technology Transfer.* Washington, D.C.: Office of Research and Development, U.S. Environmental Protection Agency, 1974.

Crowfoot, J. E., and Chesler, M. A. "Contemporary Perspectives on Planned Social Change: A Comparison." *Journal of Applied Behavioral Science,* 1974, *10*(3), 278-303.

Culbertson, J. A. (Ed.). "Changing the School." *Theory into Practice,* 1963, *2*(5), whole issue.

Culver, C. M., and Hoban, G. J. (Eds.). *The Power to Change: Issues for the Innovative Educator.* New York: McGraw-Hill, 1974.

Cummings, M. M. "Information Transfer: The Biomedical Model." *Science,* 1978, *202*(4374), 1247.

Cummings, T. G. (Ed.). *Systems Theory for Organizational Development.* New York: Wiley, 1980.

Curnow, R. C., and Moring, G. C. " 'Project SAPPHO': A Study in Industrial Innovation." *Futures,* 1968, *1*(2), 82-90.

Czepiel, J. A. "Word-of-Mouth Processes in the Diffusion of a Major Technological Innovation." *Journal of Marketing Research,* 1974, *11,* 172-180.

Dachler, H. P., Wilpert, P., and Wilpert, B. "Conceptual Dimensions and Boundaries of Participation in Organizations: A

Critical Evaluation." *Administrative Science Quarterly,* 1978, *23,* 1-39.

Daft, R. K., and Becker, S. W. *Innovation in Organizations.* New York: Elsevier, 1978.

Dahl, R. A., and Lindblom, C. E. *Politics, Economics, and Welfare.* New York: Harper & Row, 1976.

Dahling, R. L. "Shannon's Information Theory: The Spread of an Idea." In W. Schramm (Ed.), *Studies of Innovation and of Communication to the Public.* Vol. 2: *Studies in the Utilization of Behavioral Science.* Stanford, Calif.: Institute for Communication Research, Stanford University, 1962.

Dalin, P. *Strategies for Innovation in Education.* Center for Educational Research and Innovation Document 85.493. Paris: Organization for Economic Cooperation and Development, 1972.

Dalkey, N. C. *Delphi.* Santa Monica, Calif.: Rand Corporation, 1967.

Daniels, R. S. "Governance and Administration of Human Service in Urban and Low-Income Communities." *American Journal of Public Health,* 1973, *63,* 715-720.

Danziger, J. N., and Dutton, W. H. "Technical Innovation in Local Government: The Case of Computers." *Policy and Politics,* 1977, *6,* 27-49.

Dar, V., and Levis, M. "Effective Communication in Technology Sharing." *Ocean Development and International Law Journal,* 1974, *2*(4), 379-401.

Darkenwald, G. G. "Innovation in Adult Education: An Organizational Analysis." *Adult Education,* 1977, *27*(3), 156-172.

Darran, D. C., Miles, R. E., and Snow, C. C. "Organizational Adjustment to the Environment: A Review." Paper presented at 7th annual meeting of American Institute for Decision Sciences, Cincinnati, November 1975.

Datta, L.-E. "The Research and Development Programme of the National Institute of Education (United States of America)." *International Review of Applied Psychology* (Paris), 1977, *26*(2), 127-131.

Datta, L.-E. "Communicating Evaluation Results for Policy Decision Making." In R. A. Berk (Ed.), *Educational Evaluation*

*Methodology: The State of the Art.* Baltimore: Johns Hopkins University Press, 1981.

Datta, L.-E., and Perloff, R. *Improving Evaluations.* Beverly Hills, Calif.: Sage, 1979.

David, E. E., Jr. "National Policies for Science and Technology: U.S. Innovation and World Leadership—Facts and Fallacies." *Research Management,* 1977, *20*(6), 7-10.

David, P. *Technical Choice, Innovation and Economic Growth.* Cambridge, England: Cambridge University Press, 1975.

Davidson, H. F., Cetron, M. J., and Goldhar, J. D. (Eds.). *Technology Transfer.* Vol. 6. Leiden, Holland: Noordhoff, 1974.

Davidson, W. S., II, and others. *Evaluation Strategies in Criminal Justice.* New York: Pergamon, 1980.

Davies, J. *Information Services.* (ED 140 820.) London: National Foundation for Educational Research in England and Wales, 1976.

Davis, A. G. M. "EEC and Transfer of Technology." *Journal of the Patent Office Society,* 1977, *59*(7), 424-469.

Davis, H. R. "A Checklist for Change." In National Institute of Mental Health, *A Manual for Research Utilization.* Washington, D.C.: U.S. Government Printing Office, 1971.

Davis, H. R. *Mental Health Research and Development: A Report to the PSAC Panel on Health Services Research and Development.* Washington, D.C.: National Institute of Mental Health, 1972.

Davis, H. R. "Change and Innovation." In S. Feldman (Ed.), *Administration and Mental Health.* Springfield, Ill.: Thomas, 1973a.

Davis, H. R. "Four Ways to Goal Attainment." *Evaluation,* 1973b, *1*(2), 43-48, 95.

Davis, H. R. "Management of Innovation and Change in Mental Health Services." *Hospital and Community Psychiatry,* 1978, *29*(10), 649-658.

Davis, H. R., and Salasin, S. E. "The Utilization of Evaluation." In E. Struening and M. Guttentag (Eds.), *Handbook of Evaluation Research.* Vol. 1. Beverly Hills, Calif.: Sage, 1975.

Davis, H. R., and Salasin, S. E. "Applied Social Research in Combat with Waste and Suffering." *International Journal of Comparative Sociology,* 1978a, *19*(1-2), 107-113.

Davis, H. R., and Salasin, S. E. "Strengthening the Contribution of Social R&D to Policy Making." In L. E. Lynn, Jr. (Ed.), *Knowledge and Policy: The Uncertain Connection.* Washington, D.C.: National Academy of Sciences, 1978b.

Davis, H. R., and Salasin, S. E. "Change: Decisions and Their Implementation." In S. Feldman (Ed.), *The Administration of Mental Health Services.* (Rev. ed.) Springfield, Ill.: Thomas, 1979.

Davis, H. R., and Salasin, S. E. "Applying the Decision Determinants Analysis Model to Consultation in Mental Health Organizations." Unpublished paper, National Institute of Mental Health, Washington, D.C., n.d.

Davis, H. R., Windle, C., and Sharfstein, S. S. "Developing Guidelines for Program Evaluation Capability in Community Mental Health Centers." *Evaluation,* 1977, *4,* 25-29.

Davis, L. E., and Cherns, A. B. (Eds.). *The Quality of Working Life.* Vol. 1: *Problems, Prospects, and the State of the Art.* New York: Free Press, 1975a.

Davis, L. E., and Cherns, A. B. (Eds.). *The Quality of Working Life.* Vol. 2: *Cases and Commentary.* New York: Free Press, 1975b.

Davis, T. R. V., and Specht, P. S. "Citizen Participation in Community Mental-Health Programs: A Study in Intergroup Conflict and Cooperation." *Group & Organization Studies,* 1978, *3*(4), 456-466.

Deal, T. E., and Celotti, L. D. *"Loose Coupling" and the School Administrator: Some Recent Research Findings.* Stanford, Calif.: School of Education, Stanford University, 1977.

DeArman, J. W. *Investigation of the Abandonment Rate and Causes of Abandonment of Innovative Practices in Secondary Schools.* (ED 133 872.) Final Report to National Institute of Education, Grant No. 74-0005. Columbia: University of Missouri, 1975.

de Brichambaut, M. *Technological Exchange Between the United States and Europe: An Attempt in Explaining Shifting Perceptions.* (NTIS AD-A016 495.) Santa Monica, Calif.: Rand Corporation, 1974.

DeFleur, M. L. "Mass Communication and Social Change." *Social Forces,* 1966, *44*(3), 314-326.

Delbecq, A., Van de Ven, A., and Gustafson, D. *Group Techniques for Program Planning: A Guide to Nominal Group and Delphi Planning.* Glenview, Ill.: Scott, Foresman, 1975.

Denner, B., and Price, R. "Introduction." In B. Denner and R. Price (Eds.), *Community Mental Health: Social Action and Reaction.* New York: Holt, Rinehart and Winston, 1973.

Denver Research Institute. *Project for the Analysis of Technology Transfer.* National Science Foundation, Contract NSF-06-004-063. Washington, D.C.: National Science Foundation, 1970.

Denver Research Institute. *Space Benefits: The Secondary Application of Aerospace Technology in Other Sectors of the Economy.* (NTIS N76-29063.) Denver, Colo.: Denver Research Institute, 1974.

Denver Research Institute. *Benefits Briefing Notebook: The Secondary Application of Aerospace Technology in Other Sectors of the Economy.* (NTIS N76-29060.) Denver, Colo.: Denver Research Institute, 1976.

Dernberg, R. F. "Transfer of Technology to China." *Asia Quarterly,* 1974, *1974*(3), 229-252.

Derr, C. B. (Ed.). *Organizational Development in Urban School Systems.* Beverly Hills, Calif.: Sage, 1974.

Deshpande, R. "The Use, Nonuse, and the Abuse of Social Science Knowledge: A Review Essay." *Knowledge,* 1979, *1*(1), 164-176.

Deshpande, R. "Action and Enlightenment Functions of Research: Comparing Private- and Public-Sector Perspectives." *Knowledge,* 1981, *2*(3), 317-330.

Dessemontet, F. "Transfer of Technology Under UNCTAD and EEC Draft Codifications: A European View on Choice of Law in Licensing." *Journal of International Law and Economics,* 1977, *12*(1), 1-55.

Dewar, R., and Duncan, R. B. "Implications for Organizational Design of Structural Alteration as a Consequence of Growth and Innovation." *Organization and Administrative Sciences,* 1977, *8*, 203-222.

Dewey, J., and others. "Scientific Method and Social Change." *American Behavioral Scientist,* 1960, *4*, 38.

Dexter, L. A. "On the Use and Abuse of Social Science by Practitioners." *American Behavioral Scientist,* 1965, *9*(3), 25-29.

Dickey, B., and Hampton, E. "Effective Problem Solving for Evaluation Utilization." *Knowledge,* 1981, *2*(3), 361-374.

Dickman, F. B. "Work Activities, Settings, Methodologies, and Perceptions: Correlates of Evaluative Research Utilization." *Knowledge,* 1981, *2*(3), 375-387.

Dimock, H. G. *Organization Development: An Experience Report Dealing with Change.* Toronto: Ontario Council for Leadership in Educational Administration, 1975.

Dimock, H. G. *A Study of Process-Oriented, Qualitative Research Using Community Collaboration as a Social Action and Assessment Method of Community Development.* Montreal: Centre for Human Relations and Community Studies, Concordia University, 1976.

Dimock, H. G. "The Use of Systems-Improvement Research in Developing a Change Strategy for Human-Service Organizations." *Group & Organization Studies,* 1978, *3*(3), 365-375.

Dissemination Analysis Group. *Dissemination in Relation to Elementary and Secondary Education: Final Report on the Dissemination Policy Council.* Washington, D.C.: Office of the Assistant Secretary for Education, 1977.

Dobrov, G. M. "The Management of R&D Technological Progress as an Object for Applied Systems Analysis." *R&D Management,* 1978, *8*(special issue), 133-149.

Doctors, S. I. *The Role of Federal Agencies in Technology Transfer.* Cambridge, Mass.: M.I.T. Press, 1969.

Doctors, S. I. *The NASA Technology Transfer Program: An Evaluation of the Dissemination System.* Washington, D.C.: National Aeronautics and Space Administration, 1971.

Doktor, R., and Hamilton, W. F. "Cognitive Style and the Acceptance of Management Science Recommendations." *Management Science,* 1973, *19,* 884-894.

Donaldson, W. V., and others. "Technology Transfer in Tacoma, Washington: The Totem One Program." Paper presented at Urban Technology Conference, American Institute of Aeronautics and Astronautics, San Francisco, July 1972.

Donnelly, W. L. "Barriers to Educational Innovation: A Case

Study of Organizational Conflict." Doctoral dissertation, Pennsylvania State University. *Dissertation Abstracts International,* 1978, *39,* 2570A. (University Microfilms No. 78-19, 341.)

Donnison, D. "Research for Policy." *Minerva,* 1972, *10*(4), 519-536.

Dore, R. P. "The Future of Formal Education in Developing Countries." *International Development Review,* 1975, *17*(2), 7-11.

Doszkocs, T. R., Rapp, B. A., and Schoolman, H. M. "Automated Information Retrieval in Science and Technology." *Science,* 1980, *208*(4439), 25-30.

Dougharty, L., and Haggart, S. *An Information System for Educational Management.* Vol. 6: *An In-Service Training Program.* (ED 068 117.) Santa Monica, Calif.: Rand Corporation, 1971.

Downs, A. *Inside Bureaucracy.* Boston: Little, Brown, 1967.

Downs, G. W. *Bureaucracy, Innovation, and Public Policy.* Lexington, Mass.: Heath, 1976.

Downs, G. W. "Complexity and Innovation Research." In M. Radnor, I. Feller, and E. Rogers (Eds.), *The Diffusion of Innovations: An Assessment.* Evanston, Ill.: Center for the Interdisciplinary Study of Science and Technology, Northwestern University, 1978.

Downs, G. W., and Mohr, L. B. "Conceptual Issues in the Study of Innovation." *Administrative Science Quarterly,* 1976, *21* (4), 700-715.

Dressel, P. L. *Handbook of Academic Evaluation: Assessing Institutional Effectiveness, Student Progress, and Professional Performance for Decision Making in Higher Education.* San Francisco: Jossey-Bass, 1976.

Dreyfus, D. A. "The Limitations of Policy Research in Congressional Decision Making." In C. Weiss (Ed.), *Using Social Research in Public Policy Making.* Lexington, Mass.: Lexington Books, 1977.

Drucker, J. "Military Research Product Utilization." *Journal of Technology Transfer,* 1977, *2,* 9-28.

Drucker, P. F. *The Age of Discontinuity: Guidelines to our Changing Society.* New York: Harper & Row, 1968.

Drucker, P. F. *Management: Tasks, Responsibilities, Promises.* New York: Harper & Row, 1974.

Dube, S. C. "Communication, Innovation, and Planned Change in India." In D. Lerner and W. Schramm (Eds.), *Communication and Change in Developing Countries.* Honolulu: East-West Center Press, 1967.

Dubey, S. N. "Community Action Programs and Citizen Participation: Issues and Confusions." *Social Work,* 1970, *15,* 76-84.

Duchesneau, T. D., Cohn, S. F., and Dutton, J. E. *A Study of Innovation in Manufacturing: Determinants, Processes, and Methodological Issues.* Vol. 1: *A Panel Study of the Determinants of Innovation in the U.S. Footwear Industry.* Vol. 2: *Case Studies of Innovation Decision Making in the U.S. Footwear Industry.* Grant No. RDA-7423652, National Science Foundation. Orono: Social Science Research Institute, University of Maine at Orono, 1979.

Duchnesneau, T. D., Cohn, S. F., and Dutton, J. E. *A Study of Innovation in Manufacturing: Determinants, Processes, and Methodological Issues. Executive Summary.* Grant No. RDA-7423652, National Science Foundation. Orono: Social Science Research Institute, University of Maine at Orono, 1980.

Dumas, N. S. (Ed.). *Research Utilization and Dissemination: Proceedings of a Regional Conference.* Gainesville, Fla.: Regional Rehabilitation Research Institute, University of Florida, 1968.

Dumas, N. S., and Muthard, J. E. "The Consumer in the Scientific and Technical Information Market: Managing the Flow in Literature in a Professional Journal." *Rehabilitation Counseling Bulletin,* 1970, *14,* 5-13.

Dumas, N. S., and Muthard, J. E. "Coordinating Research and Practice: The Regional Rehabilitation Institutes." *Journal of Rehabilitation,* 1971, *37,* 34-37.

Duncan, M. G. "Experiment in Applying New Methods in Field Work." *Social Casework,* 1963, *44,* 179-184.

Duncan, P. "From Scientist to Manager." *The Sociological Review Monograph No. 18,* 1972, 131-146.

Duncan, R. B. "Characteristics of Organizational Environments and Perceived Environmental Uncertainty." *Administrative Science Quarterly,* 1972a, *17*(3), 313-327.

Duncan, R. B. "Organizational Climate and Climate for Change in Three Police Departments: Some Preliminary Findings." *Urban Affairs Quarterly,* 1972b, *8,* 205-246.

Duncan, R. B., and others. *An Assessment of a Structural Task Approach to Organizational Development in a School System.* Final report to National Institute of Education, Grant No. 6-003-0172. Washington, D.C.: National Institute of Education, 1977.

Duncan, W. J. "The Knowledge Utilization Process in Management and Organization." *Academy of Management Journal,* 1972, *15,* 273-288.

Duncan, W. J. "The Researcher and the Manager: A Comparative View of the Need for Mutual Understanding." *Management Science,* 1974, *20*(8), 1157-1163.

Dunn, W. E. "The Two-Communities Metaphor and Models of Knowledge Use: An Exploratory Case Survey." *Knowledge,* 1980, *1*(4), 515-536.

Dunn, W. N., and Swierczek, F. W. "Planned Organizational Change: Toward Grounded Theory." *Journal of Applied Behavioral Science,* 1977, *13*(2), 135-157.

Dykens, J. W., and others. *Strategies of Mental Hospital Change.* Boston: Massachusetts State Department of Mental Health, 1964.

Eash, M. J. "Bringing Research Findings into Classroom Practice." *Elementary School Journal,* 1968, *68*(8), 410-418.

Eaton, J. W. *Stone Walls Do Not a Prison Make: The Anatomy of Planned Administrative Change.* Springfield, Ill.: Thomas, 1962.

Eckensberger, L. H. "On Types in Social Change: A Theoretical and Empirical Investigation." *Die Dritte Welt* [*The Third World*], 1972, *1*(3), 372-397.

Eddy, E. M. "Educational Innovation and Desegregation: A Case Study of Symbolic Realignment." *Human Organization,* 1975, *34*(2), 163-172.

Edling, J. V. "Role of Newer Media in Planned Change." In W. C. Meierhenry (Ed.), *Media and Educational Innovation.*

Lincoln: University of Nebraska Extension Division and University of Nebraska Press, 1964.

Edstrom, A. "User Influence on the Development of MIS—A Contingency Approach." *Human Relations,* 1977, *30,* 589-607.

Edwards, W., Guttentag, M., and Snapper, K. "A Decision-Theoretic Approach to Evaluation Research." In E. L. Struening and M. Guttentag (Eds.), *Handbook of Evaluation Research.* Vol. 1. Beverly Hills, Calif.: Sage, 1975.

Egea, A. N. "Multinational Corporations in the Operation and Ideology of International Transfer of Technology." *Studies in Comparative International Development,* 1975, *10*(1), 11-29.

Eichholz, G. C. "Why Do Teachers Reject Change?" *Theory into Practice,* 1963, *2,* 264-268.

Eichholz, G. C., and Rogers, E. M. "Resistance to the Adoption of Audiovisual Aids by Elementary School Teachers." In M. B. Miles (Ed.), *Innovation in Education.* New York: Bureau of Publications, Teachers College, Columbia University, 1964.

Eidell, T. L. "Constraints of Information Systems: Conceptual and Technical Problems." (ED 145 807.) Paper presented at 62nd annual meeting of American Educational Research Association, New York, April 1977.

Eidell, T. L., and Kitchel, J. M. (Eds.). *Knowledge Production and Utilization in Educational Administration.* Eugene: Center for the Advanced Study of Educational Administration, University of Oregon, 1968.

Eiduson, B. T., Brooks, S. H., and Motto, R. L. "A Generalized Psychiatric Information-Processing System." *Behavioral Science,* 1966, *11*(2), 133-142.

Ein-Dor, P., and Segev, E. *Managing Management Information Systems.* Lexington, Mass.: Heath, 1978.

Eisenstadt, S. N. *Comparative Perspectives on Social Change.* Boston: Little, Brown, 1968.

Eisenstadt, S. N. (Ed.). *Readings in Social Evolution and Development.* New York: Pergamon, 1970.

Ellis, W. E. *A Joint Effort to Enhance the Dissemination Func-*

*tions of State Education Agencies.* (ED 077 544.) Columbia: South Carolina State Department of Education, 1973.

Elmore, R. *Dissemination and Implementation of Educational Innovations in Massachusetts.* Boston: Massachusetts State Department of Education, 1974.

Elmore, R. F. "Organizational Models of Social Program Implementation." *Public Policy,* 1978, *26*(2), 185-228.

Emery, F. E., and Trist, E. "The Causal Texture of Organizational Environments." *Human Relations,* 1965, *18,* 21-31.

Emrick, J. A., with Peterson, S. M., and Agarwala-Rogers, R. *Evaluation of the National Diffusion Network.* 2 vols. Menlo Park, Calif.: Stanford Research Institute, 1977.

Emrick, J. A., and Peterson, S. M. *A Synthesis of Findings Across Five Recent Studies of Educational Dissemination and Change.* Educational Knowledge Dissemination and Utilization Occasional Paper Series. San Francisco: Far West Laboratory for Educational Research and Development, 1978.

Engstrom, G. A. "Where We Stand on Research Utilization." *Rehabilitation Record,* 1969, *10,* 28-32.

Engstrom, G. A. "Research Utilization: The Challenge of Applying SRS Research." *Welfare in Review,* 1970, *2,* 1-7.

Engstrom, G. A. "Research and Research Utilization: A Many-Faceted Approach." *Rehabilitation Counseling Bulletin,* 1975, *19*(2), 357-364.

Enos, J. L. "Invention and Innovation in the Petroleum Industry." In Universities-National Bureau Committee for Economic Research, *The Rate and Direction of Inventive Activity.* Princeton, N.J.: Princeton University Press, 1962a.

Enos, J. L. *Petroleum Progress and Profits.* Cambridge, Mass.: M.I.T. Press, 1962b.

Etemad, H. E. A. "Address on Transfer of Nuclear Technology, Iran Conference, April 10-14, 1977." *Annals of Nuclear Energy,* 1977, *4*(6-8), 220-221.

Ettlie, J. E. "Technology Transfer—From Innovators to Users." *Industrial Engineering,* 1973, *5*(6), 16-23.

Ettlie, J. E. "The Timing and Sources of Information for the Adoption and Implementation of Production Innovations."

*IEEE Transactions on Engineering Management,* 1976, *23* (1), 62-68.

Etzioni, A. *Political Unification: A Comparative Study of Leaders and Forces.* New York: Holt, Rinehart and Winston, 1965.

Etzioni, A. *Studies in Social Change.* New York: Holt, Rinehart and Winston, 1966.

Etzioni, A. *The Active Society.* New York: Free Press, 1968.

Etzioni, A. "On Changing Societies." *Current Sociology,* 1975, *23*(1), 39-47.

Etzioni, A. "Reindustrialization of America." *Science,* 1980, *209,* 863.

Etzioni, A., and Etzioni-Halevy, E. (Eds.). *Social Change: Sources, Patterns, and Consequences.* (2nd ed.) New York: Basic Books, 1974.

Etzioni, A., and Remp, R. "Technical 'Shortcuts' to Social Change." *Science,* 1972, *175,* 31-38.

Evan, W. M., and Black, G. "Innovation in Business Organizations: Some Factors Associated with Success or Failure of Staff Proposals." *Journal of Business,* 1967, *40,* 519-530.

Evans, J. W. "Evaluating Social Action Programs." *Social Science Quarterly,* 1969, *50*(3), 568-581.

Evans, R. I., and Leppmann, P. K. *Resistance to Innovation in Higher Education: A Social Psychological Exploration Focused on Television and the Establishment.* San Francisco: Jossey-Bass, 1968.

Eveland, J., Rogers, E., and Klepper, C. *The Innovation Process in Public Organizations.* Final report to National Science Foundation, Grant RDA 75-17952. Ann Arbor: Department of Journalism, University of Michigan, 1977.

Everhart, R. B. "Role Development and Organizational Change: The Case of Collaborative Teaching Arrangements." *Journal of Research & Development in Education,* 1977, *10*(2), 77-86.

Ewing, A. F. "UNCTAD and the Transfer of Technology." *Journal of World Trade Law,* 1976, *10*(3), 197-214.

Experts of the Group of 77. "Draft Outline of an International Code of Conduct on Transfer of Technology." *Development and Change,* 1976, *7*(2), 175-193.

Fabun, D. *The Dynamics of Change.* Englewood Cliffs, N.J.: Prentice-Hall, 1968.

Fairweather, G. W. *Social Psychology in the Treatment of Mental Illness: An Experimental Approach.* New York: Wiley, 1964.

Fairweather, G. W. *Methods for Experimental Social Innovation.* New York: Wiley, 1967.

Fairweather, G. W. "Experimental Innovation Defined." In H. A. Hornstein and others (Eds.), *Social Intervention: A Behavioral Science Approach.* New York: Free Press, 1971.

Fairweather, G. W. "Innovation: A Necessary but Insufficient Condition for Change." *Innovations,* 1973, *1,* 25-27.

Fairweather, G. W. "The Prototype Lodge Society: Instituting Group Process Principles." In G. W. Fairweather (Ed.), *New Directions for Mental Health Services: The Fairweather Lodge: A Twenty-Five Year Retrospective,* no. 7. San Francisco: Jossey-Bass, 1980a.

Fairweather, G. W. "Spreading the Lodge Society Concept." In G. W. Fairweather (Ed.), *New Directions for Mental Health Services: The Fairweather Lodge: A Twenty-Five Year Retrospective,* no. 7. San Francisco: Jossey-Bass, 1980b.

Fairweather, G. W., Sanders, D. H., and Tornatzky, L. G. *Creating Change in Mental Health Organizations.* New York: Pergamon, 1974.

Fairweather, G. W., and Tornatzky, L. G. *Experimental Methods for Social Policy Research.* New York: Pergamon, 1977.

Fairweather, G. W., and others. *Community Life for the Mentally Ill.* Chicago: Aldine, 1969.

Fallon, B. (Ed.). *Fifty States Innovate to Improve Their Schools.* Bloomington, Ind.: Phi Delta Kappa, 1967.

Far West Laboratory for Educational Research and Development. *Educational Dissemination and Linking Agent Sourcebook: A Compendium of Product Resources.* (ED 171 260.) San Francisco: Far West Laboratory for Educational Research and Development, 1976a.

Far West Laboratory for Educational Research and Development. *Transferring Success.* (ED 151 949.) San Francisco: Far West Laboratory for Educational Research and Development, 1976b.

Far West Laboratory for Educational Research and Development. *The Research and Development Exchange, National Institute of Education.* Washington, D.C.: National Institute of Education, 1979.

Farlee, C. "The Computer as a Focus of Organizational Change in the Hospital." *Journal of Nursing Administration,* 1978, *8*(2), 20-26.

Farrar, E., DeSanctis, J. E., and Cohen, D. K. "Views from Below: Implementation Research in Education." *Teachers College Record,* 1980, *82*(1), 77-100.

Fashing, J., and Deutsch, S. E. *Academics in Retreat: The Politics of Educational Innovation.* Albuquerque: University of New Mexico Press, 1971.

Federal Coordinating Council for Science, Engineering and Technology. *Directory of Federal Technology Transfer.* Washington, D.C.: U.S. Government Printing Office, 1977.

Feldman, J. J. *The Dissemination of Health Information.* Chicago: Aldine, 1966.

Feller, I. "The Applicability of Economic Analysis to the Adoption of Innovations by Public Sector Organizations." In M. Radnor, I. Feller, and E. Rogers (Eds.), *The Diffusion of Innovations: An Assessment.* Evanston, Ill.: Center for the Interdisciplinary Study of Science and Technology, Northwestern University, 1978.

Feller, I. "Three Coigns on Diffusion Research." *Knowledge,* 1979, *1*(2), 293-312.

Feller, I., and Menzel, D. C. *Diffusion of Innovations in Municipal Governments.* University Park: Institute for Research on Human Resources, Pennsylvania State University, 1976.

Feller, I., and Menzel, D. C. "Diffusion Milieus as a Focus of Research on Innovation in the Public Sector." *Policy Science,* 1977, *8*(1), 49-68.

Feller, I., and Menzel, D. C. "The Adoption of Technological Innovations by Municipal Governments." *Urban Affairs Quarterly,* 1978, *13,* 468-488.

Feller, I., Menzel, D. C., and Engel, A. J. *Diffusion of Technology in State Mission-Oriented Agencies.* (NTIS PB-242 549/AS.) University Park: Institute for Research on Human Resources, Pennsylvania State University, 1974.

Feller, I., Menzel, D. C., and Kozak, L. A. *Diffusion of Innovations in Local Governments: Executive Summary and Final Report.* (NTIS PB-257-068, -069.) University Park: Institute for Research on Human Resources, Pennsylvania State University, 1976.

Feller, I., and others. *Sources and Uses of Scientific and Technological Information in State Legislatures.* University Park: Institute for Research on Human Resources, Pennsylvania State University, 1975a.

Feller, I., and others. *Sources and Uses of Scientific and Technological Information in State Legislatures: Summary Report.* University Park: Institute for Research on Human Resources, Pennsylvania State University, 1975b.

Ferguson, C. J. "Concerning the Nature of Human Systems and the Consultant's Role." *Journal of Applied Behavioral Science,* 1968, *4*(2), 179-193.

Ferman, L. A. "Some Perspectives on Evaluating Social Welfare Programs." *Annals of the American Academy of Political and Social Science,* 1969, *385,* 143-156.

Festinger, L. "Behavioral Support for Opinion Change." *Public Opinion Quarterly,* 1964, *28*(3), 404-417.

Festinger, L., and Maccoby, N. "On Resistance to Persuasive Communications." *Journal of Abnormal and Social Psychology,* 1964, *68*(4), 359-366.

Fields, D. "The Network of Consultants on Knowledge Transfer." *Evaluation and Change,* 1978, special issue, 36-40.

Figley, C. "The Vietnam Veteran as Survivor: An Interview with S. Salasin." *Evaluation and Change,* 1980, special issue, 135-141.

Fincher, C. "Some Straight and Positive Thinking About Schools." *Contemporary Psychology,* 1972, *17*(12), 658-660.

Fiore, C. F., and Rozwadowski, R. T. "The Implementation of Process Models." *Management Science,* 1968, *14,* B360-372.

Firestone, W. A. "Participation and Influence in the Planning of Educational Change." *Journal of Applied Behavioral Science,* 1977, *13*(2), 135-157.

Firestone, W. A. "Images of Schools and Patterns of Change." *American Journal of Education,* 1980, *88*(4), 459-487.

Fischer, W. A. "Empirical Approaches to Understanding Technology Transfer." *R&D Management,* 1976, *6,* 151-157.

Flanagan, J. C. "Case Studies on the Utilization of Behavioral Science Research." In W. Schramm (Ed.), *Case Studies in Bringing Behavioral Science into Use: Studies in the Utilization of Behavioral Science.* Vol. 1. Stanford, Calif.: Institute for Communication Research, Stanford University, 1961.

Fletcher, J. L. *Dissemination in Relation to Elementary and Secondary Education.* (ED 144 540.) Washington, D.C.: U.S. Office of Education, 1977.

Fliegel, F. C., and Kivlin, J. E. "Attributes of Innovations as Factors in Diffusion." *American Journal of Sociology,* 1966, *72*(3), 235-248.

Forecasting International, Ltd. *Technology Transfer and Technological Innovation: Annotated and Selected Bibliographies.* (NTIS COM-73-11374.) Arlington, Va.: Forecasting International, Ltd., 1973.

Foster, R. N., and Gluck, F. W. "Impact of Antitrust and Regulatory Actions on Progress of Technology." *Research Management,* 1975, *18*(4), 7-10.

Fox, R. S., and Lippitt, R. "The Innovation of Classroom Mental Health Practices." In M. B. Miles (Ed.), *Innovations in Education.* New York: Bureau of Publications, Teachers College, Columbia University, 1964.

Fox, R. S., and Lippitt, R. *The Innovation and Sharing of Teaching Practices: Stimulating Adoption and Adaptation of Selected Teaching Practices.* Ann Arbor: Institute for Social Research, University of Michigan, 1967.

Frank, L. K. "Interprofessional Communication." *American Journal of Public Health,* 1961, *51,* 1798-1804.

Frank, L. K. "Fragmentation in the Helping Professions." In W. G. Bennis, K. D. Benne, and R. Chin (Eds.), *The Planning of Change: Readings in the Applied Behavioral Sciences.* New York: Holt, Rinehart and Winston, 1962.

Frankel, C. (Ed.). *Controversies and Decisions: The Social Sciences and Public Policy.* New York: Russell Sage Foundation, 1976.

Franklin, J. L. "Characteristics of Successful and Unsuccessful Organization Development." *Journal of Applied Behavioral Science,* 1976, *12*(4), 471-492.

Freeman, C. "A Study of Success and Failure in Industrial Innovation." In B. R. Williams (Ed.), *Science and Technology in Economic Growth*. New York: Halstead, 1973.

Freeman, C. *The Economics of Industrial Innovation*. Harmondsworth, England: Penguin, 1974.

French, J. R. P., Jr. "An Experiment in Participation in a Norwegian Factory." *Human Relations*, 1960, *13*, 3-19.

French, J. R. P., Jr., and Raven, B. "The Bases of Social Power." In D. Cartwright, *Studies in Social Power*. Ann Arbor: Institute for Social Research, University of Michigan, 1959.

Friedrichs, G. "Planning Social Adjustment to Technological Change at the Level of the Undertaking." *International Labour Review*, 1965, *92*, 91-105.

Fry, B. M. *Evaluation Study of ERIC Products and Services*. Final report to U.S. Office of Education, Project No. BR00375, Grant No. OEC-0-70-3211. Washington, D.C.: U.S. Office of Education, 1972.

Fullan, M. "Overview of the Innovative Process and the User." *Interchange*, 1972, *3*(2), 1-46.

Fullan, M. "The Role of Human Agents Internal to School Districts in Knowledge Utilization." Paper presented at Program on Research and Educational Practice, National Institute of Education, Washington, D.C., April 1980.

Fullan, M., Miles, M. B., and Taylor, G. *Organization Development in Schools: The State of the Art*. Vol. 1: *Introduction and Executive Summary*. Final report to National Institute of Education, Contracts Nos. 400-77-0051, -0052. Toronto: Ontario Institute for Studies in Education, 1978.

Fullan, M., Miles, M. B., and Taylor, G. "Organization Development in Schools: The State of the Art." *Review of Educational Research*, 1980, *5*(1), 121-183.

Fullan, M., and Pomfret, A. "Research on Curriculum and Instruction Implementation." *Review of Educational Research*, 1977, *47*(2), 335-397.

Gabor, D. *Innovations: Scientific, Technological, and Social*. New York: Oxford University Press, 1970.

Galbraith, J. *Organization Design*. Reading, Mass.: Addison-Wesley, 1977.

Gallagher, A. "Directed Change in Formal Organizations: The

School System." In R. O. Carlson and others, *Change Processes in the Public Schools*. Eugene: Center for the Advanced Study of Educational Administration, University of Oregon, 1965.

Gallessich, J. "Symposium: Conceptual Bases of School Consultation Models." *Professional Psychology*, 1976, 7(4), 618-645.

Gardner, J. W. *Excellence: Can We Be Equal and Excellent Too*. New York: Harper & Row, 1961.

Gardner, J. W. *Self-Renewal: The Individual and the Innovative Society*. New York: Harper & Row, 1964.

Garfield, E. *Citation Indexing: Its Theory and Application in Science, Technology, and Humanities*. New York: Wiley-Interscience, 1979.

Garner, W. "The Acquisition and Application of Knowledge: A Symbiotic Relation." *American Psychologist*, 1972, 27, 941-946.

Gartner, A., and Riessman, F. "Strategies for Large-Scale Educational Reform." *Teachers College Record*, 1974, 75, 352.

Gartner, J., and Naiman, C. S. "Overcoming the Barriers to Technology Transfer." *Research Management*, 1976, 19(2), 22-28.

Garvey, J. J. "The National Shipbuilding Research Program, 1971-1976." Paper presented to the Philadelphia Section, Society of Naval Architects and Marine Engineers, April 1976.

Garvey, W. D., and Compton, B. E. "A Program of Research in Scientific Information Exchange: Orientation, Objections, and Results." *Information sur les Sciences Sociales*, 1967, 6 (2-3), 213-237.

Garvey, W. D., and Gottfredson, S. D. "Changing the System: Innovations in the Interactive Social System of Scientific Communication." *Information Processing & Management*, 1976, 12(3), 165-176.

Garvey, W. D., and Griffith, B. C. "Scientific Information Exchange in Psychology." *Science*, 1964, 146, 1655.

Garvey, W. D., and Griffith, B. C. "Communication in a Science: The System and Its Modification." In A. de Reuck and

J. Knight (Eds.), *Communication in Science: Documentation and Automation.* Boston: Little, Brown, 1967.

Garvey, W. D., and Griffith, B. C. "Scientific Communication: Its Role in the Conduct of Research and Creation of Knowledge." *American Psychologist,* 1971, *26,* 349-362.

Garvey, W. D., and Griffith, B. C. "Communication and Information Processing Within Scientific Disciplines: Empirical Findings for Psychology." *Information Storage and Retrieval,* 1972, *8*(3), 123-136.

Garvey, W. D., Lin, N., and Tomita, K. "Research Studies in Patterns of Scientific Communication: 3. Information-Exchange Processes Associated with the Production of Journal Articles." *Information Storage and Retrieval,* 1972a, *8*(5), 207-221.

Garvey, W. D., Lin, N., and Tomita, K. "Research Studies in Patterns of Scientific Communication: 4. The Continuity of Dissemination of Information by 'Productive Scientists.' " *Information Storage and Retrieval,* 1972b, *8*(6), 265-276.

Garvey, W. D., Tomita, K., and Woolf, P. "The Dynamic Scientific Information User." *Information Storage and Retrieval,* 1974, *10*(3-4), 115-131.

Garvey, W. D., and others. "Research Studies in Patterns of Scientific Communication: 1. General Description of Research Program." *Information Storage and Retrieval,* 1972a, *8*(3), 111-122.

Garvey, W. D., and others. "Research Studies in Patterns of Scientific Communication: 2. The Role of the National Meeting in Scientific and Technical Communication." *Information Storage and Retrieval,* 1972b, *8*(4), 159-169.

Gee, E. A. *Managing Innovation.* New York: Wiley, 1976.

Gee, S. "The Role of Technology Transfer in Innovation." *Research Management,* 1974, *17*(6), 31-36.

Gee, S. "Factors Affecting the Innovation Time-Period." *Research Management,* 1978, *21*(1), 37-42.

Gelb, J., and Polley, M. L. *The Politics of Social Change: A Reader for the 70's.* New York: Holt, Rinehart and Winston, 1971.

Gellman, A. J., and others. *Economic Regulation and Techno-*

logical Innovation: A Cross-National Literature Survey and Analysis. (NTIS PB-233 085/AS.) Washington, D.C.: National Science Foundation, 1974.

Gellman Research Associates, Inc. "Indicators of International Trends in Technological Innovation." *Science Indicators 1976.* Washington, D.C.: National Science Board, 1977.

George Washington University. *Federal Technology Transfer.* (NTIS PB-222 483.) Washington, D.C.: George Washington University, 1973.

Georgopoulos, B. S. "The Hospital as an Organization and Problem-Solving System." In B. S. Georgopolous (Ed.), *Organization Research in Health Institutions.* Ann Arbor: Institute for Social Research, University of Michigan, 1972.

Gerbner, G. "The Role of Media in Communicating Results of Research." In W. C. Meierhenry (Ed.), *Media and Educational Innovation.* Lincoln: University of Nebraska Extension Division and University of Nebraska Press, 1964.

Gerstenfeld, A. *Innovation: A Study of Technological Policy.* Washington, D.C.: University Press, 1976a.

Gerstenfeld, A. "A Study of Successful Projects, Unsuccessful Projects, and Projects in Process in West Germany." *IEEE Transactions on Engineering Management,* 1976b, *23*(3), 118-123.

Gerstenfeld, A. "Government Regulation Effects on the Direction of Innovation: A Focus on Performance Standards." *IEEE Transactions on Engineering Management,* 1977a, *24* (3), 82-86.

Gerstenfeld, A. "Interdependence and Innovation." *OMEGA, The International Journal of Management Science,* 1977b, *5*(1), 35-42.

Gery, G. J. "Equal Opportunity—Planning and Managing the Process of Change." *Personnel Journal,* 1977, *56*(4), 184-185, 188-191, 203.

Giacquinta, J. "The Process of Organizational Change in Schools." In F. Kerlinger (Ed.), *Review of Research in Education.* Vol. 1. Itasca, Ill.: Peacock, 1973.

Gilbert, J. P., Light, R. J., and Mosteller, F. In C. A. Bennett and A. A. Lumsdaine (Eds.), *Evaluation and Experiment:*

*Some Critical Issues in Assessing Social Programs.* New York: Academic Press, 1975.

Gill, P. P., and Bennis, W. G. "Science and Management: Two Cultures?" *Journal of Applied Behavioral Science,* 1968, *4,* 75-124.

Gilmore, J. S., and others. *The Channels of Technology Acquisition in Commercial Firms, and the NASA Dissemination Program.* Denver, Colo.: Denver Research Institute, 1967.

Ginzberg, E. (Ed.). *Technology and Social Change.* New York: Columbia University Press, 1964.

Gittell, M., and others. *Citizen Organizations: Citizen Participation in Educational Decision Making.* Boston, Mass.: Institute for Responsive Education, 1979.

Glancy, D. M. *Final Report on Background Study on the Impact of Federal Actions on Technology Innovation and Invention.* Washington, D.C.: National Bureau of Standards, 1973.

Glaser, E. M. "Organizational Arteriosclerosis: Its Diagnosis and Treatment." *Advanced Management Journal,* 1965, *30* (1), 21-28.

Glaser, E. M. *A Pilot Study to Determine the Feasibility of Promoting the Use of a Systematized Care Program for Patients with Chronic Obstructive Pulmonary Disease.* Final Report to Social and Rehabilitation Service, Project RD-2571-G-67. Los Angeles: Human Interaction Research Institute, 1968.

Glaser, E. M. "Knowledge Transfer and Institutional Change." *Professional Psychology,* 1973, *4,* 434-444.

Glaser, E. M. *Productivity Gains Through Worklife Improvement.* New York: The Psychological Corporation (Harcourt Brace Jovanovich), 1976.

Glaser, E. M. "If Mohammed Won't Come to the Mountain . . . ." *Evaluation and Change,* 1978a, special issue, 48-53.

Glaser, E. M. "Success in Applied Research: Improving the Odds." *Technology Transfer Times,* 1978b, *2*(3), 6, 16.

Glaser, E. M. "Participatory Management." *Science,* 1980a, *210,* 962.

Glaser, E. M. "Productivity Gains Through Worklife Improvement." *Personnel,* 1980b, *57*(1), 71-77.

Glaser, E. M. "Strategies for Enhancing the Success of Applied Research." *Professional Psychology,* 1980c, *11*(1), 5-11.

Glaser, E. M. "Strategies for Obtaining Utilizable Knowledge." In L. A. Braskamp and R. D. Brown (Eds.), *New Directions for Program Evaluation: Utilization of Evaluative Information,* no. 5. San Francisco: Jossey-Bass, 1980d.

Glaser, E. M. "Using Behavioral Science Strategies for Defining the State-of-the-Art." *Journal of Applied Behavioral Science,* 1980e, *16*(1), 79-92.

Glaser, E. M. "Durability of Innovations in Human Science Organizations." *Knowledge,* 1981a, *3*(2), 167-185.

Glaser, E. M. "There Are No Panaceas—But Let's Look at Some Promising Developments." In J. M. Joffe and G. W. Albee (Eds.), *Prevention Through Political Action and Social Change.* Hanover, Vt.: University Press of New England, 1981b.

Glaser, E. M., and Backer, T. E. "A Clinical Approach to Program Evaluation." *Evaluation,* 1972a, *1,* 54-60.

Glaser, E. M., and Backer, T. E. "Outline of Questions for Program Evaluators Utilizing the Clinical Approach." *Evaluation,* 1972b, *1*(1), 56-60.

Glaser, E. M., and Backer, T. E. "Evaluating the Research Utilization Specialist." *Rehabilitation Counseling Bulletin,* 1975, *19*(2), 387-395.

Glaser, E. M., and Backer, T. E. *Proceedings of the Workshop on Research Utilization Specialist Model Held in Pasadena, California, February 1975.* (NTIS PB-253 512.) Los Angeles: Edward Glaser & Associates, 1976.

Glaser, E. M., and Backer, T. E. "Innovations Redefined: Durability and Local Adaptation." *Evaluation,* 1977, *4,* 131-136.

Glaser, E. M., and Backer, T. E. "Organization Development in Mental Health Services." *Administration in Mental Health,* 1979, *6*(3), 195-215.

Glaser, E. M., and Backer, T. E. "Durability of Innovations: How Goal Attainment Scaling Programs Fare Over Time." *Community Mental Health Journal,* 1980, *16*(2), 130-143.

Glaser, E. M., and Backer, T. E. "Organizational Consultation:

Interviews with 18 Distinguished Consultants." *Knowledge,* 1982, *3*(4), 571-593.

Glaser, E. M., Izard, C. E., and Chenery, M. F. *Improvement in the Quality of Worklife and Productivity: A Joint Venture Between Management and Employees.* Final Report to U.S. Department of Labor, Grant No. 92-06-72-27. Los Angeles: Human Interaction Research Institute, 1976.

Glaser, E. M., and Marks, J. B. "Putting Research to Work." *Rehabilitation Record,* 1966, 7(6), 6-10.

Glaser, E. M., and Ross, H. L. *Increasing the Utilization of Applied Research Results.* Final Report to National Institute of Mental Health, Grant No. 5 R12 MH 09250-02. Los Angeles: Human Interaction Research Institute, 1971.

Glaser, E. M., and Ross, H. L. *Facilitation of Knowledge Utilization by Institutions for Child Development.* (ED 113 891.) Los Angeles: Human Interaction Research Institute, 1974.

Glaser, E. M., and Taylor, S. "Factors Influencing the Success of Applied Research." *American Psychologist,* 1973, *28,* 140-146.

Glaser, E. M., and Wrenn, C. G. *Putting Research, Experimental and Demonstration Findings to Use.* Washington, D.C.: Office of Manpower Policy, Evaluation and Research, U.S. Department of Labor, 1966.

Glaser, E. M., and others. *Utilization of Applicable Research and Demonstration Results.* Los Angeles: Human Interaction Research Institute, 1967.

Glaser, R. (Ed.). *Research and Development and School Change.* Hillsdale, N.J.: Erlbaum, 1978.

Glass, G. V. (Ed.). *Evaluation Studies Review Annual.* Vol. 1. Beverly Hills, Calif.: Sage, 1976.

Glass, G. V. "Integrating Findings: The Meta-Analysis of Research." In L. S. Schulman (Ed.), *Review of Research in Education.* Vol. 5. Itasca, Ill.: Peacock, 1978.

Glennan, T. K., and others. *The Role of Demonstrations in Federal R&D Policy.* Washington, D.C.: U.S. Government Printing Office, 1978.

Glidewell, J. C. (Ed.). *Conference on Community Mental Health Research.* Springfield, Ill.: Thomas, 1962.

Globe, S., Levy, G. W., and Schwartz, C. M. "Key Factors and Events in the Innovation Process." *Research Management,* 1973, *16*(4), 8-15.

Glock, C. Y. "Applied Social Research: Some Conditions Affecting Its Utilization." In W. Schramm (Ed.), *Case Studies in Utilization of Behavioral Science.* Vol. 1. Stanford, Calif.: Institute for Communication Research, Stanford University, 1961.

Gluckstern, N. B., and Packard, R. W. "The Internal-External Change-Agent Team: Bringing Change to a 'Closed Institution': A Case Study on a County Jail." *Journal of Applied Behavioral Science,* 1977, *13*(1), 41-52.

Gold, B. "Alternate Strategies for Advancing a Company's Technology." *Research Management,* 1975a, *18*(4), 24-29.

Gold, B. (Ed.). *Technological Change: Economics, Management, and Environment.* Oxford: Pergamon, 1975b.

Gold, B. (Ed.). *Research, Technological Change, and Economic Analysis.* Lexington, Mass.: Lexington Books, 1977.

Gold, B. "Some Shortcomings of Research on the Diffusion of Industrial Technology." In M. Radnor, I. Feller, and E. Rogers (Eds.), *The Diffusion of Innovations: An Assessment.* Evanston, Ill.: Center for the Interdisciplinary Study of Science and Technology, Northwestern University, 1978.

Gold, B., Peirce, W. S., and Rosegger, G. "Diffusion of Major Technical Innovations." In B. Gold (Ed.), *Technological Change: Economics, Management, and Environment.* Oxford: Pergamon, 1975.

Goldberg, G. S. "New Directions for the Community Service Society of New York: A Study of Organizational Change." *Social Service Review,* 1980, *54*(2), 184-219.

Goldhar, J. D., Bragaw, L. K., and Schwartz, J. H. "Information Flows, Management Styles, and Technological Innovation." *IEEE Transactions on Engineering Management,* 1976, *23*(1), 51-62.

Goldin, G. J., Margolin, K. N., and Stotsky, B. A. *The Utilization of Rehabilitation Research: Concepts, Principles, and Research.* Northeastern Studies in Vocational Rehabilitation, Monograph No. 6. Boston: Northeastern University, 1969.

Goldman, P., and Gregory, S. "PPBS and Teachers: Responses to an Educational Innovation." *Journal of Educational Administration*, 1977, *15*(2), 249-263.

Goldman, S., and Moynihan, W. J. "Initiation and Diffusion in Educational Planning." *Educational Technology*, 1976, *16* (4), 12-15.

Goldstein, B., and Farlee, C. *Hospital Organization and Computer Technology: The Challenge of Change.* New Brunswick, N.J.: Health Care Systems Research, 1972.

Golembiewski, R. J., Billingsley, K., and Yeager, S. "Measuring Change and Persistence in Human Affairs: Types of Changes Generated by OD Designs." *Journal of Applied Behavioral Science*, 1976, *12*(2), 133-157.

Goodlad, J. *Series on Educational Change.* 6 vols. New York: McGraw-Hill, 1975.

Goodman, L. H. (Ed.). *Sources and Uses of Social and Economic Data: A Manual for Lawyers.* Washington, D.C.: Bureau of Social Science Research, 1973.

Goodman, P. S., Pennings, J. M., and Associates. *New Perspectives on Organizational Effectiveness.* San Francisco: Jossey-Bass, 1977.

Goodridge, C. G. "Factors That Influence the Decision to Adopt an Educational Innovation: IGE." Doctoral dissertation, University of Wisconsin, Madison, 1975. *Dissertation Abstracts International*, 1976, *36*, 7774A. (University Microfilms No. 76-08,199.)

Goodwin, L. "Conceptualizing the Action Process: How the Actions of Individuals Relate to the Guiding of Social Change." *Sociology and Social Research*, 1966, *50*, 377-392.

Goodwin, L. *Can Social Science Help Resolve National Problems?* New York: Free Press, 1975.

Gordon, G., and Fisher, G. L. *Diffusion of Medical Technology: Policy and Research Planning Perspectives.* Cambridge, Mass.: Ballinger, 1975.

Gordon, G., and French, G. L. (Eds.). *The Diffusion of Medical Technology.* Cambridge, Mass.: Ballinger, 1975.

Gordon, G., and Marquis, S. "Freedom, Visibility of Consequences, and Scientific Innovation." *American Journal of Sociology*, 1966, *72*, 194-202.

Gordon, G., and others. "A Contingency Model for the Design of Problem-Solving Research Programs: A Perspective on Diffusion Research." *Milbank Memorial Fund Quarterly: Health and Society,* 1974a, *52,* 185-220.

Gordon, G., and others. "Organizational Structure, Environmental Diversity and Hospital Adoption of Medical Innovations." In A. Kaluzney and others, *Innovations in Health Care Organizations.* Chapel Hill, N.C.: School of Public Health, University of North Carolina, 1974b.

Gordon, W. J. *Synectics: The Development of Creative Capacity.* New York: Harper & Row, 1961.

Gottfredson, D. M. "Five Challenges." *Journal of Research in Crime and Delinquency,* 1972, *9*(2), 68-86.

Goudy, W. J., and Richards, R. O. "Citizens, Bureaucrats, and Legitimate Authority: Some Unanticipated Consequences Within the Administration of Social Action Programs." *Midwest Review of Public Administration,* 1976, *8,* 191-201.

Grabowski, H. *Drug Regulation and Innovation.* Washington, D.C.: American Enterprise Institute, 1976.

Grad, M. L., and Halpern, J. *Innovation Centers Experiment, Evaluation Status and Planning.* (NTIS PB-259 154.) Denver, Colo.: Denver Research Institute, 1975.

Graham, R. A. "Survival Means Reform. (Comments on Corwin, R. G., *Strategies of Organizational Survival: The Case of a National Program for Educational Reform.*)" *Journal of Applied Behavioral Science,* 1972, *8*(4), 481-493.

Gray, T. *A Systems Perspective on Technology Utilization.* Vol. I: *Review of the Literature.* Woodland Hills, Calif.: Perceptronics, 1980.

Gray, T., and Roberts-Gray, C. "Structuring Bureaucratic Rules to Enhance Compliance." *Psychological Reports,* 1979, *45,* 579-589.

Gray, V. "Innovation in the States: A Diffusion Study." *American Political Science Review,* 1973, *67*(4), 1174-1185.

Green, H. P. "Technology Assessment and Democracy: Uneasy Bedfellows." *Business and Society Review,* 1973, *5,* 72-80.

Greenberg, D. S. "Civilian Technology: NASA Study Finds Little 'Spinoff.' " *Science,* 1967, *157*(3792), 1016-1018.

Greenberg, P. D. *Knowledge Transfer in Mental Health Services.*

Final Report to National Institute of Mental Health, Grant No. R01-MH-22683. Los Angeles: Human Interaction Research Institute, 1977.

Greenfield, T. B. "Organizations as Social Inventions: Rethinking Assumptions About Change." *Journal of Applied Behavioral Science*, 1973, *9*(5), 551-574.

Greenwood, E. "The Practice of Science and the Science of Practice." In W. G. Bennis, K. D. Benne, and R. Chin (Eds.), *The Planning of Change: Readings in the Applied Behavioral Sciences*. New York: Holt, Rinehart and Winston, 1962.

Greenwood, P. W., Mann, D., and McLaughlin, M. W. *Federal Programs Supporting Educational Change. Vol. 3: The Process of Change*. Santa Monica, Calif.: Rand Corporation, 1975.

Greer, A. L. "Advances in the Study of Diffusion of Innovation in Health Care Organizations." *Milbank Memorial Fund Quarterly: Health and Society*, 1977, *55*, 505-532.

Greiner, L. E. "Patterns of Organizational Change." *Harvard Business Review*, 1967, *45*, 119-130.

Griffin, G. A., and Lieberman, A. "Review of Smith, L. M., and Keith, P. M., *Anatomy of Educational Innovation: Organizational Analysis of an Elementary School*." *Teachers College Record*, 1976, *77*(3), 416-423.

Griffith, B. C., and Mullins, N. C. "Coherent Social Groups in Scientific Change." *Science*, 1972, *177*, 959-964.

Griffith, D. H. S., Ramana, D. V., and Mashaal, H. "Contribution of Health to Development." *International Journal of Health Services*, 1971, *1*(3), 253-270.

Griffiths, D. E. "Administrative Theory and Change in Organizations." In M. B. Miles (Ed.), *Innovation in Education*. New York: Bureau of Publications, Teachers College, Columbia University, 1964.

Gross, N., Giacquinta, J. B., and Bernstein, M. *Implementing Organizational Innovation: A Sociological Analysis of Planned Educational Change*. New York: Basic Books, 1971.

Gruber, W. H., and Marquis, D. G. (Eds.). *Factors in the Transfer of Technology*. Cambridge, Mass.: M.I.T. Press, 1969.

Gruenberg, E. M. (Ed.). "Evaluating the Effectiveness of Mental

Health Services." *Milbank Memorial Fund Quarterly: Health and Society,* 1966, *44*(1), Part 2 (whole issue).

Guba, E. G. "Methodological Strategies for Educational Change." Paper presented to the Conference on Strategies for Educational Change, Washington, D.C., November 1965.

Guba, E. G. (Ed.). *The Role of Educational Research in Educational Change: The United States.* Bloomington, Ind.: National Institute for the Study of Educational Change, 1967.

Guba, E. G. "Development, Diffusion, and Evaluation." In T. L. Eidell and J. M. Kitchel (Eds.), *Knowledge Production and Utilization in Educational Administration.* Eugene: Center for the Advanced Study of Educational Administration, University of Oregon, 1968.

Guba, E. G. "The Failure of Educational Evaluation." *Educational Technology,* 1969, *9*(5), 29-38.

Guba, E. G. *Toward a Methodology of Naturalistic Inquiry in Educational Evaluation.* Los Angeles: Center for the Study of Evaluation, University of California, 1978.

Guba, E. G., and Brickell, H. M. *Conceptual Strategies for Utilizing Research and Development Products in Education.* (ED 098 435.) Occasional Paper No. 2. Columbus: Center for Vocational and Technical Education, Ohio State University, 1974.

Guba, E. G., and Clark, D. *The Configurational Perspective: A View of Educational Knowledge Production and Utilization.* Washington, D.C.: Council for Educational Research and Development, Inc., 1974.

Guba, E. G., and Lincoln, Y. S. *Effective Evaluation: Improving the Usefulness of Evaluation Results Through Responsive and Naturalistic Approaches.* San Francisco: Jossey-Bass, 1981.

Guest, R. H. *Organizational Change: The Effect of Successful Leadership.* Homewood, Ill.: Irwin-Dorsey, 1962.

Guest, R. H. "Quality of Work-Life—Learning from Tarrytown." *Harvard Business Review,* 1979, *57*(4), 76-87.

Guetzkow, H. "Conversion Barriers in Using the Social Sciences." *Administrative Science Quarterly,* 1959, *4*(1), 68-81.

Guetzkow, H., and Collins, B. *Social Psychology of Group Processes.* New York: Wiley, 1964.

Guskin, A. E. "Knowledge Utilization and Power in University Decision Making." In L. A. Braskamp and R. D. Brown (Eds.), *New Directions for Program Evaluation: Utilization of Evaluative Information,* no. 5. San Francisco: Jossey-Bass, 1980.

Guskin, A. E., and Chesler, M. A. "Partisan Diagnosis of Social Problems." In G. Zaltman (Ed.), *Processes and Phenomena of Social Change.* New York: Wiley, 1973.

Gutmanis, I., and others. *Transfer of Innovations in Fragmented U.S. Industries with the North Atlantic Fisheries as a Case Study.* (NTIS PB-242 188.) Washington, D.C.: National Science Foundation, 1974.

Guttentag, M. "Subjectivity and Its Use in Evaluation Research." *Evaluation,* 1973, *1*(2), 60-65.

Guttentag, M. (Ed.). *Evaluation Studies Review Annual.* Vol. 2. Beverly Hills, Calif.: Sage, 1977.

Guttentag, M., and Struening, E. L. (Eds.). *Handbook of Evaluation Research.* Vol. 2. Beverly Hills, Calif.: Sage, 1975.

Hackman, J. R., and Oldham, G. R. *Work Redesign.* Reading, Mass.: Addison-Wesley, 1980.

Hackman, J. R., and Suttle, J. L. *Improving Life at Work: Behavioral Science Approaches to Organizational Change.* Santa Monica, Calif.: Goodyear, 1977.

Haeffner, E. A. "The Innovation Process." *Technology Review,* 1973, *75*(5), 18-25.

Hage, J. *Communication and Organizational Control: Cybernetics in Health and Welfare Settings.* New York: Wiley, 1974.

Hage, J., and Aiken, M. "Program Change and Organizational Properties: A Comparative Analysis." *American Journal of Sociology,* 1967, *72*(5), 503-519.

Hage, J., and Aiken, M. *Social Change in Complex Organizations.* New York: Random House, 1970.

Hage, J., and Dewar, R. "Elite Values Vs. Organizational Structure in Predicting Innovation." *Administrative Science Quarterly,* 1974, *18*, 279-290.

Hagerstrand, T. A. "A Monte Carlo Approach to Diffusion." *European Journal of Sociology,* 1965, *6*, 43-67.

Hagerstrand, T. A. *Innovation Diffusion as a Spatial Process.* Chicago: University of Chicago Press, 1967.

Haggarty, J. J. *Spinoff 1979.* National Aeronautics and Space Administration, Office of Space and Terrestrial Applications. Washington, D.C.: U.S. Government Printing Office, 1979.

Hagstrom, W. O. *The Scientific Community.* New York: Basic Books, 1965.

Hagstrom, W. O. "Factors Related to the Use of Different Modes of Publishing Research in Four Scientific Fields." In C. Nelson and D. K. Pollock (Eds.), *Communication Among Scientists and Engineers.* Lexington, Mass.: Heath, 1970.

Hall, D. C., and Alford, S. W. *Evaluation of the National Diffusion Network.* Menlo Park, Calif.: Stanford Research Institute, 1976.

Hall, D. J. *Social Relations and Innovation. Changing the State of Play in Hospitals.* London: Routledge & Kegan Paul, 1977.

Hall, G. E. *The Concerns-Based Adoption Model: A Developmental Conceptualization of the Adoption Process Within Educational Institutions.* (ED 111 791.) Austin: Research and Development Center for Teacher Education, University of Texas, 1974a.

Hall, G. E. *Phases in the Adoption of Educational Innovations in Teacher Training Institutions.* (ED 130 390.) Austin: Research and Development Center for Teacher Education, University of Texas, 1974b.

Hall, G. E., and Loucks, S. F. "A Developmental Model for Determining Whether the Treatment Is Actually Implemented." *American Educational Research Journal,* 1977, *14*(3), 263-276.

Hall, G. E., and Loucks, S. F. "Innovation Configurations: Analyzing the Adaptations of Innovations." Paper presented at 63rd annual meeting of American Educational Research Association, Toronto, March 1978.

Hall, G. E., Wallace, R. C., and Dossett, W. A. *Developmental Conceptualization of the Adoption Process Within Educational Institutions.* Austin: Research and Development Center for Teacher Education, University of Texas, 1973.

Haller, K. B., Reynolds, M. A., and Horsley, J. A. "Developing

Research-Based Innovation Protocols: Process, Criteria, and Issues." *Research in Nursing and Health,* 1979, *2*(2), 45-51.

Halpert, H. P. "Public Relations in Mental Health Programs." *Public Health Reports,* 1965, *80*(3), 195-200.

Halpert, H. P. "Communications as a Basic Tool in Promoting Utilization of Research Findings." *Community Mental Health Journal,* 1966, *2*(3), 231-236.

Halpert, H. P. "Research Utilization, a Problem in Goal Setting: What Is the Question?" *American Journal of Public Health,* 1973, *63*(5), 377-378.

Halpin, A. W. "Problems in the Use of Communications Media in the Dissemination and Implementation of Educational Research." In K. Goldhammer and S. Elam (Eds.), *Dissemination and Implementation: Third Annual Phi Delta Kappa Symposium on Educational Research.* Bloomington, Ind.: Phi Delta Kappa, 1962.

Hamblin, R. L., Jacobsen, R. B., and Miller, J. L. *A Mathematical Theory of Social Change.* New York: Wiley, 1973.

Hamilton, L. S., and Muthard, J. E. *Research Utilization Specialists in Vocational Rehabilitation: 5 Years of Experience.* (NTIS PB-254-363.) Gainesville: Rehabilitation Research Unit, University of Florida, 1975.

Hammond, J. S. "The Roles of the Manager and Management Scientist in Successful Implementation." *Sloan Management Review,* 1974, *15*(2), 1-24.

Harer, W. B. "TEL-MED: A Public Medical Information Service by Phone." *California Medicine,* 1972, *117,* 68-70.

Hargrove, E. C. *The Missing Link: The Study of the Implementation of Social Policy.* Washington, D.C.: Urban Institute, 1975.

Harrison, E. F. *The Managerial Decision-Making Process.* Boston: Houghton Mifflin, 1975.

Harrison, R., and Hopkins, R. "The Design of Cross-Cultural Training: An Alternative to the University Model." In W. G. Bennis, K. D. Benne, and R. Chin (Eds.), *The Planning of Change.* (2nd ed.) New York: Holt, Rinehart and Winston, 1969.

Harvey, E., and Mills, R. "Patterns of Organizational Adaptation: A Political Perspective." In M. N. Zala (Ed.), *Power of*

*Organizations.* Nashville, Tenn.: Vanderbilt University Press, 1970.

Havelock, R. G. "Linking Research to Practice: What Role for the Linking Agent." Paper presented at 52nd annual meeting of American Educational Research Association, New York, February 1967.

Havelock, R. G. "Dissemination and Translation Roles." In T. L. Eidell and J. M. Kitchel (Eds.), *Knowledge Production and Utilization in Educational Administration.* Eugene: Center for the Advanced Study of Educational Administration, University of Oregon, 1968a.

Havelock, R. G. "New Developments in Translating Theory and Research into Practice." Paper presented at 96th annual meeting of American Public Health Association, Detroit, November 1968b.

Havelock, R. G. *Planning for Innovation Through Dissemination and Utilization of Knowledge.* Ann Arbor: Center for Research on Utilization of Scientific Knowledge, Institute for Social Research, University of Michigan, 1969a.

Havelock, R. G. "Translating Theory into Practice." *Rehabilitation Record,* 1969b, *10,* 24-27.

Havelock, R. G. *A Guide to Innovation in Education.* Ann Arbor: Center for Research on the Utilization of Scientific Knowledge, Institute for Social Research, University of Michigan, 1970.

Havelock, R. G. "The Utilization of Educational Research and Development." *British Journal of Educational Technology,* 1971, *2*(2), 84-98.

Havelock, R. G. *Knowledge Utilization and Dissemination: A Bibliography.* Ann Arbor: Center for Research on Utilization of Scientific Knowledge, Institute for Social Research, University of Michigan, 1972a.

Havelock, R. G. "Research Utilization in Four Federal Agencies." Paper presented at 80th annual meeting of American Psychological Association, Honolulu, September 1972b.

Havelock, R. G. *The Change Agent's Guide to Innovation in Education.* Englewood Cliffs, N.J.: Educational Technology Publications, 1973a.

Havelock, R. G. *Planning for Innovation.* Ann Arbor: Center for

Research on Utilization of Scientific Knowledge, Institute for Social Research, University of Michigan, 1973b.

Havelock, R. G. "Resource Linkage in Innovative Educational Problem Solving: Ideal vs. Actual." *Journal of Research and Development in Education,* 1973c, *6,* 76-87.

Havelock, R. G. *Ideal Systems for Research Utilization: Four Alternatives.* (NTIS PB-254 839.) Ann Arbor: Center for Research on Utilization of Scientific Knowledge, Institute for Social Research, University of Michigan, 1974a.

Havelock, R. G. "Models of the Innovative Process in the U.S. School Districts." Paper presented at 59th annual meeting of American Educational Research Association, Chicago, April 1974b.

Havelock, R. G. "Information Professionals as Change Agents." *Drexel Library Quarterly,* 1977, *13*(2), 48-61.

Havelock, R. G. "Report from the Belmont Task Force on Linking Functions." In A. Bank and others, *Dissemination and the Improvement of Practice: Cooperation and Support in the School Improvement Process.* San Francisco: Far West Laboratory for Educational Research and Development, 1979.

Havelock, R. G., and Havelock, M. C. *Educational Innovation in the United States.* Vol. 1: *The National Survey: The Substance and the Process.* Ann Arbor: Center for Research on Utilization of Scientific Knowledge, Institute for Social Research, University of Michigan, 1973a.

Havelock, R. G., and Havelock, M. C. *Training for Change Agents.* Ann Arbor: Center for Research on Utilization of Scientific Knowledge, Institute for Social Research, University of Michigan, 1973b.

Havelock, R. G., Huber, J. C., and Zimmerman, S. *Major Works on Change in Education: An Annotated Bibliography With Author and Subject Indices.* Ann Arbor: Center for Research on Utilization of Scientific Knowledge, Institute for Social Research, University of Michigan, 1969.

Havelock, R. G., and Huberman, A. M. *Solving Educational Problems: The Theory and Reality of Innovation in Developing Countries.* New York: Praeger, 1978.

Havelock, R. G., and Lingwood, D. A. *R&D Utilization Strategies and Functions: An Analytical Comparison of Four Systems.* Ann Arbor: Center for Research on Utilization of Scientific Knowledge, Institute for Social Research, University of Michigan, 1973.

Havelock, R. G., and Mann, F. C. *Research and Development Laboratory Management Knowledge Utilization Study.* Ann Arbor: Center for Research on Utilization of Scientific Knowledge, Institute for Social Research, University of Michigan, 1968.

Havelock, R. G., with Markowitz, E. *A National Problem-Solving System: Highway Safety Research and Decision Makers.* Ann Arbor: Center for Research on Utilization of Scientific Knowledge, Institute for Social Research, University of Michigan, 1971.

Havelock, R. G., and Markowitz, E. *Highway Safety Research Communication: Is There a System?* Ann Arbor: Center for Research on Utilization of Scientific Knowledge, Institute for Social Research, University of Michigan, 1973.

Havelock, R. G., and others. *Educational Innovation in the United States. Vol. II: Five Case Studies of Innovation at the School District Level.* Ann Arbor: Center for Research on Utilization of Scientific Knowledge, Institute for Social Research, University of Michigan, 1974.

Havelock, R. G., and others. *Planning for Innovation Through Dissemination and Utilization of Knowledge.* Ann Arbor: Center for Research on Utilization of Scientific Knowledge, Institute for Social Research, University of Michigan, 1976.

Hawkings, J. D., Roffman, R. A., and Osborne, P. "Decision Makers' Judgments: The Influence of Role Evaluation Criteria, and Information Access." *Evaluation Quarterly,* 1978, *2,* 435-454.

Hawley, A. H. "Presidential Address: Cumulative Change in Theory and in History." *American Sociological Review,* 1978, *43*(6), 787-796.

Hawthorne, E. P. *The Transfer of Technology.* Paris: Organization for Economic Cooperation and Development, 1971.

Hawthorne, E. P. "The Role of Infrastructure in the Transfer of Technology." *Mondes en Developpement* [*Worlds in Development*], 1976, *1976*(14), 371-385.

Hayes, F. O. R. "Innovation in State and Local Government." In F. O. R. Hayes and J. E. Rasmussen (Eds.), *Centers for Innovation in the Cities and States*. San Francisco: San Francisco Press, 1972.

Hayvaert, C. H. *Innovation Research and Product Policy: Clinical Research in 12 Belgian Industrial Enterprises*. Belgium: Catholic University of Louvain, 1973.

Hayward, G., Allen, D. H., and Masterson, J. "Characteristics and Diffusion of Technological Innovations." *R&D Management*, 1977, *7*(1), 15-24.

Hearn, N. E. "ESEA Title III: A National Model of Knowledge Utilization and Dissemination." Paper presented at 56th annual meeting of American Educational Research Association, New York, February 1971.

Heathers, G. "Influencing Change at the Elementary Level." In R. I. Miller (Ed.), *Perspectives on Educational Change*. New York: Appleton-Century-Crofts, 1967.

Heathers, G. "Planned Educational Change in Search of a Research Tradition." *Viewpoints*, 1974, *50*(3), 9-24.

Helleiner, G. K. "The Role of Multinational Corporations in the Less Developed Countries' Trade in Technology." *World Development*, 1975, *3*(4), 161-189.

Hellriegel, D., and Slocum, J. W. "Organizational Climate: Measures, Research, and Contingencies." *Academy of Management Journal*, 1974, *17*, 255-280.

Hellriegel, D., and Slocum, J. W. *Organizational Behavior: Contingency Approaches*. St. Paul, Minn.: West, 1976.

Helmer, O. *Social Technology*. New York: Basic Books, 1966.

Helmer, O. *Analysis of the Future: The Delphi Method*. Santa Monica, Calif.: Rand Corporation, 1967.

Hemphill, J., Griffiths, D., and Fredericksen, N. *Administrative Performance and Personality*. New York: Columbia University Press, 1962.

Hennigh, L. "The Overriding Problem Approach to Federal Aid to Educational Innovation." Doctoral dissertation, Washington State University, 1978. *Dissertation Abstracts Interna-*

*tional,* 1978, *39,* 3014A. (University Microfilms No. 78-20, 093).

Henning, J. F., and others. *Mandate for Change: The Impact of Law on Educational Innovation.* Boulder, Colo.: Social Science Education Consortium, 1979.

Hepworth, A. "Some Ethical and Methodological Problems for the Researcher/Consultant." *Bulletin of the British Psychological Society,* 1978, *31,* 173-174.

Herbert, E. "Information Transfer." *International Science and Technology,* 1966, *51,* 26-35.

Herlig, R. K. *National Dissemination Conference (9th).* (ED 136 784.) Washington, D.C.: Council of Chief State School Officers, 1976.

Herlig, R. K. *Linker Training Processes for the State Education Agency Dissemination System: Conference Topic Paper.* (ED 143 335.) Washington, D.C.: National Institute of Education, 1977a.

Herlig, R. K. *National Dissemination Conference (10th).* (ED 146 939.) Washington, D.C.: National Institute of Education, 1977b.

Herlig, R. K., and Vandermyn, G. *Resources for the State Education Agency Dissemination System.* (ED 143 308.) Washington, D.C.: National Institute of Education, 1976.

Hernandono. "Research Information in Process: Indonesia: Development of a Scientific Information Network." *UNESCO Bulletin for Libraries,* 1978, *32*(5), 338-341.

Herner, S., and Herner, M. "Information Needs and Uses in Science and Technology." In C. A. Cuadra and A. W. Luke (Eds.), *Annual Review of Information Science and Technology.* Vol. 2. Chicago: Encyclopaedia Britannica, 1967.

Herzog, A. J. "The Gatekeeper Hypothesis and the International Transfer of Scientific Knowledge." In Advisory Group for Aerospace Research and Development, *The Problem of Optimization of User Benefit in Scientific and Technological Information Transfer.* Paris: Advisory Group for Aerospace Research and Development, 1976.

Hetman, F. *Society and the Assessment of Technology.* Paris: Organization for Economic Cooperation and Development, 1973.

Higgins, T. "Innovation Strategies for Successful Product and Process Commercialization in Government R&D." *R&D Management,* 1977, *7*(2), 53-59.

Hill-Burnett, J. "Review of Wolcott, H. F., *Teachers Versus Technocrats: An Educational Innovation in Anthropological Perspective.*" *American Anthropologist,* 1978, *80*(4), 957-958.

Hillman, D. J. *Research Into Knowledge Transfer Systems.* Bethlehem, Penn.: Center for Information Science, Lehigh University, 1978.

Hiltz, S. R., and Turoff, M. *Network Nation: Human Communication Via Computer.* Reading, Mass.: Addison-Wesley, 1978.

Hinrichs, J. R. *Practical Management for Productivity.* New York: Van Nostrand, 1978.

Hirsch, W., and Zollschan, G. (Eds.). *Explorations in Social Change.* Boston: Houghton Mifflin, 1964.

Hlavacek, J. D., and Thompson, V. A. "The Joint Venture Approach to Technology Utilization." *IEEE Transactions on Engineering Management,* 1976, *23*(1), 35-41.

Hoberman, S., and others. "A Systems Approach to Management Training for Mental Health Professionals." *Psychiatric Quarterly,* 1977, *49*(4), 291-302.

Hodgkin, J. E., and others. "Chronic Obstructive Airway Diseases: Current Concepts in Diagnosis and Comprehensive Care." *Journal of the American Medical Association,* 1975, *232,* 1243-1260.

Hodgkin, J. E., and others. *Chronic Obstructive Pulmonary Disease: Current Concepts in Diagnosis and Comprehensive Care.* Park Ridge, Ill.: American College of Chest Physicians, 1979.

Hoffer, E. *The Ordeal of Change.* New York: Harper, 1963.

Holland, T. R., Holt, N., and Brewer, D. L. "Social Roles and Information Utilization in Parole Decision Making." *Journal of Social Psychology,* 1978, *106*(1), 111-120.

Holliday, G. D. "Western Technology Transfer to the Soviet Union, 1928-1937 and 1966-1975: With a Case Study in the Transfer of Automotive Technology." Doctoral dissertation,

George Washington University, 1978. *Dissertation Abstracts International,* 1978, *39,* 3049A. (University Microfilms No. 78-16,266.)

Hollis, P. W. (Ed.). *Comparative Theories of Social Change.* Ann Arbor, Mich.: Foundation for Research on Human Behavior, 1966.

Holloway, R. E. "Perceived Characteristics of an Innovation." (ED 150 716.) Paper presented at 63rd annual meeting of American Educational Research Association, Toronto, March 1978.

Holmes, E. H. *The Information Center: Some Selected Examples.* Santa Monica, Calif.: System Development Corporation, 1964.

Holmes, M. *The Linkage Between Research and Practice: The Case of the DTA Project.* (ED 147 375.) Chicago, Ill.: Center for New Schools, Inc., 1977.

Holt, K. *Product Innovation: Models and Methods.* Trondheim, Norway: Norwegian Institute of Technology, University of Trondheim, 1975.

Holzner, B., and Fisher, E. "Knowledge in Use: Considerations in the Sociology of Knowledge Application." *Knowledge,* 1979, *1*(2), 219-244.

Holzner, B., and Marx, J. *Knowledge Application: The Knowledge System in Society.* Boston: Allyn & Bacon, 1979.

Hood, P. D. "How Research and Development on Educational Roles and Institutional Structures Can Facilitate Communication." *Journal of Research and Development in Education,* 1973, *6*(4), 96-113.

Hood, P. D., and Blackwell, L. R. *Study of Information Requirements in Education.* Vol. 1: *Key Educational Information Users and Their Styles of Information Use.* (ED 135 411.) Santa Monica, Calif.: System Development Corporation, 1976.

Hood, P. D., and Cates, C. S. *Alternative Approaches to Analyzing Educational Dissemination and Linkage Roles and Functions.* Educational Knowledge Dissemination and Utilization Occasional Paper Series. San Francisco: Far West Laboratory for Educational Research and Development, 1978.

Hood, P. D., Mick, C., and Katter, R. V. *Study of Information Requirements in Education.* Vol. 2: *A Mail Survey of User Information Requirements.* (ED 135 411.) Santa Monica, Calif.: System Development Corporation, 1976.

Horn, B. R. "A General Systems Approach to Transnational Environmental Communication (TEC) Networks." Paper prepared for panel on "Organizational and Institutional Implications of General Systems Thinking," at joint annual meeting of Society for General Systems Research and American Association for the Advancement of Science, Washington, D.C., February 1978.

Hornstein, A., and Tichy, N. M. *Organization Diagnosis and Intervention Strategies: An Instrumented Individual and Group Approach.* Hopewell Junction, N.Y.: Behavioral Science Associates, 1973.

Hornstein, H. A., and others (Eds.). *Social Intervention: A Behavioral Science Approach.* New York: Free Press, 1971.

Horowitz, D. L. *The Courts and Social Policy.* Washington, D.C.: Brookings Institution, 1977.

Horowitz, I. L. (Ed.). *The Use and Abuse of Social Science.* New Brunswick, N.J.: Transaction, 1971.

Horowitz, I. L., and Katz, J. E. *Social Science and Public Policy in the United States.* New York: Praeger, 1975.

Horsley, J., Crane, J., and Bingle, J. D. "Research Utilization as an Organizational Process." *Journal of Nursing Administration,* 1978, *8*(7), 4-6.

Horst, D. P., and others. *Evaluation of the Field Test of Project Information Packages.* Vol. 2: *Recommendations for Revision.* Mountain View, Calif.: RMC Research Corporation, 1975.

Hough, G. W. *Technology Diffusion: Federal Programs and Procedures.* Mt. Airy, Md.: Lomond Brooks, 1975.

House, E. R. *The Politics of Educational Innovation.* Berkeley, Calif.: McCutchan, 1974.

House, E. R. "The Micropolitics of Innovation: Nine Propositions." *Phi Delta Kappan,* 1976, *57*(5), 337-340.

House, E. R. "Assumptions Underlying Evaluation Models." *Educational Researcher,* 1978, *7*(3), 4-12.

House, E. R. *Evaluating with Validity.* Beverly Hills, Calif.: Sage, 1980a.

House, E. R. "Three Perspectives on Innovation—The Technological, the Political, and the Cultural." Paper prepared for Program on Research and Educational Practice, National Institute of Education, Washington, D.C., 1980b.

House, P. W., and Jones, D. W. *Getting It Off the Shelf: A Methodology for Implementing Federal Research.* Boulder, Colo.: Westview, 1978.

Hovland, C. I., Janis, I. L., and Kelley, H. H. *Communication and Persuasion.* New Haven, Conn.: Yale University Press, 1953.

Hovland, C. I., and Weiss, W. "The Influence of Source Credibility on Communication Effectiveness." *Public Opinion Quarterly,* 1951, *15,* 635-650.

Howard, E. "How to Be Serious About Innovating." *Nation's Schools,* 1967, *79,* 89-90; 130.

Howes, N. J., and Quinn, R. E. "Implementing Change from Research to a Prescriptive Framework." *Group & Organization Studies,* 1978, *3*(1), 71-84.

Hull, W. L., and Bina, J. V. *Increasing the Impact of Federally Administered Vocational Education Exemplary Projects. Final Report.* Leadership Training Series No. 52. (ED 149 031.) Columbus: National Center for Research in Vocational Education, Ohio State University, 1977a.

Hull, W. L., and Bina, J. V. *The Influence of Selected Organizational and Administrative Variables on Continued and Extended Use of Exemplary Projects in Vocational Education.* Research and Development Series No. 116. (ED 138 814.) Columbus: National Center for Research in Vocational Education, Ohio State University, 1977b.

Human Interaction Research Institute, with National Institute of Mental Health. *Putting Knowledge to Use: A Distillation of the Literature Regarding Knowledge Transfer and Change.* Los Angeles: Human Interaction Research Institute, 1976.

Hunt, J. B. "State Involvement in Science and Technology." *Science,* 1982, *215,* 617.

Hunt, R. G. "The University Social Research Center: Its Role in the Knowledge-Making Process." *Knowledge*, 1980, *2*(1), 77-92.

Hurten, R. P., and Rubenstein, A. H. *Market Penetration by New Technology: The Technological Literature, Technological Forecasting, and Social Change.* Amsterdam: North Holland, 1978.

Huse, E. *Organizational Development and Change.* St. Paul, Minn.: West, 1975.

Husseiny, A. A. "A Strategy of Improving Nuclear Technology Transfer Processes Based on Field Experience." *Transactions of the American Nuclear Society*, 1977, *25*(Suppl. 1), 108.

Hutchins, C. L. "Review of House, E. R., *The Politics of Educational Innovation.*" *Harvard Educational Review*, 1976a, *46*(1), 134-138.

Hutchins, C. L. "Dissemination of Information in Education." In S. E. Goodman (Ed.), *Handbook on Contemporary Education.* New York: Bowker, 1976b.

Hyman, H. H., Levine, G., and Wright, C. R. *Inducing Social Change in Developing Communities.* New York: United Nations Research Institute for Social Development, 1967.

Hyman, H. H., and Wright, C. R. "Evaluating Social Action Programs." In P. F. Lazarsfeld, W. H. Sewell, and H. L. Wilensky (Eds.), *The Uses of Sociology.* New York: Basic Books, 1967.

Hyslop, M. R., and Chafe, H. D. "User Appraisal of an Information System and Services Through a Program of Joint Applied Research." In G. Schecter (Ed.), *Information Retrieval: A Critical Review.* Washington, D.C.: Thompson, 1967.

Ikonicoff, M. "Le Transfert de Technologie et les Conditions de l'Industrialisation dans le Tiers-Monde [Technology Transfer and Industrial Conditions in the Third World]." *Homme et La Société [Man and Society]*, 1974, *33*(3), 63-72.

Illinois Institute of Technology. *TRACES (Technology in Retrospect and Critical Events in Science).* 2 vols. Chicago: Illinois Institute of Technology, 1969.

Imershein, A. W. "Organizational Change as a Paradigm Shift." *Sociological Quarterly*, 1977, *18*(1), 33-43.

Institute for Development of Educational Activities. "Choosing a Model for Change." In *I/D/E/A Annual Report*. Melbourne, Fla.: Institute for Development of Educational Activities, 1970.

Interstate Project on Dissemination. *Report and Recommendations*. Washington, D.C.: National Institute of Education, 1976.

Jacobson, L., and Pellegrino, E. D. "Change Agents in a Changing System." *Preventive Medicine,* 1977, *6*(3), 379-385.

Jacobson, P. B. "The Use of Inter-Institutional Agencies in Dissemination and Implementation of Educational Research." In K. Goldhammer and S. Elam (Eds.), *Dissemination and Implementation: Third Annual Phi Delta Kappa Symposium on Educational Research*. Bloomington, Ind.: Phi Delta Kappa, 1962.

Jain, N. C. "Communication Correlates of Opinion Leadership of Professionals in a Research Dissemination Organization." (ED 120 833.) Presented at annual meeting of Central States Speech Association, Chicago, April 1976.

Jenkins, D. H. "Force Field Analysis Applied to a School Situation." In W. G. Bennis, K. D. Benne, and R. Chin (Eds.), *The Planning of Change: Readings in the Applied Behavioral Sciences*. New York: Holt, Rinehart and Winston, 1962.

Jenks, R. S. "An Action-Research Approach to Organizational Change." *Journal of Applied Behavioral Science,* 1970, *2*, 131-150.

Jenks, R. S. "An Internal Change Agent's Role in Restructuring University Governance." *Journal of Higher Education,* 1973, *44*(5), 370-379.

Jenstrom, L. L. "The National Shipbuilding Research Program: A Case Study of Innovation in the Maritime Industry." In Maritime Transportation Research Board, *Case Studies in Maritime Innovation*. Washington, D.C.: National Research Council, National Academy of Science, 1978.

Jermakowicz, W. "Organizational Structures in the R&D Sphere." *R&D Management,* 1978, *8*(special issue), 107-113.

Jervis, P. "Innovation and Technology Transfer: The Roles and

Characteristics of Individuals." *IEEE Transactions on Engineering Management,* 1975, *22*(1), 19-27.

Jewkes, J., Sawyer, D., and Stillerman, R. *The Sources of Invention.* (2nd ed.) New York: Norton, 1969.

Johansen, R., and DeGrasse, R. "Computer-Based Teleconferencing: Effects on Working Patterns." *Journal of Communication,* 1979, *29*(3), 30-41.

Johns, E. A. *The Sociology of Organizational Change.* Oxford: Pergamon, 1973.

Johnson, C. A., and Katz, R. C. "Using Parents as Change Agents for Their Children: A Review." *Journal of Child Psychology and Psychiatry and Allied Disciplines,* 1973, *14*(3), 181-200.

Johnson, D. W. *The Dynamics of Educational Change.* Sacramento: California State Department of Education, 1963.

Johnson, J. H., and others. "Organizational Preparedness for Change: Staff Acceptance of an On-Line Computer-Assisted Assessment System." *Behavior Research Methods & Instrumentation,* 1978, *10*(2), 186-190.

Johnson, K. W. "Stimulating Evaluation Use by Integrating Academia and Practice." *Knowledge,* 1980, *2*(2), 237-262.

Johnson, K. W., and Johnson, F. P. "Change Agents Working From Below: Implications for Higher Education in Criminal Justice." *Urban Education,* 1977, *12*(2), 167-188.

Johnson, K. W., Tamberrino, R., and Zuspan, K. *A Multifaceted Evaluation Strategy for the Field of Criminal Justice.* College Park: Institute of Criminal Justice and Criminology, University of Maryland, 1976.

Johnston, H. R. "A New Conceptualization of Source of Organizational Climate." *Administrative Science Quarterly,* 1976, *21,* 95-103.

Johnston, R., and Gibbons, M. "Characteristics of Information Usage in Technological Innovation." *IEEE Transactions on Engineering Management,* 1975, *22*(1), 27-34.

Joint Commission on Mental Health of Children. *Crisis in Child Mental Health: Challenge for the 70s.* New York: Harper & Row, 1969.

Joint Commission on Mental Health of Children. *The Mental*

*Health of Children: Services, Research, and Manpower.* New York: Harper & Row, 1973a.

Joint Commission on Mental Health of Children. *Social Change and the Mental Health of Children.* New York: Harper & Row, 1973b.

Joint Commission on Mental Illness and Health. "Research Resources in Mental Health." In Joint Commission on Mental Illness and Health, *Action for Mental Health.* New York: Basic Books, 1961.

Jolly, J. A. *The Technology Transfer Process: Concepts, Framework and Methodology.* (ED 127 704.) Monterey, Calif.: Naval Postgraduate School, 1974.

Jolly, J. A., and Creighton, J. W. (Eds.). *Technology Transfer in Research and Development.* Monterey, Calif.: Naval Postgraduate School, 1975.

Jolly, J. A., Creighton, J. W., and George, P. A. *Technology Transfer Process Model and Annotated Selected Bibliography.* Monterey, Calif.: Naval Postgraduate School, 1978.

Jolly, J. A., Creighton, J. W., and Moore, B. M. *Technology Transfer in Science, Technology, and Public Policy.* Monterey, Calif.: Naval Postgraduate School, 1977.

Joly, J. M. "Research and Innovation: Two Solitudes?" *Canadian Education and Research Digest,* 1967, *2,* 184-194.

Jones, G. N. "Strategies and Tactics of Planned Organizational Change: Case Examples in the Modernization Process of Traditional Societies." *Human Organization,* 1965, *24,* 192-200.

Jones, G. N. *Planned Organizational Change.* New York: Praeger, 1969.

Jones, M. "Impact of Technology Transfer on Process Engineering in Developing Countries." *R&D Management,* 1976, *6,* 179-182.

Jones, R. K., Manning, M. J., and Goldenbaum, D. M. *Final Report on a Background Study of Technology Utilization in the Field of Public Works.* 7 vols. Final Report to National Science Foundation, Grant No. DI-38422. Bloomington: University of Indiana, 1974.

Jorgenson, D. W., and Grilliches, Z. "The Explanation of Productivity Change." *Review of Economic Studies,* 1967, *34,* 249-284.

Judson, A. S. *A Manager's Guide to Making Changes.* New York: Wiley, 1966.

Jung, C. C., and Lippitt, R. "The Study of Change as a Concept in Research Utilization." *Theory into Practice,* 1966, *5*(1), 25-29.

Jwaideh, A. R., and Bhola, B. H. (Eds.). "Research in Diffusion of Educational Innovations: A Report with an Agenda." *Viewpoints,* 1974, *50*(3), iii-iv; 1-114.

Jwaideh, A. R., and Marker, G. W. *Bringing About Change in Social Studies Education.* (ED 086 205.) Boulder, Colo.: ERIC Clearinghouse for Social Studies/Social Science Education, 1973.

Kadushin, A. "Assembling Social Work Knowledge." In National Association of Social Workers, *Building Social Work Knowledge: Report of a Conference.* New York: National Association of Social Workers, 1964.

Kadushin, C. "On the Problem of Formalizing Networks Among Innovators in Education." Paper prepared for Networking Conference, School Capacity for Problem Solving Group, National Institute of Education, Washington, D.C., March 1977.

Kahn, R. L. "Organizational Development: Some Problems and Proposals." *Journal of Applied Behavioral Science,* 1974, *69* (1), 41-55.

Kahneman, D., and Schild, E. O. "Training Agents for Social Change in Israel: Definition of Objectives and a Training Approach." *Human Organization,* 1966, *25,* 71-77.

Kallen, H. M. "Innovation." In A. Etzioni and E. Etzioni (Eds.), *Social Change: Sources, Patterns, and Consequences.* New York: Basic Books, 1964.

Kaluzny, A. D., and others. "Diffusion of Innovative Health Services in the United States." *Medical Care,* 1970, *8,* 474-487.

Kamien, M. I., and Schwartz, N. *Market Structure and Innovation: A Survey.* Final Report to National Science Foundation, Grant No. RDA-7307232. Washington, D.C.: National Science Foundation, 1974.

Kaplan, B. "Dissemination of Primary Research Data in Psychology." *American Psychologist*, 1958, *13*, 53-55.

Kaplan, R. S. *Tax Policies for R&D Technological Innovation*. Final Report to National Science Foundation, Grant No. RDA-7421227. Washington, D.C.: National Science Foundation, 1975.

Kaplinsky, R. "Accumulation and the Transfer of Technology: Issues of Conflict and Mechanisms for the Exercise of Control." *World Development*, 1976, *4*(3), 197-224.

Karier, C. J. "Liberalism and the Quest for Orderly Change." In M. B. Katz (Ed.), *Education in American History*. New York: Praeger, 1973.

Karmos, J. S., and Jacko, C. M. "Innovations: A Note of Caution." *NASSP Bulletin*, 1977, *61*(411), 47-56.

Kasper, R. G. (Ed.). *Technology Assessment: Understanding the Social Consequences of Technological Applications*. New York: Praeger, 1972.

Katz, D., and Kahn, R. L. *The Social Psychology of Organizations*. (2nd ed.) New York: Wiley, 1978.

Katz, E. "The Two-Step Flow of Communication: An Up-to-Date Report on an Hypothesis." *Public Opinion Quarterly*, 1957, *21*, 61-78.

Katz, E. "The Social Itinerary of Technical Change: Two Studies on the Diffusion of Innovation." *Human Organization*, 1961, *20*, 70-82.

Katz, E. "The Characteristics of Innovations and the Concept of Compatibility." Paper presented at Rehovoth Conference of Comprehensive Planning of Agriculture in Developing Countries, Rehovoth, Israel, 1963.

Katz, E., Glock, C. Y., and Schramm, W. L. "Studies of Innovation and of Communication to the Public." In W. Schramm (Ed.), *Case Studies in the Utilization of Behavioral Science*. Vol. 2. Stanford, Calif.: Institute for Communication Research, Stanford University, 1962.

Katz, E., and Lazarsfeld, P. F. *Personal Influence: The Part Played by People in the Flow of Mass Communications*. New York: Free Press, 1955.

Katz, E., Levin, M. L., and Hamilton, H. "Traditions of Research on the Diffusion of Innovation." *American Sociological Review,* 1963, *28*(2), 237-252.

Katz, E., and others. "Innovation." *Sociological Inquiry,* 1962, *32*, 3-135.

Katzell, R. A., and Yankelovich, D. *Work, Productivity, and Job Satisfaction.* New York: The Psychological Corporation (Harcourt Brace Jovanovich), 1975.

Kaufman, I. "Change Management: The Process and the System." In G. Zaltman, P. Kotler, and I. Kaufman (Eds.), *Creating Social Change.* New York: Holt, Rinehart and Winston, 1972.

Kay, D. "International Transfer of Marine Technology: Transfer Process and International Organizations." *Ocean Development and International Law,* 1974, *2*(4), 351-377.

Keen, P. G. W., and Morton, M. S. *Decision Support Systems: An Organizational Perspective.* Reading, Mass.: Addison-Wesley, 1978.

Keith, P. M. "Administration and Faculty Turnover and Diffusion of an Educational Innovation." *Urban Education,* 1975, *10*(3), 297-304.

Keller, R. T., and Holland, W. E. *Technical Information Flows and Innovation Processes.* Final Report to National Science Foundation, Grant No. PRA-7618441. Washington, D.C.: National Science Foundation, 1978.

Kelly, P., and Kranzberg, M. (Eds.). *Technological Innovation: A Critical Review of Current Knowledge.* San Francisco: San Francisco Press, 1978.

Kelman, H. C. "Compliance, Identification, and Internalization: Three Processes of Attitude Change." *Journal of Conflict Resolution,* 1958, *2*, 51-60.

Kelman, H. C. "The Induction of Action and Attitude Change." *Proceedings of the Fourteenth International Congress of Applied Psychology,* 1961, 81-110.

Kelman, H. C. "The Relevance of Social Research to Social Issues: Promises and Pitfalls." *Sociological Review Monograph: The Sociology of Sociology,* 1970, *16*, 77-99.

Kelman, H. C. "Attitudes are Alive and Well and Gainfully Employed in the Sphere of Action." *American Psychologist,* 1974, *29*, 310-324.

Kelman, H. C. "International Interchanges: Some Contributions from Theories of Attitude Change." *Studies in Comparative International Development*, 1975, *10*(1), 83-99.

Kelman, H. C., and Warwick, D. P. "Bridging Micro and Macro Approaches to Social Change: A Social-Psychological Perspective." In G. Zaltman (Ed.), *Processes and Phenomena of Social Change*. New York: Wiley, 1973.

Keniston, K. "Accounting for Change." *Comparative Studies in Society and History*, 1965, *7*, 117-132.

Kernan, J. B., and Mojena, R. "Information Utilization and Personality." *Journal of Communication*, 1973, *23*(3), 315-327.

Ketefian, S. "Problems in the Dissemination and Utilization of Scientific Knowledge: How Can the Gap Be Bridged?" In S. Ketefian (Ed.), *Translation of Theory into Nursing Practice and Education*. New York: New York University, 1975.

Key, W. H. "Controlled Intervention: The Helping Professions and Directed Social Change." *American Journal of Orthopsychiatry*, 1966, *36*(3), 400-409.

Kiesler, C. A. "Evaluating Social Change Programs." In G. Zaltman (Ed.), *Processes and Phenomena of Social Change*. New York: Wiley, 1973.

Kiesler, S. B., and Turner, C. F. (Eds.). *Fundamental Research and the Process of Education*. Washington, D.C.: National Academy of Sciences, 1977.

Kilburg, R. "General Systems Theory and Community Mental Health: A View from the Boiler Room." *International Journal of Mental Health*, 1977, *5*(4), 73-102.

Kilmann, R. H. *Social Systems Design: Normative Theory and the MAPS Design Technology*. New York: Elsevier, 1977.

Kimbrough, R. B. "Power Structures and Educational Change." In E. L. Morphet and C. O. Ryan (Eds.), *Planning and Effecting Needed Changes in Education*. Englewood Cliffs, N.J.: Citation Press, 1967.

King, A. "Expectation Effects in Organizational Change." *Administrative Science Quarterly*, 1974, *19*(2), 221-235.

King, W. R., and Zaltman, G. (Eds.). *Marketing Scientific and Technical Information*. Boulder, Colo.: Westview, 1979.

Kinkade, R. G., and others. *Notes on Technical Reports on Science Information Requirements of Scientists*. Technical Reports 1 and 4. Washington, D.C.: American Institutes for Research, 1967.

Kiresuk, T. J. "Planned Change and Evaluation: Practitioner's Point of View." *Knowledge,* 1980, *1*(3), 405-420.

Kiresuk, T. J., and Lund, S. H. "Program Evaluation and Utilization Analysis." In R. Perloff (Ed.), *Evaluator Interventions: Pros and Cons.* Beverly Hills, Calif.: Sage, 1979.

Kiresuk, T. J., and Sherman, R. E. "Goal Attainment Scaling: A General Method for Evaluating Comprehensive Community Mental Health Programs." *Community Health Journal,* 1968, *4*(6), 443-453.

Kiresuk, T. J., and others. "Translating Theory into Practice: Change Research at the Program Evaluation Resource Center." *Evaluation,* 1977, *4,* 89-95.

Kivens, L., and Bolin, D. C. "Evaluation in a Community Mental Health Center: Hillsborough CMHC." *Evaluation,* 1976, *3*(1-2), 98-105.

Klapper, M. S., Harper, I. B., and Bridgers, W. F. "MIST—An Aide in the Delivery of Health Care." *Biosciences Communications,* 1978, *4,* 67-73.

Klarman, H. E. "Application of Cost-Benefit Analysis to the Health Services and the Special Case of Technologic Innovation." *International Journal of Health Services,* 1974, *4*(2), 325-352.

Klein, H. D. "The Missouri Story, a Chronicle of Research Utilization and Program Planning." Paper presented at 95th forum of National Conference of Social Welfare, San Francisco, May 1968.

Klein, M. W., and Teilmann, K. S. *Handbook of Criminal Justice Evaluation.* Beverly Hills, Calif.: Sage, 1980.

Klempner, I. M. "The Concept of 'National Security' and Its Effect on Information Transfer." *Special Libraries,* 1973, *64*(7), 263-269.

Kloman, H. (Ed.). "A Mini Symposium: Public Participation in Technology Assessment." *Public Administration Review,* 1975, *35*(1), 67-80.

Klonglan, G. E., and Coward, E. W., Jr. "The Concept of Symbolic Adoption: A Suggested Interpretation." *Rural Sociology,* 1970, *35*(1), 77-83.

Klonglan, G. E., and others. "Interorganizational Measurement in the Social Services Sector: Differences by Hierarchical Level." *Administrative Science Quarterly,* 1976a, *21,* 675-687.

Klonglan, G. E., and others. *Toward a Methodology for Social Indicators in Rural Development.* Sociology Report 124. Ames: Department of Sociology and Anthropology, Iowa State University, 1976b.

Knorr, K. D. "Policy Makers' Use of Social Science Knowledge: Symbolic or Instrumental?" In C. H. Weiss (Ed.), *Using Social Research in Public Policy Making.* Lexington, Mass.: Lexington Books, 1977.

Knorr, K. D. "Review of Lynn, L. E., Jr. (Ed.), *Knowledge and Policy: The Uncertain Connection." Knowledge,* 1980, *1*(4), 627-631.

Knott, J., and Wildavsky, A. "If Dissemination Is the Solution, What Is the Problem?" *Knowledge,* 1980, *1*(4), 537-578.

Knox, W. T. "Systems for Technological Information Transfer." *Science,* 1973, *181*(4098), 415-419.

Kochen, M. (Ed.). *The Growth of Knowledge: Readings on Organization and Retrieval of Information.* New York: Wiley, 1967.

Kochen, M. (Ed.). *Information for Action: From Knowledge to Wisdom.* New York: Academic Press, 1975.

Kocowski, T. "Social Engineering: Methods of Shaping Motivation." In A. Podgorecki (Ed.), *Sociotechnics: A Trend Report and Bibliography.* Hawthorne, N.Y.: Mouton, 1977.

Koestler, A. *The Act of Creation.* New York: Macmillan, 1964.

Kogan, L. S. "The Utilization of Social Work Research." *Social Casework,* 1963, *44,* 569-574.

Koizumi, T., and Kopecky, K. J. "Economic Growth, Capital Movements and International Transfer of Technical Knowledge." *Journal of International Economics,* 1977, *7*(1), 45-65.

Kojima, K. "Transfer of Technology to Developing Countries—Japanese Type Versus American Type." *Hitotsubashi Journal of Economics,* 1977, *17*(2), 1-14.

Kolb, D. A., and Frohman, A. L. "An Organizational Development Approach to Consulting." *Sloan Management Review,* 1970, *12*(1), 51-65.

Korea Institute of Science and Technology. *Proceedings of the International Seminar on Dissemination of Technology Held in Seoul, November 1972.* (NTIS PB-222 954.) Seoul: Korea Institute of Science and Technology, 1972.

Kotler, P. *Marketing Decision Making: A Model Building Approach.* New York: Holt, Rinehart, and Winston, 1971.

Kotler, P. "The Elements of Social Action." In G. Zaltman (Ed.), *Processes and Phenomena of Social Change.* New York: Wiley, 1973.

Kotter, J. P., and Schlesinger, L. A. "Choosing Strategies for Change." *Harvard Business Review,* 1979, *57*(2), 106-114.

Kraemer, K. L. "Local Government, Information Systems, and Technology Transfer: Evaluating Some Common Assertions About Computer Application Transfer." *Public Administration Review,* 1977, *37*(4), 368-382.

Kranzberg, M. "History and the Diffusion of Innovations: A Postscript." In M. Radnor, I. Feller, and E. Rogers (Eds.), *The Diffusion of Innovations: An Assessment.* Evanston, Ill.: Center for the Interdisciplinary Study of Science and Technology, Northwestern University, 1978.

Krathwohl, D. R., Bloom, B. S., and Masia, B. B. *Taxonomy of Educational Objectives. Handbook II: Affective Domain.* New York: McKay, 1964.

Krishnan, P. "Mortality Decline in India, 1951-1961: Development Versus Public Health Program Hypothesis." *Social Science and Medicine,* 1975, *9*(8/9), 475-479.

Kritek, W. J. "Lessons from the Literature on Implementation." *Educational Administration Quarterly,* 1976, *12*(3), 86-102.

Kroeber, A. L. "Diffusionism." In A. Etzioni and E. Etzioni (Eds.), *Social Change: Sources, Patterns, and Consequences.* New York: Basic Books, 1964.

Kuhn, T. S. *The Structure of Scientific Revolutions.* Chicago: University of Chicago Press, 1962.

Kuhner, A. "The Impact of Public Health Programs on Economic Development." *International Journal of Health Services,* 1971, *1*(3), 285-292.

Kunce, J. T., and Hartley, L. B. "Planned Interpersonal Informational Exchanges: The RULE Project." *Rehabilitation Counseling Bulletin,* 1975, *19*(2), 443-446.

Kunreuther, H. C., and Schoemaker, P. J. H. "Decision Analysis for Complex Systems: Integrating Descriptive and Prescriptive Components." *Knowledge,* 1981, *2*(3), 389-412.

Kurpius, D. "A Topical Bibliography on Consultation." *Personnel and Guidance Journal,* 1978, *56*(7), 442-447.

L'Abate, L., and Allison, M. Q. "Planned Change Intervention: The Enrichment Model with Couples, Families and Groups." *Transnational Mental Health Research Newsletter,* 1977, *19* (2), 11-15.

Lakhani, H. "Diffusion of Environment-Saving Technological Change." *Technological Forecasting and Social Change,* 1975, *7,* 1.

Lall, S. "The Patent System and the Transfer of Technology to Less-Developed Countries." *Journal of World Trade Law,* 1976, *10*(1), 1-15.

Lalley, T. "Some New Research Perspectives on Evaluation of Services to Victims." *Evaluation and Change,* 1980 (special issue), 90-93.

Lambright, W. H. *Technology Transfer to Cities: Processes of Choice at the Local Level.* Boulder, Colo.: Westview, 1979.

Lambright, W. H., and Carroll, J. D. *Adoption and Utilization of Urban Technology: A Decision-Making Study.* Syracuse, N.Y.: Syracuse University Research Corporation, 1977.

Lambright, W. H., and Flynn, P. J. "Bureaucratic Politics and Technological Change in Local Government." *Urban Analysis,* 1977, *4,* 93-118.

Lambright, W. H., and Teich, A. *Federal Laboratories and Technology Transfer: Institutions, Linkages, and Processes.* Syracuse, N.Y.: Syracuse University Research Corporation, 1974.

Lancaster, F. W. *Toward Paperless Information Systems.* New York: Academic Press, 1978a.

Lancaster, F. W. "Whither Libraries? Or, Wither Libraries." *College and Research Libraries,* 1978b, *39*(5), 345-357.

Landgrenbackstrom, S. "Transfer of Military Technology to 3rd World Countries." *Bulletin of Peace Proposals,* 1977, *8*(2), 110-120.

Langley Porter Institute. *Resource Materials for Community Mental Health Program Evaluation.* Washington, D.C.: National Technical Information Service, U.S. Department of Commerce, 1974.

Langrish, J., and others. *Wealth from Knowledge.* New York: Macmillan, 1972.

Lapan, H., and Bardhan, P. "Localized Technical Progress and Transfer of Technology and Economic Development." *Journal of Economic Theory,* 1973, *6*(6), 585-595.

LaPiere, R. T. "Adoption and the Adopter." In R. T. LaPiere, *Social Change.* New York: McGraw-Hill, 1965.

Larkey, P. "Process Models of Governmental Resource Allocation and Program Evaluation." *Policy Sciences,* 1977, *8,* 269-301.

Larsen, J. K. "Knowledge Utilization: What Is It?" *Knowledge,* 1980, *1*(3), 421-442.

Larsen, J. K. "Technical Assistance Consultation." Unpublished manuscript, 1981. (Available from author, Cognos Associates, 111 Main Street, Suite 5, Los Altos, CA 94022.)

Larsen, J. K., and Agarwala-Rogers, R. "Reinvention of Innovative Ideas." *Evaluation,* 1978 (special issue), 136-140.

Larsen, J. K., Arutunian, C. A., and Finley, C. J. *Diffusion of Innovations Among Community Mental Health Centers.* Palo Alto, Calif.: American Institutes for Research, 1974.

Larsen, J. K., and Nichols, D. G. "If Nobody Knows You've Done It, Have You . . . ?" *Evaluation,* 1972, *1*(1), 39-44.

Larsen, J. K., and Norris, E. L. *Getting the Most from Program-Oriented Mental Health Consultation: Guidelines for Consultants and Consultee Agency Staff.* Palo Alto, Calif.: American Institutes for Research, 1978.

Larsen, J. K., Norris, E. L., and Kroll, J. *Consultation and Its Outcome: Community Mental Health Centers.* Final Report to National Institute of Mental Health, Grant No. R12 MH25121. Palo Alto, Calif.: American Institutes for Research, 1976.

Larsen, V., and Agarwala-Rogers, R. *Reinvention in Adoption.* Palo Alto, Calif.: American Institute for Research in the Behavioral Sciences, 1977.

Lasagna, L., Wardell, W. M., and Hanson, R. W. *Technological Innovation and Government Regulation of Pharmaceuticals in the United States and Great Britain.* Final Report to National Science Foundation, Grant No. PRA-7519066. Washington, D.C.: National Science Foundation, 1978.

Lauer, R. H. (Ed.). *Social Movements and Social Change.* Carbondale: Southern Illinois University Press, 1976.

Lauer, R. H. *Perspectives on Social Change.* (2nd ed.) Boston: Allyn & Bacon, 1977.

Lavin, R. J., and Sanders, J. E. "Educational Improvement and the Function of Schools: Some Implications for Linkage Support Systems." In A. Bank and others, *Dissemination and the Improvement of Practice: Cooperation and Support in the School Improvement Process.* San Francisco: Far West Laboratory for Educational Research and Development, 1979.

Lawler, E. E., III, Nadler, D. A., and Cammann, C. (Eds.). *Organizational Assessment: Perspectives in the Measurement of Organizational Behavior and the Quality of Work Life.* New York: Wiley, 1980.

Lawler, M. R. (Ed.). *Strategies for Planned Curricular Innovation.* New York: Teachers College Press, Columbia University, 1970.

Lawless, M. W. "Implementation Issues in Criminal Justice Modeling." Paper presented at Implementation II: An International Conference on the Implementation of Management Science in Social Organizations, University of Pittsburgh, February 1976.

Lawrence, W. G. *Exploring Individual and Organizational Change: A Tavistock Open Systems Approach.* New York: Wiley-Interscience, 1978.

Layton, C. *Ten Innovations.* New York: Crane, Russak, 1972.

Lazarsfeld, P. F., Sewell, W. H., and Wilensky, H. L. (Eds.). *The Uses of Sociology.* New York: Basic Books, 1967.

Lazarus, S., and Gillespie, J. "Political Climates and the Diffusion of Innovative Instructional Materials." (ED 156 549.) Paper presented at annual meeting of National Council for the Social Studies, Cincinnati, Ohio, November 1977.

Leavitt, H. "Applied Organizational Change in Industry." In J. G. March (Ed.), *Handbook of Organizations.* Chicago: Rand McNally, 1965.

Lee, W. B., and Khumawala, B. M. "Simulation Testing of Aggregate Production Planning Models in an Implementation Methodology." *Management Science,* 1974, *20,* 903-911.

Leeper, R. R. (Ed.). *Curriculum Change: Direction and Process.* Washington, D.C.: Association for Supervision and Curriculum Development, 1966.

Lehming, R. *Improving Schools: Using What We Know.* Beverly Hills, Calif.: Sage, 1981.

Leithwood, K. A., and Montgomery, D. J. "Evaluating Program Implementation." *Evaluation Quarterly,* 1980, *4*(2), 193-214.

Leong, S. W. "Transfer of Nuclear Technology." *Transactions of the American Nuclear Society,* 1978, *29,* 314-317.

Levine, R. A., and others. *Evaluation Research and Practice: Comparative and International Perspectives.* Beverly Hills, Calif.: Sage, 1981.

Levy, G. W. *The Interactions of Science and Technology in the Innovative Process: Some Case Studies.* Washington, D.C.: National Science Foundation, 1972.

Lewicki, R. J. "Team Building in the Small Business Community: The Success and Failure of OD." In P. H. Mirvis and D. N. Berg (Eds.), *Failures in Organization Development and Change: Cases and Essays for Learning.* New York: Wiley, 1977.

Lewin, K. *Field Theory in Social Science.* New York: Harper & Row, 1951.

Lewin, K. "Group Decision and Social Change." In T. M. Newcomb and E. L. Hartley (Eds.), *Readings in Social Psychology.* New York: Holt, Rinehart and Winston, 1958.

Lewin, K. "Quasi-Stationary Social Equilibria and the Problem of Permanent Change." In W. G. Bennis, K. D. Benne, and R. Chin (Eds.), *The Planning of Change: Readings in the Applied Behavioral Sciences.* New York: Holt, Rinehart and Winston, 1962.

Lewin, K., and Grabbe, P. "Principles of Re-Education." In W. G. Bennis, K. D. Benne, and R. Chin (Eds.), *The Planning of Change: Readings in the Applied Behavioral Sciences.* New York: Holt, Rinehart and Winston, 1962.

Lewis-Beck, M. S., and Mohr, L. B. "Evaluating Effects of Independent Variables." *Political Methodology,* 1976, *3*(1), 27-48.

Lieber, A. L. "Consultation with the Police: The Psychiatrist as Organizational Change Agent." *Comprehensive Psychiatry,* 1978, *19*(1), 57-64.

Lieberman, A., and Griffin, G. A. "Educational Change: Inquiring into Problems of Implementation." *Teachers College Record,* 1976, *77*(3), 416-423.

Lighthal, F. F. "Review of Smith, L., and Keith, P., *Anatomy of Educational Innovation.*" *School Review,* 1973, *81*(2), 255-293.

Likert, R. *New Patterns of Management.* New York: McGraw-Hill, 1961.

Likert, R. "Behavioral Research: A Guide for Effective Action." In R. Likert and S. P. Hayes, Jr. (Eds.), *Some Applications of Behavioral Research.* Paris: UNESCO, 1967a.

Likert, R. *The Human Organization: Its Management and Values.* New York: McGraw-Hill, 1967b.

Likert, R., and Lippitt, R. "The Utilization of Social Science." In L. Festinger and D. Katz (Eds.), *Research Methods in the Behavioral Sciences.* Hinsdale, Ill.: Dryden, 1963.

Lin, N. "Innovative Methods for Studying Innovation." In *Research Implications for Educational Diffusion.* East Lansing: Department of Education, Michigan State University, 1968.

Lin, N., and Burt, R. S. "Differential Effects of Information Channels in the Process of Innovation Diffusion." *Social Forces,* 1975, *54,* 265-274.

Lin, N., and Zaltman, G. "Dimensions of Innovations." In G. Zaltman (Ed.), *Processes and Phenomena of Social Change.* New York: Wiley, 1973.

Lindblom, C. E. *Politics and Markets.* New York: Basic Books, 1977.

Lindblom, C. E., and Cohen, D. K. *Usable Knowledge: Social Science and Social Problem Solving.* New Haven, Conn.: Yale University Press, 1979.

Linden, M. E., and others. "Factors in the Success of a Public Mental Health Program." *American Journal of Psychiatry,* 1959, *116,* 344-351.

Lindquist, J. *Strategies for Change.* Berkeley, Calif.: Pacific Soundings Press, 1978.

Lindsey, Q. W., and Kessler, J. T. *Utilization of RANN Research Results: The Program and Its Effects. A Survey of the Research Applied to National Needs Program of the National Science Foundation.* (NTIS PB-254 466.) Research Triangle Park, N.C.: Research Triangle Institute, 1976.

Lingwood, D. A. "Producing Usable Research: The First Step in Dissemination." *American Behavioral Science,* 1979, *22*(3), 339-362.

Linhares, A. B. *An Overview of Federal Technology Transfer.* (NTIS PB-255 693.) Washington, D.C.: Office of R&D Policy, Department of Transportation, 1976.

Linstone, H., and Turoff, M. (Eds.). *The Delphi Method: Techniques and Application.* Reading, Mass.: Addison-Wesley, 1975.

Lionberger, H. F. "Diffusion of Innovations in Agricultural Research and in Schools." In R. R. Leeper (Ed.), *Strategy for Curriculum Change.* Washington, D.C.: Association for Supervision of Curriculum Development, 1965.

Lipetz, B. "Information Needs and Uses." In C. A. Caudra and A. W. Luke (Eds.), *Annual Review of Information Science and Technology.* Vol. 5. Chicago: Encyclopaedia Britannica, 1970.

Lippitt, R. O. "Dimensions of the Consultant's Job." In W. G. Bennis, K. D. Benne, and R. Chin (Eds.), *The Planning of Change: Readings in the Applied Behavioral Sciences.* New York: Holt, Rinehart and Winston, 1962.

Lippitt, R. O. "Roles and Processes in Curriculum Development and Change." In R. R. Leeper (Ed.), *Strategy for Curriculum Change.* Washington, D.C.: Association for Supervision and Curriculum Development, 1965a.

Lippitt, R. O. "The Use of Social Research to Improve Social Practice." *American Journal of Orthopsychiatry,* 1965b, *35* (4), 663-669.

Lippitt, R. O. "Processes of Curriculum Change." In R. R. Leeper (Ed.), *Curriculum Change: Direction and Process.* Washington, D.C.: Association for Supervision and Curriculum Development, 1966.

Lippitt, R. O. "The Process of Utilization of Social Research to Improve Social Practice." In W. G. Bennis, K. D. Benne, and R. Chin (Eds.), *The Planning of Change*. (2nd ed.) New York: Holt, Rinehart and Winston, 1969.

Lippitt, R. O., Benne, K. D., and Havelock, R. G. "A Comparative Analysis of the Research Utilization Process." Presentation at a symposium of American Educational Research Association, Research Utilization Committee, Chicago, February 1966.

Lippitt, R. O., and Butman, R. W. *A Pilot Study of Research Utilization Aspects of a Sample of Demonstration Research Mental Health Projects*. Final Report to National Institute of Mental Health, Contract No. PH 43651047. Rockville, Md.: National Institute of Mental Health, 1969.

Lippitt, R. O., and Fox, R. *Identifying, Documenting, Evaluating, and Sharing Innovative Classroom Practices*. Washington, D.C.: U.S. Office of Education, 1967.

Lippitt, R. O., and Havelock, R. G. "Needed Research on Research Utilization." In *Research Implications for Educational Diffusion*. East Lansing: Department of Education, Michigan State University, 1968.

Lippitt, R. O., Watson, J., and Westley, B. *The Dynamics of Planned Change*. New York: Harcourt Brace Jovanovich, 1958.

Lippitt, R. O., and others. "The Teacher as Innovator, Seeker, and Sharer of New Practices." In R. E. Miller (Ed.), *Perspectives on Educational Change*. New York: Appleton-Century-Crofts, 1967.

Liss, L. "Affirmative Action Officers—Are They Change Agents?" *Educational Record*, 1977, *58*(4), 418-428.

Liston, J., and Smith, L. "Fishing and the Fishing Industry." *Ocean Development and International Law Journal*, 1974, *2*(4), 313-334.

Litwin, G. H., and Stringer, R. A. *Motivation and Organizational Climate*. Boston: School of Management, Harvard University, 1968.

Locatis, C. N., and Gooler, D. D. "Evaluating Second-Order Consequences: Technology Assessment in Education." *Review of Educational Research*, 1975, *45*, 327-353.

Lochner, P. R., Jr. "Some Limits on the Application of Social Science Research in the Legal Process." *Law and Social Order,* 1973, 815-848.

Loeser, F. "A Revolution in Creative Thinking." *R&D Management,* 1978, *8*(special issue), 155-158.

Long, T. P. "A Case Study: Laser Processing—from Development to Application." *Research Management,* 1976, *19*(1), 15-17.

Lorenzi, N. M., and Young, K. P. "New Information Transfer Theories." *Library Trends,* 1974, *23*(1), 109-126.

Lorsch, J. W. "Contingency Theory and Organization Design." In R. H. Kilmann and others (Eds.), *The Management of Organization Design.* Vol. 1. New York: Elsevier, 1976a.

Lorsch, J. W. "Managing Change." In P. R. Lawrence, L. B. Barnes, and J. W. Lorsch, *Organizational Behavior and Administration.* Homewood, Ill.: Irwin, 1976b.

Louis, K. S. "Dissemination of Information from Centralized Bureaucracies to Local Schools: The Role of the Linking Agent." *Human Relations,* 1977, *30*(1), 25-42.

Louis, K. S. "Products and Process: Some Preliminary Findings from the R&D Utilization Program and Their Implications for Federal Dissemination Policies." Paper presented at 65th annual meeting of American Educational Research Association, Los Angeles, 1980.

Louis, K. S., Dentler, R. A., with Rosenblum, S. *Putting Knowledge to Work: An Examination of an Approach to Improvement in Education.* Cambridge, Mass.: Abt Associates, Inc., 1982.

Louis, K. S., and others. *Linking R&D with Local Schools: An Interim Report.* Cambridge, Mass.: Abt Associates, Inc., 1979.

Lowin, A. "Participative Decision Making: A Model, Literature Critique, and Prescriptions for Research." *Organizational Behavior and Human Performance,* 1968, *3*(1), 68-106.

Loy, J. W., Jr. "Social Psychological Characteristics of Innovators." *American Sociological Review,* 1969, *34*(1), 73-82.

Lucas, H. C., Jr. "The Problems and Politics of Change: Power, Conflict, and the Information Services Subunit." In F.

Gruenberger (Ed.), *Effective vs. Efficient Computing.* Englewood Cliffs, N.J.: Prentice-Hall, 1973.

Lucas, H. C., Jr. *Toward Creative Systems Design.* New York: Columbia University Press, 1974.

Lucas, H. C., Jr. *Why Information Systems Fail.* New York: Columbia University Press, 1975.

Lucas, H. C., Jr. *The Analysis, Design, and Implementation of Information Systems.* New York: McGraw-Hill, 1976.

Lucas, H. C., Jr. "The Use of an Interactive Information Storage and Retrieval System in Medical Research." *Communications of the ACM,* 1978, *21,* 197-205.

Luke, R. A., Jr., and others. "A Structural Approach to Organizational Change." *Journal of Applied Behavioral Science,* 1973, *9*(5), 610-635.

Lund, S. "How Ready Is the Mental Health System to Adopt or Expand Services for Victims?" *Evaluation and Change,* 1980 (special issue), 142-143.

Lundberg, C. C. "Middlemen in Science Utilization: Some Notes Toward Clarifying Conversion Roles." *American Behavioral Scientists,* 1966, *9,* 11-14.

Lundberg, C. C. "Images and Meta-Styles of Change Agents: An Explanatory Note." *Interpersonal Development,* 1974, *4*(2), 69-76.

Lundberg, L. B. *Future Without Shock.* New York: Norton, 1974.

Lundman, R. J., and Fox, J. C. "Maintaining Research Access in Police Organizations." *Criminology,* 1978, *16*(1), 87-98.

Lynn, F. "An Investigation of the Rate of Development and Diffusion of Technology in Our Modern Industrial Society." In National Commission on Technology, Automation, and Economic Progress, *Technology and the American Economy.* Vol. 2. Washington, D.C.: U.S. Government Printing Office, 1966.

Lynn, L. E., Jr. (Ed.). *Knowledge and Policy: The Uncertain Connection.* Washington, D.C.: National Academy of Sciences, 1978a.

Lynn, L. E., Jr. "The Question of Relevance." In L. E. Lynn, Jr. (Ed.), *Knowledge and Policy: The Uncertain Connection.* Washington, D.C.: National Academy of Sciences, 1978b.

Lynton, R. P. "Linking an Innovation Subsystem into the System." *Administrative Science Quarterly,* 1969, *14*(3), 398-416.

Lyons, G. M. *The Uneasy Partnership: Social Science and the Federal Government.* New York: Russell Sage Foundation, 1969.

McClelland, D. C. "Toward a Theory of Motive Acquisition." In W. G. Bennis, K. D. Benne, and R. Chin (Eds.), *The Planning of Change.* (2nd ed.) New York: Holt, Rinehart and Winston, 1969.

McClelland, W. A. "The Process of Effecting Change." Presidential address to Division of Military Psychology, 76th annual meeting of American Psychological Association, San Francisco, September 1968.

McCool, S. F., and Schreyer, R. M. "Research Utilization in Wildland Recreation Management: A Preliminary Analysis." *Journal of Leisure Research,* 1977, *9*(2), 98-109.

McCune, S. M. "Some Barriers to Knowledge Transfer and Planned Change." Unpublished paper, 1979. (Available from author, Sage Publications, 275 S. Beverly Drive, Beverly Hills, CA 90212.)

McCutcheon, J. R., and Sanders, J. R. *Diffusion Strategy Guide.* (ED 090 919.) Charleston, W. Va.: Appalachia Educational Laboratory, 1973.

McDonald, G. "Educational Innovation: The Case of the New Zealand Playcentre." *New Zealand Journal of Educational Studies,* 1974, *9*(2), 153-165.

McFarland, W., Nolan, R., and Norton, D. *Information Systems Administration.* New York: Holt, Rinehart and Winston, 1973.

McGinnis, R. "Research Tool." *Science,* 1980, *207*(4434), 972.

McGowan, E. F. "Rational Fantasies." *Policy Sciences,* 1976, *7*(4), 439-454.

McGuire, W. J. "The Nature of Attitudes and Attitude Change." In G. Lindzey and E. Aronson (Eds.), *The Handbook of Social Psychology.* Reading, Mass.: Addison-Wesley, 1969.

Machlup, F. *The Production and Distribution of Knowledge in the United States.* Princeton, N.J.: Princeton University Press, 1962.

MacIver, R. M. "The Role of the Precipitant." In A. Etzioni and E. Etzioni (Eds.), *Social Change: Sources, Patterns, and Consequences.* New York: Basic Books, 1964.

Mackie, R. R. "Chuckholes in the Bumpy Road from Research to Application." Paper presented at 82nd annual meeting of American Psychological Association, New Orleans, August 1974.

Mackie, R. R., and Christensen, P. R. *Translation and Application of Psychological Research.* Technical Report 716-1. Goleta, Calif.: Human Research, Inc., 1967.

McKinney, L. W., and Westbury, I. "Stability and Change: The Public Schools of Indiana, 1940-70." In W. A. Reid and D. F. Walker, *Case Studies in Curriculum Change.* New York: Routledge & Kegan Paul, 1975.

McKinsey and Co., Inc. *A Summary of Recommendations for Strengthening the RANN Private Sector Productivity Program.* (NTIS PB-256 795.) Washington, D.C.: McKinsey and Co., Inc., 1976.

McLaughlin, C., and Penchansky, R. "Diffusion of Innovation in Medicine: A Problem of Continuing Medical Education." *Journal of Medical Education,* 1965, *40,* 437-447.

McRae, D., Jr. *The Social Function of Social Science.* New Haven, Conn.: Yale University Press, 1976.

Madey, D. L., and others. *Building Capacity for Improvement of Educational Practice: An Evaluation of NIE's State Dissemination Grants Program.* Durham, N.C.: NTS Research Corporation, 1979.

Magi Educational Services, Inc. *National Diffusion/Adoption Network: A First Year Formative Look, Final Report.* (ED 157 862.) Port Chester, N.Y.: Magi Educational Services, Inc., 1975.

Magisos, J. H. *Interpretation of Target Audience Needs in the Design of Information Dissemination Systems for Vocational-Technical Education.* Columbus: National Center for Vocational Education, Ohio State University, 1971.

Maguire, L. M. *Observation and Analysis of the Literature on Change.* Philadelphia: Research for Better Schools, Inc., 1970.

Maguire, L. M., Temkin, S., and Cummings, C. P. *An Annotated*

*Bibliography on Administering for Change.* Philadelphia: Research for Better Schools, Inc., 1971.

Mahajan, V., and Schoeman, M. E. F. "Generalized Model for the Time Pattern of the Diffusion Process." *IEEE Transactions on Engineering Management,* 1977, *24*(1), 12-18.

Maier, N. R. F. *Problem-Solving Discussions and Conferences.* New York: McGraw-Hill, 1963.

Maier, N. R. F. *Psychology in Industrial Organizations.* (4th ed.) New York: Houghton Mifflin, 1973.

Maier, N. R. F., and Hoffman, L. R. "Financial Incentives and Group Decision in Motivating Change." *Journal of Social Psychology,* 1964, *64,* 369-378.

Maier, N. R. F., and Zerfoss, L. F. "MRP: A Technique for Training Large Groups of Supervisors and Its Potential Use in Social Research." In H. A. Hornstein and others (Eds.), *Social Intervention: A Behavioral Science Approach.* New York: Free Press, 1971.

Major Issues Arising from the Transfer of Technology to Developing Countries. Geneva: United Nations Conference on Trade and Development (UNCTAD), 1975.

Maloney, J. C., and Schonfeld, E. P. "Social Change and Attitude Change." In G. Zaltman (Ed.), *Processes and Phenomena of Social Change.* New York: Wiley, 1973.

Manela, R. "Notes on Innovation Diffusion." Unpublished summary of conference, Manpower Laboratory, Institute of Labor and Industrial Relations, University of Michigan, February 1969.

Mangham, I. *Interactions and Interventions in Organizations.* New York: Wiley-Interscience, 1978.

Mann, D. (Ed.). *Making Change Happen?* New York: Teachers College Press, 1978.

Mann, D., and Ingram, H. (Eds.). *Why Policies Succeed and Fail.* Beverly Hills, Calif.: Sage, 1980.

Mann, F. C. "Studying and Creating Change: A Means to Understanding Social Organization." In H. A. Hornstein and others (Eds.), *Social Intervention: A Behavioral Science Approach.* New York: Free Press, 1971.

Mann, F. C., and Neff, F. W. *Managing Major Change in Organi-*

*zations.* Ann Arbor, Mich.: Foundation for Research on Human Behavior, 1961.

Manning, B. A. *The "Trouble Shooting" Checklist for School-Based Settings (Manual).* (ED 126 095.) Austin: Research and Development Center for Teacher Education, University of Texas, 1976.

Manning, N. P., and Rapoport, R. N. "Rejection and Reincorporation: A Case Study in Social Research Utilization." *Social Science and Medicine,* 1976, *10,* 459-468.

Mannino, F., MacLennan, B. W., and Shore, M. *The Practice of Mental Health Consultation.* Washington, D.C.: U.S. Government Printing Office, 1975.

Mannino, F., and Shore, M. "Research in Mental Health Consultation." In S. E. Golann and C. Eisdorfer (Eds.), *Handbook of Community Mental Health.* New York: Appleton-Century-Crofts, 1973.

Manpower Science Services, Inc. *Putting Social Science Knowledge to Use in the Manpower System. An Overview Report.* Ann Arbor, Mich.: Manpower Science Services, Inc., 1974.

Mansfield, E. "Intrafirm Rates of Diffusion of an Innovation." *Review of Economics and Statistics,* 1963a, *45,* 348-359.

Mansfield, E. "Speed of Response of Firms to New Techniques." *Quarterly Journal of Economics,* 1963b, *77,* 290-311.

Mansfield, E. "The Process of Technical Change." In R. A. Tybout (Ed.), *Economics of Research and Development.* Columbus: Ohio State University Press, 1965.

Mansfield, E. *Econometric Studies of Industrial Research and Technological Innovation.* New York: Norton, 1967.

Mansfield, E. *The Economics of Technological Change.* New York: Norton, 1968a.

Mansfield, E. *Industrial Research and Technological Innovation: An Econometric Analysis.* New York: Norton, 1968b.

Mansfield, E. *Technological Change: An Introduction to a Vital Area of Modern Economics.* New York: Norton, 1971.

Mansfield, E. "Determinants of the Speed of Application of New Technology." In B. R. Williams (Ed.), *Science and Technology in Economic Growth.* New York: Halsted, 1973.

Mansfield, E. "Tax Policy and Innovation." *Science*, 1982, *215*, 1365-1371.

Mansfield, E., and others. *Social and Private Rates of Return from Industrial Innovations.* Vol. 1: *Analytical Report.* (NTIS PB-254 083.) Philadelphia: University of Pennsylvania, 1975a.

Mansfield, E., and others. *Social and Private Rates of Return from Industrial Innovations.* Vol. 2: *Detailed Description of 17 Case Studies.* (NTIS PB-254 084.) Philadelphia: University of Pennsylvania, 1975b.

Mansfield, E., and others. *The Production and Application of New Industrial Technology.* New York: Norton, 1977.

Manten, A. A. "A Suggested Growth Model of Science and Implications for Information Transfer." *Journal of Research Communication Studies*, 1978, *1*(1), 83-98.

Manzoor, C. "Politics of Technology Transfer (with Special Reference to the Transfer of Nuclear Technology)." *Annals of Nuclear Energy*, 1977, *4*, 225-233.

March, J. G. "Model Bias in Social Action." *Review of Educational Research*, 1972, *42*, 413-430.

March, J. G., and Simon, H. A. *Organizations.* New York: Wiley, 1958.

Marcum, R. L. *Organizational Climate and the Adoption of Educational Innovation.* Research Report for Office of Education, Contract No. OEG-4-7-078119-2901. Logan: Utah State University, 1968.

Margulies, N., and Raia, A. P. *Organizational Development: Values, Process, and Technology.* New York: McGraw-Hill, 1972.

Margulies, N., Wright, P. I., and Scholl, R. W. "Organization Development Techniques: Their Impact on Change." *Group & Organization Studies*, 1977, *2*(4), 428-448.

Marker, G. W. "Social Studies: What Happened on the Way to the Revolution?" *Indiana Social Studies Quarterly*, 1976, *29*(2), 5-13.

Markley, O. W. *The Normative Structure of Knowledge Production and Utilization in Education.* Menlo Park, Calif.: Stanford Research Institute, 1974.

Marmor, J. "Psychosocial Reactions to Social Change." *Australian and New Zealand Journal of Psychiatry*, 1975, *9*, 149-152.

Marmor, J., Bernard, V., and Ottenberg, P. "Psychodynamics of Group Opposition to Health Programs." *American Journal of Orthopsychiatry*, 1960, *30*, 330-345.

Marquis, D. G., and Allen, T. J. "Communication Patterns in Applied Technology." *American Psychologist*, 1966, *21*, 1052-1060.

Marquis, D. G., and Myers, S. *Successful Industrial Innovations.* Washington, D.C.: U.S. Government Printing Office, 1969.

Marris, P. *Loss and Change.* Garden City, N.Y.: Doubleday, 1975.

Marrow, A. J. *The Practical Theorist.* New York: Basic Books, 1969.

Marrow, A. J., Bowers, D. G., and Seashore, S. E. *Management by Participation.* New York: Harper & Row, 1967.

Marrow, A. J., and French, J. R. P., Jr. "Changing a Stereotype in Industry." In W. G. Bennis, K. D. Benne, and R. Chin (Eds.), *The Planning of Change: Readings in the Applied Behavioral Sciences.* New York: Holt, Rinehart and Winston, 1962.

Martin, G. "The French Experience of Social Planning: Evaluation and Prospects." *International Social Science Journal*, 1975, *27*(1), 87-120.

Martino, J. P. *Technological Forecasting for Decision Making.* New York: American Elsevier, 1972.

Martino, J. P., Chen, K., and Lenz, R. C., Jr. *Predicting the Diffusion Rate of Industrial Innovations.* Final Report to National Science Foundation, Grant No. PRA-7617188. Washington, D.C.: National Science Foundation, 1978.

Masters, R. "Helping Transfer Technology to Developing Countries." *Nuclear Engineering International*, 1978, *23*(268), 38-40.

Mathematica, Inc. *Quantifying the Benefits to the National Economy from Secondary Applications of NASA Technology. Executive Summary.* (NTIS N76-20033.) Princeton, N.J.: Mathematica, Inc., 1976.

Matheson, N. W., and Sundland, D. M. "Objectives of the FDI System for Mental Hospital Personnel in Missouri." Paper presented at Third International Congress of Medical Librarianship, Amsterdam, May 1969.

Matsui, S. "Transfer of Technology to Developing Countries: Some Proposals to Solve Current Problems." *Journal of the Patent Office Society*, 1977, *59*(10), 612-628.

Matula, F. V. "Factors Contributing to the Willingness of Elementary Teachers to Try Selected Classroom Innovations." (ED 066 404.) Unpublished paper, 1972.

Meadows, D. H., and others. *The Limits to Growth: A Report for the Club of Rome's Project on the Predicament of Mankind.* New York: Universe Books, 1972.

Mealiea, L. W. "Learned Behavior: The Key to Understanding and Preventing Employee Resistance to Change." *Group & Organization Studies*, 1978, *3*(2), 211-223.

Meals, D., Lavin, R., and Sanders, J. *Synthesis of Knowledge and Practice in Educational Management: Merrimack Education Center Report of Year One.* Dayton, Ohio: C. F. Kettering Foundation, 1975.

Mechanic, D. "Sources of Power of Lower Participants in Complex Organizations." *Administrative Science Quarterly*, 1962, *25*, 349-364.

Meierhenry, W. C. (Ed.). *Media and Educational Innovation.* Lincoln: University of Nebraska Extension Division and University of Nebraska Press, 1964.

Menzel, H. A. "Can Science Information Needs Be Ascertained Empirically?" In L. Thayer (Ed.), *Communication: Concepts and Perspectives.* Washington, D.C.: Spartan Books, 1966a.

Menzel, H. A. "Scientific Communication: Five Themes from Social Science Research." *American Psychologist*, 1966b, *21*, 999-1004.

Mercer, J. R., Dingman, H. F., and Tarjan, G. "Involvement, Feedback, and Mutuality: Principles for Conducting Mental Health Research in the Community." *American Journal of Psychiatry*, 1964, *121*(3), 228-237.

Merrifield, D. B. "Basic Business Concepts for R&D Management." *Research Management*, 1976, *19*(2), 33-36.

Merton, R. K. "Resistance to the Systematic Study of Multiple Discoveries in Science." *European Journal of Sociology,* 1963, *4*(2), 237-282.

Merton, R. K. *Social Theory and Social Structure.* New York: Free Press, 1967.

Merton, R. K. *The Sociology of Science.* Chicago: University of Chicago Press, 1973.

Merton, R. K. "The Self-Fulfilling Prophecy." In R. K. Merton, *Social Research and the Practicing Professions.* Cambridge, Mass.: Abt Books, 1982.

Mesthene, E. G. *Technological Change: Its Impact on Man and Society.* Cambridge, Mass.: Harvard University Press, 1970.

Metcalf, J. L. "Organizational Strategies and Interorganizational Networks." *Human Relations,* 1976, *29,* 327-343.

Meyer, M. W. *Change in Public Bureaucracies.* Cambridge, England: Cambridge University Press, 1979.

Meyer, M. W., and Associates. *Environments and Organizations: Theoretical and Empirical Perspectives.* San Francisco: Jossey-Bass, 1978.

Meyer, T. C., and others. "Providing Medical Information to Physicians by Telephone Tapes." *Journal of Medical Education,* 1970, *45,* 1060-1065.

Meyers, W. R. *The Evaluation Enterprise: A Realistic Appraisal of Evaluation Careers, Methods, and Applications.* San Francisco: Jossey-Bass, 1981.

Meyers, W. R., and others. "Organizational and Attitudinal Correlates of Citizen Board Accomplishment in Mental Health and Retardation." *Community Mental Health Journal,* 1974, *10*(2), 192-197.

Michalet, C.-A. "The International Transfer of Technology and the Multinational Enterprise." *Development and Change,* 1976, *7*(2), 157-174.

Mick, C. *Development of Training Resources for Educational Extension Service Personnel.* 3 vols. (ED 077 534, -535, -536.) Stanford, Calif.: Institute for Communication Research, Stanford University, 1973.

Midgley, D. F. *Innovation and New Product Marketing.* New York: Wiley, 1977.

Miles, M. B. "Educational Innovation: The Nature of the Prob-
lem." In M. B. Miles (Ed.), *Innovation in Education.* New
York: Bureau of Publications, Teachers College, Columbia
University, 1964a.

Miles, M. B. (Ed.). *Innovation in Education.* New York: Bureau
of Publications, Teachers College, Columbia University,
1964b.

Miles, M. B. "Innovation in Education: Some Generalizations."
In M. B. Miles (Ed.), *Innovation in Education.* New York:
Bureau of Publications, Teachers College, Columbia Univer-
sity, 1964c.

Miles, M. B. "On Temporary Systems." In M. B. Miles (Ed.),
*Innovation in Education.* New York: Bureau of Publications,
Teachers College, Columbia University, 1964d.

Miles, M. B. "Planned Change and Organizational Health: Figure
and Ground." In R. O. Carlson and others, *Change Processes
in the Public Schools.* Eugene: Center for the Advanced
Study of Educational Administration, University of Oregon,
1965.

Miles, M. B. *Designing and Starting Innovative Schools: A Field
Study of Social Architecture in Education.* Final Report to
National Institute of Education, Grant No. NIE-G-74-0051.
New York: Center for Policy Research, 1978a.

Miles, M. B. "On 'Networking.' " Paper commissioned by the
School Capacity for Problem Solving Group, National Institute of Education, Washington, D.C., January 1978b.

Miles, M. B. "Evaluation Training." In M. B. Miles, *Learning to
Work in Groups.* (2nd ed.) New York: Teachers College
Press, 1980.

Miles, M. B. "Mapping the Common Properties of Schools." In
R. Lehming (Ed.), *Improving Schools: What We Know.* Beverly Hills, Calif.: Sage, 1981.

Miles, M. B., Fullan, M., and Taylor, G. *Organization Development in Schools: The State of the Art.* Vol. 5: *Implications
for Policy, Research, and Practice.* Final Report to National
Institute of Education, Contract Nos. 500-77-0051, -0052.
New York: Center for Policy Research, 1978a.

Miles, M. B., Fullan, M., and Taylor, G. *Organization Development in Schools: The State of the Art.* Vol. 3: *OD Consul-*

*tants/OD Programs in School Districts.* Final Report to the National Institute of Education, Contract Nos. 500-77-0051, -0052. New York: Center for Policy Research, 1978b.

Miles, M. B., and Lake, D. G. "Communication Networks in the Designing and Starting of New Schools." (ED 106 972.) Paper presented at 60th annual meeting of American Educational Research Association, Washington, D.C., March 1975.

Miles, M. B., and others. "The Consequence of Survey Feedback: Theory and Evaluation." In W. G. Bennis, K. D. Benne, and R. Chin (Eds.), *The Planning of Change.* (2nd ed.) New York: Holt, Rinehart and Winston, 1969.

Miles, M. B., and others. "Data Feedback: A Rationale." In H. A. Hornstein and others (Eds.), *Social Intervention: A Behavioral Approach.* New York: Free Press, 1971.

Miller, T. C. "Review of National Research Council of the National Academy of Sciences, *The Federal Investment in Knowledge of Social Problems." Knowledge,* 1980, *1*(3), 459-464.

Milo, N. "Health Care Organizations and Innovation." *Journal of Health and Social Behavior,* 1971, *12,* 163-173.

Milstein, M. M. (Ed.). *Schools, Conflict and Change.* New York: Teachers College Press, 1980.

Mirvis, P. H., and Berg, D. N. *Failures in Organization Development and Change: Cases and Essays for Learning.* New York: Wiley, 1977.

Miskel, C. G. "A Program for Training Educational Change Agents by Increasing the R&D Technology Level." *Educational Technology,* 1973, *13*(12), 45-49.

Mitchell, D. E. "Social Science Impact on Legislative Decision Making: Process and Substance." *Educational Researcher,* 1980, *9*(10), 9-12, 17-19.

Mitchell, D. E., and others. *Social Science Impact on Legislative Decision Making.* Final Report to National Institute of Education, Grant No. NIE-G-0104. Washington, D.C.: National Institute of Education, 1979.

Mitroff, I. I., and Kilmann, R. H. *Methodological Approaches to Social Science: Integrating Divergent Concepts and Theories.* San Francisco: Jossey-Bass, 1978.

Mitroff, I. I., Kilmann, R. H., and Barabba, V. P. "Management Information Versus Misinformation Systems." In G. Zaltman (Ed.), *Management Principles for Nonprofit Agencies and Organizations.* New York: American Management Associations, 1979.

Mitroff, I. I., and Mitroff, D. D. "Interpersonal Communication for Knowledge Utilization." *Knowledge,* 1979, *1*(2), 203-217.

Mitroff, I. I., Nelson, J., and Mason, R. O. "On Management Myth-Information Systems." *Management Science,* 1974, *21,* 371-382.

Mittenthal, S. D. "Evaluation Overview—A System Approach to Services Integration." *Evaluation,* 1976, *3*(1-2), 142-148.

Moch, M. K., and Morse, E. V. "Size, Centralization, and Organizational Adoption of Innovations." *American Sociological Review,* 1977, *42*(5), 716-725.

Mogulof, M. B. "Advocates for Themselves: Citizen Participation in Federally Supported Community Organizations." *Community Mental Health Journal,* 1974, *10*(1), 66-76.

Mohr, L. B. "Determinants of Innovation in Organizations." In L. Rowe and W. Boise (Eds.), *Organizational and Managerial Innovation.* Pacific Palisades, Calif.: Goodyear, 1973a.

Mohr, L. B. "The Concept of Organizational Goal." *American Political Science Review,* 1973b, *67,* 470-481.

Mohr, L. B. "Process Theory and Variance Theory in Innovation Research." In M. Radnor, I. Feller, and E. Rogers (Eds.), *The Diffusion of Innovations: An Assessment.* Evanston, Ill.: Center for the Interdisciplinary Study of Science and Technology, Northwestern University, 1978.

Mohrman, S., and others. "A Survey Feedback and Problem-Solving Intervention in a School District: 'We'll Take the Survey But You Can Keep the Feedback.' " In P. H. Mirvis and D. N. Berg (Eds.), *Failures in Organization Development and Change: Cases and Essays for Learning.* New York: Wiley, 1977.

Mojkowski, C. "Improving Linking Processes." In A. Bank and others, *Dissemination and the Improvement of Practice: Cooperation and Support in the School Improvement Process.*

San Francisco: Far West Laboratory for Educational Research and Development, 1979.

Molitor, J. A., and Louis, K. S. *Entering the RDU Program: An Interim Analysis on Initial Problems in Managing Change at the School and District Level.* Cambridge, Mass.: Abt Associates, Inc., 1979.

Montgomery, D. "Marketing Decision Information System: Some Design Considerations." In R. Ferber (Ed.), *Handbook of Marketing Research.* New York: McGraw-Hill, 1974.

Moore, D. R. "Report from the Belmont Task Force on Linker Roles." In A. Bank and others, *Dissemination and the Improvement of Practice: Cooperation and Support in the School Improvement Process.* San Francisco: Far West Laboratory for Educational Research and Development, 1979.

Moore, D. R., and others. *Assistance Strategies of Six Groups that Facilitate Change at the School/Community Level.* 3 vols. (Prepared for the National Institute of Education.) Chicago: Center for New Schools, 1977.

Moore, J. R. "Unique Aspects of High Technology Enterprise Management." *IEEE Transactions on Engineering Management,* 1976, *23*(1), 10-20.

Moravcsik, M. J., and Murugesan, P. "Some Results on the Function and Quality of Citations." *Social Studies of Science,* 1975, *5*(1), 86.

Morell, J. A. *Program Evaluation in Social Research.* New York: Pergamon, 1979.

Moreno, J. L. *Who Shall Survive?* (Rev. ed.) Beacon, N.Y.: Beacon House, 1953.

Morgan, J. S. *Managing Change: The Strategies of Making Change Work for You.* New York: McGraw-Hill, 1972.

Moriarty, E. J. "Summary of Small Group Recommendations." In *Communication, Dissemination, and Utilization of Rehabilitation Research Information.* Washington, D.C.: Joint Liaison Committee of the Council of State Administrators of Vocational Rehabilitation and the Rehabilitation Counselor Educators, Department of Health, Education, and Welfare, 1967.

Morphet, E. L., and Ryan, C. O. (Eds.). *Planning and Effecting*

*Needed Changes in Education.* Englewood Cliffs, N.J.: Citation Press, 1967.

Morrill, R., and Manninen, D. "Critical Parameters of Spatial Diffusion Processes." *Economic Geography,* 1975, *51,* 269-278.

Morris, L. L., Fitz-Gibbon, C. T., and Henerson, M. E. *Program Evaluation Kit.* 8 vols. Beverly Hills, Calif.: Sage, 1978.

Morris, P. "Utilization of the Social Sciences in Britain and the U.S.A." *Current Sociology,* 1975, *23*(1), 129-141.

Morris, R. (Ed.). *Centrally Planned Change: Prospects and Concepts.* New York: National Association of Social Workers, 1964.

Morris, W. C., and Sashkin, M. *Organization Behavior in Action. Skill Building Experiences.* St. Paul, Minn.: West, 1976.

Morrish, I. *Aspects of Educational Change.* New York: Halsted, 1976.

Morrison, D. E. "Some Notes Toward a Theory on Relative Deprivation, Social Movements, and Social Change." In G. Zaltman (Ed.), *Processes and Phenomena of Social Change.* New York: Wiley, 1973.

Mort, P. R. "Studies in Educational Innovation from the Institute of Administrative Research." In M. B. Miles (Ed.), *Innovation in Education.* New York: Bureau of Publications, Teachers College, Columbia University, 1964.

Morton, J. A. *Organizing for Innovation: A Systems Approach to Technical Management.* New York: McGraw-Hill, 1971.

Mosteller, F. "Innovation and Evaluation." *Science,* 1981, *211*(4485), 881-886.

Moyer, D., and Clignet, R. "Social Problems in Science and for Science." *Knowledge,* 1980, *2*(1), 93-116.

Mulkay, M. J. "Conformity and Innovation in Science." *The Sociological Review Monograph,* 1972a, *18,* 5-23.

Mulkay, M. J. *The Social Process Innovation.* London: Macmillan, 1972b.

Mulkay, M. J. "Sociology of the Scientific Research Community." In I. Spiegel-Rosing and D. de Solla Price (Eds.), *Science, Technology and Society: A Cross-Disciplinary Perspective.* London: Sage, 1977.

Mullen, E. J. "The Construction of Personal Models for Effective Practice: A Method for Utilizing Research Findings to Guide Social Interventions." *Journal of Social Service Research,* 1978, *2,* 45-64.

Munro, R. G. *Innovation: Success or Failure.* London: Hodder and Stoughton, 1977.

Munson, F. C., and Pelz, D. C. *Innovating in Organizations: A Conceptual Framework.* Ann Arbor: School of Public Health and Institute for Social Research, University of Michigan, 1980.

Murphy, S. T. "Problems in Research Utilization: Review." *Rehabilitation Counseling Bulletin,* 1975, *19*(2), 365-376.

Mushkin, S. J. "Evaluations: Use with Caution." *Evaluation,* 1973, *1*(2), 30-35.

Muthard, J. E. *Personnel and Research Utilization in Rehabilitation: Six Years of Research and Service.* (NTIS PB-253 524.) Gainesville: Regional Rehabilitation Research Institute, University of Florida, 1975.

Muthard, J. E. *Putting Rehabilitation Knowledge to Use.* Rehabilitation Monograph No. 11. Gainesville: College of Health Related Professions, University of Florida, 1980.

Muthard, J. E., and Crocker, L. M. *Informational Resources for Aiding Research Utilization by Rehabilitation and Social Service Workers.* Final Report to Social and Rehabilitation Service, Grant Nos. RD 3080 and 22-P-55144. Gainesville: Regional Rehabilitation Research Institute, University of Florida, 1972.

Muthard, J. E., and Crocker, L. M. "Rehabilitation State Supervisors as Knowledge Users." *Rehabilitation Counseling Bulletin,* 1975, *19*(2), 433-446.

Muthard, J. E., Crocker, L. M., and Wells, S. A. *Rehabilitation Workers' Use and Evaluation of Research and Demonstration BRIEF Reports.* Gainesville: Regional Rehabilitation Research Institute, University of Florida, 1973.

Muthard, J. E., and Felice, K. A. *Measuring and Improving Research Utilization Practices in Rehabilitation.* Rehabilitation Monograph No. 10. Gainesville, Fla.: College of Health Related Professions, University of Florida, 1978.

Myers, S., and Marquis, D. G. *Successful Industrial Innovations: A Study of Factors Underlying Innovation in Selected Firms.* Washington, D.C.: National Science Foundation, 1969.

Myers, S., and Sweezy, E. E. *Federal Incentives for Innovation. Why Innovations Falter and Fail: A Study of 200 Cases.* (NTIS PB-259 208.) Denver, Colo.: Denver Research Institute, 1976.

Myers, S., and Sweezy, E. E. "Why Innovations Fail." *Technology Review,* 1978, *80*(5), 40-46.

Nabseth, L., and Ray, G. (Eds.). *The Diffusion of New Industrial Processes: An International Study.* Cambridge, N.Y.: Cambridge University Press, 1974.

Nadler, D. *Feedback and Organization Development.* Toronto: Addison-Wesley, 1977.

Nagi, S. Z. "The Practitioner as a Partner in Research." *Rehabilitation Record,* 1965, *4,* 1-4.

Nagi, S. Z., and Corwin, R. G. (Eds.). *The Social Contexts of Research.* New York: Wiley, 1972.

Nagle, J. *Introducing SPECS—School Planning, Evaluation, and Communication System.* Eugene: Center for Educational Policy and Management, University of Oregon, 1974.

Narris, P., and Rein, M. *Dilemmas of Social Reform.* Harmondsworth, England: Penguin, 1974.

Nash, N., and Culberson, J. (Eds.). *Linking Processes in Educational Improvement: Concepts and Applications.* Columbus, Ohio: University Council for Educational Administration, 1977.

National Academy of Engineering. *Technology Transfer and Utilization Recommendations for Redirecting the Emphasis and Correcting the Imbalance.* (NTIS PB-232 123.) Washington, D.C.: National Academy of Engineering, 1974.

National Aeronautics and Space Administration. "Technology Utilization at Work." Washington, D.C.: National Aeronautics and Space Administration, 1976.

National Institute of Education. *Databook: The State of Education, Research, and Development in the United States.* Washington, D.C.: U.S. Government Printing Office, 1969.

National Institute of Education. *Building Capacity for Renewal and Reform: An Initial Report on Knowledge Production and Utilization in Education.* Washington, D.C.: National Institute of Education, 1973.

National Institute of Education. *Catalogue of NIE Education Products.* 2 vols. Washington, D.C.: National Institute of Education, 1975.

National Institute of Education. *Program Plan, School Capacity for Problem Solving.* Washington, D.C.: National Institute of Education, 1976.

National Institute of Education. *Report of the Proceedings of the Belmont Conference on Linkage.* Washington, D.C.: National Institute of Education, 1977.

National Institute of Mental Health. *Planning for Creative Change in Mental Health Services: A Distillation of Principles on Research Utilization.* 2 vols. Rockville, Md.: National Institute of Mental Health, 1971a.

National Institute of Mental Health. *Planning for Creative Change in Mental Health Services: A Manual on Research Utilization.* (DHEW Publication HSM 73-9174.) Washington, D.C.: Health Services and Mental Health Administration, 1971b.

National Research Council of the National Academy of Sciences. *Communication Systems and Resources in the Behavioral Sciences.* Washington, D.C.: National Academy of Sciences, 1967.

National Research Council of the National Academy of Sciences. *The Federal Investment in Knowledge of Social Problems.* Washington, D.C.: National Academy of Sciences, 1978.

National Science Board. *Science Indicators.* Washington, D.C.: U.S. Government Printing Office, 1975.

National Science Foundation. *Knowledge into Action: Improving the Nation's Use of the Social Sciences.* Report of the Special Commission on the Social Sciences of the National Science Board, Report NSB 69-3. Washington, D.C.: U.S. Government Printing Office, 1969.

National Science Foundation. *Barriers to Innovation in Industry: Opportunities for Public Policy Changes.* Washington, D.C.: National Science Foundation, 1973a.

National Science Foundation. *Science, Technology, and Innovation.* Final Report on Contract No. NSF-C667. Columbus, Ohio: Battelle Columbus Laboratories, 1973b.

National Science Foundation. *Technological Innovation and Federal Government Policy.* Washington, D.C.: National Science Foundation, 1976.

National Science Foundation. *Current Research on Scientific and Technical Information.* New York: Jeffrey Norton, 1977.

Neelameghan, A., and Seetharama, S. "Information Transfer: Next 25 Years." *Library Science with a Slant to Documentation,* 1976, *13*(1), 1-15.

Neill, S. B. "The National Diffusion Network: A Success Story Ending?" *Phi Delta Kappan,* 1976, *57*(9), 589-601.

Nelkin, D. "Scientific Knowledge, Public Policy, and Democracy: A Review Essay." *Knowledge,* 1979, *1*(1), 106-122.

Nelson, C. E. *Scientific Communication in Educational Research.* (ED 073 793.) Tampa: University of South Florida, 1972.

Nelson, C. E., and Pollock, D. K. (Eds.). *Communication Among Scientists and Engineers.* Lexington, Mass.: Heath, 1970.

Nelson, C. E., and Smith, E. "Achieving Institutional Adaptation Using Diagonally Structured Information Exchange." *Human Relations,* 1974, *27*(2), 101-119.

Nelson, M., and Sieber, S. D. "Innovations in Urban Secondary Schools." *School Review,* 1976, *8*(2), 213-231.

Nelson, R. R. "A 'Diffusion' Model of International Productivity Differences in Manufacturing Industry." *American Economic Review,* 1968, *58*(5, Pt. 1), 1219-1248.

Nelson, R. R. "Organizational Requirements for a National Technology Policy." Unpublished paper prepared for Ad Hoc Committee on Science and Technology, National Academy of Sciences, Washington, D.C., 1974.

Nelson, R. R., Peck, M. T., and Kalachek, E. D. *Technology, Economic Growth, and Public Policy.* Washington, D.C.: Brookings Institution, 1967.

Nelson, R. R., and Winter, S. G. "In Search of a Useful Theory of Innovation." *Research Policy,* 1977, *6*, 36-66.

Nelson, R. R., and Yates, D. (Eds.). *Innovation and Implementation in Public Organizations.* Lexington, Mass.: Heath, 1978.

Nelson, S. D. "Knowledge Creation: An Overview." *Knowledge,* 1979, *1*(1), 123-149.

The NETWORK, Inc. *A Study of Dissemination Efforts Supporting School Improvement.* Andover, Mass.: The NETWORK, Inc., 1980.

The NETWORK, Inc. *The Configuration of Federal and State Dissemination Structures and Practice.* Andover, Mass.: The NETWORK, Inc., 1981a.

The NETWORK, Inc. *Dissemination Strategies for School Improvement.* Andover, Mass.: The NETWORK, Inc., 1981b.

The NETWORK, Inc. *The Dynamics of Successful Implementation.* Andover, Mass.: The NETWORK, Inc., 1981c.

The NETWORK, Inc. *Implementation in the National Diffusion Network.* Andover, Mass.: The NETWORK, Inc., 1981d.

The NETWORK, Inc. *Overview of Dissemination Activities in the Department of Education.* Andover, Mass.: The NETWORK, Inc., 1981e.

The NETWORK, Inc. *Resources for Evaluating Project Effectiveness: A Guidebook for Dissemination Practitioners.* Andover, Mass.: The NETWORK, Inc., 1981f.

New York State Education Department. *Educational Programs That Work, Part C.* (ED 154 511.) Albany: New York State Education Department, 1978.

Newman, D. L., Brown, R. D., and Braskamp, L. A. "Communication Theory and the Utilization of Evaluation." In L. A. Braskamp and R. D. Brown (Eds.), *New Directions for Program Evaluation: Utilization of Evaluative Information,* no. 5. San Francisco: Jossey-Bass, 1980.

Nica, I., and Birzea, C. "Educational Innovation in European Socialist Countries: Comparative Overview." *International Review of Education,* 1973, *19*(4), 446-459.

Nicholas, J. M. "Evaluation Research in Organizational Change Interventions: Considerations and Some Suggestions." *Journal of Applied Behavioral Science,* 1979, *15*(1), 23-40.

Nicosia, F., and Wind, Y. (Eds.). *Behavioral Models for Marketing Analysis.* Hinsdale, Ill.: Dryden, 1977.

Niehoff, A. H. "The Process of Innovation." In A. H. Niehoff (Ed.), *Handbook of Social Change*. Chicago: Aldine, 1966.

Niehoff, A. H. *Intra-Group Communication and Induced Change*. HumRRO Professional Paper 35-67. Washington, D.C.: Department of the Army, 1967.

Nielsen, W. R., and Kimberly, J. R. "Designing Assessment Strategies for Organization Development." *Human Resource Management*, 1976, *15*(1), 32-39.

Nielson, J., and Brazzel, J. *Evaluation as an Aid to Decision Making in the Food and Agricultural Sciences*. Joint Planning and Evaluation Staff Paper, No. 80-DD-02, Science and Education Administration. Washington, D.C.: U.S. Department of Agriculture, 1980.

Nimkoff, M. F. "Obstacles to Innovation." In F. R. Allen and others, *Technology and Social Change*. New York: Appleton-Century-Crofts, 1957.

Nisberg, J. N. "The Light at the End of the Tunnel Is a Train Coming in the Opposite Direction." In P. H. Mirvis and D. N. Berg (Eds.), *Failures in Organization Development and Change: Cases and Essays for Learning*. New York: Wiley, 1977.

Nisbet, R. A. *Social Change*. New York: Harper & Row, 1972.

Noll, R. G. *Government Policies and Technological Innovation*. 5 vols. Final Report to National Science Foundation, Grant No. RDA-7307241. Washington, D.C.: National Science Foundation, 1975.

Norman, R. "Organizational Innovations: Product Variation and Reorientation." *Administrative Science Quarterly*, 1971, *16*(2), 203-215.

Norris, E. L., and Larsen, J. K. *Allocating Resources: Priorities in Mental Health Services Delivery*. Palo Alto, Calif.: American Institutes for Research, 1975.

Northwest Regional Educational Laboratory. *Preparation of Educational Training Consultants*. 3 vols. Portland, Oreg.: Northwest Regional Educational Laboratory, 1976.

Northwest Regional Educational Laboratory. *Report of Dissemination Processes Seminar II*. Portland, Oreg.: Northwest Regional Educational Laboratory, 1979.

Null, J. A. "Water Quality Management and Political Institutions." *Policy Studies Journal,* 1976, *4*(3), 260-264.

Nunnally, J. C. "The Communication of Mental Health Information: A Comparison of Experts and the Public with Mass Media Presentations." *Behavioral Scientists,* 1957, *2,* 222-237.

Nunnally, J. C. "Experimental Studies of Communicative Effectiveness." In W. Schramm (Ed.), *Case Studies in the Utilization of Behavioral Science.* Vol. 2: *Studies of Innovation and of Communication to the Public.* Stanford, Calif.: Institute for Communication Research, Stanford University, 1962.

Nunnally, J. C., and Bobren, H. "Variables Governing the Willingness to Receive Communications on Mental Health." *Journal of Personality,* 1959, *27,* 38-46.

O'Connell, J. J. *Managing Organizational Innovation.* Homewood, Ill.: Irwin, 1968.

Office of Planning, Budgeting, and Evaluation. *Evaluation of the National Diffusion Network: Evaluation Study, Executive Summary.* (ED 147 355.) Washington, D.C.: Office of Education, 1977.

Office of Technology Assessment. *The Role of Demonstrations in Federal R&D Policy.* Washington, D.C.: Office of Technology Assessment, 1978.

Ohio State University Research Foundation. *Utilization of the Behavioral Sciences by the U.S. Arms Control and Disarmament Agency.* Vol. 1. Final Report to U.S. Arms and Disarmament Agency, ACDA/E-221. Columbus: Ohio State University Research Foundation, 1975.

Okedijim, F. O. "Overcoming Social and Cultural Resistances." *International Journal of Health Education,* 1972, *15*(3), 3-10.

O'Keefe, R. D., Kernaghan, J. A., and Rubenstein, A. H. "Group Cohesiveness: A Factor in the Adoption of Innovations Among Scientific Work Groups." *Small Group Behavior,* 1975, *6*(3), 282-292.

Olds, V. M. "Freedom Rides: A Social Movement as an Aspect of Social Change." In H. A. Hornstein and others (Eds.), *Social Intervention.* New York: Free Press, 1971.

Olsen, H. A. *The Economics of Information: Bibliography and Commentary on the Literature.* (2nd ed.) (ED 076 214.) Washington, D.C.: ERIC Clearinghouse on Library and Information Sciences, 1972.

O'Reilly, R. R., and Fish, J. C. "Dogmatism and Tenure Status as Determinants of Resistance Toward Educational Innovation." *Journal of Experimental Education,* 1976, *45*(1), 68-70.

Organization for Economic Cooperation and Development. *The Conditions for Success in Technological Innovation.* Paris: Organization for Economic Cooperation and Development, 1971.

Organization for Economic Cooperation and Development. *Proceedings of the Seminar on Technology Assessment, January, 1972.* Paris: Organization for Economic Cooperation and Development, 1972a.

Organization for Economic Cooperation and Development. *Technical Change and Economic Policy.* Washington, D.C.: Organization for Economic Cooperation and Development, 1972b.

Organization for Economic Cooperation and Development. *Case Studies of Educational Administration.* Vol. IV: *Strategies for Innovation in Education.* Paris: Centre for Educational Research and Innovation, Organization for Economic Cooperation and Development, 1973.

Organization for Economic Cooperation and Development. *Choice and Adaptation of Technology in Developing Countries.* Paris: Development Centre, Organization for Economic Cooperation and Development, 1974.

Organization for Economic Cooperation and Development. *Technical Change and Economic Policy.* Paris: Organization for Economic Cooperation and Development, 1980.

Orlans, H. *Contracting for Knowledge: Values and Limitations of Social Science Research.* San Francisco: Jossey-Bass, 1973.

Orlich, D. C., May, F. B., and Harder, R. J. "Change Agents and Instructional Innovation: Report 2." *Elementary School Journal,* 1973, *73*(7), 390-398.

Orr, J. F., and Wolfe, J. L. *Technology Transfer and the Diffusion of Innovation: A Working Bibliography with Annotations.* New York: Vance, 1979.

Osview, L., Temkin, S., and Maguire, L. *Change Capability in the School District.* Philadelphia: Research for Better Schools, 1975.

Otten, G. "Zero-Based Budgeting: Implications for Social Services." In G. Zaltman (Ed.), *Management Principles for Nonprofit Agencies and Organizations.* New York: American Management Associations, 1979.

Owens, R. G. "Conceptual Models for Research and Practice in the Administration of Change." (ED 075 907.) Paper presented at 58th annual meeting of American Educational Research Association, New Orleans, February 1973.

Ozanne, U. B., and Churchill, G. A., Jr. "Five Dimensions of the Industrial Adoption Process." *Journal of Marketing Research,* 1971, *8,* 322-328.

Paine, S. C. "Standardized Intervention Programs: Preliminary Data on Descriptive Characteristics, Methods of Dissemination, and Problems of Implementation." Paper presented at 5th annual convention of Association for Behavior Analysis, Dearborn, Mich., June 1979.

Paisley, M. B., and Paisley, W. J. *Two Papers on Educational Innovation and Dissemination. 1. Educational Innovation: Substance and Process. 2. "Post-Sputnik" Trends in Educational Dissemination Systems.* (ED 088 496.) Stanford, Calif.: Institute for Communication Research, Stanford University, 1973.

Paisley, W. J. *The Flow of (Behavioral) Science Information: A Review of the Research Literature.* Stanford, Calif.: Institute for Communication Research, Stanford University, 1965.

Paisley, W. J. "Information Needs and Uses." In C. A. Cuadra (Ed.), *Annual Review of Information Science and Technology.* Vol. 3. Chicago: Encyclopaedia Britannica, 1968.

Paisley, W. J. "Perspectives on the Utilization of Knowledge." Paper presented at 54th annual meeting of American Educational Research Association, Los Angeles, 1969.

Paisley, W. J., and others. *Developing a Sensing Network for Information Needs in Education.* Stanford, Calif.: Institute for Communication Research, Stanford University, 1972.

Paisley, W. J., and others. "Resources and Services in Support of Educational Linking Agents." In A. Bank and others, *Dis-*

*semination and the Improvement of Practice: Cooperation
and Support in the School Improvement Process.* San Francisco: Far West Laboratory for Educational Research and Development, 1979.

Palonsky, S. B. "Review of Roberts, A. D., *Educational Innovation: Alternatives in Curriculum and Instruction.*" *Educational Leadership,* 1975, *33*(3), 227.

Pareek, U., and Chattopadhyay, S. N. "Adoption Quotient: A Measure of Multipractice Adoption Behavior." *Journal of Applied Behavioral Science,* 1966, *2*(1), 95-108.

Parikh, J. K. "Assessment of Solar Applications for Transfer of Technology: A Case of Solar Pump." *Solar Energy,* 1978, *21*(2), 99-106.

Parish, R. *A Report on Facilitating Educational Change with Local School Districts Through the National Diffusion Network.* (ED 144 559.) Washington, D.C.: U.S. Office of Education, 1976.

Parker, E. B., and Paisley, W. J. "Research for Psychologists at the Interface of the Scientist and His Information System." *American Psychologist,* 1966, *21*, 1060-1071.

Parker, J. E. S. *The Economics of Innovation.* London: Longman, 1974.

Passerman, S. *Scientific and Technological Communication.* New York: Pergamon, 1969.

Patton, M. Q. *Utilization-Focused Evaluation.* Beverly Hills, Calif.: Sage, 1978.

Patton, M. Q. *Qualitative Evaluation Methods.* Beverly Hills, Calif.: Sage, 1980.

Patton, M. Q., and others. "In Search of Impact: An Analysis of the Utilization of Federal Health Evaluation Research." In C. H. Weiss (Ed.), *Using Social Research in Public Policy Making.* Lexington, Mass.: Lexington Books, 1977.

Paul, D. A. *The Concept of Structure for Describing the Diffusion of an Innovation Through Interorganizational Linkages.* (ED 102 706.) Paper presented at 60th annual meeting of American Educational Research Association, Washington, D.C., March-April, 1975.

Paul, D. A. *Change Processes at the Elementary, Secondary, and*

*Post-Secondary Levels of Education.* (ED 141 898.) Columbus, Ohio: University Council for Educational Administration, 1977.

Pavitt, K. "Government Policies Towards Innovation: A Review of Empirical Findings." *Omega,* 1976, *4*(5), 539-558.

Pavitt, K., and Wald, S. *The Conditions for Success in Technological Innovation.* Paris: Organization for Economic Cooperation and Development, 1971.

Pavitt, K., and Walker, W. "Government Policies Towards Industrial Innovation: A Review." *Research Policy,* 1976, *5*(1), 11-97.

Pedersen, P. O. "Innovation Diffusion Within and Between National Urban Systems." *Geographical Analysis,* 1970, *1*(3), 203-254.

Pedersen, P. O. "Innovation Diffusions in Urban Systems." In T. Hagerstrand and A. R. Kuklinski (Eds.), *Information Systems for Regional Development—A Seminar.* Lund Studies in Geography, Series B, No. 37. Lund, Sweden: Royal University of Lund, 1971.

Peirce, W. S. "Review of Rosenbloom, R. S., and Wolek, F. W., *Technology and Information Transfer: Survey of Practice in Industrial Organizations.*" *Technology and Culture,* 1972, *13* (3), 519-520.

Pelc, K. I. "Managerial Problems of University-Industry Interaction." *R&D Management,* 1978, *8*(special issue), 115-118.

Pellegrin, R. J. "The Place of Research in Planned Change." In R. O. Carlson and others, *Change Processes in the Public Schools.* Eugene: Center for the Advanced Study of Educational Administration, University of Oregon, 1965.

Pellegrin, R. J. "Administrative Assumptions Underlying Major Innovation." In W. W. Charters, Jr. (Ed.), *The Process of Planned Change in the School's Instructional Organization.* Eugene: Center for the Advanced Study of Educational Administration, University of Oregon, 1973.

Pellegrin, R. J. "Problems and Assumptions in the Implementation of Innovations." *Journal of Research and Development in Education,* 1975, *9*(1), 92-101.

Pellegrin, R. J. "Sociology and Policy-Oriented Research on Innovation." In M. Radnor, I. Feller, and E. Rogers (Eds.), *The Diffusion of Innovations: An Assessment.* Evanston, Ill.: Center for the Interdisciplinary Study of Science and Technology, Northwestern University, 1978.

Pelz, D. C. "Conditions for Innovation." In W. A. Hill and D. Egan (Eds.), *Organization Theory: A Behavioral Approach.* Boston: Allyn & Bacon, 1966.

Pelz, D. C. *Utilization of Knowledge on Management of R&D Units: A State of the Art Review.* Ann Arbor: Center for Research on Utilization of Scientific Knowledge, Institute of Social Research, University of Michigan, 1977.

Pelz, D. C. "Some Expanded Perspectives on the Use of Social Science in Public Policy." In J. M. Yinger and S. J. Cutler (Eds.), *Major Social Issues: A Multidisciplinary View.* New York: Free Press, 1978.

Pelz, D. C. "Use of Information in Local Government Innovation: Some Preliminary Aspects." Paper presented at meeting of Operations Research Society of America and the Institute of Management Science, Colorado Springs, November 1980.

Pelz, D. C., and Andrews, F. M. *Scientists in Organizations: Productive Climates for Research and Development.* (Rev. ed.) New York: Wiley, 1976.

Pelz, D. C., and Munson, F. C. *A Framework for Organizational Innovating.* Ann Arbor: School of Public Health and Institute for Social Research, University of Michigan, 1980.

Pelz, D. C., Munson, F. C., and Jenstrom, L. L. "Dimensions of Innovation." *Journal of Technology Transfer,* 1978, *3*(1), 35-49.

Pennings, J. M. "The Relevance of the Structural-Contingency Model for Organizational Effectiveness." *Administrative Science Quarterly,* 1975, *20*, 393-410.

Perceptronics. *Construction of a Prototype Model of Technology Utilization Oriented Toward the U.S. Army Training Environment.* Woodland Hills, Calif.: Perceptronics, 1979.

Perry, A., and others. "The Adoption Process: S Curve or J Curve." *Rural Sociology,* 1967, *32*, 220-222.

Perry, J. L., and Kraemer, K. L. *Diffusion and Adoption of*

*Computer Applications Software in Local Governments.* Irvine: Public Policy Research Organization, University of California, 1978.

Perry, R. W., and Gillespie, D. F. "Sociology and the Implementation of Microsocial Change: The Effects of Social Reinforcements." *International Behavioural Scientist,* 1975, 7(2), 1-36.

Pettigrew, A. "Towards a Political Theory of Organizational Intervention." *Human Relations,* 1975, 28(3), 191-208.

Piele, P. K. *Review and Analysis of the Role, Activities, and Training of Educational Linking Agents.* (ED 128 871.) Eugene: ERIC Clearinghouse on Educational Management, University of Oregon, 1975.

Pigg, K. "A Statement on the State-of-the-Art: Methodologies for Studying Environmental Perceptions, Attitudes, Values, Beliefs, and the Utilization of Such Studies." *Cornell Journal of Social Relations,* 1975, 10(1), 7-61.

Pincus, J. "Incentives for Innovation in the Public Schools." *Review of Educational Research,* 1974, 44(1), 133-144.

Pincus, J. (Ed.). *Educational Evaluation in the Public Policy Setting.* Santa Monica, Calif.: Rand Corporation, 1980.

Pino, R., and Emory, R. *The Consultation and Training Process and Procedures Utilized by Linker Training Services.* Portland, Oreg.: Northwest Regional Educational Laboratory, 1977.

Placek, P. J. "Welfare Workers as Family-Planning Change Agents and Perennial Problem of Heterophily with Welfare Clients." *Journal of Applied Behavioral Science,* 1975, 11(3), 299-316.

Polivka, L., and Steg, E. "Program Evaluation and Policy Development: Bridging the Gap." *Evaluation Quarterly,* 1978, 2, 696-707.

Pontecorvo, G., and Wilkinson, M. "An Economic Analysis of the International Transfer of Marine Technology." *Ocean Development and International Law Journal,* 1974, 2(3), 255-283.

Popper, K. *The Open Society and Its Enemies.* Vol. 1. London: Routledge & Kegan Paul, 1945.

Porat, M. U. *The Information Economy: Definition and Mea-*

*surement.* (ED 142 205.) Washington, D.C.: National Science Foundation, 1977.

Porras, J. I. "The Comparative Impact of Different OD Techniques and Intervention Intensities." *Journal of Applied Behavioral Science,* 1979, *15*(2), 156-178.

Porras, J. I., and Berg, P. O. "The Impact of Organization Development." *Academy of Management Review,* 1978, *3*(2), 249-266.

Porras, J. I., and Patterson, K. "Assessing Planned Change." *Group & Organization Studies,* 1979, *4*(1), 39-58.

Posavac, E. J., and Carey, R. G. *Program Evaluation: Methods and Case Studies.* New York: Prentice-Hall, 1980.

Poser, E. G., Dunn, I., and Smith, R. M. "Resolving Conflicts Between Clinical and Research Teams." *Mental Health Hospitals,* 1964, *15*(5), 278-282.

Powell, G., and Posner, B. "Managing Change: Attitudes, Targets, Problems, and Strategies." *Group & Organization Studies,* 1980, *5*(3), 310-323.

Prakash, P. "Cost-Benefit Approach to Capital Expenditure." In G. Zaltman (Ed.), *Management Principles for Nonprofit Agencies and Organizations.* New York: American Management Associations, 1979.

Price, D. de S. "Society's Needs in Scientific and Technical Information." *Annals of the New York Academy of Sciences,* 1975, *261,* 126-136.

Price, J. L. "Use of New Knowledge in Organizations." *Human Organization,* 1964, *23*(3), 224-234.

Price, W. J., and Bass, L. W. "Scientific Research and the Innovation Process." *Science,* 1969, *164,* 802-806.

Pruger, R., and Specht, H. "Assessing Theoretical Models of Community Organization Practice: Alinsky as a Case in Point." *Social Service Review,* 1969, *45,* 123-135.

Public Affairs Counseling. *Factors Involved in the Transfer of Innovations: A Summary and Organization of the Literature.* Washington, D.C.: U.S. Department of Housing and Urban Development, 1976.

Quest, R. H. *Organizational Change: The Effect of Successful Leadership.* Homewood, Ill.: Dorsey, 1962.

Quinn, J. B. "National Policies for Science and Technology: New Approaches for New Public Needs." *Research Management*, 1977, *20*(6), 11-18.

Quintelier, G. L. M. "A Technique for Problem Finding and Market Introduction." *Research Management*, 1978, *21*(5), 26-28.

Quintero-Alfaro, G. "Educational Innovation and Change in Societies with Less Advanced Technology." *Journal of Research and Development in Education*, 1972, *5*(3), 47-63.

Radnor, M., Ettlie, J., and Dutton, J. "The R&D Management Literature and Innovation Diffusion Research." In M. Radnor, I. Feller, and E. Rogers (Eds.), *The Diffusion of Innovations: An Assessment.* Evanston, Ill.: Center for the Interdisciplinary Study of Science and Technology, Northwestern University, 1978.

Radnor, M., Feller, I., and Rogers, E. (Eds.). *The Diffusion of Innovations: An Assessment.* Evanston, Ill.: Center for the Interdisciplinary Study of Science and Technology, Northwestern University, 1978a.

Radnor, M., Feller, I., and Rogers, E. "Research on the Diffusion of Innovations by Organizations: A Reappraisal." In M. Radnor, I. Feller, and E. Rogers (Eds.), *The Diffusion of Innovations: An Assessment.* Evanston, Ill.: Center for the Interdisciplinary Study of Science and Technology, Northwestern University, 1978b.

Radnor, M., Hofler, D., and Rich, R. (Eds.). *Information Dissemination and Exchange for Educational Innovation.* Evanston, Ill.: Northwestern University, 1977.

Radnor, M., Rubenstein, A. H., and Tansik, D. A. "Implementation in Operations Research and R&D in Government and Business Organizations." *Operations Research*, 1970, *18*, 967-991.

Radnor, M., Spivak, H., and Hofler, D. *Research, Development and Innovation: Contextual Analysis, Part One.* Washington, D.C.: National Institute of Education, 1977.

Ragab, A. M., Moriarty, R. J., and Guilmette, A. M. "Change Agent Research and Organizational Change." *Group & Organization Studies*, 1977, *2*(2), 216-227.

Ragano, F. P. "U.S. Roland: A Milestone in Technology Transfer." *Defense Management Journal,* 1978, *14,* 3-10.

Raizen, S. A. "The Impact of Federal Dissemination Policy." (ED 148 364.) Paper presented at 62nd annual meeting of American Educational Research Association, New York City, April 1977.

Raizen, S. A. "Dissemination Programs at the National Institute of Education: 1974 to 1979." *Knowledge,* 1979, *1*(2), 259-292.

Raizen, S., and Rossi, P. H. *Program Evaluation in Education: When? How? To What Ends?* Washington, D.C.: National Academy of Sciences, 1981.

Ramer, B. "The Relationship of Belief Systems and Personal Characteristics of Chief School Administrators and Attitudes Toward Educational Innovation." Doctoral dissertation, State University of New York, Buffalo, 1967.

Ramo, S. *America's Technology Slip.* New York: Wiley, 1980a.

Ramo, S. *The Management of Innovative Technology.* New York: Wiley, 1980b.

Rapoport, R. N. "Three Dilemmas in Action Research." *Human Relations,* 1970, *23*(6), 499-513.

Rappaport, J., Chinsky, J. M., and Cowen, E. *Innovations in Helping Chronic Patients: College Students in a Mental Institution.* New York: Academic Press, 1971.

Real Estate Research Corporation. *Factors Involved in the Transfer of Innovations: A Summary and Organization of the Literature.* (NTIS SHR-0001549.) Chicago, Ill.: Real Estate Research Corporation, 1976.

Reddin, W. J. "How to Change Things." *Executive,* June 1969, pp. 22-26.

Reddin, W. J. "Confessions of an Organizational Change Agent." *Group & Organization Studies,* 1977, *2*(1), 33-41.

Rees, A. M. "Medical Libraries and the Assessment of User Needs." *Bulletin of the Medical Library Association,* 1966, *54*(2), 99-103.

Rees, A. M., and Schultz, D. G. *A Field Experimental Approach to the Study of Relevance Assessments in Relation to Document Searching.* Cleveland, Ohio: Center for Documentation and Communication Research, Case Western Reserve University, 1967.

Rehder, R. R. "Communication and Opinion Formation in a Medical Community: The Significance of the Detail Man." *Academy of Management Journal,* 1965, *8,* 282-291.

Reiff, R. "Mental Health Manpower and Institutional Change." *American Psychologist,* 1966, *21,* 540-548.

Rein, M. "Organization for Social Change." *Social Work,* 1964, *9*(2), 32-39.

Rein, M. *Social Science and Public Policy.* New York: Penguin, 1976.

Rein, M., and Miller, S. M. "Social Action on the Installment Plan." *Trans-action,* 1966, *3*(2), 31-38.

Rein, M., and Schön, D. A. "Problem-Setting in Policy Research." In C. H. Weiss (Ed.), *Using Social Research in Public Policy Making.* Lexington, Mass.: Lexington Books, 1977.

Rein, M., and White, S. W. "Can Research Help Policy?" *The Public Interest,* 1977, *49,* 119-136.

Reitman, W. R. "Information-Processing Models in Psychology." *Science,* 1964, *144*(3623), 1192-1198.

Renehan, L. A. "The Innovation and Implementation of LASH." *Journal of Technology Transfer,* 1978, *3*(1), 71-88.

Research Triangle Institute. *RANN Utilization Experience.* (NTIS PB-247 243.) Final Report to National Science Foundation. Research Triangle Park, N.C.: Research Triangle Institute, 1975.

Resnick, H. "Effecting Internal Change in Human Service Organizations." *Social Casework,* 1977, *58*(9), 546-553.

Reston, J. *The Artillery of the Press.* New York: Harper & Row, 1966.

Rettig, R. A., Sorg, J. S., and Milwood, H. B. *Criteria for the Allocation of Resources to Research and Development: A Review of the Literature.* Columbus: School of Public Administration, Ohio State University, 1974.

Rhine, W. R. (Ed.). *Making Schools More Effective: New Directions from Follow Through.* New York: Academic Press, 1981.

Rice, A. K. "Productivity and Social Organization in an Indian Weaving Shed: An Examination of Some Aspects of the Socio-Technical System of an Experimental Automatic Loom Shed." In H. A. Hornstein and others (Eds.), *Social Intervention: A Behavioral Science Approach.* New York: Free Press, 1971.

Rice, R. E., and Rogers, E. "Reinvention in the Innovation Process." *Knowledge,* 1980, *1*(4), 499-514.

Rich, R. F. "Selective Utilization of Social Science Related Information by Federal Policy Makers." *Inquiry,* 1975, *13*(3), 239-245.

Rich, R. F. "Uses of Social Science Information by Federal Bureaucrats: Knowledge for Action Versus Knowledge for Understanding." In C. H. Weiss (Ed.), *Using Social Research in Public Policy Making.* Lexington, Mass.: Lexington Books, 1977.

Rich, R. F. "Innovation/Diffusion Research, Public Policy and Innovations." In M. Radnor, I. Feller, and E. Rogers (Eds.), *The Diffusion of Innovations: An Assessment.* Evanston, Ill.: Center for the Interdisciplinary Study of Science and Technology, Northwestern University, 1978.

Rich, R. F. "Editor's Introduction." *American Behavioral Scientist,* 1979a, *22*(3), 327-337.

Rich, R. F. *The Power of Social Science Information and Public Policy Making: The Interaction Between Bureaucratic Politics and the Use of Survey Data.* San Francisco: Jossey-Bass, 1979b.

Rich, R. F. "Problem Solving and Evaluation Research: Unemployment Insurance Policy." In R. F. Rich (Ed.), *Translating Evaluation into Policy.* Beverly Hills, Calif.: Sage, 1979c.

Rich, R. F. "The Pursuit of Knowledge." *Knowledge,* 1979d, *1*(1), 6-30.

Rich, R. F. "Systems of Analysis, Technology Assessment, and Bureaucratic Power." *American Behavioral Scientist,* 1979e, *22*(3), 393-416.

Rich, R. F. "Knowledge Utilization, Diffusion of Innovations, Public Policy, and Science Policy Making at the National Level." In J. A. Agnew (Ed.), *Innovation Research and Public Policy.* Syracuse Geographical Series #5. Syracuse, N.Y.: Syracuse University, 1980a.

Rich, R. F. "Network Consultants Create Strategies for Planned Change in Victims Services." *Evaluation and Change,* 1980b (special issue), 144.

Rich, R. F. *Social Science Information and Public Policy Making: The Interaction Between Bureaucratic Politics and the Use of Survey Data.* San Francisco: Jossey-Bass, 1981.

Rich, R. F., and Barton, E. "Research Utilization: Attitudes, Expectations, and Action of NSF/RANN Program Managers and Upper Management." Unpublished report prepared for the NSF/RANN Task Force on Research Utilization. Ann Arbor: Institute for Social Research, University of Michigan, 1976.

Rich, R. F., and Zaltman, G. "Toward a Theory of Planned Social Change: Alternate Perspectives and Ideas." *Evaluation and Change,* 1978 (special issue), 41-47.

Rich, W. *Smaller Families Through Social and Economic Progress.* Washington, D.C.: Overseas Development Council, 1973.

Richland, M. *Traveling Seminar and Conference for the Implementation of Educational Innovations.* Technical Memorandum Series 2691. Santa Monica, Calif.: System Development Corporation, 1965.

Richter, I. "Educational Innovation and Constitution." *Education and Urban Society,* 1973, *6*(1), 5-21.

Riecken, H. W., and Boruch, R. F. (Eds.). *Social Experimentation: A Method for Planning and Evaluating Social Intervention.* New York: Academic Press, 1974.

Riedel, J. "Citizen Participation: Myths and Realities." *Public Administration Review,* 1972, *32*(3), 211-220.

Rieker, P. P. "Disseminating and Using Evaluation Research." In A. Pattakos (Ed.), *Human Resource Administration.* Washington, D.C.: American Society for Public Administration, 1977.

Rieker, P. P. "Evaluation Research: The Design-to-Use Process." *Knowledge,* 1980, *2*(2), 215-235.

Riley, P., Hooker, S., and Masar, N. "Introducing RUS: A Link Between Research and Service." *Rehabilitation Record,* 1968, *9,* 22-24.

Rittenhouse, C. H. *Innovation Problems and Information Needs of Educational Practitioners.* Final Report to U.S. Office of Education, Contract No. OEC 09-099009-4590. Menlo Park, Calif.: Stanford Research Institute, 1970.

Rivlin, A. *Systematic Thinking for Social Action.* Washington, D.C.: Brookings Institution, 1971.

Rivlin, A., and Timpane, M. *Planned Variations: Should We Give Up or Try Harder?* Washington, D.C.: Brookings Institution, 1975.

Robbins, M. D., Burke, C. A., and Milliken, J. G. *Federal Incentives for Innovation. Part II: The Innovation Process in the Private and Public Sectors.* Denver, Colo.: University of Denver Research Institute, 1973.

Robbins, M. D., and Milliken, J. G. "Technology Transfer and the Process of Technological Innovation: New Concepts, New Models." *R&D Management,* 1976, *6,* 165-170.

Roberto, E. L. *Strategic Decision Making in a Social Program: The Case of Family Planning Diffusion.* Lexington, Mass.: Lexington Books, 1975.

Roberts, A. O. H., and Larsen, J. K. *Effective Use of Mental Health Research Information.* Final Report to National Institute of Mental Health, Grant No. 1R01 MH15445. Palo Alto, Calif.: American Institutes for Research, 1971.

Roberts, E. B., and Frohman, A. L. "Strategies for Improving Research Utilization." *Technology Review,* 1978, *80*(5), 32-39.

Robertson, A. B., Achilladelis, B., and Jervis, P. *Success and Failure in Industrial Innovation: Report on Project SAPPHO.* London: Centre for the Study of Industrial Innovation, 1972.

Robertson, T. S. *Innovation Behavior and Communication.* New York: Holt, Rinehart and Winston, 1971.

Robinault, I. P., and Weisinger, M. "Brief History of ICD Research Utilization Laboratory." *Rehabilitation Counseling Bulletin,* 1975, *19*(2), 426-432.

Robinson, A. C., and Madigan, J. A. *Options for Organization and Operation of Space Applications Transfer Centers.* (NTIS N77-24979.) Columbus, Ohio: Battelle Columbus Laboratory, 1976.

Robinson, R., DeMarche, D. F., and Wagle, M. K. "Community Resources in Mental Health." New York: Basic Books, 1960.

Rodman, H., and Kolodny, R. "Organizational Strains in the Researcher-Practitioner Relationship." In A. W. Gouldner and S. M. Miller (Eds.), *Applied Sociology: Opportunities and Problems.* New York: Free Press, 1965.

Roessler, R. T. "Impact of Social Programs: Issues in Implementing Research." *Knowledge,* 1980, *1*(4), 579-590.

Roessner, J. D. "Innovation in Public Organizations." Paper presented at the National Conference on Public Administration, Syracuse, N.Y., 1974.

Roessner, J. D. *Federal Technology Transfer: An Analysis of Current Program Characteristics and Practices.* (NTIS PB-253-104.) Washington, D.C.: National Science Foundation, 1975.

Roessner, J. D. "Federal Technology Policy: Innovation and Problem Solving in State and Local Governments." *Policy Analysis,* 1979, *5,* 181-200.

Roessner, J. D. "Technological Diffusion Research and National Policy Issues." *Knowledge,* 1980, *2*(2), 179-201.

Roffe, P. "International Code of Conduct on Transfer of Technology." *Journal of World Trade Law,* 1977, *11*(2), 186-191.

Roffe, P. "UNCTAD: Code of Conduct on Transfer of Technology, Progress Review." *Journal of World Trade Law,* 1978, *12*(4), 351-361.

Rogers, C. R. "The Characteristics of a Helping Relationship." In W. G. Bennis, K. D. Benne, and R. Chin (Eds.), *The Planning of Change.* (2nd ed.) New York: Holt, Rinehart and Winston, 1969.

Rogers, E. M. *Diffusion of Innovations.* New York: Free Press, 1962a.

Rogers, E. M. "How Research Can Improve Practice: A Case Study." *Theory into Practice,* 1962b, *1*(2), 89-93.

Rogers, E. M. "What Are Innovators Like?" In R. O. Carlson and others, *Change Processes in the Public Schools.* Eugene: Center for the Advanced Study of Educational Administration, University of Oregon, 1965.

Rogers, E. M. "Communication of Vocational Rehabilitation Innovations." *Communication, Dissemination and Utilization of Rehabilitation Research Information.* Washington, D.C.: Joint Liaison Committee of the Council of State Administrators of Vocational Rehabilitation and the Rehabilitation Counselor Educators, U.S. Department of Health, Education, and Welfare, 1967.

Rogers, E. M. "The Communication of Innovations in a Complex Institution." *Educational Record,* 1968, *48,* 49.

Rogers, E. M. "Research Utilization in Rehabilitation." In W. S. Neff (Ed.), *Rehabilitation Psychology.* Washington, D.C.: American Psychological Association, 1971.

Rogers, E. M. *Communication Strategies for Family Planning.* New York: Free Press, 1973a.

Rogers, E. M. "Effects of Incentives on the Diffusion of Innovations: The Case of Family Planning in Asia." In G. Zaltman (Ed.), *Processes and Phenomena of Social Change*. New York: Wiley, 1973b.

Rogers, E. M. "Social Structure and Social Change." In G. Zaltman (Ed.), *Processes and Phenomena of Social Change*. New York: Wiley, 1973c.

Rogers, E. M. (Ed.). *Communication and Development: Critical Perspectives*. Beverly Hills, Calif.: Sage, 1976a.

Rogers, E. M. "New Product Adoption and Diffusion." *Journal of Consumer Research*, 1976b, *2*, 290-301.

Rogers, E. M. "Re-Invention During the Innovation Process." In M. Radnor, I. Feller, and E. Rogers (Eds.), *The Diffusion of Innovations: An Assessment*. Evanston, Ill.: Center for the Interdisciplinary Study of Science and Technology, Northwestern University, 1978.

Rogers, E. M., and Agarwala-Rogers, R. *Communication in Organizations*. New York: Free Press, 1976.

Rogers, E. M., Agarwala-Rogers, R., and Chin, C. L. *Diffusion of Impact Innovations to University Professors*. (ED 116 707.) Ann Arbor: Department of Journalism, University of Michigan, 1975.

Rogers, E. M., and Burdge, R. L. *Social Change in Rural Society*. (2nd ed.) Englewood Cliffs, N.J.: Prentice-Hall, 1972.

Rogers, E. M., Eveland, J. D., and Klepper, C. *The Innovation Process in Public Organizations: Some Elements of a Preliminary Model*. Final Report to National Science Foundation, Grant RDA75-17952. Ann Arbor: Department of Journalism, University of Michigan, 1977.

Rogers, E. M., and Shoemaker, F. F. *Communication of Innovations: A Cross-Cultural Approach*. New York: Free Press, 1971.

Rogers, E. M., and Svenning, L. *Managing Change*. Washington, D.C.: U.S. Office of Education, 1969.

Rogers, E. M., Williams, L., and West, H. B. *Bibliography of the Diffusion of Innovations*. Monticello, Ill.: Council of Planning Librarians, 1977.

Rogers, E. M., and others. *National Seminar on the Diffusion of New Instructional Materials and Practices: Perspectives on*

*Diffusion.* (ED 083 111.) Boulder, Colo.: Social Science Education Consortium, Inc., 1973.

Rogers, E. M., and others. *The Innovation Process in Public Organizations.* Ann Arbor: Department of Journalism, University of Michigan, 1977.

Romeo, A. A. "Interindustry and Interfirm Differences in the Rate of Diffusion of an Innovation." *Review of Economics and Statistics,* 1975, *57,* 311-319.

Rose, M., and Esser, M. A. "The Impact of Recent Research Developments on Private Practice." *American Journal of Psychiatry,* 1960, *117,* 429-433.

Rose, R. "The Market for Policy Indicators." In A. Shonfield and S. Shaw (Eds.), *Social Indicators and Social Policy.* London: Heinemann, 1972.

Rosen, P. L. "Social Science and Judicial Policy Making." In C. Weiss (Ed.), *Using Social Research in Public Policy Making.* Lexington, Mass.: Lexington Books, 1977.

Rosenau, F., Hutchins, L., and Hemphill, J. *Utilization of NIE Output.* Berkeley, Calif.: Far West Laboratory for Educational Research and Development, 1971.

Rosenberg, N. "The Direction of Technological Change: Inducement Mechanisms and Focusing Devices." *Economic Development and Cultural Change,* 1969, *18,* 1-24.

Rosenberg, N. "Economic Development and the Transfer of Technology: Some Historical Perspectives." *Technology and Culture,* 1970, *11,* 550-575.

Rosenberg, N. "Factors Affecting the Diffusion of Technology." *Explorations in Economic History,* 1972, *10*(1), 3-33.

Rosenberg, N. "The Diffusion of Technology: An Economic Historian's View." In M. Radnor, I. Feller, and E. Rogers (Eds.), *The Diffusion of Innovations: An Assessment.* Evanston, Ill.: Center for the Interdisciplinary Study of Science and Technology, Northwestern University, 1978.

Rosenblatt, A. "The Practitioner's Use and Evaluation of Research." *Social Work,* 1968, *13,* 53-59.

Rosenbloom, R. S., and Wolek, F. W. *Studies of the Flow of Technical Information: An Interim Report.* Cambridge, Mass.: Graduate School of Business Administration, Harvard University, 1966.

Rosenbloom, R. S., and Wolek, F. W. *Technology and Information Transfer: A Survey of Practice in Industrial Organizations.* Boston: Graduate School of Business Administration, Harvard University, 1970.

Rosenblum, S., and Louis, K. S. *Stability and Change: Innovation in an Educational Context.* Cambridge, Mass.: Abt Associates, Inc., 1979.

Rosenfeld, E. "Social Research and Social Action in Prevention of Juvenile Delinquency." *Social Problems,* 1956, *4,* 138-148.

Rosenfeld, J. M., and Orlinsky, N. "The Effects of Research on Practice: Research and Decrease in Noncontinuance." *Archives of General Psychiatry,* 1961, *5,* 176-182.

Rosentraub, M. S., and Warren, R. "Information Utilization and Self-Evaluating Capacities for Coastal Zone Management Agencies." *Coast Zone Journal,* 1976, *2*(3), 193-222.

Rosner, M. M. "Administrative Controls and Innovation." *Behavioral Science,* 1968, *13*(1), 36-43.

Ross, D. A., and Smith, L. J. "Training and Technical Assistance in Marine Science—A Viable Transfer Product." *Ocean Development and International Law Journal,* 1974, *2*(3), 217-218.

Ross, D. H. *Administration for Adaptability.* New York: Metropolitan School Study Council, Teachers College, Columbia University, 1958.

Ross, P. D., and Halbower, C. C. *A Model for Innovation Adoption in Public School Districts.* Boston: Little, Brown, 1968.

Ross, P. F. "Innovation Adoption by Organizations." *Personnel Psychology,* 1974, *27*(1), 21-47.

Rossi, P. H. "Practice, Method, and Theory in Evaluating Social-Action Programs." In J. L. Sundquist (Ed.), *On Fighting Poverty: Perspectives from Experience.* New York: Basic Books, 1969.

Rossi, P. H. "Observations of the Organization of Social Research." In P. H. Rossi and W. Williams (Eds.), *Evaluating Social Programs.* New York: Seminar Press, 1972a.

Rossi, P. H. "Testing for Success and Failure in Social Action." In P. H. Rossi and W. Williams (Eds.), *Evaluating Social Progress.* New York: Seminar Press, 1972b.

Rossi, P. H. "Issues in the Evaluation of Human Services Delivery." *Evaluation Quarterly,* 1978, *2*(4), 573-599.

Rossi, P. H., Freeman, H. E., and Wright, S. R. *Evaluation: A Systematic Approach.* Beverly Hills, Calif.: Sage, 1979.

Rossi, P. H., and Williams, W. (Eds.). *Evaluating Social Programs.* New York: Seminar Press, 1972.

Rossini, F., and Bozeman, B. "National Strategies for Technological Innovation." *Administration and Society,* 1977, *9,* 81-110.

Rossiter, D. L. "Patterns of Change Agent Effectiveness." Doctoral dissertation, University of Colorado, 1976. *Dissertation Abstracts International,* 1976, *37,* 3690B. (University Microfilms No. 77-11,328.)

Rossman, B. B., Hober, D., and Ciarlo, J. A. "Awareness, Use, and Consequences of Evaluation Data in a Community Mental Health Center." *Community Mental Health Journal,* 1979, *15*(1), 7-16.

Rothman, J. *Planning and Organizing for Social Change: Action Principles from Social Science Research.* New York: Columbia University Press, 1974.

Rothman, J. "Gaps and Linkages in Research Utilization: Enhancing Utilization Through a Research and Development Approach." In A. Rubin and A. Rosenblatt (Eds.), *Sourcebook on Research Utilization.* New York: Council on Social Work Education, 1977.

Rothman, J. "Conversion and Design in the Research Utilization Process." *Journal of Social Science Research,* 1978a, *2* (1), 117-131.

Rothman, J. "Harnessing Research to Enhance Practice: A Research and Development Model." Paper presented at the National Conference on the Future of Social Work Research, San Antonio, Texas, October 1978b.

Rothman, J. *Getting Evaluation Research Used: Factors Conducive to the Use of Social Research in Organizations.* Ann Arbor: Center for Research on the Utilization of Scientific Knowledge, Institute for Social Research, University of Michigan, 1979a.

Rothman, J. "Three Models of Community Organization Practice, Their Mixing and Phasing." In F. Cox and others (Eds.), *Strategies of Community Organization.* (3rd ed.) Itasca, Ill.: Peacock, 1979b.

Rothman, J. "Harnessing Research to Enhance Practice: A Research and Development Model." In D. Fanshel (Ed.), *Future of Social Work Research*. New York: National Association of Social Workers, Inc., 1980a.

Rothman, J. *Using Research in Organizations: A Guide to Successful Application*. Beverly Hills, Calif.: Sage, 1980b.

Rothman, J., Erlich, J. L., and Teresa, J. G. *Promoting Innovation and Change in Organizations and Communities: A Planning Manual*. New York: Wiley, 1976.

Rothwell, R. "The Hungarian SAPPHO: Some Comments and Comparisons." *Research Policy*, 1974, *3*, 30-38.

Rothwell, R. "From Invention to New Business Via the New Venture Approach." *Management Decision*, 1975, *13*(1), 10-21.

Rothwell, R. "Innovation in UK Textile Machinery Industry: The Results of a Postal Questionnaire Survey." *R&D Management*, 1976, *6*(3), 131-138.

Rothwell, R. "The Characteristics of Successful Innovators and Technically Progressive Firms (with Some Comments on Innovation Research)." *R&D Management*, 1977, *7*(3), 191-206.

Rothwell, R., and Robertson, A. B. "The Role of Communications in Technological Innovation." *Research Policy*, 1973, *2*(3), 204.

Rothwell, R., and others. "SAPPHO Updated: Project SAPPHO Phase II." *Research Policy*, 1974, *3*(4), 258-291.

Rothwell, R., and others. "Some Methodological Aspects of Innovation Research." *Omega*, 1977, *5*(4), 415-424.

Rousseau, D. M. "Technological Differences in Job Characteristics, Employee Satisfaction, and Motivation: A Synthesis of Job Design Research and Sociotechnical Systems Theory." *Organizational Behavior and Human Performance*, 1977, *19*(1), 18-42.

Rousseau, D. M. "Assessment of Technology in Organizations: Closed Versus Open Systems Approach." *Academy of Management Review*, 1979, *4*, 531-542.

Rowe, A. P. "From Scientific Idea to Practical Use." *Minerva*, 1964, *2*, 301-320.

Rowe, L. A., and Boise, W. B. (Eds.). *Organizational and Managerial Innovation: A Reader.* Pacific Palisades, Calif.: Goodyear, 1973.

Rowe, L. A., and Boise, W. B. "Organizational Innovation: Current Research and Evolving Concepts." *Public Administration Review,* 1974, *34*(3), 284-392.

Rubenstein, A. H. *Critical Field Experiments on Uses of Scientific and Technical Information.* (ED 143 302.) Evanston, Ill.: Department of Industrial Engineering, Northwestern University, 1975.

Rubenstein, A. H. "Designing Organizations for Integrating Technology Exchange Transactions (TETS) in Developing Countries." (ED 143 301.) Paper prepared for the Caribbean Seminar on Science and Technology Planning (2nd), Port of Spain, Trinidad, January 1976.

Rubenstein, A. H., Chakrabarti, A. K., and O'Keefe, R. D. *Final Technical Report on Field Studies on Technological Innovation Process.* Report prepared for the Office of National R&D Assessment, National Science Foundation. Washington, D.C.: National Science Foundation, 1975.

Rubenstein, A. H., and Douds, C. F. "A Program of Research on Coupling Relations in Research and Development." *IEEE Transactions on Engineering Management,* 1969, *16,* 137-143.

Rubenstein, A. H., and Ettlie, J. *Barriers to Adoption of Innovations from Suppliers to the Automotive Industry.* Evanston, Ill.: Northwestern University, 1977.

Rubin, A., and Rosenblatt, A. (Eds.). *Sourcebook on Research Utilization.* New York: Council on Social Work Education, 1977.

Rubin, I., Plovnick, M., and Fry, R. "Initiating Planned Change in Health Care Systems." *Journal of Applied Behavioral Science,* 1974, *10*(1), 107-124.

Rubin, L. J. "Installing an Innovation." In R. R. Goulet (Ed.), *Educational Change: The Reality and the Promise.* New York: Citation Press, 1968.

Ruby, B. *Design for Innovation: A Cybernetic Approach.* Copenhagen: Institute for Futures Studies, 1974.

Rule, J. B. *Insight and Social Betterment: A Preface to Applied Social Science.* New York: Oxford University Press, 1978.

Rusnack, B. "Planned Change: Interdisciplinary Education for Health Care." *Journal of Education for Social Work,* 1977, *13*(1), 194-111.

Russell, L. B. *Technology in Hospitals: Medical Advances and Their Diffusion.* Washington, D.C.: Brookings Institution, 1979.

Russell, L. B., and Burke, C. S. *Technological Diffusion in the Hospital Sector.* Final Report to the National Science Foundation, Grant No. RDA75-14274. Washington, D.C.: National Science Foundation, 1975.

Rutman, L. *Planning Useful Evaluations: Evaluability Assessment.* Beverly Hills, Calif.: Sage, 1980.

Ruttan, V. W., and Hayami, Y. "Technology Transfer and Agricultural Development." *Technology and Culture,* 1973, *14* (2), 119-151.

Rutter, M., and others. *Fifteen Thousand Hours.* Cambridge, Mass.: Harvard University Press, 1979.

Ryan, B., and Gross, N. C. "The Diffusion of Hybrid Seed Corn in Two Iowa Communities." *Rural Sociology,* 1943, *8,* 15-24.

Sackman, H. *Delphi Critique: Expert Opinion, Forecasting, and Group Process.* Lexington, Mass.: Lexington Books, 1975.

Sadler, R. R., and McDevitt, C. G. *Proceedings of the Utilization Planning Conference, November 1978.* Fisherville, Va.: Research Utilization Laboratory, Woodrow Wilson Rehabilitation Center, 1979.

Sahal, D. (Ed.). *The Transfer and Utilization of Technical Knowledge.* Lexington, Mass.: Lexington Books, 1981.

Saks, M. J., and Baron, C. H. (Eds.). *The Use/Nonuse/Misuse of Applied Social Research in the Courts: Conference Proceedings.* Cambridge, Mass.: Abt Associates, Inc., 1980.

Salasin, J. (Ed.). *The Management of Federal Research and Development: An Analysis of Major Issues and Processes.* McLean, Va.: MITRE Corporation, 1977.

Salasin, J. (Ed.). *The Management of Federal Research Programs: Managers' Perceptions of Problems That May Impede the Process of Innovation.* Report prepared at the request of Joint Economic Committee, U.S. Congress. McLean, Va.: MITRE Corporation, 1978.

Salasin, J., Hattery, L., and Ramsay, T. *The Evaluation of Federal Research Programs.* McLean, Va.: MITRE Corporation, 1980.

Salasin, S. E. "Linking Knowledge to Social Policymaking: An Interview with Amitai Etzioni." *Evaluation and Change,* 1978 (special issue), 54-62.

Salasin, S. E. "Evaluation as a Tool for Restoring the Mental Health of Victims: An Interview with Frank Ochberg." *Evaluation and Change,* 1980 (special issue), 21-27.

Salasin, S. E. (Ed.). *Evaluating Victim Services.* Beverly Hills, Calif.: Sage, 1981a.

Salasin, S. E. "Information on Project Impact." Unpublished report, National Institute of Mental Health, Rockville, Md., 1981b.

Salasin, S. E., and Kivens, L. "Fostering Federal Program Evaluation: A Current OMB Initiative." *Evaluation,* 1975, *2*(2), 37-41.

Sanders, H. C. (Ed.). *The Cooperative Extension Service.* Englewood Cliffs, N.J.: Prentice-Hall, 1966.

Sands, F. F., and Glaser, E. M. (Eds.). *Proceedings of the 1977 National Symposium of the Military Services on Utilization of People-Related Research, Development, Test, and Evaluation.* NPRDC Special Report 78-3. San Diego, Calif.: Navy Personnel Research and Development Center, 1978.

Sanford, N. "Social Science on Social Reform." *Journal of Social Issues,* 1965, *21,* 54-70.

Sapolsky, H. M. "Organizational Structure and Innovation." *Journal of Business,* 1967, *40,* 597-610.

Sarason, S. B. *The Culture of the School and the Problem of Change.* Boston: Allyn & Bacon, 1971.

Sarason, S. B. *The Creation of Settings and the Future Societies.* San Francisco: Jossey-Bass, 1972.

Sarason, S. B. "The Nature of Problem Solving in Social Action." *American Psychologist,* 1978, *33,* 370-380.

Sarbaugh, L. E., and others. *A Study of the Diffusion of Ten*

*Educational Products: An Evaluation of Communication and Subsequent Action with Respect to Educational Innovations in Ten Display Modules.* (ED 083 803.) East Lansing: Department of Communication, Michigan State University, 1973.

Sartorius, N. "Priorities for Research Likely to Contribute to Better Provision of Mental Health Care." *Social Psychiatry* (Berlin), 1977, *12*(4), 171-184.

Sashkin, M., Morris, W., and Horst, L. "A Comparison of Social and Organizational Change Models: Information Flow and Data Use Processes." *Psychological Review,* 1973, *80*(6), 510-526.

Sauber, S. R. "The Human Services Delivery System." *International Journal of Mental Health,* 1977, *5*(4), 121-140.

Saunders, J. "Impact and Consequences of Military Transfer of Technology to Developing Countries." *Australian and New Zealand Journal of Sociology,* 1976, *12*(3), 204-212.

Sayles, L. R. "The Change Process in Organizations: An Applied Anthropology Analysis." In H. A. Hornstein and others (Eds.), *Social Intervention: A Behavioral Science Approach.* New York: Free Press, 1971.

Sayles, L. R. "The Innovation Process: An Organizational Analysis." *Journal of Management Studies,* 1974, *11*(2), 190-204.

Scanlon, R. G. "Building Relationships for the Dissemination of Innovations." (ED 108 302.) Paper presented at CEDaR Communications Group Workshop, Denver, Colo., July-August, 1973.

Schalock, H. D., and others. *The Oregon Studies in Educational Research, Development, Diffusion, and Evaluation.* Vol. 1. Monmouth, Oreg.: Teaching Research, 1972.

Schein, E. H. *Process Consultation: Its Role in Organization Development.* Reading, Mass.: Addison-Wesley, 1969.

Schein, E. H., and Bennis, W. G. *Personal and Organizational Change Through Group Methods.* New York: Wiley, 1965.

Scheirer, M. A. *Program Implementation: The Organizational Context.* Beverly Hills, Calif.: Sage, 1981.

Schiffel, D., and Kitti, C. "Rates of Innovation: International Patent Comparisons." *Research Policy,* 1978, *7,* 324-340.

Schindler-Rainman, E., and Lippitt, R. *Team Training for Com-*

*munity Change: Concepts, Goals, Strategies and Skills.* Riverside: University of California Extension, 1972.

Schmookler, J. "Changes in Industry and in the State of Knowledge as Determinants of Industrial Invention." In National Bureau of Economic Research, *The Rate and Direction of Inventive Activity.* Princeton, N.J.: Princeton University Press, 1962.

Schmookler, J. *Invention and Economic Growth.* Cambridge, Mass.: Harvard University Press, 1966.

Schmuck, R. A. "Social Psychological Factors in Knowledge Utilization." In T. L. Eidell and M. Kitchel (Eds.), *Knowledge Production and Utilization in Educational Administration.* Eugene: Center for the Advanced Study of Educational Administration, University of Oregon, 1968.

Schmuck, R. A. "Some Uses of Research Methods in Organization Development Projects." *Viewpoints,* 1974, *50*(3), 47-59.

Schmuck, R. A., and Miles, M. B. (Eds.). *Organization Development in Schools.* La Jolla, Calif.: University Associates, 1971.

Schmuck, R. A., and others. *The Second Handbook of Organization Development in Schools.* Palo Alto, Calif.: Mayfield, 1977.

Schoenfeld, C. A. "Communicating Research Findings." *Journal of Educational Research,* 1965, *59*(1), 13-16.

Schön, D. A. *Technology and Change: The New Heraclitus.* New York: Delacorte Press, 1967.

Schön, D. A. *Beyond the Stable State.* New York: Norton, 1971.

Schön, D. A. "Network-Related Intervention." Paper prepared for the Networking Conference, School Capacity for Problem Solving Group, National Institute of Education, Washington, D.C., March 1977.

Schramm, W. "Communication Research in the United States." In W. Schramm (Ed.), *The Science of Communication.* New York: Basic Books, 1963.

Schrank, R. *Ten Thousand Working Days.* Cambridge, Mass.: M.I.T. Press, 1978.

Schuelke, L. D. "The Processes and Effects of an Internal Technology Discovery Program Upon Management." (ED 130

344.) Paper presented at 30th International Meeting of Forest Products Research Society, Toronto, Canada, July 1976.

Schulberg, H. C., and Baker, F. "Program Evaluation Models and the Implementation of Research Findings." *American Journal of Public Health,* 1968, *58,* 1248-1254.

Schultz, R. L., and Slevin, D. (Eds.). *Implementing Operations Research/Management Science.* New York: Elsevier, 1975.

Schultz, R. L., Slevin, D. P., and Henry, M. D. *A Bibliography on the Implementation of Operations Research/Management Science.* West Lafayette, Ind.: Graduate School of Management, Institute for Research in the Behavioral, Economic, and Management Sciences, Purdue University, 1978.

Schultz, T. W. *Transforming Traditional Agriculture.* New Haven, Conn.: Yale University Press, 1964.

Schwartz, D. C. "On the Growing Popularization of Social Science: The Expanding Publics and Problems of Social Science Utilization." *American Behavioral Scientist,* 1966, *9*(10), 47-50.

Schwartzman, D. *Innovation in the Pharmaceutical Industry.* Baltimore: Johns Hopkins University Press, 1976.

Schweitzer, D. L., and Randall, R. M. "The Key to Getting Research Applied: Manager-Researcher Cooperation." *Journal of Forestry,* 1974, *72,* 418-419.

Science Policy Research Unit, University of Sussex. *Project SAPPHO, a Study of Success and Failure in Innovation.* Brighton, England: Science Policy Research Unit, University of Sussex, 1971.

Science Policy Research Unit, University of Sussex. *Success and Failure in Industrial Innovation.* London: Centre for the Study of Industrial Innovation, 1972.

Scott, J. P., and Scott, S. F. (Eds.). *Social Control and Social Change.* Chicago: University of Chicago Press, 1971.

Scribner, R., and Chalk, R. (Eds.). *Adopting Science to Social Needs.* Washington, D.C.: American Association for the Advancement of Science, 1977.

Scriven, M. "The Methodology of Evaluation." In B. R. Worthen and J. R. Sanders, *Educational Evaluations: Theory and Practice.* Worthington, Ohio: Charles A. Jones, 1973a.

Scriven, M. "Goal-Free Evaluation." In E. R. House (Ed.), *School Evaluation: The Politics and Process.* Berkeley, Calif.: McCutchan, 1973b.

Scriven, M. "Maximizing the Power of Causal Investigations: The Modus Operandi Method." *Evaluation Studies Review Annual.* Vol. 1. Beverly Hills, Calif.: Sage, 1976.

Scriven, M. *Evaluation Thesaurus.* (2nd ed.) Inverness, Calif.: Edgepress, 1980.

Search Institute. *Effecting Utilization: Experimental Use of Consultants. Phase I Report.* Minneapolis, Minn.: Search Institute, 1978.

Seashore, S. E., and Bowers, D. G. "Durability of Organizational Change." *American Psychologist,* 1970, *25,* 227-233.

Segal, J. (Ed.). *Research in Service of Mental Health: Report of the Research Task Force of National Institute of Mental Health.* Washington, D.C.: U.S. Government Printing Office, 1975.

Semple, R. K., Brown, L. A., and Brown, M. A. "Strategies for the Promotion and Diffusion of Consumer Goods and Services: An Overview." *International Regional Science Review,* 1977, *2,* 91-102.

Servi, I. S. "Information Transfer—Handle with Care." *Research Management,* 1976, *19*(1), 10-14.

Sewell, W. "Relationship Between Pharmaceutical Libraries and Pharmaceutical Information Transfer." *Lloydia, The Journal of Natural Products,* 1978, *41*(1), 78.

Shapero, A. *University-Industry Interactions: Recurring Expectations, Unwarranted Assumptions, and Feasible Policies.* Columbus: Ohio State University, 1979.

Sharp, G. "Mechanisms of Change in Nonviolent Action." In H. A. Hornstein and others (Eds.), *Social Intervention.* New York: Free Press, 1971.

Shartle, C. L. "The Occupational Research Program: An Example of Research Utilization." In W. Schramm (Ed.), *Case Studies in the Utilization of Behavioral Science.* Vol. 1. Stanford, Calif.: Institute for Communication Research, Stanford University, 1961.

Shaw, M. B., and Stubblefield, H. W. (Eds.). "Adult Basic Education: Research, Development and Dissemination." In *Proceedings of the 1976 Virginia Adult Basic Education Dissemination Conference.* (ED 138 732.) Blacksburg: Virginia Polytechnic Institute and State University, 1976.

Sheldon, E. B., and Moore, W. E. (Eds.). *Indicators of Social Change: Concepts and Measurements.* New York: Russell Sage Foundation, 1968.

Sherwin, C. W., and Isenson, R. S. "Project Hindsight: A Defense Department Study of the Utility of Research." *Science,* 1967, *156*(3782), 1571-1577.

Short, E. C. "Knowledge Production and Utilization in Curriculum: A Special Case of the General Phenomenon." *Review of Educational Research,* 1973, *43,* 237-301.

Shosteck, H. *An Evaluation of the Factors Influencing Successful Diffusion and Application of Scientific Technology under the State Technical Services Act.* (NTIS PB-262 763.) Silver Spring, Md.: Herschel Shosteck Associates, 1977.

Sidowsky, J., and others (Eds.). *Technology in Mental Health Care Delivery Systems.* Norwood, N.J.: Ablex Publishers, 1980.

Sieber, S. D. "Organizational Influences on Innovative Roles." In T. L. Eidell and J. M. Kitchell (Eds.), *Knowledge Production and Utilization in Educational Administration.* Eugene: Center for the Advanced Study of Educational Administration, University of Oregon, 1968.

Sieber, S. D. "Images of the Practitioner and Strategies of Educational Change." *Sociology of Education,* 1972, *45,* 362-385.

Sieber, S. D. "Toward a Theory of Role Accumulation." *American Sociological Review,* 1974a, *39,* 567-578.

Sieber, S. D. "Trends in Diffusion Research: Knowledge Utilization." *Viewpoints,* 1974b, *50*(3), 61-81.

Sieber, S. D. "The Requirements of a National Educational R&D System." In National Institute of Education, *R&D Funding Policies of the National Institute of Education: Review and Recommendations.* Washington, D.C.: National Institute of Education, 1975.

Sieber, S. D. "Knowledge Utilization Strategies in the Design and Implementation of New Schools—Symbolic Functions." (ED) 122 425.) Paper presented at 61st annual meeting of

American Educational Research Association, San Francisco, April 1976a.

Sieber, S. D. "Planning Change in Education." In S. Goodman (Ed.), *Handbook on Contemporary Education.* New York: Bowker, 1976b.

Sieber, S. D. "Innovation and Educational Finance." *Educational Technology,* 1977, *17*(1), 34-38.

Sieber, S. D. "The Solution as the Problem." Paper adapted from talk at Society for Sociological Study of Social Problems, San Francisco, 1978.

Sieber, S. D., Louis, K. S., and Metzger, L. *The Use of Educational Knowledge: Evaluation of the Pilot State Dissemination Program.* 2 vols. (ED 065-739, -740.) New York: Bureau of Applied Social Research, Columbia University, 1972.

Sieber, S. D., Louis, K. S., and Metzger, L. "The Use of Educational Knowledge: Evaluation of the Pilot State Dissemination Program." In H. Hug (Ed.), *Evolution/Revolution: Library-Media-Information Futures.* New York: Bowker, 1974.

Siegel, B., and Ash, C. *DEAS Information Networks Study, Phase 2, Comparison and Compatibility Analysis.* (NTIS AD-AO59 054.) Bethesda, Md.: David W. Taylor Naval Ship Research and Development Center, 1978.

Sikes, W. W., Schlesinger, L. D., and Seashore, C. "Developing Change Agent Teams on Campus." *Journal of Higher Education,* 1973, *44*(5), 399-413.

Silberston, A. "Impact of the Patent System on the Creation and Diffusion of New Technology." *Omega,* 1975, *3*(1), 9-22.

Silvern, L. C. *The Evolution of Systems Thinking in Education.* Los Angeles: Education and Training Consultants Company, 1971.

Simon, H. "The Origin of Complex Systems." In H. H. Pattee (Ed.), *Hierarchy Theory.* New York: Braziller, 1973.

Simon, H., and Newell, A. *Human Problem Solving.* New York: Prentice-Hall, 1972.

Sincoff, M. Z., and Dajani, J. S. "The Role of University Faculty in the Transfer of Technological Information." (ED 122 323.) Paper presented at 37th annual meeting of National Conference of American Society for Public Administration, Washington, D.C., April 1976.

Skelton, B. *Comparison of Results of Science User Studies with*

*"Investigation into Information Requirements of the Social Sciences."* (ED 078 866.) Bath, England: University Library, Bath University of Technology, 1971.

Slevin, D. P., and others. *Implementation Attitude Questionnaire.* Purdue, Ill.: Graduate School of Management, Purdue University, 1972.

Slocum, J. W., Jr. "Does Cognitive Style Affect Diagnosis and Intervention Strategies of Change Agents?" *Group & Organization Studies,* 1978, *3*(2), 199-210.

Smith, D. C., Jones, T. A., and Coye, J. L. "State Mental Health Institutions in the Next Decade: Illusions and Reality." *Hospital and Community Psychiatry,* 1977, *28*(8), 593-597.

Smith, L. M. "Interorganizational Structures as Educational Networks." Paper prepared for the Networking Conference, School Capacity for Problem Solving Group, National Institute of Education, Washington, D.C., March 1977.

Smith, L. M., and Keith, D. M. *Anatomy of Educational Innovation: An Organizational Analysis of an Elementary School.* New York: Wiley, 1971.

Smith, N. L. (Ed.). *Metaphors for Evaluation: Sources of New Methods.* Beverly Hills, Calif.: Sage, 1981a.

Smith, N. L. (Ed.). *New Methods for Evaluation Techniques.* Beverly Hills, Calif.: Sage, 1981b.

Smith, R. J. "Legislators Accept Fast-Paced Fusion Program." *Science,* 1980a, *210,* 290-291.

Smith, R. J. "Simon Ramo's Prescriptions for Innovation." *Science,* 1980b, *210,* 1331-1332.

Social Science Education Consortium, Inc. *National Seminar on the Diffusion of New Instructional Materials and Practices. 1.0 Are There Characteristics of Particular Subject Matters that Make Products Which Are Based on Them More or Less Likely to be Adopted? and 2.0 Are There Characteristics of Developers that Tend to Inhibit or Encourage Use of Their Ideas and Products?* (ED 083 113.) Boulder, Colo.: Social Science Education Consortium, Inc., 1973a.

Social Science Education Consortium, Inc. *National Seminar on the Diffusion of New Instructional Materials and Practices. 3.0 Product Characteristics: What Are the Characteristics of*

*Educational Products that Make Them More or Less Likely to be Diffused?* (ED 083 114.) Boulder, Colo.: Social Science Education Consortium, Inc., 1973b.

Social Science Education Consortium, Inc. *National Seminar on the Diffusion of New Instructional Materials and Practices. 4.0 Characteristics of the School: What Are the Characteristics of Schools that Discourage or Encourage the Introduction and Use of New Ideas?* (ED 083 115.) Boulder, Colo.: Social Science Education Consortium, Inc., 1973c.

Social Science Education Consortium, Inc. *National Seminar on the Diffusion of New Instructional Materials and Practices. 5.0 Characteristics of the Communications Network: What Are the Mechanisms Within the Diffusion System that Encourage or Discourage the Diffusion of Innovation?* (ED 083 116.) Boulder, Colo.: Social Science Education Consortium, Inc., 1973d.

Social Science Education Consortium, Inc. *National Seminar on the Diffusion of New Instructional Materials and Practices. 6.0 General Observations: Do You Have Some General Observations About the Whole Process of Diffusion that Would Be Useful to Others Who Are Developers or Users and Who Participate in Either Dissemination or Implementation Activities or Both?* (ED 083 112.) Boulder, Colo.: Social Science Education Consortium, Inc., 1973e.

Social Science Education Consortium, Inc. *Mandate for Change: The Impact of Law on Educational Innovation.* Boulder, Colo.: Social Science Education Consortium, Inc., 1979.

Solo, R. A. "Transfer of Technology and Developing Countries: Belgrade, September 9-11, 1975." *Technology and Culture,* 1976, *17*(3), 518-520.

Soloff, A., and others. "Running a Research Utilization Laboratory." *Rehabilitation Counseling Bulletin,* 1975, *19*(2), 416-424.

Souder, W. E. "Comparative Analysis of R&D Investment Models." *AIEE Transactions,* 1972a, *1*(2), 57-64.

Souder, W. E. "A Scoring Methodology for Assessing the Suitability of Management Science Models." *Management Science,* 1972b, *18*, B526-543.

Souder, W. E. "Autonomy, Gratification, and R&D Outputs: A Small Sample Field Study." *Management Science,* 1974, *20* (8), 1147-1156.

Souder, W. E. "Achieving Organizational Consensus with Respect to R&D Project Selection Criteria." *Management Science,* 1975a, *21*(6), 669-681.

Souder, W. E. *A Group Process Model for Portfolio Decision Making in Organizational Settings.* Technology Management Studies Group Study Paper. Pittsburgh, Pa.: University of Pittsburgh, 1975b.

Souder, W. E. "Effectiveness of Nominal and Interacting Group Decision Processes for Integrating R&D and Marketing." *Management Science,* 1977a, *23*(6), 595-605.

Souder, W. E. *An Exploratory Study of the Coordinating Mechanisms Between R&D and Marketing as an Influence on the Innovation Process.* Final Report to National Science Foundation, Grant No. 75-17195. Pittsburgh, Pa.: University of Pittsburgh, 1977b.

Souder, W. E. "A System for Using R&D Project Evaluation Methods." *Research Management,* 1978, *21*(5), 29-37.

Souder, W. E., and Chakrabarti, A. K. "Government Influence on Industrial Innovation." *Journal of Industrial Marketing Management,* 1978a, 7(2), 17-25.

Souder, W. E., and Chakrabarti, A. K. "The R&D/Marketing Interface: Results from an Empirical Study of Innovation Projects." *IEEE Transactions on Engineering Management,* 1978b, *25*(4), 88-93.

Souder, W. E., and Rubenstein, A. H. "Some Designs for Policy Experiments and Government Incentives for the R&D/Innovation Process." *IEEE Transactions on Engineering Management,* 1976, *23*(3), 129-139.

Souder, W. E., and Ziegler, R. W. "A Review of Creativity and Problem-Solving Techniques." *Research Management,* 1977, *20*(4), 34-42.

Spencer, G., and Louis, K. S. *The RDU Linking Agent Study: Role Definitions of Linking Agents.* Cambridge, Mass.: Abt Associates, Inc., 1978.

Spencer, G., and Louis, K. S. *Training and Support of Educa-*

*tional Linking Agents: Data from the RDU Program.* Cambridge, Mass.: Abt Associates, Inc., 1980.

Spicer, E. H. (Ed.). *Human Problems in Technological Change: A Casebook.* New York: Russell Sage Foundation, 1952.

Spiegel-Rosing, I. "The Study of Science, Technology, and Society (SSTS): Recent Trends and Future Challenges." In I. Spiegel-Rosing and D. de S. Price (Eds.), *Science, Technology and Society: A Cross-Disciplinary Perspective.* London: Sage, 1977.

Spooner, S. E., and Thrush, R. S. *Interagency Cooperation and Institutional Change.* Final report on a special manpower project prepared under a contract with the Manpower Administration, U.S. Department of Labor. Madison: University of Wisconsin, 1970.

Sprehe, J. T., and Speidel, J. J. "Population and Social Change." In G. Zaltman (Ed.), *Processes and Phenomena of Social Change.* New York: Wiley, 1973.

Srivastva, S., and others. *Job Satisfaction and Productivity.* Cleveland, Ohio: Case Western Reserve University, 1975.

Staats, E. "The Challenge of Evaluating Federal Social Problems." *Evaluation,* 1973, *1*(3), 50-54.

Staats, E. *Finding Out How Programs Are Working: Suggestions for Congressional Oversight.* Washington, D.C.: U.S. General Accounting Office, 1977.

Staats, E. *Assessing Social Program Impact Evaluations: A Checklist Approach.* Washington, D.C.: U.S. General Accounting Office, 1978.

Stake, R. E. (Ed.). *Evaluating the Arts in Education: A Responsive Approach.* Columbus, Ohio: Merrill, 1975.

Stanford Research Institute. *Evaluation of the National Diffusion Network: Final Report.* Vol. 1: *Findings and Recommendations.* (ED 147 327.) Menlo Park, Calif.: Stanford Research Institute, 1977.

Stearns, M. S., and others. *Evaluation of the Field Test of Project Information Packages.* 5 vols. Menlo Park, Calif.: Stanford Research Institute and RMC Research Corporation, 1975/1977.

Stedman, D. J. "The Technical Assistance System: A New Organizational Form for Improving Education." (ED 121 009.) In M. Reynolds (Ed.), *National Technical Assistance Systems in Special Education.* Minneapolis: Leadership Training Institute/Special Education, University of Minnesota, 1975.

Steele, F. *Consulting for Organizational Change.* Amherst: University of Massachusetts Press, 1975.

Steele, F. "Is the Culture Hostile to Organization Development? The U.K. Example." In P. H. Mirvis and D. N. Berg (Eds.), *Failures in Organization Development and Change: Cases and Essays for Learning.* New York: Wiley, 1977.

Steeno, T. J., Moorehead, B. B., and Smits, J. R. "Homemakers as Change Agents." *Social Casework,* 1977, *58*(5), 286-293.

Steere, B. F. "Ex-Innovators as Barriers to Change." *Educational Technology,* 1972, *12*(5), 63.

Stein, M. I. "Social Change Skills and Creativity." In Foundation for Research on Human Behavior, *Comparative Theories of Social Change.* Ann Arbor, Mich.: Foundation for Research on Human Behavior, 1966.

Stein, M. I. *Stimulating Creativity.* Vol. 1: *Individual Procedures.* New York: Academic Press, 1974.

Stein, M. I. *Stimulating Creativity.* Vol. 2: *Group Procedures.* New York: Academic Press, 1975.

Steinbruner, J. D. *The Cybernetic Theory of Decision: New Dimensions of Political Analysis.* Princeton, N.J.: Princeton University Press, 1974.

Stenberg, C. "Citizens and the Administrative State: From Participation to Power." *Public Administration Review,* 1972, *32*(3), 189-223.

Stevens, W. F., and Tornatzky, L. G. "The Dissemination of Evaluation: An Experiment." *Evaluation Review,* 1980, *4*(3), 339-354.

Stiles, L. J., and Robinson, B. "Change in Education." In G. Zaltman (Ed.), *Processes and Phenomena of Social Change.* New York: Wiley, 1973.

Stokes, T. F., and Baer, D. M. "An Implicit Technology of Generalization." *Journal of Applied Behavioral Analysis,* 1977, *10,* 349-367.

Stolz, S. B. "Adoption of Innovations from Applied Behavioral Research: 'Does Anybody Care?' " *Journal of Applied Behavioral Analysis,* 1981, *14*(4), 491-505.

Stork, K. E. *Technology Transfer in Water Research: The Interface Between Producers and Users. Proceedings of a Conference Held in Lincoln, Nebraska on September 25-26, 1972, Sponsored by Nebraska Water Resources Research Institute.* (NTIS PB-213 740.) Lincoln: Water Resources Research Institute, Nebraska University, 1972.

Strang, E. W. *Building State Capacity in Dissemination: Literature Review.* (ED 142 191.) Washington, D.C.: National Institute of Education, 1977.

Strawhorn, J. M., Omerso, R. L., and Creager, W. A. *Improving the Dissemination of Scientific and Technical Information: A Practitioner's Guide to Innovation.* (NTIS PB-247 057.) Rockville, Md.: Capital Systems Group, Inc., 1975.

Strommen, M. P. "A Planned Change Approach to Consultation and Youth Service." Paper presented at 87th annual meeting of American Psychological Association, Minneapolis, Minn., September 1979.

Struening, E., and Guttentag, M. (Eds.). *Handbook of Evaluation Research.* Vol. 1. Beverly Hills, Calif.: Sage, 1975.

Study Project on Social Research and Development. *The Federal Investment in Knowledge of Social Problems.* Washington, D.C.: National Academy of Sciences, 1978.

Stufflebeam, D. L. "Metaevaluation: Concepts, Standards, and Uses." In R. A. Berk (Ed.), *Educational Evaluation Methodology: The State of the Art.* Baltimore: Johns Hopkins University Press, 1981.

Stufflebeam, D. L., and others. *Educational Evaluation and Decision Making.* Itasca, Ill.: Peacock, 1971.

Suchman, E. A. *Evaluative Research: Principles and Practice in Public Service and Social Action Programs.* New York: Russell Sage Foundation, 1967.

Sun, M. "NIH Ponders Pitfalls of Industrial Support." *Science,* 1981, *213*(4503), 113-114.

Sundquist, J. L. "Research Brokerage: The Weak Link." In L. E.

Lynn, Jr. (Ed.), *Knowledge and Policy: The Uncertain Connection.* Washington, D.C.: National Academy of Sciences, 1978.

Suppes, P. (Ed.). *Impact of Research on Education: Some Case Studies.* Washington, D.C.: National Academy of Education, 1978.

Sutton, R. L. "Cultural Context and Change-Agent Organizations." *Administrative Science Quarterly,* 1974, *19*(4), 547-562.

Swan, W. K. "Research and the Political Process: Experience with a Plan for Deinstitutionalization." *Policy Studies Journal,* 1976, *4*(3), 254-260.

Swanson, D. R. "On Improving Communications Among Scientists." *Bulletin of the Atomic Scientists,* 1966, *22*(2), 8-12.

Swanson, G. E. *Social Change.* Glenview, Ill.: Scott, Foresman, 1971.

Sweezy, E. E., and Hopper, J. H. *Obstacles to Innovation in the Scientific and Technical Information Services Industry.* Washington, D.C.: National Science Foundation, 1975.

Swift, D. W. *Ideology and Change in the Public Schools.* Columbus, Ohio: Merrill, 1971.

Szakasits, G. E. "The Adoption of the SAPPHO Method in the Hungarian Electronics Industry." *Research Policy,* 1974, *3,* 18-28.

Szilagyi, A. D. "Review of Beckhard, R. and Harris, R. T., *Organizational Transitions: Managing Complex Change.*" *Contemporary Psychology,* 1978, *23*(11), 920-921.

Tallmadge, G. K. *The Development of Project Information Packages for Effective Approaches to Compensatory Education.* Technical Report UR-254. Mountain View, Calif.: RMC Research Corporation, 1974.

Tallmadge, G. K. *The Joint Dissemination Review Panel IDEA-BOOK.* (ED 148 329.) Washington, D.C.: National Institute of Education, 1977.

Tannenbaum, A. "A Review of 'Current Research on Scientific and Technical Information Transfer' (papers delivered at three 1976 seminars sponsored by National Science Foundation, Division of Science Information)." *Library Journal,* 1978, *103*(11), 1150.

Task Force on International and National Diffusion of Quality of Working Life Programs. "Report of the Task Force." In L. E. Davis and A. B. Cherns (Eds.), *The Quality of Working Life.* Vol. 2. New York: Free Press, 1975.

Tavistock Institute. *Social Research and a National Policy for Science.* Occasional Paper No. 7. London: Tavistock Institute of Human Relations, 1964.

Tavris, C. "The Experimenting Society—To Find Programs That Work, Government Must Measure Its Failures." *Psychology Today,* 1975, *9*(9), 47-55.

Taylor, J. B. "Introducing Social Innovation." Paper presented at 76th annual meeting of American Psychological Association, San Francisco, September 1968.

Taylor, R. "Information Systems: A Vehicle for Diffusion." In *Research Implications for Educational Diffusion.* East Lansing: Kellogg Center for Continuing Education, Michigan State University, 1968.

Terreberry, S. "The Evolution of Organizational Environments." In K. Fast and J. Rosenzweig (Eds.), *Contingency Views of Organization and Management.* Chicago: Science Research Associates, 1973.

Tetelman, A. *Technical Information Outreach Programs for Citizens and Citizen Organizations: A Review of Program Models.* (NTIS PB-266 576.) Springfield, Va.: National Technical Information Service, Department of Commerce, 1977.

Thayer, L. *Communication and Communication Systems: In Organization, Management, and Interpersonal Relations.* Homewood, Ill.: Irwin, 1968.

Thio, A. O. "A Reconsideration of the Concept of Adopter Innovation Compatibility in Diffusion Research." *The Sociological Quarterly,* 1971, *12,* 56-68.

Thomas, A. R. "Changing and Improving Educational Systems and Institutions." (ED 102 647.) Paper presented at 3rd International Intervisitation Programme on Educational Administration, Great Britain, July 1974.

Thomas, E. J. "Selecting Knowledge from Behavioral Science." In *Building Social Work Knowledge: A Report of a Conference*. New York: National Association of Social Workers, 1964.

Thomas, E. J. "Generating Innovation in Social Work: The Paradigm of Developmental Research." *Journal of Social Service Research*, 1978, *2*(1), 95-115.

Thompson, M. *Benefit-Cost Analysis for Program Evaluation*. Beverly Hills, Calif.: Sage, 1980.

Thompson, V. A. *Bureaucracy and Innovation*. University, Ala.: University of Alabama Press, 1969.

Thorsrud, E. "Socio-Technical Approach to Job Design and Organizational Development." *Management International Review*, 1968, *8*, 4-5.

Thorsrud, E. "Democracy at Work as a Process of Change Towards Non-Hierarchical Types of Organization." In G. Hofstede and M. S. Kessen (Eds.), *European Contributions to Organization Theory*. Amsterdam: Van Gorcum, 1976.

Tichy, N. M. "Agents of Planned Social Change: Congruence of Values, Cognitions, and Actions." *Administrative Science Quarterly*, 1974, *19*(2), 164-182.

Tichy, N. M. "How Different Types of Change Agents Diagnose Organizations." *Human Relations*, 1975, *28*(9), 771-799.

Tichy, N. M. "Current and Future Trends for Change Agentry." *Group & Organization Studies*, 1978a, *3*(4), 467-482.

Tichy, N. M. "Demise, Absorption, or Renewal for the Future of Organization Development." In W. Burke (Ed.), *The Cutting Edge: Current Theory and Practice in Organization Development*. La Jolla, Calif.: University Associates, 1978b.

Tichy, N. M. "A Social Network Perspective for Organization Development." In T. Cummings (Ed.), *Systems Theory for Organizational Development*. New York: Wiley-Interscience, 1979.

Tichy, N. M. "Networks in Organizations." In P. C. Nystrom and W. H. Starbuck (Eds.), *Handbook of Organizational Design*. Vol. 2: *Remodeling Organizations and Their Environments*. London: Oxford University Press, 1980a.

Tichy, N. M. "Organizational Cycles and Change Management."

In J. Kimberly and R. Miles (Eds.), *The Organizational Life Cycle: Issues in the Creation, Transformation, and Decline of Organizations.* San Francisco: Jossey-Bass, 1980b.

Tichy, N. M., and Hornstein, H. "Agents of Planned Social Change: Congruence of Values, Cognitions, and Actions." *Administrative Science Quarterly,* 1974, *19,* 164-182.

Tichy, N. M., and Hornstein, H. A. "Stand When Your Number Is Called: Empirical Attempt to Classify Types of Social Change Agents." *Human Relations,* 1976, *29*(10), 945-967.

Tichy, N. M., and Nisberg, J. "Change Agent Bias: What They View Determines What They Do." *Group & Organization Studies,* 1976, *1*(3), 286-301.

Tiffany, D. W., Tiffany, P. M., and Cowan, J. R. "A Source of Problems Between Social Science Knowledge and Practice." *Journal of Human Relations,* 1969, *19,* 239-250.

Toch, H., Grant, D. J., and Galvin, R. T. *Agents of Change: A Study in Police Reform.* Cambridge, Mass.: Schenkman, 1975.

Toffler, A. *The Third Wave.* New York: Morrow, 1980.

Torczyner, J. "The Political Context of Social Change: A Case Study of Innovation in Adversity in Jerusalem." *Journal of Applied Behavioral Science,* 1972, *8*(3), 287-317.

Tornatzky, L. G., and others. *Innovation and Social Process: A National Experiment in Implementing Social Technology.* Elmsford, N.Y.: Pergamon, 1980a.

Tornatzky, L. G., and others. *Social Processes and Social Innovation.* London: Sage, 1980b.

Toronto, R. "A General Systems Model for the Analysis of Organizational Change." *Behavioral Science,* 1975, *20*(3), 145-157.

Toulmin, S. "Innovation and the Problem of Utilization." In W. H. Gruber and D. G. Marquis (Eds.), *Factors in the Transfer of Technology.* Cambridge, Mass.: M.I.T. Press, 1969.

Towell, D. *Developing Better Services for the Mentally Ill—an Exploration of Learning and Change in Complex Agency Networks.* Bristol, England: School for Advanced Urban Studies, University of Bristol, 1979.

Townes, C. H. "Differentiation and Competition Between Uni-

versity and Other Research Laboratories in the United States."
*Daedalus,* 1973, *102*(2), 153-165.

Trapp, M. *Knowledge Utilization in Education: A Review of Significant Theories and Research.* (ED 061 468.) Iowa City: Center for the Advanced Study of Communication, University of Iowa, 1972.

Trattner, E. "Organizing Collection, Selection, and Ranking of Ideas Leading to National R&D Projects." *IEEE Transactions on Engineering Management,* 1977, *24*(2), 51-59.

Traub, J. "Futurology: The Rise of the Predicting Profession." *Saturday Review,* 1979, *6*(24), 24-30.

Traxler, A. E. (Ed.). *Innovation and Experiment in Modern Education.* Washington, D.C.: American Council on Education, 1965.

Tripodi, T. *Uses and Abuses of Social Research in Social Work.* New York: Columbia University Press, 1974.

Troldahl, V., and Powell, F. A. "A Short-Form Dogmatism Scale for Use in Field Studies." *Social Forces,* 1965, *44,* 211-215.

Turnbull, B., Thom, L. I., and Hutchins, C. L. *Promoting Change in Schools: A Diffusion Casebook.* San Francisco: Far West Laboratory for Educational Research and Development, 1974.

Turner, J. C., and Tenhoor, W. J. "The NIMH Community Support Program: Pilot Approach to a Needed Social Reform." *Schizophrenia Bulletin,* 1978, *4*(3), 309-344.

Tushman, M. L. "Special Boundary Roles in the Innovation Process." *Administrative Science Quarterly,* 1977, *22,* 587-605.

Twiss, B. C. *Managing Technological Innovation.* London: Longham, 1974.

Tymchuk, A. J. "Information Dissemination in Mental Retardation." *Mental Retardation,* 1973, *11*(3), 44.

Udis, B. "European Views on Transfer of Technology from Military to Civil Uses." *R&D Management,* 1976, *6*(1), 171-178.

Uliassi, P. D. "Research and Foreign Policy: A View from Foggy Bottom." *Policy Studies Journal,* 1976, *4*(3), 239-243.

Unco, Inc. *Communication Model for the Utilization of Technical Research (CMUTR) Study: Utilization of Advanced Management Innovations Within State Departments of Public Welfare.* Washington, D.C.: Unco, Inc., 1973a.

Unco, Inc. *Guidelines for Research Utilization.* Washington, D.C.: Social and Rehabilitation Services, 1973b.

Union for Experimenting Colleges and Universities. *Project Changeover.* Yellow Springs, Ohio: Antioch College, 1969.

United Nations. *World Plan of Action for the Application of Science and Technology to Development.* New York: United Nations, 1971.

United Nations. *Multinational Corporations in World Development.* New York: United Nations, 1973.

United Nations. "Intergovernmental Conference of Scientific and Technological Information for Development II (UNISIST II)." *UNESCO Bulletin for Libraries,* 1978, *32*(5), 350-351.

United Nations Conference on Trade and Development (UNCTAD). *The Reverse Transfer of Technology: Economic Effects of the Outflow of Trained Personnel from Developing Countries (Brain Drain).* New York: United Nations, 1975.

United Nations Conference on Trade and Development (UNCTAD) Secretariat. "Transfer of Technology." *Bulletin of Peace Proposals,* 1976, 7(3), 222-223.

U.S. Department of Defense. *Project Hindsight.* Washington, D.C.: Office of the Director of Defense Research and Engineering, U.S. Department of Defense, 1969.

U.S. Department of Education. *Introducing the Department of Education.* Washington, D.C.: U.S. Department of Education, 1980.

U.S. Department of Energy. *The Demonstration Project as a Procedure for Accelerating the Application of New Technology.* Charpie Task Force Report, Section 3. Washington, D.C.: Institute of Public Administration, 1978.

U.S. Department of Housing and Urban Development. *Factors Involved in the Transfer of Innovations: A Summary and Organization of the Literature.* (NTIS SHR-0001549.) Washington, D.C.: U.S. Department of Housing and Urban Development, 1976.

U.S. Forest Service. *Outdoor Recreation Research: Applying the Results.* General Technical Report NC-9. St. Paul, Minn.: North Central Forest Experiment Station, U.S. Forest Service, 1976.

U.S. Office of Education. *Educational Programs that Work: A Resource of Exemplary Programs Developed by Local School*

*Districts and Approved by the Joint Dissemination Review
Panel of the Department of Health, Education, and Welfare.*
(5th ed.) San Francisco: Far West Laboratory for Educational Research and Development, 1978.

U.S. Office of Education. *Educational Programs that Work: A
Resource of Exemplary Educational Programs Approved by
the Joint Dissemination Review Panel, Department of Education.* (6th ed.) San Francisco: Far West Laboratory for
Educational Research and Development, 1979.

University of Florida Rehabilitation Research Institute. "Putting Knowledge to Use." *Rehab Brief,* September 20, 1980,
*3*(12).

The Urban Institute. *The Struggle to Bring Technology to
Cities.* Washington, D.C.: The Urban Institute, 1971.

Usdane, W. M. "The State of the Art: Rehabilitation Research
Utilization." In W. S. Neff (Ed.), *Rehabilitation Psychology.* Washington, D.C.: American Psychological Association,
1971.

Useem, M. *State Production of Social Knowledge: Patterns in
Government Financing of Academic Social Research.* Paper
presented at annual meeting of American Sociological Association, San Francisco, August 1975.

Useem, M. "Government Mobilization of Academic Social Research." *Policy Studies Journal,* 1976, *4*(3), 274-280.

Useem, M. "Research Funds and Advisers: The Relationship
Between Academic Social Science and the Federal Govern-
ment." In C. Weiss (Ed.), *Using Social Research in Public
Policy Making.* Lexington, Mass.: Lexington Books, 1977.

Utech, H., and Utech, I. *The Communication of Innovations
Between Local Government Departments.* Washington, D.C.:
National Science Foundation, 1974.

Utterback, J. M. "The Process of Technological Innovation
Within the Firm." *Academy of Management Journal,* 1971,
*14*(1), 75-88.

Utterback, J. M. "Innovation in Industry and the Diffusion of
Technology." *Science,* 1974, *183*(4125), 620-626.

Utterback, J. M. "Successful Industrial Innovations: A Multi-
variate Analysis." *Decision Sciences,* 1975, *6*(1), 65-77.

Utterback, J. M., and Abernathy, W. J. "A Dynamic Model of

Process and Product Innovation by Firms." *Omega,* 1975, *3* (6), 639-656.

Utterback, J. M., and others. "The Process of Innovation in Five Industries in Europe and Japan." *IEEE Transactions on Engineering Management,* 1976, *23*(1), 3-9.

Vallance, T. R. "Processes, Problems, and Prospects for Innovating Within the University: Lessons from 45 Experiences." *Journal of Higher Education,* 1972, *43*(9), 720-736.

van de Vall, M. "A Theoretical Framework for Applied Social Research." *International Journal of Mental Health,* 1973, *2*(2), 6-25.

van de Vall, M. "Utilization and Methodology of Applied Social Research: Four Complementary Models." *Journal of Applied Behavioral Science,* 1975, *11*(1), 14-38.

van de Vall, M., Bolas, C., and Kang, T. "Applied Social Research in Industrial Organizations: An Evaluation of Functions, Theory, and Methods." *Journal of Applied Behavioral Science,* 1976, *12*(2), 158-177.

Van de Ven, A. H. "A Framework of Organizational Assessment." *Academy of Management Review,* 1976, *1*(1), 64-78.

Van de Vliert, E. "Inconsistencies in the Argyris Intervention Theory." *Journal of Applied Behavioral Science,* 1977, *13* (4), 557-564.

Van den Ban, A. W. "Utilization and Publication of Findings." In C. H. Backstrom and G. D. Hursh (Eds.), *Survey Research Methods in Developing Nations.* Evanston, Ill.: Northwestern University Press, 1963.

Van den Ban, A. W. "A Revision of the Two-Step Flow of Communications Hypothesis." *Gazette,* 1964, *10,* 237-350.

Van Meter, D. S., and Van Horn, C. E. "The Policy Implementation Process: A Conceptual Framework." *Administration and Society,* 1975, *6*(4), 445-488.

Vanvleck, E. M. *Information Transfer Satellite.* (NTIS N72-33865.) Moffett Field, Calif.: Ames Research Center, National Aeronautics and Space Administration, 1972.

Vernon, R. "International Investment and International Trade in the Product Cycle." *Quarterly Journal of Economics,* 1966, *80*(2), 190-207.

Vickers, P. H. "A Cost Survey of Mechanized Information Systems." *Journal of Documentation*, 1973, *29*(3), 258-280.

von Hippel, E. "The Dominant Role of Users in the Scientific Instrument Innovation Process." *Research Policy*, 1976, *5*, 212-239.

von Hippel, E. "Transferring Process Equipment Innovations from User-Innovators to Equipment Manufacturing Firms." *R&D Management*, 1977, *8*(1), 13-22.

von Hippel, E. *The Role of the Initial User in the Industrial Innovation Process*. Final Report to National Science Foundation, Grant No. PRA-7420435. Washington, D.C.: National Science Foundation, 1978a.

von Hippel, E. "Users as Innovators." *Technology Review*, 1978b, *80*(3), 31-39.

Wager, L. W. "Channels of Interpersonal and Mass Communication in an Organizational Setting: Studying the Diffusion of Information About a Unique Organizational Change." *Sociological Inquiry*, 1962, *32*, 88-107.

Walker, J. L. "Diffusion of Innovations Among the American States." *American Political Science Review*, 1969, *63*, 80-99.

Walker, J. L. "Innovation in State Politics." In H. Jacob and K. N. Vines (Eds.), *Politics in the American States*. Boston: Little, Brown, 1971.

Wall, J. E. *Review and Synthesis of Strategies for Effecting Change in Vocational and Technical Education*. Columbus: ERIC Clearinghouse for Vocational and Technical Education, Center for Vocational and Technical Education, Ohio State University, 1972.

Wallendorf, M. "Understanding the Client as a Consumer." In G. Zaltman (Ed.), *Management Principles for Nonprofit Agencies and Organizations*. New York: American Management Associations, 1979.

Walsh, J. "What Can Government Do for Innovation?" *Science*, 1979, *205*(4404), 378-380.

Walsh, J. "Is There a Catch to Innovation?" *Science*, 1980, *209* (4461), 1098.

Walton, R. E. "Two Strategies of Social Change and Their Dilemmas." In W. G. Bennis, K. D. Benne, and R. Chin (Eds.), *The Planning of Change*. (2nd ed.) New York: Holt, Rinehart and Winston, 1969.

Walton, R. E. "The Diffusion of New Work Structures: Explaining Why Success Didn't Take." In P. H. Mirvis and D. N. Berg (Eds.), *Failures in Organization Development and Change: Cases and Essays for Learning.* New York: Wiley, 1977a.

Walton, R. E. "Work Innovations at Topeka: After Six Years." *Journal of Applied Behavioral Science,* 1977b, *13*(3), 422-433.

Walton, R. E., and Warwick, D. P. "The Ethics of Organization Development." *Journal of Applied Behavioral Science,* 1973, *9*(6), 681-698.

Ward, J. E. *The Educational Catalyst: An Imperative for Today.* (ED 061 991.) Bloomington, Ind.: Phi Delta Kappa, 1971.

Ward, S. *A Model of the Activities and Actors in the Program Improvement Process.* Washington, D.C.: National Institute of Education, 1978.

Ward, S. "Introduction." In A. Bank and others, *Dissemination and the Improvement of Practice: Cooperation and Support in the School Improvement Process.* San Francisco: Far West Laboratory for Educational Research and Development, 1979.

Warner, K. E. "The Need for Some Innovative Concepts of Innovation: An Examination of Research on the Diffusion of Innovations." *Policy Sciences,* 1974, *5*(4), 433-451.

Warren, B. L. *Social Change and Human Purpose.* Chicago: Rand McNally, 1977.

Warren, M. Q. "The Meaning of Research in Social Action: What the Clinical Community Can Expect from Research." *Criminal Justice and Behavior,* 1974, *1,* 73-86.

Warren, R. J., Rose, S. M., and Bergunder, A. F. *The Structure of Urban Reform.* Lexington, Mass.: Heath, 1974.

Warwick, D. P., and Kelman, H. C. "Ethical Issues in Social Intervention." In G. Zaltman (Ed.), *Processes and Phenomena of Social Change.* New York: Wiley, 1973.

Wasserman, C. W., McCarthy, B. W., and Ferree, E. H. "Student Paraprofessionals as Behavior Change Agents." *Professional Psychology,* 1975, *6*(2), 217-223.

Watson, G. "How Social Engineers Came To Be." *Journal of Social Psychology,* 1945, *21,* 135-141.

Watson, G. "Utopia and Rebellion: The New College Experiment." In M. B. Miles (Ed.), *Innovation in Education.* New York: Bureau of Publications, Teachers College, Columbia University, 1964.

Watson, G. (Ed.). *Change in School Systems.* Washington, D.C.: Cooperative Project for Educational Development by National Training Laboratories, National Education Association, 1967.

Watson, G. "Resistance to Change." In G. Zaltman (Ed.), *Processes and Phenomena of Social Change.* New York: Wiley, 1973.

Watson, G., and Glaser, E. M. "What We Have Learned about Planning for Change." *Management Review,* 1965, *54*(11), 34-46.

Watzlawick, P., Weakland, J., and Fisch, R. *Change: Principles for Problem Formation and Problem Resolution.* New York: Norton, 1974.

Weber, M. *Economy and Society.* New York: Bedminster Press, 1968.

Webster, D. *The Management of Change and Improvement in Academic Library Performance.* (ED 105 832.) Washington, D.C.: Association of Research Libraries, 1974.

Weick, K. E. "Educational Organizations as Loosely Coupled Systems." *Administrative Science Quarterly,* 1976, *21,* 1-19.

Weinberg, A. M. "Criteria for Scientific Choice." *Minerva,* 1963, *1*(2), 159-171.

Weinberg, A. M. "Social Problems and National Socio-Technical Institutes." In National Academy of Sciences, *Applied Science and Technological Progress: A Report to the Committee on Science and Astronautics, U.S. House of Representatives.* Washington, D.C.: U.S. Government Printing Office, 1967.

Weisbord, M. R. "Input- Versus Output-Focused Organizations: Notes on a Contingency Theory of Practice." In W. Burke (Ed.), *The Cutting Edge: Current Theory and Practice in Organization Development.* La Jolla, Calif.: University Associates, 1978.

Weiss, C. H. (Ed.). *Evaluating Action Programs: Readings in Social Action and Education.* Boston: Allyn & Bacon, 1972a.

Weiss, C. H. *Evaluation Research: Methods for Assessing Program Effectiveness.* Englewood Cliffs, N.J.: Prentice-Hall, 1972b.

Weiss, C. H. "Utilization of Evaluation: Toward Comparative Study." In C. H. Weiss (Ed.), *Evaluating Action Programs:*

*Readings in Social Action and Education.* Boston: Allyn & Bacon, 1972c.

Weiss, C. H. "Between the Cup and Lip . . . ." *Evaluation,* 1973a, *1*(2), 49-55.

Weiss, C. H. "Where Politics and Evaluation Research Meet." *Evaluation,* 1973b, *1*(3), 37-45.

Weiss, C. H. "Policy Research in the University: Practical Aid or Academic Exercise?" *Policy Studies Journal,* 1976a, *4*(3), 224-228.

Weiss, C. H. (Ed.). "Symposium on Research Utilization Quandary: Introduction." *Policy Studies Journal,* 1976b, *4*(3), 221-224.

Weiss, C. H. "Introduction." In C. H. Weiss (Ed.), *Using Social Research in Public Policy Making.* Lexington, Mass.: Lexington Books, 1977a.

Weiss, C. H. "Research for Policy's Sake: The Enlightenment Function of Social Science Research." *Policy Analysis,* 1977b, *3*(4), 531-545.

Weiss, C. H. (Ed.). *Using Social Research in Public Policy Making.* Lexington, Mass.: Lexington Books, 1977c.

Weiss, C. H. "Broadening Concept of Research Utilization." *Sociological Symposium,* 1978, *1978*(21), 20-33.

Weiss, C. H. "The Many Meanings of Research Utilization." *Public Administration Review,* 1979, *29,* 426-431.

Weiss, C. H. "Knowledge Creep and Decision Accretion." *Knowledge,* 1980, *1*(3), 381-404.

Weiss, C. H., and Bucuvalas, M. J. "The Challenge of Social Research to Decision Making." In C. H. Weiss (Ed.), *Using Social Research in Public Policy Making.* Lexington, Mass.: Lexington Books, 1977.

Weiss, C. H., and Bucuvalas, M. J. "Truth Tests and Utility Tests: Decision-Makers' Frames of Reference for Social Science Research." *American Sociological Review,* 1980a, *45,* 302-313.

Weiss, C. H., with Bucuvalas, M. J. *Social Science Research and Decision Making.* New York: Columbia University Press, 1980b.

Weiss, J. A. "Using Social Science for Social Policy." *Policy Studies Journal,* 1976, *4*(3), 234-238.

Weiss, J. A., and Weiss, C. H. "Social Scientists and Decision

Makers Look at the Usefulness of Mental Health Research."
*American Psychologist,* 1981, *36,* 837-847.

Wellar, B. S., and Graff, T. O. *Geographic Aspects of Information Systems: Introduction and Selected Bibliography.* (ED
063 010.) Monticello, Ill.: Council of Planning Librarians,
1971.

Wenk, E., Jr. *Margins for Survival: Overcoming Political Limits
in Steering Technology.* Oxford: Pergamon, 1979.

Westley, B. H. "Communication and Social Change." In G. Zaltman (Ed.), *Processes and Phenomena of Social Change.* New
York: Wiley, 1973.

Wheeler, T. J., and Foster, A. J. "Computerized Information
Searching in Psychology." *Bulletin of the British Psychological Society,* 1977, *30,* 315-317.

Whisler, T. *Information Technology and Organizational Change.*
Belmont, Calif.: Wadsworth Publishing, 1970.

White, W. "Effective Transfer of Technology from Research to
Development." *Research Management,* 1977, *20*(3), 30-34.

Whitehead, R. R. *Transferability and Implementation of Educational Technology.* (ED 116 618.) Austin: University of
Texas, 1974.

Whitley, R., and Frost, P. "Task Type and Information Transfer
in a Government Research Laboratory." *Human Relations,*
1972, *25*(4), 537-550.

Whitten, C. F. "Evaluation of Information Transfer in Sickle
Cell Trait (SCT) Counseling." *Pediatric Research,* 1976, *10*
(4), 309.

Wholey, J. S. "Evaluability Assessment." In L. Rutman (Ed.),
*Evaluation Research Methods: A Basic Guide.* Beverly Hills,
Calif.: Sage, 1977.

Wholey, J. S. *Evaluation: Promise and Performance.* Washington, D.C.: Urban Institute, 1979.

Wholey, J. S., and White, B. F. "Federal Level Evaluation—Evaluation's Impact on Title I Elementary and Secondary Education Program Management." *Evaluation,* 1973, *1*(3), 73-76.

Wholey, J. S., and others. *Federal Evaluation Policy: Analyzing
the Effects of Public Programs.* Washington, D.C.: The Urban
Institute, 1970.

Wholey, J. S., and others. "Federal Level Evaluation—Evaluation: When Is It Really Needed?" *Evaluation,* 1975, *2*(2), 89-93.

Whyte, W. F., and Hamilton, E. L. *Action Research for Management: A Case Report on Research and Action in Industry.* Homewood, Ill.: Dorsey, 1964.

Widmer, J. *What Makes Innovation Work in Massachusetts? A Study of ESEA Title III.* (ED 119 358.) Boston: Massachusetts State Department of Education, 1975.

Wilcox, L. D., and others. *Social Indicators and Social Monitoring.* New York: Elsevier, 1972.

Wilde, D. U. "Maximizing User Benefit from a Technical Information Center." In Advisory Group for Aerospace Research and Development, *The Problem of Optimization of User Benefits in Scientific and Technological Information Transfer.* Paris: Advisory Group for Aerospace Research and Development, 1976.

Wilemon, D. L., and others. *The Role of Industry in Urban Technology Transfer: A Comparative Profile. Analysis and Conclusions.* Final Report to the National Science Foundation, Grant No. NSF-PRA-77-23746. Syracuse, N.Y.: Syracuse Research Corporation, 1979.

Wilensky, H. L. *Organizational Intelligence: Knowledge and Policy in Government and Industry.* New York: Basic Books, 1967.

Wiles, K. "Contrasts in Strategies of Change." In R. R. Leeper (Ed.), *Strategy for Curriculum Change.* Washington, D.C.: Association for the Supervision of Curriculum Development, 1965.

Wilkins, M. "The Role of Private Business in the International Diffusion of Technology." *Journal of Economic History,* 1974, *34*(1), 166-188.

Williams, C. W., and Schwartz, P. *Choosing Technological Opportunities for Innovation in the Public Sector.* Vol. 1: *Basic Report and Summary.* (NTIS PB-247 075.) Menlo Park, Calif.: Stanford Research Institute, 1975.

Williams, C. W., Schwartz, P., and Tarpey, J. *Choosing Technological Opportunities for Innovation in the Public Sector.*

Vol. 3: *Twelve Technological Case Studies.* (NTIS PB-247-077.) Menlo Park, Calif.: Stanford Research Institute, 1975.

Williams, R. C., and others. *Effecting Organizational Renewal in Schools: A Social Systems Perspective.* New York: McGraw-Hill, 1973.

Williams, W. A. "Implementation Analysis and Assessment." *Policy Analysis,* 1975, *1,* 531-566.

Williams, W., and Elmore, R. F. *Social Program Implementation.* New York: Academic Press, 1976.

Willower, D. J. "Barriers to Change in Educational Organizations." *Theory into Practice,* 1963, *2*(5), 257-263.

Wilson, E. C. "The Application of Social Research Findings." In W. Schramm (Ed.), *Case Studies in the Utilization of Behavioral Science.* Vol. 1. Stanford, Calif.: Institute for Communication Research, Stanford University, 1961.

Wilson, J. A. "The Use of Case Studies in Diffusion Research." *Viewpoints,* 1974, *50*(3), 83-106.

Wilson, J. Q. "An Overview of Theories of Planned Change." In R. Morris (Ed.), *Centrally Planned Change: Prospects and Concepts.* New York: National Association of Social Workers, 1964.

Wilson, M. L. "The Communication and Utilization of the Results of Agricultural Research by American Farmers: A Case History, 1900-1950." In W. Schramm (Ed.), *Case Studies in the Utilization of Behavioral Science.* Vol. 1. Stanford, Calif.: Institute for Communication Research, Stanford University, 1961.

Windle, C., and Ochberg, F. M. "Enhancing Program Evaluation in the Community Mental Health Centers Program." *Evaluation,* 1975, *2*(2), 31-36.

Winett, R. A. "Environmental Design: Expanded Behavioral Research Framework for School Consultation and Educational Innovation." *Professional Psychology,* 1976, *7*(4), 631-636.

Winick, C. "The Diffusion of an Innovation Among Physicians in a Large City." *Sociometry,* 1961, *24,* 384-396.

Winterton, J. A., and Rossiter, D. L. "The Community Agent and Directed Change." *Journal of the Community Development Society,* 1973, *4*(2), 53-63.

Wise, R. "The Evaluator as Educator." In L. Braskamp and R. Brown (Eds.), *New Directions for Program Evaluation: Utilization of Evaluative Information,* no. 5. San Francisco: Jossey-Bass, 1980.

Wolf, R. M. *Evaluation in Education.* New York: Praeger, 1979.

Wolf, S. "The Real Gap Between Bench and Bedside." In B. Stacey (Ed.), *Communication of Scientific Information.* New York: Karger, 1975.

Wolf, W. C., Jr. "Selected Knowledge Diffusion/Utilization Know-How: Generalizability Within Educational Practice." *Knowledge,* 1981, *2*(3), 331-340.

Wolf, W. C., Jr., and Fiorino, A. J. *A Study of Educational Knowledge Diffusion and Utilization.* (ED 061 772.) Amherst: University of Massachusetts, 1972.

Wolfensberger, W. "Dilemmas of Research in Human Management Agencies." *Rehabilitation Literature,* 1969, *31,* 161-169.

Wolman, H. "Organization Theory and Community Action Agencies." *Public Administration Review,* 1972, *32*(1), 33-42.

Woods, T. E. *The Administration of Educational Innovation.* (ED 067 768.) Eugene: Bureau of Educational Research and Service, University of Oregon, 1971.

*Work in America.* Cambridge, Mass.: M.I.T. Press, 1972.

Wright, P. "Technology Transfer and Utilization: Active Promotion or Passive Dissemination?" *Research/Development,* 1966, *9,* 34-37.

Yandell, W., Lambert, N., and Laventur, C. "Training School Psychologists and Teachers as Change Agents: Role of Mental Health Consultation Within a School of Education." *American Journal of Orthopsychiatry,* 1974, *44*(2), 234-235.

Yapa, L. S. "The Green Revolution: A Diffusion Model." *Annals of the Association of American Geographers,* 1977, *67,* 350-359.

Yapa, L. S., and Mayfield, R. C. "Nonadoption of Innovation: Evidence from Discriminant Analysis." *Economic Geography,* 1978, *54,* 145-156.

Yeracaris, C. A. "Social Factors Associated with the Acceptance of Medical Innovations: A Pilot Study." *Journal of Health and Human Behavior,* 1962, *3*(3), 193-197.

Yin, R. K. *R&D Utilization by Local Services: Problems and Proposals for Further Research.* Santa Monica, Calif.: Rand Corporation, 1976.

Yin, R. K. "Production Efficiency vs. Bureaucratic Self-Interest: Two Innovative Processes?" *Policy Sciences,* 1977, *8,* 381-399.

Yin, R. K. "Organizational Innovation: A Psychologist's View." In M. Radnor, I. Feller, and E. Rogers (Eds.), *The Diffusion of Innovations: An Assessment.* Evanston, Ill.: Center for the Interdisciplinary Study of Science and Technology, Northwestern University, 1978.

Yin, R. K. *Changing Urban Bureaucracies.* Lexington, Mass.: Lexington Books, 1979.

Yin, R. K., Heald, K., and Vogel, M. *Tinkering with the System.* Lexington, Mass.: Heath, 1977.

Yin, R. K., and others. *A Review of Case Studies of Technological Innovations in State and Local Services.* Santa Monica, Calif.: Rand Corporation, 1976.

Yin, R. K., and others. *Changing Urban Bureaucracies: How New Practices Become Routinized.* Santa Monica, Calif.: Rand Corporation, 1978.

Yinger, J. M., and Cutler, J. J. (Eds.). *Major Social Issues: A Multidisciplinary View.* New York: Free Press, 1978.

Yokote, G., and Utterback, R. A. "Time Lapses in Information Dissemination: Research Laboratory to Physician's Office." *Bulletin of the Medical Library Association,* 1974, *62* (3), 251-257.

Young, T. R. "Some Theoretical Foundations for Conflict Methodology." *Sociological Inquiry,* 1976, *46*(1), 23-29.

Young, V. *A Study of Media for Communicating Research Information.* (ED 071 721.) Ontario: Research Department, Toronto Board of Education, 1972.

Zacker, J. "Parents as Change Agents: Psychodynamic Model." *American Journal of Psychotherapy,* 1978, *32*(4), 572-582.

Zagona, S. V., Willis, J. E., and MacKinnon, W. J. "Group Effectiveness in Creative Problem-Solving Tasks: An Examination of Relevant Variables." *Journal of Psychology*, 1966, *62*, 111-137.

Zaltman, G. (Ed.). *Processes and Phenomena of Social Change.* New York: Wiley, 1973.

Zaltman, G. "Forces for and Against Change." In G. Zaltman and L. Sikorski, *Dynamic Educational Change: Models, Strategies, Tactics, and Management.* New York: Free Press, 1977.

Zaltman, G. "Knowledge Utilization as Planned Social Change." *Knowledge*, 1979a, *1*(1), 82-105.

Zaltman, G. (Ed.). *Management Principles for Nonprofit Agencies and Organizations.* New York: American Management Associations, 1979b.

Zaltman, G., and Bonoma, T. V. (Eds.). *Review of Marketing Research, 1978.* Chicago: American Marketing Association, 1978.

Zaltman, G., and Burger, P. C. *Marketing Research: Fundamentals and Dynamics.* Hinsdale, Ill.: Dryden, 1975.

Zaltman, G., and Deshpande, R. "Increasing the Utilization of Scientific and Technical Information." In W. R. King and G. Zaltman (Eds.), *Marketing Scientific and Technical Information.* Boulder, Colo.: Westview, 1979.

Zaltman, G., and Duncan, R. *Strategies for Planned Change.* New York: Wiley, 1977.

Zaltman, G., Duncan, R., and Holbek, J. *Innovations and Organizations.* New York: Wiley, 1973.

Zaltman, G., Florio, D., and Sikorski, L. *Dynamic Educational Change: Models, Strategies, Tactics, and Management.* New York: Free Press, 1977.

Zaltman, G., and King, W. R. (Eds.). *Marketing Scientific and Technical Information.* Boulder, Colo.: Westview, 1979.

Zaltman, G., Kotler, P., and Kaufman, I. *Creating Social Change.* New York: Holt, Rinehart and Winston, 1972.

Zaltman, G., and Wallendorf, M. *Consumer Behavior: Basic Findings and Managerial Implications.* New York: Wiley, 1979.

Zaltman, G., Wallendorf, M., and Hirschman, E. "Role Accumulators Versus Opinion Leaders, Innovators and Gatekeepers as Important Groups in Consumer Research." In G. Zaltman and M. Wallendorf, *Consumer Behavior: Basic Findings and Managerial Implications.* New York: Wiley, 1979.

Zaltman, G., and others. *Processes and Phenomena of Social Change.* New York: Wiley, 1973.

Zand, D. E., and Sorensen, R. E. "Theory of Change and the Effective Use of Management Science." *Administrative Science Quarterly,* 1975, *20,* 532-545.

Zander, A. "Resistance to Change: Its Analysis and Prevention." In W. G. Bennis, K. D. Benne, and R. Chin (Eds.), *The Planning of Change: Readings in the Applied Behavioral Sciences.* New York: Holt, Rinehart and Winston, 1962.

Zimmerman, J. "Neighborhoods and Citizen Involvement." *Public Administration Review,* 1972, *32*(3), 201-210.

Zollschan, G. K., and Hirsch, W. (Eds.). *Social Change: Explorations, Diagnoses, and Conjectures.* New York: Halstead, 1976.

Zurcher, L. A. "Implementing a Community Action Agency." In M. F. Shore and F. B. Mannino (Eds.), *Community Mental Health: Problems, Programs, and Strategies.* New York: Behavioral Publications, 1969.

Zurcher, L. A. *Poverty Warriors: The Human Experience of Planned Social Interventions.* Austin: University of Texas Press, 1970.

Zurcher, L. A., and Bonjean, C. M. (Eds.). *Planned Social Intervention.* Scranton, Pa.: Chandler, 1970.

Zurcher, L. A., and Key, W. H. "The Overlap Model: A Comparison of Strategies for Social Change." *Sociological Quarterly,* 1968, *8*(4), 85-97.

# Name Index

Abbott, M. C., 102-103, 437
Abelson, H. H., 42-43, 60, 156, 437
Abernathy, W. J., 437, 592-593
Abramson, M. A., 437-438
Abt, C. C., 438
Abt, P., 227, 438
Achilladelis, B., 438, 564
Adimorah, E. N. O., 337, 348, 438
Adler, N. E., 438
Agarwala-Rogers, R., 16, 197, 329, 438, 482, 524, 566
Agnew, P. C., 438
Ahmed, M., 469
Aiken, M., 72, 76, 97, 105, 106, 109-110, 158, 438, 500
Albala, A., 161-162, 438
Alderfer, C. P., 439
Aldrich, H. E., 121, 439
Aleshire, D., 439
Alford, S. W., 501
Alkin, M. C., 439
Allen, D. H., 506
Allen, T. J., 322, 411, 439, 537
Allison, M. Q., 523
Alpert, J. L., 158, 439
Al-Timini, W., 439
Altman, I., 369, 439-440
Altrocchi, J., 440
Ammerman, H. L., 440
Anderson, L. R., 82, 218, 440
Anderson, S. B., 223, 224, 227, 440
Anderson, W. A., 440
Andrew, M. D., 440
Andrews, F. M., 75-76, 440, 556

Aneja, A. P., 159, 440
Aneja, V. P., 159, 440
Anthony, R. B., 49-50, 440
Applebaum, R. P., 440
Archambault, B., 305, 469-470
Archibald, K. A., 11, 256, 314, 369, 370, 440-441
Arensberg, C. M., 441
Argyris, C., 60-61, 266, 267, 377, 441
Armenakis, A. A., 441
Aronson, S. H., 372, 441
Arutunian, C. A., 308-309, 524
Ash, C., 579
Atkeson, B. M., 442
Attkisson, C. C., 442
Austin, C. J., 442
Avellar, J. W., 442
Avery, E. L., 50, 442
Ayscough, P. B., 50, 442

Backer, T. E., 197, 202, 213-214, 216-217, 222, 235-236, 243, 246, 256, 272-273, 442-443, 493-494
Bader, M. B., 343, 353-354, 443
Baehr, P. R., 443
Baer, D. M., 28, 584
Baer, W. S., 307-308, 443
Bailey, S. K., 443
Baire, K., 443
Baker, E. L., 443
Baker, F., 576
Baker, N. R., 411, 443-444

Balasubramanyam, V. N., 337, 444
Baldridge, J. V., 120, 444
Balk, D., 198, 444
Ball, S., 223, 224, 227, 440
Banathy, B. H., 278-279, 444
Bank, A., 330-331, 444
Banks, J., 444
Barabba, V. P., 179-180, 542
Barakat, H., 464
Baranson, J., 445
Bardach, E., 445
Bardhan, P., 524
Baritsch, H., 445
Barnes, L. B., 101, 445
Barnett, H. G., 78, 144-145, 445
Baron, C. H., 572
Barringer, H. R., 445
Barry, J. R., 445
Bartlett, M. H., 445
Barton, A. H., 17-18, 445
Barton, E., 393, 460, 563
Basiuk, V., 445
Bass, G., 445
Bass, L. W., 366-367, 558
Bassett, G., 11, 445-446
Bauer, R. A., 446
Beal, G. M., 446
Bean, A. S., 446
Becker, M. H., 58-59, 70, 75, 80,
    302, 446
Becker, S. W., 446-447, 473
Beckhard, R., 87, 164-165, 171,
    267, 268, 306, 372, 447
Beckman, N., 447
Bee, R. L., 447
Beer, M., 447
Beigel, A., 447
Bell, D., 448
Bell, J. E., xi
Ben-David, J., 448
Benedict, B. A., 91-92, 237-238, 448
Benne, K. D., 115, 187-190, 191n,
    192, 195, 196-197, 257, 301,
    448, 449, 465, 529
Bennett, A. M., 448
Bennett, C. A., 448
Bennis, W. G., 87, 102, 195, 196-
    197, 258, 265, 289, 301, 448-
    449, 492, 574
Bentzen, M. M., 238, 449
Berg, D. N., 48, 449, 541
Berg, M. R., 449

Berg, P. O., 276, 558
Berger, B., 449
Bergunder, A. F., 595
Berk, R. A., 449
Berke, J. S., 449
Berkowitz, M., 450
Berlin, I. N., 59-60, 70, 81, 82,
    270, 450
Berlyne, D. E., 450
Berman, P., 51, 152, 158, 171, 195-
    196, 197, 208-209, 245, 329, 450
Bernard, V., 79, 81, 117, 537
Berne, E., 378
Bernhardt, I., 450
Bernhill, E. A., 82, 169, 467
Bernstein, I., 450
Bernstein, M., 50, 113, 238, 498
Bertelsen, K., 450
Bertrand, A. L., 451
Beyer, J. M., 72, 128, 451
Bhagat, N. A., 13, 316, 451
Bhola, B. H., 516
Bhola, H. S., 255, 451
Bice, G. R., 451
Bice, T. W., 451
Biderman, A. D., 471
Biggart, N. W., 451
Billingsley, K., 496
Bina, J. V., 245, 511
Bingham, R. D., 132-133, 451-452
Bingle, J. D., 510
Binswanger, H. P., 452
Birnbaum, M., 187-188, 448
Birzea, C., 549
Black, G., 72, 483
Blackman, A. W., Jr., 452
Blackman, C. A., 452
Blackwell, L. R., 509
Blair, J., Jr., 452
Blake, R. R., 264-265, 268-269, 452
Blanke, V. E., 451, 452
Blanksten, G. I., 445
Bloom, B. S., 522
Blum, R. H., 81, 453
Bobbe, R. A., 97, 453
Bobren, H., 551
Boguslaw, R., 453
Bohlen, J. M., 446, 453
Boise, W. B., 201-202, 571
Bolas, C., 593
Bolin, D. C., 520
Bolton, B., 453

Bonjean, C. M., 604
Bonoma, T. V., 13, 603
Booth, D. A., 453
Borich, G. D., 453
Borman, L. D., 82, 453
Boruch, R. F., 235, 453, 563
Boss, R. W., 453
Bottle, R. T., 453-454
Boucher, W. L., 454
Bowen, D., 454
Bowers, D. G., 112-113, 116, 454, 537, 577
Bowman, J. S., 382, 389, 454
Bowman, P. H., 57, 302, 454
Boyan, N. J., 454
Boyd, W. L., 142-143, 454-455
Boyer, C. J., 455
Boylan, M., 455
Bozeman, B., 569
Bragaw, L. K., 134, 173, 175, 495
Brager, G., 455
Brandl, J. E., 455
Branscomb, L. M., 362-363, 455
Braskamp, L. A., 241-242, 455, 457, 549
Braunstein, Y. M., 455
Brazzel, J., 550
Brewer, D. L., 394, 508
Brewer, G. D., 455
Brickell, H. M., 455, 499
Bridgers, W. F., 303, 520
Bright, J. R., 61, 80, 81, 82, 93, 456
Brittain, J. M., 456
Brodsky, S. L., 456
Brooks, H., 336, 456
Brooks, S. H., 481
Broudy, H. S., 456
Brown, B. S., 456
Brown, H. J., 456
Brown, L. A., 401-402, 456, 577
Brown, M., 457
Brown, M. A., 577
Brown, R. D., 241-242, 455, 457, 549
Brown, R. H., 457
Bruckmann, C. G., 457
Bruyn, S. T., 457
Bryk, A. S., 457
Buchanan, G., 457
Buchanan, P. C., 457
Bucklin, L. P., 345, 457
Bucuvalas, M. J., 383, 597

Bundegaard-Nielsen, M., 457-458
Bungay, J., 315, 458
Burchinal, J., 326, 458
Burdge, R. L., 566
Burger, P. C., 13, 603
Burke, C. A., 564
Burke, C. S., 572
Burke, W. W., 73, 265, 458
Burnham, R. A., 120, 444
Burns, E. M., 4, 458
Burns, T., 458
Burt, R. S., 324, 458, 527
Bushnell, D. S., 458
Butler, A. J., 272, 458
Butler, M., 458-459
Butman, R. W., 308, 529
Buyukcolak, U., 459

Cadwallader, M. L., 459
Cady, L. L., 307, 459
Caledrone, G. E., 459
Calsyn, R., 459
Cammann, C., 525
Campbell, D. T., 235, 459, 469
Campbell, R., 459
Canon, L. K., 459
Caplan, G., 269-270, 302, 459-460
Caplan, N., 233, 389, 392-393, 460
Caporaso, J. A., 235, 461
Carey, R. G., 558
Carey, W. D., 461
Carl, L. M., 461
Carleton, W., 461
Carlson, E. D., 461
Carlson, R. O., 461
Carlson, S., 461
Caro, F. G., 461
Carpenter-Huffman, P., 461
Carrole, J., 106, 108, 461
Carroll, J. D., 105, 523
Carter, J. E., 130
Carter, L. F., 74, 305, 306, 313, 461-462
Cartwright, D., 82, 87, 462
Cassel, J., 462
Cates, C. S., 462, 509
Cawelti, G., 82, 462
Celotti, L. D., 475
Cetron, M. J., 462, 474
Chabotar, K. J., 462
Chadwin, M. L., 462
Chafe, H. D., 512

Chakrabarti, A. K., 91, 121, 134, 171, 462-463, 571, 582
Chalk, R., 576
Chapanis, A., 463
Charpie, R. L., 463
Charters, W. W., Jr., 463
Chattopadhyay, S. N., 554
Chelimsky, E., 285-286, 463
Chen, K., 136-137, 537
Chenery, M. F., 494
Cherney, P. R., 463
Cherns, A. B., 120, 156, 172, 178-179, 273, 290-291, 299, 365, 379, 463-464, 475
Chesler, M. A., 76, 101, 115, 375, 464, 472, 500
Chin, C. L., 566
Chin, R., 188-190, 191$n$, 192, 195, 196-197, 301, 311, 420, 448, 449, 464-465
Chinsky, J. M., 560
Christensen, P. R., 256, 377, 533
Churchill, G. A., Jr., 553
Churchman, C. W., 465
Ciarlo, J. A., 226, 465, 569
Cicchinelli, L. F., 465
Clark, A. W., 259, 407, 465
Clark, D. L., 465-466, 499
Clark, M. F., 466
Clark, N., 347, 355-356, 466
Clark, P. A., 258-259, 466
Clark, R. F., 444
Clark, T. N., 466
Clarke, T. E., 466
Clausen, A. W., 337, 466
Clifford, D. L., 429-430, 466
Clignet, R., 544
Cline, M. G., 466
Clinton, A., 466
Clukey, D., 440
Coates, J. F., 239, 466
Coch, L., 115, 466-467
Cochrane, J. L., 467
Coe, R. M., 82, 169, 467
Coelho, G. V., 467
Cohen, A., 467
Cohen, D. K., 385-386, 467, 485, 527
Cohen, J., 467
Cohen, M. D., 157, 467
Cohen, M. W., 467
Cohn, S. F., 135-136, 479

Cole, J., 362, 467
Cole, N. S., 467
Cole, S., 362, 467
Coleman, D., 438
Coleman, J. S., 56, 70-71, 114, 142, 300-301, 302, 467-468
Coller, A. R., 468
Collier, K. G., 468
Collins, B., 499
Collins, H. M., 311, 468
Collins, J. F., 468
Collins, S. M., 468
Compton, B. E., 311, 489
Conner, R. F., xii, 221-251, 468
Conner, R. J., 469
Conoley, J. C., 468
Conrath, D. W., 468
Constantino, R., 469
Conway, M. E., 469
Conway, R., 469
Cook, T. D., 235, 469
Cooke, R. A., 90, 469
Coombs, P. H., 469
Cooper, C., 469
Cooper, C. R., 305, 469-470
Cooper, S., 429-430, 466
Corbett, W. T., Jr., 470
Corey, K., 195
Corwin, R. G., 70, 75, 109, 210, 470, 546
Costello, T. W., 18, 81, 93, 114-115, 470
Cottle, T. J., 86, 470
Coughlan, R. J., 469
Cowan, J. R., 589
Coward, E. W., Jr., 83, 520
Cowen, E., 205, 470, 560
Cox, F., 470
Cox, G. B., 471
Coye, J. L., 580
Crain, R. L., 471
Crandall, D. P., 331-333, 471
Crane, D., 303, 471
Crane, J., 510
Crawford, E. T., 471
Crawford, R., 471
Creager, W. A., 585
Creighton, J. W., 471, 515
Cremin, L. A., 471
Crocker, L. M., 545
Crockett, W. J., 117, 471-472
Croker, G. W., 256, 472

Cronbach, L. J., 223, 227, 472
Crowe, R. E., 287, 299, 325, 472
Crowfoot, J. E., 472
Culbertson, J. A., 472, 546
Culver, C. M., 472
Cummings, C. P., 533-534
Cummings, M. M., 472
Cummings, T. G., 472
Curnow, R. C., 472
Cutler, J. J., 602
Czepiel, J. A., 472

Dachler, H. P., 472-473
Daft, R. K., 473
Dahl, R. A., 237, 473
Dahling, R. L., 404, 473
Daillak, R., 439
Dajani, J. S., 362, 579
Dalin, P., 473
Dalkey, N. C., 96, 473
Daniels, R. S., 262-263, 473
Danziger, J. N., 473
Dar, V., 342, 473
Darkenwald, G. G., 473
Darren, D. C., 473
Datta, L.-E., 284, 473-474
David, E. E., Jr., 52, 239, 474
David, P., 474
Davidson, E., 205, 470
Davidson, H. F., 462, 474
Davidson, W. S., II, 474
Davies, J., 474
Davis, A. G. M., 474
Davis, H. R., xi, 4, 5-7, 28-30, 31,
    36-37, 58, 60, 63, 101-102, 110,
    158, 192, 216, 224-225, 246,
    271, 286, 386-387, 407, 416-
    417, 418-419, 422, 426, 474-475
Davis, L. E., 290-291, 464, 475
Davis, T. R. V., 181, 261-262, 475
Davison, W. P., 11, 445-446
Deal, T. E., 444, 475
DeArman, J. W., 475
de Brichambaut, M., 475
DeFleur, M. L., 475
DeGrasse, R., 319, 514
Delbecq, A., 476
DeMarche, D. F., 281, 564
Denner, B., 476
Dentler, R. A., 293, 530
Dernberg, R. F., 476
Derr, C. B., 476

DeSanctis, J. E., 485
Deshpande, R., 301-302, 368, 376-
    377, 476, 603
Dessemontet, F., 359, 476
Deutsch, S. E., 485
Dewar, R., 476, 500
Dewey, J., 156, 166, 476
Dexter, L. A., 377, 477
Dickey, B., 477
Dickman, F. B., 477
Dimock, H. G., 80, 260, 477
Dingman, H. F., 538
Dittmar, S., 459
Dobrov, G. M., 407, 414-415, 477
Doctors, S. I., 212, 477
Doktor, R., 477
Donaldson, W. V., 477
Donnelly, W. L., 477-478
Donnison, D., 478
Dore, R. P., 350-351, 478
Dossett, W. A., 501
Doszkocs, T. R., 317-318, 478
Douds, C. F., 571
Dougharty, L., 478
Downing, J. J., 81, 453
Downs, A., 40, 103-104, 165, 478
Downs, G. W., 24-25, 400, 478
Dressel, P. L., 478
Dreyfus, D. A., 382, 478
Drucker, J., 478
Drucker, P. F., 18, 239, 478-479
Dube, S. C., 479
Dubey, S. N., 479
Duchesneau, T. D., 135-136, 479
Dumas, N. S., 479
Duncan, M. G., 479
Duncan, P., 479
Duncan, R. B., 11, 48, 84, 190, 192,
    261, 373, 476, 479-480, 603
Duncan, W. J., 376, 480
Dunn, I., 82, 558
Dunn, W. E., 480
Dunn, W. N., 211-212, 480
Dutton, J. E., 135-136, 400, 479,
    559
Dutton, W. H., 473
Dykens, J. W., 113, 116, 480
Dynes, R. R., 440

Eash, M. J., 376, 480
Eaton, J. W., 480
Eckensberger, L. H., 24, 480

Eddy, E. M., 480
Edling, J. V., 480-481
Edstrom, A., 481
Edwards, W., 481
Egea, A. N., 15, 342, 347, 481
Eichholz, G. C., 83, 481
Eichhorn, R. L., 451
Eidell, T. L., 481
Eiduson, B. T., 481
Ein-Dor, P., 481
Eisenstadt, S. N., 481
Ellis, W. E., 481-482
Elmore, R. F., 482, 600
Emery, F. E., 482
Emory, R., 557
Emrick, J. A., 329, 330, 482
Engel, A. J., 202-203, 485
Engstrom, G. A., 282, 305, 308, 372, 482
Enos, J. L., 9-10, 482
Erlich, J. L., 201, 570
Esser, M. A., 59, 370, 567
Etemad, H. E. A., 337, 353, 355, 482
Ettlie, J. E., 180, 322-323, 400, 482-483, 559, 571
Etzioni, A., 163, 237, 407, 412-414, 424-425, 483
Etzioni-Halevy, E., 483
Evan, W. M., 72, 483
Evans, J. W., 483
Evans, R. I., 71, 483
Eveland, J. D., 165, 196-197, 385, 423, 483, 566
Everhart, R. B., 483
Ewing, A. F., 341, 357, 483

Fabun, D., 484
Fairweather, G. W., 62, 63, 75, 77, 162, 169, 190, 198, 219, 246, 325, 374, 375, 484
Fallon, B., 484
Farlee, C., 203, 485, 496
Farrar, E., 485
Farris, G. F., 75-76, 440
Fashing, J., 485
Feild, H. S., 441
Feldman, J. J., 485
Felice, K. A., 545
Feller, I., 202-203, 399, 411, 485-486, 559
Ferguson, C. J., 486

Ferman, L. A., 226, 486
Ferree, E. H., 595
Festinger, L., 486
Fiehn, P., 457-458
Fields, D., 486
Figley, C., 225, 486
Fincher, C., 486
Finley, C. J., 308-309, 524
Fiore, C. F., 486
Fiorino, A. J., 206, 601
Firestone, W. A., 58, 117, 486
Fisch, R., 596
Fischer, W. A., 16, 486
Fish, J. C., 69, 552
Fisher, E., 366, 509
Fisher, G. L., 496
Fitz-Gibbon, C. T., 544
Flanagan, J. C., 370, 374-375, 487
Flanders, M., 375, 464
Fletcher, J. L., 487
Fliegel, F. C., 58, 61, 487
Florio, D., 39, 603
Flynn, P. J., 523
Forehand, R., 442
Foster, A. J., 318-319, 598
Foster, R. N., 487
Fox, J. C., 531
Fox, R. S., 76, 78, 101, 115, 464, 487, 529
Frank, L. K., 487
Frankel, C., 487
Franklin, J. L., 454, 487
Fredericksen, N., 71, 506
Freeman, C., 487-488
Freeman, H., 450
Freeman, H. E., 569
French, G. L., 496
French, J. R. P., Jr., 115, 214, 466-467, 488, 537
Friedrichs, G., 488
Frohman, A. L., 62, 211, 257, 365, 521, 564
Frost, P., 14-15, 180, 300, 598
Fry, B. M., 488
Fry, R., 73, 74, 101, 571
Fullan, M., 43, 48, 223, 245, 273-275, 488, 540-541

Gabel, B., xii
Gabor, D., 178, 488
Galbraith, J., 488
Gallagher, A., 258, 488-489

Gallessich, J., 489
Galvin, R. T., 589
Gardner, J. W., 79-80, 110, 489
Garfield, E., 318, 489
Garner, W., 367, 374, 489
Gartner, A., 489
Gartner, J., 132, 316, 489
Garvey, J. J., 380, 489
Garvey, W. D., 305, 311, 312, 313, 316, 317, 489-490
Gee, E. A., 490
Gee, S., 8, 49, 108-109, 158, 490
Gelb, J., 490
Gellman, A. J., 490-491
George, P. A., 515
Georgopoulos, B. S., 491
Gerbner, G., 491
Gerstenfeld, A., 125-126, 137, 491
Gery, G. J., 51-52, 491
Gesten, E., 205, 470
Giacquinta, J., 50, 113, 238, 491, 498
Gibbons, M., 514
Gilbert, J. P., 491-492
Gill, P. P., 492
Gillespie, D. F., 557
Gillespie, J., 525
Gilmore, J. S., 492
Ginzberg, E., 492
Gittell, M., 492
Glancy, D. M., 492
Glaser, E. M., 3, 10, 30-32, 36-37, 51, 56, 59, 61, 69, 73, 74, 75, 76, 79, 82, 88, 93, 97, 107, 109, 111, 115, 117, 168, 190, 197, 202, 213-214, 216-217, 218, 222, 235-236, 241, 243-244, 246-249, 256, 272-273, 289-290, 301, 302, 305, 306-307, 308, 310, 313, 314, 322, 325, 374, 375, 379, 419, 433, 434, 442-443, 492-494, 573, 596
Glaser, R., 494
Glass, G. V., 494
Glennan, T. K., 494
Glidewell, J. C., 219, 494
Globe, S., 495
Glock, C. Y., 74, 369, 374, 495, 517
Gluck, F. W., 487
Gluckstern, N. B., 261, 495
Gold, B., 16-17, 49, 134, 138-139, 176-177, 183, 495

Goldberg, G. S., 99, 495
Goldenbaum, D. M., 515
Goldhar, J. D., 134, 173, 175, 462, 474, 495
Goldin, C. J., 313, 314, 377, 378, 495
Goldman, P., 84, 88, 206, 496
Goldman, S., 44, 204, 496
Goldstein, B., 496
Golembiewski, R. J., 496
Goodlad, J., 496
Goodman, L. H., 496
Goodman, P. S., 496
Goodridge, C. G., 117-118, 496
Goodwin, L., 496
Gooler, D. D., 529
Gordon, G., 496-497
Gordon, W. J., 497
Gottfredson, D. M., 497
Gottfredson, S. D., 305, 311, 316, 489
Goudy, W. J., 263, 497
Grabbe, P., 82, 218, 377, 526
Grabowski, H., 497
Grace, B. F., 461
Grad, M. L., 497
Graff, T. O., 598
Graham, R. A., 497
Grant, D. J., 589
Gray, T., 157, 213-214, 215, 497
Gray, V., 497
Green, H. P., 497
Greenberg, D. S., 312, 497
Greenberg, P. D., 65-66, 497-498
Greenfield, T. B., 498
Greenwood, E., 498
Greenwood, P. W., 498
Greer, A. L., 498
Gregory, S., 84, 88, 206, 496
Greiner, L. E., 156, 177, 214, 498
Griffin, G. A., 11-12, 238, 498, 527
Griffith, B. C., 311, 312, 313, 317, 489-490, 498
Griffith, D. H. S., 354, 498
Griffiths, D. E., 69, 71, 101, 498, 506
Grilliches, Z., 515-516
Gross, N., 50, 113, 238, 498
Gross, N. C., 300, 301, 572
Gruber, W. H., 40, 158-159, 498
Gruenberg, E. M., 498-499

Guba, E. G., 218, 227, 235, 236-237, 377, 499
Guest, R. H., 73, 109, 499
Guetzkow, H., 256, 499
Guilmette, A. M., 266, 559
Guskin, A. E., 260-261, 500
Gustafson, D., 476
Gutmanis, I., 500
Guttentag, M., 481, 500, 585
Guttinger, H. I., 470

Hackman, J. R., 93, 500
Haeffner, E. A., 15-16, 172, 500
Hage, J., 72, 76, 97, 105, 106, 109-110, 158, 438, 500
Hagerstrand, T. A., 401, 500-501
Haggart, S., 478
Haggarty, J. J., 501
Hagstrom, W. O., 311, 501
Halbower, C. C., 568
Hall, D. C., 501
Hall, D. J., 501
Hall, G. E., 501
Hall, G. R., 461
✓Haller, K. B., 313, 501-502
Halpern, J., 465, 497
Halpert, H. P., 63, 177-178, 227, 313, 314, 372, 502
Halpin, A. W., 78, 95, 369, 502
Hamblin, R. L., 502
Hamilton, E. L., 599
Hamilton, H., 517-518
Hamilton, L. S., 502
Hamilton, W. F., 477
Hammond, J. S., 502
Hampton, E., 477
Hanson, R. W., 524-525
Harder, R. J., 552
Harer, W. B., 502
Hargrove, E. C., 502
Harper, I. B., 303, 520
Harris, M. R., 450
Harris, R. T., 447
Harrison, E. F., 502
Harrison, R., 279, 502
Hartley, L. B., 309, 522
Harvey, E., 502-503
Hattery, L., 573
Havelock, M. C., 110, 277, 504
Havelock, R. G., 33-34, 36-37, 38, 40, 53, 61, 72, 73, 76, 80, 82, 99, 101, 106, 108, 109, 110, 115, 118, 169, 178, 179, 182, 255, 256, 257, 261, 277, 280, 288, 289, 302, 305-306, 312, 324, 325, 350, 371, 374, 404, 407-408, 432, 433-434, 503-505, 529
Hawkings, J. D., 505
Hawley, A. H., 147-148, 505
Hawthorne, E. P., 345-346, 349, 505-506
Hayami, Y., 572
Hayes, F. O. R., 506
Hayvaert, C. H., 506
Hayward, G., 506
Heald, K., 602
Hearn, N. E., 506
Heathers, G., 506
Helleiner, G. K., 349, 352, 506
Hellriegel, D., 506
Helmer, O., 96, 506
Hemphill, J., 71, 506, 567
Henerson, M. E., 544
Hennigh, L., 506-507
Henning, J. F., 507
Henry, M. D., 576
Hepworth, A., 507
Herbert, E., 507
Herlig, R. K., 507
Hernandono, 337, 507
Herner, M., 507
Herner, S., 507
Herzog, A. J., 507
Hetman, F., 507
Higgins, T., 508
Hill-Burnett, J., 508
Hillman, D. J., 508
Hiltz, S. R., 508
Hinrichs, J. R., 93, 94, 508
Hirsch, W., 508, 604
Hirschman, E., 603-604
Hlavacek, J. D., 508
Hoban, G. J., 472
Hober, D., 226, 465, 569
Hoberman, S., 278, 508
Hodgkin, J. E., 290, 374, 433, 508
Hoffer, E., 508
Hoffman, L. R., 534
Hofler, D., 559
Holbek, J., 11, 603
Holland, T. R., 394, 508
Holland, W. E., 518
Holley, W. H., 441

Holliday, G. D., 508-509
Hollis, P. W., 509
Holloway, R. E., 509
Holloway, S., 455
Holmes, E. H., 509
Holmes, M., 509
Holt, K., 509
Holt, N., 394, 508
Holzner, B., 366, 377, 509
Hood, P. D., 44, 509-510
Hooker, S., 256, 563
Hopkins, R., 279, 502
Hopper, J. H., 586
Hopson, A., 11, 445-446
Horn, B. R., 510
Hornstein, A., 510
Hornstein, H. A., 191n, 458, 510,
    589
Horowitz, D. L., 510
Horowitz, I. L., 510
Horsley, J., 313, 501-502, 510 ✓
Horst, D. P., 510
Horst, L., 258, 404, 574
Horst, P., 457
Hough, G. W., 510
House, E. R., 103, 114, 210-211,
    510-511
House, J. H., 466
House, P. W., 511
Hovland, C. I., 56, 511
Howard, E., 511
Howes, N. J., 171, 193-194, 511
Hsu, F. L. K., 438
Huber, J. C., 504
Huberman, A. M., 350, 504
Hull, W. L., 245, 511
Hunt, J. B., 430, 511
Hunt, R. G., 511-512
Hurten, R. P., 512
Huse, E., 447, 512
Husseiny, A. A., 351, 512
Hutchins, C. L., 512, 590
Hutchins, L., 567
Hyman, H. H., 512
Hyslop, M. R., 512

Ikonicoff, M., 357, 512
Imershein, A. W., 512
Immegart, G. L., 142-143, 455
Ingram, H., 534
Isenson, R. S., 578
Israel, B. B., 469

Izard, C. E., 494

Jacko, C. M., 81, 203-204, 517
Jacobson, L., 513
Jacobson, P. B., 513
Jacobson, R. B., 502
Jain, N. C., 513
Janis, I. L., 56, 511
Jemelka, R. P., 453
Jenkins, D. H., 156, 177, 218, 513
Jenkins, W. I., 464
Jenks, R. S., 96, 513
Jenstrom, L. L., 379-380, 408-410,
    513, 556
Jermakowicz, W., 104, 513
Jervis, P., 438, 513-514, 564
Jewkes, J., 514
Johansen, R., 319, 514
Johns, E. A., 514
Johnson, C. A., 514
Johnson, D. W., 514
Johnson, F. P., 514
Johnson, J. H., 514
Johnson, K. W., 77, 514
Johnson, L. L., 443
Johnston, H. R., 514
Johnston, R., 514
Jolly, J. A., 471, 515
Joly, J. M., 369, 515
Jones, D. W., 511
Jones, G. N., 191n, 192-193, 515
Jones, M., 344, 348, 515
Jones, R. K., 515
Jones, T. A., 580
Jorgenson, D. W., 515-516
Judson, A. S., 516
Jung, C. C., 156, 177, 377, 378, 516
Jwaideh, A. R., 516

Kadushin, A., 314, 516
Kadushin, C., 292, 516
Kahn, R. L., 516, 517
Kahneman, D., 516
Kalachek, E. D., 124, 548
Kallen, H. M., 516
Kaluzny, A. D., 516
Kamien, M. I., 516
Kang, T., 593
Kaplan, B., 317, 517
Kaplan, R. S., 517
Kaplinsky, R., 347, 351, 517
Karier, C. J., 517

Karmos, J. S., 81, 203-204, 517
Kasper, R. G., 517
Katter, R. V., 510
Katz, D., 517
Katz, E., 56, 70-71, 300-301, 302-
    303, 468, 517-518
Katz, J. E., 510
Katz, R. C., 514
Katzell, R. A., 93, 518
Kaufman, I., 17, 191n, 518, 603
Kay, D., 518
Keen, P. G. W., 518
Keith, D. M., 238, 580
Keith, P. M., 69, 518
Kell, D. G., 462
Keller, R. T., 518
Kelley, H. H., 56, 511
Kelly, P., 518
Kelman, H. C., 79, 171-172, 219,
    338, 357, 518-519, 595
Keniston, K., 519
Kernaghan, J. A., 77, 551
Kernan, J. B., 519
Kessler, J. T., 528
Ketefian, S., 519
Key, W. H., 519, 604
Khumawala, B. M., 526
Kiesler, C. A., 235, 519
Kiesler, S. B., 519
Kilburg, R., 519
Kilmann, R. H., 179-180, 519, 541-
    542
Kimberly, J. R., 550
Kimbrough, R. B., 519
King, A., 519
King, W. R., 14, 519, 603
Kinkade, R. G., 519-520
Kiresuk, T. J., 96, 246, 520
Kirkhart, K. E., xii, 221-251
Kitchel, J. M., 481
Kitti, C., 574
Kivens, L., 520, 573
Kivlin, J. E., 58, 61, 487
Klapper, M. S., 303, 520
Klarman, H. E., 520
Klein, D. A., 451
Klein, H. D., 86, 314, 315, 520
Klein, M. W., 520
Klempner, I. M., 373, 520
Klepper, C., 165, 196-197, 385,
    423, 483, 566
Kloman, H., 520

Klonglan, G. E., 83, 520-521
Knorr, K. D., 233, 389, 521
Knott, J., 521
Knox, W. T., 299-300, 310, 521
Kochen, M., 521
Kocowski, T., 521
Koestler, A., 521
Kogan, L. S., 369, 521
Koizumi, T., 521
Kojima, K., 344, 521
Kolb, D. A., 521
Kolodny, R., 369, 374, 564
Kopecky, K. J., 521
Kotler, J. P., 48, 85-86, 121, 193,
    215, 522
Kotler, P., 17, 141-142, 191n, 522,
    603
Kozak, L. A., 411, 486
Kraemer, K. L., 14, 60, 319-320,
    522, 556-557
Kranzberg, M., 399, 518, 522
Krathwohl, D. R., 522
Krishnan, P., 354, 522
Kritek, W. J., 43, 44, 143, 203, 522
Kroeber, A. L., 522
Kroll, J., 271, 524
Kuhn, T. S., 522
Kuhner, A., 354, 522
Kunce, J. T., 309, 522
Kunreuther, H. C., 523
Kurpius, D., 523

L'Abate, L., 523
Lake, D. G., 541
Lakhani, H., 523
Lall, S., 358-359, 523
Lalley, T., 523
Lambert, N., 601
Lambright, W. H., 105, 523
Lancaster, R. W., 11, 316, 523
Landgrenbackstrom, S., 523
Langrish, J., 321, 524
Lapan, H., 524
LaPiere, R. T., 70, 82, 83, 524
Larkey, P., 524
Larsen, J. K., 16, 65, 226, 271-272,
    301, 302, 308-309, 334, 524,
    550, 564
Larsen, V., 197, 524
Larson, J., 411, 443
Lasagna, L., 524-525
Lauer, R. H., 139-141, 525

Laventur, C., 601
Lavin, R. J., 525, 538
Lawler, E. E., III, 525
Lawler, M. R., 525
Lawless, M. W., 525
Lawrence, W. G., 525
Layton, C., 525
Lazarsfeld, P. F., 302, 377, 517, 525
Lazarus, S., 525
Leavitt, H., 525
Lee, W. B., 526
Leeper, R. R., 526
Lehming, R., 526
Leithwood, K. A., 526
Lenz, R. C., Jr., 136-137, 537
Leong, S. W., 353, 526
Leppmann, P. K., 71, 483
Levenson, A. I., 447
Levin, M. L., 517-518
Levine, G., 512
Levine, R. A., 526
Levinson-Rose, J., 469
Levis, M., 342, 473
Levy, G. W., 495, 526
Lewicki, R. J., 526
Lewin, K., 82, 86, 187, 218, 377, 526
Lewis-Beck, M. S., 527
Lieber, A. L., 527
Lieberman, A., 11-12, 238, 498, 527
Light, R. J., 457, 491-492
Lightal, F. F., 527
Likert, R., 117, 313, 369, 527
Lin, N., 33, 311, 324, 490, 527
Lincoln, Y. S., 227, 235, 236-237, 499
Lindblom, C. E., 237, 385-386, 473, 527
Linden, M. E., 527
Lindquist, J., 197-198, 528
Lindsey, Q. W., 528
Lingwood, D. A., 33-34, 36-37, 169, 178, 280, 408, 432, 505, 528
Linhares, A. B., 528
Linstone, H., 528
Lionberger, H. F., 528
Lipetz, B., 528
Lippitt, R. O., 61, 68-69, 71, 78, 87, 93, 97, 101, 113-114, 115, 156, 169, 177, 182, 199, 243, 256, 265, 308, 313, 325, 369,

377, 419, 433, 464, 487, 516, 527, 528-529, 574-575
Liss, L., 529
Liston, J., 62, 529
Litwin, G. H., 91, 529
Locatis, C. N., 529
Lochner, P. R., Jr., 530
Loeser, F., 530
Long, T. P., 159, 530
Lorenzi, N. M., 530
Lorsch, J. W., 85, 530
Loucks, S. F., 501
Louis, K. S., 43, 257, 293, 326, 328, 329, 530, 543, 568, 579, 582-583
Lowin, A., 530
Loy, J. W., Jr., 530
Lucas, H. C., Jr., 530-531
Luke, R. A., Jr., 48, 81, 531
Lumsdaine, A. A., 448
Lund, S., 281, 286, 531
Lund, S. H., 520
Lundberg, C. C., 258, 531
Lundberg, L. B., 531
Lundman, R. J., 531
Lynn, F., 10, 531
Lynn, L. E., Jr., 388-389, 531
Lynton, R. P., 532
Lyons, G. M., 532

McCarthy, B. W., 595
McClelland, D. C., 78, 532
McClelland, W. A., 62, 71, 108, 419-420, 532
Maccoby, N., 486
McConkie, M. L., 453
McCool, S. F., 179, 373, 532
McCormack, M., 128-130
McCune, S. M., 532
McCutcheon, J. R., 532
McDevitt, C. G., 282-283, 572
McDonald, G., 532
McFarland, W., 532
McGinnis, R., 318, 532
McGowan, E. F., 244, 532
McGuire, W. J., 82, 218, 440, 532
Machlup, F., 532
MacIver, R. M., 533
Mack, R. W., 445
MacKenzie, K. D., 450
Mackie, R. R., 256, 265, 377, 533
McKinney, L. W., 533

MacKinnon, W. J., 602-603
McLaughlin, C., 533
McLaughlin, M. W., 158, 208-209, 245, 450, 498
MacLennan, B. W., 535
McNaught, T. P., 132-133, 451-452
McRae, D., Jr., 533
Madancy, R. S., 287, 299, 325, 472
Madey, D. L., 533
Madigan, J. A., 564
Magidson, J., 227, 438
Magisos, J. H., 299, 533
Maguire, L. M., 533-534, 553
Mahajan, V., 534
Maier, N. R. F., 93-94, 218, 426, 534
Malecki, E. J., 456
Maloney, J. C., 534
Mandersloot, W. G. B., 457
Manela, R., 10-11, 99, 370, 534
Mangham, I., 534
Mann, D., 498, 534
Mann, F. C., 76-77, 111, 214-215, 219, 302, 505, 534-535
Manninen, D., 544
Manning, B. A., 46, 535
Manning, M. J., 515
Manning, N. P., 63-64, 244, 535
Mannino, F., 535
Mansfield, E., 8-9, 10, 61, 72-73, 74, 93, 108, 125, 535-536
Manten, A. A., 11, 310-311, 536
Manzoor, C., 337, 353, 536
March, J. G., 157, 467, 536
Marcum, R. L., 68, 93, 111, 536
Margolin, K. N., 313, 314, 377, 378, 495
Margulies, N., 276, 536
Marker, G. W., 65, 516, 536
Markley, O. W., 536
Markowitz, E., 305-306, 371, 408, 505
Marks, J. B., 3, 494
Marmor, J., 79, 81, 117, 537
Marquis, D. G., 40, 158-159, 411, 498, 537, 546
Marquis, S., 496
Marris, P., 537
Marrow, A. J., 115, 116, 289, 537
Martin, G., 537
Martino, J. P., 136-137, 537
Marx, J., 377, 509

Masar, N., 256, 563
Mashaal, H., 354, 498
Masia, B. B., 522
Mason, R. O., 542
Masters, R., 351, 537
Masterson, J., 506
Matheson, N. W., 314-315, 538
Matsui, S., 538
Matula, F. V., 538
May, F. B., 552
Mayfield, R. C., 601
Meadows, D. H., 339, 538
Mealiea, L. W., 44, 77, 538
Meals, D., 538
Mechanic, D., 538
Meierhenry, W. C., 538
Mense, A., 129
Menzel, D. C., 202-203, 411, 485-486
Menzel, H. A., 56, 70-71, 300-301, 302, 324, 468, 538
Mercer, J. R., 538
Merrifield, D. B., 160, 176, 538
Merrow, E. W., 443
Merton, R. K., 435, 539
Mesthene, E. G., 539
Metcalf, J. L., 539
Metzger, L., 43, 257, 326, 329, 579
Meyer, M. W., 539
Meyer, T. C., 539
Meyers, W. R., 263-264, 539
Michalet, C.-A., 343, 539
Mick, C., 510, 539
Midgley, D. F., 539
Miles, M. B., xi-xii, 48-49, 56, 57, 58, 61, 76, 92, 95, 110, 111, 112, 207-208, 219, 235, 245, 273-275, 276, 288, 289, 292-293, 294, 306, 488, 540-541, 575
Miles, R. E., 473
Miller, J. K., 456
Miller, J. L., 502
Miller, S. M., 308, 561
Miller, T. C., 541
Milliken, J. G., 160-161, 336, 340, 564
Mills, R., 502-503
Milo, N., 541
Milstein, M. M., 541
Milwood, H. B., 561
Mirvis, P. H., 48, 541

Miskel, C. G., 278, 541
Mitchell, D. E., 390-391, 541
Mitroff, D. D., 378, 542
Mitroff, I. I., 179-180, 378, 541-542
Mittenthal, S. D., 542
Moch, M. K., 106-107, 542
Mogee, M. E., 446
Mogulof, M. B., 264, 542
Mohr, L. B., 25, 400, 478, 527, 542
Mohrman, S., 542
Mojena, R., 519
Mojkowski, C., 542-543
Molitor, J. A., 543
Montgomery, D., 543
Montgomery, D. J., 526
Moore, B. M., 515
Moore, D. R., 205-206, 329, 543
Moore, J. R., 134-135, 543
Moore, M. T., 449
Moore, W. E., 578
Moorehead, B. B., 584
Moravcsik, M. J., 543
Morell, J. A., 543
Moreno, J. L., 70, 543
Morgan, J. S., 267-268, 543
Moriarty, E. J., 288, 543
Moriarty, R. J., 266, 559
Moring, G. C., 472
Morphet, E. L., 543-544
Morrill, R., 544
Morris, L. L., 544
Morris, P., 544
Morris, R., 544
Morris, W. C., 258, 404, 544, 574
Morrish, I., 544
Morrison, A., 233, 389, 392, 460
Morrison, D. E., 145-146, 544
Morse, E. V., 106-107, 542
Mort, P. R., 544
Morton, J. A., 544
Morton, M. S., 518
Mosteller, F., 10, 491-492, 544
Motto, R. L., 481
Mouton, J. S., 264-265, 268-269, 452
Moyer, D., 544
Moynihan, W. J., 44, 204, 496
Mulkay, M. J., 361, 362, 544
Mullen, E. J., 545
Mullins, N. C., 498
Munro, R. G., 545

Munson, F. C., 17, 158, 256, 407, 408-410, 545, 556
Murphy, S. T., 545
Murugesan, P., 543
Mushkin, S. J., 545
Muthard, J. E., 479, 502, 545
Myers, S., 51, 131, 159, 160, 411, 537, 546

Nabseth, L., 546
Nadler, D. A., 525, 546
Nagi, S. Z., 305, 369, 370, 546
Nagle, J., 546
Naiman, C. S., 132, 316, 489
Narris, P., 546
Nash, N., 546
Neelameghan, A., 548
Neff, F. W., 214-215, 534-535
Neill, S. B., 548
Nelkin, D., 393, 548
Nelson, C. E., 548
Nelson, J., 542
Nelson, M., 548
Nelson, R. R., 124, 346, 548-549
Nelson, S. D., 549
Newell, A., 579
Newman, D. L., 549
Nica, I., 549
Nicholas, J. M., 549
Nichols, D. G., 65, 302, 524
Nickoff, A. H., 441
Nicosia, F., 549
Niehoff, A. H., 58, 169, 302, 304-305, 306, 349, 550
Nielsen, W. R., 550
Nielson, J., 550
Nimkoff, M. F., 550
Nisberg, J. N., 550, 589
Nisbet, R. A., 550
Nitko, A. J., 467
Nolan, R., 532
Noll, R. G., 550
Norman, R., 454, 550
Norris, E. L., 271, 524, 550
Norton, D., 532
Null, J. A., 127, 551
Nunnally, J. C., 551

Ochberg, F. M., 475, 600
O'Connell, J. J., 551
Okedijim, F. O., 551
O'Keefe, R. D., 77, 551, 571

Oldham, G. R., 93, 500
Olds, V. M., 551
Olsen, H. A., 552
Olsen, J. P., 157, 467
Omerso, R. L., 585
O'Reilly, R. R., 69, 552
Orlans, H., 552
Orlich, D. C., 552
Orlinsky, N., 568
Orr, J. F., 552
Osborne, P., 505
Osview, L., 553
Otten, G., 228, 553
Ottenberg, P., 79, 81, 117, 537
Owens, R. G., 553
Ozanne, U. B., 553

Packard, R. W., 261, 495
Paine, S. C., 321-322, 553
Paisley, M. B., 325, 553
Paisley, W. J., 74, 170, 299, 304,
    313, 323, 325, 458, 553-554
Palonsky, S. B., 554
Pareek, U., 554
Parikh, J. K., 346, 554
Parish, R., 554
Parker, E. B., 304, 554
Parker, J. E. S., 554
Passerman, S., 554
Patterson, K., 276-277, 558
Patton, M. Q., 227, 241, 554
Paul, D. A., 554-555
Pavitt, K., 555
Peck, M. T., 124, 548
Pecorella, P. A., 454
Pedersen, P. O., 555
Peirce, W. S., 16-17, 134, 138-139,
    495, 555
Pelc, K. I., 363-364, 555
Pellegrin, R. J., 370, 377, 402, 463,
    555-556
Pellegrino, E. D., 513
Pelz, D. C., xii, 17, 18, 158, 233, 256,
    384, 389, 407, 408-410, 545, 556
Penchansky, R., 533
Pennings, J. M., 496, 556
Perloff, R., 474
Perry, A., 556
Perry, J. L., 556-557
Perry, R. W., 557
Peter, H. W., 449
Peterson, S. M., 329, 330, 482

Pettigrew, A., 557
Piele, P. K., 557
Pigg, K., 557
Pinchoff, D. M., 456
Pincus, J., 102, 557
Pino, R., 557
Pitts, M., 330-331, 444
Placek, P. J., 557
Plovnick, M., 73, 74, 101, 571
Polivka, L., 557
Pollard, W. E., 469
Polley, M. L., 490
Pollock, D. K., 548
Pomfret, A., 223, 488
Pontecorvo, G., 344, 557
Popper, K., 237, 557
Porat, M. U., 557-558
Porras, J. I., 276-277, 558
Posavac, E. J., 558
Poser, E. G., 82, 558
Posner, B., 558
Powell, F. A., 69, 590
Powell, G., 558
Prakash, P., 558
Price, D. de S., 337, 558
Price, J. L., 558
Price, R., 476
Price, W. J., 366-367, 558
Pruger, R., 558

Quellmalz, E. S., 443
Quest, R. H., 558
Quinn, J. B., 131, 559
Quinn, R. E., 171, 193-194, 511
Quintelier, G. L. M., 559
Quintero-Alfaro, G., 350, 559

Radnor, M., 399, 400, 559
Ragab, A. M., 266, 559
Ragano, F. P., 560
Raia, A. P., 536
Raizen, S. A., 127, 560
Ramana, D. V., 354, 498
Ramer, B., 69, 560
Ramo, S., 126-127, 560
Ramsay, T., 573
Randall, R. M., 179, 576
Rapoport, R. N., 63-64, 244, 535,
    560
Rapp, B. A., 317-318, 478
Rappaport, D., 458
Rappaport, J., 560

Rappaport, W. H., 448
Raven, B., 214, 488
Ray, G., 546
Rayman, P. M., 457
Reddin, W. J., 86, 265-266, 560
Rees, A. M., 560
Rehder, R. R., 561
Reiff, R., 561
Rein, M., 99, 308, 546, 561
Reitman, W. R., 561
Remp, R., 483
Renehan, L. A., 561
Rescher, N., 443
Resnick, H. 561
Reston, J., 561
Rettig, R. A., 561
Reynolds, M. A., 313, 501-502
Rhine, W. R., 561
Rice, A. K., 107, 561
Rice, R. E., 197, 562
Rich, R. F., 152, 226, 233, 303, 364, 389-390, 400-401, 559, 562-563
Rich, W., 354, 563
Richards, R. O., 263, 497
Richland, M., 108, 308, 563
Richter, I., 563
Riecken, H. W., 235, 563
Riedel, J., 563
Rieker, P. P., 242, 563
Riessman, F., 489
Riley, P., 256, 563
Rittenhouse, C. H., 563
Rivlin, A., 563
Robbins, M. D., 160-161, 336, 340, 564
Roberto, E. L., 564
Roberts, A. O. H., 301, 302, 312, 334, 564
Roberts, E. B., 62, 211, 257, 365, 564
Roberts-Gray, C., 157, 213-214, 215, 497
Robertson, A. B., 438, 564, 570
Robertson, T. S., 564
Robinault, I. P., 282, 564
Robinson, A. C., 564
Robinson, B., 144, 584
Robinson, R., 281, 564
Rodman, H., 369, 374, 564
Roessler, R. T., 564
Roessner, J. D., 40-42, 384-385, 446, 564-565

Roffe, P., 358, 565
Roffman, R. A., 505
Rogers, C. R., 79, 565
Rogers, E. M., 24, 40, 56, 57, 58, 60, 61, 67, 68, 70, 72, 74, 75, 76, 80, 82, 83, 87, 96, 100-101, 115, 146-147, 164, 165, 168, 196-197, 243, 256, 302, 323, 345, 374, 385, 399, 400, 401, 404, 421, 423, 433, 481, 483, 559, 562, 565-567
Romeo, A. A., 567
Roos, L. L., Jr., 235, 461
Rose, M., 59, 370, 567
Rose, R., 567
Rose, S. M., 595
Rosegger, G., 16-17, 134, 138-139, 495
Rosen, P. L., 382, 567
Rosenau, F., 567
Rosenberg, N., 49, 57, 137-138, 399, 401, 567
Rosenblatt, A., 59-60, 370, 567, 571
Rosenbloom, R. S., 72, 170-171, 172, 180-181, 303-304, 567-568
Rosenblum, S., 293, 530, 568
Rosenfeld, E., 568
Rosenfeld, J. M., 568
Rosentraub, M. S., 568
Rosner, M. M., 568
Ross, D. A., 348, 568
Ross, D. H., 99, 568
Ross, H. L., 59, 69, 75, 76, 82, 111, 115, 190, 306-307, 314, 494
Ross, P. D., 568
Ross, P. F., 13, 44-45, 322-323, 568
Rossi, P. H., 235, 560, 568-569
Rossini, F., 569
Rossiter, D. L., 264, 569, 600
Rossman, B. B., 226, 465, 569
Rothman, J., xii, 42, 119-120, 162-164, 201, 250, 257, 378-379, 569-570
Rothwell, R., 51, 173, 175, 570
Rousseau, D. M., 570
Rowe, A. P., 570
Rowe, L. A., 201-202, 571
Rozwadowski, R. T., 486
Rubenstein, A. H., 77, 121, 171, 177, 288, 341, 407, 410-412, 463, 512, 551, 559, 571, 582
Rubenstein, E. A., 467

Rubin, A., 571
Rubin, I., 73, 74, 101, 571
Rubin, L. J., 156, 177, 302, 571
Ruby, B., 571
Rule, J. B., 572
Rusnack, B., 572
Russell, L. B., 572
Rutman, L., 572
Ruttan, V. W., 572
Rutter, M., 49, 572
Ryan, B., 300, 301, 572
Ryan, C. O., 543-544

Sackman, H., 96, 184-185, 572
Sadler, R. R., 282-283, 572
Sahal, D., 572
Saks, M. J., 572
Salasin, J., 131-132, 572-573
Salasin, S. E., xi, 4, 5-7, 28-30, 31,
    158, 224-225, 246, 386-387,
    418-419, 422, 426, 427-428,
    474-475, 573
Sanders, D. H., 62, 63, 75, 77, 169,
    198, 219, 246, 325, 484
Sanders, H. C., 573
Sanders, J. E., 525, 538
Sanders, J. R., 532
Sands, F. F., 379, 573
Sanford, N., 573
Sapolsky, H. M., 93, 101, 573
Sarason, S. B., 144, 573
Sarbaugh, L. E., 309-310, 573-574
Sartorius, N., 574
Sashkin, M., 258, 404, 544, 574
Sauber, S. R., 198-199, 574
Saunders, J., 574
Sawyer, D., 514
Sayles, L. R., 574
Scanlon, J., 457, 574
Scanlon, R. G., 204-205, 574
Schaffer, R. H., 97, 453
Schalock, H. D., 574
Schein, E. H., 87, 258, 265, 289,
    449, 574
Scheirer, M. A., 574
Schiffel, D., 446, 574
Schild, E. O., 516
Schindler-Rainman, E., 87, 574-575
Schlesinger, L. A., 48, 85-86, 121,
    193, 215, 522
Schlesinger, L. D., 579

Schmidt, W. H., 73, 265, 458
Schmookler, J., 575
Schmuck, R. A., 97, 111, 275-276,
    370, 464, 575
Schoemaker, P. J. H., 523
Schoeman, M. E. F., 534
Schoenfeld, C. A., 575
Scholl, R. W., 276, 536
Schön, D. A., 61, 98, 108, 110, 153,
    266, 292, 293, 403-404, 441,
    561, 575
Schonfeld, E. P., 534
Schoolman, H. M., 317-318, 478
Schramm, W. L., 517, 575
Schrank, R., 115, 575
Schreyer, R. M., 179, 373, 532
Schuelke, L. D., 575-576
Schulberg, H. C., 576
Schultz, D. G., 560
Schultz, R. L., 576
Schultz, T. W., 576
Schwartz, C. M., 495
Schwartz, D. C., 256, 576
Schwartz, J. H., 134, 173, 175, 495
Schwartz, N., 516
Schwartz, P., 599-600
Schwartzman, D., 576
Schweitzer, D. L., 179, 576
Scott, J. P., 576
Scott, S. F., 576
Scribner, R., 576
Scriven, M., 226-227, 576-577
Seashore, C., 579
Seashore, S. E., 116, 454, 537, 577
Seetharama, S., 548
Segal, J., 577
Segev, E., 481
Seligman, E. J., 452
Semple, R. K., 577
Servi, I. S., 177, 181, 319, 364-365,
    577
Sewell, W., 577
Sewell, W. H., 302, 377, 525
Shapero, A., 577
Sharfstein, S. S., 475
Sharp, G., 577
Shartle, C. L., 577
Shaw, M. B., 577-578
Sheldon, E. B., 578
Sherman, R. E., 96, 246, 520
Sherwin, C. W., 578

Sherwood, C. C., 372, 441
Shoemaker, F. F., 40, 74, 75, 80,
    164, 243, 345, 401, 404, 566
Shore, M., 535
Short, E. C., 257, 578
Shosteck, H., 578
Sidowsky, J., 578
Sieber, S. D., 4, 43, 74, 80, 95-96,
    98, 257, 326, 329, 548, 578-
    579
Siegel, B., 579
Siegeman, J., 411, 443
Sikes, W. W., 579
Sikorski, L., 39, 603
Silberston, A., 579
Silvern, L. C., 579
Simon, H. A., 536, 579
Sinclair, R., 464
Sincoff, M. Z., 362, 579
Skelton, B., 579-580
Skinner, F. L., 448
Slevin, D. P., 576, 580
Slocum, J. W., 506
Slocum, J. W., Jr., 580
Sloma, R. L., 264-265, 452
Smith, D. C., 580
Smith, E., 548
Smith, L. J., 62, 348, 529, 568
Smith, L. M., 238, 292, 580
Smith, N. L., 580
Smith, R. J., 126, 128-130, 428, 580
Smith, R. M., 82, 558
Smits, J. R., 584
Snapper, K., 481
Snidman, N. C., 330-331, 444
Snow, C. C., 473
Sogliero, G. C., 452
Solo, R. A., 358, 581
Soloff, A., 581
Sorensen, R. E., 604
Sorg, J. S., 561
Souder, W. E., 134, 173, 174n, 177,
    183-184, 407, 410-412, 581-582
Specht, H., 558
Specht, P. S., 181, 261-262, 475
Spector, A. N., 456
Speidel, J. J., 146, 583
Spencer, G., 582-583
Spicer, E. H., 82, 83, 583
Spiegel-Rosing, I., 583
Spivak, H., 559

Spooner, S. E., 305, 583
Sprehe, J. T., 146, 583
Srivastva, S., 93, 583
Staats, E., 583
Stafford, F., 446
Stake, R. E., 227, 236-237, 583
Stalker, G. M., 458
Stambaugh, R. J., 233, 389, 392,
    460
Stanley, J. C., 235, 459
Stearns, M. S., 329, 583
Stedman, D. J., 583-584
Steele, F., 584
Steeno, T. J., 584
Steere, B. F., 584
Steg, E., 557
Stein, M. I., 185, 584
Steinbruner, J. D., 584
Stenberg, C., 584
Stevens, W. F., 584
Stiles, L. J., 144, 584
Stillerman, R., 514
Stokes, T. F., 28, 584
Stolz, S. B., 28, 387-388, 585
Stork, K. E., 585
Stotsky, B. A., 313, 314, 377, 378,
    495
Strang, E. W., 585
Strawhorn, J. M., 585
Stringer, R. A., 91, 529
Strommen, M. P., 270, 439, 585
Struening, E., 500, 585
Stubblefield, H. W., 577-578
Studer, K. E., 4, 458
Stufflebeam, D. L., 585
Suchman, E. A., 223, 224, 232, 585
Sumner, G. C., 461
Sun, M., 133, 585
Sundland, D. M., 314-315, 538
Sundquist, J. L., 391-392, 585-586
Suppes, P., 472, 586
Suttle, J. L., 93, 500
Sutton, J. A., 461
Sutton, R. L., 143-144, 586
Svenning, L., 60, 61, 70, 323, 566
Swan, W. K., 128, 304, 586
Swanson, D. R., 304, 586
Swanson, G. E., 586
Sweeny, D. J., 443-444
Sweezy, E. E., 51, 131, 160, 546,
    586

Swierczek, F. W., 211-212, 480
Swift, D. W., 586
Szakasits, G. E., 586
Szilagyi, A. D., 586

Tallmadge, G. K., 327, 586
Tamberrino, R., 514
Tannenbaum, A., 586-587
Tansik, D. A., 559
Tarjan, G., 538
Tarpey, J., 599-600
Tavris, C., 587
Taylor, G., 48, 245, 273-275, 488, 540-541
Taylor, J. B., 83, 587
Taylor, R., 587
Taylor, S., 56, 61, 75, 88, 111, 168, 301, 313, 374, 375, 494
Teich, A., 523
Teilmann, K. S., 520
Temkin, S., 533-534, 553
Tenhoor, W. J., 590
Teresa, J. G., 201, 570
Terreberry, S., 411, 587
Tetelman, A., 587
Thayer, L., 587
Thio, A. O., 587
Thom, L. I., 590
Thomas, A. R., 587
Thomas, E. J., 588
Thomas, G. P., 440
Thompson, M., 588
Thompson, V. A., 102, 508, 588
Thorndike, E. L., 70
Thorsrud, E., 61, 107, 116-117, 588
Thrush, R. S., 305, 583
Tichy, N. M., 259, 407, 415-416, 510, 588-589
Tierney, M. L., 444
Tiffany, D. W., 589
Tiffany, P. M., 589
Timpane, M., 563
Toch, H., 589
Toffler, A., 18, 435, 589
Tomita, K., 311, 490
Torczyner, J., 589
Tornatzky, L. G., 62, 63, 75, 77, 169, 198, 200-201, 219, 246, 325, 459, 484, 584, 589
Toronto, R., 589
Toulmin, S., 589
Towell, D., 199-200, 589

Townes, C. H., 589-590
Townsend, P. L., 437
Trapp, M., 590
Trattner, E., 57-58, 590
Traub, J., 18, 590
Traxler, A. E., 590
Trice, H. M., 72, 128, 451
Tripodi, T., 590
Trist, E., 482
Troldahl, V., 69, 590
Truman, H. S., 117
Turnbull, B., 590
Turner, C. F., 519
Turner, J. C., 590
Turoff, M., 508, 528
Tushman, M. L., 590
Twiss, B. C., 590
Tymchuk, A. J., 590

Udis, B., 14, 172, 212-213, 302, 590
Uliassi, P. D., 590
Usdane, W. M., 278, 282, 592
Useem, M., 372, 382, 592
Utech, H., 592
Utech, I., 592
Utterback, J. M., 137, 175, 411, 592-593
Utterback, R. A., 602

Vallance, T. R., 593
van de Vall, M., 64, 156-157, 178, 393-394, 593
Van de Ven, A. H., 476, 593
Van de Vliert, E., 593
Van den Ban, A. W., 374, 375, 593
Vandermyn, G., 507
Van Horn, C. E., 593
Van Meter, D. S., 593
Vanvleck, E. M., 593
Vernon, R., 344, 593
Vickers, P. H., 317, 593-594
Vogel, M., 602
Von Brock, R. C., 451
von Hippel, E., 160, 381-382, 594

Wager, L. W., 594
Wagle, M. K., 281, 564
Wald, S., 555
Walker, J. L., 594
Walker, W., 555
Wall, J. E., 594
Wallace, R. C., 501

Wallendorf, M., 13-14, 71, 594, 603-604
Walsh, J., 130-131, 139, 594
Walton, R. E., 94-95, 215, 594-595
Ward, J. E., 595
Ward, S., 330-331, 462, 595
Wardell, W. M., 524-525
Warner, K. E., 12, 595
Warren, B. L., 595
Warren, M. Q., 595
Warren, R., 568
Warren, R. J., 595
Warwick, D. P., 79, 191$n$, 519, 595
Wasserman, C. W., 595
Watson, G., 69, 79, 80, 82, 86-87, 97, 110, 111, 115, 117, 156, 168, 177, 256, 306, 374, 595-596
Watson, J., 97, 101, 156, 169, 177, 182, 419, 529
Watzlawick, P., 596
Weakland, J., 596
Weber, M., 215, 596
Webster, D., 596
Weick, K. E., 596
Weinberg, A. M., 373, 596
Weisbrod, M. R., 596
Weisinger, M., 282, 564
Weiss, C. H., xii, 44, 151, 223, 233, 371, 382-383, 384, 389, 427, 596-598
Weiss, J. A., 371, 384, 597-598
Weiss, W., 511
Wellar, B. S., 598
Wells, S. A., 545
Wenk, E., Jr., xii, 338, 340, 355, 407, 416, 598
West, H. B., 566
Westbury, I., 533
Westley, B. H., 97, 101, 156, 169, 177, 182, 323, 419, 529, 598
Wheeler, T. J., 318-319, 598
Whisler, L., 598
Whisler, T. L., 446-447
White, B. F., 598
White, P., 439
White, S. W., 561
White, W., 44, 115-116, 176, 380-381, 598
Whitehead, R. R., 598
Whitley, R., 14-15, 180, 300, 598
Whitten, C. F., 598

Wholey, J. S., 598-599
Whyte, W. F., 599
Widmer, J., 209-210, 599
Wilcox, L. D., 599
Wildavsky, A., 521
Wilde, D. U., 599
Wilemon, D. L., 599
Wilensky, H. L., 302, 377, 525, 599
Wiles, K., 599
Wilkins, M., 340-341, 345, 599
Wilkinson, M., 344, 557
Williams, C. W., 599-600
Williams, L., 566
Williams, R. C., 600
Williams, W., 235, 569
Williams, W. A., 600
Willis, J. E., 602-603
Willower, D. J., 600
Wilpert, B., 472-473
Wilpert, P., 472-473
Wilson, E. C., 314, 600
Wilson, J. A., 600
Wilson, J. Q., 600
Wilson, M. L., 134, 600
Wind, Y., 549
Windle, C., 475, 600
Winett, R. A., 600
Winick, C., 600
Winter, S. G., 548
Winterton, J. A., 264, 600
Wise, R., 601
Wittrock, B., 443
Wolek, F. W., 72, 170-171, 172, 180-181, 303-304, 567-568
Wolf, R. M., 601
Wolf, S., 601
Wolf, W. C., Jr., 206, 601
Wolfe, J. L., 552
Wolfensberger, W., 375, 377-378, 601
Wolman, H., 601
Woods, T. E., 601
Woolf, P., 311, 490
Wrenn, C. G., 256, 305, 308, 375, 494
Wright, C. R., 512
Wright, P., 212, 601
Wright, P. I., 276, 536
Wright, S. R., 569

Yandell, W., 601
Yankelovich, D., 93, 518

Yapa, L. S., 601
Yates, D., 549
Yeager, S., 496
Yeracaris, C. A., 601-602
Yin, R. K., 222, 244-245, 402-403, 602
Yinger, J. M., 602
Yokote, G., 602
Young, K. P., 530
Young, T. R., 602
Young, V., 602

Zacker, J., 602
Zagona, S. V., 602-603
Zalkind, S. S., 81, 93, 114-115, 470
Zaltman, G., xii, 11, 12, 13, 14, 17,

32-33, 36-37, 39-40, 48, 53, 58,
60, 61, 71, 83-84, 119, 152, 157,
172-173, 190, 191n, 192, 215,
261, 301-302, 367-368, 376-377,
519, 527, 563, 603-604
Zand, D. E., 604
Zander, A., 79, 88, 218, 604
Zeleny, M., 467
Zerfoss, L. F., 534
Ziegler, R. W., 183-184, 582
Zimmerman, J., 604
Zimmerman, S., 504
Zollschan, G. K., 508, 604
Zurcher, L. A., 604
Zuspan, K., 514

# Subject Index

Ability, and analysis of change, 4, 6, 29, 36

Abt Associates, 438

Adoption: as change factor, 45; concept of, 2-3; symbolic and use types of, 83

Advantage. *See* Relative advantage

Advocacy: as change factor, 38; internal, 32, 37; interrelationships of, 62-63; as psychosocial factor, 75

Age, as change factor, 68-69

Agency for International Development (AID), 343

Agenda setting, as change stage, 165

Alabama, University of, and Medical Information Service via Telephone (MIST), 303

Alternative solutions: clarification of, 182-183; consideration of, as change stage, 182-185; creative thinking for, 183-185

American Educational Research Association, 440

American Institutes for Research (AIR), 309

American Psychological Association, Division of Military Psychology of, 419

Application, as change stage, 159, 161

Arizona, research and policy making in, 391

Arthur D. Little, Inc., 51, 93, 441-442

Atomic Energy Commission: and government subsidy, 124; and legislative enactment, 129

Atomic Energy Forum, 129

A VICTORY: as acronym, 4-5, 28-30; as change strategy, 216; and consultation, 271; and durability, 246; as facilitative model, 416-417; features of, 418-419; illustration of, 5-7; and key determinants, 422, 426; and organizational factors, 286; and policy making, 387; stages in, 158; summary comments on, 52, 53, 67, 88; and timing of evaluation, 225

Battelle Columbus Laboratories, 7-8, 34, 35, 38, 53, 62, 98, 255-256, 446

Bell Telephone Laboratories, approaches of, 131

Belmont Conference, 258, 330-331

Berkshire County House of Corrections, and change agents, 261

Brookings Institution, 124

Bureaucratic structure, as economic change factor, 136

California, research and policy making, 391, 394

Canada, organizational factors in, 94

Capability, as change factor, 36

Capacity, as change factor, 34, 36

Capital, in technology transfer, 347

Capla Associates, 459
Catalytic role model, barriers to, 50, 113
Center for Research in Scientific Communication, 462
Central Advisory Council for Science and Technology, 462
Centralization, as organizational factor, 119
Change: analytical examination of, 4-7; aspects of, 228-234; concept of, 3; evaluation of, 221-242; maintenance of, 222, 242-250; planned and unplanned, 3; resistance to, 80-84; types of, and consultation, 267-270; utilization interrelated with, 2-3. *See also* Knowledge utilization and change
Change Action Research (CAR), 266
Change agents: analysis of, 255-297; as change factor, 45; citizens as, 261-264; concept of, 256-257; and consultation, 266-272; demographic and value-congruence differences among, 260; errors by, 266; functioning and activities of, 264-266; internal and external, 261; intervention strategies of, 258-259; and networks, 280-295; role and functioning of, 255-279; summary comments on, 295-297; training of, 277-279; types and roles of, 257-261
Charpie Task Force Report, 126
Chicago, University of: motto of, 3; Pritzker School of Medicine at, and change agents, 262-263
China, People's Republic of, educational priorities in, 351
Chronic obstructive pulmonary disease (COPD), network for, 289-290
Circumstances: and analysis of change, 4, 6, 29, 36; as change factor, 423; interrelationships of, 63-64; unplanned, as change factors, 35
Climate: nature and components of, 91-93; and quality of worklife, 93-95
Cohesiveness, as change factor, 76-78

Commerce, change stages in, 158-162
Commitment, as change factor, 33, 37
Communicability, as change factor, 32, 36
Communication of knowledge: analysis of, 298-335; background on, 298-300; comparative studies of, 321-323; as economic change factor, 136; in facilitative models, 404; by federal government, 325-333; and mass media, 323-324; multiple methods for, 324-333; networks for, 428-430; open, 111-114; personal, 300-310; between practitioners and researchers, 375; stages in, 299; and strategies, 194-195; summary comments on, 333-335; written, 310-321
Community Intervention Project, change stages in, 163
Community Service Society of New York, pressures on, 99
Comparison, as change stage, 162
Compatibility: as change factor, 31, 33, 36; of values, interrelationships of, 58-60
Complexity: as change factor, 33, 36; as organizational factor, 119
Comprehensibility, interrelationships of, 60
Computerization: claims and realities of, 320; of written communication, 317-321
Conference Board, 121
Conflict, organizational ability to deal with, 119
Conflict resolution, and technology transfer, 357-359
Consultation: application illustrations of, 270-272; change agents related to, 266-272; effectiveness of, 271-272; and organizational development, 272-277; process of, 267; teaching of, 270; and types of change, 267-270
Context sensitivity, as change factor, 37
Contingency theory, concept of, 11
Conversion, as change stage, 164

CORRECT: as acronym, 30-31; and durability, 247

Cost, as change factor, 32, 36

Council of State Governments, 470

Coupling, types of, 366-367

Creative thinking, stimulating, 183-185

Credibility, as change factor, 30, 36

Cresap, McCormick, and Paget, 471

Criminal justice, networks for, 285-286

Curiosity, as change stage, 159

Decision Determinants Analysis. *See* A VICTORY

Decision making: as economic change factor, 136; participation in, 115-116; in technology transfer, 351-352

Definition, as change stage, 162, 164

Delphi technique: and creative thinking, 184-185; for goal clarity, 96

Demonstrability, interrelationships of, 61-62

Denver Research Institute, 160, 287, 312, 476

Deprivation, relative, as sociocultural change factor, 145-146

Design, as change stage, 156-157, 164

Development, as change stage, 156-157. *See also* Research and development

Diagnosis, as change stage, 156-157, 177-179

Dialectic, as change factor, 38

Diffusion: concept of, 2-3; and networks, 291

Dissatisfaction, as change factor, 32, 36

Dissemination: concept of, 2-3; economic model of, 13; manner and extent of, 31-32

Dissemination Analysis Group, 477

Divisibility, as change factor, 31, 33, 36

Durability: and characteristics of change, 246-249; and engineering/technology assessment, 249-250; frameworks for, 245-250

Ease in understanding and installation, as change factor, 31, 36

East India Company, and scurvy prevention, 10

Economic factors: analysis of, 133-139; in industries, 135-137; profit motive as, 133-135; in successful and unsuccessful projects, 137; summary comments on, 149-150; trends in, 137-139

Education: bureaucratic structure in, 102-103; change factors in, 39-40; change strategies in, 203-211; deterrent factors in, 49-51; interrelationships of change factors in, 58, 65; networks in, 283-385; organizational development in, 273-276; psychosocial factors in, 68-69

Educational information consultant (EIC), as change agent, 278-279

Educational Innovation Attitude Scale (EIAS), 69

Educational Resources Information Center (ERIC), 284, 311, 326

Effectiveness, quality and acceptance related to, 93-94

Efficiency: as change factor, 32, 37; effects and efforts related to, 58

El Salvador, communication in, 324

Elementary and Secondary Education Act (ESEA), 208, 209, 326, 329

Empathy, as change factor, 34, 36

Energy, as change factor, 34, 37

Environment, as change factor, 35

Equal Employment Opportunity Act of 1972, 128

Europe: change strategies in, 213; need assessment in, 172; occupational specialization in, 107; and technology transfer, 337

Evaluation: analysis of, 221-242; and aspects of planned change, 228-234; background on, 221-222; and change facilitation, 240; as change stage, 162; clinical approach to, 235-236; designs for, 234-238; formative and summative, 226-227; of goals, 229; of inputs, 229, 231; issues related to, 223; misuses of, 224; of out-

comes, 232-234; of process, 231-232; purposes of, 222-225; responsive, 236-237; scope of, 227-234; sequential modes of, 237; and stakeholders, 236; timing of, 225-227; of unexpected side effects, 238-240; utilization of, 240-242
Experience, as change factor, 34, 36
Experts of the Group of 77, 358, 483
Exploration, as change stage, 161

Factors influencing change: Abelson's set of, 42-43; analysis of, 23-150; Battelle set of, 34-35, 38, 53; central theme approach to, 43-44; Davis's set of, 28-30; determining, 27-54; deterrent, 47-52; economic, 133-139; Glaser's set of, 30-32; Havelock and Lingwood's set of, 33-34; Havelock's set of, 38, 53; integrated, 36-37; interrelationships of, 56-64; issues of, 53-54; in leading-idea approaches, 44-45; miscellaneous, 46-47; multiple, studies of, 64-66; organizational, 90-122; overview of, 23-25; political, 123-133; psychosocial, 68-80; purposes of lists of, 27-28; Roessner's set of, 40-42; Rothman's set of, 42; sets of, 27-45; sociocultural, 139-148; summary comments on, 52-54, 66-67, 88-89, 121-122, 148-150; Zaltman's sets of, 32-33, 39-40, 53
Fairweather Lodge, 246
Far West Laboratory for Educational Research and Development, 328, 484-485
Federal Coordinating Council for Science, Engineering and Technology, 280, 485
Federal Water Pollution Control Act, Amendments of 1972 to, 127
Financial capacity, as change factor, 38
Florida, University of, Rehabilitation Research Institute at, 592
Follow-through. See Maintenance

Forecasting International, 315, 487
Formalization, as organizational factor, 119
Functional specialization, as change strategy, 201-202
Fundamental stage, for change, 159

Gatekeepers, as change factor, 33, 37, 74-75, 77
Gateway capacity, as change factor, 33, 37
Gateway innovations, as change factor, 33, 36
Gellman Research Associates, 491
George Washington University, 491
Germany, time lag in, 8
Goal Attainment Scaling, 96, 246
Goals: clarity of, 95-97; and social expectancies, 97-99; statement of, or job description, 97; and vulnerability to pressure, 98-99
Government: change stages in, 165-166; communication by, 325-333. See also Political factors
Growth, and organizational climate, 92

HELP SCORES, as acronym, 33-34
Homophily, as change factor, 34, 36
Hospital Improvement Plan (HIP), and change factors, 66
Hughes Act of 1970, 128
Human Interaction Research Institute (HIRI), viii, 28, 246, 511

Ideas: and analysis of change, 4, 6, 29, 36; development of, as change stage, 177; as sociocultural change factor, 145
Illinois Institute of Technology, 512
Implementation: concept of, 2-3; programmed or adaptive types of, 195-196
Incentives: as change factor, 32, 37, 45; as political change factor, 133
India, occupational specialization in, 107
Individually Guided Education (IGE), and decision sharing, 118
Industrial Research Institute, 51, 442
Industry: change strategies in, 211-

214, 216-217; economic factors in, 135-137; time lag in, 9

Information: and analysis of change, 4, 6, 29, 36; in technology transfer, 348-349

Innovation: abstraction level of, 15-16; as change stage, 162; characteristics of, 30-31; process levels of, 17; time lag for, 8, 9

Institute for Development of Educational Activities (I/D/E/A), 118-119, 513

Interagency Task Force on Information Systems (IATIS), 349

Interconnecting, as change stage, 165

Internal integration, and organizational climate, 92

International Atomic Energy Agency, 129

International transfer. See Technology transfer

Interpersonal relationships: as change factor, 33, 36, 52; as organizational factor, 119

Interstate Project on Dissemination, 513

Item readiness, as change factor, 41

Japan: government role in, 98; occupational specialization in, 107; time lag in, 8

Johns Hopkins University, Center of Research in Scientific Communication at, 311

Joint Commission on Mental Health of Children, 199, 281, 514-515

Joint Commission on Mental Illness and Health, 281, 515

Joint Dissemination Review Panel (JDRP), 327-328, 332

Knowledge: concept of, 2; as equivocal, 4; hard and soft types of, 18, 233, 384; search for, as change stage, 179-181

Knowledge creep, 383

Knowledge system, 366

Knowledge utilization and change: and acceptance variables, 55-67; and adaptation, 423, 425-426; administrative-imposed approach to, 44; assessing needs and devel-

oping plans for, 168-186; change agents for, 255-297; and change-centered conceptions, 44; character and scope of process of, 14-18; and communication, 298-335, 428-430; complexity of, 21; compliance-centered approach to, 43; concept of, 2, 366; concepts in, 2-3; conclusion on, 422-435; context, readiness, and incentives for, 426; and cooperative studies, 433-434; determinants key to, 422-426; differentiations important to, 11-18; dimensions of, 368; dissemination-centered approach to, 44; economic factors in, 133-139; economics-centered approach to, 44; evaluating and maintaining, 221-251; facilitative models and systems for, 398-421; factors influencing, 23-150; future prospects for, 432-435; guidelines for, 368, 426-431; and implementation considerations, 424-425; and information, 423; and international transfer of technical knowledge, 336-360; interrelationships of factors in, 56-64; issues in, 1-20; as knowledge- or problem-driven, 151; linkages for, 253-421; methods for studying, 18-19; nature and scope of, 1-22; need to study, 3-4; organization-centered approach to, 44; organizational factors in, 90-122; organizing subject of, 19-20; and orientation, 423; person-centered approach to, 44; personal and social influences on, 68-89; perspectives on, 399-406; political factors in, 123-133; and potential users, 430-431; process-centered approach to, 44; processes of, stages in, 155-167; progressive iteration for, 433; and research and development related to practice, 361-397; research-centered approach to, 44; and resistance, 423; resistance-centered approach to, 44; resource-centered approach to, 44; sociocultural factors in, 139-148;

and stability, 435; stages in, 151-251; strategies for, 187-220, 433; summary comments on, 20-22; systematic frameworks for, 406-417; theorem for, 434; topical application areas and settings for, 12-14; user-centered approach to, 43; and willingness and ability, 423; as worthwhile, 422

Korea Institute of Science and Technology, 522

Labor, in technology transfer, 346
Langley Porter Institute, 523-524
Laser, stages in development of, 159
Leader, personality and role of, 72-76
Leadership, as change factor, 32, 36, 44-45
Legitimation of change, as change factor, 31, 37
Linkages: analysis of, 253-421; and change agents, 255-297; as change factor, 34, 37; and communication, 298-335; concept of, 255; international, for technology transfer, 336-360; models and systems for, 398-421; of research and development to practice, 361-397

McKinsey and Co., 533
Magi Educational Services, 327, 533
Maine, government regulation in, 125-126
Maintenance: analysis of, 242-250; and burnout, 243-244; and consultation, 268; durability and routinization in, 244-250; factors in, 243-244; stages and aspects of, 242-243
Management: as change factor, 35; as economic change factor, 135
Management by objectives, as change factor, 45
Management information systems (MIS), banks of knowledge in, 180
Manpower Science Services, 324-325, 535
Marketing: barriers in, 51; as change effort, 13-14
Marketing Science Institute, 376

Maryland, University of, Office of Industrial Application at, 212
Massachusetts: change strategies in, 209-210; citizen boards in, 263-264
Massachusetts, University of, and change agents, 261
Massachusetts General Hospital, research grant to, 133
Matching: as change stage, 165; as change strategy, 195-196
Mathematica, 537
Maturity, as change stage, 159
Medical institutions, time lag in, 10-11
Medical technology, transfer of, 353-354
Mental health services: change strategies in, 198-201; interrelationships of change factors in, 59, 63, 65-66; networks in, 281; organizational development in, 272-273; resistance in, 81
Middleman, terms used for, 256
Military, change strategies in, 211-214, 216-217
Minnesota, legislative enactments in, 128
Minnesota Multiphasic Personality Inventory, 5
Models: academic disciplinary, 399-404; action research, 405-406; analysis of facilitative, 398-421; concept of, 417-418; economic, 399; formula-type, 416-417; learning-systems, 403-404; management, 400; perspectives on, 399-406; planned change, 405; problem-solving, 405; psychological, 402-404; public policy, 400-402; research, development, and diffusion, 404-405; social interaction, 405; sociological, 402; summary comments on, 421; systems, 406-417; uses of and criteria for, 417-421
Modification susceptibility, as change factor, 33, 36
Morale, as change factor, 76-78
Motivation, as change factor, 35
Multinational enterprise (MNE), in technology transfer, 342-343, 355-357

National Academy of Engineering, 132, 546

National Aeronautics and Space Administration, 121, 546; and communication, 312; and government subsidy, 124; and need assessment, 171; Technology Utilization Program of, 212, 287-288

National Diffusion Network (NDN), 284, 326-327, 328-329, 331-333, 428-429

National Institute of Education (NIE), 205, 258, 273-275, 283-285, 293, 328, 330, 390, 429, 546-547; National Center for Educational Communication of, 280; Office of Research and Development of, 283

National Institute of Handicapped Research (NIHR), 282

National Institute of Mental Health (NIMH), xi, 42, 301, 308-309, 511, 547; and advocacy, 63; and A VICTORY, 30; and communication, 315; consultants from, 5; and maintenance of change, 243; Mental Health Services Development Branch of, vii-viii, 246, 280, 281

National Institute of Technology, proposed, 125

National Institutes of Health, and government subsidy, 124

National (Military) Symposium on Research Utilization, 379

National Research Centers, 285

National Research Council of the National Academy of Sciences, 547

National Science Board, 547

National Science Foundation, 8, 34, 62, 79, 98, 132, 160, 255, 319, 370, 410, 547-548; Division of Policy Research and Analysis of, 288; Division of Science Information Service of, 288; Intergovernmental Science Program of, 315

National Seminar on the Diffusion of New Instructional Materials and Practices, 46

National Teacher Corps: and change

strategies, 210; and organizational inertia, 109; and psychosocial considerations, 70, 75

National Training Laboratory (NTL), 279

Needs: assessment of, as change stage, 168-186; awareness and assessment of, 168-173; and diagnosis, 177-179; and preassessment of research, 173-177; response to, as change factor, 45; summary comments on, 185-186

Netherlands, problem diagnosis in, 178

NETWORK, 331-333, 549

Network of Consultants on Knowledge Transfer and Change, 286

Network of Consultants on Planned Change and Knowledge Transfer, 281

Networks: and change agents, 280-288; for communication, 428-430; concept of, 291-292; for criminal justice, 285-286; in education, 283-285; as facilitative model, 415-416; guidelines for building, 293-394; in mental health services, 281; natural and deliberate types of, 292; purposes of temporary, 288-289; in rehabilitation services, 282-283; for science and technology, 286-288; and social network analysis, 291-295; temporary, 288-291

New England Rehabilitation Institute, 313-314

New International Economic Order, 337, 356

New York: change strategies in, 204; sociocultural change factors in, 143

New York State Education Department, 549

North Carolina, network strategy in, 430

Northwest Regional Educational Laboratory, 550

Norway: minimized commitment in, 61; organizational factors in, 94, 107, 116-117

Nuclear energy, technology transfer and, 353

Oak Ridge National Laboratory, 129
Obligation, and analysis of change, 4, 7, 29, 37
Observability, as change factor, 30, 36
Office of Planning, Budgeting, and Evaluation, 551
Office of Technology Assessment (OTA), 239, 551
Ohio State University Research Foundation, 551
Openness, as change factor, 34, 36
Operational development, as change stage, 161-162
Oregon, research and policy making in, 391
Organization for Economic Cooperation and Development, 80, 139, 552
Organizational Consultants, 279
Organizational development (OD): assessment of, 275-277; as change strategy, 201; and consultation, 272-277; cube, 276; routinization of, 245
Organizations: administrative and colleague support in, 114-118; analysis of change factors in, 90-122; climate of, 91-95; communication and decision making in, 111-118; deterrent factors in, 51-52; goals of, 95-99; miscellaneous factors in, 118-121; structural variables in, 100-111; summary comments on, 121-122
Origin, point of, as change factor, 33, 36
Overadoption, hazards of, 80

Patent policy, as political change factor, 124-125
Patients, readmission of, and analysis of change, 5-7
Peer group, as change factor, 35
Perceived relative advantage, as change factor, 33, 37
Perceptronics, 213, 556
Performance gaps, concept of, 40
Periodicity, as change strategy, 202
Personal communication: analysis of, 300-310; in conferences, seminars, and workshops, 305-
306; in demonstrations and visits, 306-310; gossip's role in, 304-305; informal contact in, 302-305; power of, 300-302
Personal interaction, as change factor, 31, 36. See also Interpersonal relationships
Personnel, interconnections of, 120
Pilot State Dissemination Program, as user-centered approach, 43
Planned change. See Change
Planned Parenthood, pressures on, 99
Point of origin, as change factor, 33, 36
Poland, research and development roles in, 363-364
Policy making, research and development and, 382-394, 426-428
Political factors: analysis of, 123-133; government subsidy and regulation as, 124-127; legislative enactments as, 127-130; and policy issues, 130-133; summary comments on, 149
Population ecological approach, to organizations, 121
Population growth, as sociocultural change factor, 146
Power, distribution of, 100-102
Practicability, interrelationships of, 60-61
Practitioners and researchers: analysis of relationship between, 369-382; in collaboration, 373-379, 425; in communication, 375; differences between, 369-373; examples of collaboration by, 379-382; as linkers, 374
President's Commission on the Patent System, 125
President's Council of Economic Advisers, 392
Pressures, as change factor, 32, 36
Primary Mental Health Project (PMHP), and change strategies, 205
Privateness, as change factor, 33, 36
Problem clarification, as change stage, 177-179
Problem-solver perspective, as change factor, 38

Professional qualities, as change factor, 70-72

Professional social inquiry (PSI), 386

Profit, concepts of, 57

Program and Planning Budgeting System (PPBS), 206

Project Developmental Continuity, deterrent factors in, 50

Proximity, as change factor, 34, 36

Psychological attributes, as change factor, 78-80

Public Affairs Counseling, 385, 558

Public services. See Social services

Publicness, as change factor, 33, 36

Q-sort: and creative thinking, 184; for goal clarity, 96

Quality of worklife, and climate, 93-95

Rand Corporation, 96, 124, 208, 307

Readiness, as change stage, 164-165, 171

Real Estate Research Corporation, 560

Redefining, as change stage, 165

Regional Educational Laboratories, 285

Rehabilitation services, networks in, 282-283

Rehabilitation Services Administration (RSA), 282-283, 309

Rehabilitation Utilization Specialist (RUS), 278

Relative advantage: as change factor, 30-31, 33, 37; interrelationships of, 56-58

Relative deprivation, as sociocultural change factor, 145-146

Relevance, as change factor, 30, 37

Research: basic and applied, interrelated, 364-368; brokerage of, 391-392; frames of reference for, 383-384; functions of, in policy making, 394; preassessment of, and needs, 173-177; types of, 365

Research and development: analysis of practice related to, 361-397; barriers to, guidelines for overcoming, 378-379, 386-387; basic and applied research in, 364-368; circular models of, 364-365; coaction model of, 376; coupling in, 366-367; examples of collaboration in, 379-382; perspective of, as change factor, 38; and policy making, 382-394, 426-428; practitioner/researcher relationships in, 369-382; rewards for, 362-363; summary comments on, 395-397; in technology transfer, 347-348; university role in, 361-364

Research and Development Exchange (RDX), 284, 328

Research and Development Utilization Program (RDU), 284, 328-329

Research Triangle Institute, 561

Research Utilization Laboratory (RUL), 282

Research Utilization Through Learning Experiences (RULE), 309

Researchers. See Practitioners and researchers

Resistance: and analysis of change, 4, 7, 29, 37; beliefs and values related to, 82; concept of, 40; and group dynamics, 87; and job security, 82; and need visibility, 84; as personal or social issue, 80-84; rational and irrational, 83; reducing, 85-88; and self-esteem, 82; and side effects, 83; and status loss, 81-82; and threats, 80-81; and unfamiliarity, 82-83; working through, as change factor, 37

Resource identification, as change stage, 165

Returns to investment, as change factor, 32, 37

Reversibility, as change factor, 31, 33, 36

Reward, as change factor, 34, 37

Right-to-Read Program, 208, 329

Risk and uncertainty, as change factor, 32, 37

Rochester, University of, innovation at, 105

Role accumulators, as change factor, 71
Routinization, correlates of, 244-245

School Planning, Evaluation, and Communication System (SPECS), 207
Science and technology, networks for, 286-288
Science Citation Index (SCI), 318
Scientific status, as change factor, 33, 36
Search for knowledge, as change stage, 179-181
Search Institute, 577
Seed stage, for change, 159
Social and Rehabilitation Service, 282, 433
Social contacts, as change factor, 70-71
Social network analysis. See Networks
Social Science Citation Index (SSCI), 318
Social Science Education Consortium, 46, 580-581
Social services: change stages in, 162-165; change strategies in, 201-203; interrelationships of change factors in, 57, 64
Social structure, as sociocultural change factor, 146-147
Sociocultural factors: analysis of, 139-148; psychological aspects of, 144-148; settings for, 142-144; summary comments on, 150; theoretical framework of, 139-142
Socioeconomic status, as change factor, 69-70
Stages of knowledge utilization and change: analysis of, 151-251; in commerce, 158-162; consideration of alternative solutions as, 182-185; contextual application of, 152; of evaluation and maintenance, 221-251; general considerations on, 155-158; general approaches to, 157-158; in government, 165-166; linearity of, a myth, 152-153; of need assessment and plan development, 168-

186; overview of, 151-154; and planned change, 152; and problem-solving approaches, 155-157; in processes, 155-167; purposes of understanding, 153, 167; sampling of, in settings, 158-166; search for knowledge as, 179-181; in social services, 162-165; strategies in, 187-220; summary comments on, 166-167, 185-186, 219-220, 250-251
Stanford Research Institute, 583
State Capacity Building System, 284
Strategic manipulation, as change factor, 38
Strategies: for achieving change, 187-220; adaptation in, 195-198; and advocacy formation, 190; applications of, 198-214, 216-217; chart summarizing, 216-217; and communication/utilization process, 194-195; determination of, as change stage, 165; in education, 203-211; empirical-rational, 188-189; factors affecting, 193-195; general considerations on, 187-198; intra-organizational and extraorganizational types of, 198-199; in mental health services, 198-201; normative-reeducative, 188-189, 192; power-coercive, 188-190, 192; power versus persuasion in, 214-215, 218-219; principles in, 187-193; in social services, 201-203; summary comments on, 219-220; typology of, 191; utilitarian, 192-193
Structure: bureaucratic, 102-105; as economic change factor, 135; inertia of, 109-110; innovative and productive types of, 104; and occupational specialization, 105-107; and power distribution, 100-102; and self-renewal, 110-111; size and capacity of, 107-109
Structuring: as change factor, 34, 36; as change stage, 165
Study Project on Social Research and Development, 585
Survey feedback, for open communication, 111-113

Sussex, University of, Science Policy Research Unit of, 576
Sweden, organizational factors in, 94
Synergy, as change factor, 34, 37
Syracuse University, innovation at, 105
System: client/practitioner relationship as, 407; closed or bipolar loop as, 407-408; concept of, 406-407; cybernetic societal guidance model of, 412-414; developmental stages for, 408-410; facilitating change by, 406-417; future of, 432; innovation factor, 410-412; social network model of, 415-416; and systematic assessment of new technology, 414-415; technology delivery crisis model of, 416
System Development Corporation, 308
Systematic Assessment of New Technology (SANT), 414-415
Systems Improvement Research (SIR), 260

Task accomplishment, and organizational climate, 92
Task Force on International and National Diffusion of Quality of Working Life Programs, 15, 290-291, 587
Task Force on Resources Planning and Analysis, 283-284
Tavistock Institute, 107, 379, 587
Technical assistance: as change factor, 31, 36; and change strategies, 202; in technology transfer, 343
Technical exchange transaction (TET), 341
Technical University of Wroclaw, research and development role of, 363-364
Technology: as amplifier, 355; concept of, 2, 338; embodied and disembodied, 15; horizontal and vertical transfer of, 16, 46-47
Technology assessment, and unexpected side effects, 238-240
Technology transfer: analysis of international, 336-360; and appropriate technology, 352; background on, 336-338; barriers to, 345; capital in, 347; components of, 346-352; and conflict resolution, 357-359; decision making in, 351-352; as dissemination-centered approach, 44; education and training in, 349-351; examples of, 353-354; functional criteria for, 340; information in, 348-349; infrastructure in, 349; labor in, 346; models and mechanisms of, 342-343; multinational enterprise in, 342-343, 355-357; new features in, 337-338; perspectives on, 338-340; preconditions to, 344; research and development in, 347-348; shortfall in, 345-346; side effects of, 354-355; social and economic aspects of, 344-346; social process model of, 340-342; summary comments on, 359-360; symbiosis and conflicts in, 355-357; and technical assistance, 343; technological multipliers in, 346; vertical and horizontal, 16, 46-47. See also Knowledge utilization and change
Tenure, as change factor, 69
Terminality, as change factor, 33, 36
Termination criteria, as change factor, 51
Time lag, extent of, 7-11
Timing: and analysis of change, 4, 7, 29, 37; as change factor, 423; interrelationships of, 63-64
Transfer agents, as change factor, 41
Transfer organizations, as change factor, 41
Transfer system, as change factor, 41
Trialability: as change factor, 31, 36; interrelationships of, 61-62
Trouble-Shooting Checklist (TSC), 46

Unco, 194-195, 590
UNESCO, 415
Union for Experimenting Colleges and Universities, 591
Union of Soviet Socialist Republics: government role in, 98; and technology transfer, 337
United Kingdom: communication

in, 321; government role in, 98; organizational factors in, 94, 107, 120; practitioners and researchers in, 373, 379; strategies in, 199-200; time lag in, 8, 10

United Nations, 591; Conference on Science and Technology for Development by, 340; group of 77 from, 358; New International Economic Order at, 356; and technology transfer, 339, 348-349, 358-359

United Nations Conference on Trade and Development (UNCTAD), 338, 357, 591

United Nations Environmental Program (UNEP), 339

United States: government role in, 98; organizational factors in, 94, 107; and technology transfer, 337, 343; time lag in, 8

U.S. Census Bureau, 165

U.S. Congress, Joint Economic Committee of, 131-132

U.S. Department of Commerce: and communication, 307; National Technical Information Service (NTIS) of, 315-316

U.S. Department of Defense, 124, 434, 591

U.S. Department of Education, 325-326, 327, 591

U.S. Department of Energy, 126, 129, 130, 591

U.S. Department of Health and Human Services, Research Utilization Branch of, 280

U.S. Department of Health, Education and Welfare, 124

U.S. Department of Housing and Urban Development, 591

U.S. Department of Labor, Division of R&D Utilization of, 280

U.S. Department of State, 117

U.S. Department of Transportation, Office of R&D Policy in, 46-47

U.S. Environmental Protection Agency (EPA): and communication, 325; and government regulation, 127; Technology Transfer Program of, 287

U.S. Forest Service, 591

U.S. House of Representatives: Committee on Science and Astronautics of, 239; Science and Technology Committee of, 128-130

U.S. Office of Education, 208, 211, 258, 284, 330, 429, 591-592

Universities, research and development role of, 361-364

University Associates, 279

Urban Information Systems, 319

Urban Institute, 592

Users: characteristics of, as change factor, 31, 41; involvement of, as change factor, 31, 37

Utilization, change interrelated with, 2-3. See also Knowledge utilization and change

Values: and analysis of change, 4, 6, 29, 36; compatibility of, 58-60; resistance related to, 82

Vermont Conference on the Primary Prevention of Psychopathology, 306

Vested interest, as change factor, 69

VICTORY. See A VICTORY

Violence, victims of: and evaluation, 224-225; networks for, 285-286

Vocational Education Act, 208, 329

Wants, as change factor, 78

Western Electric Company, laser development stages in, 159

Westville Assistance Group, 220

Women, barriers to change for, 51-52

Working Group on Innovation Processes and Their Management, 288

World Conservation Strategy, 339

World Health Organization, 353

Written communication: abstracts and related services for, 315-316; analysis of, 310-321; computer storage and retrieval for, 317-321; growth and use of, 310-313; improved reports for, 313-314; publishing problems for, 316-317; and readable reviews, 314-315

Yield: and analysis of change, 4, 7, 29-30, 37; interrelationships of, 56-58